W9-BUZ-921

# WORKING AMERICANS
## 1880–2015

## Volume V: Americans At War

# WORKING AMERICANS
## 1880–2015

## Volume V: Americans At War
### Second Edition

## by Scott Derks

A UNIVERSAL REFERENCE BOOK

Grey House
Publishing

PUBLISHER: Leslie Mackenzie
EDITORIAL DIRECTOR: Laura Mars
MANAGING EDITOR: Diana Delgado
PRODUCTION MANAGER: Kristen Thatcher
MARKETING DIRECTOR: Jessica Moody
COMPOSITION: David Garoogian

Grey House Publishing, Inc.
4919 Route 22
Amenia, NY 12501
518.789.8700
FAX 845.373.6390
www.greyhouse.com
e-mail: books @greyhouse.com

Publisher's Cataloging-In-Publication Data
(Prepared by The Donohue Group, Inc.)

Derks, Scott.
    Working Americans ... / by Scott Derks. — 2nd ed.

    v. : ill. ; cm.

    Date range in the title varies.
    1st ed. published in 2003. Printed in Canada.
    Content: V. 5. Americans At War  [1880-2015]
    Includes bibliographical references and indexes.
    ISBN: 978-1-61925-743-6 (v. 5)

    1. Working class—United States—History. 2. Labor—United States—History.
    3. Occupations—United States—History. 4. Social classes—United States—History.
    5. Immigrants—Employment—United States—History.

HD8066 .D47 2012
305.5/0973/0904

# TABLE OF CONTENTS

# INTRODUCTION

This second edition of *Working Americans Volume V: Americans At War,* updates the topic to 2015. It first edition, in 2003, was the fifth volume in the *Working Americans* series. Like the other titles in the series: *The Working Class; The Middle Class; The Upper Class; Their Children; Women at Work; Social Movements; Immigrants; Revolutionary to Civil Wars; Sports & Recreation; Inventors & Entrepreneurs; History Through Music;* and *Educators, At War* observes the lives of Americans, decade by decade. This new edition extends its period of examination to 2015, and includes the most recent conflicts America is facing, including those in Afghanistan and Iraq. *Americans At War* considers how war affects Americans of all economic levels—steamship magnate to inner-city teenager—and at all levels of participation—West Point graduate to a telephone engineer. By studying both those who have fought at the front lines and those at home who support (or oppose) war efforts, we examine the pulse of the nation, its reaction, and its ability to adapt to the ever-changing face of the world under the shadow of strife.

**Praise for earlier volumes—**

> *"This volume serves as an outstanding overview…highly recommended for school libraries [and] it should also be found in public libraries of every size."*

> *"The intent of this work is to profile individuals involved in music at all levels…and the publisher in large achieves that lofty goal."*
> —American Reference Books Annual

> *"[the author] adds to the genre of social history known as 'history from the bottom up,' which examines the lives of ordinary people… Recommended for all colleges and university library collections."*
> —Choice

> *"This volume engages and informs, contributing significantly and meaningfully to the historiography of the working class in America…"*
> —Library Journal

> *"These interesting, unique compilations of economic and social facts, figures, and graphs will support multiple research needs. They will engage and enlighten patrons in high school, public, and academic library collections."*
> —Booklist

Whether it be a declared conflict, an impromptu protest, a single military action, a relief effort, or a preparation for future skirmish, *Americans At War* delves into the many forms of political and social unrest. You will read about officers, civilians, enlisted personnel, and political figures, all of who play important roles in the changes effected by war and its permutations on the evolution of America.

As a "point in time" book, this volume is designed to illustrate reality during times of war. It offers first-hand accounts of men and women fighting in deplorable conditions and stories of others witnessing horrendous, violent acts.

We were concerned that graphic descriptions of warfare and social comments, not considered politically correct by today's standards, might be offensive to our audience. This notion was dispelled when previous purchasers of the series, primarily high school and public librarians, told us to not change a thing. The point of primary source material, they said, is to show others how it was…that it is crucial to show others how it was…and that the *Working Americans* series does just that.

The clippings, photographs, illustrations, and public postings reproduced in these pages are all accurate to their specific time period, and they help to demonstrate how social change impacts the ways of war, and how the ways of war enact social change, prejudices and injustices. Indeed, the realities of war often rely on predisposition and social history as the basis for conflict. Since the *Working Americans* series is based in hard facts and historical actualities, the primary documents that pertain often reflect historically valuable social outlooks.

*Americans at War* profiles Americans of all ages, ethnicities, backgrounds, and locations. Materials such as economic data, gubernatorial statistics, historiography, family archives, and publications contribute to the formation of well-researched details utilized in each chapter. The primary documents and historical matter range from excerpted song lyrics and political speeches to mementos of the era—pictorial propaganda, sociopolitical cartoons, book covers, and bottle caps.

In *Working Americans 1880-2015: Americans At War,* each of the 13 chapters begins with an overview of important events pertinent to the decade examined. Each chapter contains personal Profiles—a total of 38—plus Economic Profiles, Historical Snapshots and News Features. These common elements, as well as specialized data like Selected Prices and Average Pay, punctuate each chapter and act as statistical comparisons between decades, as well as between Americans of different socioeconomic backgrounds.

Most of the 38 Profiles are composites of real events and situations with invented names; a few, specifically the final four, use the individual's real names. The Profiles examine Life at Home, Life at Work and Life in the Community. Home ranges from California to Florida; ethnic origins, from Polish to African-American. Life at Work examines such workplaces as the cockpit of an army jet and the rooms of a French field hospital.

In nearly 700 pages, *Americans At War* offers a broad range of details intended to shed light on the actual people living through actual conflict. They include volunteer soldiers, eager to effect their patriotism in the trenches of battle; antiwar advocates decrying the disasters of discord; and those who were moved to action by the deaths of family members at the hands of war. The underlying and integral thread that links every person profiled is their first-hand experiences of what it means to be an American at war.

# PREFACE

This book is the fifth in a series examining the social and economic lives of working Americans. In this volume, the focus is on the men and women who have been impacted by the events of military actions. The first volume, *Working Americans: 1880-1999: The Working Class,* explored the struggles of the working class through the eyes and wallets of three dozen families. With pictures, stories, statistics and advertisements of the period, it studied their jobs, wages, family life, expenditures and hobbies throughout the decades. The second volume, *The Middle Class,* captured the struggles-and joys-in a similar but sometimes subtly different way, profiling the lives of everyday families who played a quiet role in building the economy of America from 1880 to 1999. Few were heroes, all felt the pressures of life, and most wanted to create a better life for themselves and their children. The third volume, *The Upper Class,* studied the fascinating and often complex world of America's upper class. Through hard work, grit, good luck or inheritance, these families were elevated to the highest pinnacle of economic prosperity. All were wealthy, though not all were well off. The fourth volume built on the concepts and social issues explored in the previous three volumes by examining the lives of children of working Americans throughout the entire spectrum of economic status. In this way, *Working Americans IV: Their Children* looked at the issues of growing up: parents, homework, child labor, education, peer pressure, food, fads and fun with friends.

This volume extends these examinations to an often life-changing event: war. Each decade explores the various ways that officers, enlisted personnel, and civilians handled the stress, boredom and brutality of war, including declared conflicts, one-time military actions, protests or preparations for future wars. This second edition of *Working Americans: At War* extends into 2015 to observe not only the pathos and drama of 9/11 but the decade long conflicts in Afghanistan and Iraq and their aftermath. This study of Americans engaged in the tumult of war features the confusion caused by long, protracted conflicts as soldiers battle to stay alive while civilians in America go forth largely untouched by war's violence. This expanded volume also examines the role of a volunteer army and of women in the modern day military. As in the first edition and, indeed, the previous volumes, each story is unique, as each of us is unique: the Marine pilot who rethinks his career, thanks to a successful bombing run in 1927 in Nicaragua; the navy pilot whose last mission lands him in the Hanoi Hilton as a POW; the Washington lobbyist who helps negotiate the first invasion of Panama in 1903; the female

MP who keeps order after the 1989 invasion of Panama; the college woman who stood for peace prior to World War II, the woman who worked to restructure Japan's economy after the war; the wounded warrior who came home in 2012 feeling like a stranger in a strange land. Yet, whether we grew up rich along the eastern shore or poor in an inner-city slum, we all experience anxiety when enemy shells begin to fall nearby.

All of the profiles are modeled on real people and events, although, as in the previous books in this series, the names often have been changed and some details have been added based on statistics, the then-current popularity of an idea, or writings of the time. Otherwise, every effort has been made to profile accurately the individuals' early life, military experience, family life, duty station and battle assignments. To ensure that each profile reflects the feelings of its subject, diaries, letters, biographies, interviews and magazine articles were consulted and used. In some cases, the featured individuals represent national trends and feelings, but most of the time, they represent only themselves. Ultimately, it is the people, events and actions of Americans—along with their investments, spending decisions, time commitments, jobs and passions—that shape society and the economy.

In many ways, this book has been a labor of both love and discovery. I grew up the son of an Air Force pilot. My uncle—an irreplaceable mentor—fought in Korea. As a child, my family experienced the tension evoked by the failed Bay of Pigs invasion; as a teen in the 1960s, I often debated with my father about the value of a continued presence in Vietnam. My memory stills holds the disappointment evoked by the failed Iranian hostage rescue attempt in 1980, and the exhilaration felt a decade later during the invasion of Iraq to free Kuwait. Now, as the calendar pushes 2015, I admit to a certain war fatigue and uncertainty of our goals in these far away lands. Yet, as I continue to meet and interview veterans of recent wars, I am struck by the pride they display in the role they play and, indeed, continue to play, in keeping Americans free. By their stories and actions, I am reminded of the price of freedom.

Unlike most books about war, *Working Americans: At War* focuses on weaponry, tactics or military structure only when it supports an individual's profile. It does not comment on victories, losses, or the wisdom or foolishness of the reasons for conflict. This is a book about the personal views and emotions of ordinary people whose lives were somehow touched by war.

*Working Americans: At War* is dedicated to my father,
Major Wayne G. Derks, and my uncle,
First Lieutenant Robert M. Hope,
both heroes to a grateful son and nephew.

# ACKNOWLEDGEMENTS

First great praise must be lavished on Jim DuPlessis for spearheading the update revisions to this new edition. His innovative thinking will certainly influence future volumes. Thanks and praise to the research and writing skills of Greg Flowers, whose dedication enriched this volume. His devotion to quality resonates throughout. Thanks also go to newcomer Sonia Montero, Linda Kelly (this is our third book together) and Elaine Alibrandi (a partner on five books), whose editing skills, enthusiasm and hard work kept this project interesting and on schedule. As in the past, my children Lucia, Marshall and Hal all made important research and writing contributions, often without the threat of bodily harm. Jan Brown stepped in to help with pictures, as did our local bookstore Dr. Books, of Columbia, South Carolina. Special thanks also go to the Interlibrary Loan, Government Documents, Circulation, and particularly the Reference departments of the University of South Carolina for their steadfast assistance, often above and beyond the call of duty.

Grey House Publishing thanks the individuals and families who are profiled in this edition for their generosity in sharing personal photographs. In addition, photographs from the following sources were used:

Associated Press
Collection of Jim DuPlessis
gocomics.typepad.com
Hawaii Office of Environmental Control
Jim DuPlessis
Library of Congress

U.S. Air Force
U.S. Army
U.S. Navy
Wikimedia/Wikipedia
www.dvidshub.net
www.pbs.org

# 1880–1899

The changes in America during these two decades were the result of events that had occurred much earlier in the nineteenth century. By 1806, Lewis and Clark had opened up the northwest to Americans, while Zebulon Pike explored the southwest, and by 1848, the United States had tripled the size of its territory. The gold rush brought statehood in 1850 to California, the western shore of the continent, and manifest destiny became a reality.

This heady period of exploration and expansion brought a profound and permanent change to the indigenous people of the land, who began to be displaced by white settlers moving West. The extreme differences between the two cultures—Native American and new American—along with the expansionist aims of the U.S. Government, caused clashes, war and, ultimately, the removal of Native Americans to designated areas in various parts of the country.

After the Civil War, the last years of the century witnessed the migration of workers from farm to factory, the explosive growth of cities, and massive immigration. The rapid expansion of railroads opened up the nation not only to transportation, but also to new industry. On the world stage, America was coming into its own as an economic force, and many Americans were beginning to take enormous pride in a new-found ability to influence their European cousins. It was a land of enormous promise, eager to test its mettle in trade, innovation—and war. The opportunity to exercise its burgeoning power arose in Cuba, where invasion by the U.S. was mainly an excuse to drive Old World power, Spain, from the tiny island. The result was the Spanish-American War, and a new sense of self in America.

# 1891 PROFILE

# THE INDIAN WARS

### Second Lieutenant

As the Indian Wars come to an end, Ohio native Second Lieutenant Eddie Rausch has been assigned the unrewarding task of patrolling the windswept lands of North Dakota, while reliving memories of the Battle of Pine Ridge and praying for a warmer assignment soon.

### Life at Home

- Second Lt. Edwin "Eddie" Rausch grew up in a small community in northeast Ohio, equidistant from Cleveland and Lake Erie.
- His childhood was filled with tales of military adventures frequently and robustly recounted by his great-uncles from their Civil War exploits.
- Rausch men, he was told repeatedly, were born to fight, ever since Johann Rausch was conscripted to serve his German princeling and found himself rented out to fight for the British against the American colonists.
- After the Revolutionary War, Johann stayed in America, settled in the middle of the vast new nation, and produced a long line of soldiers, farmers and merchants.
- Eddie Rausch was destined to be a soldier, his uncles averred.
- The third son in a family of seven, Eddie proved to be an average student, but a superb horseman who loved the outdoors.
- His father, a prosperous farmer and shopkeeper, used his political connections with their congressman to wrangle Eddie an appointment to West Point.

*Eddie Rausch participated in the Battle of Pine Ridge.*

- After a lifetime of dimestore war novels and family battle stories, Eddie envisioned himself in the midst of historic cavalry assaults.
- Instead, his first major clash was with the Corps' stringent engineering curriculum, with Eddie ending up on the losing side.
- At graduation, postings were determined by a student's class rank; Eddie Rausch, horse-lover and man of the outdoors, was not in the top half of the class of 1889, and as a result, was the last officer chosen for the cavalry.
- His assignment was the unpopular role of leading the 9th Cavalry Regiment, one of two all-black cavalry units in the army, now stationed in the West.
- Although Second Lt. Rausch was happy to be out of school and back in the saddle, he was equally uncertain about his assignment.
- No blacks lived in his section of Ohio, and he had seen few in his entire life; it was widely believed in the military that blacks made good soldiers if, and only if, led by a strong and resourceful white officer.
- When he arrived at Fort Robinson, Nebraska, Eddie was immediately impressed with the quality of his troops, finding the Negroes to be excellent soldiers.
- While many in K-Troop were planning to make a career of the military and acted accordingly, many of the white men at Fort Robinson who considered soldiering a temporary position were lazy and undisciplined.
- Months later, emergency orders arrived for K-Troop to move out immediately to Fort Buford in the Dakota Territory. Eddie was elated—a chance to engage the enemy at last!

*The Indian Wars of the American West were drawing to a close in 1891.*

- While some officers studied the Indians, their customs, background, weapons and tools, Eddie used his ample quiet time to study the military mission of each Western fort, including Fort Buford.
- Not only was it well-known as the place where Chief Sitting Bull surrendered, but it also played a significant role in keeping the Indians in check so settlers and railroads could continue westward.
- A call for additional troops could only mean one thing—an Indian uprising.

### Life at Work

- The urgent telegram arrived on November 19, 1890, at Fort Robinson, Nebraska.
- "Move out as soon as possible with the troop of cavalry at your post; bring all the wagon transportation you can spare, pack-mules and saddles; extra ammunition and rations will be provided when you reach the railroad.—By order of the Department Commander."
- The soldiers of Second Lt. Eddie Rausch's K-Troop, nicknamed "Buffalo soldiers" by the Indians because of the perceived similarity of their hair, were needed—it was time to move out.
- At the railroad station, word came that the Sioux Indians of the Dakota Territory were on the warpath and had murdered settlers.
- The rumors meshed with stories Eddie had heard about a new Indian religious movement.
- Zealots of the Ghost Shirt movement believed that soon the buffalo would return and all white men would be swallowed by the land; they also had come to believe that the special shirts they wore into battle would make them impervious to bullets.

*Chief Sitting Bull surrendered at Fort Buford, North Dakota.*

**"Steps in Building a Frontier Fort," comments of a soldier of the 11th Infantry, Fort Custer, Montana, *American Army Life*, 1877:**

I drove a mule to grind the clay to make the bricks with which the fort was built, and soldiers dug the clay, moulded the bricks and set them in the kilns, and tended the fires that burned the bricks . . . I helped to burn the lime . . . carried a hod for the plasterer . . . worked at the sawmills getting out timber from the logs brought to Fort Custer by log trains. The drivers of those log trains were soldiers. The logs were cut into timber by soldiers. The doors and the shutters were made by soldiers, and so on all down the line.

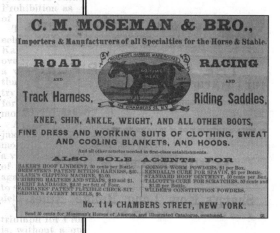

## "The Evolution of the Colored Soldier," by W. Thorton Parker, M.D., Late A. A. Surgeon, U.S. Army, *North American Review*, February 1898:

When colored troops were enrolled, soon after the close of the War of the Rebellion, the Southern states were in a chaotic condition. Troops occupied the strategic centres, and "carpet bag" politicians and adventurers swarmed into the conquered territory, their thirst for money making them willing to risk safety in order to arrive early upon the field to reap the harvest that cruel war had placed within their reach. The Negroes, freed from slavery and intoxicated with the license which they knew not how to use reasonably, were ready for almost anything except wage labor.

The war being at an end, the profession of arms, with the showy uniform and military pomp, offered them a temping experience. To recruit a colored regiment was, therefore, not a very difficult undertaking, especially when ignorance and savagery were no bar to acceptance by the recruiting officers. Hundreds of freed Negroes flocked to the recruiting stations and were quickly transformed into recruits for the U.S. colored regiments. The fiat had gone forth that the freed men were no longer to be merely enrolled as soldiers to do duty as teamsters for the quartermaster's department, but that they were to appear as soldiers, drill and do guard duty, with equal rights with the white veterans of the late war. In compliance with this idea, an expedition assembled and marched westward from Fort Leavenworth, Kansas, in the early spring of 1867, over the Santa Fe Trail, through the "Great Deserts," which were then occupied by the active and warlike Indians. Their advent astonished everyone. The frontiersmen looked upon them as a military caricature, the fruit of some political deal, unexplained and unreasonable. The officers detailed to serve with them were half ashamed to have it known. The white soldiers who came in contact with these recent slaves, now wearing their uniform of the regular army, felt insulted and injured. Their redskin adversaries heaped derision upon the Negroes by taunts and jests, loudly called them "Buffalo soldiers," and declared them "heap bad medicine" because they could not and would not scalp them. Such was the very unpromising advent of colored troops to do service as soldiers on equal terms with regular troops. . . .

- Perceptive to the ways of the world, Eddie also understood that the Ghost Shirt religion had sprung forth out of desperation.
- For months, he had been hearing stories that the once-proud Sioux, the former overlords of the Northern Plains, were starving on the reservations of North and South Dakota.
- It was well-known that many Indian agents had been stealing the majority of food supplies sent to the reservations and selling it to white travelers.
- As a result, many Indians were willing to listen intently to stories told by a Paiute Indian named Wovoka, who claimed that the ghosts would return in the spring, bringing with them the buffalo and all other game the white man had slaughtered.
- Although agents in the Pine Ridge, Rosebud, Cheyenne River, and Standing Rock reservations attempted to ignore the Ghost Dancers, thousands of Indians were now in a state of religious frenzy.
- When a new, inexperienced Indian agent at the Pine Ridge Reservation in South Dakota grew terrified of the Ghost Dancers and their threats, he desperately wired for assistance.
- Troops from the 1st, 2nd, 5th, 6th, 7th, 8th and 9th cavalry regiments, along with supporting infantry, were sent in support.

*The "Buffalo Soldiers" of company K-Troop were called out to quell the Ghost Shirt uprising.*

- The show of force was needed to calm the situation, the agent said; others saw the troop movement as the perfect opportunity to arrest aging Chief Sitting Bull, whom many blamed for the Indian tension.
- Matters only became worse when the arrest of Sitting Bull was so badly botched, the famous warrior chief was killed.
- In response, troops from the 7th Cavalry, accompanied by an artillery unit with two Hotchkiss machine guns, were called out to control a potential Indian uprising.
- When they arrived at Wounded Knee and attempted to disarm a band of Miniconjous Sioux under the leadership of Chief Big Foot, a bloodbath ensued.
- More than 200 Indian men, women and children, including Big Foot, were killed, and 26 soldiers died—many caught in the crossfire of their own men.
- The Battle of Wounded Knee, better known as a massacre, prompted both hostile and friendly Sioux factions to unite for battle near Pine Ridge—requiring the men of Eddie Rausch's K-Troop.
- More than 4,000 angry Indians had gathered.
- Eddie learned his troops were needed only after a 50-mile scouting trip through the Badlands.
- The men immediately struck camp and set out through the snowy night, arriving at Pine Ridge at 5:30 in the morning, having traveled 100 miles in a single day.
- No sooner had they dismounted when word came that the unit's supply wagons were under attack four miles away.
- The soldiers remounted, rode rapidly to the scene and dispersed the Sioux with one concentrated charge; one Buffalo soldier was lost.
- Shortly after returning to camp, word came that the exhausted K-Troop and most of the 9th Cavalry were needed once more.
- To give the men a few hours' sleep before setting out again, the 7th Cavalry was sent instead.
- While K-Troop slept, the 7th Cavalry was lured into a trap; after chasing a band of Indians caught burning a small building, they found themselves cornered in a canyon.
- The 7th Cavalry realized it was surrounded; the Indians controlled the bluffs and could fire down on the white men with impunity.
- Out of options, the 7th Cavalry took cover and hoped that reinforcements would arrive soon.

*Fort Buford was well-known as the worst assignment in the West.*

- Upon learning of their plight, the 9th Cavalry, including the Buffalo soldiers of K-Troop, was awakened and directed to the canyon, thundering into the area at 1:30 in the afternoon.
- While the Ghost Dance cult had preached that white men would be swallowed up, nothing had been said about black men.
- Uncertainty spread throughout the Sioux, with many awestruck by the sight of K-Troop.
- Quickly, the deadly Hotchkiss machine gun was set up and used to sweep the top of the canyon, after which the troops dismounted and were told to attack.
- With six officers leading 170 men, Eddie and his units ferociously charged the right canyon wall.
- A few shots were fired by the Indians, but the sight of the massed soldiers in full charge quickly scattered the Sioux.
- When the battle was won without the 9th Cavalry losing a man, the soldiers' fear before the charge was replaced with joy, pride and relief.
- The trapped soldiers of the 7th rushed from their hiding places and shamelessly hugged their rescuers.

*While pursuing the Sioux, the 7th Cavalry became trapped in a canyon.*

## "The Ghost Dance," *Chronicle of Indian Wars:*

In 1889, the [Ghost Dance] movement was suddenly revived when another Northern Paiute, Wovoka (1856-1932), was stricken with fever during a total eclipse of the sun. He recovered and reported that, during his illness, he had been transported to the afterworld, where he had seen legions of dead Indians happily at work and play, and where the Supreme Being had told him to return to his people, to tell them to love one another, to work, and to live in peace with whites. The Supreme Being promised that, if they followed these injunctions faithfully, they would be reunited with the dead, death would cease to exist, and the white race would vanish. . . .

Although Wovoka's message was explicitly specific, Teton Sioux leaders of the Pine Ridge Reservation suppressed the injunction to live peacefully and used the Ghost Dance deliberately to foment an uprising. At Pine Ridge and elsewhere, special "ghost shirts" were fashioned of white muslin and decorated with the sun, moon, stars and eagles or sage hens. The shirts, it was declared, offered protection against many dangers, especially bullets.

- Rausch was proud—very proud indeed; his first battle, and both he and his men had done well.
- That sense of pride grew when Commanding General Miles, Department of Missouri, held a parade to review all the troops involved in the Battle of Pine Ridge.
- It was thrilling for Eddie to join his soldiers, who were covered in thick coats and hats of beaver fur, riding in triumph across the snowy field for review.
- Just as his men rode by the reviewing stand, Eddie and the black troops of K-Troop, 9th Cavalry, received the ultimate compliment—General Miles raised his gloved hand in a show of respect.
- Thus was the triumph of battle.
- Having played a role in squashing the revolt gives Eddie something to think about during the long, lonely patrols that now dominate his life.

*Fort Buford was expanded numerous times to meet the needs of the Indian Wars.*

*A mule can carry up to 300 pounds of supplies.*

- Almost immediately after K-Troop's return to Fort Robinson, Major Henry began lobbying for the regiment to be transferred to Fort Myer, Virginia, for ceremonial duty—considered one of the most prestigious postings in the army.
- In April, the Secretary of War ordered Major Henry to take command at Fort Myer, and to take one troop of the 9th with him.
- Henry chose K-Troop, ordering them to prepare to embark for the nation's capital.
- Rausch could not believe his luck.
- After a hard, exhilarating winter, this duty was exactly what he needed.
- Unfortunately, as he prepared to leave with his troops, he was informed that while the black troops of K-Troop were leaving, the white officers were not.
- Second Lt. Rausch learned he was to be replaced by a cousin of the army's commanding general, who had been on recruiting duty in New York for the past two years.
- Even worse, he was to be permanently transferred to the infantry at Fort Buford—he was going back to the Dakotas.
- The change from cavalry to infantry also meant a reduction in pay from $1,500 a year to $1,400.
- So much for being a hero.
- Six months later, after endless patrols on the Great Plains watching for Indians and drinking cups of bad coffee, Eddie's greatest fear is not hostile Indians, but boredom.

## Life in the Community: Fort Buford, North Dakota

- Unwilling to cope with Indian depredations along the Bozeman Trail, the army had begun in 1866 to establish a chain of forts along the Missouri River, a major route to the newly discovered Montana gold fields.
- Fort Buford was created near the confluence of the Yellowstone and Missouri rivers, in hostile Indian territory.
- Its principal role was to protect land and river routes used by immigrants settling the West in the 1860s and 1870s.
- Shortly after construction, Fort Buford became known for having the most intolerable weather of any post in the U.S. Army.
- Its location on the plains near the Canadian border guaranteed that its summers were hot and dry, and its winters long and brutally cold; for many, a posting to Fort Buford was comparable to being sent to Siberia.
- The fort was named for Major General John Buford, a hero of the Battle of Gettysburg during the Civil War.
- Construction of the fort in the Dakota Territory was started in June 1866 under the command of Brevet Lieutenant Colonel William G. Rankin.
- By November, the finished fort consisted of a 30-foot-square stockade, enclosing log and adobe buildings constructed to house a single company garrison.
- The building of the fort and survey activities by the Northern Pacific Railway in 1871 invited attacks by the Sioux and their leader, Chief Sitting Bull, who believed that the expeditions violated the Treaty of 1868.

- By 1875, the post had been expanded numerous times to meet the growing demands of Indian retaliation, and housed six companies; new facilities often were constructed of locally made clay bricks and wood.
- That same year, the Secretary of the Interior asked the Secretary of War to force the Indians onto their respective reservations.
- This prompted the Sioux Wars of 1876-1879, in which the defeat of Gen. George Custer at the Battle of Little Big Horn occurred, as well as Sitting Bull's flight to Canada.
- Sitting Bull's trek into Canada was an attempt to maintain his independence, but a lack of natural game for hunting, and the desire of his people to be with their relatives, led him to return to the Dakota Territory.
- Thirty-five families—187 people in all—traveled with Sitting Bull in July 1881 to Fort Buford, where the Sioux chief surrendered his Winchester .44 caliber carbine to Major D. H. Brotherton, Fort Buford's commander.
- For most of the past decade, the role of the army at Fort Buford has been to protect survey and construction crews of the Great Northern Railway, prevent Indians from crossing the international boundary from Canada, and police the area against outlaws.
- Fort Buford has also been called upon to protect, from attack by the more powerful Sioux, the weaker tribes of the area: the Assiniboine, Mandan, Hidatsa and Arikira.
- Currently, it is manned by the four companies of the 25th Infantry, one of two black infantry regiments.
- Physically, the post is a collection of wooden buildings loosely grouped around a parade ground.
- With a capacity for six companies, these buildings include a large, 20-room house for the commanding officer, smaller cottages for the other married officers, barracks for the enlisted men, dining hall, kitchen, stables, hospital, magazine, storehouses and laundress quarters.
- Recently, money for maintenance has been in short supply and the buildings, although neat, look shabby.
- During the warmer months, one company of soldiers handles border duty, while a second keeps the peace between the Indian reservations and the mining camps across the Montana border—a constant and increasingly difficult problem.
- The Indians describe the long lines of infantrymen marching across the Dakota winter prairie as "walk-a-heaps" because the men's bodies, horses and long fur coats combine into one large mass.
- The long lines often include mules, the workhorses of the West.
- Packing a mule requires considerable experience, but is worth the effort; a mule, said to be the only animal Noah didn't take on the ark, can carry up to 300 pounds of supplies over rough country 30 miles a day.
- In addition to being hardier than horses, mules need less food.

# HISTORICAL SNAPSHOT
# 1890–1891

- Two-thirds of the nation's 62.9 million people still lived in rural areas, while 32.7 percent were immigrants or the children of at least one immigrant parent
- Ceresota flour was introduced by the Northwest Consolidated Milling Company
- *Literary Digest* began publication
- The population of Los Angeles reached 50,000, up 40,000 in 10 years
- The 1890 census showed that 53.5 percent of the farms in the United States comprised fewer than 100 acres
- As the demand for domestic servants grew in urban areas, women dramatically outnumbered the men emigrating from Ireland to the United States
- The Tampa Bay Hotel was completed at a cost of $3 million
- The first commercial dry cell battery was invented
- Only three percent of Americans, aged 18 to 21, attended college
- The nation's first full-service advertising agency was established in Florida
- "American Express Travelers Cheques" was copyrighted
- Thousands of Kansas farmers were bankrupted by the tight money conditions
- Restrictive "Jim Crow" laws were being enacted throughout the South
- The first electric oven for commercial sale was introduced in St. Paul, Minnesota
- America claimed 4,000 millionaires

## Monthly Pay of Army Enlisted Men in Active Service, 1890:

| Company Grade | First Year | Fifth Year |
|---|---|---|
| Private (Artillery, Cavalry and Infantry) | $13 | $16 |
| Private, Second Class (Engineers and Ordnance | 13 | 16 |
| Musician (Engineers, Artillery and Infantry) | 13 | 16 |
| Trumpeter (Cavalry) | 13 | 16 |
| Wagoner | 14 | 14 |
| Artificer | 15 | 15 |
| Corporal (Artillery, Cavalry and Infantry) | 15 | 18 |
| Blacksmith and Furrier | 15 | 18 |
| Saddler (Cavalry) | 15 | 18 |
| Sergeant (Artillery, Cavalry and Infantry) | 17 | 20 |
| Private, First Class (Engineers and Ordnance) | 17 | 20 |
| Corporal (Engineers and Ordnance) | 20 | 23 |
| First Sergeant (Artillery, Cavalry with Infantry) | 22 | 25 |
| Sergeant (Engineers, Ordnance and Signal Corps) | 34 | 37 |
| Sergeants, First Class (Signal Corps) | 45 | 48 |

"We're on the trail of Sitting Bull, And this is the way we go— Forty miles a day on beans and hay In the Regular Army, oh!"
—Dakota Marching Song

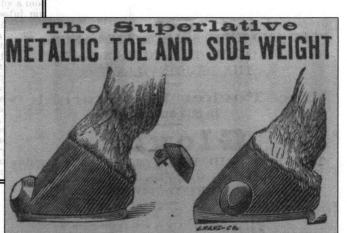

## "How Cartridges Are Made," *Harper's Weekly*, January 24, 1891:

In no other branch of industry are more ingenuity and human skill employed than in the making of instruments and materials to take life. The Patent Office is full of models of firearms and devices for the speedy changing of men from tall to long, and the number is being increased from day to day. The inventive genius of America, upon which the optimistic of coast defense rely for the protection of American ports from foreign foes in case of sudden war, is not idle. It is always busy, and just as ready to sell its product to the foreign foe as to anybody else.

If any foreign power harbored a secret design to make war upon the United States next year, it could contract today with the great rifle and ammunition manufacturers of this country for weapons and cartridges enough to equip all its soldiers and leave the United States unarmed, except with a lot of heavy, clumsy, single-shot rifles and a few tons of spoiled ammunition.

In the matter of weapons, this country would be at a great disadvantage if called upon to engage in conflict with a European power, because the machinery and tools for turning out rifles of a new model cannot be made in a day, but it would not take the great cartridge factories long to fill the belts of the largest army that was ever mustered.

The most extensive plant for the making of cartridges is in Bridgeport, Connecticut, and its capacity is two million cartridges of all kinds per day. The machinery adapted to military ammunition of the pattern now in use can turn out 750,000 loaded shells in a working day, certainly enough to carry on any ordinary single engagement.

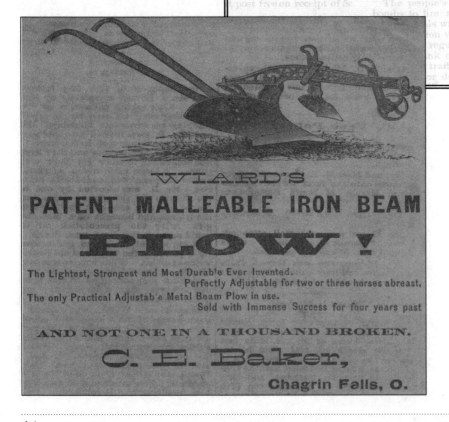

WIARD'S
PATENT MALLEABLE IRON BEAM
PLOW!

The Lightest, Strongest and Most Durable Ever Invented.
Perfectly Adjustable for two or three horses abreast.
The only Practical Adjustable Metal Beam Plow in use.
Sold with Immense Success for four years past

AND NOT ONE IN A THOUSAND BROKEN.

C. E. Baker,
Chagrin Falls, O.

PALMER'S COCOA CREAM!

Promotes Growth of the Human Hair.
Keeps the Head Free From Dandruff.
Stops Falling Hair, Thus Preventing Premature Baldness
Best and Cheapest Hair Dressing in the Market.

Prepared by
E. A. PALMER & BRO.

### Yearly and Monthly Pay of Army Officers in Active Service, 1890:

| Grade | Yearly | Monthly | "After 10 Years of Service" |
|---|---|---|---|
| Major General | $7,500 | $625 | $0 |
| Brigadier General | 5,500 | 458 | 0 |
| Colonel | 3,500 | 291 | 350 |
| Lieutenant Colonel | 3,000 | 250 | 300 |
| Major | 2,500 | 208 | 250 |
| Captain, Mounted | 2,000 | 166 | 200 |
| Captain, Not Mounted | 1,800 | 150 | 180 |
| Regimental Adjutant | 1,800 | 150 | 180 |
| Regimental Quartermaster | 1,800 | 150 | 180 |
| First Lieutenant, Mounted | 1,600 | 133 | 160 |
| First Lieutenant, Not Mounted | 1,500 | 125 | 150 |
| Second Lieutenant, Mounted | 1,500 | 125 | 150 |
| Second Lieutenant, Not Mounted | 1,400 | 116 | 140 |
| Chaplain | 1,500 | 125 | 150 |

## "How We Live at a Frontier Fort," by Maria Brace Kimball, *The Outlook*, February 5, 1898:

The soldier's day begins at sunrise. As the light breaks through the pines on the eastern horizon, the deep vibrations of the morning gun are followed by the lively march of Reveille. That half-heard, ghostly music always stirs me with awe at the thought of another day begun, and with pleasure in the lingering dream that keeps back the actualities of the day. . . .

Work in the frontier post includes all the trades from sawing of logs to mending of shoes, for the soldier is no specialist, but an all-round character, who must dig and plant, cook and scrub, as well as ride, shoot and saber. . . .

From Reveille to Retreat the day is occupied with saber practice, gymnastics and horse exercise in winter, with drills, sham battles and target practice in summer. The leisure hours of the enlisted men are also well provided for. Outdoors, he has football and baseball, hunting and fishing. Indoors, he has a reading room and library as well as concerts and balls.

In the Officers' Row the days are not less busy than in the barracks opposite. Though the average military man is not deeply interested in general literature, upon his own subjects he is well-read. He often studies, too, topics related to the comparatively unknown regions of our country which he inhabits, and becomes an expert in natural history, archaeology and Indian folklore. The officer's wife also has tactics to master in this land of no shops, no markets, no dressmakers. The daily meals require careful foresight when butter and eggs must be bought in Kansas, vegetables and fruit in California. The Thanksgiving turkey and celery and cranberries are bespoken by letter before the president has issued his proclamation. Baby's dolls and toys are ordered from catalogues two months before Christmas. The sewing is done by the mother's skillful fingers, aided by patterns and fashion plates. With all these industries she finds time to play the piano, to read, to visit and to teach the children their earliest lessons.

In the clubroom, tales of stirring Indian campaigns are told and retold by the veterans; surely those who have made the peace of the Plains should be permitted to fight their battles o'er again in the quiet of the garrison. These heroes of our Indian wars form a naïve and unworldly type—that of an American who is unruffled by the cares of the voter, the competition of the trades, or the rivalries of civil professions. . . .

Public opinion in America frowns upon the professional soldier. The man of books regards him as a medieval heguman, born out of his time; the man of affairs looks upon him as an accessory of government, useful on occasion, yet a costly and troublesome piece of machinery. A strong military power is popularly considered a menace to liberty and free institutions. A standing army, on the contrary, fosters that military spirit which tends not to destroy, but to uphold and protect government.

# 1898 Profile

## The Spanish-American War: Tampa

### Civilian

For 66-year-old Jerome Arbutney, the decision of the U.S. Army to launch its invasion against Cuba from his beloved city of Tampa, Florida, during the Spanish-American War was both a dream-come-true and a nightmare.

### Life at Home

- The past two months have been the longest of this aging man's life.
- Since the beginning of the year, businessman Jerome Arbutney has been attempting to use his political clout in support of a war against Spain—and to help his beloved Tampa, Florida.
- In telegram after telegram to his congressman and the Secretary of War, Arbutney has asserted that chasing Spain from the Caribbean will not only make the United States more secure, but also allow American companies to establish highly profitable trade opportunities with Cuba.
- Now that Spain has viciously and deliberately started a war through the sinking of the battleship *Maine,* the best way to launch an invasion of Spanish-held Cuba is through Port Tampa.
- Jerome knows a lot about trade and making money; thanks to an extensive line of steamships, he is a major importer and exporter of goods to and from Cuba.
- In addition, as he has written repeatedly in his letters, Port Tampa would be the logical place for America to launch its invasion on the Spanish.
- He should know; he owns the only rail line linking the city of Tampa with its busy port.

*Jerome Arbutney lobbied hard for Tampa to play a role in the Spanish-American War.*

*Within 45 days, 20,000 troops arrived in Tampa.*

- Now that Washington has recognized Jerome's wisdom and selected Tampa from which to dispatch the troops, much work must be done.
- The sinking of the *Maine* took place on February 15, 1898, and launched the Spanish-American War; although the explosion was of unknown origin, Americans insisted the Spanish were responsible.
- The United States, however, was unprepared for war, and an army had to be raised, war taxes created, plans drawn up, and many decisions made.
- On numerous occasions, President William McKinley has emphasized that there is a "humanitarian object to be obtained."
- According to press reports, McKinley is concerned that the condition of the starving masses in Cuba "undoubtedly has been aggravated by the outbreak of hostilities."
- It took nearly two months for Tampa to be chosen as the supply base for operations

### "Evangelists Going to Cuba," *The New York Times,* May 16, 1898:

When the United States troops at Tampa embark for Cuba, they may be followed soon after by some of the famous evangelists in the United States. Gen. O. O. Howard, retired, now an evangelist, arrived at Tampa today, accompanied by Major D. W. Whipple.

A movement was recently inaugurated by D. D. Moody, having for its object the sending of noted speakers to the various rendezvous of the soldiers, and to hold meetings for their spiritual instruction. Gen. Howard and Major Whipple have visited Chickamauga, Atlanta and Mobile. As most of the regiments are without chaplains, the sending to Cuba of several noted divines to work among the soldiers is contemplated.

It is hardly probable that they will accompany the soldiers when the expedition moves out, but once the army is settled in Cuba and the campaign against the Spanish forces is fairly on, the evangelical work will be actively begun. Gen. Howard and Major Whipple spoke at the Tampa Heights Camp Grounds tonight.

in Cuba and one of the principal mobilization points for U.S. troops.

- Then, within 45 days, 20,000 troops were shipped into the community and stationed in seven camps in and around Tampa, plunging the city, Jerome's business, and his life into turmoil.

- Some local merchants made a fortune in sales to the army, while others struggled to get any supplies at all to sell.

- Jerome was prepared; in addition to charging the military for the use of his rails and steamships, one of his smaller companies was asked to supply food—particularly fish—to the army.

- He was also the principal supplier of fresh water.

## Life at Work

- Port Tampa, where supplies arrived and troops departed, is situated at the end of a narrow, nine-mile-long peninsula, and connected to Tampa by a single wagon road and a railroad line.

*Troops prepared meals, marched and coped with Florida's heat while they waited to ship out.*

## "Hot Weather at Tampa, Soldiers Suffering in the Sun and Daily Drills Are Cut Short, Military Fever Also Burns," *The New York Times*, May 25, 1898:

Despite the fact that sunstroke is unknown under the fierce blaze of the tropical sun in this part of Florida, many of the unseasoned volunteers are suffering discomforts from excessive heat and the piercing glare of the sand. One walks here between two fires. From the cloudless sky the sun pours a flood of light as brilliant and burning as molten brass, and from the waste of sand, white and gleaming, comes a heating glare as dazzling as if each grain of sand were a refracting mirror. The skin tingles and burns in this double heat, and the brain becomes dazed.

To the young volunteers from the Northern states, the heat and glare are a severe trial. They have never before experienced such powerful sunlight, and many of them have come here from places where the snow was still lingering in the valleys and on the sides of the hills. To withstand the effects of such a sudden change from snow to fire, one must have what few of these young volunteers have, an iron frame. Even the troops from

this state, accustomed to exposure in such sun, are affected by the intense heat, and the hardened soldiers, who have been seasoned by years of baking and broiling in the alkali deserts, suffer from exhaustion. The glare pains the eyes also, and produces headache and soreness of the lids, until one is driven to the awful refuge of smoked glasses.

There have been no fatal results from the heat, however, and the officers are now looking with keen solicitude after the comfort and health of the troops. The hours of drilling have been shortened, from three and four a day to an hour and a half, and all exercises are confined to the early morning or late afternoon. For the rest of the day, lounging or sleeping in the tents, and for the night, freedom to roam over the little city and explore its half-dozen points of interest; a turn about the big hotel and its flower-burdened grounds; a glance at the queer mixture of fashionable and martial life that war has thrown together here in its crucible—and then more lounging and sleep under the white tents.

- Shortly after Tampa was selected as the army's point of embarkation, several thousand railway cars were sent south, only to be caught in a massive traffic jam extending up the East Coast, more than 500 miles; supply trains as far away as Columbia, South Carolina, were unable to leave their stations because of the backup.
- No single authority was in charge of coordinating supplies, troops and equipment as America mobilized for war against Spain.
- Worse, no system for loading and unloading supplies in Tampa had been established by the military, so that dozens of individual military units spent entire days searching for supplies, and loading and unloading boxes from the railway cars whenever they spotted materials they needed.
- Some supplies were unloaded the day they arrived, only to be unclaimed or pilfered, while railcars—including some carrying food—were sidetracked for weeks in the hot Florida sun.
- Major General Nelson Miles complained, "There were over 300 [box]cars loaded with war materiel along the [rail]roads about Tampa . . . . Fifteen cars loaded with uniforms were sidetracked 25 miles away from Tampa."
- Five thousand rifles were missing, while the ammunition for them had been found scattered among dozens of cars on the sidetracks of the railroads.
- The quartermaster general in Washington thought it unnecessary to label the railcars in advance.
- Entire regiments were then assigned the task of guarding the supplies that did arrive.
- In late April, the national media predicted the immediate invasion of Cuba; when June arrived, the pressure was building.
- Unfortunately, the hastily organized embarkation suffered a variety of other problems: Several of the volunteer regiments arrived without uniforms, while others came without weapons, blankets, tents or camp equipment.
- In addition, thousands of wives, girlfriends and mothers of newly inducted soldiers showed unrelenting enthusiasm and skill at making the trip to Tampa to see their men off.
- Some women, who had the money to pay for a first-class ticket, found they had priority over troop trains, supply shipments and other war materials.
- Women were not the only camp followers in the city.
- To control the thieves and cutthroats flooding Tampa, Jerome and other businessmen hired teams of men—mostly from the docks—to patrol the streets and "encourage" the riff-raff to leave the city immediately.

*No single authority was in charge of coordinating troops or supplies as America mobilized for war.*

- Since Jerome's rail line was the only one running from Tampa to Port Tampa, he repeatedly stated that he should decide what boxcars moved and when, but the army disagreed.
- Although Jerome was still angry at the military for threatening to take control of the railway unless he stepped aside, he worked hard to be a good host to the military, staging an elaborate gala at the grand Tampa Bay Hotel shortly after the troops arrived.
- The 511-room Moorish-style structure, which cost $2.5 million to build and $500,000 to furnish, became the perfect setting for entertaining, since all of the general officers were already lodged there.
- In fact, so many officers attended the event, it was deemed the largest assembly of regular army officers since the end of the Civil War in 1865.
- News reports also claimed the gathering included representatives of every West Point class since 1850.
- The parties were magnets for the plethora of colonels produced by the volunteer armies.
- Overnight, according to press reports, everyday businessmen were instantly "transmuted by a gubernatorial word into colonels—nothing less than colonels."
- As a result, the city was overrun with stars, bars and epaulets—all bestowed on the wearers without their ever firing a rifle or learning a single military maneuver.
- The hotel was also the temporary home of war correspondents, including Steven Crane and Richard Harding Davis, military attachés of foreign powers, and luminaries such as Clara Barton of the American Red Cross.
- All the while, officials in Washington were growing anxious, knowing the U.S. Navy's blockade of Santiago Harbor could not last forever.

## "Breaking Camp at Tampa, Great Confusion Follows the Orders for the Troops to Board the Transports. Roads and Railways Blocked. Chaotic Scenes All the Way from Camp to Dock," *The New York Times*, June 14, 1898:

After nearly two months of somewhat theatric bustle and noise, and the movement of troops hither and thither, and after a dozen orders from Washington and elsewhere to be ready to start at once, which orders were countermanded as rapidly as they were made, the army of invasion has got itself into a fleet of transports and has moved a few feet out into the bay.

The troops had been concentrated at Tampa for weeks. Their white tents lay like a pigmy city, squat amid the glaring sand waste. The heat and the labor of drilling in the soft sand were enervating them, and their spirits were sinking under the depressing toll and heat and mysterious delay. Were they getting ready? Were those who have charge of the army preparing it for the campaign, and for the kind of campaign it was expected to conduct? A single night revealed the true condition of affairs to the army itself, to the government, and to the enemy.

Tuesday, there was in the air that unnamed feeling that something was to be done or attempted soon. Before night, troops were moving. They knew not where or why, but instantly everyone was convinced that the long-expected advance on Cuba had begun. Later there was a general rush for Port Tampa and the transports. The army was certainly on the march.

### A Scene of Confusion

At once there was indescribable confusion. It was not the mere stir and bustle that must accompany even the most exact movements of an army, and which may readily be mistaken for confusion. It was confusion, unmistakable confusion.

There is one railway and one wagon road between Tampa and Port Tampa. The distance is short, not more than nine miles; but they are nine miles of sand, and the wagons sink a foot and more in the clogging white powder that has been ground beneath wheels and hoofs for weeks. The railway was blocked despite the fact that only military trains were run. Cars filled with soldiers or supplies, ammunition, and guns, stood on every sidetrack, and it was almost impossible to get even an engine through the confused mass. Trains fared worse, and only a few troops got through, although it had been estimated that at least 2,500 could be carried to the port every hour. In this emergency the sand road was used by the soldiers and by the wagon and pack trains. It was soon blocked as tight as the railway, and the nine miles lengthened to as many leagues. Wagons broke down under their heavy loads in the deep sandbeds; jaded horses and worn-out pack-mules stumbled on and on and fell by the roadside, in the way of the tolling rear. The port that seemed so near at sunset seemed as far away as the pole before midnight.

The army had been suddenly set to a task that it had not prepared for and could not perform. It began the inevitable abandonment of all impediments. The first thing to be left behind was the recruit; the next was the untrained volunteer. Then the larger tents were abandoned, and only the shelter tent was allowed the soldier. The recruit and the untrained volunteer were left to the enjoyment of the big tents and the spreading sand wastes and the drill sergeant. Rations were limited to the 14 days' regular and 10 days' travel ration;

## "Breaking Camp . . ." *(continued)*

and officers' baggage was cut down from 250 to 80 pounds. Even the horses of the officers were left, and only six were allowed to each regiment. The larger part of the cavalry was dismounted, and even the "Rough Riders" of Theodore Roosevelt—inglorious without their steeds—were ordered to go to the front on foot. Lt. Col. Roosevelt said, very gallantly, that he would gladly go to the front if he had to go on "all fours."

With all this cutting down and stripping, the army was immobile. It was apparently without sufficient guidance at this critical moment, just as it had been for weeks, apparently without a supreme head that could direct and provide. Even the regular army, so small that one would be justified in believing that it could have been handled as readily and as effectively as a missile weapon, was found to be cumbersome. It had not been supplied with light clothing, and the soldiers sweltered in their heavy winter uniforms. They had not sufficient wagon transportation and, consequently, the drivers were overworked and wearied out. Midnight Tuesday I found hundreds of them, heavy with fatigue, lying in the sand by the side of their wagons. The mules stood panting in their traces. In spite of the hurry and fever of preparation, only a few troops had reached the transports by daylight. The order had been issued that all should be ready to sail before sunrise.

*The cavalry kept fit riding through the Florida forests.*

*Loading the 35 transport ships was chaotic.*

## "Scenes in the City of Tampa," by W. J. Rouse, *The New York Times Illustrated Magazine*, May 15, 1898:

Dwellers in Northern cities at this time of excitement on the Southern coast have little or no idea of the excitement that prevails in the Florida cities, and particularly in those that are centres of military operations.

What a huge thing the army is when it is brought together, yet how small is it when compared to the standing army of other nations! The vast expanse of ground covered by the camps, the limitless number of horses, wagons and men needed to move an army, or even a regiment, can better be described by photographs than by mere words. To a civilian who has never been in an army camp, the bivouac of four or five regiments looks as if countless thousands of soldiers were quartered there. To the experienced eye of the general, however, the smallness of the real force and the magnitude of paraphernalia necessary to its use are more readily apparent.

In Tampa, in Port Tampa, and in Port Tampa City, during the last two or three weeks, everything has been of warlike character. Throngs of people surround the headquarters of the officers, eager for any item or atom of news that may be overheard or dropped. At the newspaper offices other crowds gather to discuss the meager bulletins set forth on glaring sheets of colored paper. Other crowds content themselves with reading

telegrams pasted in a frame, which was once a deck skylight of the lamented battleship *Maine*. Dark scowls lurk upon the faces of American men as Spanish is heard spoken all around them. Whether by Cuban or Spanish refugee, even the musical language is hated. A mere suspicion that a man may be a Spanish spy would be enough to cause his life to end suddenly here, for this is a cosmopolitan city, where men of all classes meet, and where only one political or national feeling is permitted to exist—a love for the Stars and Stripes . . . .

The city of Tampa proper has a population of about 5,000 souls. It is the centre of the cigar manufacturing industry, which has been constantly moving from Key West for several years. It is poor in architecture, poor in population, and worse as regards streets and highways than any city I have yet seen. It is impossible to drive half a mile out of town in a carriage. The wheels will simply mire in the soft, white sea sand. It is almost unlighted at night, and its business houses, with only a few notable exceptions, are far below what one would expect to see in a city of its size.

There are two military camps, one on the "heights," where none but infantry are encamped, and the camp on Picnic Island, at the very shores of Tampa Bay, nine miles from the town. There are quartered all the light batteries of artillery in the army, one or two entire regiments of cavalry, and several regiments of infantry . . . . They have far the advantage of the soldiers on the "heights," for they have the finest bathing facilities imaginable and, of course, take the fullest advantage of them. In the artillery camp, which is nearest the railroad tracks, long lines of frowning, slim-bodied rifles gleam in the sunlight, or in the late afternoon cast wavering shadows athwart the forms of lounging men, whose faces, lighted now and again by the wavy scintillations of the rippling water, show tanned and bronzed from service on the frontier and exposure on the sandy plains of Florida. They are a grim, Herculean lot of men, who have seen service and who are in love with their vocation . . . .

## "Scenes in the City . . ." *(continued)*

At the farther side of this encampment from the tracks is a row of single tents, in which Col. Randolph and his staff have their temporary homes. The side walls are elevated to allow the cool breeze from the bay to play through, and everything is as neat and in perfect order as in the quarters of an officer in one of the permanent garrisons. A little table, improvised from a box lid, a camp cot with its army bedding, a stand, a folding table, a water basin set on three tent pegs to form a stand, a folding table, a candle stuck in a bottle,

a sabre, an old service blouse, and a spare campaign hat complete his furnishings. . . .

Still farther from the railroad tracks lies the cavalry camp. Its duty is more diversified than that of the artillery, for theirs is a more active arm of the service. Their drills have a continuous dash and vim seen nowhere else. If one is fortunate enough to be in camp when an inspecting officer comes around, he will see an entire regiment turn out, in heavy marching order, with everything on the man and horse that is to be carried when the cavalry take the field. The vastness of an army of cavalry is then apparent. Over the broad, sandy beach for almost a mile, they spread and stand at attention until the inspection is finished. Then, with a dash and a jump, they wheel by troops and gallop off to camp, glad that the necessary trial is over. The little groups around the mess tents, the cooking outfits, the conical wall tents of the men, their songs, their jokes with each other, their sports and pastimes, their clowns, their acrobats and their story tellers—all these have a place in the camp and are a part of it. . . .

When off duty, the enlisted man, no matter what arm of the service he be in, fraternizes with his friends in other branches, and goes to town with them for a good time. With the call to arms widely wished for, the stentorian cries of "On to Cuba" mingled with "Remember the *Maine*" echo through the streets.

- The troops needed to be in Cuba, not Tampa.
- Then, almost without warning, on June 13, Army Commander Miles issued orders for the hot, tired men to board the troop ships—the invasion was about to begin.
- Because of the limited number of ships available, volunteers, horses and many supplies had to be left behind.
- In all, 35 transports carrying 20,000 men left for Cuba, along with 14 warships, which served as escorts.

- Overnight, Tampa became a veritable ghost town.
- For Jerome, it was time to slow down, count his money and get ready for the annual invasion of tourists—up to 35,000—who would soon be heading South.

## Life in the Community: Tampa, Florida

- A native of Hartford, Connecticut, Jerome Arbutney moved to Tampa in 1884 to seek his fortune.
- When he arrived in Florida's west coast community on the Gulf of Mexico, the town boasted of having 800 people.
- Since then, despite record low temperatures in 1886, an outbreak of yellow fever in 1887, and the disastrous freeze of 1895, Florida, Tampa, and Arbutney have prospered.
- Today, 14 years later, Tampa has a population of 26,000.
- The state of Florida comprises 400,000 people, 80 percent of whom live outside the cities and towns.
- The growth was driven by several major industries: phosphate processing, used in fertilizer; tourism during the months of January, February and March; and the evolution of Tampa as a center of U.S. cigar-making.
- River pebble phosphate was first discovered in 1888 along the Peace River south of Tampa, and within a few years was a major export product, thanks to many, including Jerome.
- Jerome has benefited dramatically from all of these developments; every day, his steamships carry phosphate to Eastern markets, while regularly running tobacco from Cuba to Tampa's cigar-making community in Ybor City.
- Since the 1880s, the cigar industry has shifted from Key West to Tampa, whose workers came from Cuba, Italy and Greece.
- Tampa's role in cigar production has been so significant, José Marti, the George Washington of Cuba, visited several times before his death in 1895.

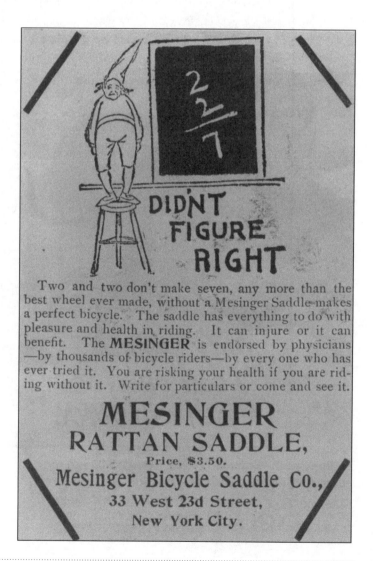

Two and two don't make seven, any more than the best wheel ever made, without a Mesinger Saddle makes a perfect bicycle. The saddle has everything to do with pleasure and health in riding. It can injure or it can benefit. The **MESINGER** is endorsed by physicians—by thousands of bicycle riders—by every one who has ever tried it. You are risking your health if you are riding without it. Write for particulars or come and see it.

**MESINGER RATTAN SADDLE,**
Price, $3.50.
**Mesinger Bicycle Saddle Co.,**
33 West 23d Street,
New York City.

## HISTORICAL SNAPSHOT
# 1898

- The production of motorcars reached 1,000 per year
- The song "Happy Birthday to You," originally composed by sisters Mildred and Patty Hill in 1893 as "Good Morning to All," was coming into common use
- The "grandfather clause" marched across the South, ushering in widespread use of Jim Crow laws and restricting most blacks from voting
- Pepsi-Cola was introduced in New Bern, North Carolina, by pharmacist Caleb Bradham
- J.P. Stevens & Company was founded in New York
- Toothpaste in collapsible metal tubes was now available, thanks to the work of Connecticut dentist Lucius Sheffield
- The trolley replaced horsedrawn cars in Boston
- Wesson Oil was introduced
- The boll weevil began spreading across cotton-growing areas of the South
- *The New York Times* dropped its price from $0.03 to $0.01, tripling circulation
- The Union Carbide Company was formed
- Uneeda Biscuit was created
- Bricklayers made $3.41 per day and worked a 48-hour week, while marble cutters made $4.22 per day
- The creation in 1892 of the crown bottle cap was hailed as being responsible for extending the shelf life of beer
- America boasted more than 300 bicycle manufacturing companies
- Cellophane was invented by Charles F. Cross and Edward J. Bevan

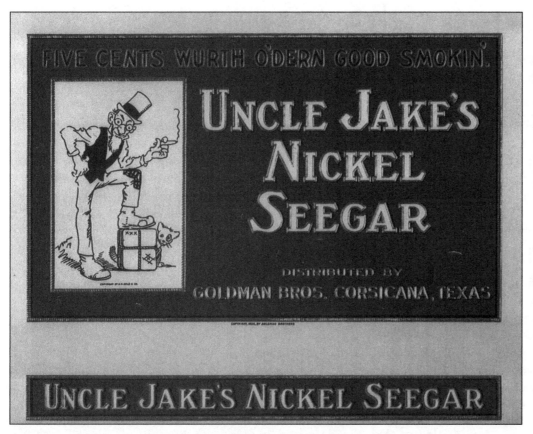

UNCLE JAKE'S NICKEL SEEGAR

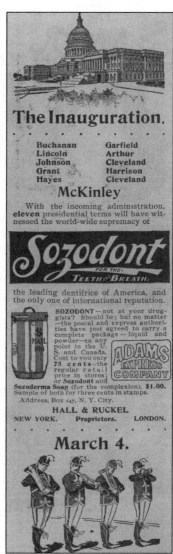
## "East Side Saloon Men Protest, Talk of Fighting the Brewers' Position on the Beer Tax," *New York Tribune*, July 1, 1898:

A lively meeting of the members of the East Side Liquor Dealers' Association was held yesterday in Liberty Hall, No. 257 East Houston Street. The association was formed last Monday, and its primary object is to fight the beer brewers in the stand which the latter have taken in relation to the war tax on beer. Speeches were made in English and German, and it was stated that the East Side saloonkeepers would suffer more from being compelled by the brewers to pay all the war tax of $1 a barrel on beer than their brethren in more favored sections of the city because they have to give big schooners and pints. They also have to compete with many cheap places where beer is sold for $0.03 a glass. The fact that the brewers charged the whole of the $1 tax on the saloonkeepers, when the government allows a rebate to the brewers of $0.07 for leakage, was also brought out . . . .

An Irishman, who was one of the speakers, advised his hearers to shorten their pints. He declared that a good way to measure a pint was to turn on the spigot and let it run until the dealer counted eight. He acknowledged that many of his customers objected to his new method of measuring, but he said he told them if they did not like it, to drink ice water.

## Letter to the Editor: "Troops with Springfield Rifles, Reasons Why They Are Put at a Disadvantage with Obsolete Weapons and Powder," *New York Tribune*, July 1, 1898:

Sir: As a regular subscriber to our valued journal, I trust you will spare me space for a few remarks relative to a subject which I look upon as of the utmost importance to us at the present time. I refer to a statement said to emanate from the War Department, and relating to small arms for our volunteer forces. The statement is that "the question of the armament of the troops with proper rifles cannot be discussed."

If this decision is final, it means sending our boys into action armed with the Springfield rifle, an obsolete weapon, and far inferior in every respect to that with which our foe is supplied. The Spanish regular arm is the Mauser magazine small-bore rifle, using smokeless powder ammunition, and having a range vastly superior to the Springfield, which is a single-shot rifle, using black

powder, giving slow velocity and high trajectory. Our men will be subject to annihilation by an enemy they cannot see, and owing to the absence of smoke, could not even approximately locate, while each puff from the Springfield would betray the shooter and be a well-defined target for concentrated fire, almost inevitably resulting in a casualty on our side.

This would be a severe test, even for veterans, one to which our boys should never be subjected, and I feel sure your attention has only to be called to the matter in order that it may receive a thorough ventilation, which will compel a reconsideration.

I ask your aid in the interest of those who have friends and relatives in the ranks, and also in the interest of the boys themselves, who, as volunteers, form the bulk of our forces, and upon whom the success of our arms will largely depend.

—F.A. Ilion, New York

Answer: The reasons the War Department is arming the volunteer forces with Springfield rifles are:

First—It was the only rifle of which the government had any considerable stock on hand.

Second—It was the only rifle with which the volunteers, largely drawn from the national guard, were familiar.

Third—The adoption of any other rifle would have required many months in which to furnish it to the volunteer forces.

# 1898 Profile

# The Spanish-American War: Cuba

### Enlisted Seaman

When the battleship *Oregon* roared into the Battle of Santiago in Cuba, Leo Knep and his team in the engine room were among the heroes.

### Life at Home

- For weeks, Leo Knep had heard conflicting messages about where the superfast battleship *Oregon* might be assigned; first, he heard the Philippines alongside Admiral Dewey, then it was Cuba in support of the battleship *Maine,* and then he heard it was needed just where it was—the Pacific Coast.
- Before he signed on with the *Oregon,* Leo had little interest in the tiny island of Cuba, off the tip of Florida, and had never heard of the Philippines.
- Like most Americans, he figured that the various revolts and revolutions during the past three decades were Spain's problem; if Spain wanted to have a colony, she could have the troubles, too.
- Besides, what could the Americans do?
- After all, when the Cuban revolutionaries won a decisive victory at the Battle of Bayamos in 1895, the Spanish brutally crushed the revolt.
- Then came the explosion and sinking of the U.S. battleship *Maine,* destroyed in Havana Harbor at 9:40 p.m., February 15, 1898.
- Now, it was personal.
- The *Maine* was located in the Cuban harbor at the request of the United States consul general in Havana, Gen. Fitzhugh Lee, a former Confederate officer and nephew of Robert E. Lee.
- President William McKinley had ordered the *Maine* to sail into Cuban waters on a friendly visit after the New York newspapers gave great play to Spanish oppression on the island.

*Leo Knep's view of the Battle of Santiago was from below decks.*

### "Bicycle 'Scorchers' Unfit Soldiers, Fast Riding Said to Enlarge the Heart and So Weaken It," *New York Tribune,* July 1, 1898:

Chicago, June 30—Dr. S. C. Stanton, who has charge of the examination of recruits for the regular army in this city, has caused a sensation among medical men by declaring that a habitual fast rider of bicycles, or a "scorcher," is unfit physically to serve as a soldier in the army.

He has made this matter the subject of his severest tests in his examination of applicants for enlistments, and many men have been rejected because of a "bicycle heart," as the surgeon terms it, caused by excessive exercise in riding a wheel. The doctor says: "Persistent scorching or fast riding has a tendency to enlarge the heart, and thus interfere with its proper action. Few enthusiastic bicyclists can resist the temptation to scorch, and as a consequence the physician believes that the hearts of a large portion of this class of riders are more or less affected. This being the case, they would be unable to endure the hardships that army life imposes, and should not be permitted to enter the service. The excitement with which war is also attended would be deleterious to those whose hearts are in any degree affected.

• When a tremendous blast below decks took the warship and her 266 men to the bottom of the harbor, opinion was divided on the cause—between an internal explosion or a Spanish mine.

• The *New York World* and *New York Journal* believed the cause was Spanish trickery and shrieked for war; Congress immediately passed a passel of new taxes to fund the military effort, including a new tax on beer.

• Leo was ready to fight the Spaniards, even if he never fired a gun.

## "The Colonies of Other Powers," *New York Tribune,* July 3, 1898:

If England, with more than 85 times as much colony as motherland, is easily the principal colonist in the world, Germany, with rapid strides, is preparing to be a good second. At present, the colonial possessions of England are 16,662,000 square miles, with a colonial population of 322 million. France comes next with 2,050,000 square miles and 44,290,000 population. Germany is third, having only recently entered upon a career of colonization. In a short time she has acquired 1,615,577 square miles of colony, containing a population of 7.4 million. The official statement issued recently by the State Department shows that only Great Britain, France, Holland and Portugal have more inhabitants in their colonial possessions and protectorates than there are at home. Spain has sunk from first to sixth power in extent of colonies, though she is fifth in population of colonies. Insignificant Portugal, once incorporated with Spain, has nearly double the territorial extent of colonies. The same remark is true of Holland. The present war is likely to wipe out entirely the colonial system of the Spanish nation.

The Spanish-American War, like its immediate predecessor, the Chino-Japanese War, doubtless revolutionizes the Eastern question. No longer do we hear of Turkey and the Danube. It is a matter of the conquest of the Philippines, the partition of China, the probable absorption of Korea, that perplexes Cabinets. A new power arises, "like a glory from afar," and may take part in the adjustment of commerce and territory in the Orient. The new power is not Japan, but the United States.

- As the number-one fireman, he is the king of the engine room, responsible for filling the boilers with coal so that his ship can cut through the waters with ease.
- He is proud that the engine room is forbidden ground to all except those working there.
- Everyone understands that speed is the result of ceaseless vigilance, and that horsepower spells fame and victory.

*Leo Knep grew up in the timbering towns of Washington.*

- He also enjoys the work, even though it can be backbreaking, dirty and hot.
- The splintering silver of the electric lamp cones illuminates some spaces, leaving other sections of the engine room deep in shadow.
- He loves to watch the men work; it's just like the teamwork required to harvest trees in the forests of Washington, where he grew up.
- Knowing that an assignment was imminent, he took his wife and family to his home in Ernest, Washington, where his mother could help look after the two girls.
- No one knew how long he would be away, but they did know there was always a chance he wouldn't come back; the men of the battleship *Maine* had had families, too.

  - Before shipping out, Leo found a gift for his two girls at a bar near the harbor—a jolly paper doll with "Daddy Drinks" written on the front of his pants.
  - His daughters loved it, but his wife was less enthusiastic.
  - Leo fell in love with his wife, a San Francisco orphan, because of her sense of fashion; she always looks great.
  - After a childhood tramping through woods harvesting trees, discovering a graceful, stylish woman who was interested in him was beyond his wildest dreams.

*Leo fell in love with his wife because of her sense of fashion.*

## Life at Work

- When Captain Charles E. Clark received last-minute orders to command the battleship *Oregon,* he had only 48 hours to learn the capacity of the most up-to-date and powerful battleship in the U.S. Navy.
- Completed in 1893, the West Coast battleship, capable of 15 sustained knots of speed, was needed in the war effort.
- The explosion aboard the battleship *Maine* made the *Oregon*'s presence on the East Coast essential, despite the risks of a long voyage from California, past the tip of South America and back up to the Caribbean—all at top speed.
- When the ship left Bremerton, Washington, Leo was not told whether they were heading to Cuba or to the Philippines.
- It didn't matter; he had little time to pen a note to his wife and girls.
- His crew toiled for almost 48 hours straight before the ship left to bring 1,600 tons of coal on board, while others loaded 500 tons of ammunition and enough supplies, or stores, for six months at sea.
- Only later did he learn that his wife and children had been aware of his every move—almost daily.
- With war fever high and newspapers competing for circulation, an anxious nation was able to follow—via sketchy telegrams published in the various papers—as the *Oregon* sped down one side of the continent and up the other to join the fight in Cuba.

> "The *Oregon's* Race"
>
> "Six thousand miles
> To the Indian Isles
> And the *Oregon*
> rushed home,
> Her wake a swirl
> Of jade and pearl,
> Her bow a bend
> of foam."
> —Arthur Guuterman,
> *The New York Times*

*The cooperation in the engine room reminds Leo of the teamwork of forestry.*

*As a parting gift, Leo bought his daughters a paper doll reading "Daddy Drinks."*

## "The Voyage of the Oregon by Sailor R. Cross," published in *My Fifty Years in the Navy*, by Rear Admiral Charles E. Clark; the complete diary begins on March 19 in San Francisco and ends on July 4 in Cuba following the Battle of Santiago:

April 4. Arived at Calao, Peru, 5:00 a.m., very pleasant trip all the way down the coast, we are doing quick work so far. Started to coal ship at 8 a.m. and as soon as we get enough on board we will pull right out for the straights of Magellan and there join the Marietta, our little Gun Boat, which will scout the straights for us in case there is a Spanish Torpedo Boat in one of the Many Coves. She can go in shallow water as she is light draft boat and at the same time order coal for us.

We have allready made one of the grandest runs on record. Just think of it, a First Class Battle ship making 4,800 miles in just 16 days and used 900 tons of Coal, That being the longest trip on record for a First Class battleship.

April 7. Got the coal on this morning at 4 a.m. there is about 1,750 tons on now, never had so much on before. Got 100 tons on deck in sacks. We are knocking some of the coal dust off the sides. She is a very dirty ship now and expect to remain so for a long time to come. There is some talk of a Spanish Gun Boat or a Torpedo Boat in the Straights waiting for us. But I think that will be all right when the Marietta gets there to patrole the place for us. We expect to go out to night some time. 7 p.m. left Port. The Capt don't know wether to go round the Horn or not. But if we do, as the Dutchman says By the Horn around, we will get a shaking up. But ever body seems to think we can take care of our selves where ever we go. Capt Clark is all right, we don't think he is afraid of the whole Spanish Navy. the weather is very fogy. Expect it to lift when we get a little ways.

April 18. Well the Marietta is hear this morning, she came in at 12.15 this morning. She was in the straights when we past her, she was laying off in one of the coves waiting for us . . . the first thing this morning we started to coal up. I havent found out how many tons we are going to take hear. But the price is $25 a ton. I think we will take about 800 tons. all

the men on the Marietta say they had a very rough trip. We are in a great rush to get out of hear . . .

April 25. 4 a.m. just came on watch and I am going on deck to get a cup of cocoa to wake me up abit. the old man is in the Chart house snoozing, so I guess it is safe to go. Every thing has settled to the same old thing except we have some Targate Practis By throwing boxes over board.

April 30. Droped anchor at 3 p.m. in the beautyfull harber of Rio de Janeiro, and befor the Mud hook stuck the botom we had the news that war was delared on the 21st of April 1898, the very day we puled out of Sandy Point. As soon as every thing was put to order we Broke out the Band to give us the Star Spangled Baner, an the Crew diden do a thing But yell and whoop her up, so they to play it over 4 times . . . started to coal up at 8.25 p.m. an we get out of hear as soon as we can. I hear the Spanish has got one of our Merchant ships, the Shanandore, loaded with English goods. I wonder how that is going to com out. Every one on his ship is crasie to get at the Spanish.

May 8. We got to Bahai, Bra. At 8:30 p.m. after making a good run and having Targete pracis with full charges of Powder, don some fine shooting with the Gig Guns. I dont think it will be a bit too healthy for the Spanish to bump up against us, for we have a good eye. We put in hear as an excuse to put on War paint saying our Engines wer Brok down and at the same time to get more coal if we can.

June 17. come down to Guantanamo Bay this morning, put some 300 tons of coal on and throde some shells over in an old Fort and then puled out right away for Santiago.

June 20. Bully for the Soldies, they are hear at last,"I thought would com tomorrow," some of the papers say there are 20,000 of them, that is enough

## "The Voyage . . ." *(continued)*

to eat the place up for lunch. Well I hope we will soon crack this not that is so hard to crack. I hear there is 15,000 Spanish soldiers over hear.

July 4. The fish has come out to see is. On the 3rd the Spanish fleet came out of the Harbor to fight and get a way if possible. (I would have put this down on the 3rd But I didn't have time and was too tired that night so put it off for today.) Well the Fleet came out and went to Davy Joneses locker. It was jus 9.25 a.m. fir call had sounded on our ship for Quraters and we all have our best dudds on; we were going to listen to the Articles of War this morning and to have chirch right affter, But we never did. all of a suden the Ordly on watch made a dive for the Cabin head first, and told the old man the Fleet was coming out of the Harbor. the old man jumpt up a standing. as son as some of the men seen the ships there, they went to there Quarters with out any further dealy.

By 9.27 the *Oregon* fired the first shot of the Battle of July 3rd, 1898 at the first ship that came out of the Harbor. I don't remember the ships as they come out, But we went in to meet them and passed them some good shots as they cep coming.

About 7 or 9 minutes after they got started good,

one of our 6 inch guns blew up one of the Torpedo Boats, struck her squar amidships, she sunk like a rock with all on board. and right here is where I had to stop for a moment to admire one of there Gunners. I do think he was one of the bravest men I ever had the pleasure to look upon. That man must have known he was going to a shure Deth, he stud on Deck and cep firing at us all the time, and the last time I seen him he was Just going up in the air. As the ships came out of the harbor they sircled to the right, or Westward, and Capt. Clark knew they were trying to escape. they did not think the old *Oregon* was such a runer as she was a fighter, so we Just tailed on with them and giving them shot for shot. In about 20 minuts the first ship went on the Beach, plumb knocked out, and 15 minuts later the secon one went on the Beach, a short ways from the first. Then came the tug of war for we had to run to catch the Vizcaya and the Colon, but we catched them both. The Vizcaya was about 4,000 yards ahead and the Colon was about 3 miles ahead, and the poor men in the fireroom was working like horses, and to cheer them up we passed the word down the ventalators how things was going on, and they passed the word back if we would cut them down they would get us to where we could do it. So we got in rainge of the Vizcaya and we sent her ashore with the secondary Battry and 6 inch guns, and then we settled down for a good chase for the Colon. I thought she was going to run a way from us. But she had to make a curv and we headed for a point that she had to come out at. We all think there is no man in the Navy like Capt. Clark, he is a Brave man, he stud on the Forward 13 inch turet through the thickest of this fight and directed his ship to the final results.

*The* Oregon *was forced to travel from California, around the tip of South America, and back to Cuba to fight in the Spanish-American War.*

- Once at sea, Leo and his fire crew were told the *Oregon's* first stop was Callao, Peru, 4,000 miles away; the goal for their progress was 250 nautical miles a day.

- Throughout the sprint, the *Oregon* belched soot from coal pumped into the furnaces by Leo's sweating stokers—most stripped naked to the waist to withstand the over 100-degree temperatures.

- Nights were spent sleeping on the deck of the rolling ship to escape the ferocity of the flames.

- Although it was fun being part of a well-working machine made up of men, the excitement of going to war shifted after a time into mind-numbing reality; whatever glory might await, tremendous work needed to be done to drive the ship's boilers at that speed for that distance.

- As the *Oregon* moved closer toward the equator, the ventilation in the fire rooms and other engineering spaces proved inadequate; temperatures rose to the range of 110 to 150 degrees.

- Because they all wanted to reach Cuba before the war was over, the men sometimes had to be forced to take breaks and walk the deck often.

- The only day off was during the 16-day run to Peru, when the *Oregon* crossed the equator; in a ceremony dating back decades, "King Neptune" was piped aboard to receive his customary honors as a traditional sign of respect for the mighty ocean.

- To keep up morale during the voyage, Capt. Clark allowed the ship's band to present a concert each evening

on the boat deck; Leo made sure his crews rotated shifts so that his men could enjoy the concerts every third day.

- Leo loved listening to the popular dance tunes and dreaming of holding his wife again—thoughts for which he had little time most of the day.
- A week out, he was gratified to learn how important the ship's speed and his men's role were in the war effort.
- Chief Engineer Milligan informed Capt. Clark that for the boilers to continue at a full head of steam, the supply of fresh water for the crew would have to be severely limited, so it could be used in powering the ship.
- Using salt water would contaminate and impair the efficiency of the boilers—resulting in less speed.
- Capt. Clark faced a difficult decision; how could he choose between the health and endurance of his crew and risking damage to the boilers driving the ship?
- To the elation of everyone in the engineering section, Clark called all the men topside and explained that salt water in the boilers meant reduced speed, which would not only delay the *Oregon,* but could impair her efficiency in battle.
- Then he announced that the very small quantity of ice on board would go to Leo's team—the firemen and coal passers—while the rest of the crew would have only lukewarm drinking water for the duration of the trip.
- The crew cheered the decision.
- Shortly after that, the chief engineer came to Leo with another idea: Why not save for emergencies the best coal on board—primarily the dusky diamonds from Cardiff, Wales—loaded in San Francisco?
- Everyone knew that purer coal meant hotter fires and more steam.
- Leo agreed to the plan without consulting Capt. Clark.
- At night, while the ship was under way, Leo led a team of willing men to redistribute the coal in the bunkers so that the best coal from Cardiff was always in a standby position.

"We shall have this war in Cuba. The interests of business and of financiers might be paramount in the Senate, but not so with the American people. Now, Senator, may we please have war?"
—Teddy Roosevelt's remarks on March 28, 1898, to Senator Mark Hanna during the Gridiron Press Dinner in Washington

- Coaling a ship in port is a filthy, backbreaking job, even with an unlimited supply of water; handling vast amounts of the black fuel at sea, aboard a rolling ship and without fresh water to wash themselves, was a true sacrifice.
- In Callao, the *Oregon* took on 1,100 tons of coal, the first of nearly a dozen stops made to refuel.
- As the ship pulled into Rio de Janeiro on April 30, two and a half months after the sinking of the *Maine,* the men of the *Oregon* learned for the first time that war had been officially declared.
- In Rio, they purchased a large supply of red ribbon to make cap bands; letters cut from brass and attached to the bands spelled out the words, "Remember the *Maine.*"
- Because of concerns that Spanish sympathizers would place bombs on the coal barges, all coal had to be examined before it was put on board.
- During the trip, 4,100 tons of coal were used to produce an average speed of 11.6 knots per hour.
- Meanwhile, the American army had been pouring into Tampa—where both tempers and supplies were growing short—and demanding that the invasion begin soon.
- On June 10, the first American troops—the Marines—landed in Cuba, supported by shore bombardment from the *Yankee.*
- Then, for the men of the *Oregon* came several anxious, silent weeks as America blockaded Santiago Harbor

*The* Oregon *dispatched the Spanish fleet in one afternoon.*

and awaited the battle between the U.S. fleet and Cervera's squadron of battle-tested ships.

- To keep the crew occupied and the Spanish enemy alert, the *Oregon* spent considerable time in target practice, including shots fired at Spain's fort, Old Morro.
- Then, on July 3, the U.S. fleet formed a semicircle three miles off the harbor, and the Spanish fleet made a run for safety.
- After 34 days, the battle of Santiago began.
- Leo and his team were ready; all boilers had already been filled and the *Oregon* was prepared for peak speed.
- As the ship passed the harbor in pursuit, two Spanish torpedo boats appeared, both receiving a volley from the *Oregon*'s six-inch guns, and were crushed.
- All the while, Leo and his crew were stoking the engine and preparing to surprise the enemy with their speed.
- The *Oregon* raced past the other American battleships and began gaining on the faster Spanish cruisers, which were being driven by special, emergency coal from England.
- In rapid succession, the *Oregon* brought down the *Teresa,* the *Almirante Oquendo* and the *Vizcaya,* driving forward at a pace of 16 knots and registering three kills in 90 minutes.
- Despite the hellish heat, the stokers fed the furnaces even as gun vibrations showered them with soot and steam from shaken pipes.
- Topside, sweating men heaved 100- to 250-pound shells into smoking guns and fired them to the sound of a slamming breechblock.
- When accurate, the projectiles tore jagged holes in the steel plates of the Spanish ships.
- Even though the U.S. fleet was still using the more primitive brown powder, while the more modern Spanish Navy had switched to the new smokeless powder, it mattered little.
- Jubilant gunners shouted gleeful progress reports to the sweating toilers in the engine room.
- As the morning wore on, all that remained was a clash with the *Cristobal Colon,* which was six miles ahead of the *Oregon.*
- As the *Oregon* gained on the Spanish ship, enthusiasm ran high.
- On several occasions, Leo ran topside to get status reports, knowing that if his crew helped the *Oregon* catch the *Colon,* the gunners could do their work with dispatch.

*While Rough Rider Teddy Roosevelt engaged the Spanish on land, the* Oregon *and its engine room battled Spanish ships.*

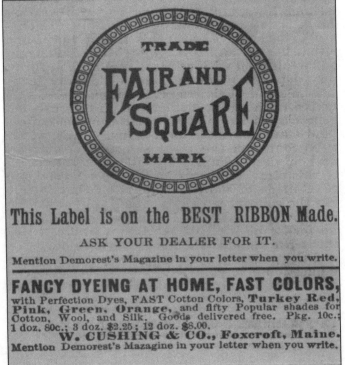

- To feed the flames, even the engineering officers were shoveling coal into the roaring furnaces to aid the exhausted firemen.
- At 12:50 p.m., almost three and a half hours after the battle had begun, the *Oregon* fired a 13-inch shell at the *Colon*, sending a 1,100-pound projectile through the air.
- When Leo's exhausted crew heard the roar of the gun, they knew the *Oregon* was in range of the *Colon* and feverishly poured on more coal.
- The seventh shot from the 13-incher, fired at a range of five miles, forced the surrender of the *Colon*.
- Almost immediately, 550 men, most bare to the waist and covered with powder, smoke and coal dust, embraced one another and celebrated victory.

### The Emergence of the U.S. Navy
- During the American Civil War, the Union Army had built some of the world's finest, most powerful warships.
- The Union Navy, with 700 ships, had introduced the

*President William McKinley promised to bring prosperity and prestige to America.*

world to armored combat vessels and perfected the rifled gun barrel, which fired projectiles farther and truer than the old, smooth bore gunnery tossed a cannon ball.

- By 1880, in the wake of a national backlash against military spending following the Civil War, the United States Navy had virtually ceased to exist as a practical fighting force.
- While the Royal Navy had more than 400 vessels, the U.S. Navy consisted of 26 ships, four with iron hulls, the rest made of wood.
- Congress eagerly subsidized the building of Western railroads, a national priority, but did not think the decline in the navy or merchant trade of great importance.
- Slowly, the rebuilding process began in 1883, when Congress appropriated funds for four new steel-hulled vessels of American design; the *Atlanta, Boston, Chicago* and *Dolphin* together became known as the ABCD fleet.
- In 1885, Congress authorized two more cruisers, the *Newark* and *Charleston,* plus two gunboats, the *Yorktown* and *Petrel.*
- Congressional approval followed in 1886 for four additional monitors and two warships, the *Texas* and the *Maine.*
- In 1890, Alfred Thayer Mahan, a 50-year-old professor at the War College, published *The Influence of Sea Power upon History,* calling upon America to build an armada capable of gaining control of the seas.
- That same year, three battleships, also known as seagoing coastal battleships, were authorized which would displace 10,000 tons each with an armor belt 18 inches thick.

"Santiago"
"Through smoke
and flame the
battle raged,
And every missile sent
Was planted where it
counted most
And where the
gunners meant
While leading all,
the *Oregon*
Dashed swiftly to
the van,
And raked and riddled
with her guns
Each deck where
dared a man."
—John Flagg, *Lyrics of New England*

*The* Oregon *and its crew gained nationwide fame for its rapid trip and fighting prowess.*

## "The Ship's Company," by J. D. Jenrod, *Scribner's Magazine*, May 1891:

When you come to measure the [engine-room] region fairly, it broadens into a wonderland; it shapes itself into a twilight island of mysteries, into a laboratory where grimy alchemists practice black magic and white. At first all seems confusion, but when the brain has coordinated certain factors, harmony is wooed from discord and order emerges from chaos. It is, in the beginning, all noise and tangled motion, and shiny steel and oily smells; then succeeds a vague sense of bars moving up and down, and down and up, with pitiless regularity; of jiggering levers, keeping time rhythmically to any stray patter you may fit to their chanting; and, at last, the interdependence of rod grasping rod, of shooting straight lines seizing curved arms, of links limping backward and wriggling forward upon queer pivots, dawns upon you, and in the end you marvel at the nicety with which lever, weight and fulcrum work, opening and closing hidden mechanisms, and functioning with an exactness that dignifies the fraction of a second into an appreciable quantity.

- The term "seagoing" was adopted to please the navy expansionists in Congress, while the word "coastal" appealed to those who valued economy and a navy designed to be largely defensive in nature.
- The *Indiana* and *Massachusetts* were built in Philadelphia, though the 348-foot *Oregon* was constructed by Irving M. Scott and Henry Scott of the Union Iron Works in San Francisco.
- The *Oregon* was launched in 1893 at a cost, fully outfitted, of $4 million; a crowd of over 100,000 witnessed its christening.
- The ship displaced 10,200 tons and was designed for a maximum speed of 16.2 knots, with a sustained speed of 15 knots.
- With the launch of coal-fueled ships, the need for secure coaling stations became essential and colonization more necessary for isolationist America.

# 1899 NEWS FEATURE

## "A Soldier's Wife in the Philippines," by Eda Blankart Funston, *Cosmopolitan*, May 1900:

Never shall I forget my first glimpse of Manila. General Miller and staff, the 1st Battalion of 20th Kansas Infantry, a detachment of California Heavy Artillery and 14 ladies had arrived in Manila Bay on the *Newport* on the evening of December 5, 1898. All but two of the ladies had come to meet their husbands. Three of us were brides who had been speculating deeply as to which one would see her husband first. Need I tell how happy I was, and how victorious, when my husband proved to be the first one on board? After having paid his respects to General Miller, my husband declared himself ready to move, and we went at once by rowboat to the *Indiana*. In consequence of lack of quarters, the two battalions of the 20th Kansas which had come on the *Indiana* had been obliged to stay on board ship. Naturally, the officers had to remain. In addition, my husband had been unable to secure a house, for good houses had become scarce by that time.

Thus it was that I got the first glimpse of Manila early on the morning after my arrival in the bay. The bright tin and tile roofs, so almost entirely prevalent in Manila, surmounted now and then by a church dome or tower, reflected the rays of the sun, which even at that early hour blazed unmercifully. The bright, rich green of the trees and foliage seemed in remarkable contrast with this baking heat, for the sun was apparently hot enough to dry up the very waters of the bay. In spite of the heat, I was most anxious to get a closer view of this remarkable city, of which we had all heard and read so much within the last six or seven months; so when the next launch came alongside, Major and Mrs. Whitman, my husband and I, boarded it and were soon approaching the Pasig.

Our little launch puffed its way up the river among the most varied and remarkable craft, from cascoes 50 to 75 feet long to little canopy-topped dugouts six to eight feet long. These boats and both banks of the river seemed literally alive with men, women and children in all stages of dress and undress. After pursuing our way about a quarter of a mile up the river, we arrived at the landing. I was surprised to see the fine stone quay and splendidly paved street, and was intensely interested in and amused at the remarkable kinds of vehicles. Large, small, open and closed, one-seater, more-seated, and from brand-new down to the most dilapidated imaginable. But the horses attached to these remarkable equipages were more remarkable still—little more than dogs, and so thin and sore that I hated the idea of riding behind them. Perhaps you have seen pictures of the typical Manila equipages. In case you have not, let me attempt to describe the one in which we drove that day. It was square, much like a gurney cab, but very light. It was higher than a gurney, was open and had but two wheels. Such a time we had getting seated for our trip to town! We drove through a number of narrow, dirty streets, over a bridge, and through another street before we reached the Escolta—a narrow street with a single car-track down the middle and just space enough on each side for a carriage. The sidewalks in some places were wide enough for two persons to walk side-by-side very comfortably, and in others barely wide enough for one. Some of the buildings, though not masterpieces of architecture, were by no means bad, and, as we soon discovered, there were at least a dozen stores in the place, where after talking for an hour you could manage to get many desired articles.

We hunted up a house-agent, an enterprising American, and late arrival, and after an hour's driving discovered a very good house. It was the district called Ermita. From a corner window we looked over the Lunetta toward the bay, the most beautiful view imaginable. We were altogether delighted with our discovery and good fortune, in spite of the fact that we should be obliged to wait at least a week before we could occupy the house. We returned to the ship that evening more than pleased with our day's doings, and counting the hours until we could take possession of our home, for the Whitmans and the Funstons were to occupy the house together. The next three days were spent aboard ship. Shall I ever forget those days? I cannot imagine anything warmer, and we suffered accordingly. By Sunday, Major Whitman and my husband devised a scheme by which we

could go ashore, even though our house was not ready for us. Regimental headquarters were in the Second Battalion barracks, where my husband had an office. This was quite a large room, and here we put up two cot-beds, which Mrs. Whitman and I occupied, while our husbands bunked with two of the officers. The three days we spent there were dreary enough. Major Whitman and Colonel Funston were extremely busy and left their wives to take care of themselves. We did not go out on the streets alone (though at that time it was safe to do so), and we thought, as we really had no right in the building, it would be wrong toward the men, embarrassing, to say the least, to have us about, so we stayed in our room—prisoners. But we could look out of the windows, the view from which almost repaid us for our imprisonment. The barracks were on Calle Analoague and in the Binondo District—one of the worst—thickly populated with Chinese. Calle Analoague was a very busy street, so that from morning until night it was most interesting to watch the numberless passersby. The men of the better classes appeared with their spotless white suits and patent-leather boots, and those of the lower classes with trousers of "any old kind" rolled up to the knees or above, and an ordinary undershirt which was always worn outside the trousers. The women were there with their odd and rather picturesque costume, consisting of a bright-colored skirt which just escaped the ground in front and in the back was made *en train* in the oddest imaginable shape about a yard or more in length. The train very much resembles the bowl of a spoon in shape, though, of course, it is flat. Over the skirt is worn a garment which looks like an apron. This for ordinary use is almost always made of a black material closely resembling our cashmere. For dress occasions, the tapis, as it is called, is made of a fine lacy material called husi, and richly embroidered about the edges. The waist, or pina, is always loose and low-necked, showing the shoulders, and the

large loose sleeves, very like those of a Japanese kimono except that they are gathered in at the armholes, are very much starched and stand out, leaving the arm bare. The ordinary children sometimes wear clothes and sometimes nature is entirely unadorned. When they do dress, their clothes are exactly like those of the grown-up people, the effect being most picturesque.

Finally, after three days of this imprisonment, we moved to our home on Calle San Luis, and now the fun of furnishing began. I shall never forget our first experience in shopping. We started out quite early in a hired victoria (worth $0.20 an hour)—not without a little trepidation, it must be confessed, for furniture-shops were conducted by the Chinese, and the streets in which they were situated were anything but inviting, being hot, dirty and full of odors. Our desire was to keep as far away from the crowd as possible, but at that time, there were so few American women in Manila that we were quite a curiosity. When we entered one of the tiny shops almost on the street, we were followed by 15 or 20 wretched specimens of humanity and stared at until it became distressing. Our purchases were all made as soon as possible, and when finally we got away and out into the more open part of the city, we marveled that we had escaped without trouble, for some of the men had been most surly. A few days after this, word came from headquarters that the officers were too far away from the regiment and must move into town. It was fully a week before a suitable house could be found in the required locality, and in the meantime, the men of the household were obliged to sleep at the barracks, coming home only to lunch and dinner. This arrangement, however, did not last very long, for we soon found a house quite close to the barracks—three blocks below and on the same street. The house being altogether too large for the four of us, we asked Major Metcalf, Mr. Walker, the adjutant, and Mr. Hull, the quartermaster, to occupy it with us, which they were only too glad to do, and we made a very merry, happy family.

This was in the latter part of December 1898, and from the time that we got fairly settled in our new quarters until the outbreak on the night of February 4, our experience was a very pleasant and agreeable one. Though the insurgents had forgotten to smile upon us and were getting more surly and sullen in their demeanor toward us every day, we continued to have the best of good times. The navy did all in its power to make things agreeable for us, and hardly a week passed without some pleasant entertainment being prepared on one or another of the warships.

Driving was our chief recreation. Many a pleasant trip we had behind our dear little white ponies; in fact, I don't know how we could have done without them. The heat between the hours of nine in the morning and four in the afternoon is so intense that one cannot do anything but lounge in the most negligée of garments, but by five it grows cooler, and then the whole city turns out on the Lunetta. The Lunetta, by the way, is a large plaza, elliptical in shape, about 600 feet in length and situated in the western part of Manila on the bay, just outside the walled city. In the middle of this pleasant expanse is the bandstand, and around it a broad driveway which on the side nearest the bay extends along the beach to the Pasig. Every evening one or another of the regimental bands gave a concert here, which began at six and lasted an hour, and here every evening were to be seen the élite of Manila city, taking their daily airing. We Americans soon fell into their ways, for not only did we find it necessary to benefit by the fresh ocean breezes, but we were attracted by the superb sunsets which were an everyday occurrence. Thus, the time was most delightfully spent, in spite of heat and discomforts, until that historic night of the 4th of February.

After a pleasant evening spent quietly in reading, my husband and I had just retired, when we were startled by a banging at the door. At the same time we heard the boom of cannon, and Major Metcalf shouted through the door, "Colonel, Colonel, the ball has begun!" Both my husband and I were on our feet in an instant, and in a few moments he was gone.

Then, gathering up the few valuables I had brought with me, I packed them with my toilet articles in a "telescope" which for some weeks past I had kept prepared—for we had been expecting an outbreak. By this time the soldiers who had been sent to take us to the barracks had arrived, and after having given our two Chinamen all necessary instructions we left the house. The night was quiet, save for the distant crackling of rifles and the heavy boom of the "Monadnock's" big guns. Halfway to the barracks we were met by the 2nd Battalion on its way to the front. With what mingled feelings of hope and fear we watched them as quickly they marched past us! Arrived at the barracks, we were shown into a little room belonging to three noncommissioned officers. Here we were told to make ourselves comfortable.

Of course, sleep for us was out of the question. The hours dragged on with only now and then an interruption by some noisy little cochero forced to give up his carromato, or an unusually loud report of the navy's guns. The next morning matters were a little more interesting. Men began to come in from the line with such long and interesting tales to tell. With what eagerness we drank in the news as each man came in during the day! By this time we had been joined by the other Kansas ladies, making our party five in all, and this made our room more crowded than ever, for we were naturally obliged to bring in more beds. This did not last long, for two of the ladies soon left us. In spite of our anxiety, we managed to make things a little lively. Mrs. Haussermann had her piano put into what we used as a parlor and sitting room. I had my violin, and together we managed to while away many a weary hour.

On the morning of the 7th, an orderly came in from the lines. I rushed to meet him, anxious for news, and received a note from my husband asking me to come to see him that day.

By the time the orderly had attended to his numerous errands, I was ready for the start. A little quelis awaited me in the court. One soldier acted as cochero, another rode on horseback in front of us, while another rode in back. Each carried his rifle. Just as we were starting, one of the ladies gave me a small pistol.

Our trip was a most interesting one, for we passed the ground which our regiment and the artillery had so bravely fought over. Ever and anon, my escort would point out a particular place where the fighting had been the hottest, or where the limbs of trees had been literally torn off by the cannon of the Utah Artillery. On either side of the road were houses fairly riddled with bullets. At length we arrived at the camp, where the officers were most kind and did everything to make me comfortable until my husband's return, which they assured me would be soon. Just then we heard a shot, and then another, and soon the bullets were falling about us. In the shortest time imaginable I was hurried off behind a large embankment, and there I stayed, with my pistol clasped tightly in my hand and feeling like a fool. The shooting lasted but a few minutes, and soon my husband put in an appearance. Then we learned that it was at him and his party that the insurgents had been firing. Almost the first thing he did, after greetings had been exchanged, was to beg of me to put my pistol away. Having safely deposited it in a carromato near at hand, we started off toward brigade headquarters, where after a few minutes' walk I was introduced to Brigadier-General Otis and his staff. After a few minutes' chat, we retraced our steps and called on the officers of the 3rd Artillery, among whom I had several friends. From this camp, which was situated on a slight eminence, we had an excellent view of the enemy, of course with the aid of field glasses. I now thought it about time for me to return to the barracks, and immediately upon reaching our camp set off. I afterward learned that I had not been gone more than half an hour when one of the fiercest battles was fought.

# 1900–1909

The dawn of the new century illuminated America as the fulfillment of economic and political freedom, and an emerging military power on the world stage. Millions of immigrants flooded to the United States, and incumbent President William McKinley campaigned in 1900 on the slogan, "The dinner pail is full." War hero and President Theodore Roosevelt proudly proclaimed in 1902, "The typical American is accumulating money more rapidly than any other man on earth." The United States had become a full participant in the world economy.

Amidst this atmosphere of prosperity, the nation came to look upon its role in world affairs as a responsibility rather than a choice. Using the military, America sought to protect its economic interests, even if it meant forcing its will upon the people and political power of another nation. In a time when countries were being annexed as the spoils of war, the U.S. had taken the Philippines from the Spanish during the Spanish-American War, and quashed the small country's independence movement. In China, America was part of an international force whose goal was to restrain the Boxers, a populist movement begun in the rural regions of China trying to eliminate foreign influence. And when the Colombian government, which claimed the Isthmus of Panama as its own, stood in the way of Teddy Roosevelt's vision of a canal built, owned and operated by America, the U.S. backed a coup by the leading citizens of Panama against Colombia.

These actions were viewed by most Americans as necessary and inevitable. From these military actions and political maneuvers came commercial expansion, as well as added prestige for the United States as an emerging world power.

# 1900 Profile

# The Boxer Rebellion

### Marine First Sergeant

The Chinese uprising known as the Boxer Rebellion is yet another opportunity for Marine First Sergeant René "Frenchy" Trimbley to demonstrate his courage, skills and joy at being a career military man doing his job across the globe.

### Life at Home

- First Sgt. René "Frenchy" Trimbley has been a Marine for 30 years.
- The thirteenth of 17 children, René was born into a French-Canadian family living on the American side of the St. John River along the Maine-Quebec border.
- In the winter, his father and older brothers would journey to the timber camps deep in the Maine woods.
- The warmer months were spent preparing the logs to be floated downriver to the sawmills and attempting to scrape a subsistence from their rocky little farm.
- When René was 12, his father lost his job as a lumberjack after his leg was crushed while he was attempting to loosen a logjam.
- As a result, the family was forced to move to Lewiston, a growing French-Canadian community where numerous textile mills had been built.
- René's father hated the boring work, mill life, and his useless leg.
- Drinking was one of his few escapes, and René was often a target of his drunken rages.
- Late one night, René fled.
- Travelling southward for several weeks, he worked odd jobs when work was available, and stole food when it was not.
- His journey ended at the Boston waterfront, where he was captivated by the teeming activity.

*René Trimbley grew up in the timber industry.*

*For the past 33 years René has been stationed around the world.*

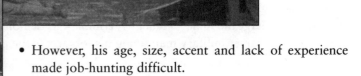

- However, his age, size, accent and lack of experience made job-hunting difficult.
- Then he discovered the naval station, which fascinated him with its sharp appearance and the discipline of the Marine Guard.
- Almost before he knew it, René was lying about his age and signing a four-year commitment to serve in the Marines.
- The Marines gave him the home, discipline and security his childhood had lacked, and he never looked back.
- Besides, most meals were hot and the pay regular.
- Only years later did he learn that only 10 percent of applicants were accepted, and almost one-third of the enlisted men deserted each year.
- For the past 33 years, René has served at stations around the world, participating in armed interventions in Nicaragua, Japan, Panama, Samoa and Egypt.
- He helped to protect the Hawaiian royal family against an attempted insurrection, fought fires in Peru, joined in an expedition to explore Alaska, raided stills in Brooklyn, and guarded the South Pacific Railroad against strikers.
- Never married, René has conducted his social life in a string of bars in port cities.
- The Corps is the only life he knows, and even though he realizes he will have to retire one day, he refuses to discuss it.
- As long as he has a warm bed, three hot squares, the rhythm of the Corps, and $32.50 a month, this Marine is happy.
- His men call him First Sergeant, those of equal rank, René or Trimbley; only the officers refer to him as Frenchy—a name he hates.

- René has never even been to Canada, let alone France.
- One night in a bar, a fellow first sergeant referred to René as Frenchy in a joking manner.
- That shattered whiskey bottle provided the man with a scar he will carry to his grave.
- Trimbley is well-known for his discipline and excellent marksmanship, but not his sense of humor.

## Life at Work

- René Trimbley's courage in dangerous situations is legendary.
- In fact, many of his most heroic acts are commemorated on his short, stocky frame, courtesy of tattoo parlors spread across the globe.
- As soon as the American contingent of 50 Marines landed in China aboard the cruiser *Newark,* he could smell the tension, and knew immediately that he was going to earn another tattoo.
- For the first three weeks, he saw little direct action, although the hair on his neck refused to lie down.
- Rebellion was in the air.
- Daily, the five foot, five inch René and his fellow Marines patrolled the Legation Quarter as part of an international force sent to Peking.
- The Quarter is occupied by the 11 foreign missions and most of the business interests of the European nations, America and Japan; it houses more than 1,000 men and women, not counting the terrified Christian refugees flooding into the protected area.
- The international contingent includes 337 officers and men from seven countries sent to the Chinese capital to defend their nations' interests from the internal rebellion.
- As May unfolds into June, René and his men are increasingly being dispatched to other parts of the city to assist refugees and to capture groups of marauding Chinese, claiming to be members of the Society of Righteous Harmony Fists, or Boxers.

*As soon as René landed in China he sensed trouble.*

# "The American Marines in the Siege of Peking," by the Rev. Courtenay Hughes Fenn, *The Independent*, November 29, 1900:

(Mr. Fenn is a missionary of the Presbyterian Board at Peking and was in the British Legation during the entire siege.)

It is hardly necessary to say that the American residents in Peking had no small share in the defense of the Legations during those fearful days from June 20 to August 14. The responsibilities, which inevitably devolved upon us in our preparations for the defense of the M. E. Mission compound, June 8-20, with few exceptions, were borne by us after our flight to the British Legation. Although the rifles loaned to us missionaries during those early days by the British Minister, that we might defend the London Mission converts as well as our own, were required by the British volunteers soon after we reached the Legation, so that but the few of our number who had rifles of their own stood guard upon the walls, yet our American Marines did enough fighting for all.

The American Legation being nearest to the city wall, it fell to the lot of our Marines, reinforced later by some of the British and Russians, to seize and to hold on to the most exposed, yet most important positions within our lines. Before the actual siege began, they had performed a noble part in the rescue of 200 Roman Catholic converts at the destruction by Boxers of the Southern Cathedral, at the risk of possible conflict with hundreds of Imperial troops on the city wall nearby. They had also maintained guard to entrench themselves in that position. The wall of the northern, or Tartar, city is about 60 feet high and 50 feet broad at the top, and is approached by a series of inclined planes, or "ramps," at intervals. One of these ramps is located directly south of the American Legation. At the head of this ramp, with the aid of the Christian Chinese, they dug a trench across the wall and threw up a

rude double barricade of the huge bricks dug from the wall, piling sandbags on the top for greater protection from the fire of the enemy. It was, of course, "loopholed" for the rifles of the Marines.

On the first day of July, in the morning, a hot shell fire was poured into this barricade by the Imperial troops from near the Ch'ien Mên (Front Gate of the City) with such accuracy of aim that it became impossible for the Marines to remain in their exposed position. One by one I watched them running down the ramp, their captain the last man to leave the wall. My heart sank within me, as I saw in a flash all the probable consequences. The Chinese would at once occupy the position, the Americans and Russians must soon abandon their Legations to destruction, we millers would be compelled to leave the mill and its store of grain, and the British Legation would be exposed on its fourth side to a closer and hotter fire than ever before. But whether the Chinese feared an infernal machine or some other "foreign devil's" device, or were merely cowards, they soon ceased to fire on the barricade, yet sent no men to take the position from which they had driven the Americans. Within less than an hour I had the joy of watching our Marines, reinforced by some of the British, stealing swiftly up the ramp to the old position, from which they were never again dislodged. Major Conger and Lieut. Squiers had insisted that it could be retaken, and must be held at all hazards. Following the Marines went a long line of our native converts, staggering under the weight of huge sandbags. Up and down, up and down, they plodded, exposed all the time to a galling fire from the east, where the Germans had been compelled to yield a similar position on the wall south of their Legation, which was speedily occupied by the Chi-

## "The American Marines . . ." *(continued)*

nese. More than one native Christian was laid low, but faithfully, perseveringly, their companions bore their burdens to be placed on the battered ramparts, working day after day, night after night, until those barricades had been made strong enough to resist shot and shell and sudden assault.

For the first month of the siege, it was often necessary for our Marines to remain on the wall, under heavy fire, for 48 hours without relief, and then, with insufficient rest, to return to this perilous position. Many almost died of fatigue and sleeplessness, and six of the seven who fell lost their lives at this place. Yet, it was a position of vital importance, the loss of which would unquestionably have rendered our destruction easy. The position first defended was, however, too narrow, the enemy's barricades approaching it within 20 feet at one point. So, in the dark, early hours of July 3rd, our men, led by Capt. Myers and assisted by a number of British and Russians, broke over our barricade and made a fierce rush for the Chinese rampart next on the west. Some of the Chinese stopped long enough to fire their rifles and were cut down, but most of them fled precipitately, leaving everything behind. Two of our men fell, while brave Capt. Myers was seriously wounded; but we had largely increased our holding on the wall, gained possession of a well-constructed fortification, including a rude tower which had overlooked our fort, and killed many Chinese soldiers. These newly acquired barricades were at once strengthened and enlarged, and were manned chiefly by the Russians. The Chinese afterward erected a much higher and stronger tower farther to the west, but gained little advantage from it. Some days after this sortie, under cover of darkness, some American Marines and native Christians stole several hundred yards to the east of the original barricade, and threw up another barricade, afterward enlarged to an elaborate and formidable system of fortifications, thus completing a strong line of defense for the entire southern side of the three Legations west of the moat. The Chinese fire from the barricade on the wall, which they had taken from the Germans, rendered it necessary to protect the ramp leading to the American barricades, which

had been christened by the Marines "Fort Myers." The only feasible protection was in the erection of alternating juts of a few feet in height, at intervals of a few feet, from top to bottom of the ramp. The source of material for these defenses, and for all barricades on the walls, was the city wall itself, whose faces and top are composed of several layers of huge bricks, weighing almost 100 pounds each, and set in a strong cement of almost pure lime. So solid are these bricks that the Marines called them "stones." The great mass of the wall consists of a filling of earth between these brick faces. The juts just mentioned could only be erected on dark nights, but when complete, rendered the approach to the wall quite safe. The street at the foot of the wall had also to be strongly barricaded to permit safe passage between the American Legation and the wall.

The American Marines were unsurpassed in courage and daring, and to those of no other nation do we owe more of our safety. No sooner had those upon the wall seen the approach of the British Indian troops, who came first to our relief on that memorable 14th of August, than they burst forth with wild yells from their own barricades, and fell with such fury upon the Chinese fortifications to the west that they drove the enemy panic-stricken before them through barricade after barricade, until the great "Front Gate" of the city was in the hands of the Americans, and the Stars and Stripes planted on its tower. This was the last finishing touch to a record of which the Marine Corps and the nation may well be proud.

- The Boxers, a populist movement begun in the rural regions of China, want to eliminate foreign influence, including the Christian religion.
- They are supported, René believes, by the arch-conservative dowager empress.
- Currently, they are being allowed to appear openly in the streets of Peking.
- During the past several months, as the Boxer movement has gained momentum in the rural countryside, the killing of many Christian missionaries has forced both missionaries and their converts to flee into the Legation Quarter in Peking.
- Walls on the north and south surround the Quarter, with wide boulevards to the east and west, making the area easy to defend.
- René's Marines are assigned, along with the Russian sailors, to defend a portion of the south wall near the American embassy, some 400 yards from the Chi'en Mên Gate.
- Tension was already at a fever pitch within the Quarter when a German diplomat was surrounded in the street and killed by Chinese Imperial soldiers.
- In response, the allies, representing Europe, America and Japan, took the Chinese forts at Taku on June 17.
- Three days later, the Imperial Court declared war on the allies; immediately, its troops joined the Boxers in besieging the Legation Quarter.
- Forces from England, Germany, Japan, Russia, Austria, Italy and America were suddenly being asked to fend off both the unpredictable Boxers and the massive Chinese army.
- René was glad his commander, Captain John T. Myers, had opted to march into Peking without baggage so that 20,000 rounds of ammunition and 8,000 rounds for the Colt machine gun could be carried by the American force.
- For the Marines, the siege of the Quarter quickly became an endurance contest for control of the Tartar Wall.
- The Chinese kept them under continuous artillery and rifle fire, making rest impossible.
- Every few days, René and his men repelled seemingly spontaneous attacks by the Boxers, and enduring the sounds of rifle fire all around them, with little opportunity to respond.

- To defend the wall with so few men, they rotated positions in 48-hour shifts; less movement also reduced the opportunity for attack by Chinese riflemen.
- Even with precautions, several Marines were brought down by snipers, who had shot each one in the head.
- During one exchange, René was grazed across the cheek by a bullet, giving him an even fiercer countenance.
- On July 1, the Chinese forces attacked and drove the American Marines and the Germans from the wall.

## A Story of the China Shop
### An Artist's View of the Complications in the Far East

Uncle Sam. "Seems ter be a little trouble at the store to-day, boys."

Uncle Sam (to France, Germany, and England). "There he goes inside, boys; guess we'd better stay out fer a while."

Uncle Sam (to China). "Be careful you don't get mixed up in it."

China. "Hellup!"
Uncle Sam. "Jinkys! they've pulled him inside too. Don't git too near, boys."

Uncle Sam. "Never mind, boys. Don't go any nearer. We'll just wait a few days."

The Kaiser, et al. "Dot looks to uncs like re vait. Uncle Sammy was right, yes?"

- René wanted to stand and fight, but his captain ordered a retreat in the face of overwhelming odds.
- Edwin Conger, the American minister and a former army officer, was indignant and ordered the wall retaken.
- Supported by a detachment of Royal Marines and Russians, the U.S. Marines staged a daring, early morning surprise attack on the wall.
- Trimbley led the charge for the Americans.
- The fighting was hand-to-hand, with spears and knives flashing.
- Thirty Chinese died as the wall was retaken in one of the major events of the rebellion.
- Two Marines were killed and several wounded, including Capt. Myers, who was badly wounded in the leg by a Chinese spear.

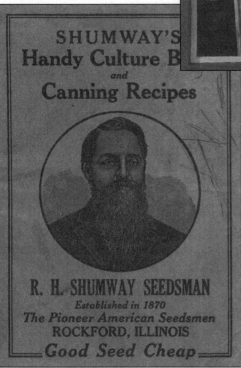

- René was also struck in the shoulder with a spear, just below the tattoo earned in Samoa, but a navy doctor patched him up quickly and sent him back to the front lines.
- While battles raged along the wall, most of the foreigners in the Quarter prayed for the arrival of the relief expedition, which was slowly making its way across China.
- Many knew about the slaughter during the 1858 Sepoy Rebellion in India and China, and feared it might be repeated.
- For the past two weeks, more than 2,000 reinforcements have been marching to Peking—delayed both by the attacks from the Chinese army and interallied bickering.
- After retaking the wall, René was in no mood to wait for anyone; trained soldiers were needed in other parts of the Quarter and René joined the fight despite his wound.
- But the long, multiweek siege and lack of supplies were taking their toll.
- Many small children within the compound became ill, with several dying of starvation.
- Horses and pet ponies were slaughtered for their meat, while trees were stripped of their leaves and bark for cooking.
- On July 17, a truce was declared.
- The exhausted troops, who had been manning the Quarter walls for four weeks without relief, could finally relax.
- For the first time, they could buy food from the Chinese and supplement their supplies.
- René was deeply suspicious of any food sold by the Chinese, and only dealt with merchants he knew; he had heard about entire teams of men being wiped out by contaminated or poisoned meat, and vowed it would not happen on his watch.
- By early August, with both sides anxious and dissatisfied, the truce was broken; sniper fire and random attacks resumed.

- Telegrams sent from the allies within the Quarter to those outside simply read: "Send relief."
- At dawn on August 14, when René heard the sounds of the guns from the relief force entering the city, he knew the fighting would be over soon, and that he should begin planning two things: the location of his new tattoo and where he could get something to drink—hard stuff with a kick.
- Shortly thereafter, the international relief force marched into the city, quickly crushing the revolt—the Imperial Court fled the city and the Boxer Rebellion was quashed.
- But the work was incomplete.
- When the dowager empress and her Court fled Peking, along with the Boxers, the international troops began looting the city.
- With their officers unwilling to stop the pillage, the soldiers freely smashed windows and began collecting souvenirs of victory.
- René considered such behavior unprofessional and reined his men in tight; no one under his command would ever dishonor the uniform of a Marine.
- The captain, still incapacitated from his leg wound, was grateful, and promised to buy the first round of drinks.
- Rumors are already circulating that René and his men will be needed shortly in the Philippines, where unrest is fomenting.

## Life in the Community: Peking, China

- The 55-day siege at Peking and the adventure of the International Relief Force are gaining tremendous publicity for the Marines in the American press.
- Until recently, there was little difference in the minds of the general public between the Marine Corps and the navy.
- The navy, on the other hand, makes it clear that the Marines do not represent them.
- Since 1895, the Marine Corps has grown from less than 2,200 to 5,240 men and 174 officers, thanks to the Spanish-American War and recent tensions in the Philippines.
- The Boxer Rebellion has been yet another opportunity for the Marines to distinguish themselves from the navy and play an important role in a military action.
- The officers of the International Relief Force think the Americans are conspicuous for their careless, casual discipline and lack of skill in small-unit tactics.
- One Japanese officer observed, "The Americans individually are probably the best fighters in the International Force, but the worst when not on the firing line."

# HISTORICAL SNAPSHOT
# 1900

- Using human volunteers, Walter Reed linked *Aedes aegypti* mosquito bites to yellow fever in Cuba, opening the way for the building of an interocean canal
- One in seven homes had a bathtub, while one in 13 had a telephone
- Orville and Wilbur Wright flew their first glider
- Albert J. Beveridge of Indiana spoke for many Americans in 1900 when he said, "God has marked the American people as his chosen nation to finally lead in the regeneration of the world. This is the divine mission of America"
- Hawaii became a United States territory
- The U.S. Navy bought its first submarine
- Hit songs included "I'm a Respectable Working Girl," "Strike Up the Band," "Here Comes a Sailor," "You Can't Keep a Good Man Down" and "I Can't Tell You Why I Love You, But I Do"
- Major books included, *Lord Jim* by Joseph Conrad, *The Wonderful Wizard of Oz* by L. Frank Baum, *The Son of the Wolf* by Jack London, *The Pains of Lowly Life* by Mark Twain and *Sister Carrie* by Theodore Dreiser
- *Who's Who in America,* the Nobel Peace Prize, the *Happy Hooligan* cartoon, and Wesson Oil all made their first appearance
- Sigmund Freud's *The Interpretation of Dreams* suggested that dream symbolism revealed the unconscious mind
- Basketball was often played on dance floors surrounded by chicken wire, resulting in the nickname "cagers" for basketball players
- The population of New York, Chicago and other major cities was exploding because of foreign immigrants and rural migrants seeking jobs
- America boasted 144 miles of roads with hard surfaces to support its 8,000 automobiles
- Diarrhea and enteritis, often caused by contaminated water and milk, were the leading causes of infant mortality
- Writer Theodore Dreiser suffered a nervous breakdown after his publisher stopped the sale of *Sister Carrie* because the publisher's wife thought the book sordid
- Two million mustangs remained on the prairie
- Casey Jones steered the Cannonball Express into a stalled freight train, saving the fireman, but losing his life and inspiring a ballad
- Women enjoyed suffrage in Colorado, Idaho, Utah and Wyoming
- Marriage between whites and persons of "Negro descent" was prohibited in 25 states

## "The Righteous Harmonious Fisters of China," by Francis E. Clark, DD., President of the Society of Christian Endeavor, *The Independent,* August 9, 1900:

[Dr. Clark, who is now on a trip around the world, left China apparently only a few days before the outbreak.—Editor]

One of the most curious phenomena of modern times is the rise and spread of the so-called "Boxers" of North China, or, as their high-sounding name would be literally translated, "The Righteous Harmonious Fisters." Another name by which they call themselves is "The Society for the Protection of the Home," as Dr. S. W. Dike will perhaps be interested to know. The whole of North China seems to be honeycombed by this secret organization. It is the one topic of conversation in Chinese inns and teahouses from one end of this vast division of the empire to the other.

Everywhere, one hears of disturbances and depredations committed upon the native Christians. In many villages the Christians are completely terrorized and do not dare to go out of doors for fear of their enemies. Near the station of Lo Fa, on the direct railway line that runs between Tientsin and Peking, is a village. The Boxers have been of late promenading three times a day, clearing the streets of Christians, and issuing proclamations that none of them shall show their faces beyond their own doorsteps. Houses have been looted and chapels destroyed. The governor of the province of Shantung has reported to the empress that 1,700 families have been looted, that nearly 10,000 people have been harassed and persecuted in that one province, with losses reaching up into the thousands of taels. Many mission premises are full of terrified refugees.

Dr. Porter, of Pang-Chuang, writes me, "Fourteen out of 17 of our little outstations have been either looted or steadily threatened with a determined purpose to root up every affiliation with the foreign religion. Four of our most interesting chapels have been practically demolished."

At almost every street corner in Peking, when I was there last week, the Boxers were going through their strange maneuvers, and as I write, I am within sight of the walls of Tung-cho, which has been the center of a most serious and determined outbreak. Here the Boxers have been drilling for weeks and a reign of terror has just been ended or at least intermitted by the governor of the city, who has arrested one of the ringleaders and condemned him to a terrible punishment of 800 blows with the bamboo.

In this particular instance, matters were brought to a head in the following curious way: The Boxers had accused the Christians of poisoning the wells. Five packages of foreign "medicines," which had been conveniently deposited there, were fished out of a public well in the presence of an excited and turbulent mob gathered for the purpose. No Christian being at hand to be charged with this enormity, a poor fellow, a stranger in the vicinity, who was known by none of the missionaries or Christians, was pounced upon and accused of being hired by the Christians to poison the wells. At first, he stoutly denied it, but was tortured in every way in order that he might make a false confession.

With red-hot branding irons, Chinese characters were written upon the bare flesh of his breast; a gaping wound was made in the hollow of his back into which was stuck a piece of incense which was then lighted and allowed to burn down slowly into his quivering flesh. No wonder that the poor fellow yielded to these persuasions and confessed that he had been hired by the "foreign devils" in the mission compound nearby to poison the well.

Then, the howling, hooting mob, with their prisoner, started for the American Board compound in the city of Tung-cho, thinking to make their victim repeat his confession there, and thus inflame the mob to utterly destroy the mission premises. But the fellow had some sparks of truthfulness left in his composition, and he would not repeat the false witness under those circumstances, so they took him to the grounds of a Buddhist temple and buried him alive. This, in the opinion of the Buddhist priest, however, was carrying mat-

## "The Righteous Harmonious . . ." (continued)

ters too far, and, fearing that some trouble might come to his temple if he allowed it to go on, before life was quite extinct in the Boxers' victim, he reported the matter to the magistrate.

This magistrate, who seems to have been a decent fellow, called for the packages of poison which had been found in the well, and discovered that they were done up, not in foreign paper, but in an old document that had actually been stolen from his own yamen.

Thus, he traced the matter home to one of his own servants or "yamen runners," and in righteous indignation at the imposture, as I have said, ordered 800 whacks from the bamboo for the rascal. The mob dispersed and, for the time being at least, the atmosphere is clearer, but no one knows when the clouds may gather again over the heads of these devoted native Christian and foreign missionaries.

This is only one instance of hundreds that might be cited. Every village where there are Christians or foreigners is threatened, and every section seems to have its band of Boxers.

# 1901 PROFILE

# THE PHILIPPINE INSURRECTION

## Officer

When news of the Philippine Insurrection reached Simon McElroy in North Platte, Nebraska, he knew he was being called to war, despite the pleas of his wife and children; it is the "white man's burden" to civilize the nations of the world.

## Life at Home

- Thirty-six-year-old Simon McElroy could not resist the call of his country one more time.
- An 1885 graduate of West Point, McElroy served in a number of posts throughout the western United States—without seeing action—before resigning his commission as a second lieutenant in 1891.
- McElroy returned to his hometown of North Platte, Nebraska, convinced he was to work at his father's dry goods store, a supplier to farmers of the area and much of western Nebraska.
- Yet, when the Spanish-American War broke out in 1898, McElroy was ready to reenlist; his country needed him in Cuba.
- His wife and father dissuaded him from volunteering, talking relentlessly about the advancing age of his father, the need to keep the business running, the welfare of the four children and the loneliness of wives during a Nebraska winter.
- They even asked him how the store could compete without his help against nationally-based mail-order companies, such as Sears, Roebuck and Company, that were stealing business from every merchant.
- To his regret, Simon relented, but followed every battle of the war in the newspapers and in magazines such as *McClure's* and *The Outlook*.

*Simon McElroy volunteered to fight in the Philippines.*

## "A Taste of War in Luzon," by Phelps Whitmarsh, *The Outlook*, March 3, 1900:

In Porac, it seemed as if the 36th was to settle for a while, and with the experience of the old campaigners, the regiment made itself comfortable with remarkable rapidity. Every bamboo and nipa shack was filled with American faces, the cool stream was constantly alive with bathers, bull-trains with commissaries blocked the marketplace, and the whole of the arboreous little town was turned into an army depot. All but a few of the inhabitants having vacated the place before our entrance, and empty houses being many, I (with my machismo) established myself in one of the ordinary native dwellings. With the exception of the hardwood window-sills and the thatch of nipa palm, the entire house was made of bamboo. The framework and rafters were bamboo poles varying in diameter according to the strength required; the walls and partitions were of the same material, split, beaten flat, and broadly plaited; and the floors were narrow bamboo strips, separated by one-quarter-inch cracks, and tied in position with bejuco strings and placed shiny side up. Doors and window-screens were woven like the sides, edged with light rods, and suspended by a simple contrivance which allowed them to be slid back and forth or propped open. This admirable arrangement was arrived at by means of large pieces of bamboo being rigidly fastened to the door or the shutter and slipped over a smaller sliding rod fixed above. The house was rectangular in shape and divided into four rooms: a living-room in front, with a little chamber off it for the elders of the family; a middle and general sleeping apartment, and a kitchen with three earthen fire-pots at the farther end. The whole

structure was raised from the ground about five feet, and entered by a bamboo ladder. The furniture of my new abode consisted of a small, hardwood table, a chest of drawers, two benches, and several stools and earthen water-vessels. Beds there were none, for the peasant class are contented with the yielding floor and a sleeping-mat. A few colored prints of saints were fastened on the inner walls, and I found several religious books, printed in the Pampangan language, in a drawer. There was also in the front room a shelf arranged for the little shrine never absent from the Tagalog house. The wealthy often possess elaborate and costly objects to decorate their place of prayer, but in the average house, as in this case, there were merely two wooden statuettes, one of the Virgin and the other representing the Crucifixion. Beyond these things, a few fishing and palay baskets and several earthen cooking utensils comprised the furnishings of the house, which in every way is typical of the ordinary central-province dwelling. The houses of the poor Filipinos, in my estimation, are more comfortable than those of the better classes. At least, one gets plenty of air in the former, and, if one has to sleep on the floor, as is often the case, bamboo is infinitely superior to hardwood boards. Compared with the dwellings of the cotters in England and Europe, or with the foul dens in which the poor of our cities crowd, the shelter of the Filipino peasant is a palace as far as ventilation, comfort and cleanliness go. It is eminently suited to the requirements of the climate, costs nothing but the peasant's own labor, and is not wanting in a picturesque quality that harmonizes with its tropical surroundings.

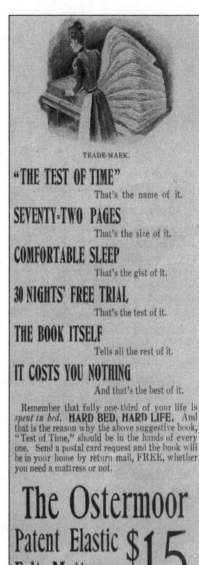

- When the fighting ended in Cuba, he was convinced his last opportunity to serve his country had been lost.
- When the newspapers brought the news of the insurrection in the Philippines, the Pacific islands captured by Admiral Dewey from the Spanish during the Spanish-American War, he felt called again.
- After all, one of his favorite poems is "The White Man's Burden," written by Rudyard Kipling to persuade Congress to annex the Philippine Islands.
- Emilio Aguinaldo, who led an unsuccessful insurrection against Spain in 1896-97, had reorganized a native army to fight America for Philippine independence.
- Clearly, America's next war was to be in the Philippines, and Simon J. McElroy was determined not to be left behind this time.
- In March 1900, Simon joined a newly formed volunteer regiment and was granted command of a company; he was delighted to be in charge of troops again.
- Because the rebel army was only equipped with ancient rifles and bolos, he was convinced that subduing it wouldn't take long.
- Two months later, he and his troops embarked from San Francisco, leaving behind a thriving business, a fine new Victorian home, four children and an angry, frightened wife.
- Simon's first wartime discovery was seasickness; having never been on a body of water larger than the Missouri River, he was unsettled by the rocking of the boat and became violently ill.
- Worse yet, as the 36-year-old commander of a troop of young men, he felt compelled to hide his sickness.
- When at long last the troop ship arrived in Manila, he discovered a city alive with activity.
- By day, the troops drilled in a camp outside the city; by night, the young soldiers frequented the bars and bordellos which had sprung up following American occupation.
- Discipline was a minor concern to the officer corps, who knew the troops would be in the countryside soon enough, where pleasures would be few and fear ever-present.

- While Simon and his men waited for orders, he attended a large number of social affairs hosted by senior and government officials.
- He was sure many of the contacts would be useful when he returned to his business in Nebraska.
- Simon writes to his wife daily, and misses her and the children more than he had anticipated, anxiously awaiting letters carrying news of his family, McElroy Supply, and life in North Platte.
- His wife Mary often encloses a clipping in each envelope—obituaries, farm news, and occasionally a mention of the presidential campaign between Nebraska native William Jennings Bryan and William McKinley.
- She knows that Simon considers Bryan a dangerous radical, and in her last letter, even enclosed an anti-Bryan campaign button inspired by the solar eclipse on May 28, 1900.
- He believes that Bryan's contention that the "have-nots" will become prosperous by the minting of large quantities of silver coins is ridiculous.
- Running the supply business, he has seen both good farmers and bad farmers, and feels that hard work—not the monetary policy in Washington—is what makes the difference.
- A recent letter from home carried news that the latest Sears, Roebuck and Co. book, billing itself as the cheapest supply house on earth, is more than 1,000 pages long.

*Simon writes home daily and misses his wife and children more than he expected.*

## Life at Work

- For the past six months, Simon's regiment has been deployed in the jungle farther down the main island of Luzon, away from the comforts, distractions and conflicts of Manila.
- Their job has been to secure the southern portion of the island.
- Simon was both ready and disappointed when the order arrived—ready to lead his men into battle, but disappointed to miss the presidential election news; America will be destroyed if President McKinley is defeated by madman Bryan.
- Since their arrival, his troop's job has been mostly to patrol, making sure the insurgents don't get out of hand.
- The hardest part is identifying who the insurgents might be.
- He knows from experience that many Filipinos who act friendly are actually freedom fighters waiting for a chance to kill.
- Often, the patrol comes under attack from unseen enemies firing from the thick jungle; worse is when his men run into rebel-laid traps that set off a flurry of poisoned spears.

*Simon left behind a successful business to seek adventure in the Philippine Islands.*

*Simon is following the presidential election closely.*

*Sears, Roebuck and Co. is offering stiff competition to stores that supply farmers' needs.*

- One of Simon's junior officers, Lt. Michaelman, a Nebraska railroad company brakeman whom Simon knew socially before the war, was caught in such a trap.
- Despite prompt medical attention, Lt. Michaelman died a horrible, painful death three days after being struck by poisoned spears.

My father said,
"Don't go
To a burlesque show;
You'll see things you
shouldn't see."
And he was right,
For the very next night
I saw Father in the
row in front of me.
—Current
burlesque song

- It fell to Simon, as the company leader, to write to Michaelman's wife of the news.
- Knowing that Michaelman was a family man with many children, but few assets other than his railroad salary, he felt inadequate writing words to comfort the widow.
- Ultimately, he was bolstered by his belief that America's cause was right and that sacrifices had to be made in the name of freedom.
- To reduce the chances of another poison spear death caused by a trap, Simon's unit now makes a prisoner—tethered to a rope—walk ahead of the troops as they patrol the jungle.
- If anyone is going to get killed with spears, it should be a rebel, most of the commanders in the field agree.
- Simon is now doubly cautious, assuming every Filipino is an insurgent.
- Over the past three months, three men in his company have been killed and seven wounded; tension is at its peak and morale is low.
- Although the rebels are only armed with old guns, bolo knives and their magic charms called "anting-anting," they possess enormous courage and willingness to strike the soldiers at any moment.
- During patrols, if there is the slightest hint of rebel activity, the company will set fire to the grass hut homes in the village, destroy the occupants' food and shoot the animals, including the lumbering caribou used for planting rice.
- Simon is unable to understand whom the Filipinos want to follow if they achieve independence.
- The Tagalog tribes were for Aguinaldo, but the Muslim-believing Moors on the island of Mindanao don't trust the Christian Filipino insurrectionists—or the Americans.
- What kind of country will the Philippines become if its people don't agree, Simon has wondered to himself and in letters home.
- Bringing Christianity to all the people will be an important first step, he is sure.
- Nonetheless, occasionally—and always quietly—Simon's soldiers are questioning why the United States is fighting in the Philippines.
- All the soldiers are counting the days until the end of their enlistment so they can return home to the wives, children, farms and townspeople they can trust.

- Most of the men are equipped with a .30 caliber, bolt-action Krag-Jorgensen rifle, the first U.S. military weapon to use smokeless powder.
- Designed in Denmark, but manufactured in the Unites States, its magazine holds five cartridges, which are loaded individually.
- The rifle has inspired a song which includes the words: "Underneath the starry flag, civilize 'em with a krag, and return us to our beloved home."
- Recently, orders came down that pleased Simon immensely; instead of simply patrolling the jungle, they were to hunt down the enemy.
- Almost immediately, Simon and his party of 18 mounted infantrymen engaged in their first major battle.
- To find the rebels, Simon positioned himself on a hilltop to look for movement or a sign of the insurgents, when he suddenly spotted in the distance a figure in a Church mission tower.
- The figure appeared, disappeared and then reappeared, indicating to Simon that the man was serving as a lookout for the rebels; the insurgents must be close by.
- With this knowledge, his men carefully and steadily approached the hill, taking pains not to be seen.
- When they drew close, the men dismounted and approached on foot.
- In this manner, they spotted the Filipino fighters standing in a trench.
- Silently, Simon and his men charged down the slope toward the trench, not firing until they were 25 yards away.
- The surprised rebels fled.
- Simon, only slightly winded from the charge, caught one rebel soldier and clubbed him to the ground with his pistol butt.
- As his troops chased the fleeing rebels, they came upon a second trench packed with men ready to fight.
- Fortunately, the insurgents did not have the firepower to withstand this charge; of a party of 85, 19 were killed and the rest surrendered.
- Simon was exhilarated; having missed the Indian Wars and opted out of the Cuban assault, he was finally in a battle to defend America's honor in the Philippines, and proud to report to headquarters that this battle opened up the area, including a nearby town, for American occupation.

*Simon's men are quietly questioning why the United States is fighting in the Philippines.*

### Testimony of former Corporal Richard O'Brien, Company M, 26th United States Volunteers, concerning a battle at Barrio la Nog, Philippine Islands, *The New York World*, April 18, 1902:

It was on the twenty-seventh day of December, the anniversary of my birth, and I shall never forget the scenes I witnessed on that day. As we approached the town, the word was passed along the line that there would be no prisoners taken. It meant that we were to shoot every living thing in sight—man, woman and child. The first shot was fired by the then first sergeant of our company. His target was a mere boy, who was coming down the mountain path into the town astride a caribou. The boy was not struck by the bullet, but that was not the sergeant's fault. The little Filipino boy slid from the back of his caribou and fled in terror up the mountainside. Half a dozen shots were fired after him. The shooting now attracted the villagers, who came out of their homes in alarm, wondering what it all meant. They offered no offense, did not display a weapon, made no hostile movement whatsoever, but they were ruthlessly shot down in cold blood—men, women and children. The poor natives huddled together or fled in terror. Many were pursued and killed on the spot. Two older men, bearing between them a white flag and clasping hands like two brothers, approached the lines. Their hair was white. They tottered; they were so feeble under the weight of years. To my horror and that of the other men in the command, the order was given to fire, and the two old men were shot down in their tracks. We entered the village. The man who had been on a sickbed appeared at the doorway of his home. He received a bullet in the abdomen and fell dead in the doorway. Dum-dum bullets were used in the massacre, but we were not told the name of the bullets. We didn't have to be told. We knew what they were.

In another part of the village a mother with a babe at her breast and two young children at her side pleaded for mercy. She feared to leave her home, which had just been torched—accidentally, I believe. She faced the flames with her children, and not a hand was raised to save her or the little ones. They perished miserably. It was sure death if she left the house—it was sure death if she remained. She feared the American soldiers, however, worse than the devouring flames.

- During the next few days, his company pushed farther into the jungle, repeatedly finding evidence that the rebels had fled before his army arrived.
- Peace, it appeared, was possible.

### Life in the Community: Manila, The Philippines
- Manila is a strange city to Simon—nothing like his native Nebraska—the people, the language, the landscape, the rules, everything.
- But the food is the worst; while many of his fellow officers speak at length about the joys of exotic foods served over rice braced with fruits, Simon is silent, hating Philippine food.
- It's just not what he is used to eating, although military food is little better; almost every letter home praises Mary and her culinary skills.
- Even worse is all the negative talk.
- Throughout the streets of Manila, he finds people questioning, with little credibility, Simon thinks, America's right to occupy the Philippines, and its campaign against freedom fighter Aguinaldo.

- When Aguinaldo's army failed to bring independence from Spain in 1896-97, before America's war with Spain, Aguinaldo and his rebel leaders were willing to take money to leave the islands.
- They ended up in Hong Kong, a British colony, living off Spain; now they want the United States to step aside while they create an independent democratic state.
- Simon knows business and the world; America won the Philippines fair and square—based on the Treaty of Paris with Spain in December 1898.
- If the United States abdicates its God-rendered requirement to civilize the natives of the Philippines, the Germans will slip in, make the Philippines an economic colony, and control trade in the Pacific Ocean.
- Besides, it is America's turn to bring Christianity to the world.
- Simon knows America saved the Filipinos from Spanish oppression; he is sure they will eventually appreciate the better life only America can bring.
- Recently, the best possible news arrived: Brigadier General Fredrick Funston and his Kansas Volunteers, masquerading as prisoners, were led into the camp of Aguinaldo; using a series of forged dispatches, they lured the rebel leader into the open and captured him.
- The rebellion appears to be at an end.
- During the two-year war, some 126,000 American soldiers have been committed to the conflict.
- In all, 4,234 American soldiers died, while more than 16,000 Filipino soldiers were killed.
- Casualties of civilians caught between the American army and Filipino insurgents were in excess of 200,000, including those who died of famine and disease.

# Historical Snapshot
# 1901

- Major movies for the year included *The Philippines and Our New Possessions, The Conquest of the Air, Drama at the Bottom of the Sea* and *Execution of Czolgosz*, the man who shot President William McKinley
- Pogroms in Russia forced many Jews to America
- The U.S. constructed a 16-inch, 130-pound breech-loading rifle that was the most powerful in the world
- Popular songs included "Ain't Dat a Shame?," "The Night We Did Not Care," "When You Loved Me in the Sweet Old Days" and "Maiden with the Dreamy Eyes"
- The first U.S. Open golf tournament under USGA rules was held at the Myopia Hunt Club in Hamilton, Massachusetts
- The U.S. granted citizenship to the five civilized tribes: the Cherokee, Creek, Choctaw, Chicasaw and Seminole
- West Point officially abolished the practice of hazing cadets
- The Boston Museum of Fine Arts was given funds to purchase Velásquez's portrait, *Don Baltazar and His Dwarf*
- Books included *Up from Slavery* by Booker T. Washington, *To a Person Sitting in Darkness* by Mark Twain, *The Psychopathology of Everyday Life* by Sigmund Freud, *The Octopus* by Frank Norris and *Springtime and Harvest* by Upton Sinclair
- North Carolina proposed a literacy amendment for voting
- *The Settlement Cookbook,* published by a Milwaukee settlement worker to help immigrant women, carried the phrase, "The way to a man's heart is through his stomach"
- Peter Cooper Hewitt created the first mercury-vapor electric lamp
- Four widows of Revolutionary War soldiers remained on pensions; one veteran of the war of 1812 still lived
- Researchers discovered a connection between obesity and heart disease
- Of the 120,000 U.S. military troops on active duty, 70,000 were stationed in the Philippines fighting the insurgency
- South Dakota passed legislation making school attendance mandatory for children eight to 14 years of age
- Jergens Lotion, over-the-counter drugs, automobile licenses, the Cadillac, the Mercedes, The U.S. Army War College and the Scholastic Aptitude Test (SAT) all made their first appearance
- The first vacuum cleaner was invented to compete with the Bissell Carpet Sweeper
- The military began placing greater emphasis on the science of nutrition after England had to reject three out of five men in its recruiting for the Boer War in 1899
- Vice President Teddy Roosevelt was made an honorary member of the Hebrew Veterans of the War with Spain; many of its members had fought as Roosevelt's Rough Riders during the Spanish-American War
- Christy Mathewson of New York pitched professional baseball's first no-hitter, defeating St. Louis 5-0
- The length of time required to cross the Atlantic Ocean shrank to one week, down from one month in 1800
- The median age of men for their first marriage was 25.9 years, while for women, it was 21.9 years

## "Filipino Responsibility," by Phelps Whitmarsh, *The Outlook*, March 24, 1900:

Responsibility for war in the Philippines lies at the door of the Filipinos. The Americans did not want war, neither did they provoke or cause the outbreak of hostilities. The Americans, it is true, had not been diplomatic, nor had they been as frank with the rebels as they should have been, but these things were not sufficient to warrant the Filipinos making war . . . .

The outbreak of February 9, which was the first recognized act of war, was begun by a Nebraskan sentry at the Santa Mesa camp, firing in self-defense at some Filipinos who were trying to dash through the American line and cut him off. In that limited sense, the first act of hostility was committed by the Filipinos, and the first shot fired by the American. But the sentry's shot was not war; sentries shoot strangers who do not halt when challenged, without this being called war. The Filipino's answering volley all along the line, however, was war.

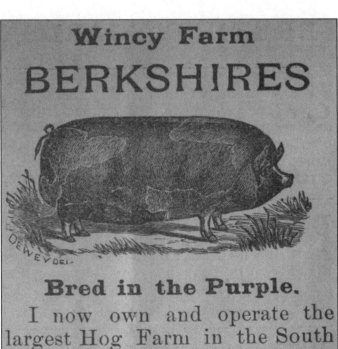

## Cincinnati, Ohio, March 6, 1900, Speech by Judge William R. Day, former Secretary of State, concerning the Philippines:

Now, since the insurrection seems practically ended, the United States enters upon the crowning duty of giving to these people a just, stable and free government. The labor of acquiring title, hampered with difficulty, was as naught compared with the labor which will be required in establishing ourselves in the confidence of the people and gradually fitting them for self-government. We shall succeed in the island by not following the policy of exploitation by which they were misruled for centuries.

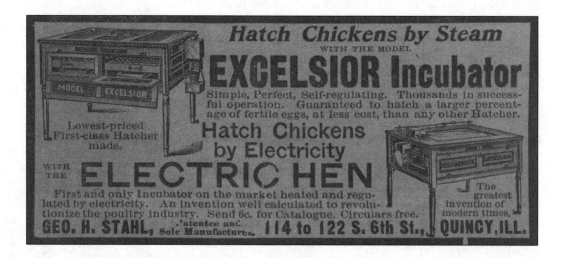

## "Some Dead Sea Fruit of Our War of Subjugation, Topics of the Times," *The Arena*, June 1902:

In his testimony before the United States Senate Committee, Governor Taft made a humiliating admission that should strike horror to the mind of every American. He admitted that the frightful torture known as the "water-cure treatment" was used occasionally by the soldiers of this Republic to force the unhappy Filipinos to disclose desired information.

This treatment consists of placing the victim on his back and then pouring water down his throat until the body is so distended as to cause exquisite suffering, which is intensified by the fear entertained by the victim that his stomach will burst.

## "How to Convert a White Man into a Savage," by Poultney Bigelow, *The Independent*, May 5, 1902:

What in other countries would be called marching, in the Philippines is creeping along like a tiger. There are no roads to speak of; we have to follow trails through a jungle so thick that one can move but in single file—and can see but a few feet in any direction.

The natives are masters of the art of making traps for wild beasts, and they hunt United States soldiers after the same fashion. They dig in our path pits skillfully masked, so that our men fall into them and are impaled on poisoned stakes. And then, at unexpected intervals, a thread is stretched in the grass at their feet, and when that is snapped, a bent sapling springs into position with several poisoned spears attached. You cannot enter a deserted cabin without running the risk of letting loose a spring of this sort with some poisoned spearheads attached; usually the mere stepping on the sill or front doorstep is the signal.

One of these traps nearly finished me. Fortunately, the spears passed me—one in front, one behind—half an inch of variation would have done the business.

I cannot tell exactly what the poison is, but it is supposed to be animal decomposition. At any rate, it is effective. Such a spear trap struck one of my men in the left side. He was treated immediately, but without effect. His extremities turned black—his nose, his feet, his fingers—and he soon died in great agony. It was hard to sit by the poor fellow and watch his torment without being able to do anything for him. After his death, our surgeon cut open where the spear had gone in and drew off several tablespoonfuls of a blackish matter, which he pronounced as something wholly strange to his experience—certainly a deadly and a swift poison.

We creep through the jungle with little worry regarding bullets, but at every step watching for the trace of a trap or a poisoned spear—an enemy more dangerous than a snake, and equally difficult to see.

After a few horrible deaths by those hidden weapons, we hit upon the device of taking a prisoner and letting him show us the way. We held him by a rope so that he could not suddenly disappear in the brush, and the poison of his fellow killed now and then even a native—possibly by the very spear he had himself placed in position! Yes, it's brutal. It's revolting to a white man, yet we're ordered to do it. If we don't, we are guilty of military insubordination—if we do, we are branded cruel!

War in the Philippines consists mainly of creeping up and down the country in search of an enemy who retires as we advance, who advances as we retire. He never attacks, save when our men are in a hopeless minority; his tactics are those of the Red Indian. So long as we confine ourselves to marching up and down after him, he has no objection to the war lasting forever. Our occupation brings a great deal of money into the country, and this money is spent mainly among the natives who pretend to be friendly, but are in truth supporting the popular cause.

President William McKinley's comments to the missionary committee of the Methodist Episcopal Church on why he decided to keep the conquered territory of the Philippines:

"I walked the floor of the White House night after night until midnight and I am not ashamed to tell you gentlemen, that I went down on my knees and prayed to Almighty God for light and guidance more than one night. And one night, late, it came to me this way—I don't know how it was, but it came. One, that we could not give the Philippines back to Spain—that would be cowardly and dishonorable. Two, that we could not turn them over to France or Germany—our commercial rivals in the Orient. Three, that we could not leave them to themselves— they were unfit for self-government—and they would soon have anarchy and misrule over there worse than Spain's was. And, four, that there was nothing left for us to do but to take them all, and to educate the Filipinos, and uplift them, civilize and Christianize them, and by God's grace do the very best we could for them, as our fellow men for whom Christ also died. And then I went to bed, and went to sleep, and slept soundly, and the next morning I sent for the chief engineer of the War Department (our mapmaker), and I told him to put the Philippines on the map of the United States, and there they are, and there they will stay while I am president."

## "More Troops Needed in the Philippines, Demands on Gen. MacArthur from Every Department," *The New York Times*, July 16, 1900:

"More soldiers" is the demand which is coming to Gen. MacArthur from every department of the islands. Recent events have worked to vindicate Gen. Lawton's judgment that 100,000 troops will be needed to establish American sovereignty over the Philippines. Until they attempted to hold provinces of 200,000 or 300,000 hostile inhabitants with a regiment or two, the American commanders hardly realized the size of the Philippine Islands. The present force is not large enough to garrison more than half of the important towns, and in some of the most important islands, among them Cebu, Panay, Samar, Leyte, and the great Mohammedan island of Mindanao, only the commercial ports are occupied. The Moors are a cloud on the horizon.

Officers best acquainted with conditions in Mindanao and the Sulu Islands say that they consider serious fighting there inevitable. If it comes, the two regiments, which are scattered in small garrisons, some of them hundreds of miles apart along the coast of Mindanao, an island nearly as large as Luzon, may have serious work. The Moors are fighters by nature, do not fear death, have many guns, though of antiquated makes, but the best execution for lying in the thick jungles and cutting down soldiers who pass through with terrible knives and spears.

Gen. Young, who is holding seven of the most mountainous provinces of Luzon with four regiments, expects severe work during the rainy season. For some two months, after his bewildering invasion of the north in December, the insurgents were paralyzed. With troops to keep an eye on the villages and prevent reconcentration, the paralysis, the general believes, would have been made permanent. Finding ample opportunities to reorganize, the insurgents have availed themselves thereof. Many troops have worn themselves and

their horses down to the limit of endurance in marching about the mountain trails, striking the Filipinos wherever they could get upon the track of an organized band. Hundreds have been slain, but much of the work has been like brushing away mosquitoes that swarm down upon a new spot.

Gen. Tinio has a nomadic command, and his warriors can hide their guns and become "amigos" if it suits their interests. As few of them wear uniforms and people combine to shield them from detection, the Americans are greatly handicapped.

The church has become a troublesome factor in Gen. Young's territory. Aglipaya, the priest who proclaimed himself as archbishop of the Philippines, is in the field as a general. His forces attacked Capt. Dodd of the Third Cavalry at Batoc. More than 200 Filipinos were slain. Aglipaya commanded in person and there is an unconfirmed report that he was among the killed. His followers fought with the recklessness of Mohammedan fanatics. They approached the Americans in three lines, with an advanced guard of women arranged with the expectation that the Americans would not fire upon them. Behind the women was a line of bolomen and others armed only with wooden swords, no more dangerous than policemen's clubs, and behind the bolomen, the riflemen. Happily, the women threw themselves flat upon the ground and sought shelter at the first fire, so that few of them were injured.

The soldiers thought they were men dressed in women's clothes. The onslaught of the bolomen was like the descent of the Mahdi fanatics upon Kitchener's squad at Khartoum. They kept coming faster than the soldiers could shoot them down, until they were so close that the cavalrymen had not time to fire and load, but went through their lines with clubbed carbines.

# 1903 Profile

# The Liberation of Panama

## Civilian

Ned Ritchie, an automobile-loving bachelor lawyer and Washington socialite, has played an important role—behind the scenes—in making sure Panama is the location of the new canal linking the Atlantic and the Pacific, even though it required the overthrow of the Colombian government to create the Republic of Panama.

## Life at Home

- For generations, the Panama Canal had been the dream of men with bold imaginations; for half a century, it had been the subject of practical effort.
- For Ned Ritchie, the value of the canal came more recently—in fact, only minutes after he was hired by a coalition of Western timber barons and shipping magnates, who simply asked Ned to make the canal a reality.
- Money was not an issue, but—they emphasized—speed was critical.
- A canal connecting the Atlantic and Pacific was essential to protecting their businesses, and it had to be in Panama, not the much-discussed route in Nicaragua.
- For a man who loved a challenge, money and, most of all, the thrill of speed—particularly when riding in an automobile—Ritchie's new clients' proposition was a dream-come-true.
- Recently, he had been able to drive a car more than 50 miles per hour and lived to tell about it—what a thrill!
- *Scientific American* insisted that one day, 55 mph would be normal, but that was hard to fathom.
- The fastest way to move cargo across the Isthmus of Panama was through the Panama Railroad, built 50 years ago by U.S. citizens and operated under the guarantee and protection of the American government.
- It had always been considered the precursor of an isthmian ship canal.
- Now it was time to take transportation between the two oceans to the next level with the construction of an American-controlled canal that need not be closed down every time some Latin country wanted to stage another revolution.

*Ned Ritchie wants to build a canal in Panama.*

*Life in Panama operates at its own pace.*

- Besides, America was now solidly behind the idea of joining the two oceans, either at Panama or Nicaragua.
- The heroic, two-month voyage in 1898 of the battleship *Oregon,* which was forced to travel from California around the tip of South America and back to Cuba to fight in the Spanish-American War, graphically brought home to America the need to complete the long-discussed canal.
- With a canal controlled by America, the trip would have been cut from 12,000 to 4,000 miles.
- The first thing Ned Ritchie did was draw up a list of impediments, the key one being the Colombian government, which claimed the Isthmus of Panama as its own.
- The second problem was the longstanding power of a coalition of railway interests that could be counted on to fight any treaty or agreement, arguing that rail was sophisticated enough to handle the job.
- In reality, the coalition knew they would lose control of the shipping revenues, including kickbacks paid by most shippers who had to have their ships unloaded to use the rail service.
- A third issue was the ongoing debate in Congress concerning the best location for the canal.
- Sites in both Nicaragua and Panama had been discussed; Admiral John Walker, head of the Walker Commission, claimed both routes were feasible from an engineering standpoint.
- However, nearly everyone agreed the canal could be constructed in Panama for less money if the French company, Compagnie Nouvelle, currently working there could be bought out for around $40 million.
- Never a fool, or one to waste time, Ned realized immediately that the man he needed to see was his good friend, Senator Mark Hanna of Ohio.
- Already a reputed "kingmaker" because of his role in the winning presidential campaigns of 1896 and 1900, Senator Hanna's support was critical to making Panama the Amer-

*Scientific American says that one day traveling 55 miles per hour will be common.*

**"The man behind the egg."**

Crane. *The New York Times*, 1903.

ican choice; he was a pragmatist who listened to reason, loved working with business, and understood the fine art of the deal.

- Ned's second stop was to Secretary of State John Hay to discuss military and business strategy; the ever-impatient President Theodore Roosevelt wanted a canal now.
- Shortly after the death of President William McKinley and the elevation of Roosevelt, the new president made it clear that he was unwilling to take the property from Colombia, but he was not above using intimidation.
- The canal, the president said, was first, last and always the indispensable path to the global destiny of the United States.
- Roosevelt envisioned America as the commanding power of two oceans, joined by a canal built, owned, operated, policed and fortified by his country.
- His ideas were influenced by the book, *The Influence of Sea Power upon History* by Alfred Thayer Mahan, who said that national greatness and commercial supremacy were directly related to supremacy at sea.
- For Ned Ritchie, this new assignment meant more time swapping gossip at Washington's Cosmos Club, where the powerful men of the city gathered to drink, think and deal.
- There, he could informally discuss world affairs with Senator John Tyler Morgan, the Chairman of the Senate Committee on Interoceanic Canals.

## Life at Work

- Senator Morgan, a 77-year-old, irritable lawyer from Alabama, was fond of saying, "A lie is an abomination unto the Lord and an ever-present help in time of need."
- He was also a great believer that the Nicaragua route was the best alternative, because it would benefit his home state of Alabama.
- World markets would open for Southern lumber, iron, cotton and manufactured goods, shifting the economic power of the nation, he believed.
- Proponents for a Panama Canal noted that it would be one-third the length of a canal at Nicaragua, have fewer curves, require less excavation in total, have fewer locks and, ultimately, cost less.

THE LADIES' HOME JOURNAL

## The Well-Dressed Woman at Middle Age

ORIGINAL DESIGNS BY VIRGINIA LOUIS RALSTON
DRAWINGS BY JEANNETTE HOPE

### "Our Future in the Pacific," *The Wall Street Journal*, October 3, 1903:

Commercially and politically, we already almost dominate the world's greatest ocean. In recent years this vast fact has been realized by the great captains of commerce more than by our public thinkers. Mr. James J. Hill, who shows in his thought and prophetic enterprises qualities of statesmanship in business (and note that in modern times the great master of business must be a statesman—the very magnitude of his operations require it), was the first to see the necessity and inevitability of American commercial expansion over the Pacific. Reasoning from this premise, the Great Northern Road was built. Again reasoning from this premise, a mighty ship line to the Orient was established. And today, the greatest vessels that float upon the face of all the waters of the world are the leviathan vessels recently launched for the Pacific trade. The value of Hawaii in this world-scheme of American commercial expansion is now clear.

- However, after years of rancorous debate, one day, the morning papers reported news that changed everything: Mount Pelee had erupted in Nicaragua, proving the area was too unstable to support a multimillion-dollar United States investment.
- Best of all, Ned remembered that Nicaragua had featured an exploding volcano on one of its postage stamps, so with the help of friends, other lobbyists and Washington insiders, 90 of the prophetic volcano stamps were purchased and placed on letters hand-delivered to every senator.
- The message inside was simple: "Panama is a safer route."
- The Senate took notice and forged a compromise to focus attention on Panama, much to the anger of Sen. Morgan and the excitement of Ned Ritchie's clients—even if William Nelson Cromwell was being given most of the credit for this deal.
- Everyone knew that Cromwell was the most powerful lobbyist in Washington, but it's invigorating for Ned to be an insider on a big deal.
- Yet, when he was hired, he never dreamed that a crucial step in guaranteeing the Panama route would be helping to orchestrate a revolution against the country of Colombia, with its outcome guaranteed by American warships.
- Staging a coup, however, was clearly within the grasp of Cromwell, hired by the French Compagnie Nouvelle to help them recover the millions spent attempting—and failing—to dig a canal across the Isthmus of Panama.
- Almost immediately, the issue shifted from the location of the route to obtaining control from Colombia of a six-mile-wide zone across the isthmus for 100 years.
- The stated price was $10 million in gold and an annual rent of $250,000.
- By the Treaty of 1846, the United States had the right and the responsibility to protect the railroad transit across the isthmus; for decades, the world had looked to the U.S. to do its duty, even in the midst of an insurrection.

*Walls are easy things to mount,*
*Sleeping aunties do not count;*
*He grows bolder by degrees—*
*Fond embraces, à la squeeze.*

### Editorial, *Boston Evening Transcript,* November 13, 1903:

Physically, socially and politically, Panama is a panhandle, a remote, slightly connected appendage of Colombia. It takes three weeks to go from the isthmus to the capital at Bogota. The interests of the two are essentially different. Colombia is a South American country, whose prosperity depends, like that of the other South American countries, on mining and agriculture. As for Panama, the one gigantic accident of nature which causes it to be a country apart is its canal possibility. That it is the narrowest part of the western hemisphere makes it *sui generis*. Its interests all hang on this, and a good government for it would be one which keeps this steadily in mind. What, to the isthmus, is the price of cattle and hides in Bogota, compared to the golden prospect of the United States spending uncounted millions in labor along the 49 miles that stretch between Colon and Panama?

I took the Canal Zone and let Congress debate.
—President Theodore Roosevelt

**Highland Linen**
Writing Paper

*HAND MADE STYLE*

Have you seen our Highland Linen with rough or deckle edges? This is the latest fine writing paper.

Highland Linen is one of our most popular papers and in Hand Made Style will be even more popular.

Every woman and most men will be delighted with the purely esthetic quality of this paper, which we have in three sizes only—Duchess—for notes, Critique—for letters, and Nelson for men's use, in White, Pearl Gray and Swiss Blue.

Your dealer should be able to show it to you. If not send his name and we will send you samples.

Twotone Linen is another popular fabric surfaced paper. Ask for samples if you are not familiar with it.

**Eaton-Hurlbut Paper Company**
Pittsfield, Mass.

- Besides, the French company was willing to exchange its rights for $40 million and relinquish its equipment, land and excavation work completed so far.
- All that was needed was for Colombia to agree to a new treaty.
- Everyone in Washington knew the cash-strapped Colombian government could be difficult, so when an argument arose over money—specifically how much Colombia would receive from the French and who would control its use—Ritchie and his colleagues were ready.
- On November 2, as a negotiation ploy, the Colombian Senate rejected the American treaty.
- It was the wrong decision.
- The next day a coup against Colombia was launched by the leading citizens of Panama with the tacit approval of the United States, including many senators with whom Ned had been dealing.
- The Panamanian revolution was supported by 4,000 rifles smuggled into the country on a cargo ship from Louisiana; $100,000 to bribe the Colombian garrison; and numerous reassuring cables from Washington confirming that American ships had been dispatched.
- Knowing American troops were on the way, Colombia made practically no effort to quell the insurrection.
- The only casualties came when a Colombian gunboat in the harbor fired a few shots, accidentally killing a Chinese man and his mule.
- Throughout the short-lived conflict, American warships were stationed on both sides of the isthmus, a reason in itself of the need for the canal, Ritchie noted.

*A stamp helped convince the Senate to pick Panama.*

THE SMALL ONE: "I'm the republic of Panama, I am!"
From the *Blade* (Toledo).

- The United States also announced that it would not permit Colombian troops to land on the isthmus and would regain by force any lost territory.
- The U.S. warships *Nashville* and *Dixie* were at the ready.
- Ned's clients rejoiced, but critics screamed about illegal colonialism on the part of America.
- According to Secretary John Hay, the United States was entitled to exercise paramount control over isthmian transit because it "runs with the land," irrespective of the personnel or central location for the government of the country.
- The United States guaranteed the freedom of isthmus transit under the Treaty of 1846 made with New Granada, but remaining in place when that country was dissolved and the isthmus fell to the control of Colombia.
- In like manner, the treaty agreements could now move to the newly created Panama.
- As Ned had predicted to his clients, Panama's M. Philipe Bunau-Varilla signed the new treaty on November 18, only 15 days after the secession movement began.
- The deal provided for a 10-mile corridor; Cromwell was reported to have received a fee of $800,000, and though Ritchie's fee was considerably less, it still topped five figures.
- The Colombian government continues to protest both the recognition of Panama by America and the loss of money which would have come to Colombia under the old treaty.
- Ritchie told his clients to expect ongoing criticism; not everyone would be pleased with America's interference in Colombia's affairs, or for finally resolving the canal dispute.
- Editorial cartoons come and go, but the canal will be there forever, protecting American interests, he likes to say.
- As part of the victory, he was invited to the White House and heard a story that made his victory even more delicious.
- According to the gossip, the president explained to War Secretary Elihu Root how he got the canal from Panama on the same terms he had proposed to Colombia.
- Root replied, "You have shown that you were accused of seduction, and you have proved conclusively you were guilty of rape."

*The French poured millions into building a ditch across Panama.*

PANAMA: "I'll just float around on this log for a while and perhaps Uncle Sam will pick me up."
From the *News-Tribune* (Duluth).

- Hay defended the deal with Panama, saying that he had "no plainer duty than to preserve for the benefit of all free transit between the oceans."

## Life in the Community: Panama

- The Republic of Panama extends about 460 miles from east to west, comprising an area of 31,500 square miles.
- Its population of 300,000 is clustered along the seacoast, most of the interior being dense jungle and largely unexplored.
- Founded by the Spanish 100 years before the Pilgrims landed at Plymouth, the city of Panama claims 25,000 people; Colon, formerly known as Aspinwall, has about 3,000 people, and dates from the building of the railroad.
- The territory remained a Spanish colony until 1821, when it declared its independence and was incorporated by the Republic of Colombia.
- In 1841, Panama seceded from Colombia; in 1885, it was forced back under the control of the Colombian regime.
- The railroad, built with foreign capital and manned by foreign labor, is the only highly developed business in the country.
- Currently, the greatest impediment to Panama's development is the prevalence of yellow fever.
- American engineers believe that with proper sanitation administration, this problem can be solved, allowing Panama to be both a water highway between the oceans and a winter resort for the wealthy.

*Ned cherishes comfort and power.*

## "The Rediscovery of America by the Automobile," R. G. Betts, *Outing*, October 1903:

Think how much more thoroughly Columbus could have discovered America had the good Queen been able to pawn an extra jewel to place an automobile or, to use the newer term, a motor-car at his command!

Thoughts of such trifles as warlike savages or trackless forests should not be permitted to distort the vision, or destroy the picture. The "leader of thought" carries you to the horseless age and the noiseless city. That's a long way forward. Columbus is merely a long way in the other direction, and the point is right here: the motor-car provides the means and is enabling Americans to really discover their own country—and some other countries—as they never have discovered, and never could discover them before. Run your finger over the list—it's a short one—human feet, the horse, the railway, the trolley, the bicycle. There you have the only means of terrestrial locomotion available to man until the advent of the motor-car.

To discover one's country it is necessary to get about—to move not within a circle or a square. Lands of promise rarely are within circumscribed lines . . . . .

The average American is more intent on touring abroad than at home. Taking a quick survey of the scenes or places in his country which fire his desire, it is reasonably safe to say that Niagara Falls, Yellowstone Park, New York City, and Washington comprise the list. He is too full of London, Paris, Brussels, Waterloo, the Rhine, the Blue Danube, the canons of Switzerland, the Cathedral of Thingumbob, or the Castle of What's-his-name, to seriously consider what America holds for him. And how does he reach these scenes of his interest? Usually in a stuffy railway coach in conjunction with a creeping horse-drawn rig. Guidebook in hand or listening to the droning description of a human guide, he gapes more or less awed at this object or that, and then hurries to his rig that he may "catch" the railroad train. Generally, he is out to see a particular object, having seen the beauties of land and water, and the charms of outdoor life are but cursory incidentals.

There is this to be said of the owner of a motor-car: Though desire to behold the scenes of promise across the sea may burn more fiercely within him than the wish to see that which is at his door, the very nature of his conveyance will, whether or no, compel him to discover the country round about. To possess a car is to become possessed of desire to go far afield. The limits of the city become narrow, contracted, cramped, cagelike. The desire, so to speak, to spread its wings is in the nature of the motor-car, if things inanimate may be said to be moved by desire.

The Tarrytowns, Valley Forges and Eagle Rocks become little more than a swoop, New York to Philadelphia a ramble, Boston to New York a mere jaunt. The motor-car is such an abridger of distance that ideas of the constitutes of a tour must be revised. But whether from New York to Tarrytown, Philadelphia to Valley Forge, or Boston to the Berkshires, the man in the motor-car must make the journey by the public road—away from the line of the railroad and trolley. He must make it, not breathing the thickened air of a public conveyance, but with the champagne of the out-of-doors dilating his nostrils and diluting his lungs, and whither he will, he cannot but discover more charm of country, more picturesqueness of scene, than he ever before thought existed so close to home. Who that ever made the trip by road from New York to Philadelphia, for instance, fancied that a journey so prosaic and uninteresting by rail was so rich in nature's paintings?

In making America more discoverable, the motor-car is destined to complete, certainly to further the work inaugurated by the bicycle—that of bettering the common roads. While few roads are so vile as to prevent the progress of the powerful car, the discoverer of today values his personal comfort, and perforce is prone to select for discovery

## "The Rediscovery . . ." *(continued)*

those routes that afford at least fair going, and when the full meaning of road reform dawns on the American populace, it will be no longer necessary to go abroad to find 500 miles of continuous good road. Then, less will be heard of the Rhine and its castles and more of the Hudson and its highlands, less of Waterloo and more of Valley Forge and Gettysburg; less of Swiss canons, more of Luray caves. If there are no castles to rebrick and restore, there are other things to remark or mark out. Our people will discover them when they are made discoverable, not by the tortuous or toiling journey, but by the easygoing rate, the desire of the average man. . . .

It was the keeper of a roadhouse in outlying New York, who, made rich by cyclists, had seen his riches take wings, who confessed that his visions of new wealth, born of automobiles, had been dis-

pelled. The men in motor-cars did not stop. Their limit is not the city's line. The open country is theirs—the wayside inn far, far from the city's streets and smoke and Sunday crowds. They may, they should, restore or build anew picturesque gables in picturesque settings of trees or hillsides. But for the clustering roadhouses, they hold small hope. Thus, not only will the man in the motor-car discover his own country, but he will add to its life and interest.

The discoverer will not hop on a train and off and on again, staring meanwhile through glass windows. He will command his own time; journey according to his own schedule or according to no schedule; he will pause when and where he will.

And whether his conveyance be termed "automobile" or "motor-car," he will make new discoveries daily of America and of the American people that will have an educational as well as a pleasure-giving value.

# Historical Snapshot
# 1903

- Thanks to the introduction of the $1.00 Brownie Box camera by Eastman Kodak Company, home photography was sweeping the nation
- The New York Society for the Suppression of Vice targeted playing cards, roulette, lotto and watches with obscene pictures
- President Roosevelt declared Pelican Island, Florida, a national wildlife refuge for birds
- The state of Florida gained title to the Everglades and began making plans to drain the swamp
- A machine that automatically cleaned a salmon and removed its head and tail was being marketed by A. K. Smith
- The dramatic action in the 12-minute-long movie, *The Great Train Robbery*, was reshaping American concepts of cinema
- The press was reporting that President Roosevelt's views of the Panama Canal were simple: "Damn the Law! I want the canal built"
- A bottle-making machine, electric locomotive, Model A Ford, the Harley-Davidson motorcycle and automobile license plates all made their first appearance
- Horace Fletcher's book, *ABC of Nutrition,* advocated chewing each bite of food 32 times before swallowing
- President Roosevelt began calling his Washington residence the "White House" rather than the Executive Mansion
- The United States Senate rejected President Roosevelt's appointment of African-American Joseph Crum as collector at the Port of Charleston
- *The New York World* publisher Joseph Pulitzer donated $2 million to Columbia's School of Journalism to fund prizes and scholarships for the encouragement of public service, public morality, American literature and the advancement of education
- Willis H. Carrier created a crude, but effective modern air-conditioner with powered ventilation, moisture control, and refrigeration by mechanical means
- The winner's share per player for the Baseball World Series was $1,316; the losers made $1,182 each
- The Women's Christian Temperance Union, which advocated temperance and general reform, claimed 300,000 members, making it the largest women's organization in America
- The St. Louis Fair spawned iced tea and ice cream cones
- Cousins Edward Binney and C. Harold Smith began marketing Crayola Crayons, with a box of eight costing $0.05
- The latest women's fashion craze featured blouses with pouched fronts and collars decorated with elaborate trim
- Post Toasties were introduced by the Postum Company
- In the first authenticated transcontinental automobile trip, a Packard Model F went from San Francisco to New York in 51 days

### Letter to the Editor, "Our National Anthem," Lucia Ames Mead, *The Outlook*, November 14, 1903:

In your issue of October 3 you refer to the decision of the army and the navy to recognize the "Star-Spangled Banner" as the national anthem, and you imply that this settles the question for the nation. But the decision of the small body of army and navy officials, though somewhat influential in shaping public opinion, can settle nothing. The rulers of the Republic—the people—must decide whether this song, written for a special time and place in the War of 1812, is to be their expression of national faith.

"I care not who makes the laws of a country if I may write its songs," said a man who knew the relation of cause and effect in history. It was a music-hall ditty 25 years ago:

"We don't want to fight,
But, by jingo, if we do,
We've got the ships,
We've got the men,
We've got the money, too."

That inflamed the English people and had tremendous weight in creating sentiment which resulted in the Berlin Treaty, one result of which today is the horrors in Macedonia. It is a matter of serious importance if children throughout our land are taught that, "Conquer we must, for cause it is just." Even if the word "for" is replaced with "when," the falsehood is the same. War is but a gigantic duel; the stronger and more skillful wins, regardless of justice. We won the Mexican War, not because we were right, but because we were strong, just as the Assyrians conquered the Jews, not because they were right, but because they were strong. Success is almost always on "the side of the heaviest battalions" in any war. Children who grow up with an ingrained notion that their country must always be right, and therefore always successful, become the zealots and hotheads who foment other wars.

The "Star-Spangled Banner," as you justly remark, "is far from being good poetry and vocally almost impossible." These two defects should prevent its adoption as a national song. But it is also unsuited to many hours and places. At sunset, when the flag is lowered, is it not rather absurd to ask, "O say, can you see by the dawn's early light"? The song deals with one incident, and that, a war incident. "The perilous night" was one special and comparatively unimportant night in our history. Whatever is special or local or refers to facts not generally known is not suited to a national anthem to be learned by heart, to be sung by millions of all classes, to shape the national ideals of a powerful people.

During our whole history we have been at war less than one-tenth of the time. War should not be the sole topic referred to in a national anthem. "My country," "sweet land of liberty," "freedom's holy light," "our fathers' God," are nobler and more universal themes than "the rockets' red glare, the bombs bursting in air." Today "America" is undeniably the American people's dearest hymn. Why should not the army respect the feeling of the people rather than the people obey the behest of a few army officers? Let this purely military air be retained, if you like, in the repertoire of military bands, where choral singing is not in order, but let the great body of teachers, preachers, editors, the mothers and the civic patriots of our land choose as their national anthem a song which does not ignore the interests, life and faith of great Christian people.

That "America" is sung to a tune of German origin, which is also used as the national heir of our "kin beyond sea," does not, to my mind, condemn it as our national anthem. One of the most thrilling experiences of many sea voyages has been the rising and singing at the close of the ship's concert of that air, common to both countries, each passenger singing the words of his own land.

National anthems cannot be written to order; they must evolve. We may be long in finding the ideal one; but let no silly shame because of the present doubt as to what our anthem shall be hasten us to accept a wholly unrepresentative and inadequate one—a work without any great or noble qualities, a compound of indifferent music and indifferent verse.

## "The Ethics of the Panama Case," *The New York Times*, December 18, 1903:

In June 1902, a law was passed authorizing the president to make a treaty with Colombia for the building of a canal across the Isthmus of Panama, and providing that, in the event of failure to make such a treaty after the lapse of a reasonable time, recourse should be had to Nicaragua. In accordance with this law, a treaty was framed, ratified by our Senate, and submitted to the Congress of Colombia. That Congress rejected it, and a few days later (November 3, 1903) the people of Panama revolted against Colombia and proclaimed their independence. On the sixth of the same month we acknowledged the de facto government; on the thirteenth, the independence of Panama; and on the eighteenth, we negotiated a treaty with the new Republic providing for the construction of a canal and guaranteeing the independence of the new-born state. This treaty has since been ratified by the Senate and is now a part of the law of the land. The independence of Panama and the guarantee of its independence by our government are accomplished facts. Discussion cannot change them. But it is eminently fitting that, as a self-governing people, we should carefully inquire whether we have observed the principles of justice in those dealings with Colombia to which Panama owes its existence as an independent state.

When the president received the new minister from Panama, he made a short speech in which he said: "It is fitting that we should do so [acknowledge the independence of Panama] as we did nearly a century ago, when the Latin peoples of America proclaimed the right of popular government, and it is equally fitting that the United States should now, as then, be the first to stretch out the hand of fellowship...toward the new-born state."

No one needs to be told that there is the sharpest contrast between our attitude toward the new Republic of Panama; we waited seven years to acknowledge the independence of the former, and 10 days to acknowledge that of the latter; we did not forcibly intervene in behalf of the former, while we have so intervened in behalf of the latter; and most important of all, our pecuniary interest in the independence of the South American republics was as nothing when compared with our pecuniary interest in the independence of Panama. The consideration of this latter fact cannot but raise the doubt whether it would not have been more fitting for the United States to have been the last rather than the first of the great powers of the world to recognize the independence of Panama.

## Selected Prices

| | |
|---|---|
| Automobile, Two-Passenger, 10-hp | $1,900.00 |
| Barber's Razor, 3.5-Inch Blade | $1.50 |
| Baseball | $1.15 |
| Breakfast Cereal, per Package | $0.15 |
| Buggy Whip, Six Inches | $0.69 |
| Broadcloth, per Yard | $1.00 |
| Flower Bulb, Calladium | $0.15 |
| Glassware, 40 Pieces | $1.75 |
| Ink, Two-Ounce Bottle | $0.04 |
| Overcoat, Man's Spring Weight | $6.50 |
| Playing Cards, per Package | $0.24 |
| Pork Sausage, per Pound | $0.10 |
| Tool Chest, Chestnut | $5.40 |
| Toothbrush | $0.04 |
| Wine, 12 Quarts | $5.00 |

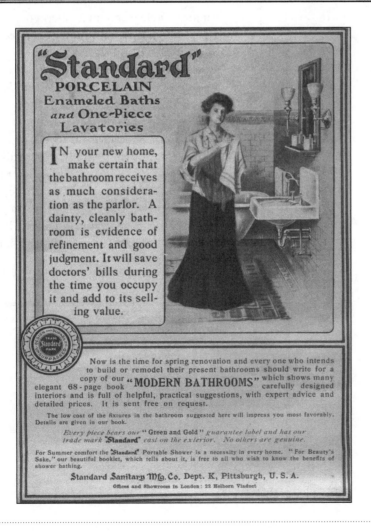

### "The Fifty Miles Order," Historicus, *The North American Review,* November 11, 1903:

Was the fifty mile order given by the Secretary of the Navy on November 2nd, 1903, many hours before there was a revolt at Panama against the government at Bogota, an illegal order if tested by the Thirty-fifth Article of the New Granada Treaty of 1846? The answer depends upon a critical historical inquiry, the nature of which I can now only give in the merest outline.

The following is a transcript of one of the orders:

Navy Department,
Washington, DC, November 2, 1903
Glass, Marblehead, Acapulco:
Proceed with all possible dispatch to Panama. Telegraph in cipher your departure. Maintain free and uninterrupted transit. If interruption is threatened by armed force, occupy the line of railroad. Prevent landing of any armed force, either Government or insurgent, with hostile intent at any point within 50 miles of Panama. If doubtful as to the intention of any armed force, occupy Ancon Hill strongly with artillery. If the *Wyoming* would delay *Concord* and *Marblehead,* her disposition must be left to your discretion. Government force reported approaching the isthmus in vessels. Prevent their landing if, in your judgment, landing would precipitate a conflict.
—Darling, *Acting*

# 1904 News Feature

**"Heart to Heart Talks with Philistines by the Pastor of His Flock,"
by Elbert Hubbard, *The Philistine, A Periodical of Protest*, February 1904:**

Richmond P. Hobson, who sank the *Merrimac,* now wants to sink $2.5 million in a navy.
    We are on to Richmond.
    The *Merrimac* was sunk with intent to block the channel to Santiago Harbor. The ship was sunk all right, but the channel was not blocked, and the hulk lies there still, a danger and a menace to commerce.

**The World's Constable**

Louis Dalrymple. *Judge,* 1905.

All good Philistines
need good pencils—thats
where Dixon comes in

Write Dept. A. M., Jos. Dixon Crucible Co., Jersey City, N. J., find your pencil affinity and be happy ever after.

Individuals like Hobson are a danger and a menace to civilization, as much so as is that hulk, around which men who go down to the ships have to carefully guard and steer. While the better part of the Christian world is talking about disarmament, this man wants to saddle upon the toilers of America the biggest and most costly implement of death this tired, bloodstained earth has ever seen.

Hobson is not a producer. He consumes, but his living is supplied him by the state. He is a pensioner—A Remittance Man. His business is death and destruction. He had his way in sinking the *Merrimac* that lies rotting in the sands of Santiago; the gulls roost on her ribs that blister in the sun, and down below, the sharks circle in and out, and the barnacles gather and wax fat on the tide that comes and goes.

If Hobson has his way in this (which God grant he never may!), this magnificent navy will rot, blister and decay as surely as did the *Merrimac,* and the end will be futile and inept. But no pen will write of the sweat and blood and work and worry of the men and women who sow and reap, who dig and delve, who toil in factory and mill until they be-

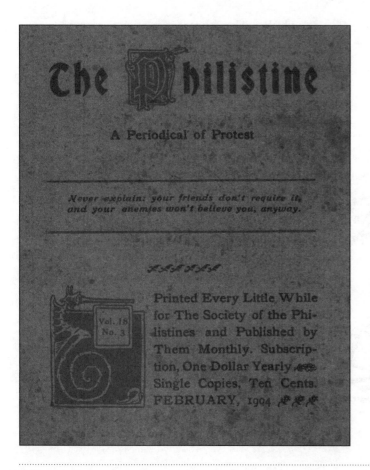

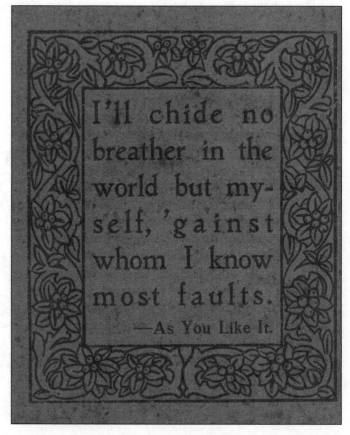

## THEIR CREED

GOOD Philistines endeavor to eliminate hate, fear, prejudice and whim. They greet the day with gladness, because it gives them an opportunity to work. They do not try to kill time, so time does not try to kill them. They take their medicine, when Fate sends it, and make no wry face; and if they possibly should have a tumble now and then, they are always up before the Referee counts ten. They seek to be truthful, simple, direct, moderate, minding their own business and not bothering other folks any more than they have to. They believe in useful industry, good cheer, fresh air, sound sleep, good digestion and kind thoughts; and they believe that the mental attitude of good will, courtesy and reciprocity will bring the best possible results that are to be obtained by anybody, either in this World or Another.

come deaf to all sweet music through the ceaseless whirr of wheels, and blind to all beauty through the one sight of flying shuttles—all that America may dominate the seas! No man will tell of this tragedy, because no man can—its terrible truth balks the pen, and De Quincy is dead.

But let these simple facts stand:

War is waste.

Where men waste, men and women must work to make good this waste.

To prepare for war is to have war. We get what we prepare for, and we get nothing else.

This country is not endangered by a foreign foe, and never will be until we adopt a policy that seemingly endangers the welfare of Europe.

When we have a navy that outclasses any one navy in Europe, there will be a combination of European Powers, and they will evolve a navy that will outclass ours.

Bullies all get bested—the wallop 'waits them all. John L. Corbett, Fitzsimmons, all get what they ask for—they are accommodated with the sedative.

The danger to this country is from within—it lies in idleness, ignorance, superstition and the false education of individuals like Hobson, so that they are experts in the inutile. Hobson does not one useful thing, and yet demands honors in inverse ratio to the square of his inefficiency. This is the warrior idea, and traces a pedigree straight back to Caius Marius, Sulla, Cato, Pompey and Crassus.

Hobson's argument is exactly and precisely the argument of Pompey, who said, "If Rome has an army large enough, and well enough trained, peace is assured, for no country or nation would dare make war upon us."

And Pompey never saw peace afterward. He was choked in his own gore, and his statue, set up in the Forum at Rome, was baptized by the blood of Julius Caesar, the greatest fighting man the world has ever known.

An army is for army officers.

A navy is for sea captains.

And death awaits them all.

The size of Hobson's proposed navy staggers the imagination, but Russia,

Italy, Germany and England could turn to and sink it, and send Hobson in chains to the rocks of St. Helena, where he could commune with the ghost of the Corsican who, too, worked for peace by overawing a world.

Napoleon would tell him that the allies did it.

And the allies lie in wait for every nation that thinks itself invincible, just as fate crouches around the corner for the man who prides himself on being supreme.

Hobson's navy would be a vast storage house full of dynamite. It might explode itself any day. Heavily armed men do not live content in peace. If there is no one else to kill, they turn on each other. Read history.

Supremacy through the power to destroy has been tried since the days of the pharaohs, and history teaches us that its end is madness and the grave.

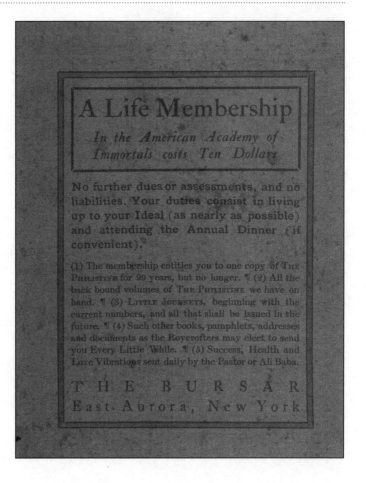

# 1910–1919

As the decade began, America was transforming economically, culturally and socially. One in 12 marriages ended in divorce in 1911, compared with one in 85 only six years earlier. In 1913, Alice Paul and a group of militant suffragists founded the Congressional Union for Woman Suffrage and organized marches, White House protests and rallies. Meanwhile, the rapidly expanding, mostly unregulated economy was still producing fabulous wealth for the few and extreme poverty for the many. When America entered World War I, two million men were drafted, and for the first time, women experienced economic independence as they were recruited into industry to fill the places formerly occupied by men. When the war ended, both men and women had acquired an expanded view of the world and of their own capabilities.

Although America entered the Great War relatively late, its resources turned the tide and dramatically elevated the nation's status. The U.S. produced arms not only for itself, but also for France and Great Britain. By 1917, when many countries could no longer pay for essential supplies, American loans worth

$7 billion to the Allied countries maintained the flow of arms and food to Europe.

By the end of the war, with U.S. casualties numbering 116,708 dead and 204,002 wounded, public opposition erupted when American soldiers were sent to Russia in 1919. They were sent after the war was over to help the European allies overthrow the Bolshevik Government and reopen the eastern front. Under the harsh conditions of a Russian winter, they served in an effort that ultimately failed, but for the first time since the Civil War, America was war-weary.

# 1916 PROFILE

# MEXICAN WARS

### Major

Major West, who toured the world as a soldier, has been called upon to lead his men into Mexico and capture bandit-political leader Pancho Villa, whose men killed 19 Americans during a raid in New Mexico.

### Life at Home

- Rudy West grew up on the Illinois side of the Mississippi River, near St. Louis, in the community of Belleville.
- He was the youngest son of a minister blacksmith and his seamstress wife, who had been born slaves but learned to read, and valued God, hard work, education and a little savings under the mattress.
- They taught their youngest child to love learning, sports and music.
- Many happy hours were spent playing the battered keyboard of an upright piano at Rudy's father's church.
- Although Rudy was an excellent student, few opportunities were available beyond his community school, until he learned about West Point.
- While working as a clerk in an insurance company, he read that his congressman was holding competitive exams for an appointment to the United States Military Academy at West Point.
- Few blacks had ever attended the academy, and fewer still had graduated.
- Relatives warned him about racism, being ostracized, hated and cursed.
- During the midst of a community prayer meeting, the calling came from the Lord, Rudy believed, to take the exam.
- After a tense day of test-taking in a drafty hall with a dozen white candidates, Rudy learned his score was the highest—the appointment was his!
- Passing the academy's entrance exam was all that lay ahead.
- His family and members of the congregation pooled their money for the trip to West Point and to hire a tutor to prepare him for the test.

*Major Rudy West has been told to track down Mexican bandit Pancho Villa.*

*Rudy is responsible for two national parks in California.*

- Instead of hostility and harassment, the other prospective cadets ignored him.
- After only a few weeks in New York, he was ready to come home; only because so many had sacrificed so much to send him there did he stay.
- He passed the test with room to spare, entered West Point in 1885, and endured four years of abusive hazing, convinced it would make him both a better man and a better soldier.
- He was only the third black student to achieve a diploma.
- His assignments were limited to the military's black units—the 9th and 10th Cavalry and the 24th and 25th Infantry.
- By 1903, the army was responsible for a number of national parks created by President Theodore Roosevelt; Rudy was made superintendent of two of the parks located in California.
- His following three-year assignment was in Port-au-Prince, Haiti, as military attaché to gather intelligence and construct maps of the island terrain.
- Then, a placement came in the newly formed Intelligence Office at Army Headquarters in Washington, DC; it was a dream assignment.
- Within the growing black middle class of the nation's capital, Rudy found friendships, comfort and a place to be himself.
- An accomplished linguist capable of speaking Greek, French, Spanish and German, he attracted a wide circle of friends.
- It was during a Washington party that he met his wife.
- Unfortunately, soon after the formerly confirmed bachelor walked down the aisle with his new bride, he was shipped to the Philippines, leaving behind his home in the capital, his friends and his pregnant wife.
- In the Philippines, he watched the slow, agonizing process of democracy forming; in 1907 under U.S. rule, the Philippines became the first Asian state to establish a national legislature.

- He also learned about exotic diseases and the songs they inspired: "I've the dobie itch and Moro stitch/The jim-jams and the fever/The burning fart and the Samar dart/And maybe a kris in my liver!"
- He discovered that Manila's San Miguel beer was excellent, but three drinks of Filipino wine were dangerous.
- When he was later assigned as attaché in Monrovia, Liberia, his wife was allowed to accompany him.
- They were finding great joy living in a nation of former slaves when new orders arrived.
- In 1916, Rudy, his wife and three sons were assigned to Fort Huachuca, Arizona; he was to command a squadron of the 10th Cavalry.
- Just as he was enjoying the chance to hunt mule deer, word arrived that American civilians had come under attack from Mexico.

## Life at Work

- Information was sketchy, but on March 9, Mexican political leader and bandit Francisco "Pancho" Villa led a force of men across the United States border and attacked the community of Columbus, New Mexico.
- Buildings were burned, stores and homes looted, women raped, and 19 soldiers and civilians killed.

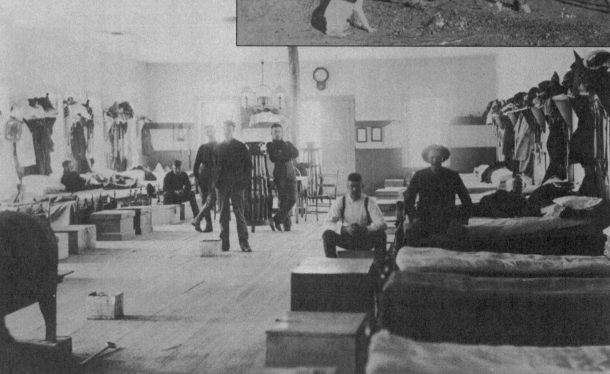

*Hunting is excellent in Arizona, especially the mule deer.*

*The barracks in Fort Huachuca, Arizona, are spacious and comfortable.*

## "The 10th Cavalry Marches into Chihuahua," by Major Charles Young, 1916:

Moonrise at midnight found us formed into a column moving silently toward the border, miles away. Daylight found us 25 miles out on the trail, and as I glanced back at my troops I could not help laughing. For hours we had plodded along at a walk across a plain that was utterly devoid of water, but was rich in white alkali dust that settled like a blanket on men and horses, and the only spots on my men where I could see their original color were their upper eyelids when they winked. All else was entirely white with alkali, and those eyelids stood out like flies in a pan of milk.

We found a little water, bad, at Carriza Springs, and that evening we reached Ojitas, 58 miles south of the line. The next day's march was hard, no water and little food, and we reached Colonia Dublan, a little Mormon settlement. That march will always stand out as an example to me of what cavalry can do in cross-country marching, and to cap it all we made camp, if one can call it that, on a prairie that was covered with a dense growth of Johnson grass five feet high and as dry as tinder, so that a single spark would have started a prairie fire and our herds would have stampeded. That night we spent fireless, each man with his horse picketed near him, waterless save for what little we had in the canteens that we used to swab out the nostrils of our jaded mounts.

*President Wilson ordered the capture of Pancho Villa.*

- President Woodrow Wilson, long troubled by uneasy relations with Mexico, immediately ordered a punitive expedition into Mexico to capture or kill Villa.
- Six regiments, including four cavalry and two infantry, under the command of Brigadier General John Pershing, were ordered out.
- Rudy West and the 10th, who were only 250 miles away from Columbus, immediately saddled up, taking care to order two wagons loaded with rations, ammunition and a double supply of horseshoes.
- As part of a tradition dating to the Indian Wars 30 years before, the band played while the troops filed off the post.

*The 10th Cavalry is only 250 miles from the action.*

## Mexican Invasion Calendar, *The Outlook*, July 5, 1916:

- March 9, 1916: Nineteen Americans were killed and about 20 wounded in a raid on Columbus, New Mexico, by Mexican bandits, supposedly led by General Villa.
- March 15: An American column under General Pershing crossed the border in pursuit of raiders. It was generally understood by the American public that this incursion was made with the consent of the Carranza government, that the Mexican de facto government would cooperate with the United States in the bandit hunt, and that American troops would be withdrawn as soon as the marauders who had attacked Columbus were killed or captured.
- April 19: General Pershing's expedition reached its "farthest south" by the arrival of two troops of the 13th Cavalry at Parral, about 400 miles from the border, where they were ambushed by Carranzista soldiers and townsmen and forced to retreat, with the loss of two killed and seven wounded. This virtually ended the pursuit of Villa by the Americans, and led to the dispatch of heavy reinforcements to General Pershing and a general contraction of his lines.
- April 29: Conferences began at Juarez, Mexico, and El Paso, Texas, between Alvaro Obregon representing Carranza, and Generals Scott and Funston representing the United States.
- May 15: Mexicans raided the "Big Bend" district of Texas, killing seven Americans.
- May 11: The conferences at Juarez and El Paso were discontinued, with no substantial agreement reached. About the same time, American

cavalrymen captured 14 Mexicans alleged to have taken part in the raid on Glen Springs in the "Big Bend," and a little later other cavalrymen killed a number of the companions of these captured bandits.
- May 31: The American government received a note from the Carranza government stating that the Pershing expedition had gone into Mexico without the consent of Carranza, and asking for "the immediate withdrawal of American troops which are now in Mexican territory."
- June 11: Mexicans raided an American ranch near Laredo, Texas, with the result that 1,600 American regulars were drawn from the Engineer Corps of the Coast Artillery to further reinforce the defenses of the U.S. border.
- June 14-21: Texas soil was twice again raided by Mexicans. President Wilson's summons to the militia of all states, except the three border states already called, resulted on June 18. Sixteen warships were sent to watch Mexican ports.
- June 20: The president's reply to Carranza's demand for the withdrawal of U.S. troops was issued. The American government refused and, while admitting that "American troops had crossed the international boundary in hot pursuit of the Columbus raiders, and without notice to or the consent of your government," served notice that any attempt by the de facto government to expel the American soldiers by force would be followed by "the gravest consequences."

## "Riding Mexican Trains through Chihuahua, Mexico, in Search of Pancho Villa," by Captain Rodney:

It was a train by courtesy, nothing else. Six cattle cars were hitched to a wood-burning engine for which there was no fuel. Our first job was to rebuild the train, for great holes had been burned in the floors. Most of the cars had no doors, and every time the engine moved, the sides of the cars opened out just as the sticks in a fan separate. When we finally got the horses loaded, we placed bales of hay along the tops of the cars so the men would not fall off when asleep; then we set to work with camp hatchets to cut a supply of fuel for the engine. In this way, we finally got started, after demolishing a set of loading pens for fuel for which the government later had to pay $1,900. Then, we started, but it was only a start. From time to time a man would roll off the roof, or sparks from the engine would set fire to the hay bales; then the engine would stop for water and we had to cut down telegraph poles for fuel, and when we got the fuel, the water was gone. It took us 24 hours to run 25 miles, and we finally reached our destination about three hours after we would have reached it had we marched. At a little wood station called Rucio, we finally got the horses off the train. As there was no ramp for unloading, the train was stopped in a railway cut and we got the horses out by the simple process of pushing them out of the open car doors. Then, we started on our cross-country march to San Miguel rancho, where rumor said Villa had been hiding.

- Both the 7th and 10th Cavalry first gathered at Colbertson's Ranch before crossing the border into the Mexican state of Chihuahua on March 16.

- In all, 1,500 men were made available to General Pershing; few expected the expedition to last a year.

- Under the command of Rudy—an excellent horseman with a love of the outdoors—the 10th Cavalry was able to move faster than its supply line and subsisted on what they brought or could buy from the locals.

- After travelling 252 miles—30 miles a day—from Huachuca, the 10th was ordered to board a Mexican train to speed their journey south.

- One lieutenant described the trip as less than pleasant: "Our troubles in patching and nailing up the cars, getting materials for camps, collecting wood for the wood-burning engine and getting started late in the afternoon with the animals inside the freight cars and officers and men on top in truly Mexican style, were exceeded, if possible, only by the troubles in keeping the engine going by having the men get off and chop mesquite to burn in it, only to find the wood must be used to send the engine someplace for water, and so on ad infinitum."

- On the morning of April 1, the 10th encountered a force of Villa's men.

Forces led by Pancho Villa attack the community of Columbus, New Mexico, burning buildings and killing nineteen people.

- Rudy felt invigorated by the brief engagement; when the Mexicans broke and ran, his troop pursued the invaders for two hours before trapping them in a ravine.
- There, the soldier in him wanted to attack, but as an officer, he knew he must wait for the remainder of the regiment to improve their position.
- When the assault occurred, the infantry controlled the rim of the canyon so they could fire down.
- A machine gun covered the ground, and the 10th was free to charge into the ravine.
- Excited by the prospect of being part of the first cavalry charge since the Spanish-American War, Rudy relished the chance to draw his .45 and yell at the top of his lungs.
- The Mexicans fled.
- None of his men was hit; the horses were the only participants who did not enjoy the skirmish.
- One horse was wounded, one dropped from exhaustion and one died the next night.

*Fifteen hundred men are made available to General Pershing for the assault on Mexico.*

- During the next few days, with rumors rampant that Villa was dead or wounded, the expedition continued.
- Chasing Villa's men required treks through mountains and high deserts at altitudes of up to 10,000 feet.
- There, the 10th Cavalry was assaulted by stinging snow and sleet, laced with sand; with freezing nights and the days filled with dust, it did not take long to discover why the region is called "the windiest place in the world."
- A dust storm could last 24 hours, making cooking impossible and sleep unlikely.
- The men were equipped with .30 caliber Springfield rifles, which weighed slightly more than eight pounds and took ammunition in five-round clips.

- The men believed the Springfield was far easier to load than the old Krag-Jorgensen rifles, the first U.S. military weapon to use smokeless powder.
- Other equipment changes, many instituted since 1910, were designed to put as much of the soldier's load as possible onto his back and remove bags that might bang against the legs.
- Reconnaissance for General Pershing was provided by four aircraft flying between the cavalry units and enemy lines, with Pershing himself delivering information.
- Mostly, though, the planes were of little use.
- Currently, Rudy and his men are faced with an unstable and dangerous foe—angry Mexican citizens inflamed by the American invasion.
- The problems began on April 12 in Parral, Villa's hometown.
- Major Frank Tompkins entered the small community, filled with Mexican government troops who were officially allied with the Americans in pursuit of Villa and his men.
- When Tompkins attempted to secure supplies, trouble broke out.
- The seething resentment against the American invasion erupted in gunfire.

- The American troops were trapped by engaged Mexican townspeople and Mexican military.
- Only a few miles away when trouble started, the 10th Cavalry immediately mounted their horses and rode into the fray, dispersing the violence without losing a man.
- When Rudy returned to camp, he was greeted with a letter from the quartermaster general, demanding to know why the hides of slaughtered animals were not sold as called for by army regulations.

## Life in the Community: Mexico

- The long presidency of Porfirio Diaz brought more than three decades of stability to Mexico; the frequent wars and uprisings were virtually eliminated under his rule.
- The stability attracted large U.S. and European investments in the country.
- By 1910, American holdings in Mexico reached $1.5 billion, triple the number in 1902.
- U.S. businesses dominated the railroad, supplied capital for the cotton, sugar, timber and cattle plantations, and controlled most of Mexico's mining operations.

### "Upheaval, the Wind That Swept Mexico," *The History of the Mexican Revolution,* Anita Brenner, 1943:

The upper classes and clergy in Mexico preferred Villa—if they had to choose among bandits. Carranza, against this, had the oil region, the best gunning territory, and he had, because Obregon was his commander-in-chief, a mobile yet unified military method. Against Villa's massive cavalry attacks, Obregon's strategy was to advance very fast, stop at some fortifiable point, set up barbed-wire entanglements and lay out trenches, in open loop shape, in which he put chiefly the Yaqui troops who were the core of his personal army. They had been fighting for generations, trained to win or commit suicide.

When the fight began, the Yaquis lay each one in a trench-hole with his wife and children, who kept handing him a reloaded gun as fast as one was finished; and if he was wounded or killed, they continued firing.

JOHNSON, WASHINGTON

JOE JACKSON, CLEVELAND - AMERICANS

## Selected Prices

| | |
|---|---|
| Automobile, Seven-Passenger | $1,395.00 |
| Blouse, Woman's Silk Embroidered | $5.50 |
| Bookcase, Oak | $8.00 |
| Comb | $0.02 |
| Hair Color, Makes One Pint | $0.25 |
| Oil, per Bottle | $0.25 |
| Pants, Man's Work Pants | $1.50 |
| Raincoat, Woman's | $10.95 |
| Room, Chicago, Illinois, per Week | $4.00 |
| Tablespoons, Silver Plate, Set of Six | $4.40 |
| Telephone | $11.28 |
| Tobacco, per Package | $0.15 |
| Toilet Paper, Large Roll | $0.09 |
| Vacuum Cleaner, Electric | $24.50 |
| Wooden Blocks, Set of 20 | $0.79 |

- As the investments grew and foreigners became wealthy using Mexican resources, natives began complaining that "Mexico was the mother of foreigners, and only a stepmother to Mexicans."
- Over half the nation's population—Indians and mestizos—were sharecroppers with little hope of climbing out of debt.
- The Mexican Revolution against foreign influence started shortly after Diaz became president of Mexico for the eighth time on October 4, 1910.
- By 1912, the country had become a battlefield of warring factions; the foreign oil companies, among many, were outraged.
- By 1913, when strongman Victoriano Huerta swept into power, the German, British and Spanish governments quickly recognized his rule, but the U.S. was more cautious.
- The Zapatistas, a peasant army that occasionally took time to look after their corn and chili patches, combined with revolutionary armies led by Pancho Villa and Venustiano Carranza under the slogan "Death to Huerta, down with the foreigners, Mexico for the Mexicans."

- By April 1914, the revolutionary armies controlled all of Mexico except the capital and a small area on the oil-rich coast.

- When the rebels took Tampico, the United States ordered the navy fleet into Veracruz, Mexico, to seize the port and occupy the city.

- Hatred of foreigners broke loose in riots everywhere; American flags were torn and stamped upon in gutters, and businesses stoned.

- Despite this, American soldiers stayed, often working in the community to improve conditions.

- In Veracruz, when Army General Frederick Funston cleaned up the water supply, improved sewage, and imported 2,500 garbage cans from the United States, the death rate among city residents plummeted.

- By July, after President Huerta had fled the country and Carranza was installed as the new president, Villa and Zapata refused to demobilized their troops or accept Carranza as their leader.

- By 1916, Mexico was again a battleground, Mexican money was worthless, and citizens were often on the move to avoid the warring factions.

- With most jobs paying in devalued currency, many men attached themselves to whatever troops were sweeping through the area.

## HISTORICAL SNAPSHOT
# 1916

- Man Ray painted *The Rope Dancer Accompanies Herself with Her Shadows*
- On the first day of the Battle of the Somme, 20,000 soldiers from Great Britain were killed, making it the bloodiest day in the British army's long history
- Joseph Goldberger showed that pellagra was a deficiency disease, not an infection
- Blood was refrigerated for safe storage for the first time
- The Piggly-Wiggly grocery store, Orange Crush, Nathan's hotdogs, Lincoln Logs, mechanical windshield wipers and the agitator washing machine all made their first appearance
- America boasted 21,000 movie theaters, with an average cost of $0.05
- Over 5,000 American Jews became British subjects in order to join the British war effort—ahead of American entry into the war—and assist in the liberation of Palestine from Turkish rule
- A polio epidemic struck 28,000 people, 6,000 of whom died
- President Woodrow Wilson continued unsuccessfully to mediate the European War
- A new mechanized home refrigerator was priced at $900, more than the cost of a car
- The United States bought the Virgin Islands from Denmark for $25 million
- Railway workers gained the right to an eight-hour day, preventing a nationwide strike
- Ring Lardner published *You Know Me Al: A Busher's Letters,* John Dewey wrote *Democracy and Education* and Carl Sandburg's *Chicago Poems* was released
- The Federal Land Bank System was created to aid farmers in acquiring loans
- Popular songs of the day included, "Ireland Must Be Heaven for My Mother Came from There" and "There's a Little Bit of Bad in Every Good Little Girl"
- Henry Ford chartered a "Peace Ship" to stop the war in Europe, caused, he said, by international Jews and Wall Street
- Margaret Sanger opened the first birth control clinic in the country and distributed information in English, Italian and Yiddish; she was arrested and charged with maintaining a "public nuisance"
- The Mercury dime and Liberty fifty-cent piece went into circulation
- High school dropout Norman Rockwell published his first illustration in *The Saturday Evening Post*
- Actor Charlie Chaplin signed with Mutual for a record salary of $675,000
- Multimillionaire businessman Rodman Wanamaker organized the Professional Golfers Association of America
- South Carolina raised the minimum working age of children from 12 to 14
- Lucky Strike cigarettes were introduced; a pack of 20 sold for $0.10

## "The Man Hunted in Mexico," by Gregory Mason, *The Outlook*, April 19, 1916:

"There's more rivers an' less water, more cows an' less milk, an' you can see further an' see less here than in any country where I've ever been."

So an ebony trooper in one of the Negro cavalry regiments described, in the terms of a common Texan story, the barren northern Chihuahua country through which the American "Punitive Expedition" is pursuing the meager trail of Pancho Villa.

Right here, let it be said that the great bandit's name is not pronounced in English as it is spelled, nor is it pronounced *Vilya*, as it would be in Spain. In Mexico and on the border, they call it *Vee-yah*.

The event which the border army has impatiently awaited for three years, the entrance into Mexico, has not been so pleasant in the realization as it was in the anticipation. Armies are made to fight, and when they fight they like to fight like men. But the first three weeks of the Mexican jaunt of our expedition brought forth only two small, running skirmishes, which were more like rabbit drives than battles. And the tawny upland desert of northwestern Chihuahua is not the course one would choose for a hare-and-hound chase such as the pursuit of Villa has been in its first stages.

The greater scarcity of water in the rivers, which are unaided through their twisting channels by man, and the greater scarcity of milk in the cows, which are left to graze on the innutritious desert uncared for, is indeed the principal difference between the part of old Mexico, where eight regiments of our army are now sweating through the sand, and the border regions of New Mexico, Arizona, and Texas, where most of the men in those regiments had spent many days prior to that crimson dawn when Villa ran amuck at Columbus. For many miles on both sides of the border, the landscape is made up of broad ribbons of yellow sand spattered with blotches of savage, thorny vegetation in buffs and browns and grays uncoiling between walls of jagged and grotesquely shaped mountains of a cool, deep blue from a distance, which melts into an arid tan on approach. But through the clear air on the American side, the eye may rest on frequent flashing windmills surrounded by fair green cottonwoods and willows, while it is true that through the eye-smarting clarity of vistas south of the line, one can see farther and yet see much less that is worth the seeing.

We Americans have conquered the frontier within our own country, and the only zone within shot of our eyes where man is still mainly bested by nature lies over the Mexican border. Columbus, New Mexico, is a typical frontier town. Half a hundred one-storied shacks of brown or white adobe, with half a dozen two-storied frames of wood, are scattered about the town's center, marked by the ashes of four of the principal buildings which Villa's rum-crazed children of nature burned.

## "The Dough-Boy and the Truck," by Gregory Mason, *The Outlook,* May 31, 1916:

"The cal-vreeman rides a big black horse
That car-ries him to fame,
The dough-boy has no horse at all,
But gets there just the same
What?
Yes, gets there just the same, boys,
He gets there just the same,
The dough-boy, he ain't got no horse,
But gets there just the same."

It was a limpid night, except for this bellowed refrain, as dead still as an Arctic tundra after a blizzard. In fact, although the scene was on a plateau in Chihuahua, farther south than Galveston or Los Angeles, and the time April, the big massed flakes of the afternoon's snow flurry were just melting around the grass roots, and the mountain peaks on every side were whitewashed pyramids. The sparks and smoke of the great bonfire of mesquite and cottonwood rose in a still column, only to break and quiver five feet above the ground from the explosive exhalations that came from the close-packed circle of mouths every three seconds, as the soldiers who stood six deep around the blaze barked hard on the second syllable of each line of this marching song of the infantry:

"The cal-vreeman rides a big black horse
That car-ries him to fame;
The dough-boy has no horse at all,
But gets there just the same."

At each detonation that came with "cal," "car," "dough," and "gets," the smoke pillar would crumble, then regather, only to writhe again before the next blare of vocal trumpets. But at the crescendo bellow of "who-wat?" shouted in all the dissonance of untrained voices roughened by night air and overuse, the cylinder of smoke was flattened into the fire and the whole plain reverberated.

These bronzed foot-soldiers who were chorusing their own praises around a campfire at General Pershing's headquarters near Colonia Dublan were part of a detachment that had "dug in" at this point to guard the sand-swept premises. They had been resting several days after the first feverish hike into Mexico, else they would not have had breath to spare in wrecking the peace of this upland evening. Little singing is done by our soldiers on the march, and after a day of tramping, the only vocal music heard at eve is of the unconscious, slumberous kind. This particular occasion was a "Vaudeville Evening" arranged by the five chaplains of the expedition.

The night before, these same chaplains, who, unlike the other men in the expedition, had not forgotten the calendar, had observed the Sabbath with services in the same temple with the sky for roof and the stars for candles. With great good sense, the chaplains had observed the day, cheering these men in a foreign country from which each knew he might never return, but not playing Billy Sunday with the men's emotions, not once lifting the lash of fear as a goad to conventional virtue.

To the audience of Baptists, Catholics, Lutherans, Methodists,

## "The Dough-Boy . . ." *(continued)*

and Jews, each chaplain spoke briefly, packing his talk with common sense and salting it well with jokes. Father Joyce, for instance, known as the "Fighting Padre" of the Fourth Artillery, took a dig at his regiment which everyone appreciated when he said, "The only way to get an artilleryman into heaven is to convert him and then shoot him quick."

After these "sermons," so refreshingly different from what the correspondents at the service expected to hear, the meeting turned into an old-fashioned Sunday night "sing," such as still flourishes in odd corners of New England. First selected were hymns like "Shall We Gather at the River?" which were thrown across the Rio Casas Grandes, twisting through the plain in silvery curves, with an excellent enthusiasm and a melodic quality not to be despised by any college glee club. But the pious atmosphere of the gathering, never too dominant, wore off by degrees, and gradually the singing drifted to "The Girl I Left Behind Me" and "The River Shannon," with the quintet of chaplains warbling as bravely as anyone. Only the clear-bugled "Taps" stopped the flow of the song. But, as one of the "sky-pilots" said, "We've all got a lot of music in our systems yet." And so the Army Vaudeville was arranged for the following night.

There were all sorts of faces in that circle around the fire, for it was a characteristic army group. There were the buff, blond faces of Scandinavian and Teutonic countries, the black, flat, grinning faces of Africa, the dark, passionate faces of Italy and Greece, the sensitive faces of Russia and Poland, the alert, self-confident face of the Jew, and the also alert but more pugnacious face of Ireland. Yes, and there were some faces that seemed to belong to Maine, Georgia, Dakota, and California.

This variety of countenance which the firelight showed moved a chaplain to comment:

"I see we've got a little of everything here tonight. The army isn't what it used to be. When I joined it, the army was all Dutch and Irish. The two elements were continually fighting, and always, after these fights, the Dutchmen would go to the hospital and the Irishmen to the guardhouse."

The roar that followed showed that the army still holds a few of Erin's sons.

## "Villa's Invasion," *The Literary Digest*, March 18, 1916:

Villa's descent of March 9 upon American soil was a surprise to readers of American newspapers, yet there has been presented evidence that it had been planned some time in advance. United States Army officers in command along the Mexican border were, of course, prepared for the worst, although in Columbus itself there had been no trouble during the past three years. An interesting story of Villa's preliminary movements, and of the ways of the man who ventured to go to war with the United States on his own account, was given in the story of an American woman who was his prisoner for several days preceding the Columbus battle. Mrs. Maud Hawk Wright, wife of an American ranch owner in Mexico, was visited on March 1 by a Villista officer Servantes. Their supplies and horses were taken, and Mr. Wright and the baby were sent away. The Villistas took Mrs. Wright prisoner, joined the main body, and compelled her to accompany them on a nine days' forced march. From the first, says Mrs. Wright:

"I knew that Villa intended to attack Columbus. It was freely discussed by the men and the officers. Some of the latter told me that Villa intended to kill every American he could find, but they pointed to me as an example of their decision not to harm women. Later, as we approached the border from Boca Grande, these same officers told me that Villa—his rage growing as he neared the boundary—would make torches of every woman and child, as well as of every man, in Columbus.

"'He intended,' they said, 'to kill everybody in the United States, and would be helped by Japan and Germany.' At Boca Grande I saw evidence of their determination. I did not see the three American cowboys named McKinney, Corbett, and O'Neill slain, but I saw officers wearing their clothing. That was after Villa had sent out 20 men to break up

the Palomas cattle roundup and supply the hungry column with meat. . . .

"We left Boca Grande yesterday and crossed the border west of Columbus before four o'clock.

"As we entered the ditch leading past the American army camp below Columbus, the captain of my company told me that he and the 20 officers had crossed the border yesterday as spies, and found that only a few American soldiers were in the camp, that the others were farther west.

"I was in the line Villa threw along the railroad tracks after his troops swept eastward through the United States cavalry. A bullet hit the saddle of my horse as I stood dismounted behind it. Villa sent his men across the tracks into the town. Soon I saw buildings on fire. Then, the American troops apparently got into action, and in a little while the Mexicans came back. . . . I went back with the retreating forces until I reached a point near the house where Mr. Moore was killed and his wife wounded. Here Villa came upon me. Again I asked him to set me free.

"'You go; you are at liberty,' he said. I went to the Moores' house and found Mr. Moore lying facing down on the steps, dead; his wife was in a nearby field, wounded. She had seen her husband shot, but did not know he was dead."

# 1918 PROFILE

# WORLD WAR I: FRANCE

## Civilian

Livia Sedgwick's lifelong passion for helping the children of her city's poor brought her to war-torn France, where she finds injured people, frightened children and a little orphan named Maria.

## Life at Home

- Livia Sedgwick has always loved children.
- Growing up in Springfield, Massachusetts, she often helped her mother with children from the town's largest mill, owned by Livia's father.
- Together, she and her mother would throw parties on special occasions, hold health and hygiene clinics and sponsor tutorials for those who had fallen behind in their schoolwork.
- Livia especially relished teaching English to immigrant children; they were always eager to learn.
- Livia's father did not understand this fascination with helping the less fortunate, but he recognized that it made for a happier and more loyal workforce.
- Even after Livia graduated—with honors—from Smith College and spent a year touring Europe, her interest continued.
- In fact, her desire to help the city's poor children only intensified after her marriage to Edward Sedgwick and their move to Hartford, Connecticut, where he was an insurance company executive.
- Her father and the Sedgwick family both held considerable interests in the company.
- Soon after moving into a large house in one of Hartford's newest and nicest neighborhoods, Livia began focusing on the needs of the city's poorest families.

*Livia Sedgwick has joined the fighting to help the children of France.*

*After marriage, Livia lives in Hartford, Connecticut.*

- She organized, lectured and recruited friends into the effort.
- When more than eight years had passed without having a child of her own, Livia increasingly began to see the city's poor as "her" children.
- The arrival of the Great War brought with it a daily barrage of death, starvation and relocation in Europe.

*America prepares for war quickly.*

### "Thousands of Aeroplanes to Break the Deadlock in Europe," *Current Opinion,* August 1917:

Why not make it the fixed aim of the United States, says Admiral Peary, to be "the first air-power in the world"? If we will only concentrate upon aircraft, he adds, as von Tirpitz concentrated on submarines, "we will not only have an answer to the submarine menace, but we will have an unequivocal decision of the war, and that within a short time." The suggestion has evidently kindled the American imagination as well as appealed to its common sense. Congress has responded by the passage, in the Lower House, without a dissenting vote, after only four hours of discussion, of a bill appropriating $640 million to build a great air fleet and train an army of aviators. Five universities started courses of instruction several months ago and began graduating students last month, 200 a week being expected to receive their certificates of graduation from now on. . . . In one month's time, 2,000 workmen have erected half a million dollars' worth of buildings at Rantoul, Illinois, for a training field; 3,000 men were at work at the same time near Dayton, Ohio; and 2,000 at work near Mt. Clemens, Michigan. The appropriation bill in Congress does not mention the number of aeroplanes or aviators to be provided. That is to remain a military secret. But the president of the Aereo Club is talking of 100,000 planes and 25,000 men to operate them.

## "Jean and Pierre See Sammy," *The Independent*, August 24, 1918:

(The following extracts from the compositions of French school children are absolutely authentic and were sent to us through the 10th Engineers. While in southwestern France they became acquainted with a village schoolmaster who asked pupils to write, without preparation, compositions on this subject: "American soldiers have been in our village for some time. You have observed them. Describe one of them. What interested you in their work and their habits? Write your personal impressions."

They are all fine men, tall, large shoulders. I know one, a big fellow. He has a scar on his right cheek, which was made by a horse kick. He has a rosy face, long hair, carefully arranged. His feet are small for his size. He has a sweet tooth. He is gay. He is good. He eats chocolates and sweets. There are some going on an errand near their camp. I met him sharing his chocolate with his comrades. Next Sunday I was playing at spinning-top with my comrades. He was looking at us. My small brother had no spinning-top. He gave him two cents to buy one.

The Americans are polite. When they shake hands, they bow down their heads a little. Before entering a house they take off their hats, and wait till they are told, "Sit down."

They have good discipline; no fault is left unpunished. They are more daring than we are; they do not fear expense.

—Jean Laberiote

I know one more particularly. He is of ordinary size. He has a fine face, round cheeks, blue eyes. He likes to laugh at others. He is intelligent. He has got the bad habit of smoking and chewing tobacco. He is fond of sweets. He bathes very often.

The Americans have been very good to France, to come to help her fight the Germans.

—Jean Gaits

I have observed them well. Most of them are close-shaved. They are almost all tall and large fellows. They have quick eyes. They are polite, but some of them are great drinkers. The Americans are very smart. They do almost everything with machines and horses. They are up-to-date in everything.

—André Proustey

The work of the Americans is certainly a curious one. I saw them raise huge logs with large pliers, as easily as they would have moved a straw. Their furnaces for their kitchens are half in the ground, in order not to waste any heat. What struck me especially about the Americans is their cleanliness. All of them are tall, healthy and strong owing to their hygiene. Their teeth are very white; and not to soil their hands, they put on gloves even at work.

—Renée Bourthe

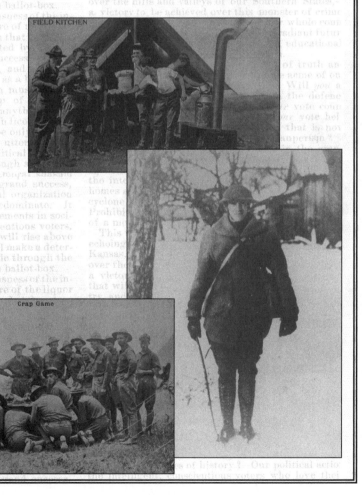

FIELD KITCHEN

Crap Game

- Livia followed every word, especially as Edward's focus on his work increased and the couple's relationship grew more distant.
- By 1916, before America's entry into World War I, Livia was convinced that her energies were needed in Europe, but was unsure of how to proceed, how it would appear to others, and how she could get across the ocean in wartime.
- Early in 1917, Edward joined the war effort as a "dollar-a-year man" in Washington, where his executive management skills were invaluable.
- His assignment was procurement—locating and purchasing the thousands of items needed for combat from ammunition and airplanes to military clothing.
- Proud as Livia was of his contribution, she was also keenly aware that the time between visits and letters grew longer.
- Just before Memorial Day, while having lunch with a Smith alumna, she learned that Harriet Boyd Hawes was leading a recruiting drive for a Smith College Relief Unit.

## Selected Prices

Baseball Glove, Horsehide.................................$3.00
Bed, Feather........................................................$8.95
Bloomers, Woman's Waist-to-Knee...................$0.90
Bust, 2.5" Bronze-plated President Wilson.........$0.10
Card Game, Rook...............................................$0.42
Clock, Winding Alarm........................................$2.00
Cup, Collapsible, Aluminum..............................$0.05
Gloves, Woman's Chamois..................................$1.19
Macaroni, Cooks in 12 Minutes.........................$0.25
Magazine, *Vanity Fair*......................................$0.25
Overcoat, Child's Winter Weight........................$5.48
Rocking Horse....................................................$2.98
Skirt, Girl's Wool...............................................$4.38
Steamship Fare, New York to Australia.............$337.50
Trunk, Wood Veneer..........................................$18.75

*The children of war-torn France love the escape of reading.*

## Life at Work

- Livia and 17 other Smith graduates—ranging in age from 20 to 40—set sail from New York in late 1917, each determined to be of service to her country during the Great War.
- Every member of the Smith College Relief Unit was fluent in French, and many possessed special expertise in health, transportation, agriculture or social work.
- To support the effort, the unit brought two trucks, a car, six portable houses, carpenter's tools, parts for the cars and trucks, cots, blankets, clothing and food for the French.
- Within weeks of arriving, the unit had established itself a few miles from the French front lines in the town of Grecourt.
- Called the "Ladies of Grecourt," their self-appointed task was to assist 16 neighboring villages, with populations totaling 1,650.
- Farms were restocked, war wounds mended, and woodworking classes created to help villagers learn how to rebuild war-torn homes.

- Designed to be independent of the much larger Red Cross, the unit's specific goal was to aid French civilians in overcoming the hardships of war.
- Livia was delighted, and wired Hawes of her interest that afternoon.
- Only the next day did she think to call Edward; he was not pleased, but said he would not stand in her way.
- Within days, she was interviewed by a panel; Hawes only wanted serious-minded women of proven ability.
- Livia's fluency in French, her knowledge of Europe and past experience in social work among the poor impressed the committee.
- She was soon notified that she would be accepted for service upon the payment of $300 for uniform, travel and sundries; she was also required to provide $55 a month for her own support.
- After closing up the houses in Hartford and Old Sagbrook on Long Island Sound, she sailed for France.
- Her parents proudly saw her off, and Edward sent a telegram from Washington.

- A sewing and knitting shop was set up to provide employment for four women.
- Livia did what she has always done—work with the children.
- She established a library for them, and found that they loved the escape of reading.
- Day after day she worked with government officials to reestablish schools and ensure the fair distribution of food.
- Some days, she was convinced that her greatest enemy was not the Germans, but French bureaucracy.
- Mostly, she listened to young children, frequently girls, talk about their lives, their families, becoming a woman, and being afraid.

*Soldiers sometimes pass through the town bringing gifts to the children.*

- She spent enormous energy planning Christmas parties for each of the villages.
- Using her own money, she purchased large quantities of food and drink.
- Most important, she made sure each and every child was able to open an individually wrapped Christmas present.
- Many of the children wept with joy—for a moment, the war had gone away.
- Livia's other project is more personal: a girl named Maria.
- Maria, whose parents were killed in an explosion, lost her right leg to an artillery shell.
- Eager, bright and resilient, Maria is devoted to Livia and wants to learn English.
- Livia began exploring the arcane and convoluted regulations of taking Maria to Hartford with her.
- She did not discuss the possibility with the little girl because, if she is unable to cut through the French bureaucracy, it would only bring one more disappointment into Maria's life.
- Occasionally, soldiers would pass through the town and offer gifts.

- Recently, a French officer sent a wagon of pigs, while an English unit provided a load of duckboard to line the muddy village streets.
- Another group of soldiers explained how the ladies could "read" their undergarments on a sunny day to rid them of lice.
- Livia was exhausted, filthy, and happier than she had ever been.
- As spring arrived, signs were everywhere that the war was drawing nearer.
- Some nights, the artillery fire was so loud, she was unable to sleep.
- Then, almost without warning, word came that the village must be abandoned.
- The relief unit was ordered to leave as the Red Cross carried out the evacuation.
- Livia and the other ladies made dozens of trips transporting the sick, the lame, and the children on muddy roads clogged with refugees, livestock and retreating soldiers.
- As each group of children was delivered to safety, Livia returned to the village for more.
- Only the crash of German shells stopped the work.
- Edward, who always wanted children, wrote of his excitement about Livia wanting to bring Maria to America.
- He began assisting with the complex paperwork involved in adopting a French orphan.
- A doctor in New York, who also has a house on Long Island Sound, has agreed to fit Maria with a prosthetic leg.

*Some nights the shooting is so near that Livia cannot sleep.*

- But first, Livia must complete her work.
- After Maria was entrusted to a group of nuns caring for children, Livia moved to a field hospital to help the many, many wounded.
- A large number of the patients came from units in New England; a few once worked in her father's mills.
- Some soldiers are missing limbs, several are suffering from mustard gas attacks, and others simply have the flu that has killed so many.
- During the day, Livia treats the wounded; at night she listens to their stories.

- Matter-of-factly, they talk of lost friends, cold trenches, and fear so strong it smells, tanks, airplane dogfights, barbed-wire battlefields and dreams of home.
- She helps them write letters and waits for word from Maria and Edward.
- Nine-year-old Maria writes often in her looping cursive handwriting, always working hard to enclose some English words in her messages.
- Edward writes that Maria's passage to America can be secured once the war ends.
- Livia writes about brave men who cry themselves to sleep.

## American Involvement in World War I

- To support the war effort, the American government amassed an army eventually totaling four million; the navy numbered 600,000 more, and the Marine Corps, nearly 80,000.
- The United States was involved with the Great War against Germany and Austria for 30 months, but played a significant battlefield role in France, Belgium and Italy for only eight months.
- Commander John "Blackjack" Pershing complained that, because most of the American troops were raised in towns and cities, many had little familiarity with firearms and were poor marksmen.
- U.S. World War I casualties were declared to be 116,516; battle deaths totaled 53,402; other deaths including disease totaled 55,114; total wounded tallied at 204,002; and fatalities worldwide for all nations were placed at 10 million.
- Artillery and machine guns, not rifles, were the biggest killers on the battlefield during World War I.
- The influenza outbreak of 1917-18 killed 52,000 American soldiers, sailors and Marines.
- Thousands of American soldiers were introduced to the concept of regular tooth-brushing by military training during the Great War.

# HISTORICAL SNAPSHOT
# 1918

- Farmers enjoyed a 25 percent jump in real income; many sold their mules to the army and plowed up pastures with their new tractors
- As an energy-saving measure, the nation adopted daylight saving time during the war, 150 years after it was first recommended by Benjamin Franklin
- Girls Scouts collected peach stones, which when heated turned into charcoal for use in gas mask filters
- Women assembled bombs in defense plants, learned to repair cars, carried the mail, directed traffic and worked as trolley car conductors
- The Committee on Public Information turned out patriotic press releases and pamphlets by the millions and drew upon a roster of 75,000 speakers to provide speeches for every occasion
- Civilians abstained from wheat on Mondays and Wednesdays, all meat on Tuesdays, and pork on Thursdays and Saturdays
- Some Americans swore off any beer that had a German name; sauerkraut become "liberty cabbage," hamburger was "Salisbury steak," and dachshunds were called "liberty pups"
- Labor unrest was at its most turbulent since 1890; inflation triggered 2,665 strikes involving over four million workers, more than 500,000 union workers staged a strike in Chicago resulting in riots and the death of 36 people, while New York City saw a strike of 300,000
- The rate of inflation reached 8.9 percent, dramatically increasing prices
- *The Economic Consequences of the Peace* by J. M. Keynes, *Ten Days That Shook the World* by John Reed and *Winesburg, Ohio* by Sherwood Anderson were all published
- Seventy lynchings occurred in the South as membership in the Ku Klux Klan increased to 100,000 across 27 states
- Herbert Hoover was named director of a relief organization for liberated countries, both neutral and enemy
- Peter Paul's Konobar, the Drake Hotel in Chicago and a state gas tax (in Oregon) all made their first appearance
- Hockey's Stanley Cup was cancelled after one player died and many others were stricken with the deadly flu

## "Flower of Nation's Younghood to Be Selected to Battle for Democracy, Ten Million Men Enrolled for Service," *Toledo Weekly Blade*, June 14, 1917:

The government at Washington now has 10 million names of citizens from which to select an army to fight for the cause which this nation represents in the world war.

Registration day, the first of its kind in the history of the United States, was a success in every way. Eligibles went quietly to the booths and had their names and ages entered on the rolls of the government. Except for a few isolated cases, there was no trouble.

Many states fell behind the Census Bureau's estimates of eligibles. In others, the registration far exceeded the estimates. In many places registration privileges were extended for two days to any who did not understand what was required of them or could not give reasonable excuses for not registering on Tuesday.

The next steps in the government's plan will be the selection of those who actually are to bear arms from others who will remain at home because of dependents or to do the work on the farm or in the factory that must be carried on to maintain the nation at war. . . .

There will be no weaklings in the armies sent to France. The flower of the nation's youth from a physical viewpoint will be selected to fight the battle for democracy. It will be an army of athletes.

In determining physical fitness, the examining physicians will observe the strict standards that have prevailed in the American army for many years. As a result of the enforcement of these physical requirements, an average of only one in four applicants for enlistment in the regular army is accepted. It is estimated, however, that the young men who have registered for the selective draft will be of a higher physical grade than those who have sought enlistment in the army hitherto, and that less than five percent will measure up to the required standard.

# TEN MILLION MEN ENROLLED FOR SERVICE

### Army Registration Day Complete Success Throughout Country — Little Trouble.

THE government at Washington now has ten million names of citizens from which to select an army to fight for the cause which this nation represents in the world war.

Registration day, the first of its kind in the history of the United States, was a success in every way. Eligibles went quietly to the booths and their names and ages entered on the rolls of the government. Except for a few isolated cases, there was no trouble.

Many states fell behind the census bureau's estimates of eligibles. In others the registration far exceeded the estimates. In many places registration privileges were extended for two days to any who did not understand what was required of them or could give reasonable excuses for not registering on Tuesday.

*Ten million men are called up for military registration and service.*

## "What Our Red Cross Is Doing in France," by Marion G. Scheitlin, *American Review of Reviews*, December 1917:

To a recent news cablegram sent by the American Red Cross Commission in France to the War Council in Washington, there was appended this sentence:

"If the American people could only get a picture of the misery among those daily driven out of their homes and dumped in poverty among other parts of the country—oftentimes terribly sick or mutilated—they would gladly do all in their power to help. . . ."

This is not an appeal for aid; it was an involuntary expression—aye, prayer—of unselfish men, drawn from them by the picture on which they had gazed since the War Council sent them to France. A ghastlier picture was never limned by the brush of Verestchagin. This picture—a panorama of France, of Belgium, created by the insensate and insatiate savagery of the Hun—is in great measure dimmed by distance to most of us in America. . . .

It has taken Prussianism nearly three and one-half years to create this picture. If peace were to come today, it would take 10 times three and one-half years to erase it; and there would still remain some ineffaceable blotches. But while the paint is still fresh and the blood-red coloring still vivid, let us try to visualize it as best we may. Perhaps the best way is to take some pages from the archives of the Red Cross in the form of communications from its workers afield. . . .

All in a day's work, a Red Cross official sends this report:

"There arrived last week at Evian, where the repatriates from France and Belgium are received back into France, a train loaded with Belgian children. There were 680 of them—thin, sickly, from four to 12 years of age—children of men who refused to work for the Germans and of mothers who let their children go rather than to let them starve. They poured off the train, little ones clinging to the older ones, girls all crying, boys trying to cheer. They had come all the long way alone. On the platform were the Red Cross workers to greet them. Those children who could walk at all marched along crying, 'Meat, meat, we are going to have meat.' Their little claw-like hands were

## "What Our . . ."(continued)

significant, but a doctor said, 'We have them in time; a few weeks of proper feeding and they will pull up.' Thirty percent of the older repatriates die the first month from exhaustion. The children can and must be saved."

Two such trains pull into Evian every day. They are laden with the too-young and the too-old—untilled grist for the Prussian industrial mill. Kultur weighs its victims only in the scale of possible usefulness to the Veterland. The humans in its power are reduced to terms of thaler, mark and pfennig. The grandchildren too young to work and the grandparents too old to work for Germany are cast into the discard and loaded for France. Germany needs its food. It cannot afford to reduce rations of its fighting men by feeding,

however meagerly, useless children and equally useless old people. If they have to starve, it were better they starved in France. And starve many of them unquestionably would were it not for Evian, Troche, and the Red Cross.

At Evian the Red Cross took over a public building, and at Troche, 20 miles from Limoges, it turned the famous monastery at La Grande Chartreuse into a haven of rest and recuperation for the very young and the very old repatriates. At these two stations, about 1,500 to 2,000 haggard, hopeless little children and aged persons arrive daily. And 30 percent of the older ones die during the first month in spite of all the tender mercies of the Red Cross can do!

## "The Fight against Venereal Disease," *The New Republic,* November 30, 1918:

When the history of America's participation in the Great War comes to be written, no finer achievement will be recorded to her credit than the unending battle against sex indulgence and venereal disease in the army. The success of the efforts to repress prostitution on this side of the Atlantic is already fairly well-known. Now that peace is at hand, some account can be given of the measures taken by General Pershing to protect the American Expeditionary Forces from this menace.

"The federal government has pledged its word that as far as care and vigilance can accomplish the result, the men committed to its charge will be returned to the homes and communities that so generously gave them with no scars except those won in honorable conflict." These were the words of President Wilson in April 1918. Through the Surgeon General of the Army and War Department Commission on Training Camp Activities, the government has carried out a programme for combating prostitution and venereal disease without parallel in any other country. It was founded on the proved principle that sexual continence was not only possible for soldiers, but was highly desirable from the standpoint of physical efficiency, morals and morale. Its chief features were education of men; repression of disorderly resorts; provision of healthful, interesting and constructive recreation; prophylaxis, or early treatment for men who had exposed themselves; punishment for those exposed who failed to take prophylaxis; and, finally, expert treatment for those who either came into the army already infected or broke through all the barriers set up by the military authorities.

On the other side of the water a similar programme was instituted, but an exception had to be made of the feature of law enforcement—repression of prostitution. The foreign governments with which it was necessary for us to deal held views about prostitution very different than ours. The French believed in "toleration" and "regulation." For generations they had been used to licensed brothels and registered prostitutes, inspected with greater or less care by medical officers. They felt that an army could not get along without sexual indulgence, and that to attempt to carry out such a policy was to court discontent, a lowering of morale and health standards, and perhaps even mutiny. So sincerely did they hold this belief that prostitution facilities for our soldiers were officially offered to the American High Command.

*The military has a formalized program to reduce venereal disease among soldiers.*

## "The Business of Clothing the Army," by Edward Hungerford, *Harper's Monthly Magazine*, April 1918:

The biggest business in the land—as well as the most versatile—has its headquarters in the rather unbusiness-like city of Washington. We Americans are accused by some of our neighbors of the habit of exaggeration, and perhaps they are right. Yet today, it is hard to find sufficient superlatives to characterize our Uncle Sam as a businessman, at least if one considers the spry old gentleman in dimensions of size. In recent years he has become rather adept in big business, despite a supposed and traditional antipathy to it. But since he plunged into the Great War, his big business has become bigger business, in all probably the biggest single business that the world has ever known. His unofficial budget for the first year of his part in the international conflict provided for an expenditure of $20 billion, or about as much as the British Empire has expended during the first three years of the war. And England had not stinted herself, in men or in money. For the second year, Uncle Sam may not spend as much—perhaps not two-thirds of his initial annual expenditure, which has bought many things that should have been purchased years before had we only been properly prepared, such as training camps, fighting ships, merchant vessels, dry docks and navy yards and coast defenses. . . .

Today, Washington is the busiest city in the land. Its Southern inertia is disappearing. Offices are open and busy until late into the evening, whole departments alight long after dark. Even through the hottest months of last summer, there was bustle in the town. The old-time official Washington has ceased explaining that things could not be done and has watched the "dollar-a-year men" go ahead and do them. . . .

In the past decade or two our manufacturing efficiency, speaking broadly, has been greatly multiplied. The practical sermons of the efficiency experts have been heeded. And some of the homelier industries, yet industries tremendously important to the fitting out of an army, have been enabled to meet their supreme test in these trying days. Today, when one hears that the spindles and the looms of the United States will be called upon to weave five million blankets for the soldiers for a coming winter, he knows that modern efficiency will render them not only able to meet the test, but will insure they absolutely do meet it. As a matter of fact, up to February 9 of the present year, more than 7.9 million blankets and 800,000 comforters had been delivered to the army as a result of its war-time contracts. Uncle Sam, in his purchases, has been a huge merchant.

We have German enemies in this country, too, and the worst of our German enemies, the most treacherous, the most menacing, are Pabst, Schlitz, and Miller.
—Wisconsin Prohibition speech, 1918

# 1918 NEWS FEATURE

**"Black Doughboy's Pride, an interview with Captain Hamilton Fish, commander of the 369th Infantry,"** *Eyewitness to War:*

When World War I was confronting the American people, I had served in the legislature three terms as a Progressive Independent, not as a Republican. I began my military career in the 71st Infantry, New York National Guard. In 1915, I went up to Plattsburg, New York, where they had a military officers' camp, having been recommended by a number of prominent people. At the end of the second year, I was recommended for the rank of captain. I studied, and at age 27 I knew all the regulations. Well, this major, who seemed to be in his 60s, and probably got his captain's rank in his 50s, told me, "You're too young to be made a captain." I told him, "Sir, I'm ready to take any test they have to offer," but he only said, "I'll find questions you can't answer—I'll give you a test on cooking." I didn't know cooking. He wanted to make me a first lieutenant, but I wouldn't accept that.

I returned to New York in disgust. There, I met Colonel William Hayward, who was in charge of a new regiment of volunteers. All to be black troops. He said, "I can make you a captain right away, if you'll accept it." I did. So on June 26, 1916, I began raising troops for the 15th Infantry, New York National Guard. My captaincy became official on January 15, 1917. . . .

They were the same as any other men. . . . they were human beings, and they had to be treated like human beings as we taught them how to per-

*Yanks in front line trench watching No Man's Land-France*

form the duties of regular soldiers. Not all of the troops were New Yorkers, but most of them came from New York, Westchester, Orange, Dutchess and Putnam counties. We drilled mostly at the Lafayette Dance Hall at 131st Street and 5th Avenue in Harlem. We had no rifles; we had to drill with broom handles. Then, in August 1917, we were shipped out—unfortunately to Camp Wadsworth, near Spartanburg, South Carolina. We got into a lot of trouble there because the Southerners resented Northern black troops. I wrote to Franklin Roosevelt, then the Assistant Secretary of the Navy, urging him to get us out of there—and he did. After 12 days at Camp Wadsworth, we were shipped back up to Camp Mills, NY. . . .

We got (to France) on the *SS Pocahontas,* after several malfunctions and damage from a collision with a British tanker on December 15, 1917, which we repaired at sea. We finally landed at Brest on December 26. . . . There was an old law against black troops serving with white troops, and the War Department didn't want to mix them, but we had no other black units with which to form a division. There were plans to form an all-black 93rd Infantry division, but it never came to be. The all-black 370th, 371st and 372nd regiments did arrive in France later, but like us, they were assigned to the French army. Then, as 1918 began, the 15th New York was re-designated the 369th U.S. Infantry and its men were put to work unloading cargo from ships at Brest—until Colonel Hayward protested to General John Pershing, "I brought fighting troops, not stevedores!" We were then given a choice: We could be shipped home, or we could be assigned to the French Fourth Army. The men were delighted—they didn't want to be sent home. . . .

We joined the 161st Division of the Fourth Army on April 13, 1918—thereby becoming the first regiment in U.S. history to serve as an integral part of a foreign army—and were assigned to Bois d'Hauza near Verdun. The Fourth Army commander, General Henri Gouraud, was a veteran who had served in Africa and had a high opinion of African troops. In the Fourth Army, the 369th fought alongside one Senegalese and two Moroccan divisions. In our first few weeks at the front, we served closely alongside French troops. I spoke French, having gone to school in France when I was eight years old, and Switzerland when I was 12. Some of the other officers could also speak French. As for the troops, the French were glad to have them, and they were glad to serve. Our men, who played baseball, could throw grenades farther than the French, which amused the French a lot. . . .

While we were attached to the French army, my men were equipped with French Chauchat rifles and ammunition, as well as French helmets and canteens. For backup fire support, the company had a lot of very good French Chauchat machine guns, also some mortars and two or three rapid-fire 75mm guns that we brought in case of a major attack.

Just before going to the trenches, I was sent to attend a three-day course on French gas school, which was most interesting and instructive. More than one-half of all the shells fired by the Germans in March 1918 were gas shells, so you could readily appreciate how frightfully important this terrible feature of modern warfare was. . . .

Every soldier near the front kept his gas mask around his neck, ready for immediate use. . . . A large percentage of the German gas shells was composed of yperite gas, which was particularly dangerous, as it was odorless and colorless, and the fumes did not take effect for 12 hours. But our gas masks provided absolute protection against infection of the lungs if put on in time and worn long enough. . . .

On April 18, 1918, we took up positions in the Bois d'Hauza, where the French knew the Germans were going to launch a big attack that day. My company was sent to some fortifications on the front line, and that was the first fighting I knew, because the German artillery knew where the fort was, and opened up on it. One of my men was wounded, so I called up the next regiment—it was a mile back—which brought up support for the wounded man. As a stretcher team came to get him out of there, I was standing 10 yards away when a 105mm shell came and landed in the middle of it. One of the stretcher-bearers was killed and three others were wounded. . . .

Then, I was ordered to move my men five miles over to join the French, because we were too far east of the German attack. So we marched over to a French advanced headquarters, which was located only 50 yards from German advanced HQ. That night, my men cooperated with the French when they sent out a raiding party to take some prisoners for interrogation. It was discovered, and came under fire from the two Germans it was approaching. One of the German bullets hit a bag of hand grenades that was being carried by one of the men and it exploded, killing three of them in-

stantly. Unable to capture the Germans, the French killed them and one Frenchman brought back a helmet and rifle, which he proudly exhibited the next day. On the way back, however, they came upon a German barrage and three were wounded. The French lieutenant, who was badly wounded in the raid by a pistol shot to the head, walked back to our dugout and reported to the captain on the failure of the raid, and was worried more about the death of his three men than about the bullet which was still in his head.

# 1919 PROFILE

# WORLD WAR I: RUSSIA

### Non-commissioned Officer

Bull Rawicz was prepared to leave his new wife and dreams of business school to fight for his country, but nothing prepared him for a journey into Russia to battle the Bolsheviks, even after World War I ended.

### Life at Home

- Bull Rawicz was enormously pleased with his life on the day the army draft notice arrived.
- Newly married, Bull was dreaming of children and a chance to attend a business school—courtesy of his new father-in-law.
- Imagine, a Rawicz in a three-piece businessman's suit!
- Born into the Polish community of Hamtramck, Michigan, a Detroit suburb, Bull was raised in a large apartment with his siblings, parents, paternal grandparents and his widowed uncle.
- Most of his extended family lived within a few blocks of him.
- Principally, their lives revolved around the family, work, the Roman Catholic Church and the traditional Polish food cooked by his mother, sisters, and grandmother.
- Bull's father was a shift supervisor at an iron foundry, his uncle the foreman of a mechanical crew at a rail yard.
- His mother had been a seamstress, but primarily managed the home, occasionally doing special jobs.
- Bull's ancestors were skilled laborers and foremen in the Polish city of Bialystok, before they immigrated in the 1890s.
- Although no Polish state had existed for 120 years, his family considered themselves Polish and spoke Polish at home.
- Bull got his name when he started school and was found to be taller and stockier than the rest of the students.

*Bull Rawicz will spend much of his service fighting in the snows of Russia.*

*Bull is eager to defend America, the country that has given his family so much.*

- His friends all agreed that Bull, although hard-working, was not an exceptional student; what he lacked, they said, was curiosity.
- After high school graduation, he joined a rivet gang, whose job was to drive the rivets manually into the steel beams holding up the tall buildings of Detroit.
- He then married Jadwiga, a girl he had known since childhood.
- Also from Bialystok, her people were small-business owners and boasted a priest in the family.
- Some neighbors whispered that marriage to Bull was beneath Jadwiga, but her father knew the Rawicz men were hard-working, frugal and respectable.
- Nevertheless, Jadwiga considered Bull's current job unsuitable for a family man, so her father offered to send Bull to management courses at the business college.
- That's when the draft notice arrived.
- Bull had been playing his accordion at a Knights of Columbus dance, a favorite social occasion for his family, when he was told to report for duty.
- He was eager to defend America—the country he felt had given him and his family so much.
- However, he was afraid.
- He had a young wife, whom he did not want to leave, and he had also never been outside of Wayne County, Michigan.
- Bull was sworn in with the other Wayne County draftees in June 1918, and soon was on his way to Camp Custer in Battle Creek, Michigan.
- A large group of friends and family—many saying they thought the war would be over quickly—saw him off at the station, wishing him a safe return.

*His assignment in Russia is to protect supplies from the Bolsheviks.*

## Life at Work

- After only three weeks of training, Bull was sent to Camp Mills on Long Island, where he was met with a telegram informing him that his wife was expecting a child.
- What a moment of excitement!
- However, Bull was worried because he would not be there to help, although he was supremely confident that the family would take good care of his bride.
- As the other regiments embarked for France, Bull's 339th Battalion waited.
- Oddly, they were ordered to exchange their rifles for the long, light, less accurate bolt-action rifles used by the Imperial Russian Infantry.
- They were also issued heavy wool clothing and Shackleton boots for use in arctic climates.

**Paul Totten of the 338th Infantry landed in Russia on October 1, 1919, as part of a detachment of replacement men in the 339th. He was 26 years old and had been in the army since July 13, 1918, serving in England and France.**

Wednesday, November 13, 1918

My sore hand was dressed again this morning. Sixteen of us were assigned to return to Archangel via the river barge. Also aboard were 25 or 30 Bolshevik prisoners under lock and key in the brig, including one woman. Of course, me with my sore hand, was assigned to brig guard at 8:00 p.m. Later that night a commotion flared up in the brig. I responded and, after some jabbering and gesturing, I finally came to as to what the trouble was. She had to "GO" and no fooling. I let her out and she "WENT," also with no fooling. Method of procedure: Left hand, grasping a davit, left foot on the rail, and the right foot out over the river. 'Twas quite a performance. After the ordeal I gave the poor woman a cigarette and let her stay out on the deck for a spell. Against the rules, of course, but felt as though I'd done my good deed for the day. Kind of a bizarre exposure, but thought you'd like to know. "Once seen, never forgotten."

Tuesday, February 11, 1919

Still on the move all day, with what rest periods the Brass deemed appropriate. But on we go, hungry, tired and with evil reflections on this, the damnedest, most exhausting trip we ever made. Finally arrived at SREDMAKRINGA at 8:00 p.m. The whole bunch about battled out. Treated well by what few civilians were there. But they were preparing to scoot to noncombative points farther north. We all wished we could join that convoy. Up the river and through the woods will be long remembered.

Wednesday, February 12, 1919

Our outfit buried 76 dead Bolos [Bolsheviks] this morning. They were killed in their raid here the day before, just prior to our arrival there yesterday. Several houses had been hit by Bolshevik artillery, but reported casualties were light. Luck was surely with them and also with us, due to our late arrival as reinforcements. . . .

Thursday, February 13, 1919

This village was slated for destruction. Today we razed buildings by burning and sheer demolition. This was the day we destroyed the post office, which was replete with stained-glass doors and other ornate czarist trappings. Discovered another dead Bolo and consigned him to the flames of a burning building. Cremation in lieu of burial in the frozen ground. This really produced a sinking, uncanny sensation. The reason for all this vandalism? WAR!—and discretionary military judgment and authority.

Friday, February 14, 1919

Still on destruction detail. More buildings razed and burned. This process seemed brutal, but will have to admit it was breathtaking. Sunshiny but bitter cold.

Saturday, February 15, 1919

Still at it, whang bang! Pangs of headache and touch of indigestion. I think a good orange would have straightened out those ailments, but had to rely on the smoke from the conflagrations as a generic substitute. Felt miserable all afternoon. The whole family where I was billeted returned from their exodus today, bringing a squalling baby, a grandfather and their livestock consisting of a small pig and several chickens. It was apparently customary to share the living quarters with the livestock and, believe it or not, they were our bedfellows for the night. They were very inquisitive and affectionate. Our rest that night would roughly compare to that lake of fire we learned about in Sunday school. The sandman never tried harder, but left early—baffled.

Wednesday, February 19, 1919

Still cold and blustery, but not disagreeable enough to let it interfere with the business at hand. So, back to the barbed wire enterprise. Started

## "Paul Totten of the 338th Infantry . . ." *(continued)*

building block houses. These structures were constructed entirely of logs, which we cut from the thousands of pine trees close by. Finally, the whistle blew and we were back in our nests—pigs, chickens et al.

Thursday, February 20, 1919

On the dug-out block houses all day. A regular convict's job. Rations growing slimmer and hardtack getting harder. To Hell with British rations! Everybody is familiar with hardtack, but this M and V! The letters stand for meat and vegetables. It was an un-Godly limey [British soldier] concoction. Putrid is the only description, so let your mind wander. Finally back to our nests with the family pig and fowls. Should have spelled this latter word—"Foul"—Correction noted.

- Quickly, a rumor spread that they were being sent to Russia, which Bull felt made no sense, considering Russia had withdrawn from the war after the overthrow of the czar.
- Nonetheless, on August 25, the 339th boarded transports in Newcastle Harbor and set off for northern Russia.
- The men were told they were not to be an offensive force, but were being sent to protect from the Bolsheviks the supplies and equipment sent by the allies to the Imperial Army.
- The equipment was now stored in the northern port cities of Murmansk and Archangel.
- The issue became confused when the 339th was placed under the command of the British.
- Their stated goal was to defeat the Bolos, as Bolsheviks were called.
- Bull has little use for Russians, who were party to splitting up Poland decades ago.
- On the bright side, as a child he had learned a fair amount of Russian from older members of his family, and preferred to be in a country where he could speak the language.

- Bull writes two letters a day—one to his parents and one to his wife—even though he cannot mail them until they make landfall.
- Through them, he is composing for his parents a chronicle of each day's events, coupled with assurances of his good health.
- To Jadwiga, he writes longer letters about their future together and about names for the baby; Bull wants the child's name to be Catholic and American.
- On September 4, 1918, his convoy arrived in Archangel Harbor.
- The first battalion, which includes Bull's company, stayed aboard ship for a couple of days while the other troops disembarked.
- When their time finally came, they did not go to guard duty in Archangel as expected, but were loaded into filthy, stinking barges.
- For five days they cruised up the river, which some of the soldiers said reminded them of the lower reaches of the Mississippi River—though few had actually ever seen the lower reaches of the Mississippi.
- Eighty-five percent of the men in the regiment are from Michigan, and 70 percent of those are from metropolitan Detroit.

## War Calendar

- March 8, 1917: The Russian Revolution began
- March 15, 1917: Tsar Nicholas II abdicated
- April 6, 1917: U.S. entered World War I
- April 16, 1917: Lenin and other exiled Bolshevik leaders arrived in Petrograd from Switzerland
- November 6-7, 1917: Bolsheviks overthrew Karensky and seized power
- January 8, 1918: Wilson's "Fourteen Points" address to Congress called for self-determination, removal of economic barriers and the League of Nations
- March 3, 1918: Russia made a separate treaty with the Central Powers at Brest-Litovsk
- July 16, 1918: Czar Nicholas and family were shot
- November 11, 1918: World War I ended
- June 28, 1919: Versailles Treaty was signed
- August 11, 1919: Germany became a republic as the Weimar Constitution was promulgated

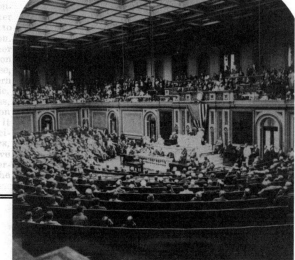

*President Woodrow Wilson addresses Congress on the war.*

- From what Bull and the company could see, the country seemed to be one giant swamp filled with vermin.
- He never could have imagined that there could be so many cockroaches; the barge swarmed with them.
- When they finally landed, his company was put on guard duty, but was soon told to back up a British unit in action a little farther south of the town.
- The fight was fierce, but the arrival of the American reinforcements soon caused the Bolos to retreat.
- Although there were no casualties in Bull's company, they felt initiated into battle.
- A few days later, half the company, including Bull, and a few allied Russian troops took a steamer up the Ovina onto the Vaga, a large tributary.
- They sought to occupy the town of Shen Kursk, a summer resort now filled with upper class refugees from St. Petersburg.
- They stayed only a short while; orders came from the British Command to proceed farther up-river to "stir up the enemy."
- The small force set out again and were soon under heavy fire from the banks.
- As bullets thumped around it, the steamer pulled close to the shore.
- The troops jumped out, waded to shore and dispersed the Bolos.
- Struggling over the marshy ground with the ever-present insects, they then embarked on a march to the interior.
- Soon, Bolsheviks from throughout the region marshaled for a battle and began pursuing the Americans.
- Finally, as their rations neared an end, Bull's battalion engaged a sizable force of the enemy, inflicting twice as many casualties as they had men.
- Again, Bull escaped injury.

## Selected Prices

| | |
|---|---|
| Camera | $2.80 |
| Chewing Gum, Wrigley's Doublemint, per Box | $0.73 |
| Cigarettes, Camel, per Pack | $0.18 |
| Dress Pattern | $0.10 |
| Dress, Baby's Long White | $1.33 |
| Hat, Man's | $5.00 |
| Mousetrap | $0.02 |
| Phonograph Record | $1.50 |
| Puffed Wheat, per Box | $0.15 |
| Shampoo | $0.50 |
| Shotgun, Remington, 12-Gauge | $32.70 |
| Streetcar Fare, New York | $0.30 |
| Suit, Woman's Velveteen | $29.75 |
| Telephone Call, Three Minutes, New York to Chicago | $14.45 |
| Travelers' Cheques | $0.50 |

- Through the fight, he was able to register his first confirmed kill; drawing a careful bead on the enemy troops, he was able to drop several of them in their tracks.
- The small force backtracked until they reached the village of Ust Padenga, about 15 miles south of Shen Kursk, where they were ordered to stop.
- They guarded the village—the southern outpost of the allied forces—until November, when they were finally relieved for a brief period to return to the relative security of Shen Kursk.
- Here, Bull took the opportunity to practice his Russian language skills.
- He was also able to play at a couple of dances on a borrowed accordion.
- He received—finally—mail from home, including a letter from Jadwiga agreeing to the names Matthew James for a boy and Mary Elizabeth for a girl; she thought the names were beautiful.
- News also arrived that the armistice had been signed; the Great War was over!
- The men rejoiced and hoped that soon, they would get their orders to go home.
- Unfortunately, the port at Archangel remained frozen and they heard they would not be able to get home until spring.
- Bull grew anxious, frustrated, and finally broke down and cried.
- If delayed until spring, he would not be able to get home in time to see his first child born.

*Following the armistice, Bull and his unit are sent back into battle in the dead of a Russian winter.*

- Soon, those concerns were washed away, as instead of going home, they were sent back into battle at Ust Padenga.
- When they arrived, they were ordered to attack the city on January 19, the dead of the Russian winter.
- First, Bull and his regiment began with a heavy artillery bombardment, followed by a charge against thousands of white-clad Bolos—almost invisible against the snow.
- Casualties rose quickly.
- After the Bolos were repulsed for the third time and the British-American force had lost half its company, orders came to abandon the town.
- On the fourth night of the engagement, Bull and the remaining troops crept from Ust Padenga, ablaze from a Bolo shell, down the frozen Vaga until they reached Shen Kursk.
- The journey took two days.
- Soon, they were nearly surrounded again by the enemy, who anticipated the allied retreat.
- One night, however, undetected by the enemy, the entire force plus a large number of civilians left Shen Kursk by a secret road and slowly retreated from town to town along the Vaga.
- They were in the town of Kitsa when spring finally broke and the Bolsheviks withdrew, afraid they would become bogged down in the melting snow.
- Spring also meant that Bolshevik boats would be able to patrol the river and attack the British-American army.
- Kitsa was abandoned.
- In mid-May, Bull's squadron was on patrol when it was swept by sniper fire, but they were able to suppress it and the sniper surrendered.

> They took him to
> the rifle range
> Way out beyond the hill,
> To teach to him the
> trigger squeeze
> And how the foe to kill.
> His rifle kicked him
> in the jaw—
> He missed the bull
> a mile!
> For the mess hall is
> the only place
> He shows off
> any style!
> —World War I
> Camp Song

## "Fact and Comment," *The Youth's Companion,* January 9, 1919:

Circumstances have combined to make saving anthracite coal a matter of urgent importance. Although last year between April 1 and October 1, much more anthracite was mined than was mined during the same period in 1917, yet since then the epidemic of influenza, which was especially virulent in the mining regions, and other conditions that followed the signing of the armistice, have reduced the production by a half million tons. In order to make the available supply meet the needs of the country, it is necessary to practice the greatest economy both in getting the most heat possible from all the coal that we burn and by mixing the regular domestic sizes with the smaller size known as buckwheat number one, which hitherto has not been used for heating houses.

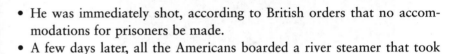

- He was immediately shot, according to British orders that no accommodations for prisoners be made.
- A few days later, all the Americans boarded a river steamer that took them to Archangel—the first leg toward home.
- There, they received a month's worth of back mail; Bull found a letter announcing the birth of his first child, Mary Elizabeth, on March 26, 1919.

### Life in the Community: Archangel, Russia

- During World War I, while the Russians fought Germany alongside the allies, their counterparts in Russia began to run out of supplies; the cost of such staples as bread rose dramatically, quickly spiraling out of control.
- Bread riots began, leading to the March Revolution.
- As a result, a provisional government was set up in 1917, but it soon fell apart.
- The Bolsheviks, under the leadership of Lenin and Trotsky, seized power.
- As a result, the Soviet government signed the Treaty of Brest-Litovsk with Germany and pulled out of the war.
- The European allies then began planning to join with the anti-Soviet forces to overthrow the Bolshevik government and reopen the eastern front.
- However, Trotsky successfully engineered the Red Army to include former officers of the Czarist government.
- The Russian army was too large and well-trained to be defeated by the paltry forces the allies had allocated.

# HISTORICAL SNAPSHOT
# 1919

- Unemployment rose to three million
- The Treaty of Versailles assigned Germany sole responsibility for causing the Great War
- The first nonstop transatlantic flight from Newfoundland to Ireland was made by J. W. Alcock and A. Whitten Brown in 16 hours and 27 minutes
- Seventy-seven percent of newspaper editors favored the ratification of the Peace Treaty, including the provision to create the League of Nations
- Enough states finally ratified the Eighteenth Amendment prohibiting the sale of alcohol, to take effect as law in 1920
- The Nineteenth Amendment, granting women suffrage, was adopted
- Attorney General Mitchell Palmer instructed the FBI to round up 249 known communists, who were then deported on the "Soviet Ark" to Finland
- The dial telephone was introduced in Norfolk, Virginia
- The Grand Canyon National Park was established
- Ice cream sales in the United States reached 150 million gallons, up from 30 million in 1909
- Henry Ford repurchased full control of Ford Motor Company for $105 million
- Seven million cars were registered nationwide
- More than 30,000 Jews marched in Baltimore to protest pogroms in Poland and other European countries
- Socialist Eugene Debs, who had called Lenin and Trotsky the "foremost statesmen of the age," was charged with sedition and sent to prison
- The mayor of Seattle set up machine guns in the streets after 45,000 strikers threatened to paralyze the city
- The Great War cost America $21.9 billion, or approximately $1 million an hour; of the total, $13.9 billion went for army expenses

## "Withdraw from Russia!" *The Dial*, December 14, 1918:

It is safe to say that the average American citizen would be thoroughly shocked at knowing the kind of imperialistic and anti-democratic game which is being played by our own and our allies' armies in Russia. These are facts and we think it high time that they be told. We do not believe that our own government wants the restoration of the monarchy in Russia or that it would support a demonstrable unpopular government forever. The American government would like to see in Russia a liberal and commercial republic like ourselves—a quiet, respectable government with which we could do business. Undoubtedly. But what we should like and what we are, as a matter of cold fact, getting are two widely different things. It is no secret that powerful parties in Japan are advocating the unostentatious annexation of large sections of Siberia, and that they have no interest in seeing any stable popular government arise east of the Urals. It is no secret that England trembles for Persia, Afghanistan, and India, and that the Tory party would gladly crush the Russian Revolution if it exhibited any tendency towards proselytism in foreign countries (as it has). It is no secret that a certain section of French governmental opinion cares not a fig what sort of a reactionary government there is in Russia, provided only that it is a government that will immediately repay the foreign loan. In a word, our intervention in Russia may have been undertaken with the best of intentions, *but the practical situation with which we are faced today is either to support reaction and imperialism or—to withdraw our troops.* Russian intervention has become for America a tragic anachronism since the defeat of Germany. We have neither a national nor an international interest which today legitimately sanctions the presence of our troops on Russian soil. It is false to our traditions to be fighting a workingman's republic, even if we do not approve of its form or its manners. It is not in accordance with any doctrine of American national policy for us to be engaged in crushing a revolution or in crucifying the hopes and aspirations of a great and mighty people. It is really difficult to believe that this is the same country which in Washington's time almost had a civil war because this government refused to intervene in the French Revolution, *on behalf of the revolutionists.* And not even the most severe critics of the present leaders of the Soviet government have said one-tenth as many bitter things as were said of Robespierre and Marat in their day. No; to help crush a revolution is not in accordance with the real American tradition.

For that reason, we demand of our government that our troops now in Russia be immediately withdrawn. We are asking no more than British Labor and French Labor and Italian Labor have already officially demanded of their governments. We are asking no more than President Wilson has again and again promised to the Russian peoples. . . . We are asking no more than most would ask, if they knew the facts, and do ask, those who are aware of them—the soldiers who entered this war inspired by an honest ideal to defeat the menace of German autocracy and to bring freedom to the oppressed peoples of this world. Those who have given their lives on the battlefields of France will rise to reproach us if we are now false to our trust.

## "America's Manpower in the Great War," *The Literary Digest*, July 12, 1919:

America put forth twice the manpower in the Great War than the North put forth in the war of the sixties. "It was almost true," writes Leonard P. Ayers, in *A Statistical Summary of the War with Germany* publication that has recently been authorized by the War Department, "that among each 100 Americans, five took up arms in defense of the country." During the Civil War, it is pointed out, 10 of every 100 inhabitants of the Northern states served as soldiers or sailors. In that struggle, 2.4 million men served in the Northern armies or in the navy. The great growth of the United States in the meantime is indicated by the fact that, in spite of a proportionate contribution in manpower of nearly two-to-one in favor of the Civil War days, a total of 4.8 million men had been gathered into the armed forces of the United States between April 6, 1917, and November 11, 1918, when the armistice went into effect. An American effort proportional to that put forth by the North during the Civil War would have produced nearly 10 million fighting men. . . .

A chapter captioned "Two Hundred Days of Battle," which is the story of St. Mihiel, and other major operations participated in by the Americans, is thus summarized by Colonel Ayers:

Two out of every three American soldiers who reached France took part in battle. The number who reached France was 2,084,000, and of them 1.3 million saw active service at the front.

Of the 42 divisions that reached France, 29 took part in active combat service. Seven of them were regular army divisions, 11 were organized from the National Guard, and 11 were made up of National Army troops.

American divisions were in battle for 200 days and engaged in 13 major operations.

From the middle of August until the end of the war, the American divisions held, during the greater part of the time, a front longer than that held by the British.

In October, the American divisions held 101 miles of line, or 23 percent of the entire Western Front.

In the battle of Mihiel, 550,000 Americans were engaged, as compared with 100,000 on the Northern side in the battle of Gettysburg. The artillery fired more than one million shells in four hours, which is the most intense concentration of artillery fire recorded in history.

The Meuse-Argonne Battle lasted 47 days, during which 1.2 million American troops were engaged.

The "Health and Casualties" of the American forces were summarized to the following effect:

Of every 100 American soldiers and sailors who served in the war with Germany, two were killed or died of disease during the period of hostilities.

The total battle deaths of all nations in this war were greater than all the deaths in all the wars in the previous 100 years.

The number of American lives lost was 122,500, of which about 10,000 were in the navy and the rest in the army and the Marines attached to it.

In the American army, the casualty rate in the infantry was higher than in any other service, and that for officers was higher than for men.

For every man killed in battle, seven were wounded.

Five out of every six men sent to hospitals on account of wounds were cured and returned to duty.

In the expeditionary forces, battle losses were twice as large as deaths from disease. . . .

## "The Germans in Defeat," *The Youth's Companion*, January 9, 1919:

Through four long years we have had an opportunity to study the German character as it revealed itself in hope of victory. The conclusions that we reached were not complimentary. Now, for two months, we have watched the bearing of Germans in defeat, and we cannot revise those conclusions. Germany in defeat is the reverse of the medal of which Germany in victory is the face; the qualities that are stamped on one determine those that are displayed on the other, in appropriately reversed form.

The arrogance that tore up the most solemn treaties and that struck blow after blow at smaller and weaker nations finds its complement in the hasty readiness to make an abject surrender when the tables at last are turned. The savage cruelty shown to those who were temporarily in the power of the Germans is replaced by a whimpering plea to be spared the hardships and suffering that must follow invasion. As the Germans fought without chivalry in victory, so they fight without spirit in defeat. Like their Bulgarian allies, they would not defend their own soil; when aggression failed they were ready to quit. The Kaiser ran away in a panic from his own army and his own people.

It is all explicable enough when you get the keyword—materialism. The Germans would fight for loot, for conquest, for material gain; they would not fight for anything else. When it began to appear that it would cost a good deal more to fight than they could hope to make by fighting, they were only too willing to stop. That may be businesslike, but is also despicable.

The case would be different if there were any reason to believe that Germany surrendered be-cause it recognized the evil it had done and the falseness of its wartime ideals. There is no such reason. There is not the slightest disposition on the part of the new German leaders to be repentant or contrite in heart. They merely recognized that Germany made a miscalculation, that it would have paid better to keep out of the war. . . .

It is even questionable whether a genuine revolution is yet possible in Germany. The material disturbance and loss that accompany such occasions frighten the German. His ingrained disposition to obey someone else is unfit for the job of revolutionary. It is dangerous to predict in such times as these, but the German soldiers returning from the front show little of the eager reforming spirit. They will give the Ebert government its chance, since the Imperial party made a mess of things; but if the moderate Socialists fail, as they very well may, a reaction to monarchy is more likely than a further decline in Bolshevism.

## "Who Are the Russian Allies of the Allies?"
### *The Fortnightly Review,* March 1919:

There was never in this country a trace of enthusiasm for allied military intervention in Russia. From bewildered acquiescence, public opinion is now passing to critical questioning. None of us know much about these Russian expeditions, but there is one thing which all of us know. The original case for them has disappeared. The strategic argument for "reconstructing the Russian front" is obsolete today. If these expeditions continue they must now be defended frankly on the ground that it is in our best interest to destroy Bolshevism by force of arms. It is evident that the undertaking will not be the easiest in the world. None of the expeditions has prospered so far. On the Murman front, we have done little more than hold the coast. The Archangel force, after an ambitious attempt to advance into the interior, has had to retire to its base.

Meanwhile, some illusions are lost and some salutary experiences gained. The legend that all Russia was eagerly awaiting the invader, and that her manhood would "fall in" when our bugles sounded, is now discarded. Some months ago the more active politicians of most of the many non-Bolshevik progressive parties were for intervention, and did call in the allies—though only, as they said, to fight the Germans. These parties were once the majority in Russia, though no one can say how strong they were then or are now. There is little doubt that many of them are now disillusioned. They do not desire foreign intervention in the internal affairs of Russia. To some extent, the more moderate socialists have even rallied in recent weeks to Lenin's government. They are not converts to Bolshevism, but they prefer native errors and excesses to foreign meddling.

# 1920–1929

The years following the Great War ushered in Women's Suffrage, Prohibition, and massive consumerism. By 1920, more than 50 percent of the population—54 million people—lived in cities, increased industrialization, and the migration of Southern blacks to the urban North. America had cast off the last remnants of the Victorian age with its idealized images of propriety, and entered a new era, one with fewer restrictions and illusions, evidenced by the growing popularity of jazz and the emergence of the flapper. Many women who had worked in industry during the war remained in the work force, although at lower wages. Now allowed to vote nationally, women were also encouraged to consider options other than marriage, such as college and a career.

As certain social issues began to be addressed, Americans were also questioning their government's foreign policy. America had invaded Haiti in 1915 to protect U.S. business interests during one of the country's revolutions and Marines were still stationed in there. In the independent nation of Nicaragua, American forces fought to keep liberal Nicaraguan revolutionaries from overthrowing the U.S.-backed conservative leader of the small country—an action which many believed reflected not only American interest in building a new canal there, but also to protect the interests of a major U.S. corporation.

The financial crash in October 1929 sobered America after its decade-long period of prosperity. Over the next few years, the U.S. Government would be obliged to focus its attention on domestic issues of poverty, unemployment, and the economic collapse of industry during the Great Depression.

# 1923 Profile

## The Occupation of Haiti

### Civilian

Eight years after the Marines landed in Haiti to stabilize the government and protect American banking interests, Lee Tully is leading an effort to bring telephone service to the island nation.

### Life at Home

- Lee Tully grew up in Eufaula, Alabama, on the banks of the Chatahoochee River.
- Each morning his father and oldest brother would drive from town to their farm, which provided the family's livelihood.
- The other three sons became professionals—one was a lawyer, another managed an insurance agency, and Lee became an electrical engineer.
- Lee attended Alabama Polytechnic in Auburn, and then went to work designing and installing systems for a telephone company in Atlanta.
- The work was rewarding, but a failed romance convinced him that a change of scenery was needed.
- When he learned that an engineer was needed to assist the entire nation of Haiti, he jumped at the chance.
- The navy had no engineer qualified for the job, opening the way for a civilian; the other Americans in the department were all naval officers.
- Accustomed to the bustling city of Atlanta, Lee was not prepared for the primitive conditions that existed in Haiti.
- The telegraph system served only a few towns between population centers, while large portions of the mountain interiors had no service at all.
- The telephone service that existed in the larger towns had few paid subscribers because service was so poor.
- At first, Lee was dismayed, but after a while he became excited by the challenge of building an entire network from the ground up.
- To meet his goals, he worked long days at the office—a pleasant, high-ceilinged room, overlooking a courtyard in downtown Port-au-Prince.
- Several times a month he traveled into the rural sections, usually by water, to in-

*Lee Tully is helping to bring telephone service to Haiti.*

155

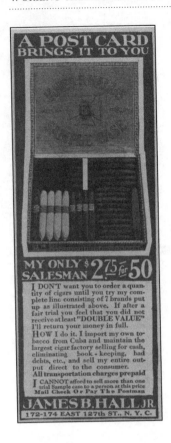

spect the telephone and telegraph systems; often he would inspect the municipal water systems for his boss.

- Water transportation was used because the roads were generally in disrepair, except where the military had constructed roads.

### Life at Work

- Lee Tully is a big man—some would say fat—who has learned to tolerate the sticky, oven heat of a Port-au-Prince summer.
- Fitting his station in life, at least in Haiti, he sports a trademark white suit and broad-brimmed Panama hat, and smokes a long, green cigar.
- The new automatic telephone system installed by the American government boasts 300 lines in operation; as new equipment is installed, the capacity will double.
- The telephone systems of Haiti being his primary responsibility, Lee views the state-of-the-art operation in the capital city of Port-au-Prince with particular pride.
- Since arriving in Haiti, he personally planned the new system, drew up the specifications, solicited the bids and oversaw the installation.
- Sometimes he even makes calls when he has very little to say just to see how well the operation works.
- Lee is a "treaty official," an American government employee paid by the Haitian government, and serves under the terms of the 1916 treaty between the United States and Haiti.
- Under that document, a large number of Americans, primarily military personnel, were assigned to assist the Haitian government.
- Many Haitians resent the power of the treaty officials, claiming they actually run the country; the men of the *de jure* government, they say, are merely puppets serving the whim of Washington.
- The treaty was negotiated following the landing of American Marines in Haiti in 1915.

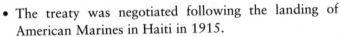

*Lee serves in Haiti as a treaty official, based on a treaty negotiated following the American occupation of the country in 1915.*

## Summary of Report of Gendarmerie d'Haiti, U.S. High Commissioner to Haiti, Annual Report, January 1, 1924:

1. Under the supervision of Lieut. Col. Douglas McDougal, United States Marine Corps, with the rank of Major General, as Chief of the Gendarmerie, are 101 officers and noncommissioned officers of the Marine Corps; 13 officers and petty officers of the United States Navy, and a contract surgeon who holds the rank of lieutenant in the Medical Corps of the navy, a total of 115 American officers. . . .

2. The Haitian commissioned and acting commissioned personnel comprises 22 lieutenants and acting lieutenants, and 22 aspirant officers in training, a total of 44.

3. The enlisted strength of 2,510, as against 2,414 for 1922, is wholly Haitian.

4. As in 1922, banditry is nonexistent, and the country has enjoyed peace and order. Routine and special patrols have proved an effective check against sporadic disorder, and have reduced minor offenses against the law.

5. Elementary school, established in 1922, has extended in scope. Daily instruction of gendarmerie is making better citizens of them and enhancing their prestige among their people.

The American landing in Haiti is based on the Monroe Doctrine, intended to keep European powers out of the Western Hemisphere.

- The landing was ostensibly to protect against any violations of the Monroe Doctrine by European Powers—principally France and Germany.
- Lee privately acknowledges that the landing was precipitated by pressure to protect U.S. business interests, especially several Wall Street banks, during one of Haiti's many revolutions.
- In addition, United States interest and involvement increased dramatically with the completion of the Panama Canal, because the waters around Haiti lie within the shipping lanes of the newly opened isthmus.
- Retired Marine Brigadier General John Russell, also known in Haiti as the American viceroy, heads the treaty officials.
- He is assisted by a legal advisor, a financial advisor, an agricultural engineer, a receiver general, the commander of the gendarmerie or police, a director for the Public Health Service and a director of the Department of Public Works.
- Lee works for the Public Works director, who employs 10 American engineers, 19 Haitian engineers, and has an overall staff of mostly Haitians numbering seasonally from 2,700 to 6,700.
- His chief assistant is Jacques Delage, the youngest son of one of Haiti's best families.

*Lee and his colleagues find conditions in Haiti to be primitive by American standards.*

It hurt. It stunk. Fairyland had turned into a pigsty. More than that, we were not welcome. We could feel it as distinctly as we could smell the rot along the gutters. . . . In the street were piles of evil-smelling offal. The stench hung over everything. Piles of mango seeds were heaped in the middle of the highway, sour-smelling. It was not merely these, prospect was filthy. . . . Haitians of the working class have the ugliest feet in the world. In my bewilderment, I somehow blamed them for the horrid things on which they stood. We were all annoyed.

—Faustin Wirkus, Marine Corps Private, describing his day ashore in Haiti

- Things are certainly different here; in Eufaula, Alabama, a Negro would never suggest to a white man that they dine together.
- Most nights Lee goes for a drink or two to the American Club, where Haitians are not allowed.
- This causes considerable friction among the natives.
- Prohibition is now the law of the land in the United States, but is universally ignored in Haiti.
- The biggest downside of Haiti is the scarcity of American women.
- For weeks, Lee watched a Red Cross nurse, who is attached to the Public Health Department, as she flirtatiously entertained a gaggle of naval and Marine Corps officers without a single look in his direction.
- The Panama hat and cigar changed all that.

- Jacques was educated in France, has a university degree in electrical engineering, and speaks flawless French and English, along with some Spanish and German.
- Typical of the Haitian ruling class, Jacques' features are largely Caucasian; only a slightly darker skin tone displays his African roots.
- He is eager to be friends with Lee, mentioning more than once that his sister Desirée is home from her studies in France, but Lee has declined all invitations to socialize.
- He fully understands that even though the Haitian élite want to be white, they still have Negro blood running through their veins.

- Recently, they have had several long conversations.
- In addition, the new look has caught the attention of the department's laborers.
- They now call him in their Creole tongue, "the man with the long, green cigar."
- Lee likes that.
- During his travels around the country, he enjoys inspecting all the improvements under way, from new schools and hospitals to roads.
- Formerly arid lands are being made fertile through irrigation, while flood-prone regions near rivers now sport sturdy dykes, increasing the amount of stable arable land.
- New lighthouses and navigational aids are being established along the coast.
- Lee also spends time looking for signs of *vodun*, the native folk religion, also called voodoo.
- From what he has seen, he believes the popular anecdote that 90 percent of Haitians are Catholic and 100 percent are believers in *vodun*.
- Lee is still astounded that this land, once the richest colony in the world under French control, has fallen into such a quagmire of anarchy and perennial revolution.
- Yet, everywhere he turns, someone wants to blame Uncle Sam for the nation's many problems.
- The dozen newspapers in Port-au-Prince—a high number for the size of the literate population—frequently rail against the American "occupation" of Haiti and the "puppet government" it created.
- Rarely do they mention that historically high foreign debt, particularly to French bondholders, amounted to $21.5 million a year, or 80 percent of government revenues, before the occupation.
- Nor do they remember their history: from 1806 to the 1915 American intervention, 17 of the 24 presidents were overthrown by revolutions, and only two of the presidents retired peacefully at the end of their terms.
- Eleven of Haiti's presidents served for less than one year.
- Besides, at the time of the intervention, German entrepreneurs were a powerful presence on the island and were a danger to nations in the Western Hemisphere once World War I got under way.

"Lips that touch liquor shall never touch mine."
"Your lips?"
"No, my liquor."
—C. C. N. Y. Mercury

*Lee has found that dressing well is gaining him considerable respect.*

- Recently, the more vocal editors of the most radical publications were thrown into jail to teach them a lesson.
- Lee knows that these measures may seem harsh to some, but he fully understands the necessity of limiting free speech when the fragile balance of power in a country is in a vulnerable and embryonic state.

## Life in the Community: Haiti

- The Republic of Haiti occupies the western third of the island of Hispaniola, which lies 60 miles across the Windward Passage from Oriente Province in Cuba.
- Haiti, which shares Hispaniola with the Dominican Republic, has a population of more than two million and a land area one-third greater than the state of New Jersey.
- After the United States, Haiti is the oldest independent nation in the Western Hemisphere.
- At the time of the French Revolution, Haiti was the wealthiest European colonial possession in the Americas, accounting for more than one-third of the foreign commerce of France; the ports on the island received 1,587 ships in 1789, a number greater than that of Marseilles.
- The chief exports were sugar, coffee, cotton, indigo, molasses and dyewoods.

- Independence was achieved during the French Revolution after a protracted slave revolt; under Jean Jacques Dessalines, Haitian slaves owned by French plantation owners defeated a contingent of French troops commanded by Napoleon's brother-in-law, General Leclerc.
- Since the overthrow of the French in 1804, Haitians with some white blood—especially French heritage—have served as the country's ruling élite.
- Currently, virtually all literate Haitians, comprising about three percent of the population, trace some of their ancestry to both Europe and Africa.
- For more than a century, nearly all the country's ruling élite have been educated in Europe, especially France.

*After the United States, Haiti is the oldest independent nation in the Western hemisphere.*

- Most are proud of their European ancestry, frequently marrying Europeans and freely associating with Germans and French—until the United States military brought "Jim Crow" thinking to the island nation during the occupation starting in 1915.
- American soldiers, particularly Southerners, believed that any trace of black blood—no matter how small—rendered a person inferior.
- The élite of Haiti, long-accustomed to their elevated role in society, quickly began to resent the American presence and their attitudes.
- The working-class Haitians, illiterate and virtually ignored by the governmental power structure, were largely indifferent to who was in control.
- This attitude changed in 1918 because of a law allowing the military to use native conscripted labor.

### "Correspondence: Haiti Today," by Mary Winsor, *The Nation*, May 21, 1924:

SIR: A cruise to the West Indies and the Caribbean Sea gave me an opportunity to stop in Haiti. Although my stay was a brief one, I was fortified with letters of introduction and was able to get much information as to what is going on in that most unhappy country. The Haitian government practically does not exist; for all intents and purposes the government in Haiti consists of Commissioner Russell, by whose will the country is ruled. Martial law prevails; the Marines are everywhere, and their heavy drinking and brutality are much complained of. A Marine recently killed an unoffending Haitian in an effort to take the latter's mule from him. It is easy to see that Americans are hated. . . .

The expenses of our occupation are bleeding the Haitians to death. As I and my Haitian companions motored through Port-au-Prince, we passed handsome villas, closed and deserted, their owners reduced to such financial straits that they can no longer afford to keep their homes open. "Persons who in America are nothing and nobody become great personages in Haiti; they live in luxury at our expense and lord over us," said my cicerone, with much feeling. American officers and their wives were passing briskly in fine motors while along every mountain road under the furious tropical sun came trudging troops of women and girls bearing great burdens on their heads and leading tiny donkeys with frail legs like match sticks and sharp, thin little bodies laden with huge pack saddles and panniers. The contrast between the prosperous air of the occupationists and the misery of the inhabitants is painful. . . .

The educated class is very highly educated, with a French culture which they do not want superseded by American culture, no matter how determined Americans may be to impose it on them. "While Haiti is a Negro civilization, it has nevertheless a civilization of its own, Negro and French, which we should be permitted to develop in our way, not subject to outside interference." This is the frank way they put it.

- In order to refurbish approximately 600 miles of roads in the country, converting dirt tracts into 18-foot gravel thoroughfares, American treaty officials pressured the Haitian government to reinstate an old law by which men were compelled to do public road work three days each year.

- Many Haitian workers claimed that three days stretched into months and that the Americans treated them as virtual slaves.

- This led to a popular uprising that was put down by the Marines—with accusations of considerable brutality.

- Despite the quality and convenience of the new roads, many Haitians believe most of the roads were designed around military, not civilian needs, since only 300 cars are reported in the entire country.

- Prior to the occupation, U.S. investments in Haiti amounted to $4 million, compared to $800 million in Mexico and $220 million in Cuba.

# Historical Snapshot
# 1923

- Even though prohibition was the law of the land, prescription liquor for those in need remained unrestricted
- Clean Book Leagues formed around the nation to protect America's youth from "smut"; debate raged about the work of D. H. Lawrence
- Clarence Darrow and William Jennings Bryan debated the issues of evolution versus fundamentalism in the *Chicago Tribune*
- Girls who dressed in the style of flappers in Tennessee were banned from public schools until they rolled their stockings back up over their knees
- Montana and Nevada became the first states to introduce old-age pensions
- The Dow-Jones Industrial Average hit a high of 105, and a low of 86
- A sign reading "HOLLYWOODLAND" was erected in Los Angeles, with each letter measuring 30 by 50 feet
- The rubber diaphragm, Pan American World Airlines, the Milky Way candy bar, Welch's grape jelly, the name Popsicle and the Hertz Drive-Ur-Self all made their first appearance
- President Warren G. Harding died in office and was mourned nationwide as his cortège traveled from San Francisco to Washington
- Evangelist Aimee Semple McPherson opened a $1.5 million temple in Los Angeles, which included a "miracle room," where the healed could discard their crutches and wheelchairs
- Music hits included "Yes! We Have No Bananas," "Who's Sorry Now?" and "That Old Gang of Mine"
- Blues singer Bessie Smith's "Downhearted Blues" sold a record two million copies
- Belt loops were added to Levi Strauss & Co. blue jeans, but the suspender buttons were retained
- The silent film *The Hunchback of Notre Dame* starring Lon Chaney was released
- The zipper, first patented in 1893 and refined in 1913 as a fastener for army clothing, was gaining in popularity
- The widespread use of the typewriter in business created standardization; a sheet of paper sized 8.5 by 11 inches came into common use
- More than 1.5 million sets of the game mah-jongg were sold as the fad swept the nation
- In fashion, women's boyish bobbed hair shifted to a shingle cut that was flat and close to the head with a center or side part

## "Haiti's Progress as a Ward of Uncle Sam,"
### *The Literary Digest*, January 10, 1920:

The United States is doing in Haiti today "just what it did in Cuba," say recent observers of conditions in the two Haitian republics of Santo Domingo and Haiti. Great improvements of various kinds are said to have been made in both these miniature republics since Uncle Sam has been keeping an eye on them. Lawlessness has been checked, it appears, and the whole island has been made safe for travelers, with some of the remote mountain locations still the stronghold of bandits. In Port-au-Prince, the capital of Haiti, much progress has been made in cleaning up the city and improving the sanitary conditions. No longer do the "distinct and original" smells, remarked upon by visitors in times gone by, assail the nostrils of the tourist who goes to Port-au-Prince. . . .

The conditions are further described in a letter from Seth H. Seelye, also a resident of Port-au-Prince, from which we quote as follows:

"Disembarking from a ship docked at the well-constructed concrete pier at Port-au-Prince, the traveler walks on clean concrete pavements to the custom-house. He then may pass out into the city, and his first impression must be that of cleanliness. A concrete paved street over a hundred feet in width borders the waterfront. Here one may hire a carriage and drive around the city for an hour without leaving similar pavements. . . . The main market is in two large, interconnected steel structures each covering a whole block.

Here on the concrete floor, the native venders sit with their produce arranged in neat piles before them. . . . Yet, in these markets one finds surprisingly few flies, and this absence of flies must surely be indicative of cleanliness and sanitation."

THE VOSE PIANO
represents 70 years of experience devoted to the attainment of an ideal. Its incomparable tone brings a lifetime of satisfaction to the lover of good music. And its price is moderate.
WE CHALLENGE COMPARISONS.
Write for illustrated catalog and easy monthly terms of payment.
Vose & Sons Piano Co., 146 Boylston St., Boston

Ask for Horlick's The ORIGINAL Malted Milk

Safe Milk
For Infants, Children, Invalids, the Aged, etc.
Avoid Imitations

TATTOOING SINCE 1910
LOWEST PRICES FOR SUPERIOR WORK

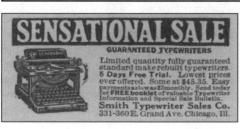

SENSATIONAL SALE
GUARANTEED TYPEWRITERS
Limited quantity fully guaranteed standard make rebuilt typewriters. 5 Days Free Trial. Lowest prices ever offered. Some at $45.35. Easy payments as low as $3 monthly. Send today for FREE booklet of valuable Typewriter Information and Special Sale Bulletin.
Smith Typewriter Sales Co.
331-360 E. Grand Ave. Chicago, Ill.

## Selected Prices

| | |
|---|---|
| Bathing Suit, Man's | $5.00 |
| Champagne, Macy's Mount Zircon Ginger | $0.19 |
| Cigars, Robert Burns Panatela | $0.10 |
| Dance Lessons, per Couple | $1.00 |
| Exercise Program, Luthy's Daily Five-minute Basic Physical Exercise | $5.00 |
| Instant Coffee | $0.10 |
| Joke Mouse | $0.19 |
| Slippers, Man's Leather | $3.65 |
| Straight Razor | $2.90 |
| Tenderloin Steak, "A" No. 1 per Pound | $0.55 |
| Tennis Racquet | $10.50 |
| Toilet | $6.95 |
| Traveling Bag, 16-inch Leather Lined | $10.50 |
| Typewriter, Remington Portable | $60.00 |
| Weekly Magazine, *Life*, per Year | $5.00 |

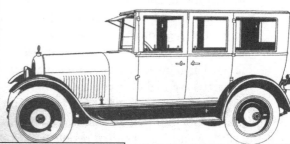

## "American Marines in Haiti Exonerated," *Current History*, August 1922:

The select committee appointed by the United States Senate to investigate the charges of misadministration in Haiti and Santo Domingo presented its formal report to the Senate on June 26, 1922. . . . The report, which is unanimous, is made up of some 26 pages, exclusive of maps. The American occupation is justified. On this subject the committee says:

"The chronic anarchy into which Haiti had fallen, the exhaustion of its credit, the threatened intervention of the German government, and the actual landing of the French naval forces, all led the government of the United States to take the successive steps set forth to establish order in Haiti, to help institute a government as nearly representative as might be, and to assure the collaboration of the governments of the United States and Haiti for the future maintenance of peace and the development of the Haitian people. . . ."

The accusations of cruelty which have been made against the Marine Corps have deeply concerned our committee, and required its full consideration. If cruelty toward the inhabitants has been countenanced or has escaped the punishment which vigilance could impose, or on the other hand, if false or groundless accusations have been made, if facts have been distorted, the true conditions should be revealed. . . .

These regions are now peaceful. There are no bandits in Haiti. The inhabitants are leaving the mountain forests to cultivate the central plains, less disturbed than they have been within the memory of living man. It is impossible to determine in exact figures the number of Haitians killed in this 18-month guerrilla campaign. A fair estimate is about 1,500. The figure includes many reports based on guesses made during combat and not on actual count. The casualties, whatever they were, undoubtedly included some non-combatants. The bandits were found resting in settlements where they were surrounded by their women and children, or in villages where they camped and were tolerated by the inhabitants through fear or friendship. When encountered they had to be instantly attacked. These conditions largely account for the deaths of the bystanders. . . .

On the evidence before it, the committee can now state:

1. That the accusations of military abuses are limited in point of time to a few months and in location to restricted areas.

2. Very few of the many Americans who have served in Haiti are thus accused. The others have restored order and tranquility under arduous conditions of service, and generally won the confidence of inhabitants of the country with whom they came in touch. . . .

3. That torture of Haitians by Americans has not in any case been established. . . .

4. That the testimony of most native witnesses is highly unreliable and must be closely scrutinized, and that many unfounded accusations have been made.

## "American Imperialism in Haiti," *World's Work*, December 1925:

The greatest problem of Haiti is poverty. While other services are giving it the fundamental machinery of civilization and organizing its finances to maintain this machinery, the agricultural service is working at the problem of increased production. This involves not only the study of soils and unusual experimental work, but also the education of the Haitian peasant in the fundamentals of agriculture. It must be remembered that cultivation had practically ceased during the Haitian regime and the natives were harvesting merely the yield of wild coffee and other plants. Haitian teachers are now being trained to go among the peasants and instruct them in the rudiments of modern agriculture. A central school of agriculture has been opened, and also a number of trade and industrial schools for both boys and girls. . . .

Of great interest to the Haitian people are the medical services. Eleven hospitals have been established, where more than a quarter million patients were treated during the last year. Rural dispensaries reach still more. Sanitary regulations are made and enforced. Streets and markets are cleaned for the first time in Haitian history. Attention is given to water supplies and sewage.

Meanwhile other Americans—navy engineers for the most part—are opening roads through the island, bridging its rivers, erecting schools and hospitals. City streets are being paved. Drains and culverts are coming to people accustomed to mud. Waterworks and electric lighting plants have been installed in the principal cities. Irrigation systems are helping to increase the productivity of the country. New wharves facilitate shipping, and lighthouses now render the coasts of Haiti safe for navigation. Telegraph and telephones have united the country as it has never been united before.

**The Round Trip to the Disarmament Conference**

Jay N. Darling. *The Des Moines Register*, 1926.

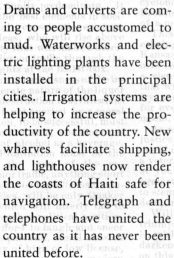

## "Haiti under American Occupation," by Ernest H. Gruening, *Century*, April 1922:

For six years American forces have controlled the two small republics that share the Caribbean island that Columbus called Hispaniola, but which is now known by the original Indian name of Haiti, "the land of mountains. . . ."

In Haiti I found the social line between Haitians and Americans rigidly drawn. When the military occupation took place in 1915, the Haitians, regardless of their feeling about the larger aspects of the invasion, extended to individual Americans a truly Haitian hospitality, inviting naval officers into their homes and their clubs. Several months later, however, when the officers' wives arrived, these social relations ceased abruptly. The officers, who had been generously fêted, never again entered the homes they had visited, nor did their wives, who instead rebuffed the kindly advances of the Haitian women. Several other episodes caused American officers to be barred from the Haitian clubs, and conversely, the newly created American club admitted no Haitians. During my stay in Haiti an American newspaper representative was requested by the management of the Hotel Montagne not to receive Haitians except on the back porch. Complaints had been made by American officers who were guests in the hotel. Jim Crow had arrived in Haiti. . . .

I am aware of the grave failures of the Haitian state, of its revolutions, of its graft, of tragic shortcomings, but I also recall certain other facts. Haiti started with no traditions or experience of self-government whatever. The tortured and debased slaves had to assume self-government in the midst of the wreckage wrought by 14 years of desperate struggle for independence in which French, British, and Spanish armies, as well as their own armies, marched and counter-marched, sacked and burned, for nearly half a generation. For nearly half a century, scarcely a nation would recognize Haitian independence for fear of the effect on its own still-enslaved blacks.

Recognition by France was bought only at the price of a heavy indemnity for the property of Frenchmen destroyed in the war of independence, and the pressures of that debt burdened the Haitian state for decades. Haiti, by reason of its color and its French culture, has been totally isolated from sympathetic neighbors in the Western Hemisphere. It has not had even the advantage of Santo Domingo, which, by virtue of its cultural ties, can count on the active sympathy of all its sister Hispanic-American states. When one recalls all this, the mere persistence of the Haitian republic as a free and independent state for 100 years seems an achievement, indeed.

# 1924 News Feature

### "Two Humorists Join the Battle of the Bonus," *The Literary Digest*, February 16, 1924:

The horrors of war begin to pale when two well-known humorists take up the cudgels on opposite sides of the adjusted compensation controversy. "Will" and "Bill" under the fighting names of "Bonus Will" and "Anti-Bonus Bill" may shortly be seen locked in deadly combat, if we are to judge from their preliminary verbal onslaughts.

"Everthing but the kitchen stove," is what you promised the soldiers, says Will, "if only they would go to war." Now a lot of our wealthy men are saying: "Oh, I am willing to do anything for the disabled, but nothing for the well." Was it these boys' fault, asks Will, that they didn't get shot? "You didn't tell him he had to come home on a stretcher before you would give him anything." Back comes "Bill" with the swift uppercut: "The silver-tongued orators call it adjustibel compinsation whatever that means. I call it a handout and handouts was over for me when I marched off the dock at Hoboken. Wages for what we went through! Wages, hell!"

"Will," of course, is the witty rope-twister from Oklahoma, Will Rogers, while "Bill" is the author of the famous "Dere Mable" letters from a buck private, which were so popular during the war. This individual in private life is Ed Streeter, an ex-artilleryman who fought through the war, and who, it appears, is against a bonus. Will Rogers, on the other hand, arguing from the civilian viewpoint, is in favor of a bonus for all our soldiers. His argument, quoted in abridged form from *The American Legion Weekly,* appeared originally in the *McNaught Syndicate* and *The New York Times*. Rogers asseverates and opines:

"We promised them EVERYTHING, and all they got was $1.25 a day and some knitted sweaters and socks. And after examining them, they wore the socks for the sweater and the sweater for the socks. They deserve a bonus just for trying to utilize what was sent to them. They got

*Will Rogers joined the Bonus Army debate with his off-beat humor.*

"EVERYTHING BUT THE KITCHEN STOVE"
Is what Will Rogers says we promised the soldiers, when they went away, but now: "You didn't tell him he had to come home on a stretcher before you would give him anything, did you?"

a dollar and a quarter a day. Out of the millions of bullets fired by the Germans every day, statistics have proved that an average of 25 bullets were fired at each man each day. That figures out at the rate of $0.05 a bullet. . . .

"Now, the only way to arrive at the worth of anything is by comparison. Take shipbuilding, wooden ones, for instance. (That's the only way they ever were taken—for instance. They were never taken for use.) Statistics show that the men working on them got, at the lowest, $12.50 per day, and, by an odd coincidence, statistics also show that each workman drove at the rate of 25 nails per day. That makes $0.50 a nail. . . .

"Now, as I say, while the soldiers got no overtime, the nail expert got time and a half for overtime, up to a certain time, then double time, and salary after that. Of course, he lost some time in the morning selecting which silk shirt he should nail in that day. And it was always a source of annoyance as to what car to go to work in. . . .

"Everybody's alibi for not giving them the bonus is, "We can't commercialize the patriotism of our noble boys." "They didn't go to war for the money, they went for glory." Then another pet argument is, "The better element of the returned soldiers are against it themselves." These wealthy men say, "All for the disabled; nothing for the well."

Will Rogers has a scheme that he says is entirely new for settling all this trouble. It is based partly, he confesses, on reading in *The Literary Digest* what both sides have to say for and against the bonus, and partly on what he heard uttered in the days when soldiers were looked on "NOT as a political organization, but as the Saviors of Civilization." At that time, he remarks, we felt that a soldier in uniform was worth "10 of us who stayed at home." Now that he has gone and done more than we ever expected of him, why isn't he worth just as much today? What has he done to lower himself in our estimation? Nothing, says Will. "He still looks like 10 to one to me, and the same to a lot of others, if they will be honest and tell the truth."

The scheme is this: Pay the bonus to all, says he. Then let the boys who don't want it give their share to a fund for the disabled ones in addition to their regular share. Suppose the number of men refusing a bonus equals the number of wounded. That would give the disabled a double share. Any surplus could be put in a fund and paid out in accordance with the degree of injury in yearly installments. This scheme, Mr. Rogers sorrowfully admits, has no political office to back it up, and "what you say for humanity doesn't have near the appeal as what you say for political purposes, especially in a presidential year." But he points out that, at any rate, it is not issued after first taking the opinions of any constituents and then stringing with the majority. At this rate, we may yet see "Will Rogers for Congress" clubs springing up. The genial philosopher sums up his proposal as follows:

"Everybody wants the disabled to be cared for first and best. That gets the disabled more than any scheme I have heard of, and also relieves any returned soldier of the embarrassment of receiving $2.50 a day. His conscience would be clear.

"In 1916, there were 1,296 men whose income was over $300,000 and they paid a billion in taxes. This year, there were only 246 whose income was supposed to be over $300,000, and they paid only $153 million.

"You mean to tell me that there are only 246 men in this country who make only $300,000! Why, say, I have spoken at dinners in New York where there were that many in one dining room, much less the United States.

"That old alibi about the country not being able to pay is all apple sauce. There is no debt in the world too big for this country to pay, if they owe it. If you owed it to some foreign nation, you would talk about honor and then pay it. Now what do you want to beat your own kin out of anything for? You say, 'Oh, it's not enough to do him any good, anyway.' If it's not enough to do him any good, it's not enough to do you any harm when you pay it. Tax-exempt securities will drive us to the poorhouse, not soldiers' bonuses. This country is not broke, automobile manufacturers are three months behind in their orders, and whisky never was as high in its life.

"And don't forget that there are many and many thousands of boys who came back and are not classed as disabled, but who will carry some effect of that terrible war as long as they live. I never met ten who were not injured in some minor way, to say nothing of the dissatisfaction. I claim we owe them everything we have got, and if they will settle for a bonus, we are lucky.

"Now, if a man is against, why don't he at least come out and tell the real truth?

'I don't want to spare the money to pay our boys.' I think the best insurance in the world against another War is to take care of the boys who fought in the last one. YOU MAY WANT TO USE THEM AGAIN."

"Dere Mable" gets a very different slant on the bonus from her devoted "Bill." "Who started all this, anyway?" exclaims Bill irritably, in a letter which we quote from a reprint issued by the City Club of the New York Post of the American Legion:

"They've been pullin' an' haulin' me from pillow to post about this thing ever since you went away. There ain't a day somebody don't come to me an' ask me for my views. It's the first time anybody's wanted 'em since the day I brought the picture post cards back from Paree. But them was views worth askin' for. Which is a French joke an' I guess you wouldn't understand.

"One day it's the Ex-Service Mens Aunty Bonus League that's after me to sign up with their outfit. Next day another bunch is tellin' me I'd be a dumbell to do that cause all I got to do is to sit tight an' holler an' Washington will have to come across with the price of a secondhand Ford Poco pronto. To use a French idiot of speech. All of which was confusin' till I got the idear of what they was talkin' about.

"It seems that accordin' to the rules of the Patryot's Union, they forgot to pay us overtime or somethin'. Maybe its for smoothin' out horses on Christmas. I don't know. I'm here to state one thing, though, an' that is I don't need no hired Napolyuns to tell me who owes me money an' who don't. Of course, they didn't pay me enough. Cause why? Cause they couldn't. If they could have, the Tresury would have gone bust the first pay day on me alone.

"Steepel Jacks that climb steepels gets 25 smackers per diem, as the lawyers say, cause their work is sposed to be dangerus. On that scale I ofen wonder

what I would have drawed that day in the Bois de Forges wood when the bullets was playin' 'she loves me, she loves me not' with the daisys right above my tin derby? And what do you 'spose me an' Angus MacDonald was worth an hour the time we sat in the Chathoe (which is a kind of French railroad station near Brillycourt) and listened to the Fritzes take the thing apart over our heads? An, Mable, I can remember times when, on a piece work basis, I've peeled $500,000 worth of govermint potatoes in one week without getting it.

"Of course I took what they handed me. I'd have took all they'd give me if not more. As it was, by the time they got through takin' deductions away from me, my Vin Rooge allowance wouldn't have kep' a Frenchman till his petty dajunay (which is a French dish eaten right after breakfast). Just the same, Mable, I'd have taken Rushin' roobles if they'd handed 'em out. An' so would the rest of the bunch.

"When I first went down to trainin' camp there was an old fat horse doctor that said I couldn't be a soldier cause I didn't have good feet. Quick as anything I says I knew they wan't much to look at but I hadn't figgered that I was enterin' 'em for no beauty contest. Fast with the comeback, that's me all over, Mable.

An' when I saw he looked kind of sheepish I says I'd used 'em for 20-odd years (barrin' a few months at the start) an' they hadn't wore off yet. But it wasn't no use. I come near tastin' my first blood that day.

"An' remember how, after that old pill-shooter had the "I-C" on my dogs, it took three months to butt my way into the army? It would be easyer for a camel to take a needle out of his eye as mister Shaksper said than it was for me to get permission to get my head blowed off in a uniform that was three sizes too big for me. But I got in, didn't I. An' I went to France. An' I ain't sorry. An' there's a few others in the same boat. About two milyun of 'em to be exack. an' *they tell me the govermint owes me money!*"

At this point we regret to say Bill lapses into a somewhat hackneyed figure of speech. He refers feelingly to the now familiar character who pulls drowning women and children out of the lake, and sends them a bill for $1.25 a year later. The war, he brightly observes, was not "fought on a contrack basis." "It's the only war I got an' I'd like to keep it decent." Of course if he had been "mussed up" admits Bill, it would have been different. But as long as we are doing our best financially for the men were "mussed up"—two "billyuns" already, says Bill, that's enough. For himself, he's on a "self-supportin' basis" and "don't need no more free movies nor Paris *Heralds,* nor feetless socks to wear my rists for nuthin'. I'm workin' now—an' it ain't the govermint nether." The genial leatherneck then proceeded to sum the situation up in the following peroration:

"The way it all looks to me is this. Either they owe us somethin' or we're lookin' for charity. Now I know they don't owe me nothin'. I didn't fight the war for the govermint. I fought it for my home and my country and for you, if you'll excuse me mentionin' it. Nobody owes me nothin' for that. Then it must be charity. Well I don't want no help just now. an' as long as things is breakin' right, what's the use of goin' round yelin' for help. Keep that for the fellows what got knocked out—An' as for them—well, Mable, I kind of feel it oughtn't to be our duty to take care of them. It ought to be our privilege.

"No—when I get to be a dodderin' old reck like your granfather, with sapnish moss hangin' from my chin an' my grandchildern (if you'll excuse my referin' to 'em) sittin' on my knee in regular order, I'm goin' to tell 'em about the war if they like it or not. An' when they ask me if I was in all the battels I'm goin' to raise my head as high as the lumbago lets me an' say "Yes, all of 'em but one—the Battle of the Bonus. I had all the war I wanted before the 11 of November 1918."

"An' that's that. Give my regards to your mother. An' to the dog if he's with you. An' to your father to for all I care.

Yours till Germany pays,
Bill

# 1925 Profile

# The Crash of the *Shenandoah*

## Aviation Rigger

Aviation rigger Jeff Bowen believes America's only military dirigible, the *Shenandoah*, represents the future of air warfare, and that ultimately the navy, not the army's airplanes, will control the skies.

## Life at Home

- Growing up in South Dakota, Jeff Bowen was wary of cities and fascinated by all things that crept, crawled, flew or ran.
- He caught frogs and toads and, with his grandfather's aid and encouragement, trapped and raised gophers, jackrabbits and a badger.
- Toads, he learned, liked attention, became quite tame after a while, and enjoyed having their backs scratched.
- Jackrabbits, on the other hand, fought one another, no matter the circumstances, often resorting to violent kicking and biting.
- The badger adored his independence, hated his corral and all things human, bringing relief to one and all when he dug his way out.
- Jeff's favorite pet was a baby antelope, which was found by a neighbor and brought as a tiny creature to him.
- Twenty inches tall, the antelope was tawny brown and creamy white.
- His grandfather constructed a moveable cage, while his mother taught him how to feed "Lope," as he was called, from a bottle.

*Jeff Bowen read stories to his children the night before the crash of the airship* Shenandoah.

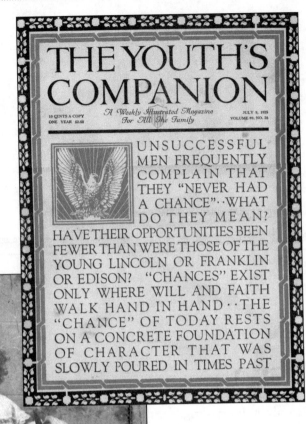

- With the advance of summer, Lope grew and focused on one activity—following Jeff wherever he went.
- In the fall, when Lope was almost grown, a small herd of antelope passed and, like a shot, he joined the herd and disappeared into the woods.
- During the winter, four antelopes came near the house, but none answered to a call or showed any sign of recognition.
- Like most country boys, Jeff learned to shoot a Remington .22 caliber rifle with deadly accuracy.
- Early on, he learned when to shoot and when to watch.
- His other fascination was the sky—how clouds formed, what created rain, and how different conditions affected the way birds flew.
- This love crystallized the first time he saw a dirigible.
- Airplanes were just noisy cars with wings, but a dirigible was truly one with the sky.
- After he graduated high school and joined the navy, Jeff had almost forgotten his fascination with the giant flying balloon, until he was asked to become an aviation rigger and assist flying America's only warship dirigible, the *Shenandoah*.

*Jeff carries a picture inside his cap of Joanna astride her hobbyhorse.*

## "Newspapers Delivered to Farm Homes by Air," *Washington Post*, September 3, 1925:

SPRINGFIELD, ILL.: Seventy-five percent perfect on the first test, airplane delivery of afternoon newspapers to the farmer's door has been attempted here. This morning three-fourths of the farmers had reported receipt of the newspapers and were informed that airplane delivery would soon come to stay.

The innovation was planned by Frederick Shuch, circulation manager of the *Illinois State Register,* of Springfield and executed by H. D. Parks.

Parks's plane was kept at a height of between 75 and 100 feet, and it was sent over the routes usually covered by motor truck. Papers were dropped as each subscriber's house was passed. Mr. Shuch said that the cost of operating the plane was $0.04 a mile, compared with $0.10 for a truck.

- It was a moment of ecstasy shared by his wife and two daughters.
- The training meant being away from his children, but he loved the challenge and the chance to fly.
- When he was home, he made it a point to read with his children, especially on evenings before a flight; they all loved the chance to be together.
- Recently, with little Emily on his lap and Joanna at his side, Jeff carefully read *The Youth's Companion,* which advertised itself as a "weekly illustrated magazine for all the family."
- As he left the house on the morning of the flight, Joanna asked if he had his good luck charm.
- Inside his hat, he keeps his favorite picture, showing young Joanna astride her hobbyhorse.

### Life at Work

- Although Jeff had flown on the *Shenandoah* dozens of times, this trip held special significance—the navy brass wanted a demonstration of the warship's range as soon as possible.
- Since weather conditions had postponed the flight for most of the summer, the navy rejected any excuses that might have caused additional delays.
- On flight day the *Shenandoah's* 20 gas bags were 91 percent full, her tanks loaded with 9,075 pounds of water and 16,620 pounds of gasoline.

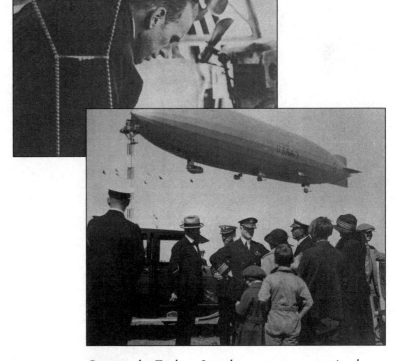

*Commander Zachary Lansdowne proposes caution before the flight, but the navy brass wants a demonstration of the* Shenandoah *as soon as possible.*

- By all accounts, the 682-foot ship appeared ready for her fifty-eighth flight—a tour of the Midwest state fairs.
- Although everyone seemed ready, Jeff knew immediately after boarding the ship that Commander Zachary Lansdowne was not happy with the orders for this trip.
- The weather was lousy.
- A native of Greenville, Ohio, Lansdowne was familiar with the line squalls that sweep over that part of the country during the summer, and he officially requested that the tour be postponed.
- However, the navy felt that too many would be disappointed; besides, the *Shenandoah* had already flown 25,000 miles in all kinds of weather.
- Also at stake was who would control the skies; the navy was in a race for funding.
- The army believed the aerial attack weapon of the next war was the airplane, but the navy insisted the dirigible would change the face of American warfare.
- Jeff was sure the dirigible would win out.
- He had seen how delicate airplanes could be, always crashing and needing repair; an airship, on the other hand, was strong and useful, as evidenced by the work of the German Zeppelin during World War I just a few short years ago.
- Like everyone on the *Shenandoah,* he was anxious to demonstrate the superiority of this wonderful machine.
- The first great rigid dirigible ever built, the *Shenandoah* made headlines every time she flew.
- At 3 p.m., as the nose of the ship slid from the socket of the mast with 41 crew members aboard and rose into the air over Lakehurst, New Jersey, Jeff's wife turned her back.
- It is considered bad luck to watch your husband's ship fade out of sight.
  - Twelve hours later, at 3 a.m., Jeff realized a storm was brewing in the northwest, causing the airship to drift from port to starboard.
  - The ship began to rise, despite the use of the *Shenandoah's* rudders, elevators and motors.
  - The tail elevated 15 degrees, rolling like a raft in the sea.
  - The rise carried it right into the squall.
  - Worse, the ship's sharp tilt disrupted the flow of gasoline and water through the fuel-supply and cooling systems.
  - All around him, men were taking action; mechanics coaxed overheating engines, while riggers scrambled down the keel ripping the covers off the automatic valves so already swollen gas bags would not burst.

*The great warship must be tethered before flight.*

**"Change in Air Program Ridiculed by Paegelow, Flying Men Have Just as Much Faith as Ever in Future of Flying,"** *Washington Post*, September 4, 1925:

Lieut. Col. J. A. Paegelow, commandant at Scott Field, says a change in the air program might result from the destruction of the *Shenandoah*.

"This talk of changing the air program is bunk," he declared. "So is the talk of scrapping dirigibles. When a railroad train smashes up and kills 30 or 40 people, we don't think of scrapping all the locomotives, do we? When a ship goes down in a storm, we don't begin to discuss throwing our navy away and staying on dry land.

"The flying men of the service have just as much faith in the air as they ever had. We never will get entirely away from accidents in the air, any more than we'll be rid of the train crashes or shipwrecks.

"We'll keep right on flying here and at all the other service stations. We believe in the ships."

- Despite the crew's best efforts, the ship continued to rise, reaching 5,500 feet, far above the *Shenandoah's* pressure height of 4,000 feet.
- To control the ascent, thousands of cubic feet of helium was valved off.
- The balancing act was under way; the ship needed to be stopped at 6,000 feet, but if too much helium was valved away, the *Shenandoah* could make a fast plunge to the ground.
- Jeff fully understood the severity of the situation when he was ordered to stand by the slip tanks and open them in case of an emergency.

*When the* Shenandoah *crashed it became a festival for souvenir hunters.*

- Cresting at 6,300 feet, the *Shenandoah* began falling at a rate of 25 feet per second; Jeff did his job and tons of water were dumped from the ship's hold.
- At 2,500 feet, the ship stopped falling.
- Jeff was exhilarated and frightened; for the first time he realized how close he was to dying.
- Engines one and two were out; the mechanic, Jeff's long-time friend, reported that engine number three was heating up badly.
- In seconds, the ship was driven back up to 3,500 feet and began turning rapidly in a circle.
- The tail was suddenly thrown up and wrenched to the right.
- Caught by opposing blasts of wind, the *Shenandoah* was driven by an enormous squall.
- Immediately, Jeff realized the struts that held the big gondola to the ship were being wrenched by the wind.
- That was when the *Shenandoah* began breaking apart.

- Horrified, Jeff watched the control car tear away from the ship and fall to earth.
- Then, something cracked in the tail, sparks shot up under the keel, and the main cable controls broke loose from the elevators and rudders.
- The gondola snapped free, carrying seven men, including Lansdowne, to their deaths.
- Largely unchurched and unsure of his faith, Jeff began to pray a simple prayer: "Let me hold my girls again; don't take their daddy away."
- Gaping holes in the ship exposed vast views of empty space as men tumbled out to certain death.
- Yet, the bow section continued to float, manipulated by the remaining helium in the tanks and one bag containing 1,600 pounds of water.
- Slowly, it drifted down onto a farm, the wreckage of the *Shenandoah* visible all around.
- Jeff grew weak as they approached the ground.
- Rescuers grabbed him first, but soon the merely curious dominated the scene.
- Everyone wanted a souvenir; as Jeff lay on the ground, helpless to stop them, women ripped yards and yards of fabric off the downed ship's frame, while men took the logbooks, fragments of the ship, blankets and specialized navigational equipment.
- Pieces of the *Shenandoah* disappeared within minutes of crashing.
- Someone even ripped Zachary Lansdowne's Annapolis class ring from his finger, after he had fallen thousands of feet to his death.
- One of 29 survivors, Jeff simply hugged the ground and whispered another prayer.

## "America Now Lacks a Dirigible for War—With the *Shenandoah* Wrecked the *Los Angeles* Is Barred by German Agreement," *The New York Times*, September 4, 1925:

The destruction of the *Shenandoah* is regarded in official circles as a very severe blow to the navy and is expected to handicap the efforts of those like Rear Admiral William A. Moffett, Chief of the Bureau of Naval Aeronautics, who have contended that huge dirigibles, properly constructed, are of great commercial and military value.

Congress, as a whole, has never cottoned very strongly to the idea of the dirigible. It is apprehended by those officers of the service who favor the construction of military dirigibles that the loss of the *Shenandoah* will render it doubly difficult, if not altogether impossible, to obtain additional appropriations from Capitol Hill for the construction of other military dirigibles.

After the loss of the ZR-2, built in England, there was a vigorous outburst in Congress against dirigibles, so much so that President Coolidge felt compelled to halt plans which the navy had prepared for sending the *Shenandoah* on a flight across the North Polar regions.

The consensus of opinion tonight is that recent events, the loss of the *Shenandoah* when considered in the light of the difficulties encountered by Commander Byrd and his companions in their futile attempt to fly from Etah to Cape Thomas Hubbard, are confirmatory of the wisdom of President Coolidge's decision to call off the polar flight of the big airship, now twisted wreckage scattered over three Ohio counties.

## War Calendar:

- January 10, 1920: The League of Nations was officially inaugurated as Versailles Treaty went into effect
- January 16, 1920: First League Council meeting in Paris with permanent members England, France, Italy and Japan
- March 19, 1920: U.S. Senate rejected Treaty of Versailles because of League of Nations proviso
- April 25, 1920: War between Russia and Poland began
- May 19, 1920: Persia (now Iran) presented first dispute to League of Nations; demanded Russia leave Azerbaijan; Russia complied
- March 8, 1921: Allies occupied Dusseldorf, Duisburg, Ruhrort because of reparations default; Germany accepted ultimatum, financed reparations on May 11
- February 6, 1922: Washington Conference guaranteed China's integrity in Nine-Power Treaty; established naval ratios of 5:5:3 for U.S., Britain and Japan
- April 16, 1922: Treaty of Rapallo provided for economic cooperation between Germany and Russia
- June 15, 1922: First meeting of Permanent Court of International Justice (World Court)
- September 21, 1922: Fordney-McCumber Tariff set highest rates in American history
- October 27, 1922: Mussolini marched on Rome
- January 11, 1923: French and Belgians occupied Ruhr because of reparations default
- November 8-9, 1923: Munich beer hall putsch led by Adolph Hitler put down; Hitler later sentenced to five years in prison, served less than one; wrote *Mein Kampf* while in prison
- November 20, 1923: German mark fell to 4.2 trillion to the dollar
- January 21, 1924: Lenin died; struggle for power began between Stalin and Trotsky
- April 9, 1924: Dawes Plan reorganized Reichsbank, revised reparations and lent Germany gold to back up currency
- May 26, 1924: Immigration quotas were set in United States; annual immigrants from each nation to be two percent of persons of that nationality residing in the U.S. in 1890

TICKLING HIS RISIBILITY

"And the last war was a war to end war."

—*The Daily Star* (Montreal).

### "Wrecked by Gale, Dirigible Plunges to Earth in Pieces," *Washington Post,* September 4, 1925:

Fourteen of the crew of the *Shenandoah*, giant dirigible, are dead and two others seriously injured early today when the pride of the United States Navy was wrecked during a severe storm on its Western cruise from the Lakehurst (NJ) airport.

Among the dead is Lieut. Comdr. Zachary Lansdowne, captain of the ship.

After battling the elements for several hours, the huge aircraft suddenly shot upward to an altitude of approximately 7,500 feet from a 3,000-foot level, where the dirigible buckled midship. The pressure and twisting was so great that it broke the ship into three sections.

The control cabin, swung beneath the fore-section of the ship proper, broke away and crashed to the ground while at an altitude of several thousand feet. It carried most of the crew who were killed.

Released from the control cabin, the fore-section, measuring about 150 feet, and bearing seven survivors free-ballooned for more than an hour, and finally landed near Sharon, 12 miles from where the control cabin crashed near Ava.

The main section, carrying 26 survivors, landed with a crash which sent several of the crew diving through the outer covering to the ground. A middle section of 15 or 20 feet settled down in pieces over the countryside.

Those aboard the nose section had a wild and thrilling ride for 12 miles.

## History of the *Shenandoah*

- The first rigid dirigible made in America, the *Shenandoah* was 682 feet long from its nose to its high mooring mast.
- Its name was adopted from an Indian phrase meaning "daughter of the stars."
- Its design, copied from a captured wartime German Zeppelin, was improved to include helium so inert it could not be set aflame with a match.
- Since the airshipman's greatest fear was fire, it was hailed as a major improvement—with limitations.
- Helium had only 93 percent of the lifting power of hydrogen, so a section 10 meters long was added to the middle of the *Shenandoah*.
- Completed, it included 20 gas bags, as well as tanks capable of carrying over 9,000 pounds of water and more than 16,500 pounds of gasoline.
- With a crew of 41 officers and men, the *Shenandoah* was positioned to take the lead among international airships.
- The men's bunks were located along the keel, a triangular tunnel running along inside the *Shenandoah's* bottom.
- Bisecting its base was a narrow catwalk, the other two sides of the triangle being bounded by the gas cells, which were usually filled to 85 percent of capacity at liftoff.
- As the ship rose, the gas expanded and the bags became swollen; at 4,000 feet, the bags were 100 percent full.

### Editorial: "The *Shenandoah* Disaster," *The New York Times,* September 4, 1925:

Two years ago today ZR-1, afterward to be christened the *Shenandoah,* was launched at Lakehurst and took to the air for her first trial. She represented the planning and labor of seven years. It was during the war, in 1916, that laboratory, engineering and fabricating experiments to form the basis for constructing the great dirigible were begun. From the moment the ZR-1 glided out of the shed, she was under perfect control. Sailing away into a sky in which the sun was sinking, America's first Zeppelin maneuvered for an hour in the presence of 15,000 people. An inspection of the ship when she returned to the hangar showed that she had undergone no strain—the fabric was sound in every part. On her many voyages, the *Shenandoah* developed no weakness of a serious character until something went wrong on her last flight to the West and she buckled and broke asunder, a complete wreck, her commander, Zachary Lansdowne, with five other commissioned officers and several of the crew losing their lives.

Speculation about the cause of the disaster would be idle, until more information of the behavior of the dirigible in the storm to which she succumbed is available. Knowing that the *Shenandoah* had weathered a gale when she tore loose from her mast at Lakehurst a year ago, and rode out a violent storm on the Pacific Coast, we may at least conjecture that the fury of the wind that tore her asunder in Ohio was of a nature that she had not encountered before. One of the survivors, Colonel C. G. Hall, the army observer, calls it a "line squall." It "enveloped us," he says, "and broke the ship into three pieces." Apparently, then, it must have wrenched and twisted the vast balloon until it could hold together no longer.

The *Shenandoah* was built with no haste and carefully, the lessons of the destruction of the British ZR-2 and the Italian semi-rigid Roma guiding the designers and artisans. The time of her construction was four years. Duralumin for fabrication of the rings, lattices and girders had to be manufactured in quantity. This necessitated production of an aluminum alloy, such as the Germans used in their Zeppelins. A light cotton cloth, with layers of goldbeater's skin cemented to it, was to be provided for the gas cells. The cement needed was unknown in this country, and it became necessary to use a rubber cement. No fewer than 150 girders, and an even greater number of individual parts, were broken up to determine stresses and safety factors before the metal skeleton was put together. The engines were another problem, and after a great deal of experimenting, a private firm furnished them. While the German war-raider L-49, brought down in France, served as a model for the American ship, the French government lending the Navy Department technical reports and blueprints, the American designers improved on the German dirigible, using ideas from other sources. Every part was elaborately tested. Nothing could have been more methodical than the assembling of the metal work. The *Shenandoah* was built "on honor," to stand every conceivable strain of weather or of attack by an enemy. But she was to be America's first war Zeppelin or dirigible, and in that sense she was, after all, an experiment.

*Magic shows are growing in popularity across America.*

- Every five meters along the keel was a triangular frame of latticed girders which bound together the circular outer ribs.
- Each was marked with phosphorescent numbers so the men would know where they were in the ship's dark interior.
- The crew's space was a plywood deck 12 feet square serving as the enlisted men's lounge and dining room.

## HISTORICAL SNAPSHOT
# 1925

- Newspaper crossword puzzles, first introduced in 1913, become a national obsession
- Johnson & Johnson perfected the first precut Band-Aid adhesive bandage
- "I'm Sitting on Top of the World," "Sweet Georgia Brown" and "Keep Your Skirts Down, Mary Ann" were among the year's top songs
- Americans enjoyed mass-produced aspirin after the federal government sold to Sterling Drugs the manufacturing rights seized from the German company Bayer during World War I
- The Dow-Jones Industrial Average reached a high of 157 for the year
- Colonel Billy Mitchell declared, "Our defense planes are the worst of any country I know. . . . Our pilots know they are going to be killed in the old floating coffins that we are still flying"
- Popular movies included *Ben-Hur, The Merry Widow, Lord Jim,* and Charlie Chaplin's *The Gold Rush*
- The Coolidge administration refused to recognize the results of a stolen election in Nicaragua and sent in the Marines, even though the country's strongman General Emiliano Chamorro Vargas was pro-American
- The Goodman Theatre in Chicago was founded by the Kenneth Sawyer Goodman family
- *The Great Gatsby* by F. Scott Fitzgerald, *In Our Time* by Ernest Hemingway, *The Professor's House* by Willa Cather, *An American Tragedy* by Theodore Dreiser, *Manhattan Transfer* by John Dos Passos and *Mrs. Dalloway* by Virginia Woolf were all published that year
- Bootleg alcohol prices appeared regularly at the end of the "Talk of the Town" section of *The New Yorker*
- Postwar prosperity spawned increased markets for cars, radios, refrigerators and vacuum cleaners
- "Yellow-Drive-It-Yourself-Systems" gained in popularity, costing $0.12 a mile for a Ford and $0.22 a mile for a six-cylinder car
- Dry ice, Wesson oil, Caterpillar tractors, compulsory auto insurance, inlaid linoleum and the Simmons Beautyrest mattress all made their first appearance
- Trinity College changed its name to Duke University after James B. Duke contributed $40 million
- The police dog became a house pet after the success of the film *Rin Tin Tin*
- The American Basketball League was organized
- Cars appeared for the first time in colors such as Florentine cream and Versailles violet
- Fads included limerick competitions, baseball cards, eating contests and marathons such as flagpole sitting and nonstop dancing
- The term "blind date" came into common usage
- Kellogg offered the first mail-away breakfast-cereal premium enticing youngsters to send a dime and boxtop in exchange for a set of printed cloth dolls
- The nation was fascinated by the debate in a Tennessee court room between Clarence Darrow and William Jennings Bryan on the subject of evolution

Lucky breakfast days !

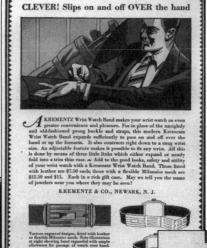

Canning Calls for the New Kind of Sink

## Fruit and Vegetable Acids Cannot Roughen or Discolor This Sink

## ... Modern

### Radio is better with *Battery Power*

## THE *New* FRESHMAN ELECTRIC RADIO

no acids trouble batteries { water excuses makeshifts

*Always Ready..Always Right*

Freshman EQUAPHASE

$185.00 COMPLETE READY TO OPERATE

Plug In Your Light Socket and Listen

CHAS. FRESHMAN CO., Inc., Freshman Building, New York

**CLEVER! Slips on and off OVER the hand**

A KREMENTZ Wrist Watch Band makes your wrist watch an even greater convenience and pleasure.

KREMENTZ & CO., NEWARK, N.J.

Krementz
WRIST WATCH B

more d.p.m.

### Cleaning *that tires you not at all...* POSITIVE AGITATION

### Editorial: "Abolish Income Tax Publicity!" *Washington Post,* September 3, 1925:

President Coolidge could perform no service more acceptable to the public than to use his influence with Congress to effect the repeal of the law requiring publicity of income tax returns.

This law is part and parcel of the spirit of intolerance and repression that has caused Congress to make serious blunders under the mistaken impression that it was responding to public sentiment.

The majority of Americans are not scandalmongers, busybodies or scoundrels. They believe in fair play. They live decent lives and cherish the idea of individual and family liberty, secure from outside intrusion.

The income tax publicity law goes directly contrary to the spirit of Americanism. It is offensive from every angle, and accomplishes no good purpose for the people or the government. On the contrary, it works harm to both. It increases the expense of tax collecting and tends to disgust the people with the operations of government. Lack of respect for all laws is increased when bad laws are foisted upon the people against their will. If the people could vote on the publicity law it would be repealed by an overwhelming majority, judging by the complaints that come from every section of the country and from all classes.

The only worthy object which the champions of this law could have had was to compel every taxpayer to make honest returns by subjecting him to public exposure in case of default. That object has not been accomplished by the law. The published return gives no evidence that the maker of the return is either honest or dishonest. A heavy return may cover items running back several years, which give a false idea of annual income. A light return may result from deductions because of losses which might not occur again, but which, when published, seriously reflect upon the status of a man's business.

Close the Book, Uncle Sam

## "Col. Mitchell to 'Rip Cover Off' Air Service—Former Chief Says New Book Is 'Only Beginning' of Exposé," *Washington Post*, Sept. 2 1925:

Col. William Mitchell, former assistant chief of the Army Air Service, today declared that "the truth about the United States air service is going to be suppressed no longer." The statement was made in connection with a review begun by War Department officials of his book, *Winged Defense*, published against War Department orders.

"I have disobeyed no orders," said Col. Mitchell, who is now commander of the 8th Corps area air forces, although admitting that he had published his book without submitting it to his superiors.

"The truth of our deplorable situation is going to be put before the American people, with what may," he continued. "If the War Department wants to start something, so much the better. Then I can get the case before Congress and the people, and then we will have a chance to remedy this unfortunate condition.

"Aviators are the only persons competent to tell what is wrong and they are going to tell. One-fourth of the shortcomings of our air service have not been told, but they are going to be.

"This book is just the beginning. I am at present preparing a series of articles which will 'rip the cover' off these deplorable conditions."

*Winged Defense*, a story of the development of commercial and military aviation, came off the press Tuesday. Its publication had been forbidden by the War Department until that branch had given approval. One chapter is devoted to bombing operations against warships bearing the caption: "United States Air Force Proves That Aircraft Dominates Seacraft."

The book is replete with cartoons, which poke jibes at the War Department. The author declared these were inserted by the publisher without his knowledge.

Is Flying Really Safe?

This plane's motor failed in a Boston fete. Sergeant Cobb barely avoided hitting a hospital and plunged into the Charles River. Miraculously both Cobb and his passenger climbed out alive

# 1927 Profile

# Fighting in Nicaragua

### Second Lieutenant

Nurtured and educated in the service, Marine pilot Ralph Field was on the verge of walking away from a military career when he was called upon to fight the Sandinistas in Nicaragua in defense of fellow Marines.

### Life at Home

- The son of a waterman in Oxford, Maryland, Ralph Field spent his life along Chesapeake Bay, where his family had crabbed and fished for generations.
- Ralph's early schooling came from his father, who explained how a waterman listened to the moving water whispering where the fish might be.
- As soon as the United States joined the Great War, Ralph and his older brothers volunteered.
- He signed up to be a Marine because he had seen Marines aboard navy ships in the harbor near his home and their uniforms looked so good.
- From his friend Jack Swinton, he learned about the joy of engines and how they operate, so when Ralph got his first military assignment, mechanics school made a lot of sense.
- He never dreamed the engines he worked on would be installed in airplanes.
- Then Frank Stanton, a Princeton-educated Baltimore pilot, asked him to ride in the observation seat on a short run.
- From the moment the plane broke through the low cloud cover, Ralph was transformed.
- When he was demobilized in 1919 as the Corps went through a postwar contraction, he reenlisted with dreams of officer and flight school.

*Career Marine Ralph Field has been called to fight the Sandinistas in Nicaragua.*

- In 1921, the Corps decided to add 150 new second lieutenants, including some from the ranks of the noncommissioned officers, and Corporal Ralph Field was selected.
- During flight school in Pensacola, Florida, where the pressure was high and the attrition rate higher, he met his future wife at a reception held in the home of a senior officer.
- Mary had recently moved to Florida to accept a teaching job; she, too, was immediately smitten.
- Although everyone in Ralph's family had married women from the Eastern Shore, Mary charmed his parents—particularly his father—and she and Ralph were married in June 1923.

*Ralph's wife Mary wants him to leave the service; he wants to stay if allowed to fly.*

- Following Corps tradition, a man was a Marine first and a pilot second; therefore, after five years of flying, pilots were given a standard Marine billet for three years.
- Ralph was afraid that would mean ground service in China or Haiti, or guard duty at a United States naval base, and he wanted to keep flying.
- Mary wanted him to leave the service.
- From 1920 to 1925, 41 Marine pilots had died in flying accidents; she wanted security for their two children.
- In 1927, Ralph had just put in an application to fly for one of the fledgling airlines when word arrived that his squadron was headed to Nicaragua.
- For years, the Central American country had been the scene of violent power struggles among rival political parties.
- For the first half of the decade, peace had been secured by the presence of U.S. Marines.

SEMPER FIDELIS

A.E.F. FRANCE 1918

FIRST MARINE AVIATION FORCE

The self-appointed cop

## "A Nicaraguan Canal?" *The Literary Digest*, April 30, 1927:

A plan to make two canals grow where only one grew before is now suspected by some people to be at the bottom of the Coolidge policy in the troublous republic of Nicaragua. The main reason why Washington has taken so much interest in Nicaragua's political affairs, the *Denver Rocky Mountain News* is convinced, is that Uncle Sam is thinking of digging another isthmian canal through Nicaragua, thus exercising an option acquired by this country under the Wilson regime. "And it goes without saying," remarks the *Springfield Union*, "that if the choice is made on a Nicaraguan canal, our government will need to provide, not only for permanent relations with a friendly Nicaraguan government, but for the complete security of the canal."

Traffic through the Panama Canal is more than double what had been forecast for this, the twelfth year of its opening; it may, we are told, reach its maximum capacity in 15 or 20 years. According to the advocates of a new canal, it is not a moment too soon to plan for the construction of such a "ditch." Ten years were required to complete the Panama Canal; a Nicaraguan route, we are assured, could not be ready before 1940, even if work began tomorrow. And work cannot be started until we have made a definite agreement with the Nicaraguan government.

- However, when in 1925 the Marines were ordered home after 13 years of peacekeeping, the country fell into civil war almost immediately.
- In Washington, fear grew that the liberal forces were gaining the upper hand through the Bolshevist element in the Mexican government.
- The U.S. Government did not want Bolshevism to gain momentum in the Western Hemisphere, and ordered 2,000 Marines to Nicaragua in late 1926 to deal with the unstable situation.

## Life at Work

- In February 1927, Ralph's squadron, consisting of eight officers, 81 enlisted men and eight DeHaviland DH-4 British-built aircraft, arrived in Managua, Nicaragua, on an airfield that had been built on a ball field.
- Small parties of Marines were dispersed throughout the country in a newly formed Nicaragua National Guard, with Marine officers occupying the senior posts.
- Ralph's squadron searched for rebel forces and reported intelligence and locations to the ground troops.
- The DeHavilands carried a pilot and an observer, each of whom had a machine gun.
- The crew also carried up to four 17-pound bombs which could be dropped by the observer.
- Occasionally, the planes strafed the rebels and took fire in return; several planes had been severely shot up, but no casualties resulted.

- In April and May, the Marines waited impatiently.
- Former Secretary of War Henry Stimson was in the country to broker a peace leading to a U.S. regulated and supervised election in 1928.
- Although Washington declared that peace was at hand when Stimson left, Liberal leader Augusto Sandino rejected the agreement others had accepted.
- Life grew tense, but remained largely quiet in Managua; Ralph's squadron used the time to practice a new concept called dive bombing.
- From a height of 1,500 feet, the planes would enter a steep dive during which a bomb would be released when the pilot reached 300 feet and had begun to pull out of the maneuver.

*Ralph flew to the rescue of fellow Marines in his first major battle as a pilot.*

- The commander said the practice would come in handy.
- Ralph was bored, and though he wrote to Mary occasionally, he spent most of his evenings in the village with the local ladies—which made him feel guilty.
- He also began to drink more than usual, especially after he received a letter saying his father had suffered a mild heart attack and was no longer able to work.
- The thought of his father sitting on the dock watching the boats go out without him haunted Ralph.
- As each day passed, he became more and more convinced that he should be helping his father or being with his wife and children.
- He was not even sure he enjoyed flying anymore.
- On July 16, while reading a letter from Mary and smoking a hand-rolled cigarette, Ralph got word that, hangover or no, he was needed in the air.

## "On to Nicaragua," by Newman Levy, *The Nation*, February 1, 1928:

I am in hearty agreement with the fellow who said "I don't care who breaks the laws of my country so long as I can write its songs." I have been working for the past few weeks on a war song for this terrible war that someone told me we are waging against Nicaragua. I am trying to do my bit by writing a stirring war song. If I can write something to cheer our gallant soldiers in this most recent War to End Wars, I shall feel that I have not entirely lived in vain.

I find that this attempt at martial balladry is not easy. My difficulty, at the start, has been to work myself up to a proper pitch of patriotic indignation against Nicaragua. We all know, of course, that the Nicaraguans mutilate babies and boil up the bodies of their victims to get fats and other valuable byproducts. We know, too, that if we don't send our Marines down there to protect the sanctity of American womanhood, it will not be long before a Nicaraguan army will be marching on to Washington, and then where will we be?

Still it is not easy to get excited about it. I wish, sometimes, that I knew a Nicaraguan so that I might hate him. It would help so much with my song. One or two of my office associates I suspect of being pro-Nicaraguan, and I have written to the Department of Justice about them. I have no proof, but it will do no harm to have them under surveillance for a while; we cannot afford to take chances. Nevertheless, it is not quite the same as knowing and hating a real Nicaraguan.

We must not allow ourselves to forget that this is war, and war is a pretty serious matter. I deplore bloodshed as much as anyone—in fact, I sometimes am afraid that I am a bit of a pacifist at heart—but when it comes to a defensive war like this one, when our homes are in danger of invasion, and the safety of our dear ones is jeopardized, then it is quite a different matter. There are certain definite precautions that must be taken at once. In the first place, Nicaraguan should not be taught in our public schools. It seems outrageous to me that the minds of our children should be poisoned by this subtle, insidious propaganda. English was good enough for Abraham Lincoln and George Washington, and it is good enough for me. Then there is the matter of hyphenates. This is no time for divided allegiance. America for Americans is my motto, and if these pro-Nicaraguans and radicals do not like it in this country, let them go back to where they came from.

One thing that distresses me is the fact that I am over military age, and that I have a wife and child dependent upon me. I am filled with envy every time I read of those lucky boys who are marching down to Nicaragua to do their bit against those dirty Huns—a little name I made up for the Nicaraguans. If only I were 10 years younger!

But to get back to that war song. If I cannot wear a uniform, at least I can write a song. At first I thought of writing a Hymn of Hate—something of this sort:

Costa Rica and Guatemala, they matter not,
A blow for a blow, a shot for a shot.
Hate by water and hate by land,
Hate of the heart and hate of the hand,
We love as one, we hate as one,
We have for one and one alone,
*Nicaragua!*

It has the right spirit but it lacks the necessary martial fervor. It would hardly do for marching. Neither would this anthem that I started to write:

Then conquer we must
When our cause it is just,
For God and our Country
And Guaranty Trust.

Nicaragua is a terrible word for rhyming. I sometimes think that those who make our wars for us should take into consideration the metrical possibilities of a country before starting a war against it. It might not make much difference to the Marine in whose jungle he is shot down, but to the bard it is a matter of vital importance whether the enemy is Nicaragua or, let us say, Chile or Peru. Considerations of far less popular consequence have been known to send a detach-

## "On to Nicaragua, . . ." *(continued)*

ment of Marines trotting double-quick to the transports. After all, we poets vote and pay taxes. We should have some rights.

Anyway, it is a glorious war. When I read in *The New York Times* of "The greatest battle that American troops engaged in since the Great War," I thrilled with patriotic exaltation. Not since the battles of Bunker Hill, San Juan Hill, and Socony Hill have I had such a kick. Perhaps I shall be able to write that song yet.

If the army and the navy
Ever look on
Heaven's scenes,
They will find the
streets are guarded
By United States Marines.
—Marine Hymn, written
in 1875

- A plane patrol had spotted several hundred Sandinistas besieging a small force of Marines and National Guardsmen in the town of Ocotal.
- Only later would he learn that when General Sandino called for the Marines' surrender, Captain Gilbert Hatfield responded, "Go to Hell—Marines don't know how to surrender!"
- Within minutes, Ralph's squadron was in the air.
- The excitement built quickly; strafing small patrols was one thing, but rescuing fellow Marines was another.
- For a moment, he felt like the air cavalry, riding to the rescue as in adventure books—the rush was glorious!
- As the airplanes crossed a ridge in the mountainous terrain, Ralph could see that the town was under a vicious assault.
- At 1,500 feet, the planes leveled off and formed a tight V-formation.
- Ralph gave the thumbs-up to his observer and touched each of the four bombs for good luck.
- Then, the planes dropped into a steep dive, their forward machine guns blazing.
- The rebel forces stopped and pointed in awe; Ralph witnessed several unable to move, simply staring at the planes.
- At 300 feet, the planes unleashed their bombs, many hitting their targets.
- On the second run, the Sandinistas began retreating.
- On the third dive, all was chaos; many rebels threw down their weapons in fear, and by the fourth run, the ground was littered with bodies.
- Ralph's fellow Marines were safe.
- For the first time, he fully understood what it meant to be a Marine pilot in the midst of war.
- Over drinks he would celebrate the final score: 360 rebels dead, American losses—one.

*Five hundred Nicaraguan rebels under General Sandino attack a band of 37 U.S. Marines at Ocotal.*

## "Is Flying Really Safe?" by George Lee Dowd, Jr., *Popular Science Monthly,* November 1927:

*The answer is: not yet—25 deaths in ocean flights a year, scores of mortalities on land prove conquest of the air remains to be achieved.*

Colonel Lindbergh, Commander Byrd and other popular heroes of aviation have recently been quoted as complaining of the difficulties of convincing the public that flying is safe. Giving those gentlemen all due credit for technical skill and splendid accomplishments, there is a growing conviction that the public should not be convinced the air today is safe.

Flying is not yet safe. Safe for Lindbergh and Byrd—so far. But the average person makes no fine discriminations. When he is told that aviation is safe, it means that flight compares in safety favorably with other transit means.

What one group of men thinks of the safety of flying is shown in a resolution recently adopted by the American Bar Association. Proposed by the Committee on Air Law, it urges Congress to empower government officials to regulate ocean flights and curb "stunt flying."

"On transoceanic flights," says C. W. Cuthell, chairman of the committee, and incidentally, general counsel of the Curtiss Aeroplane Company and the National Air Transportation Company, "approximately 25 lives have been lost during the present year. Most of the flights are not of a directly commercial nature. They are what we of the profession call stunt flight." The control Mr. Cuthell advocates is declared necessary by several flying organizations, though government departments see in it the danger of prohibiting air pioneers from necessary experiments. . . .

Today, aviation is about where railroading was before George Westinghouse invented the airbrake. And in science and invention and their application to its problems lie its hope for the future. Heroic pioneers are striving at the risk of their lives and money to make aviation safer and more practical. But no good purpose can be served by closing our eyes to the developments necessary before real safety can be achieved.

THE LESSON HE NEVER LEARNS
—Orr in the Chicago *Tribune.*

## "Nicaragua's Bloody 'Peace,' " *The Literary Digest*, January 14, 1928:

President Coolidge will face a tremendous task at the Pan-American Congress on January 16, predicts the *Camden Post*, if he should try to reconcile the peaceful hum of Colonel Lindbergh's "good-will" airplane engine with the vindictive sputter of American machine guns in Nicaragua. In fact, since January 1, when our Marines suffered a loss of five men killed and 23 wounded in "the biggest battle in which our troops have fought since the World War," the president's lot has not been a happy one. Senators to the right of him, congressmen to the left of him have volleyed and thundered. Resolutions looking toward inquiries into Nicaraguan affairs have been introduced in both Houses, and our editorial writers have had many a scathing word to say of our policy—or lack of one—in the republic. *The Boston Globe* finds that approximately 50 engagements have taken place in Nicaragua between American Marines and native forces "since active intervention by the United States began last March." And this daily expresses the gist of many another editorial when it says:

"What is all this fighting about? Why are these young men in Marine uniforms being killed?

"Two things are known. One is that the United States is not officially at war with Nicaragua. Congress alone has the power to declare war, and Congress has done no such thing. The other known fact is that clashes have been frequent. But why our men should be there at all has not been explained."

In the opinion of the *Washington News* and other Scripps-Howard papers, "The American public has been shamelessly deceived by its officials as to the real state of affairs in Nicaragua." Continues this paper:

"To sum it up in a few lines, a Liberal revolution was in full blast last year and was on the point of overthrowing our man, President Diaz, a Conservative, when President Coolidge sent Col. Henry L. Stimson down there to see what could be done to stop the bloodshed and at the same time keep Diaz in power.

"Colonel Stimson found a way. In an interview with General Moncada, the revolutionary com-

mander-in-chief, he made it plain to the general that it was either a case of surrender or fight the United States. Moncada yielded, and our forces then in Nicaragua began disarming. But one of Moncada's ablest lieutenants, General Sandino, refused to surrender. He and his command kept to the field. Sandino, Colonel Stimson reported, had only 'about 150 followers'—men whom Washington officials ever since have referred to as 'bandits.'

"Against these '150 followers' of Sandino, then, some 1,400 American Marines, along with a couple of thousand or so native troops, have been fighting ever since. But, lest you should get the idea that our Marines have lost some of their punch, let it be recorded here that the story of General Sandino and his '150 followers' was sheerest nonsense. Tabulation of casualties shows that approximately 670 'bandits' have been killed since Colonel Stimson reported. And since at least twice that number have been wounded in these same engagements, Sandino's total casualties during the same period under discussion must have been around 2,000. Yet, on December 30, this extraordinary general seems to have had with him 500 followers.

"It is perfectly patent, therefore, that the American public has been disgracefully spoofed. Not only has General Sandino's strength been grossly underestimated, but the inspiration to make it appear that he and his followers were mere bandits was equally ridiculous. And further attempts to keep up this fiction becomes an insult to the American public.

"We should at least be honest with ourselves. For the time being, at any rate, Nicaragua has become an American protectorate, and what we are doing down there is not fighting bandits, but Nicaraguans in revolt against our rule.

"Admittedly we have certain well-defined rights in Nicaragua—our canal rights, for example. But unless we wish to spoil our chances for real understanding with the rest of Latin America, we must find a better procedure than killing off vast numbers of native rebels on the pretext that they are bandits."

## "The Republic of Brown Bros.," *The Nation*, June 7, 1922:

American liberalism is no new birth. In some form it goes back to our earliest history, and almost precisely what has happened in Haiti and Santo Domingo in the past six years happened a dozen years ago in Nicaragua. Upon these three republics we have forced ruinous loans, making "free and sovereign" republics the creatures of New York banks, and in all three, the armed forces of the United States have been used to put down the attempts of the people to free themselves, and to rivet fast American financial control. The men who do the dirty work have seldom known for whom they were working; they believed that they were performing an honest police duty.

The ordinary American citizen has not even been aware that we were conquering these countries, far less that we were doing so in the interest of small groups of bankers. The people can easily follow the movement of a regiment across the border into a neighboring country, but they know little of the movements of the navy out of sight across the sea. They had no chance to advise about, to consent or not to consent to, our invasion of Haiti, of Santo Domingo, or of Nicaragua. Three successive administrations in Washington have given good evidence that they feared the verdict of the people as represented in Congress, for they made war without consulting that body. The Senate repeatedly refused to ratify the Knox-Castrillo convention regarding the financial subjection of Nicaragua, and the Bryan-Chamorro treaty was ratified in 1916 only because it disguised its real purpose behind the appearance of the purchase of canal rights, and because is was shoved through at a time when all eyes were turned to Europe.

## Life in the Community: Nicaragua

- Nicaragua, at 49,000 square miles, is slightly larger than Pennsylvania.
- Its 700,000 inhabitants are either rich or poor, although a very small middle class exists.
- The landowners operate plantations and cattle ranches.
- An individual can make as much as $100,000 on a crop of coffee, though the rich mostly invest their money abroad.
- Politics in Nicaragua often take the form of old-fashioned feuds.
- Rivalries are so intense, a girl in a Conservative family would never consider wearing a red dress, since it is the color of the Liberal cause, while Liberals scorn anything with green as the dominant color.
- A Portuguese, Antonio Galvao, made the first proposal for a shipping canal across the Isthmus of Central America in 1550, suggesting four routes, one of which was by way of Lake Nicaragua and the San Juan River.
- In 1850, the Atlantic and Pacific Ship Canal Company did extensive survey and engineering work on a Nicaragua canal route, largely promoted by Cornelius Vanderbilt.
- From 1876 to 1901, four separate interoceanic canal commissions were appointed in the United States.
- The Bryan-Chamorro Treaty of 1913 gave the United States, in return for $3 million, the right to build a canal through Nicaragua and to establish a naval base on the Gulf of Fonseca.

## HISTORICAL SNAPSHOT
# 1927

- The Ford Model A, successor to the all-black Model T, was manufactured in four colors and included a self-starter, a rumble seat and shatterproof windshield
- The National Football League was reduced from 32 teams to 12
- Charles Lindbergh flew solo, nonstop, from New York to Paris, traveling 3,610 miles in 33.3 hours
- The ticker-tape parade for Lindbergh in New York consumed 1,800 tons of shredded paper and cost the city $16,000 to sweep up
- Fifteen million Sears & Roebuck catalogs were distributed to American homes
- The take for the controversial Jack Dempsey-Gene Tunney heavyweight boxing match at Soldier's Field in Chicago was a record $2.65 million; 104,943 were in attendance for the fight that featured the "long count" for Gene Tunney
- The *New York Daily News* inaugurated the Golden Gloves program to encourage young boxers
- Coney Island introduced the world to the Cyclone rollercoaster
- Hostess Cakes, the Literary Guild of America, Delmonico's, A&W root beer, Lender bagel factory and Gerber baby food all made their first appearance
- Harvard's Philip Drinker devised the iron lung, a respirator for patients who could not breathe on their own
- "I'm Looking over a Four-Leaf Clover," "Let a Smile Be Your Umbrella," and "Me and My Shadow" were all popular songs
- The average salary nationwide was $1,312, with the average pay for teachers $1,277, and for lawyers, $5,205
- *The Jazz Singer,* the first successful talkie, opened, starring Al Jolson
- Duke Ellington's music radio program premiered from the Cotton Club in New York
- An all-black basketball team, the Harlem Globetrotters, was organized by Abe Saperstein
- Many small-town merchants were hurt by the expanding availability of the automobile, as people began traveling to the nearest city to shop or take in a movie
- The National Association of Manufacturers complained that 40 percent of high school graduates could not do simple arithmetic or use proper English
- The average annual medical expense for a family was $80, with 45 percent spent on physicians' services, seven percent for hospitals, 15 percent for dentists, three percent for nurses, and the rest for medicines and incidentals
- Violinist Yehudi Menuhin debuted at age 10

# "The Bloodshed in Nicaragua, Topics of the Day," *The Literary Digest*, July 30, 1927:

The bloody affray at Ocotal, where 500 Nicaraguan rebels under General Sandino, attacking a little band of 37 United States Marines and 47 native constabulary, were repulsed with a loss of more than 300 dead, has fanned into fresh flames the smoldering criticism of our policy in Nicaragua and has also aroused the Administration's friends to rally to its defense. The criticism is directed, not against our greatly outnumbered Marines and airmen who met the attack with such amazing and deadly efficiency, but against the policy in Washington which has borne fruit in this sudden blood-spilling. . . .

"Secretary Kellogg's stupendous and stupid folly in plunging this country into armed intervention in Nicaragua is now bearing its fresh fruit of blood and slaughter," avers the independent *Washington News,* a Scripps-Howard newspaper, which predicts that our spilling of Nicaraguan blood "will rouse peoples against us all the way from the Rio Grande to Cape Horn."

And it asks, "How are we to justify this slaughter of Nicaraguans? Nicaragua is sup-

THE DISAPPOINTED LADY

WORLD PEACE: "O, Samuel!"

—A. G. Racey in *The Daily Star* (Montreal)

posed to be an independent nation, as sovereign within her territory as the United States. Under international law, what right have we to be there? Are we at war with her? Have we annexed her that we may kill her people as 'rebels' against our rule? Or what?

"The world—not just Americans—awaits an answer to these questions."

The dramatic happenings at Ocotal on July 16 and 17, as gathered from dispatches, are as follows: In this little Nicaraguan town, 110 miles north of Managua, a scant twosome of United States Marines under Capt. G. D. Hatfield and about the same number of Marine-trained native constabulary were surrounded and attacked by the forces of the insurgent General Sandino, the only Nicaraguan general who refused to accept the terms of peace and disarmament submitted in May by Henry L. Stimson, President Coolidge's personal emissary. The attack began from all sides at one o'clock in the morning, and the fighting continued for 17 hours, when the remnant of Sandino's force scattered before the attack of five bombing planes under Major Ross E. Rowell sent to the rescue from Managua, where news of the battle had been brought by two scout planes. . . . After the battle, Captain Hatfield and his men, according to a Managua correspondent of the *New York Herald Tribune,* "counted and assisted in burying 360 members of Sandino's force and attended about a hundred wounded." Two-thirds of the losses of the Nicaraguans were inflicted by the five Marine bombing planes. Captain Hatfield's forces suffered only three casualties. To quote Mr. Linton Wells, the *Herald Tribune* correspondent, further, "Nicaragua is in a turmoil over the battle. So great was the death-toll that Nicaraguans are amazed. To them it is almost unbelievable that five airplanes and 87 men could have destroyed or wounded so many and suffered only three casualties—one dead and two wounded—themselves."

## "This Is War, Gentlemen!" by Carleton Beals, *The Nation,* April 11, 1928:

We met the first Nicaraguan refugees in Danli, Honduras, on our way into Sandino's territory. In fact, we had supper in the house of a bearded carver of saints who had had his house burned in the battle of Ocotal. And on the trail from Escuapa to the frontier, we met long trails of émigrés, some coming with merely the clothes on their backs, others with a few salvaged possessions in gunnysacks, some with chickens; one bent old woman came driving a pig. Others, being comfortable ranchers, came with many belongings packed on mules, came driving cattle, came accompanied by all the appurtenances of their normal patriarchal life. Clear to the frontier in Honduras, indeed clear to the flanks of El Chipote and beyond, we met these same straggling lines of homeless and dispossessed.

With all these refugees I talked, often at length. All were filled with deep bitterness, not toward the "bandit" Sandino, whom they considered their friend, but toward the American Marines. And on their tongues were tales of Marine atrocities, most of them, I imagine, grossly exaggerated. But men do not leave their homes and their belongings and fly into the wilderness or into a foreign country with their families without grave provocation. Men do not hide in the darkness of narrow canyons and seek shelter in inhospitable crags and cower at the approach of a stranger like frightened animals without having suffered violations.

Nearly all of these people are from the Department of Nueva Segovia, in which is situated in El Chipote, the fortified height which for six months served as the bulwark of General Augusto C. Sandino. Over most of this region Sandino for a time held sway, not only in the imaginations of the people, but in the military sense. From El Chipote his *retenes* or military outposts radiated clear to the frontier. And he had the unbounded loyalty of the inhabitants who were safe in person and property. Women of the region came voluntarily to El Chipote to wash the clothes of the soldiers, to grind corn for the tortillas, and prepare the meals. The husbandmen of the locality brought food and provisions. And every man was a newspaper to keep Sandino informed of the movements of the Marines.

Against not merely the armed contingents of Sandino, but against an obviously hostile country-

**"This Is War . . ."** *(continued)*

side, the American forces could only consider every civilian a combatant and treat him accordingly.

The Marines are not accustomed to fight in tropical forests, and they are dealing with a tricky opponent who declares "God and my native mountains are fighting for me." It is perhaps only prudence before advancing into a dense growth of these hostile mountains—especially since ammunition is plentiful and the American taxpayer generous—to blaze away with machine-guns. But in these mountains and in these forests, people have their homes, humble to be sure, and their little clearings, both invisible a few yards away. One of the *Juanas,* or camp women, wounded in the forehead by a piece of shrapnel in an aerial bombardment of El Chipote, put it to me: "The Machos [Americans] have killed many civilians, but they've been careful to kill few Sandino soldiers.

## Selected Prices

| | |
|---|---|
| Ax, Official Boy Scouts of America | $1.65 |
| Book, *Winnie The Pooh* | $2.00 |
| Ceiling Fan, Hunter, 52" | $52.00 |
| Cigars, Box of 50 | $3.98 |
| Crayons, Box of 24 | $0.30 |
| Fishing Reel, 100 Yards | $4.37 |
| Grave Marker | $1.50 |
| Lincoln Logs, Set of 53 | $1.00 |
| Milk Chocolate, Hershey's Box of 24 | $0.97 |
| Milk of Magnesia | $0.25 |
| Motorbike | $25.75 |
| Plow, One-Horse, 4' Deep by 7' Wide | $8.25 |
| Pocketknife, Remington, Three Blades | $3.50 |
| Rifle, Winchester | $31.98 |
| Sombrero, Man's Wool Felt | $1.98 |

### Take a Kodak with you

You'd like to remember a day like this and pictures won't let you forget.

Any Kodak is convenient to carry, easy to work and fun to use; you'll get good pictures from the first.

*Autographic Kodaks $6.50 up At your dealer's*

Kodak Company, Rochester, N. Y., *The Kodak City*

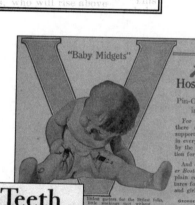
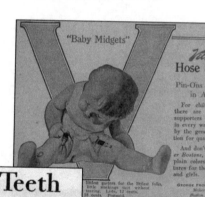

"Baby Midgets"

### Velvet Grip Hose Supporters

Pin-Ons and Sew-Ons in All Lengths

For children of all ages, there are Velvet Grip hose supporters of every type and in every wanted style—backed by the generations-old reputation for quality and service.

And don't forget the Knickerbocker Bostons, just like Dad's, in plain colors and heather mixtures for the knicker-clad boys and girls. Fifty cents a pair.

GEORGE FROST COMPANY, BOSTON
*Makers of the famous Boston Garter for Men*

### Her Pretty Teeth
### a social asset

# 1930–1939

The decade of the 1930s was marked by the most severe depression in United States history. Economic collapse gripped the country as banks failed, railways became insolvent, unemployment rose, factories closed, and foreign trade declined. By 1932, one in four Americans was jobless. Five thousand banks closed, wiping out the lifetime savings of millions of Americans. Bread lines became a common sight.

Meanwhile, the nation continued to defend its interests elsewhere. In China, where various factions vied for power in a bloody civil war, several countries including Japan, the major European powers—and the United States—all maintained a naval presence on the Yangtze River to protect commercial activity. At home, a different kind of army was being mobilized. In 1924, World War I veterans had been granted a "bonus"—certificates that would be worth about $1,000 in 1945—to compensate them for the low wages they had received during their military service. As the depression worsened, many veterans wanted the bonus to be paid immediately. Although the House approved the early payment, the Senate dragged its feet. As a result, the veterans formed quasi-military units—called the "Bonus Army"—and marched on Washington.

As the decade drew to a close, the spectrum of public opinion was reflected by those who felt war was the only response to escalating events in Europe, and on the other side, those involved in nationwide programs such as the Emergency Peace Campaign, aimed at promoting world peace and keeping America out of war.

# 1930 PROFILE

## PROTECTING AMERICAN INTERESTS IN CHINA

### Naval Executive Officer

For many years, the navy has accommodated Vance Patterson's desire to travel; now in China, amidst major cultural changes, he has fallen in love with a woman who fled the Russian Revolution.

### Life at Home

- Since he was a small boy, Vance Patterson has loved the water and dreamed of traveling the world.
- Growing up in Dubuque, Iowa, on the banks of the Mississippi River, he fished, swam and learned the currents of the greatest of American waterways.
- When he was not at the river, he was reading books on adventure and travel.
- After exhausting the modest collection at the Dubuque library, he began begging his father for money to buy books through the mail.
- An attorney who represented many of the large commercial interests in the city, his father could not understand how he had produced not a worker, but a dreamer.
- Vance's three siblings, all older brothers, were respectable professionals who made the family proud: one an attorney who practiced with his father, one a surgeon and one a banker.
- The family lived in a comfortable two-story wooden house on a tree-lined street in the city's most established neighborhood.
- Vance's favorite place was the cool of the garage, where he looked for roly-poly bugs and imagined what India or Burma might be like.
- He also spent considerable time looking at stereographic travel cards which showed the wonders of the Orient, the strangeness of Africa and the luxury of Paris.

*Vance Patterson loves to travel.*

## "I'd Sail 'Round the World and See Everything," advertising booklet of Belgenland Seventh World Cruise, Red Star Line, 1930:

CHINA: There are many places and things to see in China, too—the Chinaman himself—and the China woman and all the jolly little China children. The Chinese are charmingly naïve, natural and friendly. Peiking, the capital of China, is a great Asiatic mart, its shops being filled with fascinating things from all parts of the continent. Here the Temple of Heaven and Confucian Temple will be viewed with pleasure.

Your visits to the Chinese markets and theaters and cabarets, the native tea rooms and restaurants and racetracks, all these neighborly contacts with the people of China will help you to a deeper and more human understanding of Chinese affairs.

One particularly memorable day you will have in China, the day of your motor drive from Hong Kong over the justly famous Repulse Bay Drive to the delightfully situated Repulse Bay Hotel.

«I'd Sail 'Round the World and See Everything»

- His ambition to join the Merchant Marines and see the world upset his father, who insisted—loudly, at times—that he had worked hard all his life so that his sons could have college degrees and positions in the community; he had not raised a mere "sailor boy."
- Thus, it was agreed that Vance would apply for an appointment to the Naval Academy.
- A military education and an officer's position would provide Vance with some needed discipline and satisfy his ambition to travel.
- Life at the Naval Academy was harder than he had imagined, but at least he was away from his father.

- Quickly, he learned how to play the system, and by the time he graduated, Vance knew how to spend as much time as possible at sea, roaming from port to port.
- In a very short time, he was able to see much of Europe, South America, the Caribbean and the Pacific Rim.
- While assigned to the Asiatic Fleet based in Cavite, Philippines, in 1928, he began jockeying for an assignment in China, especially YangPat, where the naval patrols protected American interests along the Yangtze River.

- Since the fall of the last Chinese emperor in 1911, the country lacked a central government.
- The Nationalists under Chiang Kai-shek, the Communists supported by Moscow, and a variety of regional warlords all competed for power.
- The major European powers, the United States, and Japan all had a naval presence on the Yangtze River, China's commercial lifeline.
- For Vance and others on a steady government paycheck, the standard of living and rates of exchange combined to make China an attractive duty station.
- Enlisted men could afford to keep both a house and a personal servant, while officers fared even better.
- Menial tasks on board the gunboat were often performed by Chinese men in exchange for 10 percent of the enlisted men's pay.
- The largest cities along the river boasted foreign districts offering clubs, parks, bars and other diversions.

*Vance Patterson is currently patrolling Chinese waters to protect American interests.*

*The Red Star Line advertised cruises to China even as battles raged in the ancient country.*

*Vance has fallen in love with a White Russian, who is well educated.*

### "Shall We Leave China to Its Fate?" *The Literary Digest,* October 25, 1930:

Should China be abandoned by those who have befriended her in the past? Is there any use in trying to help a country torn by civil strife, subject to all forms of banditry, endangering the lives of missionaries and often driving them from their posts?

This is the question which the *Reformed Church Messenger* puts to itself. To desert China now, it thinks, would be the counsel of despair, and *The Messenger* asserts emphatically: "We simply cannot afford to let China alone. Never has that great land been more in need of true friendship. Even if the overtures of helpfulness are despised and neglected, they must be offered with greater urgency.

"For one thing, we must not even for a single moment forget the 'fact of China.' It is a tremendous fact, an inescapable reality. Within the borders of that country, now so wracked with travail, are approximately one-fourth of all the people in the world. Who can doubt the influence which a rapidly developing China will have upon the wealth of the world?

"Here, indeed, is a case of Christ or chaos. If a godless philosophy dominates in the building of a new China, it may well spell the doom of mankind."

- Always available in these spots were women from China and White Russia, many avoiding abject poverty only through prostitution.
- The White Russians, a large number of whom were prosperous before the fall of the czar, had fled Russia during and after the Russian Revolution.
- Vance considered White Russian women more desirable than their Chinese counterparts because they were both European and well-educated.
- Also, they helped Vance avoid marrying a local Chinese woman, as many sailors did, thereby losing the opportunity to travel.

### Life at Work
- Vance Patterson's gunboat is 160 feet long, displaces 370 tons, has two three-inch guns and eight .30 caliber machine guns.
- The boat carries a complement of 60, including four officers, one of whom is a doctor.
- Vance's assignment is to patrol a stretch of the Yangtze between Chungking and Ichang and to protect American missionaries, tankers and freighters that fly the American flag.

- Occasionally, parties of Marines would be transported up the river, normally in support of American missionaries.
- Vance is the executive officer, often heading vessel protection assignments, as well as offering assistance to missionaries.
- Raised a Presbyterian, Vance has been surprised how much he enjoys his encounters with the Catholic missionaries, finding them to be well-educated people whose minds are full of ideas and knowledge.
- Vance also admires the many medical missionaries, working against formidable odds.
- On the other hand, he cannot stomach the piety of some missionaries, particularly those who seem to be from small towns with small minds and a narrow view of the world.
- They seemed determined, at times, to impose their will and religion on the Chinese people no matter the circumstances, perennially convinced their way is the only way.
- Thanks to his position and the relatively low cost of housing, Vance rents an apartment in Chungking for when he is not patrolling the river.
- He has filled it with books covering all aspects of the Chinese people and their cultural heritage.
- He has also amassed an impressive collection of Chinese artwork, much of it purchased personally, and books on the archeology under way in western China under the leadership of Sven Hedin and Aurel Stien.

## "Rights of 'Extrality," *Outlook* and *Independent,* September 18, 1929:

Asked by the youthful Nanking government for permission to administer justice throughout China, the United States recalls that it has never sought to seize Chinese territory, that it recently allowed China to fix its own tariffs, and that it has always respected Chinese aspirations. More pertinently, it announces its readiness to negotiate on abandoning rights of extraterritoriality, or "extrality," under which, since an American sailor was executed in China a hundred years ago for a crime he did not commit, American defendants have been tried in courts controlled by their own consular representatives.

The decision is prudent and as progressive as conditions permit. The Chinese have a way of denouncing and ignoring treaties they no longer respect. Agreeing to relinquish these rights little by little—in a community here, in certain types of cases there—the United States safeguards its dignity and again demonstrates friendliness toward Chinese nationalism. Drawing upon the report of the Commission on Extraterritoriality, which went to China in 1926 headed by Silas Strawn of Chicago, the State Department points out that "extrality" rights were established with the consent of both governments, that legal theory and practice in China and America are still dissimilar, and that the consular courts must be maintained until Nanking creates an independent Chinese Judiciary fairly interpreting known codes of law.

While China doubtless believes that its newly drawn but still untested civil and commercial codes meet all reasonable requirements, it may be content if the United States, seemingly conceding much, actually concedes little; it is not unaware that, however unsatisfactory the American reply, it is more liberal than the British answer to a similar request. In befriending China, the United States is apparently second to no other power with interests in the Orient.

*Various factions have fought for control in China since 1911.*

- Shortly after his arrival, he began learning the language.
- Soon, he was being tutored by Ykaterina Loshilov, a White Russian refugee whose father had been a professor of modern languages.
- She and her mother manage to eke out a living by providing translation services and giving language lessons to foreigners like Vance.
- Thanks to her father, Ykaterina speaks Russian, Chinese, English, German, French and Spanish.
- Quite unexpectedly, while learning Chinese from Katya, Vance also found romance.
- He has taught her to ride horses, and they often go for long trips into the countryside.
- They also frequent restaurants and bars which cater to Europeans.
- Katya shares his sense of adventure and dreams of traveling beyond the bounds of China.
- They have talked of marriage, even though it would mean Vance must resign his commission.
- Recently, while debating their future, Vance received a new mission—leading a party to protect a small American-owned freighter on a trip to Ichang and back.
- Although the freighter sports a U.S. flag, the captain was the only other American on board; all the rest were Chinese.
- Protection was needed, since the freighter would pass through the territory of several warlords, any one of whom had an interest in seizing the cargo outright or holding the ship for local taxation, a form of extortion.
- Vance's party consisted of himself, a petty officer and two seamen.
- They were armed with a Lewis .30 caliber machine gun, two Thompson submachine guns, a Springfield rifle, a sawed-off 12-gauge shotgun and two Colt .45 automatic pistols.
- Vance and all his men wore civilian clothes aboard the freighter so as not to be obvious targets, and occupied the three passenger cabins on the ship.
- Days were spent cleaning their weapons, smelling the opium constantly smoked by the crew, and admiring the landscape of China as it rolled by.
- One member of the group was always on lookout duty.
- Vance and the petty officer, who lives with a Chinese woman, looked forward to the meals prepared by the Chinese cook.

- Most of the enlisted men complained that Chinese food got tiresome very quickly, and longed for steak and potatoes.
- The trip passed peacefully; the Chinese warlords always seem to know which ships are heavily guarded.
- On the trip back, Vance enjoyed the river's passage through dramatic gorges and breathtaking scenery.
- The peaceful passage also allowed him time to read more about China's culture, and to contemplate a life with Katya.
- Asking her to marry him would be exciting; telling his father what he had done would not.
- The ship was less than 100 miles from Chungking when the river took a particularly sharp bend.
- There on a precipice was a man waving a large banner as a signal to pull ashore.

*Vance is intrigued by the culture and beauty of China.*

- Grabbing a Thompson submachine gun and a Colt pistol, Vance immediately told the American captain to speed up the boat and ordered his men to collect their arms.
- When the ship rounded the bend, they saw that both banks of the river were defended with hundreds of armed men; numerous sampans were heading from the shore to intercept the freighter.
- The men on the shore rained a wall of fire at the ship, shooting with many different kinds of weapons.
- Bullet holes appeared throughout the superstructure of the ship as the navy men returned fire.
- They didn't need to aim carefully; so many men swarmed the banks, nearly every shot hit a target.

*Life along the Yangtze River is delightfully diverse and picturesque.*

### Selected Prices

| | |
|---|---|
| Binoculars | $33.48 |
| Cards, 3" x 4" | $0.10 |
| Cigarettes, Kool Mild Menthol, per Pack | $0.15 |
| Girdle, 12-Inch Length | $1.74 |
| Grapefruit | $0.05 |
| Haircut | $0.20 |
| Handkerchief, Cotton, per Dozen | $0.58 |
| Icebox | $18.75 |
| Mattress, 54-Inch Cotton | $4.65 |
| Memory Course, Bott 15-Minute | $1.00 |
| Motor Oil, per Gallon | $0.49 |
| Radio, Automobile | $55.00 |
| Sanitary Napkins, Kotex, per Dozen | $0.85 |
| Shotgun | $36.98 |
| Thermometer | $0.79 |

- Most of the Chinese crew huddled below deck in terror.
- Vance began to fire at the approaching boats, then turned his attention to the main deck to fend off men attempting to board the ship.
- That's when a grappling hook came over the side and caught.
- Vance reached over to cut the line, when he felt the presence of someone over him—a large, muscular Chinese man was poised to slice him in two with an axe.
- In that moment, he wished he had told Katya good-bye.
- Behind him came a roar and his assailant flew off the ship into the water; Vance's petty office had killed him with the riot gun.

- Vance then turned his attention to the other boarders using the rapid-fire Thompson.
- Dozens died aboard ship before the momentum of the freighter carried them past the army on the shore and their sampans.
- Two crewmen were dead, several wounded; bullet holes covered the ship.
- One enlisted man took a shot in the forearm, but was soon patched up well enough until a doctor could be found.
- One tough day.
- One more day to Chungking—and Katya.

### Life in the Community: China

- Currently, China struggles from a complete lack of modern communications and an underdeveloped transportation system.
- Compared to the 250,000 miles of railway in America, China only possesses 7,000 miles.
- The mileage of modern roads is negligible.
- It takes more time to travel between some provinces of China than to go from America to Europe.
- The movement of large bodies of troops and munitions over the more distant and mountainous sections of the country is difficult, limiting the enacting of nationwide military campaigns.
- Generals in remote sections of China feel free to declare their independence from the central government, knowing that government troops cannot easily reach them or, in the event of a defeat, that they can withdraw to a still more remote district.
- During the past 20 years, China has gone through more changes in government than in the previous 10 centuries.
- Wen Ying Peng writes, "In these circumstances, China's wars represent merely the most acute and violent phases of the rapid social, economic, political and ideological transformation."
- Ninety-percent of China's population is engaged in small-scale farming, domestic handicrafts or purely local trade.

# HISTORICAL SNAPSHOT
## 1930

- Unemployment passed four million
- The International Apple Shippers Association gave 6,000 jobless men surplus apples on credit to sell for $0.05 a piece on street corners
- More than 1,350 banks closed in a single year
- The United States had one passenger car for every 5.5 persons; in the wake of the depression the car boom was collapsing
- Advertisers spent $60 million on radio commercials
- *All Quiet on the Western Front, The Blue Angel, Monte Carlo, Hell's Angels* and *The Big Trail,* starring John Wayne, all premiered
- Jean Harlow became a blonde for her role in *Hell's Angels*
- The Eiffel Tower in Paris ceased to be the world's tallest building when the Chrysler Building went up in New York
- Hostess Twinkies, Snickers, sliced Wonder bread, Jiffy biscuits, windshield wipers, Plexiglas and *Fortune* magazine all made their first appearance
- The University of Southern California polo team refused to play against the University of California at Los Angeles until its one female member was replaced with a male
- Laurette Schimmoler of Ohio became the first woman airport manager, earning a salary of $510 a year
- The movie industry employed 100,000 people
- In fashion, the sophisticated Greta Garbo look was replacing the now passé flapper style of Clara Bow
- *As I Lay Dying* by William Faulkner and *The 42nd Parallel* by John Dos Passos were published; *Lincoln* by Emil Ludwig was a bestseller
- The first all-air commercial New York to Los Angeles transport was begun by Transcontinental and West Airlines
- "Georgia on My Mind," "What Is This Thing Called Love?" and "On the Sunny Side of the Street" were all popular songs
- A *Literary Digest* poll showed that 40 percent favored repeal of Prohibition, while 29 percent wanted modification to the law
- Tree-sitting and contract bridge were current fads, along with knitting and playing backgammon and "Sorry"
- America's illiteracy rate fell to 4.3 percent

## "The World Over," *The Living Age*, September 1930:

Accumulating evidence tends to show that influences are at work both in Shanghai and Wall Street to persuade the United States to put an end to the present chaos in China by active intervention. George Bronson Rea, editor of the *Far Eastern Review,* a lavish illustrated monthly published in Shanghai and packed with advertisements of foreign companies that do business out there, has taken a recent dispatch by Mr. Hallett Abend, chief correspondent of *The New York Times* in China, as a text to promote American interference.

Mr. Abend, just back from a visit to the States, asserted that "foreign business leaders consider that, if China could enjoy a few years of peace, security and alleviation from crushing war taxes, it would be able and eager to buy vast quantities of things which could profitably be produced by factories now idle." From this simple and obvious statement, Mr. Rea then elaborates a moral quite his own. He explains, "Unemployment in Great Britain, in the United States, in nearby Japan, and in other manufacturing countries has become an ominous problem. It is fast assuming portentous proportions that menace the very stability of the governments concerned." And now follows the kernel of his case:

China has the right to be mistress in her own house, to settle her problems in her own way, to indulge in continuous and indecisive civil wars, to ruin her own country, to bring misery, starvation, and death to millions of her own people, but when these prerogatives of sovereignty are carried to the point where the chaos of China imperils the stability of other governments and the livelihood of millions of workers in other parts of the world, the day must dawn when the Chinese will be politely but firmly invited to put their house in order. Continued civil warfare in China, boycotts, interference with trade, and the general impoverishment of the country have already brought Japan to the brink of economic disaster. The collapse of Japan or any great diminution of her purchasing power would affect every other nation in the world.

American business is keenly alive to these conditions so far as the pendulum swung in the other direction, that the sentiment in Wall Street is now strongly and openly in favor of joint international pressure upon China to put a stop to these exhausting civil wars. China is a sovereign state. Her territorial integrity is guaranteed under treaties subscribed to by all the principal Powers, except Russia. No nation covets her territory. Japan's policy toward China is in full harmony and accord with that of the United States. China has no real enemy in the world today. She has nothing but friends and well-wishers. She has appealed for a square deal and has received it. In return, she has assumed responsibilities that cannot be shirked.

The inability of China to discharge her obligations to the rest of the world, the wracking and ruin of her country, and the plunging of millions into a state of hopeless misery, make her as much an instrument of Moscow as though she was an integral part of the Soviet system of Socialist Republics. The prolongation of conditions which close the markets of China to the manufacturing nations of the world and intensify the present unemployment problem abroad only serves to advance the cause of world revolution.

Stability and peace in China, with a revival of the purchasing power of its people and the credit of its government, will help to solve the problem of world unemployment and bring happiness and a full dinner pail to millions of human beings. The drift of world opinion is unmistakable. The collapse of Nanking, the triumph of communism in this country, will affect the whole world. These facts are being slowly grasped and when the influence of big business, international finance, capitalism, if you will, is brought to bear on governments, there will be no hesitancy when it comes to the choice between communism and demanding that China put her house in order.

*China has gone through more changes in government in the past 20 years than in the previous 10 centuries.*

### "Chinese Outcry against Scientific Spoilation," *The Literary Digest*, November 2, 1929:

If a Chinese expedition should proceed to dig up our Indian mounds and carry off what they found to enrich Chinese museums, we should doubtless object, and probably interfere. Just at present, the boot is on the other leg in China. *The Science News-Letter,* A Science Service publication (Washington), tells us that the expeditionary work of the American Museum of Natural History in Mongolia, led by Roy Chapman Andrews, has been interrupted by a Chinese organization, the Society for the Preservation of Cultural Objects. Dr. Henry Fairfield Osborn, president of the museum, has recently described what has happened, says *The News-Letter:*

"The expeditions of the Museum, of which the present was intended to be the seventh, have attracted worldwide attention because of their sensational discoveries of dinosaur eggs and fossils, and for their hope of finding the original home of the human race."

The Chinese Society for the Preservation of Cultural Objects is not in any way an official body, but it possesses great influence and has apparently been able to bend officers of the Chinese government to its will. Roy Chapman Andrews, leader of the American field party, describes much antiforeign propaganda which this organization has been carrying on through the press and other media, charging American and European scientific expeditions with "stealing China's priceless treasures," "infringing her sovereign rights," "seeking for oil and minerals," "being spies against the government," and so on.

At the beginning of the 1929 season, Mr. Andrews states, the Chinese demanded joint participation in and control over the field expedition, the retention in China of much of the material obtained, and the eventual return of all specimens sent to the United States for study, and payment by the American Museum of all expenses for Chinese experts sent to this country to carry on research in the museum. After prolonged negotiations in an endeavor to obtain a modification of these demands, the American Museum authorities decided to suspend operations.

## "The Causes and Cures of Civil War in China" by Wen Ying Peng, *Current History,* January 1930:

Once again, civil war is harassing China, a country already exhausted by internecine strife during the last dozen years. The present struggle promises to be more extended, if not more bloody, than any in recent years. What are the causes that have led to it?

The present war was averted several times in one way or another during the two years before its outbreak, and its postponement has rendered it more serious, more unmanageable and more devastating. On the one side, there is President Chiang Kai-shek, head of the Nanking government and of the conservative section of the Kuomintang, ruling over the richest sections of the country. On the other side, there is General Feng Yu-hsiang, once known as the "Christian General," the most spectacular figure in China today, also the most astute and the most ruthless, leading the best-disciplined and most personally loyal army of 200,000 strong, descending from north China to the rich Yangtze Valley. Is it a mere personal struggle for power between two military leaders? What will be the effects in China, if one or the other should prevail?

The high hopes for a long period of peace and progress under the Kuomintang regime, entertained not only by the supporters of Nanking, but also by many who do not entirely agree with them, have now been so thoroughly shattered that recovery must be held to be extremely doubtful. When can China have peace? Under what conditions can real peace, and not six or 12 months' truce, be finally established in China?

To understand the civil war in China, the best approach is perhaps that of the historian, for China today is making history just as any other nation is, and the present situation is properly to be regarded as but one stage in a great historical evolution. The remarkable feature of the situation is that China is making history at breakneck speed and under conditions peculiarly its own. What then are the characteristics of this period of transition?

Within the last 20 years, China has probably gone through more changes than all the changes during the previous 20 centuries. Not one, but several great historical revolutions are taking place simultaneously. A 4,000-year-old monarchy is being changed to a republic; autocracy to democracy; an international "semicolony" to a sovereign state; medieval agricultural-handicraft economy to modern industrialism; family loyalty to individualism; Buddhism, Confucianism and superstition to Christianity, perhaps, but to science eventually; order to disorder, and to order again; everything old to something new—a thousand changes, a thousand conflicts and a thousand struggles, in ideas, institutions, groups and individuals. In these circumstances, China's wars represent merely the most acute and violent phase of the rapid social, economic, political and ideological transformation. The present outbreak of hostilities is simply an episode in the struggle for final supremacy or an unfinished act in the long-drawn campaigns and battles, nor will it be the last unless conditions for real peace are established and an early victory is assured to the forces and ideas that are destined eventually to triumph.

### Transportation Difficulties

The forces led by General Feng, for instance, after being defeated near Peking in 1926, retreated to Inner Mongolia and the borders of Chinese Turkestan. A year later, Feng reemerged as one of the strongest factors in China. When Chiang Kai-shek was successfully leading his northern expedition three years ago, crushing one enemy after another, he might then have dealt a blow at Feng had it not been for difficulties of transportation. Chiang, however, compromised and incorporated the entire army of Feng, giving the latter the vice presidency in the government. Now that the truce is over, Chiang Kai-shek is again facing the problem that confronted him three years ago. With troops mostly of doubtful loyalty, it is highly problematical whether he can overcome Feng's army, which is the best-disciplined China has. Even if Chiang could prevail, the story of 1926 might be repeated with another reappearance of Feng in the arena of conflict.

## "The Causes and Cures . . ." (continued)

Besides Feng's army, there are various other independent armies in the north, south, and west of China which owe their existence chiefly to their being inaccessible. Almost completely isolated from the rest of China, the big province of Szechuan, with an estimated population of about 50 million, has been a constant battlefield during the last decade among the petty local generals.

Unless, therefore, a good system of railways and roads is developed, knitting all parts of China into one, it is difficult to imagine how civil wars can be eliminated and real peace achieved.

A second, equally important cause arises from defective army organization. There is actually no one army in China, only numerous armies each responsible solely to its own leaders. Any adventurer who can gather a large enough following of armed men creates an army of his own. The officers and the men are then taught to be loyal only to their commanders—that is, the hands that feed them. These leaders, knowing nothing of civil responsibility and control, take power of the local government into their hands and use it to oppress and plunder the people. They are ever struggling for greater power and gain. Sometimes they are on one side, sometimes on another, only soon to desert it to join a third, or perhaps declare themselves neutral in a pending conflict. Frequently, these local generals enter into bargains to sell themselves to the highest bidder. At their best, they resemble the fighting noblemen and petty princes of medieval Europe; at their worst, they are little better than organized banditry.

*Civil war continues to harass China, sparing neither city nor rural area.*

# 1932 PROFILE

# THE BONUS ARMY MARCHES ON WASHINGTON

### First Sergeant

Thirty-year veteran Clay Montgomery is faced with the distasteful task of defending Washington from the onslaught of the rag-tag, desperate Bonus Army, composed of fellow World War I veterans.

### Life at Home

- In 1885, when Clay Montgomery's mother was pregnant with him, the family left their tiny holdings in the Ozark foothills in Arkansas for the promise of a better life.
- They eventually settled on a strip of "no man's land" separating Texas from Colorado and western Kansas, where Clay was born.
- There, at 4,000 feet above sea level, land was plentiful, cheap and inhospitable.
- His father bought a parcel along the Cimarron River near what was to become the town of Kenton, where he operated a modest cattle operation.
- The entire family worked to make the ranch a success, and though wealth was never a possibility, neither was starvation.
- Methodists by tradition, the Montgomery family gravitated toward the Pentecostal movement sweeping the West.
- The entire family would travel long distances, neglecting ranch and self, to hear the word of the Lord from traveling preachers passing through the area.
- The first luxury purchase the family made was an upright piano, which they ordered through the Sears Roebuck Catalog and had shipped to their ranch by rail.
- The piano was placed in an honored spot in the house.
- After supper, the family would gather in the living room for scripture reading, hymns and prayer.

*Clay Montgomery has spent a lifetime in the army.*

- One Easter, Clay decided to memorize all of the psalms, spending three years in the valiant effort.
- Drinking, smoking, swearing, dancing, kissing, gambling, card playing and lots of things he never knew about were prohibited in his home.
- He loved working outdoors, eating his Momma's cooking and singing hymns.
- Fortunately for all concerned, he was blessed with a rich baritone voice.
- On his seventeenth birthday, knowing his older brother would inherit the ranch, Clay gathered his savings and sought his fortune in Texas, taking one bundle of clothing and a King James Bible—a gift from his parents.
- In Texas, he worked a variety of jobs before deciding to enlist in the army, a decision he has never regretted.
- Twice he was sent to the Philippine Islands; both times his unit was assigned garrison duty and saw no action.

## Selected Prices

| | |
|---|---|
| Baby Powder, Johnson & Johnson | $0.29 |
| Bicycle | $17.50 |
| Clock, Mahogany Finish | $5.95 |
| Hair Color Treatment, Slate Color | $1.29 |
| Highway Flare Torches, per Dozen | $24.00 |
| Hog Trough, 20-Gauge Steel, Lot of Six | $0.48 |
| Iron, Electric | $1.00 |
| Marshmallows, Kraft Box of 200 | $0.65 |
| Pocket Watch, Ingersoll Mickey Mouse | $1.50 |
| Shaving Cream, Colgate Rapid | $0.25 |
| Shoes, Man's Oxford | $2.48 |
| Telephone Call, New York to London, Three Minutes | $30.00 |
| Tent, 5' x 7' | $4.95 |
| Valentines, 16 Cards | $0.25 |
| Wrenches, Complete Set | $15.00 |

- While on leave in North Carolina, he was passing by a church picnic when a pastor asked him to join in the feast.
- There, he met Eula Potman; in a single afternoon he found both a wife and a church home.
- In 1917, Sergeant Montgomery was assigned to a training camp to prepare wet-behind-the-ears recruits to be soldiers who could fight for the honor of America against the German Huns.
- In the spring of 1918, he was reassigned to an infantry division in France, where he learned the intricacies and dangers of trench warfare, mustard gas, bombs dropped by giant balloons and the smell of blood three days old.
- Late at night, troops on both sides listened to the sound of a clear baritone belting out "Blessed Assurance."

- Despite the horrors of war, Clay spent considerable time telling young conscripts they should be honored to be serving both God and America in such a way.
- Late in the war, he took shrapnel from an artillery shell, enough to take him off the front line, but not enough to change his mind about a career in the military.

## Life at Work

- In the spring of 1932, First Sergeant Montgomery was thinking about retirement after nearly 30 years in the army.
- He is now assigned to a company of the 112th Infantry stationed in Fort Washington, Maryland, near the nation's capital.
- His daughter, the wife of a Department of Labor clerk, and his grandchildren live in a neat bungalow nearby.
- Yet his thoughts keep returning to Eula's family land in North Carolina, where their oldest son has a tobacco farm and a church where he is pastor.
- Clay's duty is light, his captain easy to please, and his soldiers all volunteers who respect discipline and know the value of a steady paycheck during these depressed economic times.
- Across the nation, jobs are scarce, even for veterans who fought gallantly for their country during the Great War.
- In 1924, legislation was passed granting most veterans certificates worth about $1,000 in 1945, theoretically to compensate them for the lower-than-market rates they received during their time in service.
- As the depression deepened, many men desperate for ways to feed their families wanted the certificates to be paid immediately.
- Congressman Wright Patman of Texas even proposed legislation to that effect, which gained approval in the House.
- But the Senate was slow to act; with employment down, the accompanying tax revenues are down—hardly a good time to make billions in early pension payments.
- So, like good soldiers, this army of unemployed organized themselves into quasi-military units.
- Their goal was simple: March on Washington and force the federal government to support immediate payment of their bonus.
- Clay was appalled; serving one's country was a privilege, and the bonus a reward, not an entitlement.
- He thought it shameful that the perfectly fit were demanding special treatment while an entire nation of men and women were struggling with the depression.
- Even worse, the governors of Indiana and Ohio supplied the bonus marchers with transportation, and food was donated by patriotic organizations.
- Then, as the Bonus Army approached Washington, Clay's battalion was ordered to receive intensive training in riot control.

*Clay grew up in a close-knit family in the West.*

### "On to Washington with the Bonus Hikers," *The Literary Digest,* June 11, 1932:

Mulligan, bread, and coffee—coffee, bread and beans—so it goes, ringing the changes. Three times a day on the road to Washington, when the people are kind, as they have been hitherto, and three times a day in Washington itself.

Men must eat, Washington argues. Somebody must feed them, even at a time when producing mulligan for a thousand or more men is harder than pulling rabbits out of a silk hat.

And yet, the general opinion seems to be that these gaunt, travel-stained veterans have created a most embarrassing situation for Congress by hitchhiking from the ends of the land to the national capital, under circumstances of piercing publicity—incidentally kidnapping a freight-train for a few hours while passing through Illinois—to make a seemingly impossible demand upon the nation.

Two billion dollars for ex-servicemen—immediately—in cash!

Nice news for a distracted Congress!

Rolling-kitchens and bed-sacks from the War Department for veterans barracked in vacant stores and a garage. Talk of pup-tents in open spaces near Bolling Field. "Bonus Camp."

One contingent all the way from Portland, Oregon, with the help of motor-trucks lent by the governors of various states. Other contingents reported "on the road" from New Orleans, Philadelphia, Cleveland, Albany, El Paso, and way off in Nevada, "waiting for a train over the desert."

"Isn't there some way of turning them back," twitters Washington. . . .

The veterans' campaign was described by Representative Henry T. Rainey, Democratic House leader, as "useless." He said, "It is too bad these men were not advised against this useless journey. There isn't a chance for the bonus. If the bill passes, it will be vetoed. It can't get a two-thirds vote to pass over a veto. I never heard of a more useless trip than this being made to Washington."

## "Communications," *The Commonwealth,* November 16, 1932:

To the Editor: May I suggest an argument in favor of the bonus payment which I have not seen advanced so far. Indeed, the argument is good for the payment of pensions to all veterans, widows of veterans, husbands of remarried widows of veterans, their children and grandchildren. The argument is this: The more we pay for the last war, the more likely we are to think twice before starting or being drawn into another war. Let's make war so burdensome for ourselves and the generations to come that it will become financially impossible.

And as for the immediate payment of the bonus, I think that a little inflation will be just the thing. The vast body of American debtors, cracking under the strain of debts incurred under inflated valuation, have a right to relief by being allowed to pay with inflated currency.

—A.R. Bandini, Crockett, California

The Lincoln Memorial and regular flights over Washington symbolize the modern District of Columbia.

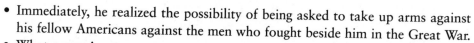

- Immediately, he realized the possibility of being asked to take up arms against his fellow Americans against the men who fought beside him in the Great War.
- What a mess!
- As marchers, many of whom were unemployed, arrived from around the country, the government found vacant buildings where the protestors could sleep.
- The military provided mobile kitchens and supplies to keep the Bonus Expeditionary Force alive.
- When the vacant buildings were filled, a camp was established across the river in Anacostia.
- Soon, the Bonus Army grew to 20,000, including some wives and children who came with their husbands to demand the payment of the $2 billion bonus.
- Immediately, city officials became concerned that epidemic disease might sweep the city.
- Most days, the Bonus Army would peacefully march the capital in an orderly manner carrying placards, but those marchers with a different agenda, especially those espousing communism or radical ideas, were driven from the group.
- On several Sundays, Clay and his wife visited the Anacostia camp to talk with the men.

## "The Pension Racket," by Orland Kay Armstrong,
### *The North American Review,* June 1931:

There is no better illustration of the rapid drift of our national government into the whirlpools of lawmaking at the demands of and for the benefit of organized minorities than legislation for the veterans of the World War.

Since the Armistice, that legislation has moved forward, gaining momentum with each session of Congress, and shifting its emphasis from the original efforts to pay, in some measure, the debt our nation owed the wounded and disabled, to a free-for-all fight to see who should head the procession in passing laws for "veterans' relief" of any kind and character, whatever the cost and however absurd the provisions by which the veterans are to be relieved.

"No pensions to follow this war!" was the announcement of the government while the war was in progress. A liberal war risk insurance was to take the place of the old-fashioned pensions that had followed in an endless and irksome train behind all past wars of the United States.

A war without pensioned soldiers? The history of America has been written in her pensions. Land grants for the soldiers of the Revolutionary War. Grants and money for the veterans of 1812 and the Indian Wars. Pensions for Civil War veterans, beginning at a $6-a-month minimum back in 1895 and growing to $100 for the survivors of the Union Army today, with widows' pensions to be paid on and on a generation from today. Pensions for Spanish-American veterans—but not in such amounts comparable to Civil War pensions. The war did not last so long and there were fewer troops, consequently, less organized pressure.

And now the World War, with its businesslike system of insurance. No more pension bills by congressmen for worthy and neglected constituents. No more heavy burden of taxation to go rolling on from the backs of one genera-

tion to another. Once the insurance obligations were taken off, and disabled veterans provided for, the task would be done.

Congress old at the business in those years just following 1918 must have smiled at all this. Nearly three and a half million veterans! No pensions? Some of them in service only a few weeks or months; only about half of them overseas; comparatively few in trench warfare longer than a few weeks; about 80 untouched by wounds of war to one wounded; but all veterans, nonetheless. An average of 8,000 to the congressional district. All voters with families and friends. *What? No pensions?*

Through progressive steps, the foundation for a pensions system was laid from 1918 to the sessions of the Seventy-first Congress. And this Congress, which came to an end last March fourth, started the system off on its long journey down the years.

As a World War veteran, and one intensely interested in legislation for the benefit of veterans sick or disabled as a result of military or naval service, I have watched the efforts of Congress to swing veterans' relief into a channel where its flow can be an ever-increasing political asset, with amazement. I have been chagrined to see the appropriation of money for veterans reach the plane of a tremendous racket.

- Often, disagreements arose when he told them they were wrong, but offered to pray for their souls.
- His wife Eula always brought a basket of food for the children, who must be taken care of no matter what, she believed.
- In early June, despite the presence of men from across the nation camping nearby, the U.S. Senate soundly defeated the Bonus Army Bill.
- With nowhere to go and no backup strategy, the Bonus Army simply stayed in Washington and waited for a different result.

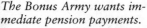
*The Bonus Army wants immediate pension payments.*

- Rumors flew that the men were planning a violent overthrow of the government, although Clay saw no evidence of a conspiracy—just desperate men with too few ideas and too little leadership.
- On the morning of July 28, District of Columbia policemen attempted to evict the marchers from the vacant buildings so the structures could be demolished.
- The police action, mixed with pent-up frustration and the humid air, set off a riot—the first major disturbance of the Bonus Army Movement.
- The men began throwing bricks, injuring several District policemen.
- President Hoover was asked to provide assistance, an action Clay had been dreading.
- Almost immediately, Clay's captain told him to assemble the troops and load them into waiting trucks.

- When their trucks stopped in Washington, Clay found an assembled force of 600 consisting of a squadron of cavalry, a platoon of tanks and a battalion of the 12th Infantry.
- This assembly was under the direct command of Brigadier General Perry Miles, an officer with whom Clay had served, while the overall Commander of the Army for this operation was General Douglas MacArthur.
- At 5:10 p.m. on the same day the riot had begun, the troops led by the cavalry, followed by the tanks and supported by the infantry, moved in to disperse the rioters.

- Token resistance offered by the Bonus Army was put down with tear gas grenades.
- The cavalry moved the marchers off government property with the flats of their sabers.
- Thank God, thought Clay, there was little for the infantry to do but simply march with their bayonets fixed behind the fleeing men.
- As wrong as they may have been, he could not stomach the idea of harming a fellow war veteran in the shadow of the nation's Capitol Building.
- When the property was clear, the troops broke for dinner; no apparent injuries had taken place on either side of the lines.

- Shortly after 9:00 p.m., orders were given to reform the units and evict the marchers from the Anacostia Camp.
- Clay knew that if violence was to occur, it would take place there.
- To keep their minds off the task ahead, his troops marched with a steady cadence toward the camp.
- As they approached, they were met by a man who claimed to be a leader, asking for one hour to evacuate the remaining stragglers.
- Gen. MacArthur agreed, and the troops set up camp for the night.
- A few old veterans who had fought in France smiled as they heard a familiar baritone singing "Just a Closer Walk with Thee."
- The next morning, the troops marched into a deserted Bonus Army Camp; approximately 20,000 members of the Bonus Army had left the city without a serious injury or a shot being fired.

## Life in the Community: Washington, DC

- Eight cities in four different states sheltered the Continental Congress and its successor, the Congress of the Confederation.
- Washington became the seat of United States Government in 1790 as a result of a bargain made by Alexander Hamilton at a dinner arranged by Thomas Jefferson.
- As a result, the seat of Congress was fixed for 10 years in Philadelphia, and after that was permanently located on the Potomac River.
- The original territory set aside by George Washington was four and a half miles from east to west and two and a half miles from south to north, or roughly the size of Paris, then a city of 800,000 people.
- Work on the nation's Capitol Building began in 1792; buildings and additions have continued until present day, in a sense symbolizing "the evolution of the country," *National Geographic* said in 1923.
- The District of Columbia now has a population of more than half a million people.
- The Lincoln Memorial, which witnessed the Bonus Army Movement, was completed a decade ago following 10 years of construction.

## HISTORICAL SNAPSHOT
# 1932

- *Forbes* magazine predicted that the number of television receivers would reach 100,000 this year, up from 15,000 in 1931
- As the depression worsened, wages dropped 60 percent in only three years
- Wages for picking figs were $0.10 per 50-pound box, $1.50 a day for 15 boxes; for picking peas the pay was $0.14 cents a pound
- New York's Radio City Music Hall, with 6,200 seats, opened as the world's largest movie theater
- An interest in snow skiing was stimulated by the Winter Olympics in Lake Placid, New York
- The Zippo lighter, Mounds candy bar, Fritos corn chips, Johnson Glo-Coat wax, and tax on gasoline all made their first appearance
- Reacting to the depression, President Herbert Hoover reduced his own salary by 20 percent
- The FBI created a list of "public enemies"
- *Light in August* by William Faulkner, *The Good Earth* by Pearl S. Buck, *Death in the Afternoon* by Ernest Hemingway and *Sweeney Agonistes* by T. S. Eliot were all published
- James Chadwick discovered the neutron
- Radio premieres included "The George Burns and Gracie Allen Show," "National Barn Dance," "The Jack Benny Program" and "Tom Mix"
- Unemployment was officially recorded at 23.6 percent
- Across America, 31 percent of homes had telephones
- Amelia Earhart became the first woman to make a solo transatlantic flight
- Movie openings included *Mata Hari, Scarface, Dr. Jekyll and Mr. Hyde* and *Tarzan, the Ape Man*
- President Hoover declared: "Grass will grow in the streets of 100 cities" if Franklin Roosevelt was elected
- The "Great I Am" Movement, promising wealth to its followers, gained popularity
- The Federal Reserve Board's index of production was down 55 percent from 1929
- Most of America could now benefit from some type of ambulance service, though most were operated by funeral directors
- Baseball cards began to appear in packages of bubble gum, accompanied by tips on how to improve one's game

## "Facts about the Soldiers' Bonus" by General Frank T. Hines, Administrator of Veterans' Affairs, *Review of Reviews* and *World's Work*, December 1932:

From the close of the Revolutionary War up to May 31, 1932, the government disbursed for veterans' relief approximately $14,346,962,000. Of this account, $8.618 billion represented the amount paid as pension to veterans of all wars prior to the World War, and to those soldiers of the regular establishment who have been pensioned for injuries or disease resulting in the line of duty in the regular army, navy or Marine Corps.

The net disbursements for direct monetary benefits to the World War veterans and their dependents, up to May 31, 1932, amounted to $4.17 billion. The balance of the disbursements on account of World War veterans, amounting to $1.559 billion, is because of indirect benefits such as hospitalization, domiciliary care, travel expenses to veterans, burials, etc., and administration costs.

It is well to review briefly the history of adjusted compensation. The question of legislating on this matter was before the Congress from 1920 to 1924. It was the desire of Congress to make some adjustment in the remuneration given to men who served in the army, navy, and Marine Corps, adjusting their wages to some extent to compare with those who labored at home. . . .

The bill which finally became a law was passed over President Coolidge's veto. It provided that each veteran having held a rank below that of lieutenant-commander in the navy or major in the army should receive as adjusted compensation (after deduction for the first 60 days of service, for which a cash settlement had been made at the time of discharge) credit at the rate of $1 per day for service in the United States and $1.25 for service overseas. . . .

As a concrete example: A veteran with 178 days' service in the United States and 176 days' service overseas, on the basis of $1 and $1.25 per day, secured an adjustment in a net amount of $398. To this adjusted service credit there was added 25 percent because of the deferred payment. Thus, the gross credit to be used as a net single premium amounted to $498, which was sufficient to procure an adjusted service certificate in the average case with an amount shown on the face thereof of $1,000. . . .

Certainly, no reasonable person holding a 20-year endowment life insurance policy with a commercial insurance company would seriously press a claim for payment thereof before the policy could normally mature.

## "Correspondence: It Is Not a Bonus," by F. W. Burgess, *The Nation*, March 11, 1931:

To the Editor of *The Nation*:

Sir: I am much chagrined that *The Nation* should have published the two editorials, "Cash for the Veterans" and "The Bonus Raid."

In the first place, the word "bonus" is misleading for what has been properly and legislatively called adjusted compensation. The stipulated pay in the army was $30 per month and board. Qualified men within the age limits were compelled to enter the army regardless of their profession or earning capacity, and to take their chances of becoming cannon fodder or permanent inmates of hospitals. At the same time, common laborers were receiving from $4 to $6 a day and mechanics from $6 to $10, with nearly unlimited overtime, which was not allowed in the service. Let the profiteers be left out of the reckoning.

After five years, Congress enacted legislation providing compensation at the rate of $1 per day for service in this country and $1.25 per day for service overseas. But in spite of the fact that this compensation constituted wages for services rendered, and wages are recognized as having the first lien on capital in nearly all states of the Union, the federal government, on the advice of the greatest Secretary of the Treasury since Hamilton, evaded responsibility by issuing certificates of indebtedness to the veterans, now worth only 22.5 percent of their face value with interest computed at six percent. The face value, by the way, varies from $30 to $1,789, not $1,000 to $2,000 as stated in your editorial.

"Hard-headed" businessmen foresee economic disaster if the veterans are paid now. But how foresighted are they? It was they who recommended the reduction of super taxes to stimulate business. Yet general business went steadily down while stock brokerage went up until it was so top-heavy, it fell of its own weight. As for the forecasts of our perennial Secretary of the Treasury, in spite of his annual predictions of a deficit, the government has paid off $3.5 billion of United States Bonds out of annual surpluses and returned to large corporations and wealthy individuals $1.25 billion in supposedly overpaid income taxes—although there is no doubt that the incomes were very carefully scrutinized by batteries of overpaid lawyers and underpaid accountants. Forecasts, in fact, have failed so repeatedly and completely that it would be safer to class them with dreams, mules, and weather predictions and go contrary.

As I see it, there is no proposal which would stimulate business so much as the liquidation by the government of its obligation to the veterans in small amounts that were due 11 years ago. The money would be distributed in almost every channel of trade, mainly through the lower strata of society, and afford relief from what will be a continued depression if heroic measures are not taken to change the business methods now operating this country.

When You
BUY an AUTOMOBILE
You GIVE
3 Months' Work
to Someone

Which Allows Him to BUY OTHER PRODUCTS

BUY A CAR NOW—HELP BRING BACK PROSPERITY

## "The 'Ghost Parade' of the Bonus Seekers," *The Literary Digest,* June 18, 1932:

"They marched in the dark like ghosts out of the forgotten past."

That's how they looked to Floyd Gibbons, these worn and ragged World War veterans, as they staged their bonus parade through the streets of a nervous Washington.

But there was no disorder—welcome news to a nation which had half-expected some outbreak of violence among these thousands of men who had hitchhiked, walked, or ridden freight trains to the capital to demand a bonus.

This time there was no more disorder than that other time these men marched. Then, as Mr. Gibbons tells us in his sympathetic description—"In the light of day and the glory of youth, and with the prayers and hopes of the nation pinned above their khaki-clad breasts, they marched that same route between thousands of proud and admiring public officials and civilians."

But now, continues this copyrighted article for Universal Service, they marched like ghosts—

"Four abreast they marched—5,000 strong.

"Few uniforms tonight and those ragged and wear-worn.

"The grease-stained overalls of jobless factory workers.

"The frayed straw hats of unemployed farm hands.

"The shoddy, elbow-patched garments of idle clerks.

"All were down at the heel. All were slim and gaunt, and their eyes had a light in them. There were empty sleeves and limping men with canes.

"They were 5,000 hungry ghosts of the heroes of 1917. Not so young now. They came back triumphant from the smoke of battle in distant wars, only to go down in the battle of life with their own kind. Their own people. Their own Government. The Government they fought for.

"They did not march in the light of day. They marched in darkness. The moving-picture record of the march of the 5,000 ghosts will be dim and obscure, if any at all.

"That's why they marched at night, with their shoes worn thin and their boots run down at the heel. They marched without hats, many of them because they have no hats. Many were without coats.

"But they were clean-shaven, every man of them. And the shirts they wore, though patched and torn and thin and cheap, were clean from their own washing.

"And they marched, proud and unashamed, carrying the flag they fought for."

One hundred thousand watched this strange demonstration of the "Bonus Expeditionary Forces," whose members already had alarmed or angered many officials, legislators and editors by congregating at Washington, but also had won the plaudits of a few.

"First came the colors and pro-bonus banners of the massed units," writes the correspondent of *The New York Times,* "and after them, in a place of honor, the veterans who had received medals for heroism. There were scores of these."

And now the *Washington Post* gives us a glimpse of the parade:

"Gone was the jauntiness that everyone saw in these men when they marched away to the World War. Many of them limped, seemed tired, and the rigors of distress were written hard into their sun-baked faces.

"Their thoughts were written on the placards they carried: 'Remember 1917-1918—Pay the Bonus Now,' 'Pay the Bonus,' 'We Want the Bonus,' 'Here We Stay, till the Bonus They Pay,' 'Suppose the Kaiser Had Won the War? Would the Bonus Have Paid the Bill?'

"On and on the marchers stepped. More banners. 'Millions for War—Not One Cent for the Hungry Vets,' 'Remember November,' 'No Bonus—No Votes,' 'Who Won the War? We Haven't Won Anything.'

"Their leaders have harangued them throughout the day with the watchwords—'Every man walk who can, and carry those who can't.'

"Their leaders told them to help police should an outbreak occur."

For the police had received reports that communists were planning a fight. But nothing happened then.

The situation on the Washington "front" was

## "The 'Ghost Parade' . . ." *(continued)*

complex and rapidly becoming more so. Over thousands of veterans were converging on the capital from all points of the compass. Here and there, state and local authorities helped them on their way. Those already on the ground were sleeping in hastily built shacks, or in the open, on the sun-baked mud flats of south Washington.

Divided into six regiments, they were maintaining military discipline, and the chief rules were: "No panhandling; no liquor; no radical talk; stay until we get paid."

Although the men were getting but two three-cent meals a day, the "army's" money was running out. Police had served notice that they must leave the city on a certain day, and that they would be given a 50-mile ride to start them back home. They had refused to go. Meanwhile, they were lobbying intensively, doing their utmost to win the bonus votes of congressmen.

But the payment of their 1945 adjusted compensation certificates now, involving the expenditure of $2.4 billion, would be disastrous, according to the Administration.

This bonus march is "a disgrace to the name of veteran," declares the *Sacramento Bee,* and "the country is in no mood to be coerced in this fashion." Agreeing, the *Springfield Union* asserts that "the country has not yet sunk to the level of mob rule."

"If disorder and bloodshed should ensue," says the *Washington Post,* "the responsibility will rest primarily upon the individuals in Congress who have deliberately misled the veterans."

"It requires no army to bring honest and fair legislation out of Washington," remarks the *Omaha World-Herald.* "If it did require an army, then free government would be lost, and we should live no longer by law, but by ukase."

A bonus, many papers point out, would be in the interest of a special class, while hundreds of thousands of others also are unemployed.

"Nothing is too good for the veteran actually disabled in the war," asserts the *Boston Herald,* "and for the dependents of those who gave 'the last full measure of devotion,' but this bonus is a malicious raid."

An interesting summary of what the United States has done for its veterans in comparison with other countries is provided by the *New Haven Register:*

"This year's American Relief Bill for ex-soldiers is $1,072,064,527. Great Britain, France, Italy, Canada, and Germany combined will spend on their veterans' relief $891,190,360. For the approximately 34 million men mobilized by all these countries, about 10 percent less is being spent than for the approximately four million men mobilized by the United States.

"This year's American Relief Bill for the ex-soldiers shakes down to about $223 for every man mobilized. Great Britain's bill averages down to about $26 per man. France's payments will be about $33 per man. And the most generous of the lot of those principal belligerents is Canada, which will give out about $98 per man on the basis of the number mobilized to fight in the allied forces.

"With such comparisons in mind, it is impossible to become much bothered about the serious grounds these bonus-hikers have for their demands for more cash. The comparisons are not absolutely parallel in all ways. Payments have taken different forms in the different countries; scales vary, and other considerations besides cash outlays enter in the question. But on the whole, such differences add to, not detract from, the impropriety of the American bonus-hikers' demands."

## "Remarkable Remarks," *Outlook* and *Independent*, January 7, 1931:

The trying experiences through which we are passing may ultimately be a fine thing for us.
—Thomas W. Lamont

If we do not get what we want, we probably get more of what we ought to have.
—Calvin Coolidge

I believe that the remedy for unemployment is employment.
—Charles H. Tuttle

There have been a great number of wars, but the fight for prohibition means more to me than all the wars we have fought, and it should mean the same to every American.
—Thomas A. Edison

Reform in general is all right. Individual reformers are all hell.
—Sinclair Lewis

At heart, "Red" [Sinclair] Lewis is almost fanatical in his idealism and his evangelism.
—Prof. William Lyon Phelps

I do not care for money, and owe to the somewhat vainglorious boast of never having consciously written a line with any thought of its marketability.
—George Jean Nathan

In women, courage and a majority of the other good qualities are more highly developed than in men. Conceit, which is useful because it encourages us, keeps men from knowing it.
—Arthur Brisbane

No other business in New York is so in need of the feminine touch as the taxi industry.
—O. O. McIntyre

The aristocratic look in the eyes of a Pekingese is not convincing evidence that he is free from fleas. He may be just too refined to scratch.
—Roy W. Howard

**No. 1018N. Pillow Slips.** Lovely Morning-Glory pattern in simple cutwork. Design stamped on ready-made pillow slips, 42-by-36 inches, with hemstitched hem. Price per pair, stamped, **69 cents.** Floss to embroider, 24 cents.
**Send to NEEDLECRAFT MAGAZINE, Augusta, Maine**

## 1937 PROFILE

## FIGHTING FOR PEACE

### Civilian

Adele Morrison has found new freedom and excitement by joining with other students at the Colby Junior College for Women in fighting for peace through the Emergency Peace Campaign.

### Life at Home

- Adele Morrison was crushed when her mother told her—very firmly—that she would be attending Colby Junior College for Women and not the University of New Hampshire as she had planned.
- She knew that her mother's talk about "a more stable environment" was code for little social life and no boys.
- When she appealed to her father, he deferred; he was late for a business meeting.
- Where his children are concerned, he is content with his role as provider, generally agreeing with his wife's decisions.
- Occasionally—but only occasionally—he takes a stand and demonstrates he is the real seat of power in the house.
- This was not to be one of those times.
- Jack Morrison had worked hard to rise from being a car mechanic to owning one of the largest car dealerships in Manchester, New Hampshire.
- He liked to describe himself as the embodiment of the American dream.
- After all, he had achieved his life goals: a brick, two-story home, a new car every three years, and all his children with college degrees—especially the three boys.
- And now that he is able to be active in the Optimist Club and donate regularly to the church, the rumors concerning his involvement with liquor bootlegging from nearby Canada during Prohibition are dying down.

*Adele Morrison is an advocate for peace.*

Guns will make us powerful; butter will only make us fat.
—Hermann Goering, 1936 radio address

Let the PEOPLE VOTE ON WAR! Who else can decide so momentous a question? Write your Congressman!

WHAT ARE YOU GOING TO DO ABOUT IT?

THE CASE FOR CONSTRUCTIVE PEACE

BY ALDOUS HUXLEY

PRICE THREEPENCE

## Life at Work

- Adele Morrison dissolved into tears watching her parents drive away from Colby Junior College for Women that first day.
- It was bad enough that her three brothers and all her friends got to attend the University of New Hampshire, but Colby was located in New London, close to nothing but cows.
- Even when classes were under way, Adele felt miserable, spending considerable time composing desperate, tear-stained letters to her friends at the University.
- Her roommate is a quiet, deeply religious girl from near Boston named Evelyn, who frequently asks Adele to participate in activities of the "Commission."
- Adele had heard that the group was involved with the peace movement, but didn't care; she wanted out of Colby, and although war was bad, it wasn't her problem.
- The closest Adele had come to politics was hearing her parents discuss the chances that Franklin Roosevelt will be defeated by a good Republican before he names himself dictator.
- For years, she has heard that the president is a dangerous man, destined to give away America's wealth—and eventually its freedom.
- She also knew from listening to her father that most peace activists were at least leftists, if not outright communists.
- Yet, it was equally obvious that the Commission was one of the most active groups on campus.
- When Adele accompanied Evelyn to her first discussion group gathering of the Commission, she realized it was populated by girls considered to be campus leaders.
- The meeting turned out to be primarily a strategy session for the student mass meeting planned for November 11, Armistice Day.
- The goal was for students to speak about peace to various groups of townspeople.
- The Commission, as it turns out, is one of more than 150 campus units of the Emergency Peace Campaign.
- The campaign got its start in late 1935 after the American Friends Service Committee attracted the involvement of a number of prominent Americans, including First Lady Eleanor Roosevelt and Admiral Byrd, the polar explorer.

- Conceived as a two-year program, its goal is to assure United States neutrality in the event of another European war.
- The American Service Committee preaches that the use of American armed forces should be restricted to defending U.S. territory.
- Its opposition to war is mixed with a heavy dose of isolationism and a strong anti-communist outlook.
- The Emergency Peace Campaign's primary, short-term goal is educating Americans on the horrors of war; its long-range plan is a grass roots foundation that can impact national policy.
- The passion of the speakers immediately captured Adele's attention.
- Even her roommate Evelyn seemed to shed her shyness when she spoke to the gathering of her unflinching fervor for peace through the work of the Commission.
- Back in their dorm room, Evelyn shared with Adele some tracts filled with figures and pictures on the horrors of the Great War and the revolution under way in Spain.
- Over the next several days, Adele read everything available on war and peace.
- A couple of student leaders are mentoring Adele, taking her on walks to extol the importance of their work.
- Adele is now convinced that working with the Commission is the most important thing she can do; if she can help shape a little community's attitude about peace, anything is possible in the wider world.
- She is so convinced of her mission, Adele is no longer concerned what her parents might think.
- Besides, once her mother learned that girls from nice families were talking about peace, all would be fine.
- Adele quickly became active in speaking at local town meetings.
- Never shy about speaking in public, Adele is on fire now that she has something important to say.
- Almost the entire student body of 300 girls showed up at the main building on Armistice Day.
- Adele felt wonderful when her speech received enthusiastic applause.

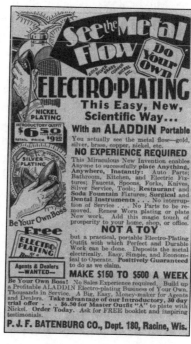

- Next, the Colby Commission held a joint meeting with the Dartmouth Commission to develop plans to reach much of western New Hampshire.
- Several of the Dartmouth boys, whom Adele had been dying to meet months ago, asked her out.
- Surprising even herself, she decided she did not have time to socialize; boys would have to wait.
- Her room is adorned with pictures of women peace activists such as Eleanor Roosevelt and Jane Addams.
- She is still not exactly sure why she took them down when her father and mother came to visit.
- Maybe it was because she told her mother that day she was not coming home for the summer, but would instead be teaching vacation school through the Commission in a town near the college.
- To further the peace effort, the summer school combines fun and discussions of world affairs.
- Five days a week, the teachers assemble their charges, averaging 75 each day, at the town meeting hall, where they entertain the students with traditional activities such as crafts, games and music.
- Adele is even trying her hand at the piano after years of being out of practice.
- The key element of the program is the importance of world peace, imparted through discussions, plays, dances, movies and study projects, some of which come from the national office, while others are being developed by Adele and her fellow teachers.
- As the summer draws to a close, Adele is delighted by their work.
- During an exhibition for the town, her students showed their handiwork, sang songs and performed skits—many on the subject of peace.
- The reception among students and townspeople alike was overwhelmingly enthusiastic; even members of the local American Legion Post applauded with gusto.

### Life in the Community: New London, New Hampshire

- New London, 1,300 feet up in the Sunapee hills of New Hampshire, boasts 1,000 residents, including the 300 women of Colby College.
- The community is 100 miles from Boston, 40 miles from Concord, and eight miles from the railroad.
- New London is clustered along both sides of an elm-shaded main street and includes a white-spire church, a brick town hall, an inn, which once served stagecoach travelers, and a war memorial.
- Except for the growth at the college, New London has changed little in three generations.

## "Who Wants Peace?" Dorothy Thompson, *Survey Graphic*, February 1937:

More than any other movement in the United States, that represented by the peace societies is a cross-section of the American mind. At some point it touches all of American liberal opinion, some of the conservative, and much of the radical. For it starts with a premise that few dispute: Peace is the desideratum of all political activity; the condition of freedom, the necessity of sound prosperity, the parent of culture, the demand of orderly social progress.

On the side of peace, therefore, are not only those who hate uniforms and militarism as a primary cause of war, but those who think that peace depends upon international armament against aggressors; for peace, are those who believe that there will be wars until national sovereignties are eliminated in a socialistically organized world, and those who think war will end when every nation has equality. On the side of peace are those who believe wars can be quarantined, and those who think that neutrality is immoral. The result is usually coupled in the mind of its advocate with something else: "Peace and Freedom, against War and Fascism."

**The Only Way We Can Save Her**

Carey Orr. *The Tribune* (Chicago), 1939.

*Peace advocates believe America will be harmed by war, an angry Europe and leaders like Joseph Stalin.*

- Garages for automobiles exist alongside a large and busy livery stable.
- A chain store is located in New London, but part of it remains dominated by yard goods, house dresses and notions.
- Residents pride themselves on the number of out-of-town papers read in the city and how hard the radio is worked for information.
- The Emergency Peace Campaign became part of the fabric of community discussion in 1936.
- In late 1935, the American Friends Service Committee and other pacifists such as Devere Allen, Frederick J. Libby, Ray Newton, John Nevin Sayre and E. Raymond Wilson initiated the Emergency Peace Campaign, a nationwide program to keep the United States out of war and to promote world peace.
- Its focus included a desire to promote world peace through strengthening pacifist alternatives to armed conflict, bringing about political and economic changes as essential to a just and peaceable world order, and recruiting in one dynamic movement all organizations determined not to approve of or participate in war.

## HISTORICAL SNAPSHOT
# 1937

- Scottsboro defendant Clarence Norris was sentenced to death for the third time on a charge of rape
- As the depression continued, unemployment reached 14.3 percent
- Howard Hughes flew from Los Angeles to Newark in a record seven hours, 28 minutes and five seconds
- The crash of the dirigible *Hindenburg,* witnessed by hundreds who had come to see its landing at Lakehurst, New Jersey, killed 38 people
- Spam was introduced by George A. Hormel & Company
- President Franklin D. Roosevelt called for an investigation of "immoral" tax evasion by the wealthy
- The principle of a minimum wage for women was upheld by the United States Supreme Court
- General Motors introduced the automatic transmission for automobiles
- Radio quiz shows grew in popularity, including "Melody Puzzles," "Professor Quiz," "Spelling Bee" and "Uncle Jim's Question Bee"
- "Nice Work if You Can Get It," "Whistle While You Work" and "The Lady Is a Tramp" were all popular songs
- Nylon, Santa Claus school, the trampoline, Pepperidge Farm and the Lincoln Tunnel all made their first appearance
- Several thousand Americans, including authors Dorothy Parker, John Dos Passos, Ernest Hemingway, Malcolm Cowley and Upton Sinclair, joined the Abraham Lincoln Brigade to fight with the Loyalists against fascist-supported Franco forces
- Spinach growers erected a statue to Popeye in Wisconsin
- John D. Rockefeller died, leaving an estate of approximately $1 billion
- *Popular Photography* magazine began publication
- After 70 years of failure, the first successful instant coffee was formulated by the Nestlé Company
- A *Harper's Monthly* article concluded that today's young people behaved "without thought of social responsibility"
- Numerous federal parks and fish and game sanctuaries were set up by the National Park Service, which set aside some 600,000 acres
- A revolt against progressive education was under way, led by Robert M. Hutchins, president of the University of Chicago
- Pro-Nazi Bund societies were forming in Germany, ostensibly devoted to social and athletic pursuits
- Studies showed that people were spending 4.5 hours daily listening to the radio
- A *Fortune* magazine story reported, "As for sex...the campus takes it more casually than it did 10 years ago. . . . It is news that it is no longer news"
- *Life* magazine reported that one out of 10 Americans had a tattoo
- Icemen made regular deliveries to more than 50 percent of middle-class households

## "CCC Speeds Up: Spring Brings Renewed Activity in 2,000 Camps," *Grit*, April 18, 1937:

The advent of spring sees work swinging into full stride in about 2,000 camps of the Civilian Conservation Corps scattered across the nation, while Congress studies a proposal that the corps be made a permanent arm of the federal government.

The act of Congress under which the corps has been operating for four years expires June 30. President Roosevelt has asked Congress to make the CCC permanent, with an enrollment of 300,000 young men and veterans.

On a permanent basis, the corps would continue indefinitely its program of reforestation, road building, and park development, it is explained.

The CCC has been one of the least criticized "New Deal" agencies, although charges have been made that the work it has done has not justified its cost, and assertions have been heard that politics has been allowed to interfere with the direction of the corps. . . .

The cost per man of the CCC is estimated at about $1,000 a year. Thus, a permanent corps would cost $300,000 annually to maintain.

The record of the CCC is one of almost staggering figures.

It has provided temporary jobs for two million men, including men recruited from cities and towns, war veterans and Indians.

Out of their $30 monthly pay, enrollees in the corps have sent some $360 million to their families. Each member of the corps is required to send a percentage of his pay to his home.

Two thousand camps have been established in all parts of the country, with an average of about 200 men in each camp now in operation.

Enlistments are limited to a period of six months, but an enrollee is permitted to enlist once.

*The CCC has been one of the least criticized of the New Deal agencies.*

*In England, children prepare for war.*

"I have seen war. I have seen war on land and sea. I have seen blood running from the wounded. I have seen men coughing out their gassed lungs. I have seen the dead in the mud. I have seen cities destroyed. I have seen 200 limping; exhausted men come out of the line—the survivors of a regiment of 1,000 that went forward 48 hours before. I have seen children starving. I have seen the agony of mothers and wives. I hate war."

—President Franklin D. Roosevelt, during an appearance in August 1936 in the great outdoor pavilion at Chautauqua, New York, where William Jennings Bryan had often preached pacifism before America entered World War I

### Selected Prices

| | |
|---|---|
| Corset, Maternity | $2.98 |
| Dog Food, per Eight Pounds | $1.00 |
| Fishing Reel | $8.25 |
| Hamburger, per Pound | $0.24 |
| Hotel Room, Copley Plaza Boston, per Night | $4.00 |
| Laundry Cleaning for 15 Pounds Damp Wash | $0.49 |
| Light Bulb, 150-Watt | $0.20 |
| Pitchfork, 11 Tines | $1.35 |
| Pocket Telescope | $1.00 |
| Radio, Full-Size | $16.50 |
| Stockings, Silk | $0.21 |
| Table Tennis Set, Four-Paddle | $2.95 |
| Table, 45"x36" Gateleg | $8.69 |
| Tire, Goodyear All-Weather | $15.55 |
| Traveler's Checks, American Express, per $100 | $0.75 |

## "In the Name of Peace," William Frederick Bigelow, *Good Housekeeping*, December 1939:

Looking back over the records, we find that on this page, 25 years ago, we advocated a women's war upon war. The First World War was then digging in for its long and bloody struggle, but it had already put an end to what had been called the "Women's War"—fight for suffrage. In England, particularly, this fight had been a bitter one, or so it seemed to a world that took the fabled gaiety of Vienna as something to emulate, ignoring sights and sounds that it did not care to understand. It was rude of women to make such a fuss over the vote in the mistaken belief that they could make the world better and safer if they had it. Some of the things the women had done had shocked the same complacent world. They had "battled" with the police; they had hurled stones through windows; they had chained themselves to grating, from which they had been removed forcibly, screaming and scratching. Such violence—in a world that seemed all right, until an Austrian archduke went motoring on a Sunday morning.

We said then: "Now the Women's War is at a truce because a men's war is on, and when men fight, everything else has to be subordinated to that business. Never mind the broken hearts and the mangled, bleeding bodies; without them a man's war would be a fizzle. The more blood is shed, the greater the glory of the victor. Some of the most marvelous devices of this wonderful age of invention have only one purpose, the wholesale destruction of men in war, and day by day the evidence grows that the devices are working devilishly well. . . ."

Women, some women, had seen the menace in the world's bristling guns, and were hoping they could somehow be kept silent. But "it will never come" had been the denial for a generation of Europe's preparation for war: It would be too horrible to contemplate. But it did come, and as it grew in intensity and spread its hatreds over the world, people said hopefully, "It will be the last great war." To that we replied: "Why will it be the last great war? Not because of the horror or the carnage or the cost of it. Other wars have been relatively as great, and still men fight. If this really is, as some say, a war against war, if the battled flags go from the last red field in this conflict to be forever furled, it will be because a finer, completer democracy than we have yet known is seeded in it—a democracy that shall not arbitrarily reduce to voicelessness the mothers of its men, but shall take counsel of them, whether they will permit the doing of anything that kills men or debauches them or makes them less than free."

And the Second World War came—with everyone aware of its cost, of its uselessness, of the brutality it would let loose. It came because it is the perfect flowing of the seeds sown in the first one—seeded, not of democracy, whose fruitage would be some sort of brotherhood of man, but seeds of vindictiveness, of despair, of worldwide economic confusion. It—this Second World War—will end with the same old policies strengthened, with Hate sitting at the head of the council table and everything taught by the last war forgotten. Men will say, "We did not go far enough before; this time we will make harsher terms and enforce them."

We hope the United States sits at that council table—not, please God, as a participant in the war, but as one nation wise enough, unbiased enough to make our plea for a lasting peace not go again unheeded. We shall strengthen our position, if, as the conflict drags on its bloody, costly way, we make it clear we are unalterably opposed to war—this war or any other—and will not be drawn in unless we are forced to defend ourselves. This may not be so easy as it sounds, for emotions are easily aroused, and we should be building up a wall of calm determination that cannot easily be broken down. And to that task we call the Women of America. Peace for our country is in their hands; if they will grasp it firmly, they can assure it. Let them be propagandists for peace; here, there, and everywhere let them talk peace. And with their talk let them mingle prayers for peace. And let them make sure that their senators and congressmen know that they are working and praying, praying and working. With these two powerful weapons—propaganda and prayer—at their command, our women can make peace seem, as it really is, so precious that we as a nation will do our best to keep it.

## "Peace, Inc.," Stanley High, *Saturday Evening Post*, March 1938:

When Andrew Carnegie set aside the income from $10 million worth of first-mortgage bonds to be used "to hasten the abolition of war," it looked as though that might be enough. The year was 1910 and the prevalent opinion seemed to be that the abolition of war was a pushover. It was only the hastening of it that required so munificent a gift. "When war is abolished," Mr. Carnegie wrote to his trustees, "please consider what is the next most degrading evil."

Mr. Carnegie's trustees have not yet had to come to grips with that problem. The funds at their disposal have grown through the years. In 1938 their expenditures for peace will total more than $800,000. But the prospect that they can close out their account with war and move on to the next evil is as remote as ever. At present there appears to be nothing permanent about peace, save the quest for it.

As far as the quest for it is concerned, that undoubtedly has come to stay. The success of the peace movement in the United States is debatable. But since the war, it has espoused many important causes. From the League of Nations to the World Court and disarmament, it has gone down to defeat almost every one of them. Its major objective has not changed. But every year, for at least the last 10 years, it has become more distant. And yet, for all this almost unbroken record of setbacks, the peace movement, as distinguished from peace, has not been set back. On the contrary, the state of its health is probably better at present than at any

time since this holy aspiration became a budgeted crusade. . . .

There are, for one thing, more peace organizations today. There is an organization for every conceivable taste and every known shade of opinion from the Youth Communist League, which considers itself a political body but probably is not, to the Foreign Policy Association, which does not consider itself a political body, but undoubtedly is. The National Peace Conference—which aims to endow the movement with some coordination—lists 40 participating organizations on its letterhead. To the left and right of these 40 there are probably 20 more that find the program of the National Peace Conference too conservative or not conservative enough. That means a minimum of 60 organizations devoted, in whole or in part, to the business of peace—which is unquestionably the largest number of organizations devoted to a single reform in the whole history of moral uplift. . . .

It is the radio that has been the greatest boon to the budgets of the peace movement. It is not easy for the program director of a local radio station—or, for that matter, of a network of stations—to refuse a request for free time on the air for a cause so undeniably worthy as peace. To refuse such a request is to run the risk of being branded unfriendly to the cause and thereby to incur the hostility of the good, but often exceedingly articulate, people who sponsor. Radio executives are peculiarly sensitive to such risks. The result is that peace goes on the air often and extensively.

# 1939 NEWS FEATURE

**"Germany, Background for the War,"** *Time*, **May 22, 1939:**

Wehrwirtschaft. As of the spring of 1939, the country which balances Europe's fate on its brown back is Nazi Germany. At the heart of the question of whether Europe will have war or peace lies the riddle not of Germany's military might or expanding totalitarian ideology, but of Germany's internal economy. Deliberately geared for war for the past five years, is it an economy that can withstand peace? Is further territorial expansion a necessity for Germany's economic survival? And if that expansion should bring Germany into armed conflict, could the economy of the Third Reich withstand a prolonged war?

Bismark to Stinnes. In 1913, Kaiser Wilhelm II received from the Association for International Conciliation congratulations on his reign of peace. Within the next 25 years, Germany had fought the greatest war in history, seen its Kaiser flee to Holland, gone through the most harrowing political, social and economic disorders in modern times, and emerged the scar-covered bully-boy of the world. The Germany of Kaiser Wilhelm's day differs from the Germany of Adolf Hitler's day in that it had 18,778,491 fewer people and 50,545 fewer square miles in Europe. Aggrandizer Hitler's Germany does not to date possess Kaiser Wilhelm's Germany's African and Asiatic colonies, but since these accounted for less than five percent of prewar Germany's export and import trade, they are not the major factors in the altered economic picture.

The salient fact about Germany then and now remains that she has few natural resources except for her people. In important raw materials, Germany has an exportable surplus of only two things: coal and chemicals. With a few industries (such as the electrical and dyestuff industries), the Germans have worked wonders. But ever since Germany ceased after 1871 to be a collection of medieval agrarian principalities, she has had to import wool, cotton, rubber, metals, wood, oil and foodstuffs from beyond her territory.

Pragmatic economists have pointed out that fascism is a reflex of the lean and bony ridges and sandy or sparse soil of Central Europe. Socialists insist that fascism is not inevitable anywhere, and that a different system of property, political and consequent international relations would result in plenty for the German people even though their soil and raw materials are poor. But whatever the truth of the socialist argument, it is ax-

iomatic that a nation's total well-being under any economic system is limited by two things: the nature of the land and what is under the land, and the number and ingenuity of the population. A nation of clever and ambitious people with scant natural resources has but one recourse: It must sell its services by fabricating and transporting raw materials supplied by others. The economic history of Germany since the third quarter of the last century has been the history of a people consciously and steadfastly steered by their State to sell services. "We must export," recently said Herr Hitler, a legitimate heir to this tradition, "or die."

In the rush to catch up to western industrial powers, Germany has tried ever since 1871 to syncopate history. A patron saint among German economists is Friedrich List, who spent seven years in the U.S., learned to admire Alexander Hamilton's protectionist philosophy and went home to write his *National System of Political Economy* (1841). While Prussia was busy consolidating the German nation by successive wars with Denmark, Austria and France, no one paid much attention to List. But after 1871, he provided justification for what Aggrandizer Bismarck wanted to do.

An aristocratic landowner from Pomerania in the backward German east, Bismarck cared little for the doctrines of economic freedom from feudal interference that were popular in free-trade England. He made German capitalism an "assisted" capitalism, far more consciously purposeful than the economic systems of the West. Price-fixing and market-sharing cartels were encouraged; protection was granted to both agriculture and industry. The Prussian railroads were bought for the Prussian State, and the social democratic trade unions were won over to the paternalistic system partly because of the general prewar prosperity and partly because Bismarck had introduced sickness, accident and old-age insurance for wage earners.

By the time of the World War, the German steel cartel, or *Stahlwerksverband,* which included the Krupp armament works, was practically co-terminus with the entire German steel industry. Fettered at home, competition was directed outward against the industries of other nations; and throughout Germany the professors were quarreling over the concepts of State Socialism and State Capitalism, and wondering which was which. Meanwhile, the Kaiser and court were fearful that the Socialists in the Reichstag (the Social Democratic party had 112 seats out of 397 in 1912) might forget their "revisionist" doctrines and adopt the naked class war propounded by Karl Marx. Lacking internal flexibility and with the shaky Austro-Hungarian Empire messing up the possibilities of progress to the east, the German economic system had seemingly reached its limits of growth as far back as 1914; Germany's "assisted capitalism" had run head-on into Germany's poverty of resources—a circumstance which was to have an ominous parallel 25 years later.

Before the World War, Germany was a rich creditor nation, with an estimated 35 billion marks invested abroad. Although she imported more than she exported, income from this overseas capital and revenues from a merchant marine second only to England's were more than enough to make up the difference. To back a note circulation of 1.8 billion marks, the Reichsbank held 1.37 billion marks in gold—double the coverage considered normal in 1914. Another two billion marks in gold currency were in circulation among the people. These liquid reserves made it easy for Germany to market her war bonds— and had she won, there would never have been an inflation as insane as that of 1923.

As it was, defeat gutted the German economy. Colonies, working capital, merchant marine, chattel and domestic animals were taken by the Allies. Lorraine's minette iron ore, historic complement to Ruhr coking coal, reverted to France. Some of the gold had gone for raw materials, shipped in via Holland and Scandinavia, and the rest went after the war in the year in which Germany could get no credit. A strained industrial machine deteriorated still further during the chaotic years of sporadic revolution and French occupation of the Ruhr, and when the inflation came there were no marginal producers to be jogged into action by the rise in prices. So the rise in prices failed to stimulate increased production of real wealth. It worked only to impoverish the nation by making its money valueless.

In 1933, the sinister fruits of 1923 were finally plucked by Hitler, who spent the stabilization year of 1924 in jail working on *Mein Kampf*. The appeal of the dynamic jailbird, however, fell flat throughout the late '20's, for a still democratic Germany was able to buy herself five years of Indian summer prosperity with the aid of $1.377 billion bor-

rowed from the U.S. and $2.373 billion from the rest of the world, chiefly Great Britain. The equivalent of two-thirds of the borrowed funds went out again as reparation payments, but the rest was spent to finance a local boom. Those were the fat years in which Germany revamped her industrial machine, built 1,432,843 (1926-30) houses, and dotted her cities with parks, athletic stadia, modernistic churches, skyscrapers, new city halls, post offices and monuments.

The depression called a halt to all that. And with other nations holding up their internal price levels by prohibitive tariffs, import quotas and preference systems, the German exporter began to lose hope that he would ever recover. Currency devaluation in England, Japan and the U.S. compounded the difficulties, for changed relations in the value of money left the German price level too high to appeal to the foreign buyer. And the Germans themselves did not dare tinker with the mark to meet the competition in depreciation. Memories of the 1923 inflation were too strong.

Enter the Nazis. Unable to compete abroad, the German business class cried weakly for a directing savior. In their happiest times they had always had one. The immediate pre-Hitler years were the years of the phenomenon of "tired capitalism"; the German cartelized business structure, which was inextricably merged with five big banks, did not know the rules of intramural competition. Then came the first Nazi experiments with a rigidly controlled system, with businessmen retrained as managers in their own plants, but with the government allocating raw materials, dictating wages and prices, and limiting and forcing new investments in accordance with Nazi conceptions of national welfare. Capital surpluses went into armaments; the Nazis ceased to build houses. The peasant was bound to his land by laws prohibiting the sale or mortgaging of hereditary homesteads, and farm production was indirectly managed through price-fixing boards. The great drive of *Wehrwirtschaft,* or war economy, was on the way.

During the World War, Walther Rathenau, industrialist and economist, had taken hold of the German economic machine and coordinated it after the fashion of Bernard M. Baruch's later U.S. War Industries Board. A Jew, Rathenau was assassinated after the war by anti-Semitic, anti-liberal nationalists. But Rathenau's secret dream of a completely rationalized and goosestep-clicking German industry was remembered by some of his young disciples who became Nazis. Hitler's first and second Four-Year Plans owe more to Rathenau's social thinking than any Nazi would dare to admit.

Schacht to Funk. Even before Hitler, the Germans had been forced to experiment with foreign exchange control. With exports falling in 1933, Hjalmar Horace Greeley Schacht, head of the Nazified Reichsbank, first prohibited the transfer of interest on German foreign debts and then evolved a system of control boards to balance imports and exports. Out of these equilibrist schemes grew the blocked currency accounts and the barter devices, with the Germans paying foreign exporters in special marks good only for German goods at a price lower than the internal price level. Boycotts and currency difficulties kept lopping off chunks of normal German trade with England, the U.S., and Soviet Russia, but export subsidies to the extent of 30 percent of the value of all German exports enabled Nazi businessmen to quote speciously attractive prices to the Balkans and South America, regions with surpluses of grain, tobacco, oil, cotton, coffee and cocoa. . . .

The overall German standard of living has, however, fallen by at least 20 percent since the depression. And if extended work hours, decreased quality of goods and the recent failure to build houses or to replace obsolescent railroad equipment are considered, the decline has been even more precipitous. Money that formerly went into dwellings and the making of machines for producing articles that could be enjoyed is now funneled off by government commands into industrially sterile armaments and showy public monuments. Before the War only five percent of the national income was spent on armaments—and that was a time when Colonel Haus was reporting that Berlin presented a spectacle of "militarism run stark mad." Today, one-fourth of the national income goes for guns, fortresses and stadia for the self-glorification of the Nazi party meetings.

By comparison with 1932 standards, the Nazis have raised the level of overall German consumption. But immediate consumption (which omits money spent for housing construction) is still 10 percent below that of 1927. Moreover, Nazi economists themselves predict a decline of purchasing power for this year. The regime gains acquiescence from the majority because the industrial working class (approximately 40 percent of the population) has lost relatively less income than the upper, upper middle and lower middle classes—and with the unemployed now at work the class as a whole has gained. The farmers (approximately 21 percent of the population) receive about what they were getting per capita in 1927. Hence, it can be argued that Nazism has a mass base, even though forced contributions (party dues, winter relief, etc.) subtract considerably from workers' incomes. The decline in quality is most noticeable in upper and middle class goods; working class goods are maintained in comparative quality and abundance. The German lower class diet has always been heavily weighted with potatoes, cabbage and bread, and in consequence working class food standards have not had very much room in which to fall. The one real gain the "little man" in Germany has over his 1932 condition is assurance of employment.

Enter Goering. Since General Goering took control of the entire German economy in 1936, the Nazis have made some progress towards their goal of wartime self-sufficiency in Central and Eastern Europe. Low-grade iron ores are being worked by the state-owned Hermann Goering Iron Works; by 1940, the Nazis expect that perhaps 35 percent of the iron consumption of greater Germany will be supplied from domestic sources. Aluminum from bauxite imported from Hungary and the Balkans is supplementing heavier metals, such as copper and nickel. Artificial rubber sufficient for 25 to 30 percent of the peacetime rubber requirements is being conjured out of limestone and coal.

Welfare and Warfare. Yet, though Reich chemists are worked night and day, Germany is less able today to support a long war than she was in 1914. With

Lorraine gone, the iron ore supply is not enough. The available soil, even including the Bohemian and what could be seized in Poland, Hungary and Rumania, is not sufficient to produce both fodder crops for the cattle and breadstuffs, sugar beets, potatoes, vegetables, flax and hemp for the 152,300,000 population of a middle European empire. Intensive grain cultivation operations are now being set up in East Prussia, but most of the acres available for agricultural production are even now under intensive cultivation.

On the whole, Germany's agricultural situation is no better and no worse than it was in 1914. But one thing has changed very much for the worse: the fuel oil needs for a modern mechanized army and air service. In the event of a major war, Germany will need 15 to 20 million tons of oil each year. The entire annual yield of the nearby Rumanian fields, assuming Germany could and would quickly take Rumania through Hungary, is short seven million tons, and synthetic production in Germany can hardly exceed a million tons. Furthermore, the number one truism of writers on military problems is that the next long war will be won by the nation with the greatest industrial potential behind the lines. The ability to mass-produce and to service guns, tanks, planes, ships and motors will, so the military theoreticians predict, be the crucial factor. Her lack of home metallurgical supplies would indicate that here, too, a warring Germany would be behind the eight ball.

In deliberately abandoning an economy of welfare—in which, as in the richer democracies, a variety of goods is produced for universal consumption and the productive machinery is merely tapped, not regimented, for the use or revenue of the State—for an economy of warfare, Germany has developed out of her economic past a new and unique type of economy. The Italians have, to a lesser extent, followed the same method, and the eagerly imitative Japanese have copied Nazi Procedure since their Chinese Adventure.

The Nazis' economic invention has organized Germany from top to bottom for war. The "unemployed" have been at work for years on strategic roads, airports and military structures. The farmer has been directed to produce cheap bulk crops for the masses instead of money-making high-quality vegetables and fats, and priority in raw materials has gone either to the armaments makers or to the export manufacturers, who bring in needed foreign exchange which can be turned into imported materials of military value. But the Nazi effort is a frenzied effort to build out an insufficient natural base, and indications are that, like German efforts in the past, it is probably doomed to splinter on the harsh facts of Central European geography.

It is possible that, with belt-tightening and abandonment of the 25 percent of German effort now going into armament and public works, Germany could sell its services to a mollified world and live at home. Given a decade of peace, the ability of the Nazis to remain in power rests partly on psychological factors (how many economic sacrifices the German people will bear) and partly on economic factors (how high a standard of living Nazi economics can give). Continued "bloodless" victories over the races of Eastern Europe will increase Germany's economic self-sufficiency, but at the cost of new political difficulties of a sort that led to the disintegration of old Austria-Hungary.

Moreover, the need for industrial and military manpower is draining the German farms of needed labor, and hopelessness is spreading in the rural villages. In the old Reich alone, the number of male farm workers has fallen by 800,000—which adds to the burden of farm women and children. Peasants have traditionally been the backbone of the State in Central Europe; and if the peasantry becomes disaffected, a war-making Nazi government might find itself defeated on the field of morale. The chances of Germany's winning a long war are even slimmer in view of one further factor which lies outside of Germany or Germany's economy: the German lines of communication are even more vulnerable than Britain's. The British Isles front has many coastal miles on the open ocean, while Germany's ports are all on semi-landlocked seas. During the World War the British effectively blockaded Germany and starved her by keeping the fleet in readiness in the home waters.

The moral: If she fights soon, Germany, unless she can team up with Russia, must win by a *Blitzkrieg,* or "lightning war," or she will lose, as in 1914-18, to the silent pressure of human and industrial starvation and the British fleet. If she chooses to postpone war, she must keep her people imbued with the belief that continued belt-tightening now will mean a stronger industrial machine—and a reversion to a welfare economy—later on.

# 1940–1949

During the turbulent World War II years, Americans were consumed with the national war effort and recovery. Slow at first to mobilize before the growing threat of war from Germany and Japan, America responded forcefully to the Japanese bombing of Pearl Harbor in December 1941. People from every social stratum either signed up for the military or went to work supplying the military machine. Children collected scrap and planted the Victory Gardens that symbolized America's willingness to do anything to defeat the Nazis. Enormous amounts of money and food were sent abroad not only to support U.S. and Allied forces, but to satisfy civilian needs in Europe as well, as Americans observed meatless Tuesdays, gas rationing, and other shortages to feed the war machine. By 1944, the U.S. was producing twice the total war output of the Axis powers combined.

Following Germany's unconditional surrender on May 4, 1945, Japan continued fighting. To prevent the loss of more American lives defeating the Japanese, President Truman, in a still controversial decision, dropped atomic bombs on the Japanese cities of Hiroshima and Nagasaki, thus ending the war in the Pacific. Subsequently, the U.S. spent millions of dollars and sent thousands of workers to rebuild Europe and Japan.

America emerged from the war as the world power. Millions had served overseas; millions more had listened to broadcasts about the battles from France and the Pacific and watched the newsreels in movie theatres. As a result, Americans became more conscious of the world outside their own country. But the war had exacted a high price. In all, the United States lost 405,000 men and women in combat, while the cost in dollars totaled $350 billion.

# 1940 NEWS FEATURE

*Some Notes on War and Peace,* **by Walter Lippmann,
The Macmillan Company, 1940:**

It is inordinately difficult, I find, even to begin thinking about the peace that is to follow this war. There must be others who are laboring under the same difficulty. There must be others who, when they broach the problem, are as baffled as if in a dark jungle they had come face-to-face with an angry elephant, and were then told it was their duty to tame the elephant.

How does one begin to tame an angry elephant? Does one climb a tree and from a safe height deliver an oration on the bad habits of elephants? Does one tickle the elephant's snout and offer him a handful of hay every time he gets angry? Or would it perhaps be better to retire from his presence and take a course in elephant taming, a course which any really up-to-the-minute college would no doubt be glad to offer?

For myself, I do not know how to tame an elephant, or how to abolish war and establish perpetual peace. But for more than 20 years I have been worrying about the peace that was signed at Versailles, and have been criticizing it, and listening to plans for reconstructing it, and going as a newspaper man to conferences which were revising it. The only thing I know for certain about the next peace is that I know no one who can sit down at his desk and devise a plan which will tell the survivors of this war just what they ought to do.

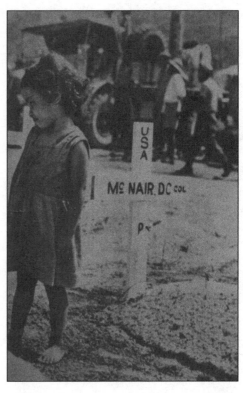

So it has dawned upon me that a more modest approach to this great question might at this time prove to be more useful, and that before beginning to think about the settlement of this war, it might be better to think about how one thinks about the settlement of such a war. In this way one might eventually discover how to take hold of the problem, where and how to begin to think about such a problem.

I shall not start, therefore, with a set of principles for making peace, not with a plan and a program, but with a summary of what I believe are fallacies into which we tend to fall when we think about making peace.

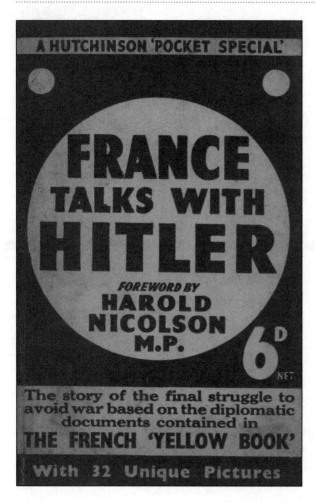

1. The Fallacy of Our Own Eventual Omnipotence

When we are under the spell of this fallacy, we image ourselves, sometimes crudely but more often subtly and unconsciously, as playing the part of the victorious masters of the world. We are Hitler in his dream castle, only we are still our own noble selves. We draw frontiers on maps. We make combinations of people. We dispose grandly and easily of the lives, the fortunes, the wishes and the prejudices of mankind. The underlying assumption is that we are in a position to impose upon mankind the constitution that we have decided is good for them.

This is, however, sheer fantasy—in Hitler's case a lunatic fantasy, in our case perhaps only an amiable daydream. For nobody in all history, not Alexander, Caesar, or Napoleon, not the Congress of Vienna or the Peace Conference at Paris, has ever remotely approached omnipotence of this order. It is, therefore, a fundamental error to think about peace on the assumption, however concealed, that someone, or even some group of men, is not going to arrange the world according to his heart's desire; and that this someone, or one of the someones, is oneself.

2. The Belief in the Miracle of Universal Consent

Many attractive schemes, of which the Kellogg Pact to Outlaw War is a classic example, are based on the assumption that all men will not only acknowledge the same principles of conduct (which is just conceivable), but that all men will draw the same practical conclusions from the principles. This is not, I think, conceivable—even theoretically—in practical affairs to act as if it were possible to ignore the problem of war and peace and then to call this ignorance a solution.

For the problem is not how men should act if they were all in fundamental agreement; if they were in fundamental agreement, there would be no problem and, therefore, no need of a solution. The problem is how to obtain more agreement than there is, and how to get on without wrecking our civilization by the conflicts that arise out of disagreement. Yet there are an astonishing number of fine plans in circulation today which tacitly assume that the plan is so attractive that the whole competing and fighting world will find it too rational, too just, and too inspiring to reject.

Some Notes on

# WAR and PEACE

BY

Walter Lippmann

3. The Fallacy of the Exaggerated and Isolated Cause

In this category are to be found all the plans that isolate some issue as the "fundamental" and "underlying" cause of the whole disorder. There are innumerable cults, each with its separate diagnosis: The cause, we are told, is lack of raw materials, or lack of living space, or lack of colonies, or lack of national self-determination.

When this fallacy is disinterested, it arises from intellectual specialization: We all like to think that the most important things in the world are the things we know about the world. When this fallacy is not disinterested, as is often the case, it is a device of the propagandist.

4. The Fallacy of Overvaluing Our Good Intentions

The problem of war and peace has baffled the greatest minds for more than two thousand years; we must not, therefore, imagine that to hate war and desire peace, however passionately, is a qualification for solving the problem. . . .

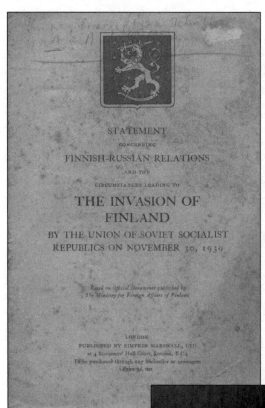

Peace is as desirable, and just about as indefinable and elusive, as good health. And war is as undesirable as a bad disease, but there are many kinds and causes of war, as there are many kinds of disease. No disease is curable by thinking how horrible it is, nor is a robust constitution achieved by wishing for it. . . .

5. The Fallacy of Not Understanding That the Character of the Peace Is Shaped by the Course of the War

There are many who think that the settlement is made by the diplomats who write the peace treaty. During a war, this error provides an agreeable escape from its grim realities. For when we accept this error we feel that we can think about "the peace," ignoring the deplorable war that precedes it. This is, I think, the great popular illusion both about the Versailles settlement of 1919 and about what is to be the settlement which ends this war.

To get rid of this illusion is perhaps to begin to prepare to think about peace.

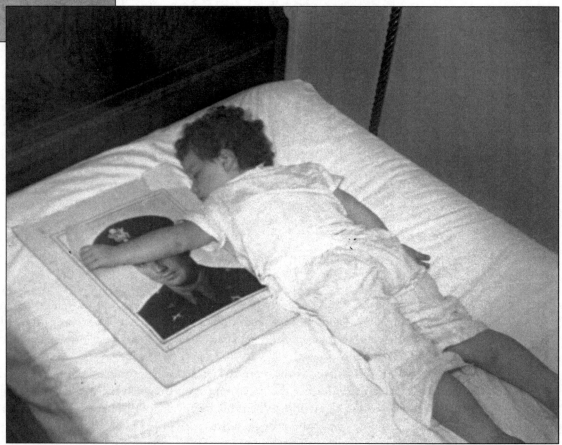

# 1944 Profile

# World War II

### Aerial Gunner

Trained as a radio operator for a B-17 bomber crew, Bernard Gunn, nicknamed Blue Tick by his buddies, left the quiet mountains of North Carolina for the flak-filled skies over Germany as a member of the 8th Air Force.

### Life at Home

- Even Bernard Gunn was unsure why he chose to be a radio operator-aerial gunner on a B-17 airplane crew.
- This was scary business; during the past two years, more than 3,000 bombers—and often their crews—had been lost fighting the Nazis.
- Initial flight training took place in Salt Lake City, Utah, followed by a troop train ride to Alexandria, Louisiana, for overseas training.
- For Bernard, it felt like a trip to the ends of the earth.
- Five large army training camps and two air bases were located in the immediate vicinity; some weekends as many as 50,000 GIs invaded the town.
- The townspeople—even those getting rich on overpriced and watered-down drinks—were resentful.
- Airmen like Bernard stay away from the town bars on weekends, when they are considered fresh meat by the fight-hungry ground troops who comprise the majority of the soldiers.
- He was not used to running from any fight, but the odds against whipping an entire unit were pretty high—even for a mountain boy from North Carolina.
- Besides, at this stage of training for war, everyone was scared and ready to fight to prove they weren't.
- To keep up his courage during flight training, Bernard wore a pilot's cap, smoked big black cigars and confidently drank boilermakers—a drink he'd never met in dry Polk Country, North Carolina.
- It made him look tough, the way he had looked in his football uniform at Saluda High School.
- The planes available for training were exhausted war veterans prone to malfunctioning.

*Bernard "Blue Tick" Gunn is a B-17 radio operator.*

## "Gifts for U.S. Prisoners Sent to German Camps," *New York Herald Tribune*, December 21, 1944:

Official word has been received that American Red Cross Christmas packages for prisoners of war arrived several weeks ago in the distribution centers in Europe and were sent to German camps, it was announced today by Basil O'Connor, chairman of the American Red Cross.

The packages were shipped from Philadelphia in August so that normal delays in transportation through war areas would not prevent their arriving at the camps in time for Christmas. A large reserve was included in the shipments to allow for men who might be captured during the months between August and December.

The packages contain turkey, plum pudding, sausages, strawberry jam, nuts, fruit bars, dates, canned cherries, chewing gum, deviled ham, cheddar cheese, butter, bouillon cubes, tea, honey, cigarettes, smoking tobacco, a pipe, a washcloth, playing cards, a game and two pictures of American scenes.

*Five large army camps and two air bases are located close together in Alexandria, Louisiana.*

- On one of his first cross-country training flights, two engines caught fire nearly forcing the plane down before the flames could be extinguished.
- Once his training ended, he went home on furlough, visiting his family in Saluda and giving everyone the impression he was ready to beat the Germans single-handedly.
- Actually, he was terrified about going to Europe; in preparation for war he revisited familiar scenes of his youth and even borrowed his father's car so he could visit several of his former teachers at the high school.
- He also stopped to reminisce at Porter's, a familiar nightspot in Hendersonville.
- Over a beer, he put a nickel in the jukebox and played "Cherry" by Erskine Hawkins, and then "Summit Ridge Drive" by Artie Shaw, but there was no one to dance with that night.

## Selected Prices

| | |
|---|---|
| Bedroom Suite, Four Pieces | $49.50 |
| Billfold, Leather | $2.50 |
| Casserole Dish, Pyrex | $0.50 |
| Denture Adhesive, Polident | $0.30 |
| Flour, Pillsbury, 24.5-Pound Bag | $1.09 |
| Gin, Seagram's, per Fifth | $1.70 |
| Globe, 10-Inch | $2.95 |
| Golf Clubs, Set of Five Irons | $12.95 |
| Iron | $12.95 |
| Lipstick, Almay | $1.10 |
| Paint, Dupont, Gallon | $2.45 |
| Record, "Porgy and Bess" | $4.72 |
| Shoes, Children's Saddle Oxfords | $1.69 |
| Tie | $1.00 |
| Wedding Ring, 18-K White Gold | $9.75 |

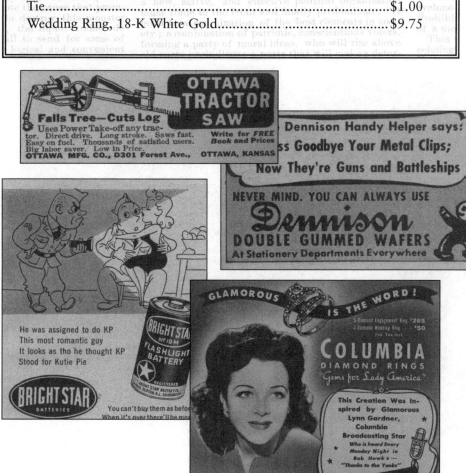

### My War, A Love Story in Letters and Drawings, Tracy Sugarman:

(The author is a sailor stationed on a troopship bound for England, part of the massive Allied buildup for the D-Day liberation of Europe; he is writing to his wife, June.)

May 16, 1944:

It's 11:45 and I'm sleepy, but I want to write you a bit anyhow. This is a most dreadful situation and I don't know what to do about it. As of May 1st, we've been told, no mail has left the country for the States. No mail will leave until further notice. I received five wonderful letters from you today and noted that the last one of mine you received was sent out April 29. I'm afraid that will be the last you receive for a while, although I've kept on writing. I know somehow that you feel I'm all right.

Don't let the incessant commentators and sensation mongers touch your mind and spirit, Junie. I can sense the growing tension and anxiety in your heart. No wonder. While we here are almost oblivious to news, developments, prognostications, you're enmeshed in them. This fever that is growing in the States is felt somehow by all of us here. Living here each day is completely unemotional. You're too busy doing your work with your men or your materiel to indulge in this psychological war dance that is increasing in tempo at home. Keep cool. It's just a job I must and want to do. I count on your common sense and sound values as I do on my own aptitude, training and ability. Together, we can lick this thing to a frazzle.

## Life at Work

- The B-17 crew with whom Bernard Gunn has been assigned in England includes an Italian pilot, a Jewish copilot, a Irish bombardier who talks non-stop, a Hungarian tough guy from New Jersey for a waist gunner and a Scot from Chicago as tail gunner; truly, the crew likes to say, "an all-American bunch."
- Stationed at Molesworth, England, they were sent to a barracks shared by three other crews, where they were assigned the cots of a crew who had been shot down the previous week.
- The bombardment group at Molesworth has four squadrons, each dispersed in a different location on the base; on combat missions it is customary to put up three squadrons of 12 aircraft each and stand one squadron down for rest.
- Many of the company commanders, including generals, are young, and it is common to see full colonels in their twenties and some generals in their thirties, while the average age of the flight crews is about 20 years old.
- One of Bernard's first lessons was that much of the radio procedures learned in stateside training are useless in the war zone, and the hours and days spent learning how to repair radios proved worthless for high-altitude, subzero weather conditions.
- His first mission was a shock: Berlin.
- He felt like a condemned man—it was April 1944, the war was raging, and 361 heavy U.S. bombers were lost that month alone over Europe.

- At breakfast, the cooks were jovial, offering pancakes, eggs and toast, but Bernard felt like it was his last meal.
- Before the flight, all the crews, officers and noncoms were briefed together; afterwards, radio operators received a separate briefing, along with a canvas packet of coded data.
- When the briefing began, the target remained covered up; once it was revealed, the entire room groaned.
- When told to expect heavy fighter opposition with considerable flak, Bernard knew the target was both valuable and heavily defended.
- During the flight, enemy flak was so heavy it blackened the sky from one end to the other.
- Once, the B-17 lurched suddenly as the plane took a direct hit that left a hole two feet in diameter through the port wing.

- Bernard was too occupied to know about the damage until they returned.
- They were also subject to a frontal attack by 40 German FW 190s.
- Silver with black crosses, they flew between planes in formation, attempting to take down the bombers before they dropped their payload.
- Bernard is able to fire point-blank at them, and is always amazed when they keep on going.
- Because of his hillbilly twang and origins, he is now known as Blue Tick, as in the Blue Tick Hound—one of the finest hunting creatures on earth.
- He is proud that he has a nickname—a sign of acceptance—but prouder that he can send $100 home each month to be put into savings.
- To relax after missions, he drinks with his buddies or goes hunting for rabbits with his .45 automatic pistol.
- Most of the time, he misses the fast-moving targets, but when he is successful, the rabbits are taken to the Red Cross where a woman prepares a special feast.
- At Molesworth, there is almost no distinction between officers and noncoms, who often go on pass together, and some officers even lobbied for invites to the noncom bar.
- Seldom are uniforms worn; dress consists of flight overalls and leather A-2 jackets, while feet are shod mostly in flight boots, especially in the latrine.
- Bernard goes bareheaded most of the year, only occasionally donning his leather, fleece-lined gunner's cap.
- Nearly everyone, including Bernard, has at least one English bicycle.
- When word arrives that a crew has been shot down and will not be returning, there is a mad dash to claim the dead men's bikes.
- In letters home, he has explained to his wife that this is not a show of disrespect, but only reflects the need to keep the company's corral of bikes intact.
- His wife says she understands, but really doesn't.
- Infrequent showers are something else his wife wouldn't understand, so he doesn't tell her.
- The distance to the showers is great and hot water is a rarity, so few people bother.
- Mostly, the men can't smell themselves, and everyone else smells, anyway.
- Crews tend to be clannish, protective and as close as brothers—except when it comes to poker.
- The constant poker game in the barracks is a source of unending battles—especially when no one can stand to lose.

*Crews tend to be clannish, protective, and as close as brothers.*

## Pamphlet: "Women Are Funny That Way, I Will Win the War," compliments of Horton Moving Van Company, 1943:

My wife told me that she would like to do some Red Cross work, but that a neighbor woman told her that the Red Cross was just a lot of society dames playing nurse to get their pictures in the paper. "They won't let you do anything unless you are Sassiety with a big S," she says to me. I says to my wife, "Now if that's so, it's all wet."

And I told her to go over to the Red Cross and see what the score was. Well, that rumor was dead wrong. They signed up my wife in no time to take a course in volunteer nursing. She's now taking a course washing babies—I thought she knew all about that—making beds, bandaging, treating burns, shock. They even gave her the dope on reviving shocked or half-drowned people. You know—the old prone pressure stuff which we learned at the plant safety meetin's. Thought everybody knew that, but my wife had never heard of it.

- When every mission can be your last, gambling with money doesn't seem much of a gamble—besides, every barracks has a loan shark, known as a shylock, who will lend you enough to make payday.
- Of course, if the shylock's plane goes down, all debts are cancelled.

## Life in the Community: The 8th Air Force in Germany

- The saga of the 8th Air Force was written from August 17, 1942, to April 25, 1945, when more than 4,500 B-17s were lost over Europe.
- One of 10 Americans killed in World War II was a member of the 8th Air Force, which recorded 43,782 men killed or missing in action out of 405,399 Americans killed in the war.
- In 1944, it was commonplace to see great armadas of up to 2,000 planes flying a mission over Germany.
- Most of the men have a personal pin-up such as Betty Grable or Chili Williams in a two-piece polka-dot bathing suit, but Bernard prefers Ginger Rogers in a silk negligée.
- He has found that the tenuous existence of the combat crews produces enormous generosity, with the men sharing everything—especially boxes from home.
- The finest mail-call boxes arrive for the Jewish men, whose care packages are loaded with salami, knockwurst, gefiltefisch (stuffed carp), pumpernickel, bagels, kosher dills and Manischewitz.
- The flight crews also share with the children of the English countryside, doling out chewing gum and chocolates.

*American industry met the president's call for 60,000 planes in 1942 and 125,000 in 1943.*

- When WWII started in 1939, the United States had plans for military aircraft, but few machines on hand or in production.
- Many questions were unanswered: Could an airplane sink a battleship? Would air power render ground troops obsolete? Could air speed bring overseas lands within range of attack?
- By the time Pearl Harbor was attacked by the Japanese two years later, many of the questions had been answered.
- American leaders knew how the German Stuka dive-bombers aided panzer units in blitzkrieg tactics, and how English Spitfires had won the Battle of Britain.
- As a result, America's military visualized heavy bombing of enemy industrial sites, and designed accordingly.
- When the U.S. entered the war, the Army Air Forces and American manufacturers had developed a variety of aircraft: the B-17 heavy bomber (Flying Fortress); the B-24 medium bomber (Liberator), the B-25 medium bomber (Mitchell); the B-26 light bomber (Marauder); the A-24 light bomber (Dauntless); the P-38 fighter (Lightning), and the P-40 (Tomahawk).
- In July 1941, the army had about 2,500 planes and the navy about 4,000.
- When President Roosevelt set a goal of 60,000 planes in 1942 and 125,000 in 1943, the aircraft industry met the demand.

## HISTORICAL SNAPSHOT
# 1944

- On D-Day, June 6, the Normandy invasion was mounted by 6,939 naval vessels, 15,040 aircraft, and 156,000 troops; casualties numbered 16,434 killed, 76,535 wounded, and 19,704 missing
- Jell-O became a popular dessert substitute for canned fruit
- Baking powder sales fell as women continued to join the work force
- Bill Mauldin's cartoon *Willie & Joe,* originally in *Yank* and *Stars and Stripes,* was picked up by the domestic press and achieved wide acclaim
- More than 81,000 GIs were killed, wounded or captured in the Battle of the Bulge, Germany's last big offensive of the war
- Because of a shortage of cheese and tomato sauce, the sale of pasta fell dramatically
- Gen. Douglas MacArthur returned to the Philippines; his American army annihilated the troops commanded by Gen. Tomoyuki Yamashita, the Tiger of Malaya; 50,000 Japanese were killed, and fewer than 400 were captured
- Nearly 372,000 German POWs were being held in the United States
- The Dow-Jones reached a high of 152 and a low of 135; unemployment stood at 1.2 percent
- Victory bonds became an obsession, with actress Hedy Lamarr offering to kiss any man who bought $25,000 worth and Jack Benny auctioning his $75 violin—Old Love in Bloom—for $1 million worth of bonds
- Herr Adolf Hitler was among the citizens of enemy nations whose assets were frozen during the war; $22,666 from the sale of *Mein Kampf* was later used to pay Americans' claims against enemy nationals
- Chiquita brand bananas were introduced
- Expenditures for spectator sports hit record levels, topping 80 million; the nation had 409 golf courses and 910,000 bowlers
- The first give-away items appeared in a cereal box when Pep put paper airplane cutouts in some packages; robots, rings, iron-ons, balancing clowns and cars soon followed

## "Ex-Pastor Held as Agent for Nazi Saboteur"

Newark, N.J.—A mild-mannered little former minister was arrested today as a Nazi spy helper after he had been under surveillance ever since his name and address were reportedly found two years ago on the handkerchief of a German saboteur who landed on the Atlantic coast from a U-Boat. The prisoner, 60-year-old Emil Ludwig Krepper, lately a bookkeeper at Newark's Downtown Club, was held on $30,000 bail, while the Federal Bureau of Investigation here and in Washington described him as a German agent commissioned to help Nazi spies and saboteurs.

The arrest of Krepper, born in Germany and naturalized as an American citizen in Philadelphia in 1922, preceded the opening in United States District Court of three sealed indictments returned against him here on Friday.

It also disclosed that for nearly 30 months, the black-haired, round-faced Krepper has been trailed night and day by F.B.I. agents who indicated today, with satisfaction, their dogged surveillance may have turned up news of other German agents to be disclosed later.

The downfall of Krepper, who lived at 68 James Street, Newark, and who formerly held Lutheran pastorates here and in Rahway and Carteret, began in June 1942, when eight German saboteurs landed from U-boats on the shores of Long Island and Florida.

All of the eight were caught and convicted, and six of them were executed, but before that the white pocket handkerchief of one of them—he was apprehended in New York but whose name the F.B.I. withholds—yielded the invisible ink message:

"Pas. Krepper, Route 2, Rahway, New Jersey."

"Pas." stood for pastor. The Rahway address was one at which Krepper received mail. Instead of pouncing at once, the F.B.I. shadowed Krepper for nearly 30 months—until today when he was arrested at an unannounced place.

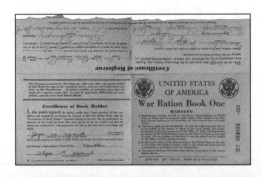

WAR BONDS·STAMPS
Buy MORE
WE MUST WIN !

OUR FIRST DUTY

Buy MORE WAR BONDS★STAMPS

CLOSE COVER BEFORE STRIKING

UNIVERSAL MATCH CORP., NEW YORK

Buy WAR SAVINGS BONDS and STAMPS

V for VICTORY

★ ★ ★ ★ ★ ★ ★ ★

THE OHIO MATCH CO., WADSWORTH, OHIO
MADE IN U.S.A.

CLOSE COVER BEFORE STRIKING

Buy WAR BONDS AND STAMPS

Own a Share in AMERICA

STEP ON IT

CRUSH THE AXIS

CLOSE COVER BEFORE STRIKING

DO NOT BURN THEM

Save PAPER
SALVAGE PAPER AND PAPER CONTAINERS

HELP WIN THE WAR

SAVE FATS

AMERICA'S BULLETS ARE FIRED BY EXPLOSIVES MADE FROM YOUR WASTE FATS AND GREASES
Save A Tablespoonful Every Day

THE OHIO MATCH CO., WADSWORTH, OHIO
MADE IN U. S. A.

CLOSE COVER BEFORE STRIKING

# Diary of a Tail Gunner, *John Gabay*, 1943:

*Gelsenkirchen, Germany 11/5/43 (B-17 382— Horrible Hanks) Target: Ruhr Valley refineries. Temp: -43 FT (flight time): 5:15 ET (time over enemy territory): 1:35 Altitude: 28,000 feet*

We went over Holland and immediately saw three ME (Meserschmitt) 109s. Later on, we saw 10 FW (Focke-Wolf) 190s. I fired at a 109 coming in at 6 o'clock. . . . Flak was very intense and pretty accurate (14 solid minutes). Our ship was hit several times (two holes in left wing flaps, several in fuse lodge, severed oil line in number three engine and bent prop). Oil covered ball turret and wheels. I could hear pieces of flak hit—concussion driving the ship several feet upward. . . . A waist gunner got the bends. He screamed with the pain. Now the 109s moved in for another battle. My guns worked perfectly. I was holding them off pretty good . . . our P-47s met us and scattered the enemy fighters. We lost one bomber on that last fight. Bombs went through the wing of another ship but they made it back OK. This was my first raid and it was with an old crew. They had 24 millions and were uneasy to have a rookie flying tail gun. But when we landed, they all came back and shook hands with me and said I did OK.

*Munster, Germany 11/11/43 (B-17 846— Lucky 13) Target: Mashalling yards in the heart of the city. -28 FT: 6:00 ET: 1:55 Altitude 24,000*

Our escort stayed as long as they could—engaging in several dogfights. They had to leave us over Holland and then the fun began. About 50 FW 190s and ME 109s attacked us from every direction. We couldn't close our bomb-bay doors so they picked on us thinking we were crippled. One FW dove straight down from 1 o'clock high and let go with his cannons. He put a hole in our left wing big enough to crawl through. He also blew off a piece of the vertical stabilizer over my head. The Fort on our wing burst into flames and only five got out—one chute was on fire. They were from our barracks. A 109 came directly at me and I know I hit him as he rolled over

in a dive and disappeared. Another came in low at 8 o'clock and Chauncy, our ball gunner, hit him and he burst into flames and went down. Several FW 190s kept coming in at the tail and I hit one. . . . The Fort on our other wing burst into flames and went into a spin. Didn't see any chutes. Flak burst under our ship and concussion knocked us up about 50 feet . . . an FW 190 followed up low and Chauncy knocked him into the water. We made it back OK but our new ship was a wreck . . . our crew's first raid together.

*Bremen, German 11/29/43 (B-17 846—Lucky 13) Target: Docks in city. –64 FT: 7:45 ET: 2:20 Alt. 28,500*

Flak was heavy. Ship on our left had its wing blown off . . . fighters hit us hard. Our P-47 escort jumped on them and the battle began. I called out a ME 210 at 5 o'clock low to Chauncy: he almost got him. I fired at an FW 190 and saw him blow up just as a P-47 pulled over the tail . . . dogfights all over the sky. Vapor trails were heavy and broke up our formation . . . Our commo and radio compass were shot out. I never saw so many different types of enemy fighters . . . about 150 in all, trying to outdo each other. It must have been an Iron Cross day. The 87s tried dropping parachute bombs. All our guns were going at the same time. It felt like the ship would come apart. . . . I know I hit a few as I saw several break off and dive. We made it back OK, but I had frostbite on my face, chin and knees. They wanted to put me in the hospital but I went into a fit and got off with only one day grounding. Went to confession. . . .

## "Hell's Angels over Germany," *Chick's Crew, A Tale of the 8th Air Force,* Ben Smith, Jr., 1978:

Dogfights were going on between our escort and their fighters right among the bomber formations. The tail gunner and the ball-turret gunner, having the best vantage points, kept calling out at intervals the falling aircraft, friend and foe. There was not even a brief lull in the fighting, not a single instant when some aircraft was not departing the conflict in flames. Up ahead of us, Lt. Determan's B-17 got a direct hit from flak and disintegrated. Unbelievably, three parachutes came out of the inferno. Nearby, a P-47 collided head-on with a P-51, which exploded in flames. The P-47 went into a spin, and the pilot parachuted. No chute came from the P-51.

To make it a Wagnerian apocalypse, the lurid skyscape was lit up every so often by spectacular rocket explosions. I couldn't see where they were coming from. Sometimes they were fired from the ground, but more often twin-engine German fighters launched these at the formation from a distance.

We were flying into a corridor where most of the synthetic oil industry was located, and it was protected by the greatest concentration of flak guns in the Third Reich. Dessau, Merseburg and Leipzig, three of the most infamous targets in Germany, were all right there together. We began a bomb run on the primary target at Dessau, but did not drop our bombs because it was obscured with haze. We looked for the secondary, but could not find it either. Finally, we bombed a target of opportunity, a refinery at Rotha. We ranged over this hell's cauldron for 25 minutes, flying through a curtain of shellfire seemingly without end.

Suddenly, as I gazed out on this, a feeling of exaltation swept over me. It was magnificent. I had the sudden revelation: This would not be happening if men didn't love it.

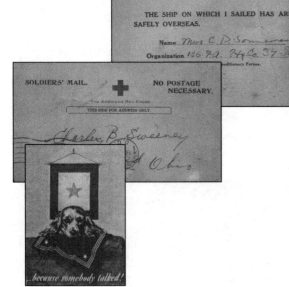

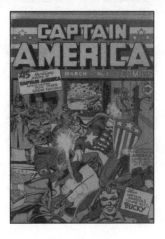

## "Don't I Know You? Experience of War," Lloyd Bentsen, MHQ, *The Quarterly Journal of Military History*, Autumn 1989:

I was a major and commanding officer of the 717th Squadron of the 449th Bomb Group in 1944. I was only 23, but they called me "the old man." We were stationed in Grottaglie, Italy, very near Taranto and very far from the area around McAllen, Texas, where I grew up.

One bombing run we made over Austria in February of that year will live forever in my memory. Our target had been a railroad marshalling yard in Vienna. There was a great deal of flak on this run. We were being fired on by 88-millimeter antiaircraft guns.

The flight from Grottaglie to Vienna normally would have taken 11 hours, round-trip, but after we dropped our bombs, we lost two engines. Flames were shooting out of one of them. By the time I got the plane under control, I had lost several thousand feet and had given up the lead of the mission. We were not able to keep up with the formation, even though we threw overboard everything that could be dumped to lighten our aircraft.

Before long, it became obvious that we had lost—and were continuing to lose—so much altitude that we would not be able to get back across the Adriatic Sea. I asked the navigator to find a place where we could go down, in hopes that we would not have to bail out. He advised that there was an island available in case of emergency. The island, which was named Vis, had changed hands in the past, but he understood it was presently Allied.

I told him I hoped that was the case, but I knew I would have to try to land there, regardless. There was no way we could have made it to the coast of Italy; had we gone down in the Adriatic, we probably would not have lasted over five minutes in the freezing water.

We crossed the Yugoslav coast and were able to locate the island, but by then we were at a very low altitude, and it was only at the last moment that we found the emergency strip. After spotting the runway, I had to make a very sharp turn to line up with it, since there were hills all around. As a result, I made a poor landing and washed out the nose gear.

At that point I still wasn't certain we were on friendly soil—and when the plane slid to a stop, I saw some women wearing grenade belts coming toward us.

I climbed out of the plane and walked toward them, hoping they were friendly, only to have a man about my age emerge from the group and come toward me.

I said, "Don't I know you?"

He looked at me and said, "Sure, you're Bentsen. I used to sack groceries for your mother when she went to the store in McAllen."

The man had returned to his homeland before the war and had become one of General Tito's partisans. He and his friends cared for my crew until a British bomber came in and flew us to safety.

## "The New Crew," *Chick's Crew, A Tale of the 8th Air Force,* Ben Smith, Jr., 1978:

Finally it was our turn. We did not fly to our base; we took the train from Bovingdon to a station near Molesworth and were ignominiously carried there in trucks. When we came to our squadron area, we were not greeted by the familiar, "You'll be sorry," the customary greeting on the State side. The men we saw gave us only a few incurious glances and said nothing to us. Our hearts sank. We were assigned a barracks shared by two or three other crews. Six empty cots gaped at us. These had been occupied by a crew that had not returned from the mission the day before. We were not prepared for this sobering reality.

In progress was a non-stop poker game. The players did not look up or acknowledge our presence in any way. We were accorded a few glum nods from some others who were lying in their sacks reading. About that time the door flew open, and a bevy of uproarious drunks fell inside. It was the lead crew—Captain Brinkley's crew. I had seen many drunks, but this was a different kind of drunkenness. These men were veterans of the great missions of Schweinfurt and Oschersleben. They had seen too much, and it showed. I had the sudden feeling that things were far different from what I had been led to believe. I was right.

The lead crews were specially trained crews used to lead the missions. Only the bombardier in the lead crew used the bomb site along with a deputy lead in case the lead crew was shot down. All of the other airplanes dropped their bombs simultaneously with the lead ship, it being the point of the formation. In addition, the navigator in the lead ship navigated for the entire group. The lead radio operator did all of the transmitting from air to ground, his first transmission being the strike message after "Bombs Away."

We were not referred to as Lt. Cecchini's crew. Instead, we were called the "new crew," which continued to be our status until we had flown about eight combat missions. New crews were given the most vulnerable places in the formation and had a way of disappearing after a few missions. We heartily resented this callous treatment, but, after winning our spurs, we were as bad as the rest. We flew practice missions for a while, mostly out over the ocean on gunnery exercises. The place was called the Wash. The Wash was a large indentation on the bay on the northern coast of East Anglia. All the gunnery missions were flown there, as it was an isolated spot and reasonably safe from incursions of enemy aircraft.

One day the waist gunner and I were firing at the tow target when, to our amazement, holes began appearing in the horizontal stabilizer. The end of it buckled, and the aircraft set up a violent trembling. We thought the gun had a cut-off when

### "The New Crew . . ." *(continued)*

it was pointed at something vulnerable. That was not the last thing we learned the hard way. Chick, our pilot, somehow got us down in one piece.

Chick and Bachy flew several combat missions to get experience before the rest of us were allowed to go along. Their first mission was a 12-hour marathon to Marienburg, which ended in a crash-landing. Chick had flown as copilot with Captain Bob Lunch, one of the veteran pilots. Bachy's description of his initiation to the Big League dampened our enthusiasm considerably. He did not paint a pretty picture of what was in store for us.

# 1944 Profile

# Fighting with Merrill's Marauders

### First Lieutenant

Mining engineer-trained Joe Pukinin is one of the famous Merrill's Marauders assigned the job of clearing a path for the Chinese army in Japanese-controlled Burma.

### Life at Home

- Joe Pukinin volunteered for military service on December 8, 1941—one day after the attack on Pearl Harbor.
- A recent college graduate, Joe was happily working as a mining engineer when Japan staged a sneak attack on the United States military bases in Hawaii on Sunday morning, December 7.
- After college, he had returned to his hometown of Hibbing, Minnesota, planning to live his life there forever.
- He had no taste for adventure or travel, but was more interested in the family traditions of mining and raising horses.
- Joe's paternal grandparents were Finnish and his mother's family Cornish.
- Both grandfathers had worked as miners in the great open pit mines of the area.
- As a child, Joe dreamed of working in the mines; after college he got his opportunity.
- On the day he enlisted, he was living in a small but comfortable apartment above the grocery store where he had worked as a child, only a few minutes' walk from his parents' home.
- He was dating Athena Tsokas, whom he has known since the third grade, and whose father managed the nicest hotel in Hibbing.
- Joe and Athena shared a love of the land and riding horses.
- Soon after Joe finished basic training, a decision was made to send him to officer candidate's school to take advantage of both his college degree and his engineering expertise.

*Joe Pukinin, third from left, volunteered the day after the attack on Pearl Harbor.*

## Selected Prices

| | |
|---|---|
| Alka Seltzer, Eight Tablets | $0.24 |
| Automobile, Chevrolet Fleetline Aerosedan | $880.00 |
| Bandages, Box of 36 | $0.19 |
| Business School Fee, per Week | $1.00 |
| Coca-Cola, Six-Pack | $0.25 |
| Fur Coat, Ladies' Muskrat | $245.00 |
| Ice-Cube Tray | $1.50 |
| Listerine | $0.27 |
| Magazine, Time, per Year | $4.50 |
| Parking, New York Theater District, per Day | $0.50 |
| Shotgun, Remington 20/26, Automatic | $39.30 |
| Tattoo, Snake Design on Arm | $0.25 |
| Theatre Ticket, *Porgy & Bess* | $2.75 |
| Whiskey, Seagram's Five Crown Blended, per Fifth | $2.25 |
| Whitman's Sampler, Five-Pound Box | $5.00 |

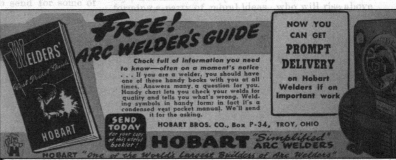
## From the News Editor's Desk, Popular Science, October 1942:

All-out war effort by cows, to increase milk production for supplying our allies, may be promoted by administering chemical hormones. Research in England has shown that stilbestrol6, a sex hormone in the laboratory, and anterior pituitary extract, a glandular substance obtained from the ox, both stimulate the flow of milk even in virgin animals. In one experiment, a scrub goatling that had never given birth was brought into lactation by merely rubbing the udder with an ointment of stilbestrol.

- Initially slated for the school leading to the U.S. Army Corps of Engineers, Joe worked to be assigned to the Infantry School at Fort Benning, Georgia, instead—thanks to his persistence and his family's small amount of political influence.
- While engineering was his chosen profession, he wanted to be where he could have the greatest immediate impact.
- After being commissioned, he waited impatiently to be assigned.
- Considered an excellent officer, Joe was named a first lieutenant in 1943, increasing his annual pay from $1,950 to $2,166 a year.
- Only weeks later, he was assigned to the Caribbean Defense Command and posted to Trinidad, where he underwent extensive training in jungle warfare, but no battle experience—the enemy was across the ocean.
- Joe became so discouraged, even Athena's packages of baklava did not cheer him up.
- Finally, in September the letter arrived that he had been waiting for—an assignment in combat.
- Joe had been selected for a special jungle warfare unit being formed in Burma.
- Even though the war with Germany and Japan had dramatically expanded most Americans' knowledge of world geography, he had to check an atlas to find Burma.
- Tucked away in the northwestern portion of Southeast Asia, Burma had been a British colony until it was recently overrun by the Japanese.
- Now, the Allies decided to strike into north Burma from India.
- Joe's assignment was to help clear the way for the construction of a road which would connect with the old Burma Road into China and provide a supply route for Chiang Kai-shek and his Chinese army—currently America's ally against the Japanese.

*Joe Pukinin was trained in jungle warfare in Trinidad; his girlfriend, Athena, sent him baklava.*

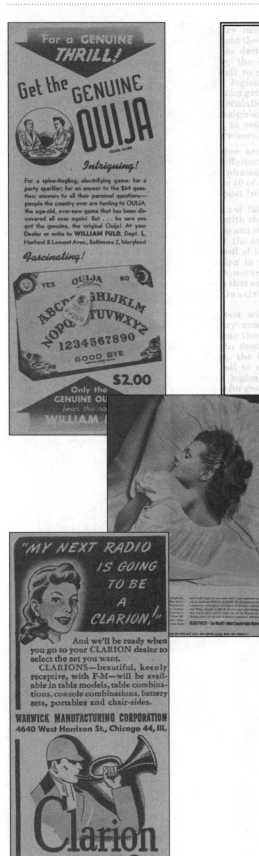

### "Consumers Set 97-Billion High in '44 Spending," *New York Herald Tribune*, December 21, 1944:

American consumers are ringing up a new spending record this year. The Department of Commerce estimated today that $97 billion will have been spent for goods and services in 1944. That's six percent bigger than last year. It's more than half again as big as 1939 spending, which totaled $61.7 billion.

There's a war on, but the department said enough civilian goods were produced in 1944 to satisfy most consumers' wants. There were "some inconveniences, but no hardships."

Rising prices account for some of the increased spending, but not all. The actual quantity of goods and services bought this year has been somewhat larger than in 1943. Civilians spent $2 billion more for food than they did last year, even though prices averaged slightly less than in 1943, according to the report. . . .

It was increasingly harder to buy some items in 1944, such as radios and low-priced children's clothing. Such items either weren't being made or were produced in insufficient volume and stocks were low.

There were "temporary shortages" in certain other items, like high-grade meats and cigarettes.

- The drive through north Burma was to be accomplished by two Chinese divisions and the regiment-sized United States unit, which was being formed from some 1,000 jungle-trained troops from the Caribbean, about 1,000 from the United States, and a like number from the Pacific.
- In November, the 3,000-man unit was assembled in Deograh, India, and put through two months of intensive training.
- The battle ahead was expected to be fierce.

*Burma was a British colony until it was overrun by the Japanese.*

## Life at Work

- Frustrated for almost two years by his inability to join the fight, First Lt. Joe Pukinin was pleased to be given command of the Pioneer and Demolition Platoon of the 3rd Battalion in Burma.
- As a trained mining engineer, he knows a great deal about demolition and blowing rock.
- Now, thanks to his training, he and his unit are prepared to operate for long periods without support or supplies.
- Although most of the travel in Burma is by pack animals, all other supplies must be airlifted to the unit.
- From the jumping-off point at the town of Ledo, India, to the designated intersection with the Burma Road are about 300 miles of rugged hill country covered by tropical rain forest.
- There are few roads and fewer towns of any size.
- Before he left India, Joe wrote home to say he would not be able to write often from then on, but not to worry—he was now in the fight for freedom.
- He even said he preferred the mild dry air of India to the January snows of northern Minnesota—but he wasn't serious.
- In January 1944, the U.S. unit was named the 5307th Composite Unit (Provisional) and placed under the command of Brigadier General Frank D. Merrill, a 39-year-old New Hampshire native.

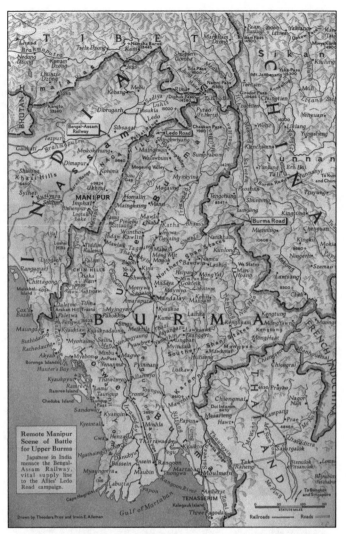

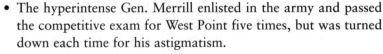

*Before Joe left for Burma, he wrote home to say he would be difficult to reach once fighting began.*

- The hyperintense Gen. Merrill enlisted in the army and passed the competitive exam for West Point five times, but was turned down each time for his astigmatism.
- He was accepted on the sixth try.
- Gen. Merrill's 5307th, which the press has dubbed Merrill's Marauders, is the only American combat unit in the Southeast Asia Command.
- Most of the troops in Burma are British, Indian or Chinese.
- Joe was tingling with excitement when the unit moved into Burma in February; before the month was out the 5307th had met significant resistance from the Japanese 18th Division.

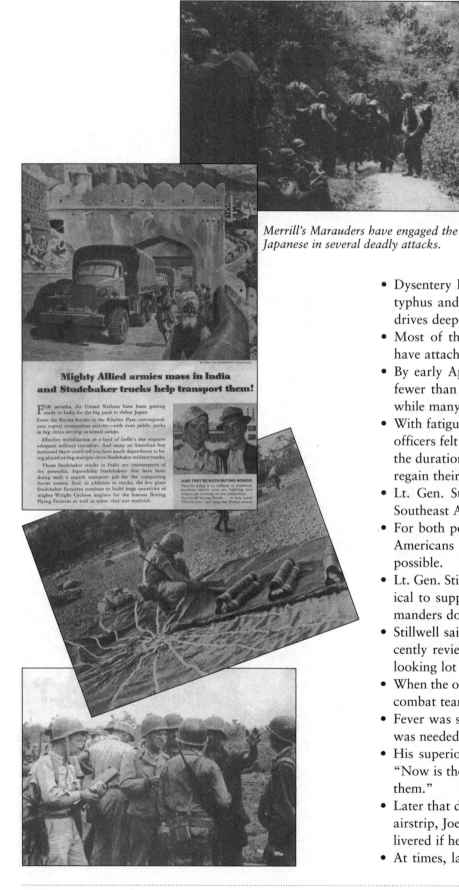

Merrill's Marauders have engaged the Japanese in several deadly attacks.

**Mighty Allied armies mass in India and Studebaker trucks help transport them!**

FOR months, the United Nations have been getting ready in India for the big push to defeat Japan.

From the Burma border to the Khyber Pass, correspondents report tremendous activity—with even public parks in big cities serving as armed camps.

Effective mobilization in a land of India's size requires adequate military transport. And many an American boy stationed there could tell you how much dependence is being placed on big multiple-drive Studebaker military trucks.

Those Studebaker trucks in India are counterparts of the powerful, dependable Studebakers that have been doing such a superb transport job for the conquering Soviet armies. And, in addition to trucks, the five great Studebaker factories continue to build huge quantities of mighty Wright Cyclone engines for the famous Boeing Flying Fortress as well as other vital war matériel.

**AND THEY'RE BOTH BUYING BONDS!** They're doing it in millions of American families—where sons are fighting and fathers are working on war production they're all buying Bonds ... to help speed Victory now—and keep our Nation sound.

- Dozens of times, they engaged the Japanese in firefights, which were deadly for both sides.
- The Americans are being aided by the native population of Kachin, who serve as scouts, guides and interpreters.
- On more than one occasion, the Kachins, whom both the U.S. and British troops have taken pains to recruit, have prevented the Marauders from walking into a trap.
- But all is not going well in the jungles of Burma.
- While battle wounds and combat deaths are considerably fewer than expected, disease is taking its toll.
- Dysentery has felled large numbers of men, and fever, typhus and malaria are also decimating the force as it drives deeper into Burma.
- Most of the men sport bloody patches where leeches have attached themselves to their skin.
- By early April, the health of the unit was doubtful as fewer than half of Joe's men were still on active duty, while many others were below par.
- With fatigue lingering from the siege at Nhpum Ga, the officers felt the 5307th should establish a base camp for the duration of the monsoon season and use the time to regain their strength.
- Lt. Gen. Stillwell, the senior American officer in the Southeast Asia Command, felt otherwise.
- For both political and strategic reasons, he wanted the Americans to take the Myitkyina airstrip as soon as possible.
- Lt. Gen. Stillwell believed the airstrip's capture was critical to supplying the war in the south, but some commanders doubted that the facility could be taken.
- Stillwell said he knew the risks and the assets; after recently reviewing the 5307th, he called them a "tough-looking lot of babies."
- When the order arrived, Joe immediately went to see the combat team commanders.
- Fever was sapping morale; a break, not another battle, was needed, Joe told them.
- His superiors were sympathetic but stern, telling him, "Now is the time to follow orders, soldier, not question them."
- Later that day when a supply plane landed at the jungle airstrip, Joe gave the pilot a letter for Athena—to be delivered if he did not make it back.
- At times, late at night in the Burmese jungle, Joe's en-

thusiasm for service was tempered by his fear of dying from a tropical disease he could not see or fight.

- On April 21 the assault force on Myitkyina was assembled.
- Because the 5307th was at less than half strength, it was augmented by Chinese forces.
- Seven days later, K Force, consisting of the remainder of the 3rd Battalion and the 88th Chinese Infantry Regiment, set out.
- Although ill with the worst stomachache of his life, Joe was determined to clear roads, direct his team and lead his men into battle.
- He had been promised that if the airstrip could be taken, the 5307th would be eligible for immediate furlough.
- He needed all the inspiration he could get.
- As they marched south over rugged terrain, the conditions were worse than expected.
- Insects—including giant buffalo flies and three types of leeches—as well as disease attacked every part of their bodies; groups of men were left behind on the trail with promises they would be helped as soon as possible.
- Many members of the platoon cut away the seats of their jungle trousers so that dysentery would not impair their efficiency in combat.
- Repeatedly, they were told Myitkyina must be captured before the full force of the monsoon rains arrived.
- The plan called for the Chinese 22nd Division to drive down the Mogaung Valley with a strong show of strength to attract the attention of the Japanese.
- Meanwhile, the 5307th plus two Chinese regiments were to conduct an end run and strike over the Kumon mountain range through the 6,100-foot Naura Hkyet Pass and into Myitkyina.
- The trail had not been used for 10 years, and the going was rough, especially in a steady rain that turned the trail into a quagmire.
- On the steeper slopes, even the mules sometimes fell and slid 50 yards on their haunches, while some dropped to their deaths into the valley below.
- In one day, the 3rd Battalion lost 20 mules and two tons of equipment.
- It was the most taxing march undertaken in the 500 miles the 5307th had covered since February.
- In the early morning hours of May 16, the Kachin guide was bitten by a snake, but two officers of the 5307th alternately sucking blood from his foot saved his life.

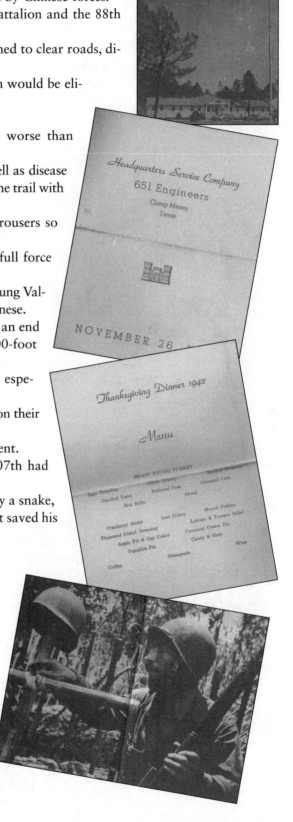

- The assault on the airstrip took place the next day; by marching across the remote mountain pass while the Japanese were still concentrating on the Chinese, the Marauders' attack achieved complete surprise, and the airfield was captured.
- Within hours, the Marauders gave the signal that transports could be landed.
- By afternoon, reinforcements had arrived: The 879th Aviation Engineer Battalion came in by glider, while two troops of British light antiaircraft guns, together with the 2nd Battalion of the Chinese 89th Regiment, arrived by transport aircraft.
- But no supplies came for the Marauder units on the ground, though they were urgently needed.
- That's when all attempts to capture the nearby town and wrestle it from the grasp of the Japanese turned into a battle of attrition.
- Many of the men in Joe's unit were in pitiful shape, covered with various jungle sores; several could do little more than stagger along because of weakness and fatigue.
- In the midst of one engagement with the Japanese, several men went to sleep from exhaustion.
- It was decided that the men were no longer fit for action and should be relieved.
- The 3rd Battalion, which had started off with almost 1,000 men, was down to 12 men in action; Joe and several of his men were flown to a hospital in India for treatment—each pleased to be a Marauder and excited about a momentary rest from war.

## Life in the Community: Hibbing, Minnesota

- Joe Pukinin's hometown of Hibbing, Minnesota, is the self-proclaimed "Iron Ore Capital of the World."
- Hibbing has a population of about 16,000 and is the largest town on the Mesabi Range, which supplies the raw material for the iron and steel industry around the Great Lakes.
- The town grew rapidly after its founding in 1893—largely because of the mining opportunities.
- More than 30 nationalities live and work together in Hibbing, although in recent years the number of immigrants has been declining, as has the town's overall population.

## HISTORICAL SNAPSHOT
# 1944

- College football was becoming the number-one sporting event, replacing professional baseball, whose teams had been significantly depleted by the war
- Approximately 350,000 pounds of DDT was shipped monthly to the military to fight typhus and malaria
- The second atomic pile was built in Clinton, Tennessee, for the manufacture of plutonium for the atomic bomb
- The city of Boston banned the distribution of *Strange Fruit,* a novel about the love between a white man and a black woman
- DNA, the basic material of heredity, was isolated by Oswald Avery at the Rockefeller Institute
- U.S. grocers began testing self-service meat markets
- A New York judge ruled that *Lady Chatterley's Lover* was obscene and ordered to trial the publisher, Dial Press
- Horseracing was banned during the war
- Graffiti reading "Kilroy was here" was seen on buildings, phone booths and construction fences as a symbol of the valor of American GIs
- A mathematical robot with a 50-foot panel of knobs, gears and switches was created at Harvard by Howard Aiken and IBM engineers
- The price of gasoline averaged $0.21 per gallon
- Since the Japanese attacked Pearl Harbor on December 7, 1941, the Army Air Corps' fleet of 10,329 planes expanded to 79,908 planes and 2,403,000 officers and men
- The War Refugee Board revealed the first details of the mass murders at Birkenau and Auschwitz, estimating that 1.7 million people had been killed
- Half the steel, tin and paper needed for the war effort was being provided by people recycling goods
- Paper shortages stimulated publishers' experiments with softcover books
- The war cost $250 million per day
- The U.S. Army announced the development of a jet-propelled, propless plane
- Lt. John F. Kennedy received the Navy and Marine Corps Medal for "extreme heroism" in rescuing two sailors after a Japanese destroyer cut his PT boat in half
- The GI Bill of Rights was enacted to finance college educations for veterans and four percent home loans with no down payment

## "Merrill's Marauders: Combined Operations in Northern Burma in 1944," Gary J. Bjorge, U.S. Command and General Staff College, Fort Leavenworth, Kansas:

Unfortunately for the 5307th, however, even as the Chinese were helping them fight the Japanese at Walawbum, they were seriously degrading the health of the unit by unintentionally contaminating the drinking water. Hunter notes that before the 5307th pulled out of Walawbum, 350 cases of amoebic dysentery were diagnosed because of contaminated drinking water: "Only too late at Walawbum did we learn that the Chinese units were using the stream, from which we obtained our drinking water, as a latrine. Those men who, through force of circumstance or by choice, relied on halizone tablets to purify their drinking water soon became the victims of amoebic dysentery of the worse type." This situation was undoubtedly exacerbated by a difference in Chinese and American habits. [Author Charlton] Ogburn states the Chinese "took time to boil all their drinking water, [while]. . . . far from boiling what they drank, many of the Marauders could not even be bothered to await the action of the halizone tablets in their canteens, but would pop the tablets into their mouths like aspirin and wash them down with a pint of water dipped out of a trailside stream. . . ."

After the battle at Nhpum Ga, the 5307th was given several days' rest, and new outfits of clothing were issued. In addition, nutritious 10-in-1 rations were delivered, and mail was received for the first time in two months. But baths and new clothes could not alter reality; the unit was worn out, according to James H. Stone, writing in *Crisis Fleeting*:

"Terribly exhausted; suffering extensively and persistently from malaria, diarrhea, and both bacillary and amoebic dysentery; beset by festering skin lesions, infected scratches and bites; depleted by 500 miles of marching on packaged rations, the Marauders were sorely stricken. They had lost 700 men, killed, wounded, disabled by non-battle injuries, and, most of all, sick. Over half of this number had been evacuated from the 2nd Battalion alone. Many remaining in the regiment were more or less ill, and their physical condition was too poor to respond quickly to medication and rest."

## "Merrill's Marauders," *The Pan/Ballantine Illustrated History of World War II*, Alan Baker, 1972:

The western slopes of the mountains of north Burma are covered with tropical rain forests, with trees between 80 and 100 feet high obscuring the sun, and the ground beneath covered by rotting vegetation, often three to four feet deep.

In the valleys the trees are smaller, but the undergrowth is so tangled as to make progress by military forces unbearably slow. Even the clearings are filled with the tough and very sharp kunai grass standing about six feet high, while the bamboo requires cutting both near the ground and at the top below the matted and tangled leaves in order to make a tunnel through which columns of troops could pass. Unexpectedly, the area was not lush and fruitful, and provided little additional food for the troops who were now approaching it, for the native Burmans grew only sufficient rice for their own needs.

"After a series of successful engagements in the Hukawng and Mogaung valleys of north Burma, in March and April 1944, the unit was called on to lead a march over jungle trails through extremely difficult mountain terrain against stubborn resistance in a surprise attack on Myitkyina. The unit proved equal to its task, and after a brilliant operation on 17 May 1944, seized the airfield at Myitkyina, an objective of great tactical importance in the campaign, and assisted in the capture of the town of Myitkyina on 3 August 1944."

—Distinguished Unit Citation

## "The Yanks Came: Descent on Myitkyina Brings Land Link with China Near," *Newsweek*, May 29, 1944:

"Cafeteria lunch!"

This message crackled over the radio to Brig. Gen. Frank Merrill's jungle headquarters deep in Burma. It meant that the Allies had won one of the most startling victories of the war in the Far East. Striking out of the dark jungle, like avenging hosts, Chinese and Americans captured the chief airdrome at Myitkyina, main Jap base in Northern Burma, and swarmed into the town itself.

The assault on Myitkyina was part of a general attack on the Jap defense triangle formed by that base plus Kamaing and Mogaung. For weeks, Lt. Gen. Joseph W. Stilwell's men had seemed to be mired in the jungle, progressing feebly from one unpronounceable village to another. Then came the lightning stroke against Myitkyina spear-headed by those fabulous troops, Merrill's Marauders. At almost the same time a new Chinese Army attacked the Japanese across the Salween River and drove toward Burma.

In three weeks Merrill's Marauders had marched 112 miles over 8,000-foot mountains which native tribesmen told them could not be crossed. Their nimble-footed pack mules had fallen off the heights; the men themselves had to scramble up on all fours. Three columns slogged through ankle-deep red mud from the pre-monsoon rains. They fought two pitched battles, killed more than 2,000 Japanese, and lost 60 killed and 300 wounded.

When the Chinese and Americans neared Myitkyina, they blasted the rail and road bridges between it and Mogaung, 37 miles to the west. Then, the dirty, tired men burst forth upon the air-field, with its 5,000-foot landing strip and its neatly contrived dispersal bays. The surprised Japanese defenders barely took time to litter the field with oil drums and logs before they fled.

In 37 minutes the Marauders cleared the field. Twenty minutes later, Brig. Gen. William Old, troop carrier commander piloting an American transport, loosed the first gliders brought in and let them dip down on the runway. From then on, gliders and transports disgorged Chinese soldiers, American engineers, equipment and mortars. The gun crews trained the mortars on Myitkyina, two miles north, while the Marauders pressed on to take the town. General Stilwell arrived on the scene while the Allies were still in the outskirts.

## "Largest of the Automatics," John Walker, *Popular Science*, October 1942:

It's the newest thing in American antiaircraft defense—a gun that aims itself and hits hard. There may be one in your own back yard, guarding some vital area slanting upward from a carefully concealed position spotted around our seacoast cities and industrial areas, sleek gun barrels with odd flared muzzles that rake the sky. Around the guns, artillerymen stand always on the alert, ready to blast any enemy plane that might appear. Theirs is a powerful weapon against raiding planes—the Bofors 40-millimeter automatic cannon, hooked to a magic director mechanism that will hold the gun on a hostile bomber while it pumps shells as fast as the clips can be fed into it.

A neatly streamlined combat team, known informally as the "40-50," has been organized recently for the specific job of guarding American installations against one of the most dangerous forms of air attack—low-level or diving bombing. The tag "40-50" is entirely unofficial and comes from the fact that one defense section or emplacement has two supplementary weapons—the sleek Bofors 40-millimeter automatic cannon and the blunt, ugly, efficient .50-caliber machine gun. . . .

# 1947 Profile

# Occupied Japan

## Civilian

When Nora Steiner decided to put away her travel magazines and start visiting some of the places she'd read about, her life was opened to possibilities she had never even considered.

## Life at Home

- Nora Steiner was at work in the spring of 1945 when she received the news that her brother Tom had been shot during a minor battle near the Elbe River.
- Her mother had called to tell her that he was taken to a field hospital with a chest wound, but did not make it.
- Two years later, Nora decided it was time to pursue her lifelong interest in travel—with or without her father's permission.
- Since she was a small girl growing up in Wildrose, North Dakota, she had dreamed of traveling the world.
- The money she earned from the eggs laid by her chickens paid for a subscription to *National Geographic Magazine* and travelogues by female writers.
- Upon taking a job as a clerk for the federal government in Bismark, she embarked on a saving campaign that would allow her to travel.
- Ready to make those countries on the map come alive, her first step was to investigate the availability of jobs overseas.
- Nora first considered positions associated with the occupation in Germany, but when word arrived of clerical jobs with the occupation forces in Japan, she couldn't contain her excitement.
- In an uncharacteristic display of emotion, she squealed out loud with delight when the letter arrived offering her a position.
- For her grand adventure, she packed carefully—including all of her travel books.
- For weeks she carefully constructed list after list of places she wanted to visit.
- And the trip—when it became reality—was better than the dream; her first train ride across the country was a thrill.

*Nora Steiner is headed to occupied Japan.*

## Selected Prices

| | |
|---|---|
| Adding Machine | $120.00 |
| Aftershave, Mennen Skin Bracer | $0.98 |
| Board Game, Ouija | $1.59 |
| Cereal, Nabisco Honey Grahams | $0.27 |
| Chemise, Frederick's Gay Paree | $5.98 |
| Chicks, Box of 100 | $4.95 |
| China, Wedgwood Woodstock, 20-Piece Starter Set | $75.60 |
| Cycle Goggles | $3.49 |
| Hairstyling | $6.50 |
| Hatchet, Craftsman | $1.69 |
| Lotion, Jergens | $1.00 |
| Mirror, Full-length | $14.90 |
| Television, Emerson, 10-Inch | $295.00 |
| Vacuum Cleaner, General Electric | $39.95 |
| Washer, Kenmore | $119.95 |

## "The Reconversion of Douglas MacArthur," Martin Summers, *Saturday Evening Post*, May 25, 1946:

The Douglas MacArthur you are thinking about when you arrive here, the one you expect to find, is the relentless warrior who fought the Southwest Pacific war. You recall an unforgettable picture, MacArthur, on the shell-torn sands of bloody Los Negros, in the Admiralties, standing over the naked body of a Jap—one looking thoroughly dead, as only a Jap can look dead—and saying with satisfaction, "This is the way I like to see them."

But that is not the MacArthur you find here, not at all. You find a Douglas MacArthur who is, mirabile dictum, one of the most popular men in Japan, whose fan mail includes letters from intelligent (by Jap standards) Japanese women who want to have a son sired by him because they believe in some fashion this will fuse superior virtue into the Japanese people. You find a MacArthur who is working so hard at the systematic pacification of the Japanese people through constitutional government that his thoughts have turned away not only from killing and the art of war, but also from any presidential ambitions he may have had. You find a Douglas MacArthur who has come to take his job as overseer of 60 million obedient and peaceful people so seriously that he believes he may, through leading them in the creation of a sort of model democratic state without an army or navy, eventually point the way to world peace.

---

- The Rocky Mountains were taller than she had expected, San Francisco more charming and exciting, the ocean vastly larger than the books had said.
- After days of haunting the library and bookstores of San Francisco for literature on Japan, she felt prepared.
- On the date her ship arrived in Tokyo harbor, she stayed up all night, too excited to sleep.
- But even with all the reading, she was unprepared for postwar Tokyo, once the world's third-largest city.
  - Nearly all of the wooden buildings in the city had been destroyed during the wartime bombing.
  - For miles in every direction, she found only a desert landscape, where once seven million people had lived.
  - Three million people were crammed into the buildings that survived the bombing and subsequent flames.

### Life at Work

- Downtown Tokyo is filled with people from the Allied nations, especially Americans, and is the headquarters of the occupation forces, including 20,000 civilian War Department employees like Nora, one of 4,000 American women in clerical jobs.
- Japan has established a national government, but Gen. Douglas MacArthur, whose authority is absolute, exercises the real power.
- He is assisted by a large civilian staff.
- Since arriving, Nora has been assigned to the Surugadai Hotel, one of 10 downtown hotels where single women are housed.

General
Information
for
DEPENDENTS
Coming to the
TOKYO AREA

- The Surugadai is considered particularly desirable.
- Because of her newcomer status, she shares a large room with two other women of similar age—Midge Arndt, whose father manages a small fertilizer plant outside Spokane, Washington, and Celeste Amato, whose father is a stevedore in Bagonne, New Jersey.
  - In addition, they have the services of room girls—young Japanese women who work as personal servants.
  - Nora quickly learned that their room girl would wake her in the morning, tend to her clothes, clean the room, help her dress and even give massages.
  - Nora's job requires that she work from 9 a.m. to 5 p.m. five days a week, similar to her stateside government job.
  - All three roommates work in offices close to the hotel.
  - Celeste is a typist/stenographer for the medical supply division in the Public Health and Welfare Section.
  - A small, almost silent girl whose olive skin, large brown eyes and devout Catholicism advertise her Sicilian origins, she felt called by God to work in Japan.
  - Even though her assigned job is largely clerical, Celeste envisions her efforts bringing healing drugs and supplies to the most destitute people of Japan.
  - At 5 p.m., when others are heading home, Celeste catches a bus to the Our Lady of Lourdes Home in Yokohama, a Catholic orphanage specializing in occupation babies—children with Japanese mothers and occupation-force fathers, including Americans.
- These mixed-race children are often deserted by the fathers and rejected by the family and community of the mothers.
- Many of the babies are abandoned on the steps of the orphanage.
- The hardest lot, Celeste believes, falls to children with black fathers, since most Japanese consider blacks to be an inferior race.
- For several hours each evening and all day on Saturday, Celeste helps the nuns with the 130 babies in their care, taking time to feed them, change their diapers, play games and teach them to walk and talk.
- The half-black children are her special focus; she thinks they need her help most.

*Nora has two roommates in Tokyo, a city heavily damaged by war bombing.*

- Nora wonders whether Celeste secretly yearns to be a nun.
- Their other roommate, Midge, works for the government section responsible for transforming Japan into a self-governing democracy, including universal suffrage.
- Her actual goal is to meet men; work is simply a way to pass time between dates.
- Midge volunteered for duty in Japan because she had heard there would be 20 men for every single woman.

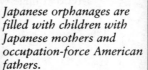

*Japanese orphanages are filled with children with Japanese mothers and occupation-force American fathers.*

- A tall blonde with a full figure and vivacious personality, Midge does not need 20-to-1 odds to be popular; nearly every night is spent out partying at bars, restaurants and private homes.
- A current focus of her attention is a divorced, balding major with a pot belly and vast tracts of land in his native Virginia.
- She often remarks that she would have no contact with the Japanese people were it not for the servants who wait on her.
- The best thing about Midge, in Nora's opinion, is that she isn't in the room often.
- Nora's job is with the information division of the Civil Information and Education Section, the function of which is to improve the status of women in Japan.
- In America, Nora had never considered the status of women.
- The rigidity of Japan's patriarchal society is not only shocking, but is a mirror of her own life.
- Since she was five years old, she has known that—merely because of his gender—her older brother was her father's favorite.
- College was affordable for her brother, but not for her, and good grades were discouraged because "boys don't like girls that are too smart for their own good," her mother had whispered like a close friend.
- For the first time, she is angry that she accepted this underclass status without a fight.
- In Japan, many of the women around her are professionals—graduates of prestigious colleges—who are in charge and making decisions without having to ask for permission every time something needs to be done.
- Nora finds herself eavesdropping on the conversations of these intelligent women, and has even asked their advice on reading lists and colleges to attend.
- Several times a week, mostly in the evenings, she attends Japanese-language colleges or lectures on Japanese art and culture.

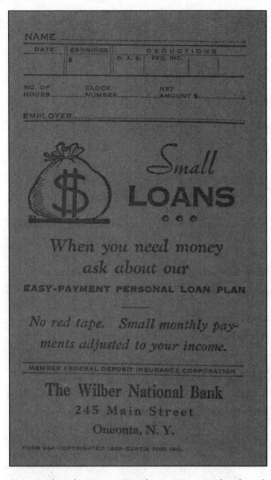

On weekends, Nora travels to Japanese landmarks and museums to understand the culture. She is also saving for college—a new dream.

- On weekends, she journeys to museums or nearby historical sites that have survived the war.
- She is growing to love the quiet beauty of Japan, and has invested in a Leica camera so she can capture the incredible world around her.
- During these trips, she takes every opportunity to practice her Japanese on natives, who are almost universally friendly and pleased that one of the "conquerors" is willing to learn their language—even while giggling politely behind their hands.
- Clearly, she has come to understand that the rural areas suffered less destruction than the cities did, but that economic hardship is everywhere.
- Her letters home, which include pictures she has taken, describe a nation struggling to rise from the ashes of absolute defeat.
- She does not mention her growing savings account, or her plans to attend college when she returns.

## Life in the Community: Japan

- During the Second World War, over a third of Tokyo was devastated.
- In Hiroshima and Nagasaki, almost a quarter of a million people lost their lives under the atom bombs; millions more were killed, maimed, or made homeless in the ruins.
- The bombing of the steel mills of Yawata, the shipyard of Kobe, and the aircraft factories of Yokohama resulted in the destruction of most of the country's major industries.
- In the "new" Japan, many small manufacturing plants—which were not targeted—are now up, running and competitive in the national economy.
- Like Americans, many Japanese citizens want to buy the goods that were unavailable during the war, allowing factories to switch smoothly from manufacturing planes to making aluminum kitchenware.

*Under American occupation, Japan's caste system is being transformed.*

- With the dismantling of the social caste system, American officials believe a great leveling is under way which will completely destroy the power of the upper class who controlled Japan—and with that, the country's power to wage war.
- As part of this process, the lowly are being raised; the farmer, once a poor peasant, is discovering that his needs and welfare are of interest to his government.
- In addition, young men both rich and poor have lost their lives in the fighting.
- One wealthy Japanese businessman says, "The past year has dealt no more lightly with me than it has my gardener. Truly, the war has made him my equal."
- Another blow to the roots of the social system is the passage of the Election Bill, which lowered the voting age from 25 to 20 and gave women the right to vote for the first time.
- In the first election after the voting reforms, 66 percent of the eligible women voters cast their ballots.
- To provide economic equality, no person is allowed to draw out more than 1,800 yen per month—no matter their wage.
- Anything workers make over that sum is deposited to their accounts and frozen, to become available at some time in the future.
- American soldiers are contributing to this equality; observers say, "You Americans don't seem to care about a man's social position at all. You would just as soon joke with a common laborer as with the chief of police."

# HISTORICAL SNAPSHOT
# 1947

- A Gallup poll reported that 94 percent of Americans believed in God
- Gerber Products Company sold two million jars of baby food weekly
- *A Streetcar Named Desire* by Tennessee Williams opened on Broadway
- The Freedom Train, carrying 100 of America's greatest documents, toured the United States
- The American Meat Institute reported that Americans abandoned wartime casseroles for meat five nights a week
- Seventy-five percent of all corn production was now hybrid
- *Esquire* magazine promoted the "bold look" for the man of "self-confidence and good taste," featuring wide tie clasps, heavy gold key chains, bold striped ties, big buttons and the coordination of hair color and clothing
- Bikini bathing suits arrived on American beaches to great excitement
- The American Friends Service Committee won the Nobel Peace Prize
- One million homes now had television sets
- Gillette and Ford paid $65,000 to sponsor the first televised World Series, during which an estimated 3.7 million people watched the Brooklyn Dodgers fall to the New York Yankees
- Returning GI veterans took advantage of the GI Bill, sending college enrollment to an all-time high
- New York began a fluoridation program for 50,000 children
- The new innovation of drive-in facilities at banks was spreading rapidly
- A house costing $4,440 in 1939 retailed for $9,060; the price of clothing was up 93 percent over the same period
- Minute Maid Corp., Ajax, Everglades National Park, the Cannes Film Festival and the Tony Awards all made their first appearance
- The United States was urged by the American Association of Scientific Workers to study bacteriological warfare

## "Are the Japs Really Licked?" Report to the Editor, Will Oursler, *True, The Man's Magazine*, January 1946:

This occupation of Japan is turning out to be the greatest weekend party in history.

People ask me plenty of questions since my return from Tokio [sic]. Do the Japs know they were beaten? Will they stay beaten and how does it look close-up?

Well—the Japs know they lost. But what they lost—at least in the minds of the smart-money boys and saber-rattling crew—was only a battle, not a war. Jap propaganda for a long time was telling the folks this would be a hundred years' conflict. Many of the Nips believe it. They think this peace is only a pause between the quarters.

Meanwhile, guests have arrived in the sacred homeland. American boys with plenty of cash and a healthy love of saki [sic], women and souvenirs. Jap propaganda in the early days of occupation contained instructions on how to treat the "guests"—remember, no violence, no disorders and don't make the prices too high.

That's the way of the Japs in this Alice in Wonderland occupation. Stores in Tokio are doing a rush business in souvenirs, raking in the yen, although one Jap girl in a department store on the Ginza, Tokio's Fifth Avenue, told me they were saving what good material they had and only brought out the "junk" for the GIs.

Of course, not all the GIs caught on to this host-guest arrangement with their former enemies. A few say after our landings began, a Jap lady showed up before the MPs quite distressed. She ran a geisha hangout in Yokohama and the night previous some Americans had appeared. That was okay. But it seems when the boys left, they took along the girls' kimonos as souvenirs. What with surrender and shortages, she explained, she couldn't get new kimonos for her girls and faced a difficult problem with a flock of girls and no clothes. The MPs promptly put the place out of bounds. I understand it is back on bounds now, but the MPs give a careful once-over to all GIs coming out, to make sure nobody's trying to get away with a kimono.

It isn't all laughter. A lot of people—among them newspapermen with whom I lived when I was in Tokio—are wondering just what is happening in Japan—and why. Everything has gone smoothly. The Japs have followed every order. There has been no trouble and I doubt that there will be unless some radical change occurs.

Japan, while she knows she has been licked, is certainly not suffering too greatly. There has been no attempt at punishment of any kind, beyond the arrest of a number of top war criminals. MacArthur, however, has ordered that the big Jap industrial combines be broken up. Stock owned or held by the eight powerful families who controlled all of Japan's industries and financed the war likely will go on public sale.

There have been changes, but the whole mood seems to be not to weaken Japan too greatly, not to upset her economy any more than necessary, not to carry the social revolution too far too fast.

But we heard some ugly reports in Tokio that the real reason we were allowing Japan to remain comparatively strong is that we want a buffer nation should we ever become involved in war with another nation. Facts on this have not come to light. I do not believe that this policy is MacArthur's. But I do believe that the American people deserve to have the whole story of the peace and our plans for Japan told to them by responsible officials.

For I am certain, also, that the Japanese are playing a waiting game. Their hope is that if they carry out all the orders carefully, we won't stay too long—and when we leave, the boys can start all over again, building up a war machine and making ready for new "expansion."

On the surface, it's sweetness and light. But you don't have to look too far to realize it's a fake. The Japs hate us now as they hated us before. If they get a chance—if we are trying to carry out some policy of building them up as a buffer against anybody else—I believe that someday we will have to fight them again.

## "What the Japanese Think of Us," Nora Waln, *Saturday Evening Press*, April 30, 1945:

A good way to try to understand the Japanese people is to understand first the mysteries of Fujiyama, the small mountain they love so well. Sometimes, below a crescent moon, it appears from nowhere. Sometimes, against a blue sky, you will find it floating in flawless white and silver, phantomlike, without base on earth. Its color changes with the seasons and the light from the Firmament—green, rose, purple and gold-tinted.

Fujisan can be seen from 22 of Japan's prefectures. Not at all shackled by the mundane matter of mileage, the mountain can appear very near or very far off. I have seen Fuji stand still in plain view—and then slowly disappear. It hides for days in veils of gray mist. It can be invisible when the weather is clear. Often it rises before me in beauty when I least expect to see its slopes.

I have found the Japanese people as varied in character as are the views of their mysterious mountain. And each Japanese whom I have met during my 18 months here has given me a new view into the mysteries of his nation. During much of my time in these islands, I have been staying at the homes of laborers, teachers and farmers; meeting purgees, the new rich and postal clerks; spending days with repatriates, getting acquainted with people in all walks of life. New arrivals from America and those who write to me always ask: "What do the Japanese really think of the occupation?"

In this article I will let the women and men of Japan tell you for themselves, as so many of them told me. We will visit many at some length. . . .

A suitable stop for our first visit is the monthly meeting of the Young Mothers' League. We are in Hanna's house, which stands by the sea, west of Hayama, and the room is filled with carefully groomed young women with dark hair, soft brown eyes and smooth complexions. Nearly all are the daughters or granddaughters of once-wealthy industrialists, diplomats and the nobility. Several were titled before the occupation took away the special privileges of their birth. Today, their graceful hands show the signs of housework in homes where warm water and good soap are scarce.

It is Mieko's turn to read a paper this month, and I have a copy. Mieko pauses to tend the baby on her back, since he was pulling at her hair. We are sitting on the floor because Hanna's house has no chairs, but each of us has a large square cushion filled with soft fiber from the silkworm's cocoon. Some young mothers wear kimonos of beautiful material with handsome obis girdling their waists. Others are in western dress. Many have their babies tied on their backs, where a child is usually quieter than in the lap. All the children are prettily and neatly dressed in harmonious colors. Some sleep. Others watch wide-eyed, even when cuddled down on the mothers' necks.

"We are free if we want to be free," said Mieko. "Those who have the courage can speak up to parents and husbands and have their say about the education of their children. This is now the law—there shall be no more discrimination in social, economic or political relations because of sex, social status or family origin, race or creed. Marriages shall not be arranged by parents or guardians against the wishes of those to be married. After the wedding, the wife shall be equal to the husband in all matters, including those which relate to their home. Any sin which is a sin done by the wife is a sin when done by the husband, too."

Here audience stirred, several exchanging glances.

"These ideas are not new in Japan. We had them early in our history. Then they were lost. Not until less

## "What the Japanese . . ." *(continued)*

than a century ago did a movement start to regain them. Some of our mothers and grandmothers worked in a vain attempt to secure an honorable position for us. They failed. In too many families submission to father by instruction given through the mother, and then submission to the husband and his parents were taught as the virtues of well-bred girls. The daughter was not to try to reason. In middle- and upper-class families it was generally believed that the female mind is not equal to the masculine mind. The working people were led to copy us."

Mieko drew in her breath. Her voice was pleading as she went on, "I do have to say something which is disrespectful to our fathers. When you and I were growing up, our nation's armed forces were succeeding in aggressive warfare on land and sea. But as conquest after conquest abroad was proclaimed, the regulations on girls and women were tightened at home. We were not to question. We were to praise.

"Disgrace and defeat were our nation's fate. Many of us were stunned when we heard our Emperor's broadcast. I remember that my mother and I were so tired that when the word came that war was over, we slept most of the time for two days. The defeat brought us all relief, but our nation had never been invaded. What would happen when the victors landed and made their control secure? A miracle occurred. The dread enemy surprised us by presenting to the women of Japan the very same rights that their own women have. Was there ever, in the whole history of mankind, a nobler gesture?

"Liberty brings new responsibilities and new opportunities," said Mieko. "Some are bewildered by our new rights. Let us here resolve that the faith which the citizens of the United States have shown in the women of Japan shall make us faithful to them. We can be partners for good in the world. Something fine is possible. Japan is the testing ground where Orient and Occident can truly meet in a great common adventure."

## "Japan's Occupation Babies," Darrell Berrigan,
### *Saturday Evening Post*, June 19, 1948:

For somewhat more than 300 years, white conquerors from the West have been mixing their blood with the conquered people of the East, creating a minority of unhappy misfits belonging neither to the East nor to the West. In long-occupied countries like India, Indonesia and Indo-China, the Eurasian population, fathered by European military and civilian administrators, has grown into a troublesome minority of millions living in a political and social limbo between the native populations and the Western nationals. Such a minority is growing in Japan under the Allied occupation.

But neither the Japanese nor the occupation authorities are going to wait 300 years to try to find a solution to the problem of what to do with what is called here the "occupation baby." The attempt is being made now—while the babies are still in their cribs, ignorant of their differences from the majority of the pure Japanese with whom most of them will have to live out their lives—to prepare them for a fairly normal existence in Japan or to send them to the countries from which their fathers came.

It is impossible to say how many occupation babies—black, white, brown and yellow—there are in Japan today, after almost three years of occupation. Estimates range from 1,000 to 4,000, but there are no official figures. There never will be so long as the Allied authorities have anything to say about it. Even if the authorities were interested in counting heads, they could not. Mothers of what the Japanese call "half-half" babies attempt to hide the child's paternity or kill or abandon it because of the stigma attached to occupation motherhood. Whatever the statistics, the number of occupation babies abandoned and turned over to institutions is so large now that public groups have begun to take an interest in their future. That future is a matter for considerable indirect argument between SCAP—Supreme Commander Allied Powers—officials and missionary and other groups interested in the welfare of the half-half children of white and black Americans, Russians, Australians, British, Indians and Chinese.

There is very little that can be done to prevent the continued increase in the number of occupation babies as long as the Allied armies are in Japan. Armies have for untold centuries left traces of their blood in every country, friend or enemy. Sex education, among the American forces at least—and they, being the most numerous, are the ones most concerned—has limited to a certain extent the number of children of mixed blood who will be left behind when the occupation armies move out some time in the undecided future. Military law, however, frees the soldier or its officer unless he wishes to admit paternity, and moral responsibility is difficult to cultivate in a barracks full of lonely young men feeling the full force of manhood. No "Off Limits" signs or bans on "public displays of affection" are going to keep men from finding female companionship among the only people available in any numbers, the Japanese.

Women, too, have always found their way to the tents of soldiers, whether enemy or ally. In Japan, the material rewards of the camp follower are supplemented by the treatment they receive at the hands of foreigners accustomed to considering women as something several ranks above a work animal. If the foreigner happens to be an American and shows up with a box of candy from the PX and a little respect and courtesy, the girl usually falls in love with the paragon. Few Japanese males would pay her such honor or treat her with such kindness....

Other mothers of occupation babies come from ordinary farm or village homes near a military base. The excitement the gallant foreigner brings to their drab lives is the realization of a dream too beautiful to resist. At least that is the way Akiko, who is one of them, reacted to her Lochinvar.

Akiko is a homely, pink-cheeked little girl with a couple of silver teeth in the middle of her mouth.

## "Japan's Occupation . . ." *(continued)*

She lives in a small village near Hiratsuka, an industrial center south of Tokyo which American bombers flattened level with the sea beside which it stands. Chuck, the lanky soldier from New England, ambled into her yard one day when she was helping her mother make sembei, the salty cakes they sell for a living. He asked for a glass of water in very amusing Japanese. Akiko and her mother sat with the soldier until he had rested, and walked with him to the tiny gate when he left. He came often after that with gifts and, at last, asked her to go to a dance. The mother did not object.

Before the little fatherless family knew exactly how it came about, they had a foreigner living with them whenever he was off duty. It seemed a very happy arrangement. Akiko treasures a collection of dim snapshots taken then—pictures of Chuck, a bitter-looking young man, homely and gaunt, helping Akiko thresh rice by hand, slouching on the floor in a kimono with a cigarette dangling from his mouth; holding a neighbor's baby in his arms to pose with Akiko and her mother and two brothers in front of their cramped little house.

When Chuck brought his last box of candy and told Akiko he had to go back to America, and didn't know whether he would be able to return or not, he gave her an envelope with his address on it. He asked her to let him know whether his child was a boy or a girl. Then he disappeared into the dimness that is America in the imagination of the Japanese, and hasn't been heard of since. Akiko's baby is a girl, a lively child with white skin, brown eyes and silky, light brown hair. Otherwise, it is like any other Japanese child with a dirty, padded kimono, chapped cheeks and hands, and a running nose. Akiko named her Lily. . . .

# "Foreign Affairs: An Estimate of MacArthur's Success in Japan," *Newsweek*, January 7, 1946:

Never before in the history of Japan has anyone except the emperor himself or a returning conqueror in a carefully staged triumph been able to attract a voluntary crowd. Now nearly every day, numbers of Japanese gather before the Dai Ichi Building, General of the Army MacArthur's headquarters, in downtown Tokyo. That is the measure of the success MacArthur and his advisers have had in smashing the old fabric of Japanese life and starting the Japs on the road to a democratic state.

Two weeks ago General MacArthur said that the initial stage had been accomplished. Last week the Moscow agreements gave 10 other nations a say in the further development of Japan. Newsweek asked a contributing editor and expert on Japan, Maj. Compton Pakenham, to draw up the following estimate of what has already been done and the basis on which the Japs will now go forward under 11 flags.

Military: To one who has served in the Japanese Army, as I have, the military master stroke of the Americans was successfully using the authority of the emperor to tame a people ready for last-ditch defense and obtain the surrender of the Japanese forces scattered all over Asia. Thereafter, MacArthur in Japan proper quickly moved to root out the foundations of Jap militarism.

So far so good. But the key to whether those reforms can be maintained in the future lies in what happens to the demobilized Jap officer corps. The mass of Jap officers came from the lower edge of the middle class to which they will return as did their predecessors, the samurai, when the Meiji emperor did away with their privileges in the last century. Their state of mind in the aftermath of defeat will be important, for it must be remembered that the foundations of modern Japan were laid by samurai out of jobs.

Financial: MacArthur demonstrated quickly that the domination of Japanese finance and industry, both private and governmental, by the Zaibatsu, the ruling clique of great families, could be dispensed with. Japanese industry and finance had been reduced to a state of chaos anyway, so that the time was ripe to break up the combines. The abolition of these interlocking trusts should make it impossible for any Japanese government ever again to form the cohesive war machine that was set up during the late conflict.

At the same time, Japanese peasants have been released from age-old bonds by the abolition of absentee landlordism and the ruinous system of rents in kind. This is especially significant because the peasant probably represents the Allies' best chance for achieving some kind of democracy in Japan. He has been less warped in mind and spirit than the industrial proletariat.

Politics: Political parties in Japan have seldom represented much more than the power and prestige of their leaders. There were really only two of any importance, the Seiyukai and the Minseito. Both of them have had their days of respect and their days of corruption. During the war, all the parties were swept into the catch-all Dai Nippon Seijikai (Political Association of Great Japan).

Now, MacArthur has either named as war criminals most of the leaders of the Dai Nippon Seijikai or has in effect scared them out of public life with the threat of being so named. This should enable the Japs to start out on a fresh political basis. The franchise has also been extended by lowering the male voting age from 25 to 20 and introducing women's suffrage. Even so, the Japs are probably not ready for elections, and those scheduled for January will probably wisely be postponed.

Educational and Religious: The reform of the educational system and the press and radio has already borne its first fruits. The press itself is bringing home to the Japanese the full enormity of their defeat and their responsibility for the war.

Last on MacArthur's program was an order sweeping away the cancer at the core, State Shinto, by cutting off its support from the government. Distinguishing between the simple pantheis-

## "Foreign Affairs . . ." (continued)

tic faith of the conservatives, Sect Shinto, and the monstrous distortion created to unite the people under the throne for imperial domination of the world, the directive undermined the ludicrous mumbo-jumbo of divinity and national destiny. The proof of the pudding appeared this week. In a

New Year's Eve prescript, the emperor renounced his own divinity as a "myth" and urged the development of a true constitutional monarchy. He also advised the Japanese to abandon any pretensions to being a "master race" and to accept the fact of their defeat.

## "Main Street Moves to Japan," Wedon James, *Colliers*, June 14, 1947:

Occupation forces and their civilian colleagues in Japan live in a world of their own. It's even better than home, and the entire expense of it is charged to reparations. Nobody's worried but the Japs.

The charming young woman with the blue eyes and the freckled nose stared moodily at the orange groves and rice paddies of Kyushu as the Allied Express thundered along the rickety roadbed of Japan's southernmost island. She was having none of it.

"I tell you," she said with vehemence, "they've found the one weak chink in our American armor, and they're cracking away at it. They know we're absolutely dependent on plumbing that works, and they're damned well determined we shan't have it. It's psychological warfare, that's what it is."

Her army officer husband nodded in weary agreement. He had heard this, off and on, ever since his wife arrived in Japan. He had long before taken over an army-requisitioned Western-style house, supervised repairs, painting and furnishing, and felt complacently that Mrs. Smith and little daughter Mary could not have been welcomed to a nicer home, not even in the States.

But the plumbing had never worked, not for more than a week at a time. The water supply would fail. On days when it didn't fail, it flooded, when the supply on the first floor was all right, the pipes on the third would burst and soak the house. Or, when guests for the weekend arrived, the heat would fail, and no one could bathe.

The Smiths had had it. And were ready to go home. They would have to stay a year or more, of course, the army being what it is, but they wouldn't have to like it. And if anyone ever dared to say anything like, "Never had it so good!" Well. . . .

The Smiths are a pleasant if saddened fraction of the 160,000-odd Americans currently running Japan (or being run by the Japanese). And for some, despite plumbing and lingual difficulties, it must be said, in truth, that they never had it so good.

General MacArthur has only about 130,000 GIs and officers in his incredibly small U.S. occupation force, bolstered by some 35,000 British troops. But his civilian charges are increasing apace. By July he'll have more than 20,000 War Department civilian employees in Japan, and by December, with more than 1,100 wives and children arriving monthly, a "dependent" population of 26,000.

These Americans are a foreign society sitting on top of the Japanese body politic and economic, a flock of democrats living under army rule and by army Grace, creating a new kind of Little America.

Aside from the GI, who has it good enough by anyone's overseas standards, most of the Americans live in the best parts of whatever region they occupy, possessing the best private houses, and best of the relatively few hotels and apartment buildings thoughtfully left around by the B-29 boys, or the spanking new Quonset cottages and houses put up by the army with Japanese labor. The highest price even a general can pay for a mansion complete with army-furnished heating systems, refrigerators, furniture and five Japanese servants: $100.50 per month, the maximum in the War Department Scale. The average: closer to $51.

The heart of the American capital is the mile or two of modern office buildings and hotels miraculously spared by the B-29s, an oasis of solidity and comfort in the burned or blown-out wreckage of Tokyo's 750,000 "missing" buildings. It stretches roughly from the Imperial Palace, upon which General MacArthur can look down from his marble offices in the great Dai Ichi building to the Ginza, and up and down "MacArthur Boulevard," and weaves across occasional ruins to include scattered smaller cases of London-like office buildings or hotels.

Here, thousands of Americans live and work, and here their thousands of jeeps, trucks, buses and increasing numbers of shiny new autos, fresh from the States, make the sight of a rickshaw a rarity and give the heart of the city an incredibly

### "Main Street Moves . . ." *(continued)*

Americanized look. (The Americans already have almost as many motor vehicles on the roads as all the 74 million native Japanese put together.)

If he wants to, the American can be as insulated against contact with real Japan (except for servants) as though he was in New York. The GIs have luxurious clubs, with beer and dancing, and plenty of American girls to dance with—at least in Tokyo or Yokohama. The officers have comfortable hotels, overheated and staffed with countless servants, and every billet has a good and well-used cocktail bar. Civilians live comparably, depending on their real or simulated rank; a CAF-15 can, like a general, live in the supposedly splendid Imperial Hotel, have a staff car and driver, and pay only $28 per month for a suite with bath; the lesser lights will be in somewhat humbler, less expensive, and more crowded quarters, as will the junior officers or the GIs.

Even with PD, the Americans are all a flock of millionaires to the Japanese. A GI corporal gets $108 a month, the lowest-paid civilian at least $200 (minus no more than $45 for army food, shelter and service). And worth its weight in yen if not gold is the individual ration of cigarettes, candy, snack food and other PX items; a carton of cigarettes traded on the black market fetches a price legally valued at about $30 but actually worth about $5 in black-market trade. Army blankets, PX clothing (especially women's wear), food, gasoline and other occupation naturals fetch similarly high prices. But the army thinks it has the black market fairly well under control, or at least limited to small-time operations.

That backbone of the American community, the GI, has been getting a cleaner bill of health lately, too. GI crimes in the Tokyo area, major and minor, have decreased 400 percent in the last three months. Indeed, according to the Tokyo Provost Marshal, two-war veteran Brigadier General C.S. Ferrin, today's GI is a vast improvement over what he calls "last year's drugstore cowboys—the reluctant postwar draftees who just wanted to get home again, and to hell with it all."

# 1950–1959

As World War II was drawing to a close, America was pushing east to free Europe from Nazi rule, while the Soviet Union was advancing west with the same objective. However, the geographic point at which the U.S. and the U.S.S.R. met in Berlin was to have a profound effect on Europe for over four decades. The Soviet Union claimed the east side of Berlin, and eventually built the Berlin Wall, while closing off most of Eastern Europe behind an imaginary "Iron Curtain."

The far-reaching consequence of this "remapping" of the globe between Soviet Russia and the West—between communism and capitalism—was the Cold War. Government policies were rewritten according to the difference in philosophy between the U.S. and the U.S.S.R. and, it seemed, no conflict could occur anywhere in the world without involving either of these two superpowers in some way. Thus, the Korean War in the early part of the decade, the overthrow of Guatemala's elected president, and at home, the paranoia and subsequent witch hunts spurred by McCarthyism overshadowed the entire decade.

Americans became obsessed with the threat of the atomic bomb, the need for building fallout shelters, and the weeding out of suspected communists. The Screen Actors Guild banned suspected communists from membership, and libraries were harassed to remove books by authors who had the slightest leftwing leanings. Propaganda and harassment drove such popular figures as Charlie Chaplin from the country, and ruined the careers of many Hollywood writers, actors, artists and directors. Friends and colleagues were pressured to inform on them or be branded communists themselves. Universities similarly expelled faculty whose personal beliefs or professional writings were suspect. Conservative politics and social conformity ruled the day as women were assigned a rigid role centered on home and family.

On the bright side, the war years' high employment and optimism stimulated the longest sustained period of peacetime prosperity in the nation's history. A decade of high employment and consumerism produced demands for all types of goods. Businesses prospered, while rapidly swelling families, new suburban homes, televisions and most of all, big, powerful, shiny automobiles symbolized the hopes of the era.

# 1950 NEWS FEATURE

**"The Big Plot," published by the National Non-Partisan Committee to Defend the Rights of the 12 Communist Leaders, Co-Chairmen Paul Robeson and Judge Norval K. Harris, 1950:**

A plan to impose a police state on America has already been drawn up.

It is not the ranting of Rankin, but the cold sober calculation of the Justice Department of the United States.

The plan, disclosed on Thursday, January 12, 1950, by Mr. Raymond P. Whearty, Acting Assistant Attorney General, calls for the arrest and trial of 21,105 people who "appear to be acting in concert with Russian interests"!

According to Senator McCarthy and the FBI, this could include Judge Dorothy Kenyon, Albert Einstein and the shop steward who asks for $0.10 an hour more.

Certainly, it would include people who want peace, trade unions fighting Taft-Hartley, and individuals opposed to the remilitarization of Germany.

The housewife against high prices, the tenant who wants rent control, the college professor who demands the right to think and speak for himself, all come under its terms.

Here is the official transcript of Mr. Whearty's testimony before the House Subcommittee on Appropriations:

MR. ROONEY: (John J. Rooney, Representative from New York, Chairman of Subcommittee)

With regard to the Internal Security Section, your chart shows there are pending at the end of the first six months of this fiscal year 21,105 cases. What sort of matters are these?

MR. WHEARTY: . . .The bulk of the cases involve subversive activity as applied to individuals or organizations. By that I mean persons who are active members of the Communist Party and similar organizations, or who appear to be acting in concert with Russian interests. Does that answer your question sufficiently?

MR. ROONEY: I am still at a loss to understand the large number, 21,105 cases pending.

MR. WHEARTY: Let me explain it this way, sir. The Federal Bureau of Investigation furnishes to this Department and the Internal Security Section reports on individuals engaged in subversive activities. I would say that these reports come in volumes ranging

THE BIG PLOT

Proof of the Justice Department's
plan to jail 21,105 Americans

Published and Circulated by:
**NATIONAL NON-PARTISAN COMMITTEE**
To Defend the Rights of the 12 Communist Leaders
DUE PROCESS IN A POLITICAL TRIAL
The Record vs. The Press      25¢ per copy. Orders of 25
                              and more — 10¢ per copy.
A 64-page abstract of the Record in the trial of the 12 Communist Leaders in the U.S. District Court for the Southern District of New York, prepared by a group of New York attorneys
who examined more than 21,000 pages of the record, with a
view of determining whether the press reports of the proceed-
ings were substantiated by the record.
   Direct from the record, this document raises serious questions
in relation to the administration of justice.

THE COMMUNIST TRIAL: An American Crossroads
by George Marion                        $1.25 per copy
   *"An Exciting Book."*—O. JOHN ROGGE, *former U.S. Assistant
                              Attorney General*
FREEDOM IS EVERYBODY'S JOB: by George Crockett
   The crime of the Government Against the Negro People.
   Summation in the Trial of the 11 Communist Leaders.
                  $.10 per copy. 12 copies for $1.00

----------- ORDER YOUR COPIES NOW! -----------
NATIONAL NON-PARTISAN COMMITTEE
23 West 26th Street
New York 10, N. Y.

Enclosed please find $ .............. for which send me
.......... copies of "THE BIG PLOT."

(Bundle orders of 100 at 3½¢ per copy; 1000 at 3¢ per copy. Special
rates for organizations ordering 5000 or more. All postage prepaid.)

I also enclose $ ............. for .......... copies of DUE
PROCESS, .......... copies of THE COMMUNIST TRIAL and
.......... copies of FREEDOM IS EVERYBODY'S JOB.

Name ...............................................
Address ............................................
City ..................... Zone ...... State ...............

from 20 to 200 per day. They involve different individuals. Each one has to be read and screened to determine whether there is any action required, criminal or otherwise.

MR. ROONEY: . . .The figure 21,105 represents the number of reports?

MR. WHEARTY: No, sir. They represent the number of subjects covered by the reports, whether those subjects be individuals or organizations. . . . I should also say that with respect to many of these persons engaged in subversive activities, such as the Communist case in New York, in line with our appearance before the committee last year, there is a program of extensive suits to prosecute members of the Communist Party who can be shown to be sympathetic and appreciative of its views. We prosecute them as individuals under the Smith Act.

I will call your attention to the fact that in New York, the defendants in the Communist trials have been directed to file their briefs before the Circuit Court of Appeals by May 1. . . .

I feel that if the case is decided in the lower court, it will be in the Supreme Court of the United States next fall. I cannot conceive of the Supreme Court not taking this case, and we will have an ultimate decision one way or the other. If the government is sustained in the Supreme Court of the United States, it will be about the fiscal year 1951 when that program will come up. This is the workload which we must look forward to as possible, and indeed very probable.

MR. ROONEY: Of the 21,105 cases now pending, how many of them would you say depend upon the outcome of the Communist trial in New York?

MR. WHEARTY: Roughly 12,000.

MR. ROONEY: What about the others?

MR. WHEARTY: The others are cases in which action may or may not be possible. I would like to elaborate a little bit more. There are a number of cases in the Department which are perfectly good trial cases, but can't be proven for the reason that the sole witnesses to the cases are confidential informants and cannot be used as witnesses and those cases have to be canceled out.

### THE NEW CRIME—THINKING

Mr. Whearty's language is so calm that the significance of what he is proposing can easily be overlooked.

He is not outlining a plan for the trial of 21,105 people because of what they have done. He is proposing to try them for their ideas—21,105 people hauled into court for thinking!

At the same time that Mr. Whearty was asking for

money to bring these people to trial, J. Edgar Hoover, head of the FBI, asked for funds for 702 additional agents.

Since Mr. Whearty indicated that the 21,105 cases are already processed, the additional agents must be to go after thousands more.

And, in the Mundt-Ferguson Bill, the dragnet that will sweep millions into courts and concentration camps is being prepared.

Commenting on the Mundt-Ferguson Bill, the conservative *San Francisco Chronicle* said: ". . . a law requiring members of the Communist Party to register their names with the government would imperil the civil rights of every American, Communist and non-Communist."

While Administration forces try to push the Mundt Bill through Congress, the Department is basing its thought-control trials on the Smith Act, which has been on the statute books since 1940.

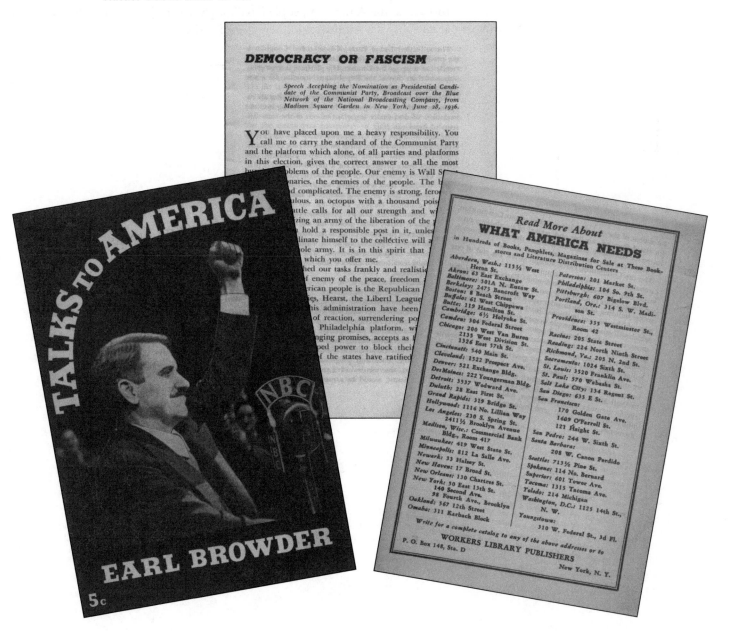

Now, there is no mention in the Smith Act of acts of force and violence. On the contrary, the Smith Act makes the teaching and advocating of ideas a crime. But if it is now a crime to teach and advocate ideas, what happens to the first Amendment to the Constitution?

The First Amendment says clearly:

"Congress shall make no law respecting an establishment of religion, or prohibition the free exercise thereof; or abridging the freedom of speech, or of the press, or the right of the people peaceably to assemble, and to petition the government for a redress of grievances."

"No law," says the First Amendment. But Congress has made a law—the Smith Act—and the Smith Act is being used by the government today to subvert the Bill of Rights, which guarantees Americans their right to think, to speak, to advocate, to trial by jury, to bail, etc.

For over 150 years, the American people have fought to enforce these rights. Now, in three short paragraphs, the Smith Act blithely destroys them.

# 1951 Profile

## Aboard a Minesweeper: Korean Waters

### Navy Crewman

Under the slogan "Where the Fleet Goes, We've Been," Edwin Sherman Webber from California is fighting the Communists in Korea aboard a minesweeper, a tiny wooden ship critical to a naval assault.

### Life at Home

- When Ed Webber first learned he was going into the navy, his head was filled with dynamic destroyers and elegant, super ship carriers; the last assignment he expected was minesweeping in Korea.
- In fact, when he finished high school in Salinas, California, he wasn't sure he even knew where Korea was; he was just trying to impress his girlfriend Jane by going into the navy.
- Ed grew up in a small home located in a new development outside Salinas.
- As he grew, so did Salinas, as new subdivisions surrounded his development and flooded the area with kids to play with.
- In Ed's junior year in high school, his father, who worked on road construction, was made foreman of a large grading crew.
- Ed's father, a smart, proud man who understood math and how to make a crew work hard, could barely read.
- He and his wife, a part-time beautician, were determined that all five children would finish high school, because they had been told that working class kids who were educated could be rich one day.
- Starting in the ninth grade, Ed did his part to build the wealth by working afternoons and summers at a neighborhood grocery.
- Enlisting in the navy, however, was a ticket to the GI Bill and college.
- But getting in wasn't easy.

*Edwin Sherman Webber grew up in Salinas, California.*

COMMUNIST KHRUSHCHEV

- The first time he went for his physical, he was told he was underweight and his blood pressure was too high.
- The doctor told him: "Go home, eat a lot of bananas, drink lots of milk and take some tranquilizers."
- He did as he was told, and was accepted on the second try.

### Life at Work

- Minesweeping was not what Ed had been promised upon enlisting, but that's what he got.
- Within the navy, the assignment is considered a poor relation to those of other surface warfare duties.
- Minesweeping does, however, represent a regular paycheck.
- Quickly, Ed found it also presents steel-handed challenges: No amphibious landing is undertaken until the minesweepers have done their dangerous work.
- Upon completion of his final course, he took a short leave, which gave him time enough to marry Jane before he shipped out to the Far East.

## HOW COULD SOVIET ATTACK COME?

### THE REDS, WHOSE WAR PRODUCTION FAR OUTSTRIPS OURS, MIGHT BASE STRATEGY ON A QUICK KNOCKOUT

The danger of war is seen best in one compelling fact: the Soviets are preparing for war (chart, *left*). They are spending tremendous manpower and a qua... mad... mo... civi... ler's... rez... seel... ten...  vas... can... wea... new... tria... The... typ... but... of t... a n... flee...

ful undersea fleet than Germany had at the start of the last war. Its 270 submarines include the latest Schnorkel-equipped U-boats which Germany de...

as a scare gesture shelled the Oregon and California coasts from submarines and sent bomb-laden balloons floating aimlessly toward the Pacific Coast. ...ock ...arn- ...orce ...ight ...ange ...ities ... far ...ight ...sive ...first ...aps, ...  So- ...uld ...ars, ...ex- ...suf- ...U.S. ...Rus- ...rld.

### "War, Sea, Death for the *Magpie*," *Time*, October 16, 1950:

Before she became a minesweeper, the *USS Magpie* worked in the California fishing fleet as a dragger, or purse seiner, and she was known as the *City of San Pedro*. In 1936 the navy bought her and 20 sister boats, gave them each a three-inch gun, gear to catch something more deadly than tuna, and names from the birds, such as *Bunting, Crossbill, Crow, Puffin* and *Heath Hen*. They all had wooden hulls so thin that a dummy torpedo dropped in practice from a plane once sank one. Still, the *Magpie* and her sisters, not without casualties, served in World War II, sweeping up enemy mines off Palau, Okinawa, the Philippines and Normandy.

Last week, while clearing the waters off the east Korean shore, the *Magpie's* wooden hull bumped a floating mine. The explosion sent her to the bottom, with her crew, including her commander, Lieut. Warren Roy Person; only 12 survivors were picked up.

The *Magpie* was the third U.S. warship hit by floating mines off Korea. . . . In Washington, Chief of Naval Operations Admiral Forrest P. Sherman said the mines were Russian-made, "only recently from the warehouse," probably set adrift in Korean rivers. More than 65 have been swept up so far. They are illegal under The Hague Convention of 1907, which forbids unmoored mines. Russia, however, had never signed the convention.

- The honeymoon was too short, the voyage from San Diego to Japan too quick.
- In Japan, introductions were succinct; the *Yellowhammer*, a 136-foot wooden-hull vessel, was now home.
- The *Yellowhammer* began life as a tuna fishing boat in California.
- Since the late 1930s, she has served as a minesweeper in the Philippines during the darkest days of World War II.
- Commanded by a reserve lieutenant who has been called into active service for the Korean conflict, she now carries a crew of 29 men and four officers.
- Ed lives for letters from his new bride, but those from his little brother, Cotten, are a wonderfully mundane godsend.
- One of the first told how Cotten was crowned the red-hot cinnamon jaw-breaker king after he kept one in his mouth the longest—almost 20 minutes.
- Cotten is also assembling the world's largest bottle-cap collection by hanging around the gas station where folks buy lots of drinks; the collection includes dozens of rare caps, but is still missing a Vernor's ginger ale cap.
- No one would drink a Vernor's—too gingery—making the cap even more rare.
- The *Yellowhammer's* assignment, now that the Korean conflict is well under way, is patrolling the east coast of the Korean peninsula.
- On small missions, she operates alone; on larger jobs, the *Yellowhammer* is part of a flotilla of minesweepers acting in concert to clear the waters before the destroyers arrive.
- In the larger operations, several of the vessels sweep the water for mines using steel wires extending from the beams.
- The wires are stretched out and kept submerged with steel "kites."
- Every 250 feet, the wires have cutters capable of severing the mooring cables of contact mines, allowing them to float to the surface.

*Ed and Jane married before he shipped out.*

- One vessel acts as the "destruct," following the sweepers to detonate or destroy the mines using rifle or machine-gun fire.
- The one or two remaining vessels have "dunning" duty, marking the cleared area with buoys.
- The majority of the mines used by the North Koreans are contact mines; however, Ed must always be alert for Russian-made magnetic mines which lie at the bottom of a body of water and are set off by the magnetic field of a passing ship.
- These mines are swept by streaming two large cables—one 1,200 feet long, the other shorter with a copper electrode—from the stern of the sweeper.
- When the cables are extended to their full length, a generator on the vessel sends a powerful current through the cable, creating a magnetic field capable of detonating the mine.
- Unfortunately for the sweepers, the Russian magnetic mines can be calibrated to detonate only after several ships had passed over—to ensure an explosion takes place in the middle of a convoy.
- This forces minesweepers to work a section of water numerous times to make sure all the mines have been found.
- On the *Yellowhammer,* the entire mine-related work, including the sweeping, marking of the buoys and destruction of floating mines, is part of Ed's duty.
- Every member of a minesweeper knows the statistics: Minesweepers comprise only two percent of naval personnel, but 20 percent of deaths.
- When sweeping is not required, maintenance of the gear and drilling take priority.
- Since arriving in Korea, Ed has experienced some long, tense days.
- During an operation, his crew may clear mines for 24 to 36 hours at a stretch, especially if a major amphibious landing is planned.
- In April, the *Yellowhammer* received orders to sweep the mouth of a small river, where military intelligence indicated that mines had been laid by small sampans, or fishing boats, during the previous three, nearly moonless nights.

### "U.S. Will Base Road Building on War Needs," *New York Herald Tribune*, November 11, 1950:

Plans for a sweeping revision of the federal-state road construction program to meet the nation's military needs are rapidly shaping up.

The new program follows President Truman's request that all government agencies coordinate their activities, insofar as possible, with the military preparedness program.

Federal Bureau of Roads officials say a state-by-state survey shows that half of the projects scheduled for construction on the 400,000 mile secondary system can be eliminated. . . .

However, officials said plans for reconstruction and expansion of the 40,000-mile interstate system will go ahead as originally scheduled.

The substituted projects in the secondary system will include highways to hitherto untapped mineral and agricultural resources vital to the nation's military needs.

**Starting Something?**

Edwin Marcus. *The New York Times*, 1950.

- After weeks of tough assignments, this one sounded easy—a small job with no known major enemy forces in the area, so the *Yellowhammer* went alone.
- After she had covered over half the area and disposed of six mines, a loud crack was heard from the shore, followed by the splash of an artillery shell 30 yards to starboard.
- The *Yellowhammer* employed her three-inch guns with little impact.
- Still with a mission to complete, the vessel continued to sweep.
- To provide cover, the captain called for air support, but with the closest aircraft carrier nearly 60 miles away, the crew's best hope was the Korean soldiers' poor marksmanship.
- As the number of shots from the jungle-covered shore continued to increase, Ed tried to focus on the task at hand—making sure the kites were kept taut from the stern.
- Like everyone on the boat, he was also keeping one eye on the sky, hoping for air support.
- The captain had already said the *Yellowhammer* was not running from a small artillery piece, but he pulled the boat farther from shore.
- About the time two more severed mines floated to the surface, the crew heard a low rumble and saw two specks in the sky.

*War dominates the lives of the people in Korea.*

- The explosion of the two mines blended with the sound of a bombing run on the enemy artillery positions, followed by a machine-gun strafing by the low-flying planes.
- As the planes turned back to the ship, Ed checked the coordinates; two more hours of sweeping were ahead.
- Maybe the rest of the ride would be quiet.

## Life in the Community: Korea

- Korea is a peninsula, about the size of Great Britain, lying between Japan and the mainland countries of China and Russia in eastern Asia.
- Its location as a small country surrounded by powerful neighbors has directed its history.
- One Korean proverb points out, "The shrimp is broken when the whales fight."
- From the sixteenth century on, both Japan and China have invaded the country, with Japan winning wars with China and Russia over Korea during the latter part of the nineteenth century.
- By 1905, Japan had declared Korea a protectorate subject to Japanese control, which the United States recognized.

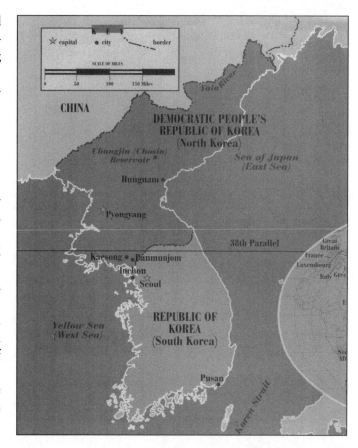

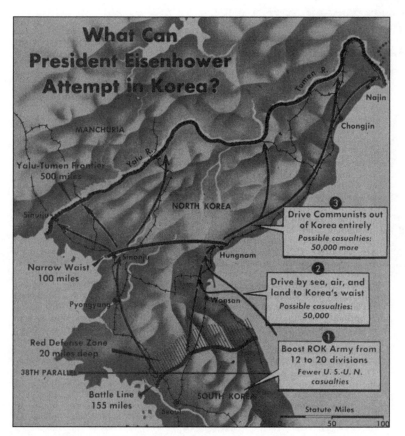

- In 1910, Japan had annexed Korea and installed a colonial governor.
- The majority of Koreans detested Japanese rule.
- By the 1930s, guerrilla leader Kim Il Sung organized a resistance movement.
- In 1937, Japan launched an assimilation program in the country designed to eliminate Korean culture; Korean schools could only teach in Japanese, and Koreans were compelled to change their names to Japanese names.
- When World War II erupted, half a million Koreans were conscripted to serve in the Japanese military, while 150,000 young Korean women were forced into sexual servitude in Japanese military brothels.
- After the defeat of the Japanese, Korea became entwined in a power struggle between the United States and Russia.
- In 1945, when the Allies reclaimed Korea from its Japanese invaders, they divided it at the 38th parallel.
- The land north of that line became a Communist country under the influence and protection of the Soviet Union, while South Korea came under the protection and sponsorship of the United States.

- On June 25, 1950, the North Koreans attacked South Korea in the first real hot-war confrontation of the new Cold War era.
- President Harry Truman met the challenge instantly, fearing the next target would be America's oil sources in the Middle East.
- Determined to take a stand against communism, he deployed troops held over from occupied Japan, though many were poorly trained and equipped.
- In contrast, the North Korean forces were extremely well-trained and possessed Russia's sophisticated tank, the T-34.
- During the first months of the conflict, it seemed possible that North Korea would defeat both South Korea and America.
- When better-trained U.S. troops arrived in August, the tide began to turn.
- Then, in November 1950, as many as 300,000 Chinese Communists joined the fight.

## HISTORICAL SNAPSHOT
# 1951

- Women comprised 28.9 percent of the American workforce outside the home, up from 14.7 percent in 1880 and 21.4 percent in 1920
- The odds that military personnel would die in combat had reduced dramatically during the past century; in the Civil War, one in 16 soldiers died, and in World War II, one in 55, while in Korea, the fatality ratio dropped to one in 170
- Color television was first introduced
- H&R Block, formed in 1946 in Kansas City, began offering tax-preparation services because the IRS had stopped preparing tax returns
- Margaret Sanger urged the development of an oral contraceptive
- The Topps Chewing Gum Company added statistics and biographic information to its colorful baseball cards for the first time
- The Univac computer was introduced
- Metropolitan Life Insurance Company reported a link between obesity and early mortality rates
- Massive flooding covered more than a million acres of land in Oklahoma, Kansas, Missouri and Illinois
- The Twenty-second Amendment to the U.S. Constitution passed Congress, limiting the service of the president to two terms
- The latest census reported that eight percent of the population was more than 65 years old, up from four percent in 1900
- For the first time in history, women outnumbered men in the United States; Washington DC had the highest percentage of single women (27 percent), Nevada the lowest (13 percent)
- Julius and Ethel Rosenberg were sentenced to death for espionage against the United States
- President Truman dispatched an air force plane when Sioux City Memorial Park in Iowa refused to bury John Rice, a Native-American who had died in combat; his remains were interred in Arlington National Cemetery
- Sugarless chewing gum, Dacron suits, push-button-controlled garage doors, a telephone company answering service, college credit courses on TV and power steering all made their first appearance
- The median age at first marriage was 23 years for men and 19.8 years for women; in 1900, the average age for men had been 25.9 years and for women, 21.9 years
- Entertainer Milton Berle signed a 30-year, million-dollar-plus contract with NBC
- New York and other major cities increased the cost of a five-cent phone call to $0.10

## Selected Prices

| | |
|---|---:|
| Automatic Toaster, General Electric | $21.95 |
| Automobile, Buick Skylark | $5,000.00 |
| Basketball, Official Size | $2.98 |
| Bra, Maidenform | $2.00 |
| Cake Mix, Betty Crocker | $0.35 |
| Christmas Set, Old Spice | $1.65 |
| Cough Drops, Luden's Menthol | $0.05 |
| Gas Range | $99.00 |
| Gun Rack, Six-Gun Capacity | $17.95 |
| Hope Chest, Lane | $47.95 |
| Mop | $5.95 |
| Parker Brothers' Monopoly | $4.00 |
| Sheet, Double Bed | $10.50 |
| Stapler | $2.60 |
| Tinkertoy, 149 Color Pieces | $1.98 |

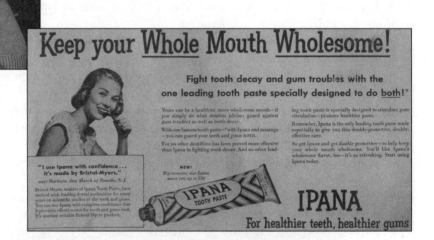

## "The U.S. Navy's Korean War: Dull, Dirty, and They Die, Too," *Newsweek*, January 12, 1953:

Shortly after sunrise one morning last week, a small wooden ship flying the U.S. flag slipped quietly into Wonsan Harbor. At her bow, on the lookout for mines, stood a seaman wearing a steel helmet, a flak vest, and a life jacket. Other seamen in helmets, flak vests and life jackets stood by her guns. This day, as every day the weather permits, the 136-foot *U.S.S. Waxbill* was on a dull, yet dangerous mission. We were sweeping the channel into Wonsan so that other and bigger United Nations ships could enter it safely to shell the Communist installations there.

ROK Marines, under the command of U.S. Marines, hold eight of the islands in Wonsan Harbor but the Communists have many more. The hills ringing the harbor are pock-marked with caves, and every cave hides a gun. The men aboard the *Waxbill* made no bones about it: This was not their idea of a full life. There was always the chance of running into a mine before they spotted it. And every now and then, whenever the Communists felt they could spare the ammunition, they liked to use the *Waxbill* for target practice. They had done so only the day before, bracketing her with gunfire. One shell had fallen in her wake, another off her port bow, and another off her starboard bow. She has been able to escape only by cutting loose her minesweeping gear and laying a smokescreen.

This particular morning, in hopes that the Communists again would open up, two U.S. destroyers were hovering outside the harbor. If the Communists did fire, they would reveal their positions, and the destroyers could then get to work on them. It didn't make the *Waxbill's* crew any less nervous to know that they were being used as decoys. . . .

On the bridge, the *Waxbill's* youthful skipper, Lieutenant Thomas R. Allen of Sioux City, Iowa, peered through his glasses at the Communist caves. "A ship as small as this one is pretty hard to hit," observed Lt. Allen. "However, if the Communists keep trying long enough, they are obviously bound to, eventually."

The morning wore on and nothing happened, but still the men couldn't relax. Those Communist guns were too close. And then, a few minutes before noon, the plotter, Chief Quartermaster Angelo John Zanoni of Walsenburg, Colorado, told Lt. Allen: "Sir, we've covered the channel." The lieutenant gave the order to leave the harbor. Smiles broke out all over the ship. A youngster joked: "Man, we'll never earn our combat pay if the Reds don't cooperate more." A seaman gets $45 extra if his ship is under fire on six days of the month. "Listen, stupid," said Hospital Corpsman Ivan Bently Owen of Senath, Missouri, "I'd be willing to pay Uncle Sam $45 a month if he'd just get me out of here."

## What Course Now in Korea?

U.N. offensive held impractical if not impossible;
Double ROK forces and let 'Asiatic fight Asiatic'

*by Lt. Gen. Robert L. Eichelberger, USA, Ret.*

# KOREAN WAR CALENDAR

**August 10, 1945:** U.S. officials select the 38th parallel as the dividing line across Korea. Americans accept the Japanese surrender south of the 38th parallel; the Soviets will receive the surrender north of the line

**August 15, 1945:** As Japan surrenders, Korean leaders prepare an interim government, forming the Committee for the Preparation of Korean Independence

**September 5, 1945:** American troops arrive in South Korea to establish a U.S. military government

**October 1945:** Exiled Korean leader Syngman Rhee arrives in Seoul

**September 1947:** The United States passes the matter of Korea to the United Nations

**May 1948:** Members of the United Nations' Temporary Commission on Korea arrive to supervise elections; the North Koreans refuse to allow them north of the 38th parallel

**May 10, 1948:** The Republic of Korea's first National Assembly is elected without participation of the North

**August 15, 1948:** Rhee is inaugurated as president of the Republic of Korea, representing South Korea

**December 1948:** The Soviet Union withdraws its troops from North Korea

**1949:** Guerilla resistance to the rule of Rhee rages in the southern provinces of the Republic of Korea

**October 1949:** Mao Zedong establishes the People's Republic of China after driving Chinese Nationalist leader Chiang Kai-shek and his forces to the island of Taiwan

**December 1949:** The United States withdraws from Korea

**June 25, 1950:** Ninety thousand North Korean People's Army troops cross the 38th parallel, attacking the Republic of Korea's Army at five key locations

**June 26, 1950:** The UN Security Council condemns North Korea's armed attack

**June 27, 1950:** Seoul falls to the North Koreans

**June 30, 1950:** President Truman authorizes General Douglas MacArthur to use ground forces; a naval blockade of North Korea is approved

**July 5, 1950:** A small U.S. unit of 406 men is shattered by the North Koreans at Osan

**July 10, 1950:** The UN Security Council creates a unified Korean command under MacArthur

**July 14-16, 1950:** North Koreans crush two regiments of the 24th Division at the Kum River

**July 19, 1950:** The city of Taejon falls to North Korea

**August 1950:** The People's Republic of China begins to move troops into Manchuria; UN forces retreat to the Pusan perimeter

**August 17, 1950:** U.S. Marines strike the North Koreans at the Naktong Bulge, scattering them

## "Korean War . . ." *(continued)*

September 15, 1950: MacArthur leads a successful amphibious assault on the port city of Inchon

September 24, 1950: China protests the strafing of sites in Manchuria by U.S. aircraft

September 27, 1950: UN troops recapture Seoul

September 30, 1950: Republic of Korea forces cross the 38th parallel, followed by UN troops

October 14, 1950: Communist Chinese forces, numbering 180,000, move from Manchuria into North Korea

October 20, 1950: UN forces capture the North Korean capital of Pyongyang and continue toward the Chinese border

October 26, 1950: Chinese Communist troops attack UN forces

November 25, 1950: The Chinese aggressively attack the 8th Army

November 27, 1950: The Chinese strike at seven different fronts near the Choson Reservoir; the 8th Army begins withdrawal

December 3, 1950: MacArthur orders a withdrawal of all UN forces to the 38th parallel

January 1, 1951: The Chinese launch their third offensive, pushing UN forces 50 miles south of the 38th parallel

January 4, 1951: Seoul is recaptured by Communist forces

March 14, 1951: Seoul returns to UN control

April 11, 1951: MacArthur is relieved of command; General Matthew Ridgway is named commander of the UN forces

April 21, 1951: UN forces successfully battle Chinese and North Koreans

June 1951: Chinese and UN forces dig in across from each other at the crater known as the Punchbowl

July 10, 1951: The first armistice meeting convenes

July 16, 1951: Korean officials declare their unwillingness to accept cease-fire while Korea remains divided

August 1951: Communists call off the armistice talks, claiming UN aircraft are bombing neutral zones

September 13-26, 1951: The battle at Heartbreak Ridge results in many deaths on both sides, but little territory is exchanged

November 23, 1951: During armistice negotiations, a demilitarized zone stretching two kilometers on each side of the 38th parallel is established

January 1952: Armistice talks enter a long stalemate over the issue of repatriating prisoners of war who do not wish to return to their country

May 1952: Mark W. Clark replaces General Matthew B. Ridgway as commander of the Far East Force and the UN Command

March 5, 1953: Soviet Premier Joseph Stalin dies and is replaced by Georgy M. Malenkov, who quickly expresses the Soviet Union's desire for peace in Asia

April-May 1953: The first exchanges of Korean War POWs begin with the transfer of sick and wounded prisoners

June 18, 1953: As truce negotiations near completion, South Korean President Syngman Rhee secretly orders the release of about 25,000 North Korean POWs who do not wish to be repatriated, effectively sabotaging the armistice agreements

July 11, 1953: With promises of enormous economic aid and the continued security role of U.S. troops in South Korea, Rhee agrees not to obstruct the armistice

July 27, 1953: The armistice agreement is signed by both sides

## "Men of the Minesweepers: Where the Fleet Goes, We've Been!" Charlotte Knight, *Collier's*, November 10, 1951:

It was a grim morning and an even grimmer mission. Cold, driving rain stung our faces and beat hard on the decks of our plucky little minesweeper, the *Osprey*, as we left Korea's "unswept" channel in the Yellow Sea. We were on the hunt for the most insidious weapon UN forces have encountered in 17 months of the Korean war: the magnetic underwater mine. Like most minesweep missions in this war, this was another urgent, top-priority, sweep-it-right-now assignment.

Intelligence sources, evaluated as reliable, had produced information that Communist forces had laid several magnetic mines in the channel of Chawol-to, one of the approaches to the vital UN supply port of Inchon. The *Osprey* and two of her sister sweepers, the *Swallow* and the *Waxbill*, had been suddenly diverted from their major sweeping operation off Wonsan on the east coast and ordered to steam full-speed for the Yellow Sea to take care of the situation. It was up to them to locate and explode the dreaded mines—or be able to assure our high command that the mines had become inactive and were therefore no longer a threat to UN warships.

A few mines, stealthily laid at night by innocent-appearing sampans and fishing junks could put an immediate and very likely disastrous end to our naval operations in the vicinity, unless we first took appropriate means to counter them. Of these methods, that of physically sweeping a given area clear of all types of mines still is, after almost half a century of coping with the mine as an offensive weapon, the most effective countermeasure.

It is hazardous work—as navy casualty figures offer somber proof—but danger is the *Osprey's* business and her crew takes it in stride. . . .

Not that anybody on the *Osprey* had any doubts about what could happen. For these are the sobering statistics to date: 17 of our ships have been hit by Communist mines since the start of the Korean war; the deadliness of the weapon can be attested to by the fact that 12 of these vessels sank, and one of them, the destroyer *Walke*, suffered se-

vere damage and 26 of her crew killed in the navy's worst single disaster in Korean waters. Six of the ships sunk were UN minesweepers; four were American. The *Magpie*, the first U.S. Navy sweeper lost, went down a year ago, with 21 of her small crew of four officers and 29 men missing in action.

Since then (although those who man the sweepers comprise less than two percent of naval personnel in the Far East), more than 20 percent of all naval dead or missing have been minesweeping people.

### No Push-Button Gadgets for This Job

"Until we can come up with a classy, remote-control, push-button sweeper, looks like we'll have to keep on doing it the hard way," said one of the *Osprey's* officers as the little ship rocked and rolled on our way toward Chawol-to, past the stately *Los Angeles*, the *Eldorado* and some of the other great gray warships. Our 136-foot wooden craft suddenly seemed absurdly small. As though he read my thoughts, Lieutenant David A. Beadling of Prospect Park, Pennsylvania, the *Osprey's* executive officer, sprang to her defense. "Yeah, I know. I suppose we do look pretty silly alongside those steel jobs." (I was shortly to discover that to all minesweep personnel, everything from a small destroyer to a battleship falls under the simple classification "steel job.")

### "Men of the Minesweepers . . ." *(continued)*

"I suppose they have a right to think they're pretty important—they're the only ones you read about; and nobody ever heard about the *Osprey*. But you ought to see 'em run for cover the minute they smell a minefield. Yes, sir," reflected Beadling, with what appeared to be some satisfaction, "there's nothing like a few mines strewn about to cut the big boys down to size."

"Don't forget our motto," prompted Lieutenant Gordon Shoolman of Rochester, New York, " 'Where the Fleet Goes, *We've* Been!'"

"It may become apparent after a while that we don't quite consider ourselves part of the regular navy—or maybe it's vice versa," continued Beadling, known aboard the *Osprey* only as "the Beadle." . . .

Like any group of proud people whose jobs are specialized, dangerous, virtually unpublicized, and frequently unrecognized even in their own service, the minesweep personnel are inclined to be a bit hypersensitive. Slights and rebuffs are apt to be long-remembered. . . .

"Mines are easy to mass-produce. Why, any toy factory or typewriter plant could turn 'em out in quantity and at very low cost. It's damned frightening."

The commander's words were reminiscent of those of the late Admiral Forrest P. Sherman in his testimony before a congressional committee shortly before his death. When the committee chairman pointed out that the several hundred mines the U.S. Navy had swept in Korean waters must have made serious inroads in the Communist mine supply, Admiral Sherman said: "Well, sir, I would like to be that optimistic, but I'm afraid they can probably be manufactured at a rate just as fast as our recovery of them."

The enemy has laid thousands of mines around the coasts of Korea, of which we have so far swept less than half, despite continuous dawn-to-dark operations. Ninety-eight mines were "cut" recently in one day, just off Wonsan alone.

"The whole idea gets grisly after a bit," said Commander Shouldice. "Some mines weigh as lit-

tle as 750 pounds. So, a few coolies can pick one up and walk off with it. They can put four of them on a fishing boat with no strain at all. Or they can suspend a magnetic mine underneath an ordinary sampan by putting a few lines (which look like fishing lines, of course) over the side and conceal it that way. When they get the boat in position, they merely cut the lines and drop the mines." . . .

With few exceptions, all the mines swept have been the common, moored "contact" mines— mammoth spheres with protruding "horns" which detonate the explosive charge when they come in contact with a ship.

To date, the best method of sweeping these moored mines is for a vessel to tow from her stern two Oropesa or "O"-type sweeps: These are steel wires stretched out from the port and starboard beams by steel "kites" or "otters" which are designed to submerge the sweep wires at the required depth and keep them there; they are attached to Oropesa floats, torpedo-shaped affairs known in minesweep parlance as "pigs." These floating "pigs" stream out at an angle from the ship and keep taut the kite lines, along which are arranged, about 250 feet apart, a series of cutters capable of severing the mooring lines holding the mines in position.

When these lines have been cut, the buoyancy chamber within the submerged contact mine brings it to the surface, where it bobs about until destroyed by minesweep crews, usually by rifle fire. (It isn't necessary to hit the horns or explode the mine; filling the buoyancy chamber with rifle holes is sufficient to send the mine to the bottom, where it stays.)

"We kept on getting orders: 'Sweep this area instantly!'" said one of the mine people, "when sometimes we wouldn't even know if the beaches

## "Men of the Minesweepers . . ." *(continued)*

were in friendly hands. We're small so that we can maneuver close to shore, but we're also slow. We'd ask the brass; 'What if the shore batteries start firing?' 'Very simple,' they'd say, 'Duck 'em. Take evasive action.' At *eight* knots? Good grief!"

Sweeping up enemy mines is unpleasant enough even when the beaches are "ours." Add to this the ever-present fire from enemy shore batteries and you have Wonsan—exactly as it has been for the better part of a whole year, except for the comparatively short time when UN forces held that important North Korean port. Neither Dusty nor anyone else in the mine force here is likely to forget those first sweeps. . . .

Lieutenant Edward P. Flynn, Jr., of Ozone Park, New York, skipper of the *Incredible*, told me what happened on October 12, 1950:

"It was the third day of our Wonsan sweeping operation. We were determined to get our nose in. By about 10:00 a.m. we had got in between Rei-to and Kodo-to a couple of the islands that guard the approaches. The *Pirate*, commanded by Lieutenant Commander Bruce Hyatt, of Albuquerque, New Mexico, the OTC (officer in tactical command) was lead ship; the *Pledge*. . . . was second in the formation; the *Incredible* followed. The *Kite* and the *Redhead* were dunning. The *Kite* and the *Redhead* were going to get in as far as they could. He was getting sonar 'pips' and echoes all over the place, so he knew he had a good field.

"At 11:54, the *Pirate* cut six moored mines with her gear," he continued. "Three or four minutes later, the *Pledge* cut three and the *Incredible* cut four. And then, suddenly, the *Pirate* got hit in the starboard quarter. She foundered awfully fast, thrashed from side to side and sank in three minutes. Six men were lost and there were a lot of wounded.

"Then the formation really started to have trouble. The shore batteries opened up from Sin-do and Rei-to with their 75-millimeters," Flynn went on. "They had an angle on the ends of the two islands and, therefore, had us bracketed pretty closely. The *Pledge* took Sin-do under fire with her three-inch gun and the *Incredible* took Rei-to. The *Endicott* (our fire-support vessel) stayed outside the mine line and opened up with her five-inch guns, but still couldn't silence the island batteries. We called for air and, 45 minutes later, our planes knocked them out. . . .

"Finally, by October 18, the date which had been set as D-day for the landings of our troops at Wonsan, the minesweepers had cut what they had every reason to believe was a clear channel right to the beach, but on that day, minesweeping suddenly took a new and terrifying turn.

"It had been duck soup all day," Dusty recalled. "We had one hour to go to give the high command the go-ahead to let the big ships come in. They had said; 'We want it by 16:00 hours, Dusty,' and I said: 'I'll give it to you by 15:00' and we would've, too—and then, damn it, we ran into this 'influence' field. I was in the *Mockingbird*; the *Redhead* was ahead of us and the magnetic field around one of her otters triggered an influence mine and set it off. That explosion set off a second mine next to it. Then a couple of ROK (Republic of Korea) minesweepers got it, and one of them blew sky-high. And, of course, there went the 'clear channel' we'd promised the brass. It was sure disappointin'."

Plenty of time for resting. Plenty of time for hull soldiers. Plenty of ocean.

## "How Rich Can Your Children Be?" Milo Perkins, *Harper's Magazine*, July 1949:

They can be twice as rich as you are 25 years from now—if the military situation becomes no worse and if all of us can hold our greed in check. The present "adjustment" period is one of deep uneasiness for all of us. It promises to become more painful before it becomes less painful. But the long-range future is full of hope.

During the past 25 years, we have increased our output of goods per person somewhere between two and 2.5 percent a year. We don't know exactly, because there are gaps in the statistics. Looking ahead, Sumner Slichter feels that we should be able to increase our future output some three or four percent a year for each hour worked. Louis Bean calculates that our total output of goods and services has gone up at an average rate of 3.5 percent a year for decades, doubling every 20 years. He sees no reason for believing that there will be much change in this pattern in the future. . . .

Since our increase in productivity each year is based on the progress made in the year before, a three percent annual gain means a 100 percent increase in a quarter of a century. The advance won't be even each year but it ought to average out over the 25-year period. No nation ever faced a brighter future.

Now let's look at the next 10 years. We are presently producing about $240 billion of goods and services a year; a three percent increase will add $7 billion-plus the first year—and a little more than that the second year. We shall start the third year with nearly $15 billion more in goods and services than we had at the beginning of the first year. By the end of the tenth year, we can have about $80 billion more.

That will be nearly $2,000 a family. . . . The prospect of marketing $80 billion worth of additional goods and services is startling when we jump 10 years ahead, but it represents less of an increase than we have taken in our stride during the past 10 years. With our large and growing labor force, we can get this increased production. A growing population with rising living standards can consume the extra output. We must move in this direction if we are to avoid mass unemployment. The key to success is intelligent action each year.

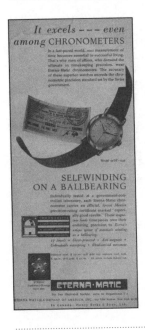

# 1953 PROFILE

# THE KOREAN WAR

### Second Lieutenant

With the signing of an armistice only days away, Robert Hope led a counterattack up Pork Chop Hill in Korea—despite being wounded three times—to turn back an assault by the Chinese communists.

### Life at Home

- News of the invasion of Korea in June 1950 arrived while Robert Hope was attending an eight-week summer camp for infantry platoon leaders in Fort Benning, Georgia.
- Still a student at Clemson College in South Carolina, Robert had assumed that military exercise was simply the completion of his ROTC obligation.
- Suddenly, he was actually training for battle; America was at war with North Korea, the first hot conflict of the Cold War.
- He knew immediately that his plans to establish a chicken farm could be impacted.
- At first, it was hard to understand why America was willing to fight over land in a place like Korea.
- At the end of World War II and the defeat of the Japanese, half the country had been assigned to the communists, and half to the United States.
- Now, with no warning, the North Korean Army, backed by China, had crossed the 38th parallel—the official dividing line—and attacked South Korea.
- That fall, Robert was at Clemson completing his degree in chicken husbandry and cheering his beloved Clemson Tigers on the football field; by March, he was back at Fort Benning with his entire ROTC unit from college.

*Robert Hope prepares to ship out to Korea.*

> "As we were moving through the field, we started to receive some fire from the Chinese. But, you know, I was tired and cold, just plain miserable, I didn't care. You can get that way."
> —Sergeant Joseph DeMarco, B Company, 1st Battalion, 7th Marines

## The Korean War Casualty Totals:

**United Nations Forces:**
United States: 36,913 dead, 103,248 wounded, 8,142 missing
South Korea: 58,127 dead, 175,743 wounded, 166,297 missing
Other Nations: 3,194 dead, 11,297 wounded, 2,769 missing
**Communist Forces:**
North Korea: 214,899 dead, 303,685 wounded, 101,680 missing
China: 401,401 dead, 486,995 wounded, 21,211 missing
**Civilians:**
An estimated 2 to 2.6 million dead, wounded and missing

- This time, it was no longer eight weeks of playing soldier; training became the difference between living or dying in combat.
- By July, he and his classmates were assigned to duty at Fort Jackson, South Carolina; most were placed in rifle units, but Robert was assigned to be a trial lawyer in the judge advocate's office.
- Most of his cases involved soldiers who had gone AWOL—absent without leave—resulting in court marshal.
- As Robert quickly became aware, in the military a soldier was guilty before he was tried; thus, it was the job of the defense to prove the defendant not guilty.
- Robert knew little about the court system and less about trying people, but he did know that his desk job kept him from getting up at 4 a.m. for duty on the rifle range.
  - The onset of war had upset not only his establishment of a poultry business, but also his marriage plans.
  - He and his girlfriend Sadie decided to marry immediately so that she would be financially provided for if he was killed in action.
  - His last month stateside was spent in a small apartment off-base with Sadie, dreaming of life after his tour ended.

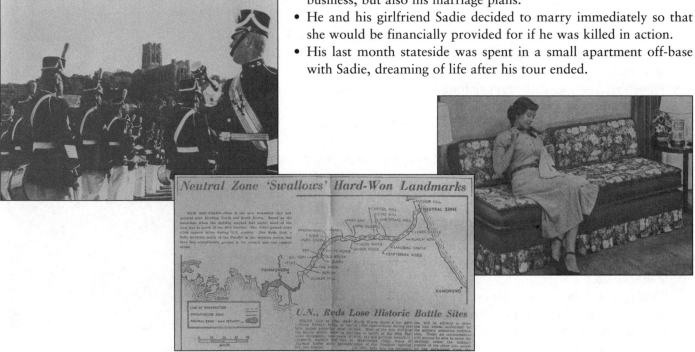

Neutral Zone 'Swallows' Hard-Won Landmarks

U.N., Reds Lose Historic Battle Sites

### "U.S. Donates Huge Rice, Ration Supply to Korean People," *Stars and Stripes*, Korean Edition, July 30, 1953:

The first distribution of 10,000 tons of food donated by President Dwight D. Eisenhower in appreciation of the valiant courage and fighting ability of the Korean people was made to the citizens of Pusan today.

More than 600 tons of rice and C-rations were trucked to the eight docks of Pusan. . . . The gift, not part of any present aid or relief program, was withdrawn from military stocks.

Broken down it will mean one C-ration, or eight cans of meat, and five hops of rice to every five people.

- When his orders arrived to report overseas, he realized that his court training at Jackson had prepared him poorly for the job ahead as an infantry platoon leader.
- He was shipped out of San Francisco aboard the *U.S.S. Black*, which had been brought out of mothballs for the Korean conflict.
- The trip from the U.S. to Yokohama took 16 days; Robert's job as a second lieutenant was to guard the hole, where enlisted soldiers were housed during the long boat ride.
- The bunks were stacked four or five layers deep, and if one soldier vomited from seasickness, a dozen men could be affected.

### Life at Work

- When Robert arrived in Japan, he was assigned to the 17th Infantry, 7th Division, which was defending the hills in Korea.
- On April 17, 1953, with rumors of an armistice in the air, the *U.S.S. Black* arrived at the harbor in Inchon—a city that had experienced at least three major battles since the fighting began.
- People were still debating whether General Douglas MacArthur should have been allowed to invade China—the source of many of the communist troops—and end the war quickly.
- Opinion was sharply divided about President Harry Truman's decision to remove MacArthur.
- While still in the harbor, Robert experienced his first taste of war.

*Robert left San Francisco aboard the* U.S.S. Black.

- As he and the troops watched, a steady stream of helicopters flew the wounded to a Swiss hospital ship—two litters per chopper.
- Rumors circulated that the 7th Division was in Korea to replace the wounded he had seen that day.
- On the troop transport train, he was assigned guard duty to prevent frightened men from jumping off the train.
- None did, but he was still relieved when the journey ended.
- Equally disturbing, though, was the sight of hordes of Korean children begging for food along the rail line.
- Giving them a small amount of food set off riots, but providing no food resulted in the children throwing rocks through the windows of the train.
- Robert's first duty was "graves registration" for the dead being shipped in by the truckload for processing.
- Two days were spent handling dead bodies—some in bags, many not—to ensure that all were identified and the bodies boxed for shipment back to the States.
- Robert learned that the slot on each end of a dog tag was there for a purpose—so it could be inserted between the teeth of the dead.
- When Robert arrived at his outpost, he discovered that the rumors were true: Every officer in Easy Company had been wounded, and warm bodies—even untrained Clemson men—were desperately needed as platoon leaders.
- When Robert was asked to take over the company, he was terrified; not only was he untrained to lead a platoon, but he had not used live ammunition in nine months.
- It didn't matter—a war was on—so for the next several weeks, he and his troops prepared, despite rumors of a truce.
- Generally, the weather was pleasant, between 75 and 80 degrees during the day and 45 to 50 at night.
- When he was blue, he ate cans of fruit cocktail.
- The biggest problem was the dust turning to mud when it rained.
- Any word from home was a gift; a letter written from the East Coast took six to seven days to reach Easy Company in Korea.
- Everyone assigned a different date to when the shooting would stop, while the battle for a series of Korean hills intensified.
- Even with the obvious buildup toward a major battle, Robert continued to think about home.

- Letters to his mother and wife mentioned the 20,000 chickens his farm would boast next year, and he is willing to pledge all of his monthly pay to make it happen.
- Following 10 tough days in the field with little sleep, his biggest worry was a $300 bill to repair the roof of the farmhouse.
- Many of his letters were written using light from a gasoline lantern—a step up from a flickering candle in a dusty tent.

- But some days, with constant patrols and fighting in the area, writing was difficult to fit into his schedule.
- During a skirmish in mid-May, he lost three soldiers in battle.
- Much time was spent protecting his men, keeping back the Chinese troops, or trying to capture them.
- With both sides eager for intelligence, his company tried anything to get an enemy prisoner so they could obtain advance warning of battle plans.
- On one occasion, they even dropped a dummy from a low-flying plane to lure the Chinese from their hiding places in order to capture them.
- To coax deserters, American planes dropped thousands of brochures urging the soldiers to put down their weapons and return home.
- By June, Robert had lost nine men in battle and came to respect the toughness of the Ethiopian soldiers assigned to a regiment attached to the 7th.
- Several times, he had seen them return from a patrol carrying a souvenir ear of a Chinese or North Korean soldier they had killed.
- He was less trusting of the South Korean soldiers, who seemed to switch sides on a whim.
- During an April night patrol on Pork Chop Hill, Robert saw the Chinese preparing to attack; immediately, he recalled his outguards, requested illumination and called for a flash fire all around the perimeter.
- Quickly, the artillery responded with direct hits on the massed Chinese troops.
- By the light of the explosions, Robert watched as gaps were blown in the Chinese lines by the artillery assault.
- Later, it was estimated that the Chinese lost 1,400 men that day.
- Like most soldiers on the front, he kept close track of his points: 36 points gets a man home.
- Every frontline soldier earns four points a month, while a clerk away from the action earns only two points a month.

> "The wounded were all loaded down and the 'copters gone. The dead would go down in the morning with the gook train, silent slumps being carried down the hill to the battalion and the morgue. You didn't waste chopper space on the dead."
> —James Brady,
> *The Coldest War: A Memoir of Korea*

*As a member of the Buffalo Brigade, Robert visited orphanages in Korea to distribute food and clothing.*

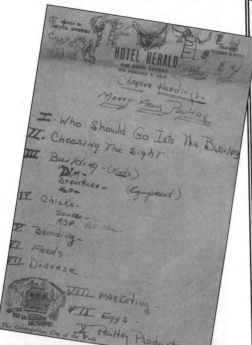

IF YOU WANTA PRODUCE

You Gotta Stay On The Job!

*Despite the press of battle, Robert dreams about the chicken farm he will create.*

## Buffalo Bugle, May 28, 1953:

It was a mere coincidence, but to PFC Dale Erickson, a machine gunner in "A" Company, 17th Infantry "Buffalo" Regiment, is sent a happy birthday.

Erickson was 21 the twelfth of May. It was his first birthday overseas, and he hadn't received a scrap of mail in more than a week. He was feeling "pretty low," until the company mailman made his rounds.

Addressed to this mother's young Buffalo were a birthday cake, six congratulatory cards and five letters.

Although the chocolate cake was smashed to a one-inch mound of crumbs, Erickson and the rest of his squad still agreed it was "number one."

- By early July, when the peace talks had resumed, no one wanted to be the soldier who died on the day the treaty was signed.
- When the Chinese forces took the elevated positions on Pork Chop Hill, Robert's regiment was called out on a counterattack.
- It was clear that the Chinese held a superior strategic position against the outnumbered American forces, and casualties mounted quickly, including Easy Company's commander.
- Robert immediately assumed control, and after securing his men in the trenches, began planning a way to attack, even though his hand was wounded.
- Screaming at the top of his lungs, he led an attack on the enemy position where small grenades, known as potato smashers, were being tossed down 10 at a time.
- He then called on the mortars to fire from a distant hill and provide cover while the wounded were collected.
- Dozens of men were on the ground with no unoccupied trenches available for cover, and though Robert was wounded a second time in the leg and buttocks, he kept command as the fighting intensified.
- The next morning, orders arrived to send two men out on a scouting mission to pinpoint the Chinese positions, but both were killed almost instantly after leaving cover.
- Against orders, Robert did not send anymore.

- The number of wounded in the trenches became a problem as the healthy had to walk over the dead to reach the wounded.
- On July 10, while attempting to remove the wounded, Robert was hit for the third time with shrapnel.
- This time, he was ordered off Pork Chop Hill for rest and initial treatment at the command post.
- There, he awoke to a horrible vision: A captured Chinese soldier was standing over his bed.
- For several minutes, Robert did not know where he was or if the enemy had captured him.
- Later, at a nearby MASH unit, the shrapnel was removed, and by July 17, he was back with his unit.
- After word got back to his home town that he had been injured, more than a dozen friends and relatives wrote letters.
- Everyone said they were sorry, then went on to rag him about being injured in the buttocks.
- For weeks, he kept explaining, "It's possible, you know, for a mortar to hit behind you! It wasn't that I was pulling a withdrawal."
- He knew he was getting teased because he has played tricks on everyone else.
- Talk of a truce continues.

## Life in the Community: Pork Chop Hill, Korea
- To provide entertainment for the troops early in his tour, Robert made a volleyball court and organized a tournament.
- His other recreation is shooting pheasant and deer—providing a special treat for his company.

*During the battle of Pork Chop Hill, Robert was wounded three times, earning the Purple Heart.*

- A month after he and over 100 men were wounded or killed in the battle on Pork Chop Hill, he is pleased that base camp is being moved 20 miles back to a location only 20 miles from Seoul.
- At the new location, Robert is planning to keep the men occupied with sports: horseshoes, volleyball, softball, basketball, touch football and boxing.
- Trips around South Korea include visits with American POWs recently released by the Chinese.
- Next on his agenda is organizing a search of Pork Chop Hill to find his company's missing; following the prisoner exchange, approximately 130 men are still unaccounted for.
- The plan is for both Americans and Chinese to visit the battleground in search of their missing and presumed dead soldiers.

*To entertain the troops, Robert organized sports events and kept a small dog for company.*

## HISTORICAL SNAPSHOT
# 1953

- The Screen Actors Guild adopted by-laws banning communists from membership
- For the first time, a link was made between coronary heart disease and a diet high in animal fats
- New York subway fares rose $0.05 to $0.15
- Nationwide, 30 million Americans attended performances of classical music, and 7.2 million children took music lessons
- The Dow-Jones Industrial Average reached a high of 293 and a low of 255
- Per-capita state taxes averaged $68.04
- An airmail stamp cost $0.07 per ounce, and a postcard, $0.02
- All-black military units had nearly disappeared; 90 percent were now integrated
- Leland Kirdel wrote in *Coronet* magazine: "The smart woman will keep herself desirable. It is her duty to be feminine and desirable at all times in the eyes of the opposite sex"
- In the wave of McCarthyism, libraries were ordered to remove books by "communists, fellow travelers and the like"
- Lucille Ball and Desi Arnaz signed an $8 million contract to continue *I Love Lucy* for 30 months
- *TV Guide* and *Playboy* began publication
- The number of comic books surged, comprising about 650 titles
- Twenty-five percent of young Americans were attending college, thanks to the GI Bill—an increase of 65 percent from before the Second World War
- During his inaugural address, President Dwight D. Eisenhower called on Americans to make whatever sacrifices may be necessary to meet the threat of Soviet aggression, and defined the Cold War as freedom against slavery
- Charlie Chaplin said it was "virtually impossible" to continue working in the United States because of the propaganda by powerful reactionary groups
- General Motors introduced the Chevrolet Corvette, the first plastic laminated fiberglass sports car; the cost was $3,250
- Elvis Presley paid $4.00 to cut "My Happiness" in Memphis for his mother's birthday
- Joseph Stalin died in May; Queen Elizabeth II was coronated in June
- Bell Aircraft Corporation landed a $35 million contract to make a guided missile
- Four out of five men's shirts sold in America were white
- The DC-7 propeller plane, Sugar Smacks, 3-D cartoons and movies, and Irish coffee all made their first appearance

TAPE-recorder fans will soon be able to buy hour-long concerts to play on their machines. Webster-Chicago Corp. and Pentron Corp., are planning to market prerecorded tapes of classics, eventually hope to put out two-hour tapes.

"The son-of-a-bitch isn't going to resign on me! I want him fired."
—President Harry Truman in dismissing General Douglas MacArthur as commander of United Nations forces in Korea, 1951

## "World's Future Lies in Hands of GOP," *Newsweek*, January 26, 1953:

After 20 years of impatient waiting, the Republicans have had their celebration. The era of the Deals, New and Fair, is ended. General Dwight D. Eisenhower has taken the oath making him President Dwight D. Eisenhower. The triumphant inaugural parade has flashed its color along Pennsylvania Avenue. The confetti has been swept up and the stands are coming down.

Today, the United States Government is operating under new management. This management stands pledged to clean up corruption in Washington, restore some of the American freedoms which have been curtailed in recent years, and bring new blood and new methods into the Washington councils. Yet, the new managers must deal with old problems.

These problems can't be swept away or torn down. They constitute a challenge of unprecedented proportions to the determination and ingenuity of American statesmanship. Nothing less than the world's future hangs on the new administration's success.

The basic problems confronting President Eisenhower are these:

- To organize the free world in such a way that it can and will resist the continuous spread of Russian communism, make itself strong, and keep itself free.
- To achieve this without allowing the clash between the free world and the communist world to degenerate into a third world war, which, fought as it would be with atomic weapons, would be unspeakably destructive to both sides.
- To guard the immediate prosperity and opportunity for happiness of 160 million Americans at home while protecting their long-range interests abroad.

Whereas the Democrats throughout the Roosevelt and Truman administrations relied primarily upon academic advisers and trained politicians to make policy, the incoming Republicans will rely most heavily upon a professional soldier and a group of trained business executives. Therefore, the government's approach to the old problems will be essentially different.

### *The Coldest War: A Memoir of Korea,* James Brady, 1990:

All along the front the snow fell, deep here in the real hills and on the high ridges, and the battle fell into halfhearted feints and jabs with no hard fighting. Even the North Koreans, whose land this was, huddled against the snow and sheltered out of the wind. On the third day of the storm, the snow petered out and stopped. More than three feet had fallen, and now a colder, drier wind swept down from the north, ignoring the line of battle on its cruel, neutral passage from Siberia to the sea.

I was having bowel trouble again. Not as severe this time, only frequent, and five or six times a day, I slid down the slope to the holed ammo box set into the hill, to sit there and empty myself while I tried to keep the snow from drifting down into my furled trousers. Even (Capt. John) Chafee was grounded by the snow. He held his daily company meeting by telephone, transmitting the password, giving a brief account of the fighting elsewhere, checking on the condition of the men and irregularities in supply. There were no patrols. But Chafee urged us over and over not to be lulled, not to relax, to be alert when everyone else might nod, to scout out the ground each day whatever the weather, to see to it the weapons were clean and lightly oiled. Oil froze in the cold; you couldn't use much. In this snow it was easier to duck into the bunkers to talk, to inspect weapons, to question men at the firing ports. They brewed cocoa or coffee, and I took it. Odd, I'd never liked coffee, not even coffee ice cream, and now I was sluicing it down black and strong, cup after cup.

## Award of the Silver Star for Gallantry in Action, 1953:

First Lieutenant Robert M. Hope, 02004641, Infantry, United States Army, a member of Company E, 17th Infantry, distinguished himself by gallantry in action near Sokkogae, Korea. During the period 8 July 1953 to 10 July 1953, when his company commander was wounded during an attack against a strategic enemy-held outpost, Lieutenant Hope grasped the reins of command, maintained control, and led a well-coordinated attack. Lieutenant Hope was wounded on three separate occasions, but although suffering from his wounds and disregarding his own personal safety, inspiring his men by a show of valiant courage above that expected in the normal line of duty. On one occasion, Lieutenant Hope led a group of men up the hillside to annihilate a contingent of enemy soldiers who were rolling grenades down the slope of the hill on friendly positions. Through the singular courage of Lieutenant Hope, a breach in the numerically superior enemy line was effected, enabling the friendly attacking force to consolidate their positions and stave off the relentless enemy attacks. The gallantry displayed by Lieutenant Hope reflects great credit on himself and is in keeping with the highest traditions of the military service.

## "Austin Stack: The Brewmaster from Queens, Hey, Mac, Where Ya Been?"
### *Living Memories of the U.S. Marines in the Korean War*, Henry Berry:

At any rate, after the Chinese drive was stopped, we started moving back into what I'd call north-central Korea. We took a hill without any opposition, which was a blessing. (Lt. Jim) Cronin told us to dig in because we'd be there for a few days. I first dug a hole where I put the machine gun. Then I started to dig a hooch for myself.

Much to my surprise, there was a little hole right near the gun. I jumped in and conked off. The next day Cronin came by.

"Stack," he said, "you better dig your hole deeper; we might catch some incoming mail tonight."

So I went to work. I hadn't dug very far when I saw what looked like a sweater. I yanked at the cloth and this body broke through. For Christ's sake, I was sleeping on top of a dead chink. This was late April, but it was still cold enough that he hadn't begun to really decompose.

The minute the rest of the squad found out about it, they began to give me the needle.

"Hey, Stack, double rations; you have to feed your pal." Or, "Stack's got a friend for tea," things like that.

I dug deeper, put the stiff in as deep as I could, and dug myself another hole.

## Letters from Lt. Robert M. Hope to his mother Edna Hope:

*April 10, 1953:*

Dearest Mother and all,

Well, here I am in Korea—The Land of the Morning Calm. It doesn't show me much. Nothing but hills. We landed at Inchon about 2:30. I got a deal on the train. I was on the staff. Had a train commander, executive officer and I was mess officer. We had the only car with heat, lights, etc. We had 17 cars. Got eight or 10 windows broken out. The Korean kids will throw rocks at the train if they don't get any food. Rock-throwing is a great sport over here. . . .

*April 17, 1953:*

I've been tempted to buy a camera. The only way you can appreciate the country is to see this place. . . . I'm getting along okay with my razor; however, cold water doesn't make for the best shaving. No bathing facilities close by. Oh, I could use my electric razor if I wanted to use the power in the staff officer's tent. This is quite different from what I expected. The thing you have to watch here is the Koreans stealing everything you have. They won't hurt you, but just want to steal and they are professional, I've been told. All that we have around here are attached to the company. The staff officers have a Korean (Christian) preacher for their houseboy. Reads his Bible every chance he gets.

*April 29, 1953:*

My platoon is shaping up pretty good. We are full strength now and I have a wonderful platoon sergeant. We had a big feed tonight. Had the CO (Commanding Officer) and CO's brother for supper. I was right in with the wheels. Our CO is tops.

Both he and his brother are West Pointers. Pay Day tomorrow so I spent my first money tonight. Bought a box of cigars, candy, etc. I get toothpaste, cig, chewing gum in rations so no sweat there. My platoon is on guard tonight so I had better close and check on them.

*May 17, 1953:*

I'm all by my lonesome tonight. All the other officers went to Division CP tonight to a movie. I had the guard for tonight so couldn't go. Went to church today. A Hall boy from Hickory (SC) preached . . . I hear the other officers coming in now—we all played canasta last night. Me and my partner won, of course. We had two bad accidents in the company yesterday—three boys got hit with one machine gun bullet. The weapon has been hit with shrapnel and wouldn't operate. Two boys were fooling with it—one pulled the trigger and it discharged hitting three men outside working. . . . How is your garden coming along? I would sure like to have some of those radishes. We are getting fine chow. Haven't had to eat too many "C" rations. Best close and go check my guard—5 o'clock comes pretty early. Don't worry about me, I'm fine.

*June 4, 1953:*

I talked with Stoney (a friend from home) this afternoon for the first time in 12 days. He has himself a deal now—managing the regimental baseball team. He is trying to get me back there to play ball for him. A few catches stand in the way. First, they only allow one officer to play and that is Stoney. We don't have any extra officers in the company to take

## "Letters from Lt. Robert M. Hope . . ." *(continued)*

my place. If they want me bad enough those things can be arranged. Just keep my fingers crossed I guess. I would duplicate Daddy's feat in World War I if a peace was signed and I got to play ball.

*June 7, 1953:*

I got to church today. Didn't get to go last Sunday. I go every chance I get. War really makes a lot of new believers, not that I wasn't a firm believer before but it just helps out. I'm kinda looking for some kind of truce by and by. I'm kinda disgusted with all these postponements. I hope something is done before long. I'm fine and know I'm happy as long as I can play ball. I don't have much of a team but we may develop. I got several Puerto Ricans and they can't understand English. I have to take an interpreter along to get things across to them. All pretty good ball players.

*June 10, 1953:*

Have just been listening to the news. I just don't know what to think. I still predict there will be a truce by the 20th. Everyone is mad at [South Korean President Syngman] Rhee. I think they will come across—wish they would do it and get it over with. . . . I shouldn't have to serve my full time if an agreement is reached.

*June 19, 1953:*

Peace talks are disgusting. We don't even bother to listen to the news anymore. My prediction has fallen through, I guess. I predicted a cease-fire would be in effect by 20 June.

*July 10, 1953:*

Just a note for now. I want to get a jump ahead of the Red Cross and Dept. of Army—I have been slightly wounded. I have about 15 small pieces of steel in my thigh, my hand and buttocks. None of them went deep and all are in fleshier parts. You may get a telegram from Dept. of Army saying I regret to inform you that your son has been wounded in action. I expect you will get one but I want you to disregard it because I'm fine. It is no more than small grains of sand under the skin. Yes, it was the Pork Chop deal. Don't believe that's my favorite place anymore. We went up about 3:15 p.m. on the 8th and I came off this morning. The remaining men are coming off this afternoon. The

## "Letters from Lt. Robert M. Hope . . ." *(continued)*

CO got hit right at first so I had charge of the company. We suffered some pretty heavy losses. We have five officers wounded and about 25-30 men left out of the 189 we took on the hill with us. Most of them are just wounded.

*July 13, 1953:*

Just a note this morning to tell you I am fine. I will begin where I left my last letter. I came to the hospital and they cleaned my hand and leg. I had to rest for two hours. They then put me to sleep to cut the pieces out. I didn't know a thing for four hours. I was on the table about one and a half hours. I woke up in the officers' ward. The thing they do when they cut is to open the wound and allow it to drain. Four days later (tomorrow for me) they sew them up. I don't have but three or four openings. I'm able to get around pretty good. The bandage on my hand is so big it is hard to write. The thing is I don't want you to worry about me. I will be back to duty in about another week. I have a job ahead of me when I get back. See, I was the only officer left and I was right in all the action from beginning to end, so I'm the only one that knows what every man did—award and decorations, etc. I just thank God I'm here. I've never seen anything like it. Where's that truce?

## Selected Prices

| | |
|---|---|
| Carbon Paper | $1.19 |
| Clock | $3.98 |
| Curling Iron | $1.79 |
| Diamond, per Caret, DeBeers | $857.50 |
| Hair Dryer | $21.50 |
| Lawnmower | $88.00 |
| Razor, Gillette | $1.00 |
| Record, "Kiss Me Kate" | $4.85 |
| Refrigerator, Admiral | $189.95 |
| Roller Skates | $2.45 |
| Sleeping Bag | $4.88 |
| Stationery, 48-Piece Set | $0.49 |
| Wieners, per Pound, Oscar Mayer | $0.49 |

# 1954 Profile

## Guatemala Battle

### Civilian

Playwright Randall Hatfield has found that working with the CIA is rewarding, especially when the assignment is the overthrow of Guatemala's elected president.

### Life at Home

- Almost as soon as Randall Hatfield learned to write, he started creating stories of his own.
- As a young boy, he loved listening to tales spun by his grandfather during camping trips to the woods of Michigan's Upper Peninsula.
- He dreamed of being a famous playwright whose stories would move millions.
- In 1946, when he turned 18, he was taken by his parents to attend the University of Chicago.
- There, he fell in love with Latin American literature and the Spanish language; in his sophomore year he began intensively studying Spanish so he could read the stories in the original language.
- His evening hours were consumed by discussions with fellow students on what constituted the perfect play.
- During one of these barroom conversations, he met Elizabeth Holst, an intense Northwestern student from Waukegan, Illinois, who shared his enthusiasm for the Spanish language and culture.
- Married in the winter of 1949, they worked their way through their senior years in college; Randall did copyediting for several small newspapers in town, while Elizabeth tutored students in Spanish.
- Upon graduation, they packed their belongings in an elderly Studebaker—a hand-me-down from Randall's father—and set off for Mexico City.
- Elizabeth had a good job lined up teaching English, and Randall had been in contact with an avant-garde theater group which was very interested in several of his more abstract plays, and also needed a part-time manager.

*Randall Hatfield loves to write plays.*

## "The Americas: The Problem of Guatemala," *Time*, January 11, 1954:

Because the U.S. views communism in Guatemala as a menace to hemisphere security, it wants the 21 American Republics to take joint action against this danger at the Inter-American Conference in Caracas next March. But the U.S. is running into trouble trying to get Latin America to agree to anything like a strong line against Guatemala's fellow-traveling government. It is even having difficulty finding a suitable neighbor to take the lead in presenting the case under the 1947 Rio pact provision for joint measures against "an aggression which is not an armed attack."

Like many Europeans, the Latinos are not nearly so roused against the dangers of world communism as people in the U.S.; in fact, a large body of non-Communist leftist opinion holds that the U.S. is too upset about the Reds and not bothered enough about right-wing dictatorships. Latin America's powerful nationalist sentiment, moreover, tends to sympathize with Guatemala's Red-led harassment of U.S. companies.

**Old Ghosts:** At bottom the trouble is that any U.S. proposal for strong action against Guatemalan communism raises the old spectre of U.S. intervention, which scares the Latinos more than communism—even after a generation of U.S. goodwill, loans and trade agreements. Said a pro-U.S. South American president: "Nonintervention is essential to continental solidarity." The intervention of Moscow-controlled communism apparently does not bother them yet. Even such neighbors of Guatemala as El Salvador and Honduras, while turning up evidences of Communist infiltration, are reluctant to step forward with accusations.

MOSCOW DESIGN FOR LIVING

*In college, Randall began to study Latin literature and Spanish.*

- For Randall and Elizabeth, Mexico was a dream: the food, music and atmosphere all exceeded their expectations.
- To increase his income, Randall also picked up editing and writing jobs from anyone willing to pay for his services.
- It was an idyllic life, disturbed only by news from his parents that inquiries were being made in Wausau, Wisconsin, about him and Elizabeth by people claiming to be conducting a credit check.
- Randall's parents were afraid he was in trouble—possibly running with the wrong people in Mexico.
- One day, Randall was startled to receive a lunch invitation from Al Stevenson, a reserved, middle-aged man from the U.S. Embassy.
- They had met twice at parties, but Randall could not recall any meaningful conversation.
- After a pleasant lunch, they took a long ride into the country, where Al told him he was the CIA station chief in Mexico and needed Randall's help.
- The agency had already conducted extensive background checks, Randall was told, and the CIA was sure he could be of help to the Central Intelligence Agency.

- He then asked Randall to be a courier, who would write pieces for placement in the Mexican press and relay information he learned from his left-leaning artistic friends.
- Randall and Elizabeth were confused, flattered and unsure; neither of them had been very interested in politics, but ultimately, they became convinced they would be fighting for the future of their country against communism.
- Besides, with Elizabeth pregnant, they could use another $50 a month.

## Life at Work

- Since Randall and Elizabeth said yes to the CIA, life has been a whirlwind of activity.
- First came the birth of their daughter Sonia, the growth of the theater community, the critical approval for several of Randall's plays, and an increasing number of assignments from the CIA.
- By late 1953, he traveled to Washington, where he was offered a full-time position with the agency.
- He had been ready; his writing career was stalled, Elizabeth was pregnant again, and the threat of communism was growing across Latin America.
- Besides, he enjoyed intelligence work—it appealed to his sense of the dramatic.
- After a carefully worded phone call to Elizabeth in Mexico, he accepted the new position.
- His first major assignment came in March 1954, when he received simple instructions: Report to Miami, expect to be gone for several months.
- At the Miami airport, he was met by a nondescript man who drove an unmarked sedan.
- They drove in silence to what appeared to be a deserted air field.

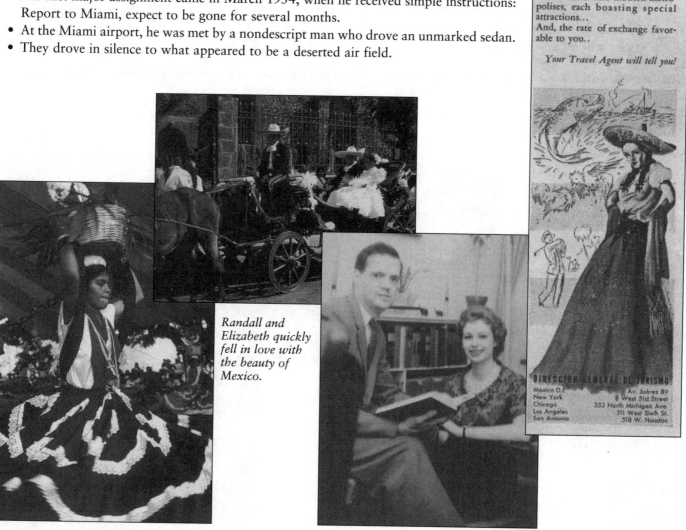

*Randall and Elizabeth quickly fell in love with the beauty of Mexico.*

## "The New Junta," *Time*, July 12, 1954:

Colonel Carlos Castillo Armas, the deadpan little insurgent who overthrew the pro-Communist government of Guatemala, came back in triumph last week in his country's capital. Guatemalans greeted him with firecrackers, kisses and backslapping embraces. At the bunting-draped central plaza, where 20,000 people yelled themselves hoarse, a huge picture of the rebel leader hung from the palace and cathedral bells pealed joyously. Later, as he had said he would, Castillo Armas dined in the palace.

Castillo Armas was not yet boss. In peace negotiations, the presidency of the ruling junta had been won, temporarily, by a fellow officer and an old schoolmate, Colonel Elfego Monzon, who had taken the leading part in the palace revolution that followed Castillo Armas' armed invasion. But the crowd went wild for Castillo Armas alone.

How much did the U.S. have to do with the turn of events? No matter who furnished the arms to Castillo Armas, it was abundantly clear that the U.S. Ambassador John E. Peurifoy masterminded most of the changes once Castillo Armas began his revolt. It was he who helped spot the phoniness of the first palace change, and it was he who saw to it that the new government was solidly anti-Communist.

**Tubeless Radio**

The first fully transistorized radio was claimed this week by Regency, a division of Industrial Development Engineering Associates. It is not quite the wristwatch radio of the comics, but it is only a small pocketful (3 by 5 by 1¼ in.), and it makes loud music on a single hearing-aid battery. Inside, instead of vacuum tubes, it has four transistors.

The chief advantage of transistors—besides their smallness—is that they have no glowing filament and therefore need no "A current" to keep the filament hot. All they need is the "B current," and very little of that. According to Edward C. Tudor, president of I.D.E.A., the 22½-volt B battery (cost: $1.15) lasts 20 to 30 hours if used continuously, longer when played intermittently.

- There, at Opa-Locka Marine Air Base, Randall learned about Operation PB Success and his role in Guatemala.
- Since the election of President Jacobo Arbenz in 1950, the threat of communism was growing, he was told; already, thousands of acres of land had been transferred from the nation's large landowners to the peasants.
- The U.S. Government decided to overthrow Arbenz and replace him with former Colonel Carlos Castillo Armas.
- The CIA pledged to help the coup by providing arms, air support and propaganda.
- Randall's job was to be deputy head of the radio propaganda team.
- He and the team leader would supervise, advise and write for a group of young Guatemalans whose goal was to destabilize the Arbenz government through radio broadcasts.
- After a month, Randall and his team left Opa-Locka and flew to Nicaragua where they would broadcast into Guatemala from a barn located on the estate of dictator Somoza.
- Listeners were told that the broadcasts were coming from deep in the jungles of Guatemala.
- To gain an audience, newspaper ads were placed in the major Guatemalan papers announcing a broadcast featuring major Latin stars on May 1, Labor Day, which was an opportune time because everyone was on holiday and few other broadcasts were planned.
- The many who tuned in heard not only their favorite stars, but also an announcer who reported that a revolution was scheduled on June 18.
- The broadcast then set forth the goals—carefully worded by Randall—of the revolution.
- During the broadcast, he was both nervous and elated.
- The radio programs then evolved into special-interest programming aimed at workers, students and women.
- Randall and his team had worked well into the night to accurately craft additional messages and scripts; a single misstatement of fact could undermine the entire operation.
- As reports arrived of unrest in Guatemala City, he was thrilled by the power of his written words.

*Using a primitive radio set-up in Nicaragua, Randall helped orchestrate the overthrow of the government in Guatemala.*

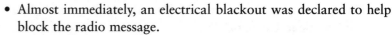

- Almost immediately, an electrical blackout was declared to help block the radio message.
- Using batteries and generators, the farmers in the countryside continued to listen, sharing the information with the cities.
- Randall and his team even broadcast sounds that made it appear government forces had found the radio transmitter and were forcing the brave men to seek a new location deeper in the jungles.
- This image was then reinforced by government radio, which proudly announced that the station had been overrun.
- On June 18, Randall and his team, acting as the Voice of Liberation, announced the invasion of a massive armed force, carefully ignoring the fact that the army consisted of fewer than 100 men led by a battered station wagon.
- The invasion force moved only six miles inside the country before setting up camp.
- Meanwhile, the radio broadcasts falsely announced that 5,000 men were headed for the capital, and relayed bogus orders transferring hundreds of men from one command to another.
- Broadcasts stating that Lake Atitlán had been poisoned sent many into panic, and within hours, the population of Guatemala City began to flee.
- It was one of the finest plays Randall ever wrote.
- The Voice of Liberation then made appeals to the escaping refugees, calling for them to make way for the rebel columns advancing on the city.
  - On June 27, with the imaginary rebel forces still only six miles inside the country, President Arbenz stepped down.
    - The revolutionary army was quickly flown to a landing strip outside the capital.
      - Several of the Guatemalan broadcasters were rushed to the city from Nicaragua to be a part of the triumphant parade and celebration.
  - Communism had been halted in Guatemala.
- Randall knows his work will keep the Reds out of the Panama Canal and the rest of his beloved Latin America.

### Life in the Community: Guatemala

- The nation of Guatemala was ruled by unelected dictators for most of its history.
- In 1944, a military junta overthrew the dictator and called for the first elections in decades.
- Juan José Arevalo, an exiled professor, won the election, and was succeeded in the election of 1950 by Jacobo Arbenz.
- Arbenz, although not a communist, was friendly to the small Guatemalan Communist Party.
- Soon after taking office, he initiated a land reform program to purchase land—with or without consent—from the handful of large landowners nationwide, and distribute it among the peasants.

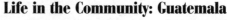

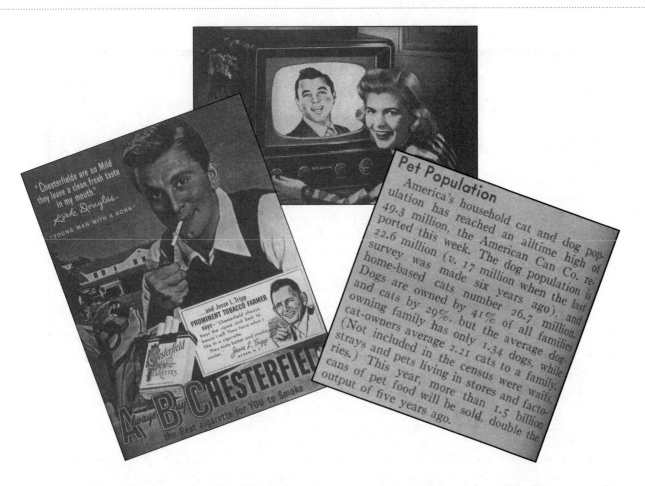

- In March 1953, more than 200,000 acres were expropriated from the politically connected, Boston-based United Fruit Company.
- The land was purchased at its stated value for tax purposes, which was a fraction of its actual value.
- The company immediately raised the spectre of encroaching communism in the Western Hemisphere; communism in Guatemala could threaten the future of the Panama Canal.
- As a result, a decision was made for the CIA to overthrow Arbenz.

# HISTORICAL SNAPSHOT
# 1954

- President Dwight D. Eisenhower personally drove a bulldozer to break ground for the nation's first commercial nuclear power plant in Shippingport, Pennsylvania
- American Airlines cut the customary 11-hour flight time from New York to the West Coast to eight hours with the introduction of the new Douglas DC-7s
- The government reported that 154 Americans had an income of more than $1 million, down from 513 in 1929
- RCA sold the first color TV sets at $1,000 each
- Felt skirts with poodle appliqués swept the teenage fashion world
- Disney's TV program *Davy Crockett* ignited a national demand for coonskin caps
- A Gallup poll reported that a family of four could live on $60 a week
- Newspaper vending machines, the breath-inhaler alcoholism detector, Miami's Fontainebleau Hotel, the Mercedes 300 SL with fuel injection, Trix cereal, frozen TV dinners and Levi's faded blue denims all made their first appearance
- Elvis Presley made his first commercial recording
- Unemployment rose to 5.5 percent, inflation was only 0.4 percent and the GNP was five percent
- *On the Waterfront* with Marlon Brando won the Academy Award for Best Picture; *The Teahouse of the August Moon* by John Patrick captured the Pulitzer Prize for best play
- A record $3 billion was spent on new construction
- Disk jockey Alan Freed introduced the "rock'n'roll" format on radio station WINS
- The American thermonuclear tests at Bikini Atoll wounded 31 Americans, 236 natives and 23 Japanese fishermen; the U.S. offered an $800,000 indemnity
- The Supreme Court ruled that the doctrine of "separate but equal" had no place in public education; separate facilities, the court said, were "inherently unequal"
- Ernest Hemingway won the Nobel Prize for literature; the Pulitzer Prize in fiction went to William Faulkner for *A Fable,* and to Wallace Stevens in poetry for *Collected Poems*
- President Eisenhower modified the Pledge of Allegiance from "one nation, indivisible" to "one nation, under God, indivisible"
- Polls showed that 78 percent of Americans thought it was important to report to the FBI relatives or acquaintances suspected of being communists
- Mississippi voters approved a constitutional amendment to abolish public schools if required to racially desegregate their classrooms
- The Tobacco Industry Research Committee reported that there was "no proof" that cigarette smoking was a cause of lung cancer
- Sales were high for the newly introduced tranquilizers Milltown and Equanil
- Paul Landis wrote in *Your Marriage and Family Living* that, "College women in general have greater difficulty marrying. . . . Men still want wives who will bolster their egos rather than detract from them"

## Selected Prices

| | |
|---|---|
| Automatic Coffee Maker, General Electric | $29.50 |
| Buffalo Bill Costume, Child's | $2.98 |
| Camera Film | $0.46 |
| Candy Bars, for Two | $0.13 |
| Coffee, per Pound | $0.83 |
| Crib | $49.95 |
| Electric Tool Kit, Black and Decker | $29.95 |
| Hair Coloring, Clairol | $0.95 |
| House, Three-Bedroom Brick Ranch | $13,800.00 |
| Lighter Fluid | $0.25 |
| Lip Balm, Chapstick | $0.25 |
| Pinking Shears | $3.95 |
| Refrigerator, Frigidaire | $199.75 |
| Shotgun, Double-Barrel | $1.98 |
| Television, 17" | $140.00 |

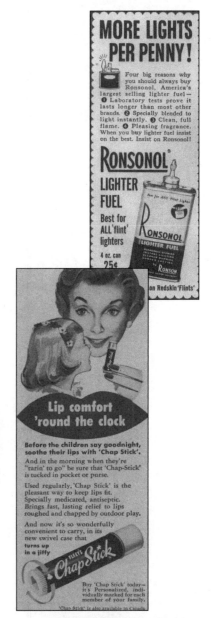

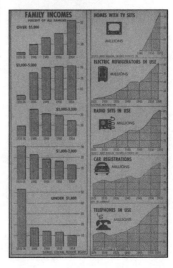

### The Old Boys, The American Elite and the Origins of the CIA, Burton Hersh, Charles Scribner's Sons, New York, 1992:

(Jacobo) Arbenz was 37, quick, difficult to approach, high-strung, with a sharply etched Scott-Fitzgeraldian profile. The child of an unstable Swiss pharmacist and a Latina woman, Arbenz had married the vivacious daughter of a wealthy Salvadoran coffee grower, who stimulated her inward husband with fantasies of remedial social experiment. Several of Senora Arbenz's intimates were already celebrated Latin-American Communists. . . .

Arbenz pledged "to convert Guatemala from a backward country with a predominantly feudal economy into a modern capitalist state." He meant to construct a second port on the Atlantic coast, cut through a highway to break the International Railways of Central America transportation monopoly, and compete with the endemic foreign ownership until control of production and distribution gravitated into Guatemalan hands. Arbenz inaugurated a hydroelectric plan to offset the hegemony of the American and Foreign Power Company, a Foster Dulles client since the 1920s. In June of 1952 he squeezed through the legislature his agricultural reform bill, which expropriated the uncultivated segment of the latifundi-size plantations and repaid their owners with two percent, 25-year bonds based on the evaluation of the properties for tax purposes. Since United Fruit had connived to force down the assessment of its properties to an insignificant fraction of their obvious worth, this turn of events electrified the management in Boston, which regarded the nefarious Decree 900 as tantamount to confiscation.

## "The Tempest in the Coffee Pot," *The American Mercury*, July 1954:

The little lady legislator from Illinois had no idea of helping the Communists in Guatemala, or anywhere else, when she took the rostrum of Congress for one of her rare speeches last January and proceeded to stir up a tempest in the Inter-American coffee pot. She simply wanted to know why the American housewife had to pay more than a dollar a pound for coffee, and why it was that one cannot get a decent cup of coffee for a nickel, or even a dime, in a restaurant anymore, and she very obviously suspected something sinister about the whole thing. Besides, a tight election was in the offing, and a lot of votes are cast by American housewives. American housewives have been getting madder and madder for a long time about rising prices—especially coffee.

Politically, the little lady's speech was a natural. It had press appeal and it had voter appeal. All over the country, astute newspaper editors—who also had no thought of giving the Commies a helping hand—spotted the coffee speech out of the dreary welter of news about A-bombs and H-bombs, taxes and budgets, Malenkov and Molotov, Korea and Indo-China, and correctly assessed it as a good "relief story." They assigned their best feature writers to blow it up and keep it alive, and got their crack editorial writers to wax indignant about the 15-cent cup of coffee.

Certainly there was no subversive thought in the minds of the U.S. senators who sniffed those coffee-scented breezes, found them laden with aromatic political possibilities, and proceeded to whip them into a whirlwind with the inevitable senatorial investigation. But the net result of all of these works, the hubbub in the United States over coffee prices and the proposals to boycott Latin American coffee, proved to be the greatest piece of sheer good luck that has fallen to the Communists since they opened their campaign to gain a firm foothold in the Western Hemisphere some 30 years ago. It enabled them to scuttle the most promising, and from their standpoint, the most threatening effort that has been made to date to dislodge them from the one firm foothold they

have gained, the neighboring Central American Republic of Guatemala.

And therein lies the hitherto untold story—a story that just goes to show how complicated life and politics and editing have become since Lenin and his small band of Bolsheviks seized control of a disorganized revolution in a huge, sprawling country halfway around the world from us.

Few residents of the United States have any conception of the bitterness and concern that the coffee tempest up here aroused throughout Latin America, especially in those countries whose economies are heavily dependent on coffee. One of the deep-seated grievances in Latin America is the conviction of all of those countries that they do not receive from the United States and other industrial nations prices for their raw materials that are commensurate with the prices they pay for the manufactured products they must buy in return. That is one of the things they mean when they talk so bitterly about "economic colonialism."

## "The Tempest in the Coffee Pot . . ." *(continued)*

Our Latin American neighbors complain, and with considerable justice, that when the raw materials and agricultural products which they export are in surplus in the world markets, the United States preaches "free enterprise" and allows prices to seek the natural level. But when raw materials are scarce, we use our tremendous economic power to bring the prices down.

Thus, just as we had done throughout World War II, when raw materials became tight after the outbreak of war in Korea and the launching of our big rearmament program, the U.S. forced prices down by the establishment of intensive domestic controls on distribution. Increased production in Latin America finished the job. There was one notable exception, though, from the decline in commodity prices—coffee. Partly as a result of the Brazilian drought together with rising world demands, and to some extent as a result of speculation, coffee prices continued to rise—and that was the one drop of solace in the bitter cup of Latin American woes. The economies of Brazil, Colombia, Nicaragua, El Salvador, Haiti, Costa Rica, the Dominican Republic and Guatemala are heavily dependent on the price of coffee. A serious drop in coffee prices would bring economic disaster, or at least depression, to nearly all of those nations. But probably the most vulnerable country to any fluctuation of the price of coffee in the U.S. market is the Republic of Guatemala, which for the past several years has been under the almost complete domination of the Kremlin. Not only have the Communists gained control there, but they are using that foothold to launch an intensive drive to capture all Central America.

For several years, these neighboring countries have been becoming increasingly exasperated at Guatemala's flagrant intervention in their internal affairs. And shortly before the recent Caracas Conference of the Organization of American States, they decided to do something about it. The governments of Nicaragua, El Salvador and Honduras agreed to present to the Caracas Conference a formal resolution denouncing the Guatemalan government as Communist-controlled and charging it with intervening in their domestic affairs. The ambassadors of those countries in Washington consulted with their Latin American colleagues and were pledged a total of 14 supporting votes.

The OAS charter sets up specific punitive actions that can be taken against any member nation that is found to have violated the treaty by intervening in the domestic affairs of its neighbors: diplomatic isolation, economic sanctions, and finally, even military action. A few weeks prior to the Caracas Conference, the possibility of economic sanctions against Guatemala was being seriously discussed among Latin American diplomats. The consternation of the Guatemalan Communists to all of this was clearly revealed in their almost frantic efforts to bolster up their own position and to muddy up the diplomatic waters. They recalled the Guatemalan ambassador to Washington, Guillermo Toriello, a tough, articulate follower of the Communist line (whether he carries a Party card or not), and promoted him to Foreign Minister to head the Guatemalan delegation to Caracas. Then, in a typical Communist diversionary maneuver, Guatemala charged that the leaders in the diplomatic attack, Nicaragua, El Salvador and Honduras, were conspiring with the United States and the Dominican Republic to invade their country and unseat their "democratic" government. In a further effort to muddy things up, Costa Rica, where the Communists are rapidly gaining control, brought vague charges in the OAS against the Dominican Republic and threatened to boycott the Caracas Conference unless Venezuela released certain political prisoners (mostly Communists). Then, just as the Guatemalan Communists were progressing from deep concern to outright consternation, the coffee tempest blew up in the United States. The U.S. press became filled with talk about a coffee boycott. Egged on by the Senate investigating committee, the Department of Agriculture slapped controls on the coffee exchange.

All talk of economic sanctions against

## "The Tempest in the Coffee Pot . . ." *(continued)*

Guatemala, of course, was automatically dropped. For all practical purposes, economic sanctions against Guatemala by the OAS would amount to nothing more or less than a boycott of Guatemalan coffee by the United States.

Needless to say, a boycott of Guatemalan coffee by the U.S. would be a crippling blow and might possibly upset the Communist-controlled government. Certainly the example would slow down the drift of the Costa Rican government towards the Kremlin.

But so severe was the shock throughout the coffee-producing states to the loose proposals in Congress and the press of a general coffee boycott to bring prices down that it is impossible to even mention the word "boycott" in Latin America, now, in regards to Guatemala, or even the Soviet Union for that matter. Each country feels that it is, itself, too vulnerable. And the whole success of the proposed resolution denouncing Guatemalan intervention depended on the firm support of the other coffee-producing countries. . . .

## "Guatemala Battle of the Backyard," *Time*, June 28, 1954:

In Guatemala, a lush, green little country only 1,000 miles from the U.S., anti-Communist and pro-Communist forces were locked in battle this week. What kind of war was it? Guatemala's Communist-line Government called it "aggression" and "invasion," and shrilled accusations against its neighbors, including the U.S. The lightly armed insurgents who moved in over the eastern border from Honduras called themselves the Army of Liberation, took for their motto "God and Honor," and urged all true Guatemalans to join them against the government and its Red friends. The first actual shooting came as insurgent aircraft strafed fuel tanks and airfields and dropped a few homemade bombs. Days later, two infantry task forces of a few hundred men each fumbled their way toward each other in the bush near a sleepy town called Zacapa and opened the ground fighting. The battle picture was obscure, but the government claimed that it had 3,000 men in "a general offensive" against 2,000 rebels along a line north and south of Zacapa.

Neither side had rushed headlong into combat. Both knew that the outcome would almost certainly depend on whether the regular Guatemalan army, some 6,000 strong and not at all Communist, stuck by the government or swung over to the anti-Communist cause. But whether the Guatemalan clash swelled into bitter and prolonged civil bloodshed or petered out in anticlimax and frustration, the issue was nonetheless clearly drawn. Guatemala, in its special way, was a small-scale sequel to Korea and Indo-China, and the world knew it. Even the United Nations Security Council was stirred into action; it held its first Sunday emergency meeting since the June 1950 session on Korea.

**"Supreme Chief."** The invading anti-Communist rebels were mainly Guatemalans who had been driven into exile in recent years. Their leader, emerging from almost total obscurity, was Carlos Castillo Armas, 40, sometime colonel in the Guatemalan army, who had been jailed in Guatemala City in 1950 after an attempted revolt, but tunneled spectacularly out of prison and fled. Living in Tegucigalpa, Honduras, he made himself a symbol of the exiled right-wing opposition to Guatemala's Communists. He also began quietly collecting arms, money and men.

No one had given his plans for "liberating" Guatemala much chance. But suddenly last week he was calling himself "Supreme Chief of the Movement of National Liberation," doing his best to look like it. From his Tegucigalpa house, boxes of arms appeared and were loaded into trucks. Soldiers were recruited, and promised pay of $2.50 a day. The force thus swiftly mobilized was uniformed in fresh sunfans, and airlifted (in commercial DC-3s, at $400 a flight) to Macuelizo, Copan and Nueva Ocotepeque, Honduran hamlets on the Guatemalan frontier.

The way of the campaign's beginning was certainly unlike any hot war fighting of recent times. There were no tanks or artillery, and for that matter, no roads for such luxurious military equipment to move on. The army that gathered along the unpatrolled jungle border that first afternoon could have made no sense except against the background of Central America, where history has been made before by a handful of angry men with rusty Mausers and machetes.

"I shall be with you very soon," Castillo Armas radioed to the Guatemalan people. Then he strapped a string of hand grenades around his waist and clapped a steel helmet on his head. Unopposed, his men quickly crossed the border and seized Esquipulas with its famed old church.

**"The Other Colonel."** In Guatemala City, that day, another colonel strode tight-lipped along the underground tunnel that leads from the executive mansion via an elevator to the presidential office on the second floor of the city's avocado-green National Palace. President Jacobo Arbenz, the stubborn, enigmatic career soldier who had started the trouble in the first place by flinging wide the palace doors and welcoming Communists into his government, had plenty to think about. But he may have taken a moment to recall

## "Guatemala Battle . . ." *(continued)*

that Castillo Armas had once been a schoolmate, a fellow graduate of the country's West Point, the *Escuela Politécnica.*

For the first day or two, Arbenz seemed curiously unwilling to move his troops or put his army officers to the test. Reports indicated that officers and men alike were being confined to barracks. Finally, Arbenz made his decision and announced that he was taking personal command of the armed forces. He cautiously organized a picked force of 500 men from the three forts within the capital, put a trusted colonel in command, and started them on, all in slowly crawling trucks toward Zacapa 70 miles away. With that spearhead force on the way, he gave command of his field force to a St. Cyr-educated officer, and hoped for the best.

Once off the road, the army forces' might have trouble keeping contact with the rebels. This would be particularly true if the rebels tried to avoid combat and play for time in the hope that throngs of Guatemalans within the country might be won over to them. As a hedge against that, the government passed out guns to some of its Red-led unions of workers and peasants, and sent them to police roads and villages in the interior.

**"Grenades & Thunderbolts."** In the air, meanwhile, Castillo Armas' pilots were scoring successes. His air force was tiny but effective. It took only a small Cessna plane, carrying hand grenades and a light machine gun to blow up the gasoline tanks at the Pacific port of San Jose, thus forcing Arbenz into immediate and drastic gas rationing. F-47 thunderbolts—Castillo Armas would not say where they were flying from—strafed Guatemala City and Puerto Barrios. Arbenz was embarrassingly unable to fight back. His air force, made up of a few lightly armed trainers, was no match for F-47s, even if he could trust his pilots. But four of them, at least, had defected, taking refuge in the Salvadoran Embassy.

"Somewhere over the border," Castillo Armas this week proclaimed a "provisional government"

and issued his first fiery statements. "The dawn of liberation illuminates our land," it said. "The glorious struggle has begun against tyranny, treason, deceit and shame. . . . Assault the garrisons of the Communists and capture them. They are cowards!"

A certain amount of hyperbole is doubtless permissible in a manifesto issued on such an emotional occasion; Castillo Armas probably knows quite well that some Communists are cowards and some are nothing of the sort. And while he may regard Fellow Traveler Arbenz as a tyrant or a traitor, he could scarcely consider him a coward. On the contrary, military attachés, diplomats and journalists who have met the Guatemalan president are in striking agreement that the mainspring of his character is dogged, stubborn, self-willed courage. If there is perhaps the higher degree of courage that could enable a man to look into his own heart and see what his reckless flirtation with communism has done—and may yet do—to his country and his people. . . .

## "Guatemala's 'Strong Man,'" J. Alvarez Del Vayo, *The Nation,* August 14, 1954:

Colonel Castillo Armas needed no more than a month to prove that, apart from Ambassador Peurifoy and perhaps the Archbishop of Guatemala and the representative of the United Fruit Company, he had few dependable supporters. The whole propaganda tale of a country miraculously "liberated" from the claws of communism, which four weeks earlier had monopolized the headlines in the American press, fell to pieces when a handful of army cadets obliged the strong man to knuckle under and pledge to immediate disarming and disbanding of his "liberation" forces in the capital. That was the exact wording of the second point of the agreement concluded on August 2 between Castillo Armas and the rebellious cadets. The first point was a government guarantee that the young rebels would not be punished. The third was a promise by the regular army to accept the authority of the ruling junta—not a very impressive conquest for a chief of state who is supposed to be also the commander-in-chief of the army.

The whole affair had the quality of *opéra bouffe*—the more so since the revolt seems to have begun in the congenial surroundings of a *maison de tolerance* in Guatemala City—and one could treat it accordingly were it not that it involves the fate and hopes of the Guatemalan people. Actually, the explosion of the cadets was only spectacular surface evidence of a deep dissatisfaction within the army. Seven top leaders of the regular army have been seized and placed under arrest, including Colonel Adolfo Garcia Montenego, former ambassador to Cuba; Colonel Federico Fuentes Giron, former director of communications; and Colonel Daniel Caceres, former secretary of the armed forces. Castillo Armas has charged the officers with plotting to restore former President Arbenz to power. This accusation no one takes seriously.

Feeling justifiably insecure as to the attitude of the army, Castillo has now called upon a handful of union leaders who had been at odds with the Arbenz regime to rally to his assistance—an act reminiscent of Peron. These "labor" recruits have threatened a general strike unless the regular army forswears any role in the government and Castillo Armas is made sole boss. They demand not only "unification of power" but a Cabinet composed entirely of "certified anti-Reds." The main target of the group is Colonel Monzon, who with the agreement of Ambassador Peurifoy headed the governing junta before Castillo Armas became president.

In spite of the unrest it is most unlikely, at least for the time being, that the Arbenz government will return to power, but it is probable that the army will presently assume the task of creating a caretaker regime to put an end to the existing ridiculous state of things. No matter how many "victories" Castillo Armas may announce, he is obviously no longer in a position to resist a real ultimatum from the army. He has lost his freedom of action—along with whatever prestige may have surrounded a man who, before his exile and return, carried no weight. His recent behavior has revealed his character. For instance, he invited two emissaries of La Aurora garrison to come to see him to discuss a compromise, and when they arrived he had them both arrested. According to reliable reports it was necessary for Ambassador Peurifoy to bring to bear on the other members of the junta, Colonel Elfego Monzon and Major Enrique Oliva, all the weight of his—and his government's—influence to hold the trio together. But as an Associated Press dispatch from Guatemala reported, the three are governing the nation through a "shaky shotgun political union."

## Who Won

In Guatemala and Honduras last week, voters went to the polls to elect their next Presidents, and Brazil neared the end of the slow, complex tally (TIME, Oct. 18) of its off-year congressional vote. In all three nations, the overall pattern of results was reassuring for Western Hemisphere stability: with minor local exceptions, the voting was peaceful and orderly, and moderates and anti-Communists did better with the voters than extremists of either the left or right wing. The big winners:

¶ Brazil's conservative President João Café Filho, though not on any ballot, significantly bested the politically potent ghost of the late President Getulio Vargas. After Vargas' suicide in August, ultra-nationalists and Communists rallied around congressional candidates running in Vargas' name; pro-U.S. moderates backed Café Filho. But not even Vargas' rabble-rousing former Labor Minister, João ("Jango") Goulart, succeeded in winning his race for Senator, and as the votes piled up, the net effect was a green light for Café Filho to steer Brazil down the middle of the road.

¶ Guatemala's President Carlos Castillo Armas, who seized power in June's anti-Communist revolution, was legally confirmed in office. By having the voters asked out loud whether they wanted him to continue in office and requiring an oral answer, he managed to roll up the vote in the proportion of 1,000 to one. Concurrent elections for an assembly to write a new constitution produced some possibly troublesome opposition for the future—not from the well-beaten Communists, but from ambitious politicos of the extreme right wing.

¶ Honduras went anxiously to the poll fearing armed revolution as the like upshot of a three-way presidential ra that looked like a three-way standoff. B Ramón Villeda Morales, a socially prom nent pediatrician and a pro-U.S. liber got 48% of the vote. Because he miss an absolute majority, a newly elect Congress must choose the next Presider but the talk of revolt dwindled rapidly the face of such a clear verdict. Ho durans, whose history lists 134 revol tions in 130 years, pinched themselv and wondered if democracy had perha arrived at last.

# 1960–1969

No aspect of American society escaped the tumult of the 1960s. Sexual mores, education, the role of the family, the purpose of college and even the need for parents came into question. Following the placid era of the 1950s, the seventh decade of the twentieth century contained tragic assassinations, momentous social movements, remarkable scientific achievements, and the longest war in American history. Civil Rights leader Martin Luther King, Jr., would deliver his "I have a dream" speech in 1963, the same year President John F. Kennedy was killed. Five years later in 1968, King, along with John Kennedy's influential brother Bobby, would be killed. Violent protests against American involvement in Vietnam would be led and heavily supported by the educated middle class, which had grown and prospered enormously in the healthy economy.

Internationally, the power of the United States was immense. Congress gave the young President John F. Kennedy the defense and space-related programs Americans wanted, but few of the welfare programs he proposed. The Cold War became hotter during conflicts over Cuba and Berlin. Fears over the international spread of communism led to America's intervention in a foreign conflict that would become a defining event of the decade: Vietnam.

Military involvement in this small Asian country grew from advisory status to full-scale war. By 1968, Vietnam had become a divisive issue leading to President Lyndon Johnson's decision not to run for another term. Antiwar marches, which had drawn only a few thousand in 1965, grew in size until millions of marchers filled the streets of nearly every major city in the U.S. By the spring of 1970, students on 448 college campuses made ROTC voluntary or abolished it.

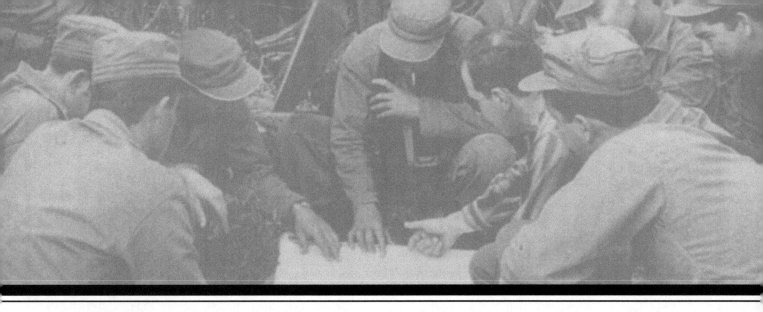

# 1961 Profile

# Bay of Pigs, Cuba

### Air National Guard Pilot

Attorney Taylor Pendarvis from Huntsville, Alabama, is willing to leave his family and join an all-volunteer army of revolutionaries if it means eliminating communism in Cuba.

### Life at Home

- Huntsville, Alabama-based attorney Taylor Pendarvis was preparing for an important meeting with a new client when the call came in.
- His long-time secretary knew he was willing to be interrupted by the Alabama Air National Guard, headquartered in Birmingham.
- Taylor, a 38-year-old World War II veteran, placed America first, his wife and four children second, and flying planes a close two and a half.
- Since leaving the service 16 years ago, he had flown for the Air National Guard.
- He was told a jet trainer was on the way to pick him up, and that he should be ready to leave for Birmingham in 15 minutes.
- His new client would have to wait.
- Following a quick flight, Taylor was shown into the office of the commander of the Alabama Air National Guard and told that his country needed him to serve in a secret mission that would last up to three months; he must be prepared to leave in under 30 days.
- He was told the mission was outside the continental limits of the United States, but in the Western Hemisphere.
- The commander added that shooting may be involved.
- Taylor knew this mission involved Fidel Castro, with whom the U.S. had severed diplomatic relations 15 months ago.
- Taylor was being asked to act as a private citizen, not as an Air Guard officer.
- Rumors of this type of mission had been swirling for weeks; one newspaper even carried a story about an American contractor who was building an airstrip in Guatemala—an extremely hush-hush operation under tight controls.

*Taylor Pendarvis has joined an all-volunteer army to fight communism.*

## "New Packages," *Business Week*, October 8, 1960:

Coca-Cola is continuing to expand its distribution of Coke in cans, a weighty step for a company that has made a bottle familiar around the world. The company is doing this despite its long-held doubts about the wisdom of raising the price of its product through increase in the cost of the package. In part, it is yielding to the desire of some consumers for the convenience of the throwaway can.

Another factor that motivates the company is pressure from big food chains over the cost of handling returnable bottles. Food chains prefer cans, which don't have to be returned.

To meet these problems, Coke reportedly is planning to offer Coke in a throwaway bottle, which will about split the cost difference between regular bottles and cans. One industry guess is that Coke will offer cartons of six throwaway bottles at about $0.04 to $0.06 under the price of six returnable bottles, plus deposit. Confronted with the apparently lower price of throwaways, consumers may not care that getting back their deposit actually makes the returnable bottle cheaper.

- The next steps included the creation of a cover story, saying goodbye to his wife Anne, convincing 16-year-old Hugh he could not drive his father's car while he was away, and attending a meeting in Birmingham with a man who told Taylor that a privately financed invasion of Cuba was being planned.
- Experienced American pilots, preferably those not in the service, were needed for both training and combat roles.
- The pay was $2,800 per month, similar to Taylor's legal earnings, plus an opportunity to buy insurance that provided $15,000 and $550 a month to his wife for life if he was killed.
  - At this meeting, Taylor was paid in advance in hundred-dollar bills.
  - He then selected his new identity: Harry Clark from Monroe, Louisiana, a community he knew well from childhood trips to relatives, and very fitting, since his assignment required that he defend the Monroe Doctrine.
  - With the phony name came a phony driver's license, Social Security card and birth certificate.
  - Taylor noticed that several of the other pilots at the meeting, some from the Alabama Air Guard, specialized in C-54 heavy transport planes, while the rest were like himself—qualified in the aging B-26 bomber flown by the Cuban Air Force.

"There should be no misunderstanding of our position: We shall render the Cuban people and their government all necessary assistance. . . . We are sincerely interested in a relaxation of international tension, but, if others aggravate it, we shall reply in full measure."
—Soviet Union Premier Nikita Khrushchev, April 18, 1961

- During their briefing, the American pilots were told that the revolutionary force had sufficient planes and pilots; what they lacked was confidence.
- Since April 1960—almost a year ago—the Movement of Revolutionary Recovery had been calling for all Cubans to take up arms against Castro.
- A few months later, Assistant Secretary of State A. A. Berle said, "For all practical purposes, Cuba is just as much a communist nation as Hungary or North Korea. The island republic has been converted into not only a spearhead of Soviet and Chinese propaganda, but also a potential base for Soviet and Chinese power."
- Recently, both *Time* and *U.S. News & World Report* have been filled with stories about communist Cuba and its eminent demise, while *Parade* ran an article by Pedro Luis Diaz Lanz, once head of the Cuban Air Force, headlined, "Why I Fight Fidel Castro."
- In the midst of this saber-rattling, one thing was clear: The privately financed invasion was under the exclusive control of the CIA.
- During the briefing, Taylor was told only that "this operation is being planned by professionals in whom you can place complete trust and confidence."
- While Cubans, referred to consistently as foreign nationals, would do the vast majority of the flying, the most minute details were under the control of the American advisors.

*Popular magazines are filled with stories linking Russia's Nikita Khrushchev and Cuba's Fidel Castro.*

### Life at Work

- The makeshift airbase in Retalhuleu, Guatemala, where Taylor Pendarvis trained Cuban pilots, was carved out of the jungle.
- The 4,800-foot runway was oriented northwest to southeast; it was not only short, but barely wide enough to accommodate a C-54 or a B-26, and would have been illegal to use for heavy aircraft landings in the U.S.
- The Cuban pilots were enthusiastic, but inexperienced; most had never flown in formation and had no skills in aerial gunnery.
- They were so bad, Taylor laughed, "Most can't hit the side of a barn; hell, some can't hit the pasture the barn is standing in."
- To improve their skills, the Cubans constructed a target of bamboo poles, pine boards and some 50-gallon drums, which was set afloat in a small lake a few miles from the base.
- But trouble of another type was brewing—the media.
- *The New York Times* reported a story very accurately describing the base, including the presence of large numbers of American advisors.
- The Guatemalan government insisted the military activity at the base was a response to the threats made by Castro.
- Also, lives were lost; four Cuban soldiers were killed by sharks while swimming on a beach as American pilots circled overhead, helpless to intervene in the tragedy.
- In general, the work was interesting, the food bad, the scorpions plentiful, and the chance to fight communism exciting.
- To add adrenaline to each day, the area was inhabited by a very small snake whose venom was said to be so poisonous that a man, if bitten, would die in minutes.
- As a result, many of the pilots showered with their boots on.
- Based on the plans provided to Taylor, the first strike was to take place sometime in April, prior to the amphibious landing at the Bay of Pigs.
- This mission was critical; Castro's air power had to be neutralized for the invasion to succeed.
  - Two planes flown by American-trained Cubans were to attack each of Cuba's three major airports and destroy all of the aircraft and fuel supplies found there.
  - For weeks, Taylor ran the Cubans through mock bombing runs, providing practical flying advice, tactical tips and personal thoughts.
  - While they trained, cries for the ouster of Castro grew louder; some anti-Castro leaders predicted his defeat before summer's end.
  - Many of the pilots were passionate about retaking Cuba from communism so they could return to friends, family and familiar places.

*Taylor and his men were concerned that Castro's forces would attack first.*

  - In the days leading to the invasion, all of the American pilots slept with sidearms, fearful that Castro's forces would attack first.
  - Taylor did not trust the Guatemalan guards, either, whose mission was to turn back a possible guerrilla assault on the base.
  - In addition, the mission was strewn with cultural clashes between American and Cuban pilots, which grew worse after the construction of a club and bar open only to Americans and their invited guests.

"Cuba is not an island unto itself, and our concern is not ended by mere expressions of nonintervention and regret. . . . The American people are not complacent about Iron Curtain tanks and planes less than 90 miles from our shores. . . . Our security may be lost without the firing of a single missile or the crossing of a single border. . . . As your president, I am determined upon our system's survival and success, regardless of the cost and regardless of the peril.

—President John Kennedy, April 20, 1961

- The restriction was initiated to prevent Cuban infiltrators from learning critical secrets, but that had been lost on the emotional Cubans, Taylor thought.
- However, when it came time for the assault, it was the Cubans who took to the air; during the initial wave, the American B-26 pilots were left behind, causing a storm of protest and frustration.
- Taylor had been told the Cubans were so sure of success, they insisted on doing all their own fighting, which he does not entirely understand or believe.
- Despite the clashes, on April 15, the day of the invasion, everyone was tense as the planes left the ground; Taylor felt as if his children were taking flight.
- The planes, loaded with 500-pound bombs and rockets under their wings, left a base in Puerto Cabezas, Nicaragua, several hours before dawn; Taylor stayed by the radio all day.
- Of 22 available planes at the base, nine were sent out.
- In the days leading to the invasion, the advisors told the ground troops that they would enjoy complete air superiority, pledging, "The skies over Cuba will be blotted out."
- At sunrise, the planes hit their targets, but Castro's forces fought back.
- Of the nine planes that went out, five came back to Puerto Cabezas and three landed at other bases; all were spattered with bullet holes.
- Twelve of Castro's aircraft had been destroyed, but his entire air force could have been destroyed if all 22 planes had been deployed.
- A second assault on a heavy concentration of armored equipment was cancelled.
- Rumors were rampant that newly elected President John Kennedy cut the size of the initial attack force because he feared political repercussions if American involvement was detected.
- From what Taylor could see, America was running from Soviet threats instead of showing the communists who was boss in the Western Hemisphere.
- Clearly, they had knocked a big hole in the Cuban air force, but more could have been done prior to the landing planned for Monday, April 17.
- Word was, the U.S. would not fly in support of the assault.
- When 1,300 anti-Castro invaders—most trained by Americans—invaded their native land, they were confident of support from B-26 air and U.S. Navy fighters from the carrier *Essex* patrolling off the Cuban coast.
- No one knew until after the invasion began that Kennedy had forbidden American support, even though his military planner made it clear that air support of the amphibious operation was critical.

*Anti-Castro troops were quickly gunned down during the Bay of Pigs Invasion.*

## "The Inquest," *Time*, May 5, 1961:

The early editorial cheers that accompanied the anti-Castro rebels had subsided, along with the chorus of dismay that followed the news of disaster. Last week, it was time for the inquest, and the U.S. press turned to the gloomy business of explaining what went wrong.

"We Americans," wrote C.L. Sulzberger in *The New York Times*, "look like fools to our friends, rascals to our enemies and incompetents to the rest." The *Times*'s Washington Bureau Chief James Reston was equally embarrassed: "For the first time in his life, John F. Kennedy has taken a public licking. Cuba was a clumsy and humiliating one, which makes it worse." *The New York Post*'s Max Lerner wallowed in despair, "Love is never enough when pitted against death in an unequal struggle." In the *New York Daily News*, Ted Lewis sounded almost grateful that "a little of the self-assurance of the Kennedy administration has rubbed off as a result of the Cuban invasion fiasco." Concluded columnist Russell Reeves in the *Cleveland Plain Dealer*, "Cuba even last week demonstrated that life is unlike the television westerns. The good guys do not always win."

- The brigade forces had been transported from Puerto Cabezas on six ships, of which two were sunk by Castro's planes soon after daylight.
- The heavy equipment needed by the brigade parachute troops was lost in the swamps; one unit was also tangled there.
- The battalion of Cuban freedom fighters that occupied the town of Playa Larga ran out of ammunition.
- Taylor and most of the American advisors were frustrated—and worried about the Cuban invaders.
- Then, on the day of the landing, orders were changed again; the B-26s would fly and many would be piloted by American volunteers in support of the assault.
- Taylor was nervous climbing into the pilot's seat; if he were shot down, the only identification he carried said he was Harry Clark of Monroe, Louisiana.
- To calm himself, he carefully reviewed the flight check list and chatted with his crew.
- As he taxied down the runway, Taylor was convinced that defending Cuba was the right and necessary step toward defeating communism.
- His only wish was that he could be defending America as an Alabama Air National Guardsman.
- Quickly, his thoughts turned to helping the invading Cuban forces.
- He knew that if no support from the *Essex* was allowed, the slow, lumbering B-26s would be easy targets for the Cuban jets.
- Flying in tandem with another B-26, Taylor spotted a column of 1,000 highly concentrated soldiers and trucks assembled behind several Soviet-made tanks—the perfect target for the napalm he was carrying.

- Within minutes, the area was ablaze; his napalm had landed in the midst of the foot soldiers, while the second plane dropped conventional bombs on the trucks.
- They both then strafed the Castro troops with machine gun fire and rockets, making three runs.
- As they turned toward home base, bodies and burning hulks of vehicles littered the ground.
- They passed jets from the *Essex,* which were only allowed to be near the action, not enter into battle.
- For the next several days, the bad news came in waves.
- Four fellow guardsmen had been shot down and were presumed dead.
- Without air support, the revolutionaries were being hammered at the Bay of Pigs.
- Castro compared the bombing to the air attack on Pearl Harbor, only "twice as treacherous and a thousand times more cowardly."
- The mission, beleaguered by poor planning and American indecision, was a failure.
- Within days, 250,000 suspected revolutionaries were rounded up in Cuba to be hung.
- Taylor knows he can't say a word about his role or America's betrayal by its own president.

## Life in the Community: Cuba

- The Bay of Pigs is a 20-mile indentation in the south coast of Cuba, 75 miles southeast of Havana.
- It is entirely surrounded by dense swamps; Playa Larga is located at the farthermost reach of the bay.
- A major highway connects Playa Larga with Barra de Potosí, where a large sugar plantation and airport is located.
- Another highway parallels the east shore of the Bay of Pigs, connecting Playa Larga with Giron.
- Except for two narrow-gauge railroads, these highways provide the only access to Giron and the Bay of Pigs.
- It was on these roads and in the air above that the battle at the Bay of Pigs took place.

*More than 22 million pamphlets on building fallout shelters were distributed.*

# HISTORICAL SNAPSHOT
# 1961

- The NFL championship game at Green Bay, Wisconsin, drew the first million-dollar gate
- Four thousand servicemen were sent to Vietnam as advisors
- Civil Defense officials distributed 22 million copies of the pamphlet "Family Fallout Shelter"
- Fixed-term certificates of deposit, the IBM Selectric typewriter, tab-opening aluminum drink cans and electric toothbrushes all made their first appearance
- Popular movies included *West Side Story, The Hustler,* and *Judgment at Nuremberg*
- Harper & Row was created through a merger
- Two months after his inauguration, President Kennedy established the Peace Corps
- The right-wing activities of the John Birch Society stirred concerns in Congress
- Alan Shepard became the first American in space on a 15-minute suborbital flight aboard *Freedom 7*
- Both black and white "Freedom Riders" tested integration in the South; many were attacked and beaten in Alabama
- Cigarette producers spent $115 million on television advertising; R.J. Reynolds acquired Pacific Hawaiian Products Company in an attempt to diversify away from tobacco products
- Sprite was introduced by the Coca-Cola Company
- The top 10 television shows of the year included *Wagon Train, Bonanza, Gunsmoke, Hazel, Perry Mason, The Red Skelton Show, The Andy Griffith Show* and *Candid Camera*
- Canned pet foods were among the three top-selling categories in grocery stores
- Kennedy reduced tariff duties to stimulate foreign trade
- Popular songs included "Big Bad John," "Moon River," "Tossin' and Turnin'," "I Fall to Pieces" and "Runaway"
- Ninety percent of American households had at least one television set
- Approximately 44 percent of the world's adult population of 1.6 billion were illiterate
- The American Broadcasting Company (ABC) began color telecasts for 3.5 hours each week
- Joseph Heller's *Catch 22,* John Cheever's *Some People, Places and Things* and Henry Miller's *Tropic of Cancer* were published
- Diet-Rite Cola was introduced as the first sugar-free soft drink

The vital 1/10th
of your appearance
**BEAR BRAND** hosiery
75c to $1.25

Every Home Needs This 'All-Purpose' Oil
Clean · Lubricate · Prevent Rust
**3-IN-ONE® OIL**
REGULAR – OIL SPRAY – ELECTRIC MOTOR

THE BEST-GROOMED PEOPLE USE...
**TRIM**
MANICURE IMPLEMENTS
Look for the TRIM display in stores everywhere
THE W. E. BASSETT CO. · Derby, Conn.

Live it up!

Did you see this Kellogg's Frosted Flakes advertisement in this issue?

Taste-tickling reminder: you can get those gr-r-r-eat "Live It Up" flakes in Kellogg's Variety Pack.

You also get these other favorites:

America's best-liked cereal assortment

21 GREAT TOBACCOS make 20 WONDERFUL SMOKES!!

**Chesterfield** KING CIGARETTES

They Satisfy!

HOW LONG HAS IT BEEN

SINCE YOU'VE HAD A CUP OF **REAL** COCOA?

Aren't you tired of warmed-up kid's stuff? Nestlé's EverReady® is the only instant that gives real old-fashioned hot chocolate flavor, with just hot water. Whole milk and sugar's already in it. Have a real cup of cocoa—instantly! Get Nestlé's deluxe cocoa in the bright red package!

EVERREADY
**NESTLÉ'S**
SWEET MILK COCOA

**NESTLÉS**
MAKES THE VERY BEST CHOCOLATE!
Copyright 1962, The Nestlé Company, inc.

LIPS SORE?
**Blistex**
BEST FOR COLD SORES · CHAPPED LIPS · FEVER BLISTERS
POCKET SIZE 39c HIGHER IN CANADA

It's the happiest marriage of quality and value in the history of Television to date!

Special during October only...

**NEVER BEFORE SO MANY STANDOUT FEATURES in a 23" genuine wood console classic** for only **199.88**
And it's designed and engineered for finest fringe area reception!

Western Auto

**KRYLON** SPRAY PAINT
You have a use for
In Ready-to-Use Aerosol
IF YOU PRIZE IT... KRYLON-IZE IT!

1961

## " 'I Give Castro Six Months': An exclusive interview with a former high official of Castro's government," *U.S. News & World Report,* January 16, 1961:

**Is Cuba about to blow up in Castro's face?**

Break with the U.S. came when Castro's troubles were mounting, his enemies growing bolder. How come? What about all the massive assistance he's supposed to be getting? Did Russia double-cross him? Where can he turn for the financing he needs to keep going?

For the full story of what goes on in Cuba, *U.S. News & World Report* interviewed a former high official of Castro's regime. Dr. Justo Carrillo Hernandez headed Cuba's Bank for Development of Agriculture and Industry until a year ago. He is now a refugee in Miami—plotting Castro's downfall.

Q. Dr. Carrillo, what were your connections with Fidel Castro?

A. My connections with Fidel and his regime were intimate. I supported Castro in 1955 when he was alone in Mexico with few supporters and no money. At that time I contributed $5,000 to his cause, and went to Yucatan to meet him. Throughout the period of his revolution against Batista, I worked with his movement.

When Castro came to power, I became president of the Bank for Development of Agriculture and Industry, a post from which I had resigned on March 10, 1952, when Batista seized power. . . .

Q. What caused your final break with him?

A. I abandoned him only after his actions and policies as ruler of Cuba convinced me that Fidel was determined to give over six million Cubans to the service of international communism. In January of 1960, I left Cuba and began work in my fourth revolution.

And let me say that this fourth revolution is the most important of them all. That is because by overthrowing Fidel Castro, Cuba and the Cuban people will have the honor of being the first in the world to destroy a communist regime since the Soviets consolidated their power inside Russia.

Q. Are you convinced Castro will be overthrown?

A. Absolutely. He will be finished by next June. Already he has lost the initiative and is on the defensive. His economic problems are enormous, but they stem from the political mistakes and ineptitude of the Castro regime.

The root cause of this, in my opinion, is that Castro did not study and prepare in advance the ways to impose communism on Cuba. Without a plan, he was obligated to destroy the system that existed before he was ready to replace it with something that would work. His lack of a plan left him unable to replace what he destroyed. . . .

Q. Does Castro have any of the elements of economic strength needed to stay in power?

A. Yes, he has some. In the international field he has whatever strength Soviet Russia chooses to let him have. He depends wholly on full Soviet backing politically, and the Soviets have to supply Cuba with the last ounce of everything the Cubans need for their economy.

*Many Cubans predicted that Fidel Castro would be ousted from office in 1961.*

## "When U.S. Has Intervened in Latin America," *U.S. News & World Report,* May 1, 1961:

*Not since 1934 have U.S. troops intervened directly in a Latin-American country. Between 1900 and 1934, U.S. troops went into Latin America 31 times to protect U.S. lives and property in times of revolution and disorder. Here is the record, country by country:*

Cuba—3 times. U.S. sent troops into Cuba in 1906, and kept them there until 1909 to help restore a stable government after a revolution. In 1912, troops went into Havana and Oriente Province to protect American interests. Again, in 1917, U.S. troops went to Cuba during an insurrection. Some of the troops remained there until 1922.

Haiti—4 times. U.S. troops entered Haiti on three occasions in 1914. Then, in 1915, the troops returned and stayed through 19 years of chronic unrest. Their withdrawal in 1934 ended U.S. military intervention in Latin America.

Nicaragua—4 times. During a civil war in 1910, U.S. troops entered Nicaragua twice. They returned during an attempted revolution in 1912 and stayed until 1925. They went back in 1926 after a coup d'état and remained until 1933.

Dominican Republic—4 times. U.S. sent troops into the Dominican Republic during one revolution in 1903 and another in 1904. U.S. naval forces established a neutral zone in a 1914 revolution. Then, the U.S. kept troops there continually from 1916 to 1924, through a period of chronic insurrection.

Honduras—6 times. Repeated upheaval in Honduras brought U.S. troops into that country in 1903, 1907, 1911, 1919, 1924, and 1925.

Colombia—3 times. Once in 1901 and twice in 1902, U.S. troops entered strife-torn Colombia.

Panama—3 times. U.S. troops were based in Panama continuously from 1903 to 1914, during construction of the Panama Canal. They returned for police duty during disturbances from 1918 to 1920, then went in again during rioting in 1925.

Mexico—3 times. Marines landed to evacuate U.S. citizens threatened by civil strife in 1913. After the seizure of seven unarmed U.S. seamen, U.S. troops captured Vera Cruz in 1914, and held it nearly seven months. General Pershing led a military expedition into Mexico in 1916-1917 in pursuit of the bandit leader, Pancho Villa.

Guatemala—1 time. U.S. troops entered Guatemala to guard the U.S. legation and U.S interests during an outbreak of fighting in 1920.

## Selected Prices

| | |
|---|---|
| Boy Scout Uniform | $10.75 |
| Camera, Polaroid 100 | $99.95 |
| Crackers, Nabisco, per Pound | $0.25 |
| Doll Clothes, Barbie Airline Stewardess | $3.50 |
| Driving Lessons | $46.88 |
| Flag, 3' by 5' | $3.95 |
| Flower Delivery, FTD | $7.50 |
| Hat, Woman's Pillbox with Veil | $3.97 |
| Lunch, Walgreen's Cafeteria | $0.49 |
| Peanut Butter, Jif | $0.51 |
| Radio | $29.95 |
| Slide Rule | $2.95 |
| Subway Token, New York City | $0.15 |
| Suit, Man's | $90.00 |
| Typewriter, Royalite | $49.95 |

"Just at the moment I am so angry with that infernal little Cuban republic that I would like to wipe its people off the face of the earth. All that we wanted from them was that they would behave themselves and be prosperous and happy so that we would not have to interfere. And now, lo and behold, they have started an utterly unjustifiable and pointless revolution and may get things into such a snarl that we have no alternative save to intervene—which will at once convince the suspicious idiots in South America that we do wish to interfere after all, and perhaps have some land hunger."

—President Theodore Roosevelt, in a letter written concerning Cuba in 1906, eight years after the U.S. set Cuba free in the war with Spain

## "Castro's Triumph," *Time*, May 5, 1961:

Perhaps unintentionally, the Cuban press gave eloquent testimony that the rebels, so docile in captivity, had fought a ferocious battle. Splashed across the pages of the government's mouthpiece *Revolucion* were dozens of photographs from the Bay of Pigs. A youthful invader, too small for his oversized camouflage fatigues, lay dead in some weeds; another lay on his stomach among rocks; a third was on his back, knees sticking up, cut down where he sat behind his machine gun. And then there were the militia losses: a body burned black by a flamethrower; two more militiamen draped across each other beside a fallen tree.

Neither Castro nor the exiles put out casualty figures. The best estimate was that 1,300 landed, possibly 90 were killed in combat. A handful—perhaps 50 men, no more—may have made it to the rugged Escambray Mountains; another 100 to 200 were evacuated from the beachhead. The rest were captured when their ammunition gave out. Castro's casualties were much higher. Before being destroyed by Castro's jet fighters, B-26s wiped out two columns of advancing militia, totaling three tanks, two armored cars, 31 militia-crammed trucks and buses. Castro's militia dead may have run to 2,000 or more. . . .

Watching it all in stunned horror, 65,000 anti-Castro exiles turned Miami into a city of grief. The brick house on Biscayne Boulevard that served as headquarters of the Frente [front] was besieged by hysterical women asking news of sons, brothers, sweethearts in the ill-fated invasion force. In the confusion, no one could be sure which men were dead, wounded, captured or evacuated.

### "Cuban Post-Mortem," *U.S. News & World Report,* May 8, 1961:

From bitter young refugees, you get this story of the bungled attempt to overthrow Fidel Castro.

These men put most of the blame on the U.S. Central Intelligence Agency, which, they say, masterminded the attack from beginning to end. Among the charges the refugees make:

Communist double agents infiltrated the circle of refugees that worked closely with the CIA. Castro knew everything that was going on.

As a result, mass arrests in Cuba have now destroyed an underground force that had been built up carefully for more than a year. When the time of invasion came, there was no advance signal to the underground—and Castro struck before its members got into action.

"Castro may have wiped out our entire underground," said Rafael Lorie, an official of one refugee force that was excluded from the invasion attempt. "We cannot reach our people, have not been able to do so since the invasion. Castro has arrested so many people—60,000—that he has caught many of the underground fighters, whether he knows who they are or not. . . ."

The invaders were supposed to have air and naval support. The Cubans claim this support was promised to them by CIA agents. The soldiers were told not to worry about Soviet MIGs, that if they came, U.S. F-104s or other warplanes would shoot down the Castro planes.

But when the attack was launched, air and sea support were withheld. The Cuban landing force was left on its own to battle against heavily armed troops of Castro. Some of the refugees insist this lack of support doomed the invasion from the outset. Said one of them: "If you have air support in that flat swampy country, you're all right. If you don't, you're a dead duck."

# 1966 Profile

## Fighting in Vietnam

### Private

As an inner-city kid raised by his grandmother, Orlando Wright spent little time thinking about politics in southeast Asia; as an army private in the jungles of Vietnam, he was forced to confront the brutality of war and the death of a friend.

### Life at Home

- When Orlando Wright arrived at Fort Jackson Army Base for basic training camp, he learned immediately that the drill instructor treated all the men, black or white, the same—badly.
- Also, marching through the sparsely wooded sandhills of Columbia, South Carolina, in the heat of August while carrying a full pack bore few similarities to the picture painted at his recruitment.
- Not only was he miserable, the always equally unkind drill instructor insisted that the jungles of Vietnam would only be worse.
- Imagine—worse than August at Fort Jackson!
- All the while, his grandmother continued to write regularly, reminding him often about everyone at his church praying for his safety and how proud she was that he was following in the footsteps of his grandfather, who had served in the 369th Infantry during World War I.
- Prior to joining the service and being shipped to South Carolina, Orlando had never traveled more than 30 miles from his home in Washington, DC.
- He grew up in the Anacostia neighborhood of the nation's capital.
- His father was never in the picture; Wright was the family name of Orlando's mother, who had persistent problems with drugs and alcohol.
- Orlando's maternal grandmother, "Mama Clem," took responsibility for his upbringing.
- Clementina Wright, who had cooked for a family in Georgetown for decades, was a prominent member of the African Methodist Episcopal (AME) Church, and a tough taskmaster.

*Orlando Wright traded inner-city Washington for a tour in Vietnam.*

"As the United States Government has frequently stated, we seek no wider war. Whether or not this course can be maintained lies with the North Vietnamese aggressors."
—President Lyndon Johnson, 1965

- Even though her household consisted of an ever-changing number of children, grandchildren and great-grandchildren, she expected everyone to do chores and never, ever, use drugs, alcohol, tobacco or strong language in her home.
- In addition to God, she also worshipped education for her grandchildren and made Orlando finish high school, even after all his friends had dropped out.
- When he arrived at Fort Jackson, he knew nothing about the Viet Cong or communism, but being a soldier appealed to him; he had always been known for his toughness.
- At only 12 years old, he earned his nickname, "Hard Head," when a much larger boy had repeatedly smashed his head on the asphalt.
- As the older boy walked away, Orlando struggled to his feet demanding to finish the fight.
- His antagonist shouted back for all to hear, "Man, you got a hard head!"
- The biggest adjustment was dealing with white people.
- Everyone in his school, church and neighborhood had been black.
- Even though his drill instructor was not prejudiced, others saw black and white as an issue.
- At the end of training, Orlando was assigned to the 25th Infantry Battalion headed to Vietnam.
- His platoon, which included six African-Americans, was commanded by an Italian second lieutenant from Rhode Island, who had had no experience with blacks.
- However, the hostility he sensed from the commander didn't last long; they were all equally scared of what was ahead of them in the jungles of southeast Asia.

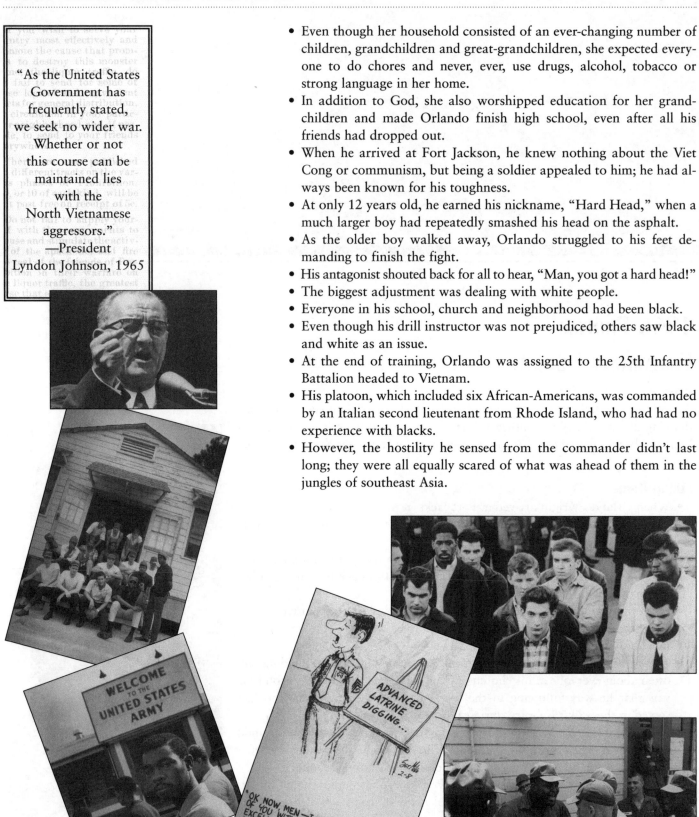

### "Only One Color," *Newsweek*, December 6, 1965:

On a bloodstained field in the Ia Drang Valley, a white American soldier lay wounded, his leg in a bandage. Despite fierce enemy fire, a Negro GI broke cover, ran to the side of the wounded man and began dragging him through the tall elephant grass. Next day, after the enemy withdrew, the two Americans were found dead side-by-side, the Negro's arm still outstretched to the white man he tried to save.

Poignant episodes like this symbolize one of the least noted aspects of the Vietnam conflict: For the first time in its history, the U.S. is fighting a truly "integrated" war. Negroes, of course, have served in every American war since the Revolution, but generally they have fought in segregated units. And though President Truman officially banned segregation in the armed services in 1948, the army still had some all-Negro units as late as the Korean War.

All that is changed in Vietnam. Negroes have become so thoroughly integrated in the armed forces that officers, both Negro and white, insist it is impossible to describe their fighting performance as any better—or worse—than that of their white comrades. Declares Capt. Brigade: "I see only one color. And that's olive drab."

### Life at Work

- During his first months in Vietnam, Private Orlando Wright's biggest shock was the brutality.
- During his first two weeks in the country, his unit entered a village looking for Viet Cong.
- It appeared to be clean, just old men, tired women and cautious children trying to eke out a living.
- But when the villagers would not answer questions, two women were beaten and a child shot when the soldier interrogating them was startled by something that turned out to be a stick.
- Then, when the men were leaving the village, a new guy tripped a booby trap wire and got a load of steel balls in his legs and gut.
- Immediately, the soldiers returned to the village for revenge, burning everything in sight and beating those who did not cooperate.
- Over time, Orlando has come to understand survival in Vietnam.
- He has seen several members of his unit—men he viewed as brothers—killed or maimed by ambush, infectious pongie stakes, or landmines.

"IT'S OK — ALL'S THEY GOT WUZ TH' AMMO DUMP!! TH' BEER'S OKEY!!"

- Though he tried to steel himself, he was revolted when, after a fire fight, two of the men in his squad—one white and one black—calmly cut the ears off the dead enemy and strung them from their dog tags like trophies.
- The lieutenant ordered the practice to stop when the ears began to stink; after that the men kept their collections hidden.
- As days ever so slowly became weeks, Orlando was deeply depressed.
- The fever and loneliness were inescapable.
- He couldn't wait for each day to end, but especially feared the Viet Cong at night; for the first time in his life, he was unable to sleep more than an hour at a time.
- Only alcohol and marijuana—both in plentiful supply—made the time go more quickly.
- Another issue was the load he had to carry.
- It was not unusual to see a rifle company moving out of an operation with men carrying 50 to 60 pounds of equipment.
- Orlando himself carried his weapon, a double basic load of ammunition, two to four grenades, two canteens of water, and three to four C-rations.
- These were the essentials.
- When soldiers added to the pack a Claymore mine, smoke grenades and a few other "nice-to-have" items, mobility was reduced.
- Then there was the guilt.
- When the unit was pulled back to base camp for rest, Orlando found himself drawn to Cousin Eddie's, a club exclusively patronized by black soldiers, which featured attractive prostitutes, some of the best hash Orlando had ever smoked, and the chance to gamble with his paycheck.
- Mama Clem wrote him a letter three times a week, often including a prayer.
- Orlando found it hard to write back.

*Orlando was shocked by the violence of war in Vietnam.*

- With only eight weeks to go in his tour of duty, Orlando was confused, hurt and angry.
- He accomplished his first goal—staying alive—but everything else about his life and future was a jigsaw puzzle like the one his Mama Clem kept on a card table in her bedroom.
- Recently, as the unit moved through a narrow jungle trail, Orlando realized that he was still slightly stoned, but believed he had the experience to handle pot and the VC at the same time.
- In front of him was his friend Darryl Burrows, a guy from Harlem with a silly sense of humor and an innate goodness.
- When Darryl suddenly froze, Orlando stopped immediately.
- With a slight grin and immense calm, Darryl explained that he had just stepped on the plunger of a land mine.
- If he allowed his foot to rise, he and anyone around him would be blown up.
- Cautiously, the soldiers gathered around.
- The platoon sergeant, a crusty Jewish New Yorker, cautiously dug around the mine with his bayonet and decided the mine could not be defused.
- All the while, Darryl was cracking jokes, acting cool—and sweating profusely.
- He was only 28 days from his tour's end.
- Quietly, the rest of the platoon eased back 30 yards, while the sergeant radioed for assistance.
- The sun beating through the leaves made the jungle feel like a sauna.
- The soldiers stared at Darryl as if he were a bad accident.
- Forty-five minutes into the ordeal, and in the middle of a wise crack, Darryl's foot slipped.
- The silence of the jungle was shattered with the explosion.
- Darryl was lifted into the air; most of him was deposited in a lifeless heap at the feet of the platoon.
- Orlando was there and had done nothing; now that Darryl was gone, all he could do was scream.
- At camp, his first instinct was to get stoned.

- Before he had gotten a solid start, the chaplain arrived.
- First, Orlando screamed about a God who didn't care and loved cruelty.
- Then, he cried.
- Together, the two men began to sing hymns Orlando had learned growing up.
- When the chaplain departed, he left a copy of the Bible and a recommendation that Orlando tell God his thoughts and feelings.
- Orlando was not sure he knew how to talk with God, but he wanted to talk with his Mama Clem, so he wrote to her about all the good, the bad and the horrible of Vietnam.
- He confessed that he had indulged in drugs, alcohol and sex.
- Over and over in the letter, he said he wanted to come home.
- He also said he had decided to give up marijuana, and was ready to start a new life.
- Believing he had found his calling, he asked Mama Clem to show him how to become a minister.
- The loving letter he received in reply was stained with tears.

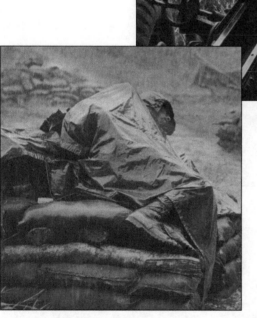

## Life in the Community: Vietnam

- America's involvement in Vietnam began during WWII when American Office of Strategic Services (OSS) teams joined with Vietnamese guerrillas in fighting the Japanese invaders.
- Leading the guerrillas was a Vietnamese revolutionary named Nguyen Ai Quoc, widely known as Ho Chi Minh.
- After the Japanese were defeated, President Franklin Roosevelt declared that the country should not be handed back to the French, but to the Chinese, who declined the offer.
- After the death of Roosevelt, President Harry Truman was unwilling to risk a split with France and chose not to oppose the French occupation, despite Ho Chin Minh's desire for an independent Vietnam.
- In 1950, Truman officially recognized the French-supported Saigon government of Emperor Bao Dai and began sending aid to the country.
- The first Indochina war ended in May 1954 with the defeat of the French at Dien Bien Phu in northwest Vietnam.

- The Geneva Conference of 1954, which officially ended the war, divided Indochina into four parts; Vietnam was divided along the 17th parallel with Ho Chi Minh's government ruling the north; the Saigon government in the south; and Laos and Cambodia again made separate countries.
- By 1956, after France had withdrawn all of its troops from South Vietnam, the United States remained the only foreign power supporting the new regime of Ngo Dinh Diem.
- By 1959, the United States maintained in the country only 300 military advisors, whose main task was to prepare Diem's forces for the day the North Vietnamese invaded South Vietnam.
- During the next two years, the war heated up steadily.
- In 1961, President Diem requested newly elected President Kennedy to send more aid to fight the communist offensives of North Vietnam.

*Presidents Truman, Eisenhower, and Kennedy all had difficult decisions to make about Vietnam.*

- Kennedy decided in December of that year to send 33 H-21C helicopters, bringing the total U.S. personnel to 1,500.
- Eleven days later, the first American soldier was killed by a Viet Cong bullet.
- On June 11, 1963, a 73-year-old Vietnamese monk immolated himself in front of a crowd of Buddhist monks to protest the Diem government.
- In response, Diem raided hundreds of temples and arrested thousands of Buddhist monks and nuns, thereby slowly losing the support of the United States.
- In November 1963, 14 dissident Vietnamese generals staged a coup, assured that the United States would support the new regime.
- Kennedy then ordered U.S. military forces from the 7th Fleet to protect the 16,500 American troops and 3,563 civilians in the country.
- Over the next 18 months, the Saigon government would change hands several times.
- By March 1964, approximately 20,000 troops were in the country, all of them restricted to advisory roles; soldiers arriving in Vietnam were told they were there only to help the South Vietnamese.

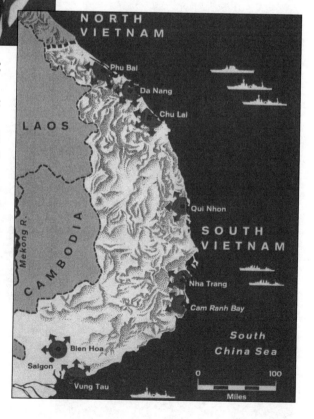

- By August 1964, nearly 300 Americans had died in Vietnam and 1,000 had been wounded.
- That same month, the *U.S.S. Maddox* reported a torpedo attack by North Vietnamese PT boats in the Gulf of Tonkin.
- In response, President Lyndon Johnson ordered air strikes against North Vietnam and called on Congress "to take all necessary measures to repel any armed attack against the forces of the United States and to prevent further aggression."
- In November, Viet Cong gunners hit Bien Hoa Air Base north of Saigon with mortars, killing five Americans and wounding 76.
- On Christmas Eve, terrorists bombed a Saigon hotel where American officers were staying, killing two and wounding 98.
- Responding to the coordinated attacks on bases in February 1965, U.S. fighter-bombers from the carriers *Coral Sea, Hancock* and *Ranger* attacked a guerrilla staging area in North Vietnam.

- The attack marked the official start of the American air war against North Vietnam and an expansion of U.S. involvement.
- Following a car-bomb attack on the American embassy in Saigon that killed or wounded more than 200, President Johnson tripled American troop strength in Vietnam to 75,000.
- In June 1965, the White House disclosed that General Westmoreland had the authority to send American troops into combat; the United States was no longer in an advisory role and could pursue the enemy.
- By the end of 1965, American troop strength topped 181,000.
- In the first three months of 1965, 71 Americans had been killed in Vietnam, and by the last quarter, the total was 920.
- In 1966, an average of 400 U.S. soldiers per month lost their lives.

# HISTORICAL SNAPSHOT
# 1966

- *Time* magazine named the "Twenty-five and Under Generation" its "Man of the Year"
- Blanket student military deferments were abolished; draft calls for the Vietnam War reached 50,000 a month
- A study showed that food prices were higher in poor neighborhoods than in affluent areas, where more variety was available
- The National Organization for Women was founded
- The per capita consumption of processed potato chips rose from 4.2 pounds a year in 1958 to 6.3 pounds
- Jimi Hendrix popularized the electric guitar
- The words "abort," "big-bang theory," "cable TV," "flashcube," "flower children," "miniskirt," "Third World" and "psychedelic" entered the language
- To combat smog, California imposed car-exhaust standards to take effect in 1969
- Bestsellers included *In Cold Blood* by Truman Capote, *A Thousand Days* by Arthur M. Schlesinger, Jr., *Valley of the Dolls* by Jacqueline Susann, *Capable of Honor* by Allen Drury and *All in the Family* by Edwin O'Connor
- Heavyweight boxing champion Cassius Clay became a Muslim and changed his name to Muhammed Ali
- Television premieres included *The Newlywed Game, Mission: Impossible, Star Trek, The Monkees, That Girl, The Dating Game* and *The Smothers Brothers Comedy Hour*
- Stokely Carmichael was elected head of the Student Nonviolent Coordinating Committee
- Sears introduced the Allstate Radial Tire with steel-cord tread plies for $30.80 to replace the unpopular two-ply tire.
- The approximately 80 million Americans born between 1946 and 1964 came to be called the Baby Boomer Generation
- Computer programming languages included FORTRAN for scientific and engineering applications, COBOL and ALGOL for business use, and BASIC for general use
- Procter & Gamble researchers Robert Duncan and Norma Baker came up with the wholly disposable diaper, test-launched as Pampers
- Total U.S. car registrations reached 78 million passenger cars and 16 million trucks and buses
- Black Power was introduced into the civil rights movement, differentiating SNCC and CORE from the pacifist followers of Martin Luther King, Jr.
- After years of debate, Congress passed the Traffic Safety Act to provide for auto safety standards and recalls
- The National Association of Broadcasters instructed all disc jockeys to screen records for hidden drug or sexual messages

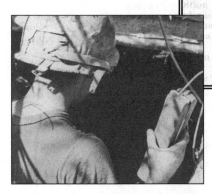

## "Basic Pay," *The Noncom's Guide*, Sixteenth Edition, The Military Service Division:

| Pay Grade | Monthly Basic Pay | |
|---|---|---|
| | Under two years | Over 10 years |
| Sergeant Major, E-9 | $380 | $380 |
| Master Sergeant, E-8 | 310 | 320 |
| Platoon Sergeant, E-7 | 206 | 285 |
| Staff Sergeant, E-6 | 175 | 255 |
| Sergeant, E-5 | 145 | 240 |
| Corporal, E-4 | 122 | 190 |
| Private, E-3 | 99 | 141 |
| Private, E-2 | 86 | 108 |
| Private, E-1 | 83 | 105 |

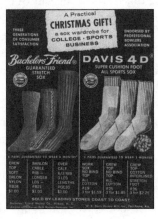

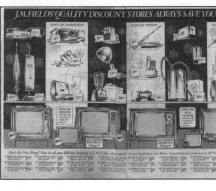

## *. . . and a Hard Rain Fell, A GI's true story of the War in Vietnam,* John Ketwig:

Captain Benedict ordered a search-and-destroy patrol through the marshland outside what would be our new perimeter. I tried to talk my way out of it, to no avail. We lined up about six feet apart and headed into the tall grass in a pouring rain. Even at six feet, it was hard to keep track of the guy next to you. It was imperative that we maintain eye contact on both sides, because if you got ahead, you could be blown away by your own guys. I soon discovered that the elephant grass hid a tangle of twisted vines, thorns and razor-sharp leaves. You couldn't see your feet. You couldn't tell what you were stepping on, if it was solid or not. The wall of vegetation hid everything. We inched forward.

Whump! To my left, an explosion. I crouched, listening to sickening, heartrending screams. "Oh my God! Oh, God, it hurts! Momma! Oh, please! Momma, please! Oh, it hurts so bad! Pleeese help me!" I could feel my heart thumping against my ribs, the familiar shaking starting again. From the left came the cry, "Stay in place! Don't anybody move! We got a booby trap. Look for thin, clear wire, trip wire. Don't anybody move 'til we find out what they want us to do!" I could feel the cold rain dripping down the back of my neck, adding to the shivers already wracking my body. A thin, clear wire. I strained my eyes at the tall grass inches from my face. Crystal clear beads of water clung to the edges of the vertical blades, gathered, and trickled downward. The movement resembled a wire. A million straight edges of a zillion six-foot fronds, and I had to trust my water-spotted army-issue glasses to pick out a thread of clear wire or be blown away. If there was one booby trap, there were bound to be more. Jesus Christ.

"Move out! Stay awake!" Who could fall asleep? We edged forward, trying to inspect each waving blade of grass, but not wanting to take too much time and fall behind. You sure wouldn't want to be out here alone. We came to a stream. "Count off by twos. Ones cross, twos cover 'em. I slipped the safety off, and aimed blindly at the wall of shimmering green and brown while the two guys on my flanks plunged into the muck. I took off my ammo belt and held it and my rifle, safetied again, above my head. The stream was reddish-brown, swirling in and out among the base of the grasses. I waded forward, gritting my teeth, waiting for a pongie stick's point to drive itself into my leg or groin. Waiting for the big bang that would cut me in half. Praying for it to be over. My head went under. I clambered forward, more than a little panicky. There was a sharp bank of slimy mud on the other side, and I slipped twice before I hauled myself and my heavy, wet clothes up out of the goo. I wiped the grit off the lenses of my glasses, buckled the belt around my waist. I could only half-see. In the distance I heard the approach of an ambulance siren, coming to pick up the wounded. I thought they used helicopters. Next time I would tuck a clean rag inside my helmet so I could clean my glasses. We reached another stream. I was soaked. It was surprising how much heavier the wet gear had become, and how the belt seemed to have stretched 'til it was dragging my pants down off my waist. The pant legs were glued to my skin, a ponderous extra layer pulling my tired legs into the goo. My feet seemed to have shrunk, and the slipping from side to side was wearing blisters. Christ, how do some guys do this every day for a year?

## "Reflections of a Battalion S3," *A Distant Challenge,* by Lieutenant Colonel Garold L. Tippin:

One of the enemy's favorite battlegrounds was the fortified village. This usually consisted of hamlets prepared with extensive fighting positions, trenchworks, connecting tunnels and spiderholes. The fighting bunkers often had five to seven feet of overhead cover and could take a direct hit from a 155-mm howitzer round.

The bunkers were placed to cover avenues of approach and were interspersed throughout the village with tunnels connecting the bunkers and trenches, thereby allowing the enemy to disappear and reappear firing from another location. Trees, shrubs and even the earth itself were reshaped to conceal these positions.

At first glance, there seemed to be no logic or method to these defensive works. But upon closer investigation, one could find an intricate, well-planned defensive position that took advantage of existing cover and concealment, natural barriers and avenues of approach into and within the village.

The enemy elected to use a hamlet or a village as a battleground for one or more reasons:

- He expected to inflict enough casualties on U.S. troops during the attack to justify his making a stand.
- He knew that the U.S. soldier does not like to fire upon villages and populated areas.
- The village offered the enemy a labor source to prepare the fortifications.
- In the open valleys and coastal lowlands, the villages contained a great deal of natural cover and concealment.
- The hamlets in a village were usually spread out and their arrangement offered many avenues of escape.

The enemy's usual plan of battle followed the same pattern:

- He would allow U.S. troops to get as close as possible before opening fire, usually 15 to 25 meters. The purpose of these hugging tactics was to get the U.S. soldiers so closely engaged that they could not effectively use artillery and tactical air support.
- The enemy felt if he inflicted several casualties in his initial burst, the U.S. soldier would become involved in trying to get the wounded back to the rear for evacuation. He believed that when the U.S. troops started worrying more about getting their wounded buddies to safety than about the battle, they would become easy targets; in this respect, he was correct.
- Another facet of his battle plan was to fight viciously until dark; then, using the cover of darkness, he escaped by using one of his many preplanned escape routes, carrying off his dead, wounded, their weapons and even empty cartridges. . . . The enemy knew that we placed great emphasis on body count and weapons.

## *NAM, The Vietnam War in the Words of the Soldiers Who Fought There:*

My platoon was pulled to do sentry duty at a place called Anu Tan, a rice mill surrounded by huts. Things weren't so safe at Anu Tan. People got killed. I was living in a bunker, but couldn't go in there at night because the rats were so bad you'd get bitten. If a rat bites you, you're sure not going to catch the rat and turn him over to find out if he has rabies. It was just assumed that all rats had rabies. You would undergo the shots. . . .

Once, early in the evening, before it was really dark yet, I was by myself on the top of the bunker when they started shooting at us. I didn't panic by this point in time. Calmly and methodically, but disconnected, like you're watching yourself do it—Clint Eastwood would have been proud of me—I moved my M-16 so that eventually the muzzle flashes from the graveyard lined up through my sights. The guy fired and I fired back on top of him, emptied eight or nine rounds right back at him.

I heard this scream, high in volume but like the stuff you use to scream with had been disconnected. I knew that I had really blasted somebody for the first time. The gurgling went on for 30 or 40 seconds, a retching scream for a long time. I felt strange. The consequences of pulling the trigger came home to me the next day when I found blood, hair and tissue all over this one tombstone. I probably killed the guy.

## "AWOL," *The Noncom's Guide:*

When a man goes AWOL, he puts a black mark on your record as a leader. You may not be directly to blame, but you are responsible for "all our unit does or fails to do." A soldier absent without leave has committed a serious breach of discipline, and it is your duty to see that discipline is never broken.

During the war, a detailed study was made of the reasons why men go AWOL. Based on thousands of cases, this survey revealed that soldiers with little education and low mental ability are more likely to go "over the hill."

There is nothing the matter with this type of man except that he is not bright enough to make the grade in the army, even though he may not look "dumb" and may be strong, healthy and pleasant. The things that an average soldier learns easily, however, this man finds so difficult that he may become afraid and go AWOL. He does not seem to understand orders, he repeats mistakes over and over despite correction, and he is usually forgetful. Since he is unable to solve his personal problems, he takes what seems to be the easiest way out.

Accordingly, pay close attention to the least educated, least intelligent men in your outfit. They are the weakest and will need the most help and understanding.

## Swanson N. Hudson, U.S. Army:

As a black kid straight from the farm in North Carolina, coming to Vietnam was a great adventure to me. I was looking forward to seeing the sights of southeast Asia. After all, what little I knew about Asia I had learned from movies such as *The World of Suzie Wong*. I knew there was some fighting going on, and I knew U.S. Marines had made a "peaceful landing" up in Da Nang, but to me, all this was exciting stuff. . . .

My platoon spent Christmas 1965 in guard duty up by the Man Yang Pass on Highway 19. We were guarding the few bridges that hadn't been blown up by roving bands of VC. In January, we started patrolling northeast of An Khe in places like Vinh Thanh Valley. I guess they were priming us new guys for the upcoming operation in Bong Son. At that time we "cherries" had never heard of the place. It wouldn't take long before we would never forget it.

After a few days of insignificant contacts, our company was flown back to base camp for rest. We were then choppered over to Qui Nhon on the coast for several more days. Then we went northwest to LZ [Landing Zone] Dog, about 2.5 miles north of Bong Son along Highway 1.

At LZ Dog, it really started looking like a war was going on. To this day, after three tours in Vietnam and more than 30 years later, the scene at Dog is still vivid in my mind. I remember setting up our pup tents in the cemetery. Heavy artillery was firing day and night, and an occasional incoming enemy mortar round was hitting in the distance. What really sticks in my mind, though, were the large piles of bloody G equipment, web belts, boots and helmets with bullet holes in them. Even now, that's what I remember about the Bong Son area. Seeing those piles gave me my first glimpses of death.

## Selected Prices

| | |
|---|---|
| Automobile, Volkswagen Station Wagon | $2,602.00 |
| Baseball Cards, Topps Complete Set | $11.95 |
| Beer, Six-Pack | $0.99 |
| Carpet, per Yard | $10.95 |
| Catcher's Mask, Wilson | $11.50 |
| Coffee, Folger's, Two Pounds | $1.27 |
| Electric Shaver | $13.97 |
| Film Developing | $5.99 |
| Gun Scope | $34.50 |
| Lawn Flamingo | $3.69 |
| Table Tennis Set | $10.00 |
| Table Tennis Table | $43.95 |
| Tap Shoes, Child's | $5.77 |
| Tool Set, Craftsman, 155 Pieces | $128.60 |
| Tricycle | $7.95 |

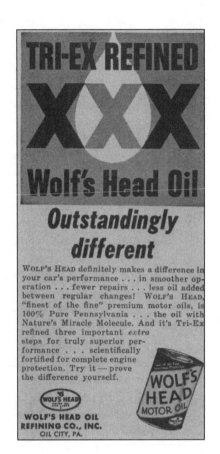

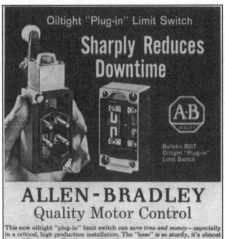

## "One War," *The Nation*, October 14, 1968:

"You have a home in the Army," the slogan that was echoed with resigned bitterness by black GIs as they reenlisted in the years after World War II, no longer seems to lure the Negro soldier. According to Robert Terrell, writing in the *New York Post*, rates for Negro reenlistment are down in the last year from 66.5 percent to 32.7 percent. Terrell talked to a number of black GIs whose terms were coming to an end and heard two main reasons for the reluctance to stay in the service. The first, according to his respondents, is that Negroes are dying in disproportionate numbers in Vietnam. No statistics were offered, but the blacks look around them and see that the company typewriters and supply rooms are manned by white boys. The Negroes feel themselves field hands once more—in fields of blood.

The other reason given is that the DMZ and the Mekong Delta are poor places to go hunting for freedom when the soul brothers are stalking it in the streets of urban America. Incredibly, and ironically beyond comment, the black troops in the rice paddies yearn to be where the action is.

Corroborating this picture of Negro disillusionment with the army game in Vietnam, Lee Lescage tells in the *The Washington Post* of a recent riot of military prisoners at Long Binh Jail (known with sweet brevity as LBJ). Sixty-three men, including five guards, were injured; one white prisoner was killed. When the uproar had burned itself out—and most of the stockade's buildings with it—all the white prisoners and 100 of the Negroes cooperated in restoring order. But 220 others, all Negro except for the three Puerto Ricans, refused and were placed in a special compound, where they improvised African-style garments and beat on metal drums. They were fed a diet of C-rations until, one by one, they agreed to

form up for roll call and otherwise obey confinement routine.

Army spokesmen dismiss this demonstration as atypical: Everyone in the jail was already out of step with the army. But army spokesmen make a practice of dismissing whatever seems to contradict their image of a holy war fought by golden youths. The fact is that the riot in the LBJ was not directed against the authorities; it was fought by prisoners against prisoners, blacks against whites, with Negroes apparently on the offensive. Another thing that army spokesmen would certainly deny (if they could be made even to understand the question) is that Vietnam and the ghetto, Saigon and Harlem, are two fronts of one war. But the blacks don't deny it, and neither will history.

### "Negroes in Vietnam," *American*, August 6, 1966:

Night after night, as we watch TV reports from Vietnam, even the least observant must notice that the ratio of Negro fighting men there is much higher than the Negro 11 percent of the national population. Statistics, in fact, show that their percentage of combat dead is seven points above their population percentage. The discrepancy stands out even more sharply when we remember how much less than 11 percent of our national affluence is theirs.

When the Urban League's executive director Whitney M. Young, Jr. visited military posts in Vietnam last month, we wondered what he would come up with. At a Saigon press conference, July 23, he stated that he had found morale high among the Negro combatants. They were, by and large, content, worked well with their white comrades, and judged Negro rioting in America damaging to the Negro community.

Nor were the Negro servicemen at all impressed with "slogans that the media have built up, such as Black Power." What they were concerned about, stated Mr. Young, was "black progress." There were some criticisms, but in general, they said the Negro lot was better than during World War II and the Korean War. However, he frankly added, "We're going to be in for a rough time if these servicemen come home to find the old racial problems are still unsolved." It shouldn't be hard to see why.

# "When the Negroes in Vietnam Come Home," Whitney M. Young, Jr., *Harper's*, June 1967:

When I returned from visiting the American Negro GIs in Vietnam last July, I was surprised to learn that my trip had caused consternation among some of the press and public who maintained, among other things, that the place to be addressing myself to the Negro struggle for equality was at home, not in some far-flung, war-torn land.

It is true that the Negro victory for equal opportunity and the full desserts of democracy must and will be won on American soil. But it is equally true that what has happened—and is happening—to the Negro and white soldier in Vietnam will have a profound and far-reaching effect on the whole race situation in America during the next decade. For in this war there is a degree of integration among black and white Americans far exceeding that of any other war in our history, as well as any other time or place in our domestic life. The impact of this experience on both white and Negro servicemen in Vietnam has formidable ramifications for the future of all Americans. . . .

When asked what was the most significant impression he had from this new integrated condition, one Negro GI summed up the situation: "To find out for the first time that all white people are not geniuses and all Negroes are not idiots." At the same time, the white soldier cannot help observing and coming to respect the courage, intelligence and effectiveness of his Negro fellows. One white American general in Saigon told me: "My people in the army were made to integrate in the early 1950s long before the rest of the country. But we are sure glad it happened. Today, here in Vietnam, there is absolutely no difference between the caliber of white and Negro soldiers. The Negroes are good. In fact, I think they try just a little harder. They won't let that white guy in the foxhole with them do better than they. . . ."

"In a tight situation over here, the race thing just doesn't exist," said Negro Sergeant Otis Curry. "Sure, you find guys with chips on their shoulders. But when this happens, they are ostracized by their own kind. And, man, you can't make it over here alone. . . ."

The first question is, naturally: What can the discharged Negro GI expect when he returns? In talking with many of the Negro soldiers, I found this thought to be foremost. Many expressed bitter concern about the condition of their parents, wives and children in semisegregated America while they were risking their lives in the service of the country. Sergeant Andrew May, a 29-year-old Negro squad leader from Rocky Mount, North Carolina, who has been more than once decorated for bravery, said, "It does make you feel funny sometimes, fighting here for things we're denied at home. But you just got to shake your head and hope the situation will change."

# 1969 Profile

## Protesting Vietnam

### Civilians

Greg and Ellen Watson of Charleston, West Virginia, have found that the decision to voice their opposition to the Vietnam War, even at the risk of social, financial and professional consequences, has yielded some unexpected results.

### Life at Home

- Ellen Watson was never considered a radical, not even a quality rabble-rouser on a cranky day.
- She rarely attended public meetings, except for the PTA and Women's Club at the church, and never, ever spoke up, unless it was to volunteer for the food committee.
- Her husband, Greg, was even less flamboyant.
- Greg always preached to Ellen and the three girls that he was performing his civic duty when he got up every day and worked hard to support those who didn't.
- So, the Watsons speaking at an antiwar rally was a strange sight indeed.
- After all, Greg had served in World War II, and Ellen's father had been decorated for his service in France during World War I.
- Ellen would claim that their daughter Carol led them to this decision, but Greg insisted the momentum had been building for a while.
- A sophomore at Marshall College in Huntington, West Virginia, Carol had been talking about the nationwide moratorium planned for October 15.
- The youngest of three girls, Carol was polite, adventurous, challenging—and always Carol.
- Moratorium participants were asked to stay home from school, and for businesses to close on October 15 to send a message to President Nixon that the war should end now.

*Greg and Ellen Watson were concerned about the direction of war in Vietnam.*

## B52s Hammer Suspected Viet Jungle Base

### U.S Pushes Buildup; 4th Division Men Fly to Highlands

SAIGON, South Viet Nam (AP) — High-altitude B52s from Guam poured 750-pound bombs today into a suspected Viet Cong jungle base south of Da Nang where the Communists are believed massing for operations.

A military spokesman said the eight-engine jets hit almost the same region plastered by a B52 strike yesterday. The target today was a suspected Viet Cong concentration and base camp area.

Da Nang, site of a big U.S. air base, is about 380 miles north of Saigon.

Although the air war continued unabated, no significant ground action was reported either early today or late yesterday, a U.S. spokesman

**Infantry Sweep End**

One military op named Kolo, ended Sa night, U.S. military he ters said. The two-week by the U.S. 25th Infantr sion about 25 miles north the capital accounted for Cong dead and 25 capture

In the central highland 000-man U.S. infantry fresh from the United flew in yesterday to b American forces block Communist attempt to South Viet Nam in two T troops raised U.S. manp

- After first broaching the subject to her parents of cutting class in protest, Carol asked how they would feel if she attended a rally and maybe was arrested.
- Clearly, this was not the type of thing children from Charleston, West Virginia, had been raised to do.
- Greg had been willing to support the war for President Johnson, believing the president knew things he couldn't reveal, but when the death toll continued to mount, Greg grew silent.
- He recalled that Eisenhower had misled America on the U2 incident, Kennedy on the Bay of Pigs, Johnson on the Gulf of Tonkin, and now Nixon was talking peace and acting war.
- It did not help that America was spending $2 billion a month to help a South Vietnamese government that appeared authoritarian and corrupt; at this pace, inflation would definitely be right around the corner.
- Besides, during the 1968 election, Nixon announced he had a plan to end the war.
- Greg was a man who took politicians at their word, and wanted to see the plan.
- For the first time, the Watsons talked about the war and the nearly 1,000 soldiers who had died in combat during the past two months.
- They began reading the *Washington Post* to see what the big city papers had to say about it.
- None of it was good.
- The peace talks were in disarray, drug use among soldiers was rising, the politicians and generals were fighting each other, and the Negro civil rights leaders said that too many black men were dying in southeast Asia.
- The Hiltons down the road still were unable to believe they had lost to the war their oldest son, who was supposed to take over the hardware store.
- Big Bob had trained Little Bob in everything from fertilizer to plumbing supplies.
- Everyone in town, it seemed, was at the funeral.

- Since the Hiltons were just simple folks who worked hard and minded their own business, they didn't know how to protest.
- When Ellen decided that Carol was leading them in the right direction, she finally found the courage to tell Mary Sue Hilton that she was planning to attend the moratorium and read out the name of William Edward Hilton, among others.
- Ellen held her breath waiting for a reaction.
- Mary Sue simply said that would be fine.
- Greg was experiencing similar struggles: How do you tell your coworkers at a car dealership you think America should tuck tail and run from a fight?
- As parts manager, he was well-respected for his work, knowledge and cooperative spirit, but he was hardly an opinion leader.
- What would people say when he didn't show up for work? Or should he just take the day off? Or be really bold and tell the boss to shut down that day?
- He was afraid they would think he'd turned hippie.
- The moratorium began as a campus-based program, with college-town canvassing, leaflet distribution, class-cutting, seminars, candlelight processions and readings of the names of the war dead at colleges and universities.
- The aim of the activities was to pressure President Nixon into altering his course and bring the troops home faster than he intended.
- Carol was pleased with her parents' decision, but her oldest sister Helen was furious.
- Helen vented over the phone to her father: This type of thing could harm her husband's law practice; the Watson name would be mud; her children—their grandchildren—would be shunned; could her parents even be trusted to keep the kids anymore? Wasn't he aware that bank loans could disappear because of his weirdo ideas?
- Greg finally told his daughter to grow up, and hung up the phone on her ranting.
- Neither Ellen nor Greg expected Helen and the kids to appear for customary Sunday supper after church.

## Life at Work

- The night before the moratorium, Ellen created black crepe paper armbands as a sign of solidarity, and though Greg said it was silly, he wore one anyway.
- Shortly after Ellen and Greg Watson arrived at the gathering site near the town's war memorial, several people tried to start an antiwar chant, "Out Now, Out Now," but it died at birth.
- A few moments later, efforts to sing "Blowin' in the Wind" fared little better.
- Ellen knew she needed all her energy just to read the alphabetized E through J names of the war dead.
- When the moratorium organizers learned that Ellen was willing to participate, they offered to let her go first with the A through D names, but she knew that would be too hard.
- Being second would suit her just fine, if she could get through the Hs without tearing up at the name William Edward Hilton.

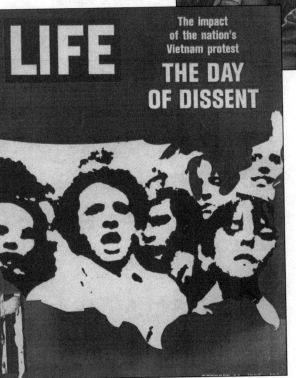

- Clearly, this group was not gathering for fun; most attendees had never opposed anything before, especially nothing as significant as the U.S. president and his policy in Vietnam.
- For about 10 minutes, they simply stood awkwardly.
- Then, as the first candle was lit, Greg knew there was no turning back.
- For a moment, he wished he could have mustered the courage to read the names himself, but then he looked at Ellen and realized how nervous she was.
- Unsure of what was proper etiquette at an antiwar rally, it had been decided in advance that church candles would be lit first, then an Episcopal priest would lead the Lord's Prayer, followed by the reading of names.
- The first name read was one Ellen did not know, but the second, Alfred Allen Anderson, was the son of a high school classmate.
- She hadn't even known of her friend's loss, but realized she had no time to mourn now.

- The first reader was nearly through the D names; Edmund Perry Dallas . . . David Templeton Dukes. . .
- For Ellen, these moments were terrifying and exhilarating.
- She wanted to throw up, but couldn't possibly consider such an act in public.
- When she started reading the names out, she was startled by the flash of a photographer's camera, and realized that tomorrow, all of Charleston would know what she had done.
- "Ellen the activist and the quiet Greg are now a hippie couple. . . . What do you think of that?"
- Well, let them talk, she thought; Greg and Ellen Watson want the war to end.
- Then, she saw Mary Sue Hilton, still wearing black and carrying the American flag that had been draped on Little Bob's casket.
- Big Bob wasn't there and Mary Sue seemed unsteady in her mission.
- She had come to hear the name of her son read out in public as one of America's war dead, while she clutched the flag.
- Old Mrs. Rice, dressed in her Sunday best, stood defiantly with a sign taped to her pocketbook reading, "God Bless our President."
- Two teenagers drove by, yelling, "Dirty commies!" but did not stop.
- The next morning, the *Washington Post* reported that "uncounted and uncountable thousands of Americans demonstrated their opposition to the Vietnam War yesterday in one fashion or another all across the nation."
- According to the story, crowds ranged from 100,000 on Boston Common to a rain-drenched 1,500 in San Francisco, 30,000 on the New Haven Green to 10,000 at Rutgers University, about 5,000 in the center of Minneapolis to 50,000 on the grounds of the Washington Monument.
- The reporters said: "3,500 braved a six-inch snowfall in front of the state Capitol in Denver to hear speeches and the reading of names of the state's 567 war dead."
- Despite snow and 15-degree temperatures, 20 stood through the night in front of a war memorial on the Wyoming University campus at Laramie.

*On October 15, spectators came to support the President and the war; others, like Eugene McCarthy, came to condemn the fighting.*

*Some students protested by ringing a bell for each life lost in Vietnam.*

- Sixty-five people in small, conservative Charleston, West Virginia, felt about right, Greg told Carol, as she relayed her own protest activities.
- Carol had helped ring an old church bell for three days, striking the bell once every four seconds in memory of each U.S. soldier killed in Vietnam.
- There were only minor incidents of violence nationwide, and few arrests.
- In Phoenix, Texas, a mother of a sailor killed in the war demanded that his name be excluded from a list being read at a moratorium rally.
- The crowds were overwhelmingly white, generally but not always predominantly young, and included a number of middle-class, middle-aged "respectables" who now believed direct action was necessary to end the war.
- After the rally at the Monument grounds in Washington, DC, 30,000 marched past the White House carrying candles.
- According to aides, President Nixon kept a business-as-usual schedule, having stated that he does not propose to be the first American president to lose a war.
- He has begun a unilateral withdrawal of the bulk of American forces in Vietnam, and some military commanders have been reined in so tightly, a unilateral cease-fire prevails.
- *Life* magazine is calling the one-day moratorium "a display without historical parallel, the largest expression of public dissent ever seen in the country."

### The October 15 Vietnam Moratorium
- The nationwide protest was initiated by three activists: David Hawk, Sam Brown and David Mixner.
- They raised $75,000 and enlisted the pledged support of more than 100 student-body presidents.
- Brown is 25 years old and the main fundraiser, beginning as a National Student Association activist during the "Dump President Johnson" movement that lead to Sen. Eugene McCarthy's presidential challenge.

- He has won a reputation as a first-rate choreographer of mass movements.
- Twenty-four-year-old Hawk, whose primary focus is opposing the draft, has a background in civil rights work in Georgia and staff work for Allard Lowenstein, the student protest leader.
- Currently, he faces imprisonment as a draft-resister; last spring, he directed a we-won't-go letter to President Nixon from 250 student presidents and editors.
- Mixner, also 24 years old, is a union organizer with a specialization in farm laborers—his father being one.
- Mixner is also a member of the McGovern Commission for Reform of the Democratic Party.
- In addition, the moratorium gained support from nationally recognized individuals such as baby doctor Benjamin Spock and Coretta King, wife of the civil rights leader, Martin Luther King, Jr.
- In Washington, thousands gathered to participate in a candlelight parade led by Mrs. King.
- In her remarks, she said, "Forty thousand Americans have been given as sacrificial lambs to a godless cause. When will it cease? While we spend billions of dollars in Vietnam, we have ignored our problems at home."
- Sam Brown is planning another massive demonstration for November 14 and 15 if Nixon refuses to change the present policy and accelerate withdrawal.

# HISTORICAL SNAPSHOT
# 1969

- To protest the Miss America Pageant, feminists dropped girdles and bras in the trash
- Approximately 484,000 U.S. soldiers were fighting in Vietnam
- After weeks of debate, the delegates from the United States and Vietnam were only able to agree on the shape of the table to be used when South Vietnam and the National Liberation Front joined the talks
- Black militant defendant Bobby Seale was ordered bound and gagged by Judge Julius Hoffmann when Seale repeatedly disrupted the Chicago Seven Conspiracy Trial
- Rock concerts drew millions as groups such as the Rolling Stones, the Who, Joan Baez, Jimi Hendrix and the Jefferson Airplane launched tours
- A copy of the first printing of the Declaration of Independence sold for $404,000
- One study of deferment policies showed that a high-school dropout from a low-income family had a 70 percent chance of serving in Vietnam, 64 percent for a high school graduate, and 42 percent for a college graduate
- *The Johnny Cash Show, Hee Haw* with Buck Owens and Roy Clark, and *The Bill Cosby Show* premiered on television
- U.S. universities made ROTC voluntary or abolished the program altogether following student protests
- Neil Armstrong, Buzz Aldrin and Michael Collins landed on the moon; Armstrong and Aldrin collected nine pounds, 12 ounces of rock and soil, and remained on the moon 21 hours, 31 minutes
- Richard Schechner's *Dionysus in 69* emphasized group participation in the theater: Each night a woman from the audience was selected to have sex on stage
- John Lennon and Yoko Ono married
- Nationwide, 448 universities experienced strikes or were forced to close; student demands included revision of admissions policies and the reorganization of academic programs
- *Penthouse* magazine, vasectomy outpatient service and automated teller machines made their first appearance
- The 17-point underdog New York Jets, led by quarterback Joe Namath, upset the Baltimore Colts to become the first AFL Super Bowl winner
- Robert Lehman bequeathed 3,000 works valued at more than $100 million to the Metropolitan Museum of Art
- Bestsellers for the year included *Portnoy's Complaint* by Philip Roth, *The Love Machine* by Jacqueline Susann, *The Godfather* by Mario Puzo and *Naked Came the Stranger* by Penelope Ashe
- Hippie cult leader Charles Manson and followers were charged with the Hollywood murders of pregnant Sharon Tate Polanski and six others
- The first draft lottery was held

## Selected Prices

| | |
|---|---|
| Acne Solution | $2.98 |
| Airline Fare, Delta | $74.70 |
| Camera, Polaroid | $50.00 |
| Dinette Set, Five Pieces | $119.88 |
| Flag Set | $44.88 |
| Food Processor | $39.95 |
| Guitar | $97.95 |
| Locomotive, Tyco | $16.77 |
| Pepsi, Six Bottles | $0.59 |
| Sewing Machine, Kenmore | $149.95 |
| Shoes, Women's Flats | $6.97 |
| Spray Paint | $1.49 |
| Television, Magnavox | $650.00 |
| Tile, Vinyl Asbestos Floor | $12.50 |
| Vitamins, 100 Tablets | $1.49 |

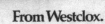

### "In Duluth, a Mother of Five Joins the Campaign against War," Nan Robertson, *The New York Times*, October 16, 1969:

Mary Carolyn Lennon Fleege shivered in the frigid wind off Lake Superior at her first peace rally today, whispered a few "Hail Marys" to herself and tied a bit of white rag to her sleeve in public mourning for the men who died in Vietnam.

She sang antiwar songs and "America the Beautiful" in a light soprano in front of the county courthouse and confessed that never in her life had she done anything nearly so daring.

Mrs. Fleege is a 34-year-old housewife with a broad, open Irish face, the mother of five small children and the wife of an engineer for the Minnesota Highway Department. She describes herself as a "ghetto Catholic" who has just begun to move out into a world of new and sometimes painful ideas.

Today, she took her children out of classes for 90 minutes to go to a memorial service at the Duluth campus of the University of Minnesota and later joined several thousand persons, mostly high school and college students, at the downtown demonstration. Her actions climaxed a year of private worry about the war.

For 30 minutes, Mrs. Fleege and the others sat mutely on the cold ground before the courthouse. When the rally dispersed, after the Mayor of Duluth had complimented those present on their good behavior, Mrs. Fleege went home to tend her children, put another load of washing through the machine and bake the supper casserole.

### "Antiwar for Everyman," *The New Republic*, September 6, 1969:

On the nation's campuses, when young men still face the draft, the antiwar clock has begun to tick again. Beginning October 15 with a one-day "moratorium" (to sidestep the more inflammatory word "strike"), the Vietnam Moratorium Committee plans to retool the dormant campus antiwar machine and launch it on a campaign to pressure the Nixon administration to do either of two things: Negotiate a Vietnam settlement or get out fast. The emphasis in both cases is speed.

Moving from the teach-in of 1967-68 to the teach-out, college students this year will be asked to forsake the homogeneous campus and go out into the community, where the door-to-door canvassing techniques that worked so well for Sen. Eugene McCarthy in New Hampshire will be used. The committee hopes to involve labor, business, professional and academic groups in a revived antiwar effort which would escalate to a two-day moratorium in November, a three-day affair in December and so on. The goal is a national moratorium to protest the war—a day when normal activity ceases and everyone's business is some sort of antiwar activity.

The purpose of the October 15 Moratorium is that of "putting an end to the most tragic mistake in our national history—the cruel and futile war in Vietnam. We meet today to call our government away from folly into the paths that lead to peace."

## "The Search for a Nexus—Vietnam and the Negroes," William F. Buckley, Jr., *National Review*, August 22, 1967:

There is a shift in the making—a shift in public opinion on the question of the Vietnam War, and in the strange way it relates to the Negro problem, or rather is being made to relate to the Negro problem. There are signs everywhere, and from very important people. The most significant, in my judgment, is the recent declaration of Bishop Fulton Sheen that we should unilaterally pull out of Vietnam. Bishop Sheen is neither senile nor loose-minded. His anti-Communism is unalloyed, and his knowledge of the strategic realities is unsentimental. I put off for another day an analysis of the bishop's reasoning—for the present purposes it is significant to note merely that he has taken that position, and that he is an enormously influential priest.

Moreover, a priest who is grimly engaged at the moment, as Bishop of Rochester, in attempting a substantive reconciliation between the Negro and white people in that tense city. Notwithstanding his great urbanity and learning, he is at heart an evangelist—and he is asking for nothing less than reconciliation, between white and Negro, but also between white and yellow.

At this point, the mind sets out doggedly in search of a nexus. Is there one between the Negro problem and the Vietnam War? The effort is being made to find one, and we can trust to the ingenuity of the politician to discover one. During the weekend, Senator Robert Kennedy went on a paralogistic spree. The occasion was a Democratic fundraising dinner in San Francisco, the immediate purpose of which was to show the great big biceps of Speaker Jesse Unruh, who was recently worsted at the O.K. Corral by the deft gunmanship of Ronald Reagan. Senator Kennedy got his usual running ovation. But it was interrupted by a special ovation when he called on the American people to note the "monstrous disproportion of

anyone willing to spend billions for the freedom of others while denying it to our own people." That is one of the political effusions which are the highest testimony to the moral and intellectual emptiness of the political idiom.

The costliest riot in United States history took place a few weeks ago in Detroit, whose Democratic mayor, a long-time hero of the National Association for the Advancement of Colored People, can hardly be said to have conspired against the freedom of the Negro people. But the senator was just warming up. "We cannot allow involvement in the name of independence and democracy in Vietnam to interfere with democracy for our own people." Another burst of applause, more testimony to non-thought. Who is asking that democracy for the Negroes be put off until the end of the Vietnam War? Lyndon Johnson? Ronald Reagan? Abigail Van Buren?

And then the old blackmail: "We must reject the counsel of those willing to pass laws against violence while refusing to eliminate rats." It's sentences like that one that discredit the democratic process. Sentences like that one plus the applause they receive.

But the outline emerges. Somehow, our commitment in Vietnam is one cause of the riots in the United States. Get it? Remember it: The one-two will be very prominent in the rhetoric to come. This is to begin with the sick-at-heartness over the Vietnam war of which Bishop Sheen's manifesto is the expression. Then there is the dazed American attitude towards the riots. . . . why? why? why? There are politicians around who think they can supply a viable answer.

## "From GIs in Vietnam, Unexpected Cheer," *Life,* October 24, 1969:

To find out how American troops fighting in Vietnam regard the moratorium, *Life* correspondent Hal Wingo interviewed about 100 men in eight different units scattered from I Corps in the north to III Corps in the provinces around Saigon. He concentrated on young draftees and enlisted men who had been in combat recently. Here is his report:

My conversations led me to four main conclusions:

- Many soldiers regard the organized antiwar campaign in the U.S. with open and outspoken sympathy.
- The protests in the U.S. are not demoralizing troops in the field.
- Nearly all feel the Paris peace talks are a fraud.
- The troops believe President Nixon has done a good job so far in pulling Americans out of Vietnam.

The biggest frustration comes from the feeling that nothing has been accomplished in Vietnam, and that nothing is likely to be. To some men, the moratorium makes particular sense because they feel forgotten. "Outside our families," says Army Pfc. Chris Yapp, a 4th Division civil affairs team member in a Montagnard village, "I think the protesters may be the only ones who really give a damn about what's happening."

Repeatedly, even those opposed to the idea of peace demonstrations at home admit to uncertainty about what the United States has bought with its investment of 39,000 lives. "I don't even know what I'm fighting for," says Marine Pfc. Sam Benson. "I'm just out in the bushes getting shot at." Few men argue that we are here to stop communism and give the Vietnamese a chance for a better life. Most feel the Vietnamese themselves couldn't care less what kind of government they have. "I don't see the threat to these people if they do have a communist government," says SP4 Richard Beshi, 25th Division infantryman at Cuchi. "They're going to be rice farmers regardless of who is running Saigon. . . ."

For some of these young men, the disillusionment has been far more painful than for others. Pvt. Jim Beck, 19, from Philadelphia, had high personal motives for coming to Vietnam. His brother was killed at Khesan on July 4 last year. The brothers were Italian immigrants who hoped to gain American citizenship more quickly by volunteering for military service. "I came partly for revenge," says Beck, a 101st Division medic. "but now I have lost all faith. The demonstrators are right to speak up because this war is wrong and it must be stopped."

By no means are all the troops opposed to the war. Some would like to get on with it in a bigger way, and one repeated complaint heard against the demonstrators was that voiced by Marine Sgt. Howard Clarke, who is on his second tour in Vietnam. "People who haven't been here and suffered," Clarke argues, "have no right to bitch and moan about what is going on." First Division Infantryman Hascal Dennison, 21, sees the protests only slightly differently. "They have the right," he says, "but they are wrong."

## "Vietnam Debate, Will it Help or Hinder Peace?" *U.S. News & World Report,* October 20, 1969:

"NEVER MIND HOW FAST TH' WAR IS WINDING DOWN !!"

Fighting dropped off in Vietnam—but there was no breathing spell in Washington. Pressures, protests and discussion swirled around the White House. Critics—of all stripes—demanded the president "do something to end the war." There was argument, too, whether the protesters were doing more harm than good in the hazardous search for peace.

Almost before many realized what was happening, Richard Nixon found himself in the vortex of a Vietnam "Great Debate" not unlike the one that dogged Lyndon Johnson's last year in the White House.

President Nixon wanted a "60-day moratorium" on national discussion of Vietnam in hope that he could use the time to break the deadlock with the communists.

What Mr. Nixon got, instead, was a torrent of public reaction from prominent men in both of the major political parties, from the military, from campuses and elsewhere.

The president was confronted with a variety of demands.

Some insisted the war be stopped immediately, at whatever cost. Others wanted the president to set a rigid deadline for troop withdrawal—or risk having Congress set one for him.

At the other extreme, there were demands that the president reverse course, step up the war and strike a decisive blow against North Vietnam.

Through the swelling debate and argument ran only one common thread: "Do something."

Accompanying all this was a parallel and important issue: Will the mounting debate over Vietnam help or hinder the search for peace?

On October 7, the view of the Nixon administration was presented by Defense Secretary Melvin R. Laird, who charged that antiwar forces were trying to pressure the White House "into capitulation on Hanoi's terms."

Said the defense chief in a speech to the AFL-CIO in Atlantic City:

"Hanoi's strategy is clear: Expect to achieve victory by waiting for us to abandon the conflict as a result of the antiwar protest in this country."

Other administration sources, speaking privately, were deeply embittered by the outburst of dissent in Congress and on the campuses. One official emphasized: "There is no doubt that each and every speech, and each and every demonstration helps the communist cause."

The president's critics gave no sign of letting up. A massive nationwide "Vietnam Moratorium" on October 15 won the open support of a group of senators and congressmen who urged that the demonstrations continue until all troops are brought home.

On October 8, Senator Frank Church (Dem.), of Idaho, and Senator Mark Hatfield (Rep.) of Oregon, teamed up to introduce in the Senate a resolution demanding complete disengagement from Vietnam.

The Church-Hatfield move, one of several of a similar nature, was regarded as a key proposal because of its bipartisan basis. At the heart of the resolution was a complaint that President Nixon was moving too slowly in bringing home the troops-a total of 60,000 during all of 1969.

"At the present rate of withdrawal," the resolution said, "American troops will be engaged in Vietnam for the next eight to 10 years."

The essential argument of "doves" is this: It has been decided to get out of the war, so let's get out right now.

# 1967 News Feature

## "Longer Hair Is Not Necessarily Hippie," *Time*, October 27, 1967:

The hair of the male human animal grows more slowly than crabgrass—about a quarter inch to one inch a month. But it never stops growing this side of the grave. Were it not for the tyranny of fashion, which insistently summons men to the barber, they might all conform to the Book of Leviticus, which commands that "Ye shall not round the corners of your heads, neither shalt thou mar the corners of thy beard." In these shaggy times, which can produce a Van Cliburn, an Allen Ginsberg and a Joe Namath, not to mention the Beatles, the Monkees, the Rolling Stones and the entire male population of Haight-Ashbury, Leviticus' 2,500-year-old injunction seems astonishingly up-to-date.

The Beatles may have triggered the trend; the hippies may be making a scissorless, combless and soapless travesty of it. But long hair has outgrown its parameters, traditionally described by the rebelliousness of youth and the self-consciousness of show business. It has become grey, middle-aged, ubiquitous and eminently respectable, a coast-to-coast phenomenon that has infiltrated even the U.S. Army, the last bastion of the butch. Last March at Fort Ord, Calif., by command of the commanding officer, the compulsory 30-second scalp job for all recruits was succeeded by a permissive repertory of six hairstyles.

These days, it seems, nobody wants to look like Hank Bauer except Hank Bauer. Certainly not Richard Nixon: Despite a hereditary sparseness in front, his coiffure now rolls luxuriantly down the neck and trespasses on the ears. And certainly, certainly not Bobby Kennedy, who was once neat and trim but who lately resembles a sheep dog—or maybe a sheep. Presumably, long hair is now a political asset, although Washington's most notorious tousle, Everett Dirksen, declines comment as "below the pale." Dirksen is at least known to have visited his barber before the 1952 Republican Convention, at which he appeared in a hairdo that would have thawed a drill sergeant's heart.

### Now He's a Stylist

The barber is changing to accommodate the trend. Until 1957 his professional bible was called the *Barber's Journal*. But that year its name was changed to the *Barber's Journal & Men's Hairstylist,* and seven years later the name changed

again. It is now the *Men's Hairstylist & Barber's Journal*—a title eloquently testifying to the ascendancy of a less ruthless tonsorial breed.

It is possible, of course, to get an ordinary old-fangled hair cropping at a decent price. But in increasing numbers, men are demanding more. The new hairstylists give it to them, at prices ranging from $6 to $100. The new shops do not even look like the old ones; they look like beauty parlors. Figuratively, and in some cases, they are. Manhattan's Hair Design Associates, on St. Mark's Place, caters to both men and women, although once the clients have been swaddled up to their necks in hair cloths it is difficult to tell. These lush and costly emporiums attract a surprisingly conservative trade. Roger, a hairstylist on East 58th Street in New York City, estimates that 75 percent of his customers are doctors, lawyers and businessmen. . . .

**And Beards, Too**

Whatever the Freudian significance of hair and its style fluctuations, it seems probable that the root causes of the new trend are neither deep or esoteric. Any understanding of it must begin by making a distinction between the hippie and the respectable non-hippie with longish hair.

The hippie is all juvenile protest. He wears his hair extravagantly long because short hair was once the Establishment's style, and he opposes the Establishment. In a predominantly long-haired society—the African Bushman's, for example—he would doubtless shave his skull. The respectable longhair, on the other hand, is protesting nothing, and, what's more, his hair is only respectably long.

To be sure, the respectable longhair stands slightly in the hippie's debt. The equivalence of long hair and youth appeals to middle age; the 50-year-old may not look any younger or more like an actor if he lets his hair grow out—or asks his stylist to tease a bit more body into it—but he thinks he does. So do many women, the ultimate style-setters for men. Long hair is also a way of advertising the distance a man has moved upward in a culture now more than ever devoted, in a time of expanding income and leisure, to the luxuries both provide. Good grooming is only part of it. The new American male also goes to the opera, masters a few French phrases, perhaps buys an elegant Edwardian suit and tours the Continent—where many of the latest styles, including long hair, originated. Good grooming is only the most visible part of it; any investment, however steep, pays off just beyond the hairstylist's door. It is worth noting that, since 1953, the U.S. male has spent more money—and conceivably more time-in the beauty shop. The manufacture of perfumed products for men has risen 400 percent since 1950; some colognes are now sold by the gallon. In 1948, two out of three men used aftershave lotions; today nine out of 10 do.

The test of any trend is acceptance. Long hair passes the test. During the protest stage some three years ago, when brow-shrouding males' tresses bloomed all over the classroom, they drew down a withering fire from the academic Establishment. Today, most of the hirsute scholars are back at their desks, tolerated if not entirely approved. "We ignore it," says C. W. McDonald, dean of men at Western Washington State College. "We do absolutely nothing against long hair even if it's down to their heels."

Will it go that far? It seems unlikely, but there are sociologists as well as barbers who believe that still more men will start growing more hair and the moustache and beard will proliferate. However, in light of historical evidence that how men wear their hair is cyclical, it may turn out that the next generation will feel an urge to be clean-cheeked and crew-cut—or even bald.

# 1970–1979

The Vietnam War finally came to an end during the 1970s. For more than 10 years, it had been fought on two fronts: at home and abroad. As a result, U.S. policymakers conducted the war with one eye always focused on public opinion. The Vietnam War had been the longest war in American history, with a loss of 56,000 dead and 300,000 wounded. The total cost was $118 billion—plus the loss of American prestige abroad. For the remainder of the century, all military conflicts were decided and fought in the shadow of the lessons of Vietnam.

Though the Vietnam War was over, the Cold War continued. The U.S. cargo ship *Mayaguez* was fired upon and boarded by Cambodian armed forces, necessitating a rescue by the Marines. In another incident, President Jimmy Carter sent 1,800 Marines and a squadron of Skyhawk attack warplanes to beef up U.S. forces in Guantanamo Bay when the Kremlin refused to withdraw a Soviet combat brigade recently discovered in Cuba.

At home in America, the Women's Movement was reenergized by the legal case in 1973 of Roe v. Wade, in which the U.S. Supreme Court deemed that criminalizing abortion violated a woman's constitutional right of privacy. Harvard University had only begun granting degrees to women in 1963, and women still had many battles to fight, such as limited opportunities in career choice, inequities in salary compared to their male colleagues; lower expectations in education; and segregation in certain restaurants, bars, and even golf clubs.

The economy during the decade was marked by inflation and recession. Job security could no longer be relied upon as thousands were laid off due to the massive downsizing of companies. Trust in government was largely damaged after the Watergate scandal, which led to the resignation of President Nixon in 1974.

# 1973 Profile

# North Vietnam Prison

### Navy Lieutenant Commander

Navy pilot Lieutenant Commander William Ellis spent nearly six years as a POW in North Vietnam, dreaming of life back in the States with his wife and four children.

### Life at Home

- On June 30, 1967, William Ellis carefully placed a letter from his wife in a box, the contents of which were carefully arranged by date and included a letter for each day of his absence.
- Twelve years of marriage had not dimmed their devotion.
- Besides, he needed to keep abreast of the activities of his four children.
- William, 10, wanted to spend the summer swimming and playing.
- Lucius, seven, was being tutored during the summer so he could catch up in school and calm down his temper.
- Elizabeth, four, loved horses and was pestering her grandparents to buy her a pony.
- Anne, two, was determined to be the center of attention.
- William's wife, Elizabeth, and the four children were spending the summer with her parents in the mountains of North Carolina.
- June 30, 1967, was also the day William flew his 200th combat mission.
- When William and his wingman took off from the *USS Constellation* in their A4-C Skyhawks, the mission was described as a routine armed reconnaissance over North Vietnam.
- The flight was uneventful, and the two pilots were returning when an explosion caused William to lose control of the plane.
- He pulled the ejector handle and was thrust from the craft as it plummeted into the jungle.
- Within moments of landing, he was assaulted by villagers who tore at his clothes while kicking and screaming at him.
- Six men and women dragged him, nearly naked, through the North Vietnamese village, hitting him for show and sport.

*Navy Pilot William Ellis was a prisoner of war for six years.*

*After William's capture, children took delight in kicking his badly sprained ankle.*

- Particular delight was taken in kicking his badly sprained and rapidly swelling ankle, while children were encouraged to throw rocks at him.
- When uniformed North Vietnamese soldiers arrived, the villagers were praised for their bravery.
- William was taken by truck to the "Hanoi Hilton," the central prisoner-of-war facility in North Vietnam.
- Immediately, a fierce interrogation began.
- Training told William to provide only his name, rank and serial number in accordance with the Geneva Convention.
- The North Vietnamese responded that Vietnam was not a declared war, and that he was a war criminal.
- Then he was beaten with hoses.
- His right arm was pulled behind his back so severely, his shoulder dislocated; the pain was excruciating.
- As long as he refused to talk or to denounce his country, the North Vietnamese withheld medical treatment.
- After four days of interrogation, he was placed in a cell measuring seven by nine feet and furnished with only a mat on the floor and a dented bucket for his waste.
- His ankle was broken, his many bruises were healing badly and his shoulder would not stop throbbing.
- For weeks, he was unable to sit and barely able to eat, while his body became covered with boils and sores.
- He was in solitary confinement—no talks with fellow fliers, no letters from home, no news of Elizabeth and the four children.
- For 18 months the days passed slowly, the loneliness was beyond words, and despair lingered constantly.
- Guards occasionally passed him food and allowed him out into the courtyard to empty his waste bucket; on seven occasions over 18 months he was allowed to take a cold bath from a sink.
- Quickly, he learned that whenever he encountered one of his keepers, he must bow; failure to show respect resulted in another beating.
- After the North Vietnamese attempted to set his broken ankle and failed, William rebroke the ankle and set it himself.
- Some prisoners were still on crutches months after being captured.

- Through trial and error, William learned that he could communicate with his neighboring cell by tapping out messages in code and writing notes using the rough toilet paper, ink made from cigarette ashes and a pen fashioned from bamboo.
- But most days were spent quietly, with nothing—absolutely nothing—to do.
- William passed the time thinking about how the children were growing up, what they might be doing and how they were coping without a father.
- He reassured himself that Elizabeth was a strong woman; in addition, his in-laws, Colonel and Mrs. DesChamps, were not people to be trifled with.
- He knew they were praying for him, and that his government was trying to gain his release.

## The Tap Code

The tap code was the principal means POWs used to communicate. POWs who did not know the code needed a written copy of the letter scheme at first either on paper or scratched somewhere in their cell. Eventually they all memorized the order of the letters in their head. To use the code, the sender would tap first to denote the row; the second set of taps denoted the column. Each letter required two sets of taps. For example, for the letter S, four taps, a pause, then three taps meant row four, column three.

|  | | **Columns** | | | | |
|---|---|---|---|---|---|---|
|  | | 1 | 2 | 3 | 4 | 5 |
| **Rows** | 1 | A | B | C | D | E |
|  | 2 | F | G | H | I | J |
|  | 3 | L | M | N | O | P |
|  | 4 | Q | R | S | T | U |
|  | 5 | V | W | X | Y | Z |

### You Had to Keep Busy

Discipline and activity were needed to fuel the minds and emotions of the prisoners. Doing something, anything, not only took their minds off of their despair, but provided energy and hope. Some prisoners practiced memorizing the names of other inmates so that they could tell military officials who else was in the prison, should they ever escape or be released. In an interview with the author, Commander James Stockdale said:

You had to keep busy. You didn't just lie around and wait for them to ring the gong, you had a lot of things to do. Contrived things, but they filled the day. You had to have an exercise program, and that took about forty-five minutes. I did 400 push-ups a day, and it helped with my self-respect. Later I discovered it helped with my physical health for years to come. You had to go over your names. Each one of us kept an individual roster of names that eventually went over four hundred, and you recited these every day. If you forgot one, you went on the wall and asked your neighbor to give you his list for the letter in the group. You had a prayer period. And you did the same things at the same time every day.

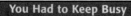

Memorizing other prisoners' names was just one activity that kept POWs busy and focused on something other than their desperate situation.

*Most days at the Hotel Hilton passed slowly, with absolutely nothing to do.*

### Life at Work

- Three years after his capture, conditions for William were improving at the Hanoi Hilton.
- He was moved out of solitary confinement and placed in a room with 55 other men—mostly pilots shot down on a mission.
- Food and baths were scheduled, he could occasionally shave, and was allowed to receive and send letters home—letters that tried to reassure his family that he was fine and would be home soon.
- All correspondence needed to be on a piece of paper no larger than a postcard.

- He was told he could receive one postcard-sized letter a month, but received far, far fewer.
- He believed his captors must have been holding some mail, but there did not appear to be any pattern to it.
- Even with better conditions, he was periodically tortured on the flimsiest excuse—made to kneel on a small pebble for hours, bamboo slivers were inserted under his fingernails, and he was beaten with a strap.
- To maintain his health through the long ordeal, he exercised regularly, doing 100 pushups and sit-ups twice a day and running in place.
- On a diet of either pumpkin or cabbage soup, he lost 60 pounds.
- He knew from experience that if he did not eat his food quickly, it would be stolen by the rats infesting the prison.
- The prisoners exercised together, played games and "saw" movies through the eyes of a narrator.
- William's rendition of *To Kill a Mockingbird* was a particular favorite on movie night.

- Another favorite pastime was "grapevine"; when new prisoners were brought into any of the half-dozen POW camps in the area, they were exhaustively debriefed and the information passed from camp to camp.
- As a result, William knew about the navy's sweeping changes in hair regulations, the skin index of *Playboy* magazine, and how the World Series turned out.
- Letters from home indicated that his mother was doing well, his oldest son William started the prep school attended by Col. DesChamps, Lucius had been held back and was out of control, Elizabeth was quite the equestrian, and Anne loved to read.
- Elizabeth spent her time calling and writing to the wives of the other POWs.
- As a result of her visits to Washington, dozens of congressmen knew her on a first-name basis.
- By the end of 1972, word was spreading at the prison camp that something was afoot.

Things the POWs tell

REG MANNING
*Courtesy Arizona Republic*

- The loudspeaker in the dormitory still spewed English-language propaganda, but the guards had lost interest in the strict enforcement of prisoner routines.
- William was excited and scared; after more than five years, he might actually go home, but to what?
- Would he recognize his own children? Did his wife still love him? What would he do when he returned to the States? Certainly, he would never be able to fly again.
- The days went by faster, while the nights—when fears leapt up—dragged.
- In early 1973, the release of POWs was official; they were to be set free in stages during the next several months.
- The very ill were to go first, the remainder in order of their capture.
- William was able to say good-bye to several men who had been granted release.

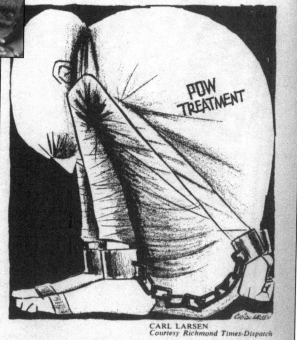

The True Picture Begins to Take Form

POW TREATMENT

CARL LARSEN
*Courtesy Richmond Times-Dispatch*

- In March, he was on a truck to the Hanoi airport with no ceremony, no emotion, and many of his guards absent.
- Yet, fear remained; the North Vietnamese could stop the release at any moment.
- All of the men were cautioned to act with reserve and decorum.
- It was not until William was aboard the Air Force C-141 and felt its wheels leave the ground that he could finally relax.
  - Inside the plane, a cheer rang out.
  - "Home, take me home," was all William could think.
  - However, the first stop was Clark Air Force Base, Philippines, where the former POWs were admitted to the hospital for a checkup.
  - For the first time in years, William put on a new navy uniform.
  - He learned that, during his time as a POW, he had been promoted to commander.
  - He now could look forward to quality food, rest in a real bed, and then a stopover in Hawaii.
  - Ahead is Elizabeth, their children, and the future William thought he had lost.

### Life in the Community: The Hanoi Hilton

- The Hanoi Hilton was named by the American fliers imprisoned there.
- Located on the outskirts of Hanoi, it was originally a French prison built shortly after World War II.
- It was surrounded by a red wall topped by several strands of barbed wire, with an entrance gate on a quiet street of the North Vietnamese capital.
  - Inside was a large courtyard, and a long, low building that housed the camp and a special "interview room."
  - In this room, the myriad of propaganda films were made that included interviews with communist journalists from Poland, East Germany and Cuba.
  - North Vietnam was reportedly making money selling these films, along with pictures of downed pilots.
  - Film footage of captured U.S. airmen, much of it obviously staged, was distributed widely in Iron Curtain countries and sold to Western outlets through East German and Japanese firms.
  - In most of these films, the same prisoners were shown time after time being paraded through the streets, playing table tennis, carrying trays of food and attending church services.
- Inside the compound were clusters of buildings containing cells for one or two of the Americans.
- The crowded sleeping rooms were furnished with wooden pallets and straw mats.
- Every building had a loudspeaker that broadcast English-language news and propaganda.
- American prisoners were fed twice a day, and permitted to wash six times a week and shave twice a week.
- During the 1970s, a prisoner's day at the Hanoi Hilton started at 6 a.m.
- For the next four hours, the men washed, exercised and attended morning language classes.
- By 10 a.m., the first meal was served, eaten from porcelain-covered tin plates and cups.
- This was followed by more classes and exercise.
- At 3:30 p.m., prisoners listened to a news broadcast in English, a strong focus being the antiwar movement in America.

- The second and final meal of the day was brought at 4 p.m. and usually consisted of cabbage or pumpkin soup with bread or rice.
- The prisoners were not allowed access to the Red Cross parcels of concentrated food.
- Communist-style books translated into English were available.
- The first American shot down was captured in August 1964; by 1969, 200 Americans had been missing for more than three and a half years—longer than any U.S. serviceman was held prisoner in World War II.
- More than 1,600 Americans are listed as missing.
- The mass deaths of the Korean War, when 2,700 American prisoners died in captivity, have not been repeated in North Vietnam; currently, only 55 of the acknowledged POWs in Vietnam are reported to have died in captivity.

## HISTORICAL SNAPSHOT
# 1973

- The last of the federal price controls were lifted; 25 percent of Americans said they had participated in various boycotts against the high cost of food
- The Nobel Peace Prize was awarded to Henry Kissinger and North Vietnamese Le Duc Tho, who refused the honor because the war had not ended
- Television premieres included *Barnaby Jones, Police Story, The Young and the Restless* and *The Six-Million-Dollar Man*
- *Pioneer 10* produced significant details of Jupiter and its great red spot
- *The Sting* with Paul Newman and Robert Redford captured the Academy Award for best picture; other popular movies included *The Paper Chase, Scenes from a Marriage, The Last Detail, The Exorcist* and *American Graffiti*
- A computerized brain scanner known as CAT (computed axial tomography) was marketed
- Hit songs for the year were "Tie A Yellow Ribbon," "Delta Dawn," "Let's Get it On," "Me and Mrs. Jones," "Rocky Mountain High," "Could It Be I'm Falling in Love?"; Roberta Flack won the Grammy Award for best record with "Killing Me Softly with His Song"
- Richard Nixon resigned the presidency of the United States; he was succeeded by his vice president, Gerald Ford
- The OPEC oil embargo raised the price for crude oil by 300 percent, causing shortages and long lines at the nation's gasoline pumps
- Skylab, juggernaut, biofeedback, ego trip, let it all hang out, and nouvelle cuisine entered the vernacular
- The "pet rock" became a fad
- The U.S. Supreme Court ruled that employment advertisements could not longer specify gender
- A cigarette pack-size electronic brainwave reader was developed that could detect and signal lapses in concentration
- The median sale price of a single-family house was $28,900, up from $20,000 in 1968
- Oregon became the first state to decriminalize marijuana
- The percentage of foreign-born Americans fell to 4.7 percent
- Frederick Smith invested $72 million in a mail service to deliver international packages within 24 hours; for $5 a package customers could buy Federal Express service
- Fifty rock stars each earned from $2 to $6 million a year
- An estimated 600,000 people attended the Watkins Glen Rock Music Festival to hear the Grateful Dead and the Allman Brothers
- The American Psychiatric Association revised its categorization of homosexuality, no longer declaring it a mental disorder
- The University of Miami provided an athletic scholarship to a woman

## Selected Prices

| | |
|---|---|
| Bed-Wetting Alarm | $19.95 |
| Cassette Tapes, Set of Three 60-Minute | $1.99 |
| Christmas Tree, Six-Foot | $29.95 |
| Cocktail Shaker | $47.00 |
| Doll, Smokey the Bear | $4.94 |
| Eggs, Dozen | $0.39 |
| Eye Drops, Visine | $0.99 |
| Fabric Softener, Downy | $0.99 |
| Hairspray | $1.09 |
| Jeans, Lady Wrangler | $15.00 |
| Magazine, *Penthouse*, Monthly | $1.00 |
| Slide Rule | $2.95 |
| Theater Ticket, *Hair*, Orchestra | $12.00 |
| Trip, Las Vegas, Three Nights, Four Days | $149.00 |
| Weight Bench | $35.87 |

"DARLING, WE CAN'T GO ON MEETING LIKE THIS!"

## "POW, North Vietnam: Are U.S. Prisoners Mistreated?" Warren Rogers, *Look*, July 25, 1967:

American officials are facing up to a chilling new development in the Vietnam War: evidence that the North Vietnamese are systematically brainwashing the scores, perhaps hundreds, of Americans they hold as prisoners. Amid fanfare, some of these men have been brought from secret cells, trotted through anti-American "confessions," and locked up again. Like Pavlovian dogs salivating on cue, they apparently live in a very narrow world, rewarded when they cooperate, punished when they don't.

It is not clear exactly how many American POWs there are in Vietnam. Neither the Hanoi Government nor the Vietcong had provided lists of names or numbers of prisoners, as required by the 1949 Geneva Convention on Prisoners of War. Current American estimates are that 158 U.S. servicemen, mostly air force and navy fliers, are imprisoned in North Vietnam. Approximately 300 more are missing and possibly held captive, for a total of 458 imprisoned or missing in the North. Twenty-one U.S. soldiers are believed to be POWs in South Vietnam, with another 128 missing, for a total of 149.

What is clear is that Ho Chi Minh at least at one time regarded the Americans in his hands as "war criminals," covered by the 1945 Nuremberg Charter under which some Nazi leaders were tried and sentenced to death or imprisonment, and not as prisoners of war protected by the Geneva Convention. When Ho signed the Convention in 1957, like many other signatories, he added a reservation. His was a declaration "that prisoners of war prosecuted and convicted for war crimes or for crimes against humanity, in accordance with the principles laid down by the Nuremberg Court of Justice, shall not benefit from the present Convention." Last year, when Ho paraded captured American pilots through the streets of Hanoi and threatened to try them as war criminals, his spokesman cited the Nuremberg Charter. Article 6 says that "crimes against peace" included "waging a war of aggression, or a war in violation of international treaties, agreements or assurances." The North Vietnamese contend that the United States, by fighting, violates the 1954 Geneva accords on Indochina calling for the withdrawal of foreign troops. . . .

Two recent examples, from other than American sources, point up the Orwellian ordeal of two U.S. airmen after they were shot down and captured. To protect them against possible reprisal and to spare their families further anguish, no names are used here. But they are actual cases, uniquely providing "before" and "after" pictures of the brainwashing process—a complete turnabout in one instance and the collapse of resistance in the other, each apparently the result of pressure, certainly mental and perhaps physical:

One pilot, interviewed for Japanese television on a program shown in May 1966, looked drawn and haggard, his eyes heavily lidded. He spoke slowly, rolling his eyes or closing tightly when pondering a question, at times looking blankly at the ceiling. He asked his interviewer for word on how the war was going in Vietnam, saying, "I

"YOU PEACENIKS BURN ME UP!"

## "POW, North Vietnam . . ." *(continued)*

don't know what is happening (there) but whatever my government's policy is, I support it." On July 8, 1966, Peking Radio broadcast in English what it said was a statement by this man. In rhetoric as foreign to Americans anywhere as it is familiar to communists everywhere, the statement confessed to "the revolting crimes of bombing the innocent people and civilian buildings of the Democratic Republic of Vietnam." It praised "the brave and determined men of an antiaircraft battery (who) shot down my aircraft." And it added: "The local people treated me most humanely, although I am a criminal. I have received adequate food and medical care for injuries and sickness. This great treatment is derived from the kindness of heart of the Vietnamese Government and people in spite of my vicious crimes against them. These crimes were carried out in obedience to orders from the aggressive American Government."

In November 1966, a Czech radio reporter broadcast an eyewitness account of the interrogation in Hanoi of another American pilot. As he reported, an American voice was heard to mutter, "I feel sad and lonely." The Czech said the prisoner seemed "mixed up in his mind" and unable to respond to questions. "He was certainly the quietest American I had ever met," he commented. But the North Vietnamese interrogator assured him, "We are patient people—after some time, they all will tell everything." A few days later, the Czech said he met the interrogating officer and asked him what happened to the quiet American. "We have transported him to a camp with the other prisoners," he replied. "And did he start talking?" asked the Czech. "Of course, he talked," the North Vietnamese said. "I

told you that all of them would start talking." He took out a small parcel. "Here, I have got him on tape," he said. "Do you want to listen to him?" The tape was played. "If a majority of the people in South Vietnam want a certain type of government, it is their right. The United States should not interfere in the internal affairs of the Vietnamese people and should leave it to the Vietnamese to settle their own affairs. I pray that the U.S. will stop the destructive bombing of North Vietnam as soon as possible and withdraw its troops from the country. . . ."

The situation is painfully reminiscent of the spate of brainwashed "confessions" in the Korean War, when the American people and their government wrestled with the moral dilemma: "Were such men weaklings, to be shunned and even punished, or was there a breaking point for all of us?"

## "Living with Uncertainty: The Families Who Wait Back Home," *Time*, December 7, 1970:

Navy Lieut. Charlie Zuhoski, 25, and his attractive girlfriend of a year, Patty Highley, 20, decided to get married in June 1967. They waited for an hour outside a post exchange until it opened, he bought a $5.95 silver wedding ring, and they drove to a justice of the peace. The honeymoon took place at the Miramar Naval Air Station—in the bachelor-officers' quarters. Ten days later he sailed to the war: The next month he was shot down.

The impact on young Patty Zuhoski was fast and hard. She says, "Before he left we discussed the possibility. If it happens, it happens. But we were kind of joking; every third sentence was a joke. But we knew what we were talking about."

The resources of a 20-year-old, living in the world of the half-married, half-widowed, were slight supports. She tried going back to her bank teller's job but had to quit; living in San Diego, a naval town where every uniform made her edgy, was too much. Finally, she achieved a bearable situation at her parents' Southern California home. Talks with her father, a retired air force colonel, and a friend who had been a World War II POW at least reduced the unknown terrors.

She has done volunteer Red Cross work, audited college courses, played bridge, read a good deal. "I go to a lot of movies. I've had more than one lady say when I've gone out with friends, "Good heavens, what are you doing out?" And I say, "What am I supposed to do? He left a very alive individual and that's what he expects to find when he comes back. I can't go out and date. But I can only put up with these wives [of other POWs] once or twice a week. They are so depressing. It's a very lonely existence. You're married, but you're not married. You're not single. You're not divorced or widowed. Where does that put you in society? That puts you in your own world."

Charlie Zuhoski must have had his agile wit working when his Navy Crusader was hit. He survived, and Patty got her first letter last February, 30 months after he went down. Since then, there have been six others; in a recent letter he spent one of his precious six lines talking about the grandchildren he was going to have. Patty's literary criticism: "He was probably just horny." She has sent him letters and packages; one contained a gift that brings a rare laugh from her, and may have been her response to his musing about grandchildren: some scandalous, yellow-striped underwear. "But I don't think he got them," she says. "Maybe some V.C. or North Vietnamese is walking around looking pretty. . . ."

Before her marriage, Patty Zuhoski says, she "probably didn't even realize there was a Vietnam War. Now sometimes I feel like—well, just give me back my husband and you can keep that damn war going for 10 more years. We used to park on the flight line and watch the planes bounce [practice landing]. I'd get more jealous over his airplanes than anything else. I never realized what war was. I know now. . . . If things don't work out, I have less to lose than some people. Sure, I'll lose a wonderful individual, but I can't lose the memories. You couldn't pay me 10 million dollars for those 10 days."

Patty Zuhoski has changed in some ways. She has gained 20 pounds since her marriage because of a medical diet. At 23, she has a bleeding ulcer.

## "The Navy War in Vietnam," *Look*, November 30, 1965:

Every war has its "new breed" of fighting man. In Vietnam, the breed is embodied in the pilots of Coral Sea. Cdr. "Wes" McDonald, for one, is a brave and patriotic man; chances are that if he were a youngster and his country needed him, he would rush to Vietnam anyway. That fact is, he is 41, a navy professional with 19 years of service, and a wife and four children (the oldest, 18) back home in San Diego, California. He gets paid roughly $18,000 a year for being ready to go anyplace, and his own, unspoken ideas on geopolitical struggles have little to do with it. Regulars like him, in all the services, still make up the bulk of our manpower in Vietnam. For the first time, the United States is fighting a war with professionals.

"Bombing's a job," says another of the pilots, a powerfully built, graying man, whose paunch disappears under 75 pounds of G-suit, flak jacket, survival gear, revolver and a mystifying tangle of harness. "We've had the best training in the world, we've got the best equipment, and we're good. I've dropped 40 tons of bombs on North Vietnam because it's what I've been training to do for the last 20 years. Results? We never see them. They're someone else's job."

"Gently, Mother..."

DRAPER HILL
Courtesy Memphis
Commercial Appeal

THE LIGHT AT THE END OF THE TUNNEL...

"WE HAVE TURNED THE CORNER..."

"A SOLUTION IS NEAR."

"VICTORY IS IN SIGHT."

"PEACE IS AT HAND."

## The Hanoi March

### Editorial: "The Cruelty of North Vietnam," David Lawrence, *U.S. News & World Report*, March 8, 1971:

Senators who want to tie the hands of the President and force the withdrawal of all American troops from Vietnam by a certain date never seem to put any conditions upon North Vietnam as a first requirement. Yet, the handling of prisoners of war by North Vietnam is a story of cruelty rarely matched by history. President Nixon, in his comprehensive report to Congress on February 25 on U.S. policy, said:

"We have the deepest concern for the plight of our prisoners of war in Indo-China. Some 1,600 Americans, including pilots and soldiers and some 40 civilians, are missing or held in North Vietnam, South Vietnam, Laos and Cambodia. Some have been held as long as six years, longer than any other prisoners of war in our history. . . .

"I repeat my October 7 proposal for the immediate and unconditional release of all prisoners of war held by both sides. All prisoners, journalists and other civilian captives should be released now to return to the place of their choice. Such action would not only meet humanitarian concerns; it might also lead to progress on other aspects of a peace settlement. . . .

"War and imprisonment should be over for all these prisoners. They and their families have already suffered too much. . . ."

The cruelty shown in this instance is one that is rare in all of history. The International Red Cross, which for many years has served as a neutral agency to see that prisoners are humanely treated, has not been permitted to visit the camps in which these persons are held. . . . The Hanoi Government has consistently declined to reveal the names of captives, and families do not know whether their missing relatives are alive or dead.

The North Vietnamese show no signs of relenting and apparently intend to continue their policy until the American forces are out of Indo-China. Meanwhile, the question remains: How many of the missing men are prisoners and what is their condition?

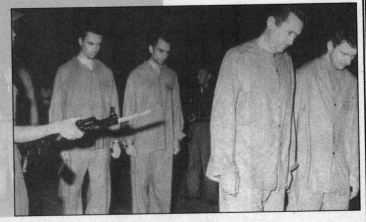

# 1973 NEWS FEATURE

## "Ask a Marine," David Harris, *Rolling Stone*, July 19, 1973:

Ron Kovic was born on the Fourth of July, 1946, and spent much of his youth laying cap pistol ambushes for the Long Island Railway trains that clanked in and out of Massapequa. In those days, the Fourth of July still meant something in the state of New York. Every year the American Legion marched and Ron's birthday shone through it all as a blessing, if not a small miracle, in the family. Being born like that wasn't something the Kovics took lightly. Ron's father had left the family farm to work for A&P and Ron's Uncle Jim fought all over Korea with the United States Marine Corps. The two of them sat in the kitchen behind beers and talked. Uncle Jim said he'd seen good men splattered for the birthday of his nephew, which had been given as a gift from God. Ron's dad nodded his head.

After overhearing a few of these family discussions, Ron had his heart set. He ran his body until it was a young bunch of ropes. He was Massapequa High's finest wrestler and the American Legion's biggest fan. The sign by the road said, MARINE CORPS BUILDS MEN: BODY, MIND AND SPIRIT, and Ron knew it was true. No one in the neighborhood was surprised when Ron Kovic finished high school and joined up. He was meant for the Marines. They were just in his stars.

When Ron signed his life over to the bald eagle, he went to Parris Island with all the others just like himself. His dream commenced with the drill instructor lining all 82 up on the parade deck. Their heads were shaved and they wore their khaki in wrinkles and lumps. The DI introduced himself and told them were a bunch of maggots. He would address them as "the herd" and they would respond with "aye, aye, sir." They would say "aye, aye sir" when they opened their mouths and they would say "aye, aye, sir" before they closed them. If they did everything he said and did it quicker than he could say it, then he would transform them from lowly maggots into something the Marine Corps could use. That was the DI's first promise. His second promise was to beat their asses if they didn't. Ron listened hard. The walls of his stomach grew hair and he settled into his life. He was going to be a Marine. . . .

After boot camp, Private Kovic was sent to Camp Lejeune and then to Radio School

at Norfolk Marine Barracks. When he was done in Norfolk, the private was first class and assigned to the Second Field Artillery. It chafed Ron a little. He wanted to charge up a hill, but mostly he cleaned radios. It was getting hard on him, being ready and not asked, and then he heard about Vietnam. Right away he wanted to go. That's where the Marines are fighting and that's what a Marine is supposed to do.

PFC Kovic requested immediate transfer to WESPAC, Vietnam. When the form asked why, he wrote, "to serve my country." It's so much later now that it's hard to believe, but back then Ron and everybody in the battalion office had no doubts. PFC Kovic got orders in 10 days and flew to Camp Pendleton, to Okinawa, to Da Nang Airfield and into his dreams.

Ron Kovic really did like it. Just like he knew he would back in Massapequa. He liked it so much he went right for its middle. After three months, PFC Kovic was a lance corporal and he volunteered for what was called "Recon." It was April and Sgt. Jimmy Howard had a platoon from Delta Company that had been surrounded on Hill 488 west of Chu Lai. Only eight grunts got back so the reconnaissance outfit had to be what was called "rebuilt." The sergeant asked for volunteers and Ron was the first to step forward. He'd heard about Recon.

Recon were studs. They were jungle thugs and said they ate Cong for lunch. Every mean thing Ron had ever heard, he'd heard about Recon. They were the light of the West in an ocean of darkness. Ron was ready for it.

When he got home, the Marine Corps gave Ron Kovic a Commendation medal for combat and a promotion to E-4.

Ron had a good taste in his mouth right up to the time he left. He was tied in a knot with the second platoon and he loved them the same way he loved his gun. It was tight, hairy, silent work they did together and it made them close. Only one last memory had an edge on it.

Ron was sitting on his sea bag in the middle of base camp waiting for the jeep ride to his plane. He was right by the sign that said DUNN'S RAIDERS. That was his outfit, Dunn's Raiders, like the sign said: WE CAME TO KILL. NEVER HAVE SO FEW DONE SO FOUL TO SO MANY. There was a skull and crossbones on its bottom edge.

The heat was burrowing into his back when someone called him.

"Hey, Kovic," they said. "Come here and see what we got."

Ron walked over to one of the tents with three Marines inside. The grunt in the middle had a jar in his hands. Inside the jar were two fingers and an ear.

"Look at this," he said. "Nice, huh? I'm gonna mail 'em back to the States. Wheatstraw says he knows how to get 'em through."

Ron got stiff and a strap tightened around his gut. The fingers hung halfway up in the fluid and the ear was floating on the top. Since he was about to leave, no one held his reaction against him. It was to be expected.

Charging up the runway to the plane back to the States, Ron forgot about the jar and sailed home to Massapequa to show the neighborhood his yellow boots.

The C-130 took him to a different world, miles away. It got old quick and Ron missed Recon. His memories burned at him. Ron Kovic was stationed with a Hawk Missile Battalion and his buddies were getting cut up in the middle of the jungle. That was no good. It pushed at him and pushed at him until it finally pushed him over.

A copy of the New York Daily News did the trick. The front page was covered with four long-hairs burning a flag in Central Park. That pissed Ron off so bad, he sat on his foot locker and cried for the first time since he's become a Marine. When he finished, E-4 Kovic went down to the Admin office and requested a transfer back to Vietnam. Transfer was denied four days later. Going back had come to be thought of as insane and the sergeant stared when Kovic came in 14 more times to repeat his request. By then he was considered crazy enough to return.

His new orders made Ron Kovic a full sergeant with three stripes on his arm. When the sergeant was honest, he copped that his future had him worried. His orders wouldn't let him join his old outfit. He was going to the Third Division in the DMZ instead. From what he'd heard, the DMZ was a different kind of place from the one he remembered.

It sure enough looked that way on the plane he took to Dong Ha. No one talked. The only sounds were the Marines loading their ammo magazines. When speaking broke out, the dirty ones said there was lots of "arty" up there and Ron had never been under arty before. Not that it took long to find out what arty meant. He looked out the window and Dong Ha airfield was full of rocket holes. People there said the s*** was coming in every day, a hundred at a time.

Ron's base was at the mouth of Qua Viet River, past Geo Lin. The country was all sand and stumpy pine trees and the Marines worked mostly off amtracs: steel boxes with a cave inside big enough to carry a squad. The camp was dug into bunkers, eight sandbags high. At night, Ron led a scout team outside the perimeter and laid ambushes 1,000 meters from the wire. They sat in the rain and watched for the NVA. During the day, the scouts slept. At least they tried to. They had to ask arty's permission first. When it was arty's turn to talk, nobody slept.

As soon as the Marines heard the crack with the whistle on the end of it, everyone with any sense ran for the bunkers. The rounds came in right on top of each other, each one sounding like it had a ticket for the hairs on your ass. Noses bled and ears ached. A lot of the Third Marines got to keeping rosaries close by, to use in the shelters. It was nothing but scary. The worst Ron ever saw was when they took 150 hits, right after lunch.

As soon as the arty lifted, Ron grabbed a medic bag and ran out on the compound. He saw his own tent first and it was just shrapnel holes held together with canvas threads. Past that there was a crowd where Sgt. Bodigga's supply tent had once been. Ron pushed through the ring of Marines and found a hole. No tent. Just a hole. In the bottom was something that looked like five or six bodies. They were all powder-burned and torn up. Ron reached in to find IDs and could only find Bodigga's wallet. After looking again, Sgt. Kovic realized that Bodigga was all there was in the hole . . . all those pieces were just Bodigga. Ron stacked Sgt. Bodigga on a stretcher and cried. Over his shoulder, in the motor pool, someone was screaming.

"McCarthy," they screamed. "They got McCarthy. . . . They got McCarthy."

McCarthy was from Boston and he had blue eyes. When he was laid out with the rest of the dead, stripped naked in front of the command bunker with his loose parts piled next to him, McCarthy's eyes were open and looked straight up into the rain.

Ron saw him there and wanted to kill somebody. He wanted to kill somebody and use them to paste McCarthy and Bodigga back together.

It didn't turn out that simple. As soon as Ron Kovic got to wanting that, something happened to make him feel just the opposite. It was a night patrol.

A lieutenant took Ron's detail out to search for sappers across the river. There was a village on the far bank and the colonel was worried someone would dive in and put a mine to the Marine boats. A hundred meters from the village, the patrol saw the light of a small fire. It was inside a hootch and it wasn't supposed to be there. The village had been ordered to keep lights out. The platoon spread out along a paddy dike and watched. Word was passed to hold fire and the lieutenant set off an illumination flare. Just as the flare lit, someone to Ron's left . . . [screwed] up and let go. That shot set the whole line on fire for 30 seconds at full automatic. When they finished, Ron and Leroy were sent up to check the hootch.

Inside the broken bamboo, there was an old man with the top of his head shot away. Two kids were on either side of him. One's foot just dangled. The other had taken a round in the stomach. . . . The hootch's floor was covered with blood.

When the platoon crossed the paddy and saw it, the Marines melted into lumps. Some dropped their weapons and only Leroy talked.

"Jesus Christ," he whined. "What'd we do? We've killed an old man and some kids."

The lieutenant yelled to form up in a 360 but Leroy kept moaning and no one else moved. The villagers started to come out of their huts and scream at the Marines. It took the lieutenant five minutes to round the patrol into shape. After they called a chopper for the kid who was still breathing, the platoon went inside the wire. Sgt. Kovic laid in his bunker all night and wanted to give it up. He wanted the referee to blow the whistle and call time out until he'd had a chance to think it over.

But wars don't work that way. Ron reported to the colonel in the morning and asked to be taken off patrol. The colonel said no. Instead, the platoon got a week in camp and Sgt. Kovic was ordered to get his act together and be a Marine.

The platoon didn't go back into action until January 20. When they did, it was in the afternoon. January 20 started late but turned into a big day, about as big a day as there will ever be in the life of Sgt. Ron Kovic. It was a day that made all the others after it very different from the ones that went before.

"The people on the amtracs got hit first" is the way he remembers it. "I heard the pop . . . pop . . . pop as the mortars left their tubes and the crashing as they hit around the tracks. Then rounds started cracking around us. I couldn't tell if they were coming from the village or the treeline, so I fired at both places. I was completely out in the open.

"All we could do was take ground and return fire. After a little bit, I heard a loud crack right next to me and my whole leg went numb. A .30 caliber bullet had gone in the front of my foot and come out the heel. It took a piece the size of a silver dollar. My foot was all smashed. I stayed standing as long as I could, but then it began to feel like it was on fire. I went to a prone position and kept using my rifle until it jammed from the sand.

"When I couldn't get a round into the chamber, I decided to stand and see where the rest of my platoon was. I slammed the rifle down and pushed myself up with it. Just as I got my arms straight, I heard a huge crack next to my ear. It was like getting hit with an express train. My whole body started vibrating. Another .30 caliber bullet had hit my right shoulder, passed through my lung and severed my spinal cord in two places. My whole body seemed to have left me. I felt like I was somewhere up in the air.

"I closed my eyes for just a second, then I started to breathe. My lung was collapsed so I just took little breaths. Slow little sucks. All I could think was that I didn't want to die. I could think of nothing else. I waited to die. I mean I just waited for it all to black out, for all the things that are supposed to happen when you die. I couldn't believe what was going on. Where was my body? I must've been hit with a mortar. That was it, a mortar. It had ground up everything below my chest. . . .

"I lay there for what seemed like hours. Once somebody ran up in back of me. 'Hey,' he said. 'Hey Sarge, you all right? Then I heard another crack and he seemed to fall on the back of me. I couldn't feel it but heard. Someone from my left yelled, 'He's dead, Sarge. They shot him through the heart.' He was a Marine from the company who'd run all the way up. I yelled for everyone to stop coming. I don't know if they heard, but I yelled. I was being used as bait. Other than that, I felt nothing. I just wanted to live. I tried to calm myself. I felt cheated. I felt cheated to die. Twenty years old and they were taking my life away from me."

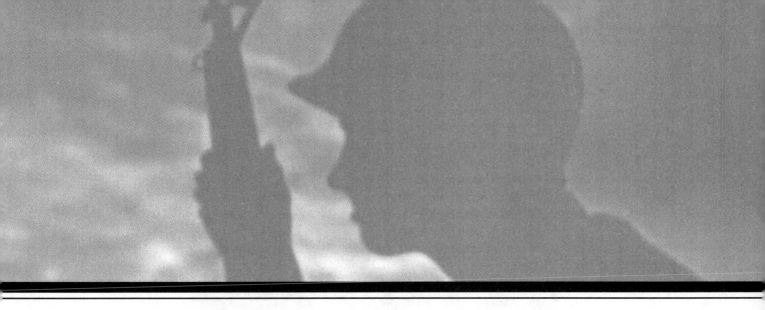

# 1975 NEWS FEATURE

## "3 Days of Drama in the Gulf of Siam: Story of the Rescue of Merchant Vessel *Mayaguez*," *U. S. News & World Report*, May 26, 1975:

Monday, May 12

In the Gulf of Siam, it was 2:18 p.m.—local time—when the U.S. cargo ship *Mayaguez* radioed a mayday distress signal followed by this terse message:

"Have been fired upon and boarded by Cambodian armed forces. . . . Ship being towed to unknown Cambodian port."

The signal was picked up at listening posts in the Far East. Word first reached the national Military Command Center in the Pentagon at 5:13 a.m., eastern daylight time, almost two hours after the seizure. President Ford was told of the incident at 7 a.m. in a phone call from Lt. Gen. Brent Scowcroft, Deputy Director of the National Security Council. Almost four hours had elapsed.

Within minutes, the president was meeting with General Scowcroft in the Oval Office. It was just the first of almost continuous strategy sessions that morning. At noon the National Security Council met for 45 minutes.

In the Gulf of Siam, where the time is 11 hours later than in Washington, midnight was approaching. The *Mayaguez* radio was silent. There had been no further word.

In the highest levels of the government there were urgent questions. Why had the ship been taken? Was it involved in surveillance? On a secret mission? Or was it just what it claimed to be—an unarmed merchant vessel owned by Sea-Land Service Corporation of Menlo Park, N.J., on a routine voyage from Hong Kong to Sattahip, Thailand, with a mixed cargo? The safety of the 39-man crew was paramount. How could it be assured? The nearest U.S. warships were at least two days away.

It was at 1:50 p.m., Monday—with an announcement at the White House by Press Secretary Ron Nessen—that the world first learned officially of the *Mayaguez* seizure. The president, said Mr. Nessen, felt it to be an "act of piracy."

The State Department was instructed to seek immediate release of the ship and its crew through diplomatic channels. The chief of the Chinese liaison mission in Washing-

ton came to the White House to pick up a message to the new Communist Regime in Cambodia, and then returned it—unanswered—24 hours later.

Tuesday, May 13

By dawn, Washington time, on Tuesday, U.S. military aircraft had spotted the *Mayaguez* "dead in the water" off Tang Island, 34 miles from the Cambodian mainland. Two Cambodian patrol boats were on guard. There was no sign of the American crew.

In midmorning, the National Security Council convened again. The aircraft carrier *Coral Sea* and two destroyers were ordered to the Gulf of Siam and 1,100 Marines were dispatched to the U.S. air base at U-Tapao in southern Thailand.

The Thai Government immediately protested. The Marines, it said, were not welcome, and bases in Thailand must not be used for any action against neighboring Cambodia. Publicly, at least, the Thai protests were ignored by the U.S.

Secretary of State Henry Kissinger, in Kansas City for a speech, told a news conference: "The United States will not accept harassment of its ships on international sea lanes."

By 5 p.m., Tuesday, the congressional-liaison office of the White House was notifying legislative leaders that some form of military action was planned. In fact, as Mr. Ford later informed Congress, U.S. planes had fired warning shots across the bow of the *Mayaguez* as early as 6:20 a.m., Tuesday, Washington time. Force was to be used if the Cambodians attempted to move the ship or its crew.

The first showdown came at 8:30 a.m., EDT, not long after sunup Wednesday on Tang Island. A patrol boat heading away from the island was sunk by American planes. Within four hours, two more patrol boats were sunk. Four others were damaged and immobilized. One boat, which pilots said appeared to be carrying Americans, reached the mainland.

*The Pusher*

While these attacks were going on, the National Security Council met for the third time within 34 hours. The session lasted until after midnight.

Wednesday, May 14

This was a day of almost continuous meetings in the White House between Mr. Ford and his advisers.

One final diplomatic appeal was made—to United Nations Secretary-General Kurt Waldheim. But by 3:52 p.m., Wednesday, when the president again summoned the Security Council, the course of action was set.

The destroyer *Holt* had reached the scene. Marines from U-Tapao were flown to the *Holt* aboard three helicopters. The rescue operation was to begin at dawn Thursday, Cambodian time—early Wednesday night in Washington.

Events moved swiftly. At 7:20 p.m., the first wave of Marines landed under fire by helicopter on Tang Island. Seven more helicopters followed. Three of the eight crash-landed, apparently hit by small-arms fire. At 8:30 p.m., Marines from the *Holt* boarded the *Mayaguez* and found it deserted. One hour later, they ran up the American flag.

Even as the assault started, the Pnompenh radio was broadcasting a 19-minute message suggesting the Cambodians might release the ship. No mention was made of the crew. The U.S. Government replied by radio that it welcomed the development, "if true," and asked for immediate and unconditional release of the crew members.

By then, planes had been launched from the *Coral Sea* against targets on the Cambodian mainland around Kompong Som and the military airfield at Ream. The aim: to cut off possible reinforcements.

At 10:45 p.m., the guided-missile destroyer *Wilson* radioed that a small vessel flying a white flag was approaching from the direction of the mainland. The 39 American crewmen were returning. At 11:16 p.m., Secretary of Defense James R. Schlesinger notified President Ford that the entire *Mayaguez* crew was safe aboard the *Wilson*.

Thursday, May 15

At 12:27 a.m., the president announced the rescue on national television and praised the valor of those who participated. By 4:40 a.m., the *Mayaguez* resumed its voyage. But Marines on Tang were still under fire. It was not until 9:10 a.m., Washington time—almost 14 hours after the landing—that the last contingent left by helicopter. Ten minutes later, they arrived aboard the *Coral Sea*. Casualties: one dead, 13 missing, 22 wounded. The episode was over.

# 1979 Profile

# Guantanamo Bay, Cuba

## Marine

For Leon Purvis, the Marine Corps offered an escape from both Mississippi and a drunken father; he never dreamed it would also be his ticket to the luxuries of Guantanamo Bay in Cuba, which harbors the largest communist threat in the Western Hemisphere.

## Life at Home

- The second time Leon Purvis journeyed outside his home of Tunicia, Mississippi, was to join the Marines at a recruiting station in Memphis.
- Even the poorest white families managed to send their children to a private academy to avoid court-ordered integration, but being one of six white kids in his senior class had its challenges.
- More than one black kid wanted to make his mark by whipping the white boy.
- Leon was not always the clear winner, but he did gain a measure of respect; by the time he was a senior, almost no one challenged him to meet after school by the football stadium.
- Leon's father spent some of his time doing odd farming jobs and the rest of the time drinking.
- His mother, who could not read, worked at the dry cleaner's pressing rich men's suits all day.
- Leon was the third of seven children, five of whom made it to adulthood.
- The family moved often, usually for nonpayment of rent, but never left the county.
- All Leon knew growing up was that he wanted to be somebody, somewhere else.
- At best an average-to-uninspired student, Leon began thinking in his sophomore year about the Marines.
- When a Marine recruiter visited the school, Leon learned about the places he would visit on active duty, the skills he could acquire, and the educational opportunities that awaited him.

*The Marines offered Leon Purvis an escape from Mississippi.*

*Leon's father did odd jobs around the farm.*

- The next day, after his older brother got fired from the cotton mill and his father came home drunk, Leon cut school, borrowed a friend's car and drove to Memphis to enlist in the Marines following graduation.
- Three days after his father got arrested for public drunkenness at Leon's high school graduation, the boy was on his way to boot camp at Parris Island, South Carolina.
- There, his ideas about his toughness were immediately tested.
- After a particularly grueling march with full packs in the summer heat and humidity of coastal South Carolina, Leon asked his drill instructor if he could call home.
- Leon had never been away this long.
- The sergeant smiled reassuringly and said of course he could call home.
- Leon was told to meet the drill instructor after supper.
- Leon found himself in marsh water up to his neck, screaming "Home, Home!" as salt-water mosquitoes swarmed about his head in a dense cloud.
- After his voice gave out, he was made to continue calling home for what seemed like hours, his words coming out as a rasping noise.
- It was the last favor he asked anyone at Parris Island.
- At first, he was devastated by his failures at the rifle range and obstacle course, but slowly he started to feel like a Marine.
- He began to understand discipline, structure and being part of a team.
- It was impressed upon him that he was part of a noble effort, waged by only a qualified few, to defend America from communism and all the forces that were plotting to bring down the greatest country in the world.
- Therefore, he was pleased that, following basic and some additional training in California, he was assigned to help guard Guantanamo Bay, Cuba—the most dangerous communist threat in the Western Hemisphere.
- In his bunk, late at night, he envisioned himself standing between America and the godless hordes of communists in Cuba.

## Life at Work

- When Leon Purvis arrived at Guantanamo Bay, his first reaction was joy—he was the first person in his family to leave the shores of America.
- His second reaction was discomfort at the oppressive heat and humidity.
- While on the ferry crossing the bay to Gitmo, his base, Leon decided the weather was similar to Mississippi, but better than the hellhole of Parris Island.
- Seventeen miles of high, barbed-wire fence surrounded the entire base.
- In response, Cuba had constructed a barrier line approximately one mile from the American fence.
- Numerous watchtowers were erected on both sides of the line.
- Behind the American fence was the world's largest minefield, measuring 723 acres.
- Tooling down Sherman Avenue, the main street, Leon thought Guantanamo looked like most bases—littered with long metal Quonset huts, bowling alleys and government-designed parade fields.

*Life at boot camp in Parris Island was a great challenge.*

*Guantanamo Bay was like a small city, containing 6,000 Americans, mostly civilian workers.*

- Gitmo is like a small city, containing 6,000 Americans, nearly 1,000 Jamaicans, several hundred Filipinos and about 400 Cubans, of whom 260 live on base.
- The remaining 140 Cubans commute each day, despite Castro's efforts to stop them.
- All have worked at the base since before the revolution in 1959.
- Each day, they travel to the Cuban line, remove their clothes, walk to a separate room to don their work clothes, and walk one mile to the American gate, where they are inspected, admitted and transported to their jobs.
- At the end of the day, the process is repeated in reverse.
- Of the Americans, most are civilian workers or dependents; the naval force totals 1,800, while the Marines number 420.
- The navy operates a deep-water training base for 75 to 80 ships each year, while the Marines are responsible for guarding the 17-mile fence and defending the base from attack, with patrols maintained along the fence itself.
- After a few weeks into the new duty, Leon's enthusiasm was waning.
- Guard duty on the communist front was not as dramatic as he had anticipated; thus far, he has not seen a Cuban who does not work at the base.
- Yet, he knows that without the Marines, the Cubans would have overrun Guantanamo years ago.
- Just when he thought he was going to go crazy from boredom, word rocketed through the base that a Russian brigade had arrived in Cuba.
- Some speculated that this could be the first wave of Cossack attackers preparing to retake Guantanamo.
- World War III could start right here!
- Leon, now well-schooled in his role as a Marine, kept his mouth shut and did his job.
- If his superiors wanted him to know something or attack anything, he would be told.
- Then, the newspapers reported that President Jimmy Carter had ordered a mock landing of 1,800 Marines for October as a show of force for the Russians and Cubans.
- Leon wasn't sure that that many Marines were needed, but he grew excited to learn the invading American troops would remain on the base for a month to conduct joint exercises.
- The purpose, he was told, was to prove Guantanamo Bay's ground defense could be quickly reinforced.

- That would shake up the monotony of guarding Gitmo.
- Not that there wasn't a lot to do, especially for a poor boy from Mississippi.
- Because the base is located in a hostile country, soldiers are not allowed to leave the base; therefore, every luxury possible has been provided.
- Leon has taken a course in auto mechanics and learned to scuba dive, play golf and ride horses.
- The only animal he had ever ridden was a mean-as-a-snake mule who loved to bite.
- Through the post exchange, Leon bought a camera and regularly shoots pictures of the horses he has ridden, the fish he has caught and the boats he crewed on.
- He now has choices he never had: to reenlist, buy an auto repair garage back home, or even attend college.
- Imagine, a Purvis in college!
- For the time being, he is awaiting the mock invasion while he patrols the fence dividing democracy from communism.

### Life in the Community: Guantanamo Bay, Cuba

- Guantanamo Bay came under the control of the United States following the Spanish-American War in 1898; the first treaty was signed in 1903, leasing the bay to America for $2,000 a year.

- In 1934, the terms of the agreement were extended in perpetuity, and the annual rent for the 32 square miles of land doubled to $4,000.
- A check for the agreed-upon amount has been sent to the Cuban Government every year since then, though none have been cashed since the year after the Castro Government assumed power in 1959.
- The facility is divided into sections on either side of the bay, one containing the airfield and the other the naval station, with a ferry connecting the two.
- The base has facilities for docking, ship repair, ordnance, training, communications, supplies, and medical and administrative functions.

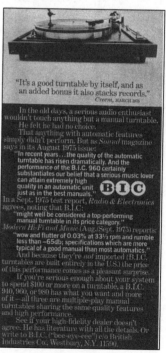

## HISTORICAL SNAPSHOT
# 1979

- The Broadway play *Grease* reached 3,243 performances, passing *Fiddler on the Roof* as the longest-running show
- The rate of inflation totaled 13.3 percent; the prime rate was 15.75 percent
- The United States established diplomatic relations with China and severed those with Taiwan
- An industrial accident at Three Mile Island, Pennsylvania, dramatically increased fears concerning the use of nuclear-powered energy
- Movie openings included *Kramer vs. Kramer, Apocalypse Now, Norma Rae, The China Syndrome, Star Trek—The Motion Picture* and *10* with Dudley Moore, Julie Andrews and Bo Derek
- The federal government approved a $1.5 billion bailout loan guarantee program for the Chrysler Corporation
- Television premieres included *The Dukes of Hazzard, Archie Bunker's Place, Knot's Landing* and *Hart to Hart*
- Hit songs included "I Will Survive," "Reunited," "Hot Stuff," "Too Much Heaven," "Mama Can't Buy You Love"
- Eleven people were trampled to death rushing for seats at a Cincinnati concert performed by the Who
- Norman Mailer's *The Executioner's Song* received the Pulitzer Prize for fiction, while Edmund Morris won the biography award for *The Rise of Theodore Roosevelt*
- Electronic games such as Chess Challenger, Microvision, Speak and Spell, and Little Professor became popular
- *Marvel Comic, No. 1* was purchased for a record price of $43,000
- Video digital sound discs, electronic blackboards, throwaway toothbrushes and Cracker Jack ice cream bars made their first appearance
- Polls reported that 55 percent of the population saw nothing wrong with premarital sex, up from 23 percent in 1969
- The price of gold reached $524 per ounce, up from $223 in 1978
- *Pioneer 11* reached Saturn and showed that its rings were composed of ice-covered rocks and moonlets
- Americans purchased 315,000 microcomputers, up from 172,000 the previous year
- California was the first state to initiate gas rationing using a method of alternate-day purchasing
- The sale of health foods topped $1.6 billion, up from $140 million in 1970
- U.S. Trust reported that 520,000 Americans were millionaires, or one in every 424
- The divorce rate increased 69 percent during the decade; the median duration of marriage stood at 6.6 years

## Selected Prices

| | |
|---|---|
| Alaskan King Crab, per Pound | $2.50 |
| Bean Bag Chair | $37.95 |
| Calculator, Texas Instruments | $29.00 |
| Car Battery, Firestone Forever | $59.00 |
| Fruitcake, Three Loaves | $6.00 |
| Hotel Room, New York City, per Day | $31.00 |
| Hummingbird Feeder | $13.50 |
| Makeup, Revlon Ultima II Foundation | $8.50 |
| Massage Shower Head | $26.95 |
| Microwave Oven | $168.00 |
| Swimsuit, Bikini | $13.00 |
| Turntable | $199.95 |
| Vacuum Cleaner, Eureka | $49.88 |
| Viewer, Viewmaster 3-D | $17.44 |
| Vodka, Smirnoff | $8.59 |

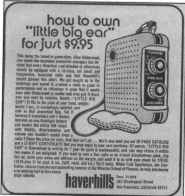

## "The Sun Sometimes Sets on the American Empire," Tom Miller, *Esquire*, September 1973:

*What is it about Guantanamo Bay that makes it everybody's favorite, longed-for duty station? Perhaps because it is one of those rare places in the world that seems to exist in everybody's dream vocabulary. Guantanamo evokes visions of a long-ago and faraway sort of place, a languid Caribbean paradise where the waves break on pristine beaches, and where the islanders shake down coconuts from trees when they want something to eat. Guantanamo today combines the nostalgia of the past with the adventure of a busy, growing naval base. There is just no other place like it in the world.*

*—Rules of the Road, a U.S. Navy publication*

Well, there is just no other place like it in the world. When the Cubans finally get the land back someday, land the U.S. Navy has used for 70 years, they will not inherit a military installation, although it is in part that, they will not find numerous secret espionage centers, although there is that also, nor will they be able instantly to convert the grounds into a port town, although the potential for that exists, too; no, the Cubans will inherit a 28,000-acre amusement park. It comes equipped with a yacht club, three horseback-riding corrals, some bowling alleys, numerous outdoor movie theatres and, of course, miles of Caribbean beaches. There are also swimming pools, libraries, taxis, nightclubs, servants and traffic jams. There is a

newspaper, a jail, a ruling class and a lovers' lane. What we have right on the island of Cuba, 500 miles southeast of Havana, firmly implanted on the first communist country in the Western Hemisphere, is an "American City."

The base admiral is not the most indispensable man here. To find the man who really runs things, the essential man, you drive up past the soccer field on your right, pass the bowling alleys on the left, turn right, and in 50 yards a vintage warehouse appears. In the back room shared with others sits Chief Petty Officer John Harris. He is a friendly, portly fellow, and like others on base, hardly ever wears his uniform unless he has to. He is essential at Guantanamo Bay Navy Base, because every hour he isn't at the Chief's Club Stag Bar drinking and fraternizing, John Harris oversees Special Services Operations. He is what amounts to the base recreation director, for he and his staff make reservations for the cabanas, keep up the golf course, rent cars and drive the cabs. They maintain the ceramics center, along with the auto, photography and carpentry shops. Without Special Services on base, there would be low morale, dissention in the ranks, deep frustration, and possible mutiny. Special Services at Gitmo, as the base is called, must compensate for the lack of off-island action. Outside most military bases there is a strip of go-go joints, third-rate restaurants, cheapo used-car lots, dirty-book stores, pornhouses and, lately, massage parlors. But getting off-base at Gitmo is a little more difficult than

## "The Sun Sometimes Sets . . ." *(continued)*

at, say, Great Lakes or San Diego—to the south there is the Caribbean and in the other three directions there more than 17 miles of eight-foot-high fence patrolled by Marines armed with M-16s. Chief Harris admits, "It doesn't take much to amuse people here. If you find someone who likes fishing and warm weather, this place is a paradise."

A paradise indeed. Conditions are ideal for fishing, snorkeling, yachting, cruising the clear waters of Guantanamo Bay in a rented sailboat, swimming in one of the nine pools, or just relaxing with fleet personnel at Cable Beach. And if you're good enough, diving with the Reef Raiders Club is not to be missed.

Meet Terry Chaney. You wouldn't recognize him as a Marine by his job or his uniform, but Terry is one of the most useful servicemen on base. He is a Marine cowboy. From dawn until dusk, Terry serves his country and serves it well running the Family Corral, one of three stables on base. Years ago, Marines rode horseback on guard duty along the base perimeter, but today servicemen

and their families alike can ride through miles and miles of open trails without coming in sight of the fence. Twenty-four-year-old Terry grew up riding horses in Arizona, so his job today is just a militarized extension of childhood cowboy fantasies. Gitmo has four other Marine cowboys who, along with Terry, groom, care for and break in horses during stable hours (nine to six) and even assist with base horse shows.

## "On 'The Rock,' " *Newsweek*, October 15, 1979:

*Cuban President Fidel Castro*

When the Marines land on Windmill Beach on Guantanamo Bay next week, they will be staging an exercise at one of the oldest and most isolated U.S. bases in the world, and the only one on communist soil. *Newsweek's* David C. Martin flew to Guantanamo last week and filed this on-scene report:

Seventeen miles of fence, 420 Marines and the world's largest active minefield are all that stand between the Guantanamo naval base and the entire Cuban Army. But the reports of a Soviet combat brigade somewhere on the island caused less of a stir here than in Washington. Col. Mark Fennessy, commander of the Marine Corps detachment at Guantanamo, says the first he heard of the troops was when he read about them in the base newspaper, The *Guantanamo Bay Gazette.* Guantanamo's commanding officer, Navy Capt. John Fetterman, adds: "It's been business as usual down here."

Business is slow at "Gitmo." Christopher Columbus anchored here one day in 1494 to look for fresh water but left the next day, and many of Gitmo's 5,000 Americans wish they could do the same. "There are civilians as well as military people who are most unhappy here, who just can't stand the confinement," says Florence Franz, whose husband works for the U.S. Navy. More than 80 percent of the married personnel assigned to Guantanamo extend their tours. But with only 250 single women to go around, and with square dancing the principal action at the misnamed Gitmo Swingers Club, few bachelors volunteer to stay more than a year on "The Rock."

Despite its questionable charms, Guantanamo Bay is an important strategic asset for the U.S. The base serves as a beachhead on Castro's island. With its deep harbor and command of 14,000 square miles of open water, it also provides an ideal training area for the Navy's Atlantic fleet. Each year, about 75 U.S. naval vessels put into Gitmo for five to eight weeks of training in the Caribbean.

Next week's Marine exercise has both a political and military purpose. With the Cubans holding most of the high ground around the camp, the Marines could not withstand a major assault. "They say we're supposed to hold on for 48 hours before reinforcements arrive," says Steve Hesselgrave, a Navy technician. "But the Marines can't do it. The base is not defendable."

Guantanamo was captured by the Marines in 1898 during the Spanish-American War, and the U.S. held it ever since under a lease signed with Cuba in 1903. A second treaty, signed in 1934, made the lease perpetual and specified that it could be voided only by mutual consent or if the U.S. abandoned the base and its 45 square miles of Cuban territory. Fidel Castro likes to bluster about U.S. "imperialism" at Guantanamo Bay, but his troops have not tried to throw the Americans out. "We've had no trouble from them," says Marine Capt. Carlton Carter. "We carry out our duties and they carry out theirs."

## "With U.S. Marines at Guantanamo," *U.S. News & World Report*, October 29, 1979:

The 1,800 battle-clad Marines who swarmed ashore on the communist island of Cuba on October 17 signaled this message to Moscow and Havana:

The United States is ready and able to counter threatening adventures by the Soviet-Cuban alliance in the Western Hemisphere.

The landing at the U.S. naval base at Guantanamo was advertised as Jimmy Carter's response to the Kremlin's refusal to withdraw a Soviet combat brigade discovered in Cuba in August—in short, the president's way of altering what he called an "unacceptable status quo."

Military men monitoring the reinforcement exercise describe it as "technically flawless."

In a heavy squall, the Marines—together with their tanks and other heavy equipment—were lifted by amphibious craft and helicopter from the three warships that transported them from Camp Lejeune, NC.

Only minutes after the first troops landed, they were clambering into bunkers overlooking Cuban territory and patrolling the 17-mile perimeter fence, which is supported by a 723-acre minefield.

These troops reinforced the 420 Marines who comprise the permanent garrison in the 45-square-mile American base on this communist island.

Besides the temporary beefing up of the Guantanamo garrison, its air defenses were reinforced by a squadron of Skyhawk attack warplanes that were flown in from North Carolina.

The whole operation was completed in only

two hours, with the results summed up by one observer: "No mishaps, no casualties, no hitches."

As precise as this operation proved to be, the officers in charge emphasize this point: In a real crisis involving the Guantanamo base, the U.S. response would take a different form.

If the base were threatened, American troops would be airlifted directly from the U.S. mainland into Guantanamo. America's trump card, officials say, would be a naval blockade similar to the one clamped around the island by the U.S. in the 1962 missile crisis.

But the real purpose of the Marine operation was not to prove that the U.S. can hold Guantanamo against a 159,000-man army. Rather, the aim was to demonstrate that Cuban-Soviet adventurism in this region would face a powerful American challenge.

Despite the obvious vulnerability of their tight enclave, the 6,000 Americans in Guantanamo—sailors, civilian workers and dependents, as well as the Marine garrison—seem unflustered. Even while the well-publicized Marine reinforcement exercise was being organized, there were no threats from Cuba's President Fidel Castro.

There were reports, in the days before the landing, that the Cuban Army called up about 3,000 reservists near Guantanamo and increased its tank and antiaircraft deployments nearby. Cuban aerial surveillance was intensified, although no flights over the base were detected.

Marine detachments patrolling the perimeter began noticing increased numbers of Cubans from Havana's Frontier, a quasi-military unit.

Just before the first Marines disembarked, an unidentified vessel drew within 2,000 yards of the *Nassau*, one of the three American warships participating in the exercise. Presumably Cuban, it tracked the progress of the American naval vessels but disappeared into the mist when approached by an American destroyer that was leaving Guantanamo.

The Americans stationed at this base are not concerned with the danger from the Cubans so

### "With U.S. Marines at Guantanamo, . . ." *(continued)*

much as the disruption of their ordinary routine caused by the Marine reinforcements who are scheduled to remain here until mid-November. The mood was reflected in the comment of a Navy enlisted man, William Norton, who works at the base airfield. "Castro," he said, as the reinforcements moved in, "probably is sitting there on one of those mountains laughing about all of us crazy fools down here wasting our tax money by bringing in the Marines."

Laughing or not, Castro will have to get used to the presence of a more substantial American military presence at Guantanamo and in his neighborhood generally. Besides the Marine reinforcement exercise, the navy is planning other displays of military prowess in the region.

These moves are calculated by President Carter to demonstrate that the United States has the capacity—and the will—to bring its armed strength to bear in defense of its interests in the Western Hemisphere.

Is the message getting through to Castro and his Soviet patrons? Col. Mark Fennessy, the Marine commander at Guantanamo, has one answer: "We are not in an aggressive mode. But I'm sure they are showing a logical interest in what we're doing."

## "Making Marines, Boot Camp Is Still the Meanest 11 Weeks of a Recruit's Life," Richard Lawrence Stack, *Life*, November 24, 1972:

These Marine recruits at Parris Island, SC, have just finished a four-hour "motivation" (read punishment) march, crawling the last 500 yards through mud and slime while trying to keep their mock weapons dry. One look at them and even the first-day rookie, rigid in his civvies, gets the message: Shape up or else.

While the other branches of the service woo volunteers by offering civilian comforts, the Marines are determined to stay "lean and mean" as ever. For the trainee, usually a teen-ager, that means surviving 11 weeks of relentlessly "hostile" environments in which he is pushed to the brink of physical and psychological endurance. What the Marines want is "a few good men." They don't get them; they make them.

### The DI's Code: First humiliate, then motivate

Feared and hated, a consummate actor, the drill instructor plays angry god to his recruits. Even at mealtime he is there to harass—"Move your stupid butt"—as the recruit sidesteps down the chowline, trying to hold his tray at attention just below eye level. The DI's aim is absolute mental and physical domination over his men. First he humiliates, then he motivates. Since the sorry night in 1956 when a DI marched his platoon into a swampy creek, drowning six of them, even DIs have had to live with certain restrictions. Physical training is more systematic now—the daily run in the Carolina sun is only three miles instead of open-ended. And a DI can no longer beat up a recruit—at least not in public.

### Individuality is out—and so is hair

Shorn of their hair, and as much individuality as the Marines can drum out of them, the recruits pay avid attention as an instructor describes how to club an enemy from behind. Soon they will be practicing on each other. To make them think and act as a group, the recruits are isolated from the outside world of television, beer, phone calls and girlfriends. Often, they are punished collectively for one man's mistake. They may speak only to their instructors—and then only when spoken to. If they blunder, they end up like the recruit in the mud, learning the hard way "to live to be an old man."

### Breaking down a rookie with words alone

Physical abuse is forbidden, but the drill instructor can break a man with his tongue alone. . . . Three DIs take turns verbally slicing up a recruit guilty of poor marksmanship on the rifle range. "Get yourself together, dummy, or we'll send you to the 'motivation' platoon." The recruit's lip quavers. He'd already been there. "What do you want then, to go home to Mommy?" The recruit whimpers and the DIs zero in for the kill. "What's this? You're crying? The little girl is crying for Momma. Come on, girlie, let's have a big smile." But the recruit now is in tears.

"We call them names," explains a senior DI, "because if they ever become prisoners of war, they'll be called worse things than we call them. If they can't take it now, they won't be able to take it then."

# 1980–1989

The tumultuous 1980s began with the hostage crisis in Iran, and ended with the invasion of Panama to capture Manuel Noriega. Major changes involving women in the military were apparent in that, for the first time in history, women were included in the Naval Academy's graduating class, and they played an active role in combat during "Operation Just Cause" in Panama.

The decade witnessed an attack on the Battalion Landing Team Headquarters of the U.S. Marines in Lebanon which left 229 dead and 81 wounded. The suicide bombing which successfully drove U.S. troops out of Lebanon, followed an almost identical attack on the U.S. embassy in Beirut that had killed 63 a year earlier. Meanwhile, a large-scale mission was organized, with Marines diverted from Lebanon to Grenada, obstensibly to protect U.S. medical students.

The War on Drugs at home and abroad utilized vast amounts of law enforcement and financial resources. Stiff prison sentences were pronounced even for first time offenses involving marijuana. The strict enforcement of laws concerning marijuana had the unforeseen effect of dealers introducing a different type of drug—a purer, cheaper form of cocaine—crack—which brought with it a rapid increase in violent crime. Other battles included the hotly contested right of women to have an abortion, with the conservative Reagan administration taking a stand to abolish abortion rights, dubbed "pro-life." The AIDS epidemic—acquired immune deficiency syndrome—began in the homosexual population and spread to intravenous drug users and the heterosexual population. Initially ignored by the Federal government, the fight against AIDS put ads for condoms on television and radio, and caused some to lobby for needle-exchange programs to ensure that drug addicts did not share their needles.

As the end of the decade approached, many Eastern bloc countries staged revolts against communist rule, and the Berlin Wall fell. Within two years, the Soviet Union would collapse, replaced by 15 newly independent nations, and the Cold War would come to an end.

# 1980 Profile

# Desert One Mission, Iran

### Sergeant First Class

After years of preparation, Sergeant First Class Alberto Enriquez was ready and willing when his Delta unit was called to Iran to rescue 53 hostages in the American Embassy.

### Life at Home

- Alberto Enriquez was a professional and proud of it.
- While many of his friends were scheming to avoid the draft, Alberto volunteered to serve his country.
- He enjoyed his time in the 101st Airborne Division, and when the opportunity presented itself, was quick to join the 75th Ranger Regiment—the men called upon for the really tough jobs.
- When he heard a new unit called Delta was being formed to specialize in counter-terrorism, he knew where he belonged.
- He especially loved the challenge of the new unit: The physical requirements were rigorous, only men of sergeant rank and above were eligible, and excellent performance reviews were needed.
- Alberto had grown up in the Mexican section of Denver; his grandparents had been illegal immigrants from Mexico.
- His father served in the Second World War, earning a bronze star for bravery.
- A small pair of American flags and a picture of the current American president—Democrat or Republican—always hung in his house.
- In school, Alberto earned better-than-average grades, played some football and ran track.
- After school and most Saturdays he worked in his father's suburban landscaping business, the success of which paralleled the growth of rapidly expanding Denver.
- When Alberto joined the army following graduation, he realized almost immediately that he had found his place, and after a few years set sights on being the best sergeant in the army.

*Sergeant First Class Alberto Enriquez is a professional soldier.*

## "8 U.S. Dead as Rescue Try Fails in Iran," William Greider, *The Washington Post*, April 25, 1980:

The United States tried and failed to rescue the American hostages in Iran with a commando-style raid in which eight U.S. crewmen were killed, the White House announced today.

The military operation, according to a post-midnight statement from the White House, was "aborted" because of an equipment failure, followed by a collision of two aircraft, at a remote desert location, in which the eight were killed and others injured.

The American troops, including the injured, were then airlifted safely from the unknown staging site in Iran, according to the statement issued by White House Press Secretary Jody Powell.

The statement, issued shortly after 1 a.m., said:

"This mission was not motivated by hostility toward Iran or the Iranian people, and there were no Iranian casualties. Preparations for the rescue mission were ordered for humanitarian reasons, to protect the national interests of this country and to alleviate the international tensions."

- Yet his father was unhappy; he wanted his son to be an officer.
- Alberto demurred; sergeants, he knew from experience, were the guys who got the real work done in the military.
- His wife had grown up in the same neighborhood in Denver, graduated from the University of Colorado and became a nurse.
- Over the years, Alberto had also attended college classes under various training programs, but getting a degree remained secondary to his military career.
- They both loved the military life—its discipline, purpose and focus.
- Most of all, Alberto enjoyed the opportunity to fight on behalf of his country—even for the ones who, he felt, did not fully appreciate what it took to have a great military to protect America.
- The selection process for Delta, or 1st Special Forces Operation D, as it was known, was both exhilarating and the most grueling experience of Alberto's life.
- Each candidate had to perform a 40-yard inverted crawl in 25 seconds, 37 sit-ups in a minute, 33 pushups in a minute, a run-dodge-jump obstacle course in 24 seconds, a two-mile run in 16 minutes, 30 seconds, and a 100-meter swim fully clothed, including boots.
- Those who met these standards were then subjected to an 18-mile speed march followed by an exercise in which each man, equipped with a map, a compass and a 55-pound pack, traversed heavily wooded mountain terrain from one rendezvous point to another in a prescribed time.
- Then came a psychological evaluation lasting four hours.
- In addition, each prospective Delta Force member was required to have a special skill.

*The selection process for Delta is both exhilarating and the most grueling experience of Alberto's life.*

- Alberto speaks Spanish, Portuguese and Italian; he is also a skilled rock climber.
- His acceptance into Delta was one of the high points of his life.
- His wife arranged for a romantic celebration dinner—without their 10-year-old son—at one of Fayetteville's finest restaurants.
- Even Alberto's father said he was proud, although he continued to talk about son Ricardo, who was now a partner in an insurance company.

## Life at Work

- A basic Delta operating group consists of four men armed with light weapons, pistols, rifles, machine guns and grenade launchers.
- Each is given latitude in selecting the weapons that best suit his style and the demands of the mission.
- Alberto prefers a German-made machine gun that can fire fully automatic or single-shot at a rate of 900 rounds per minute with an effective range of 1,200 meters.
- Alberto was proud of his efficiency and skill.
- One exercise that demonstrated his judgment involved entering a multi-room structure filled with both "captors" and "captives."
- Without warning, silhouettes pop up representing the enemy or a hostage; Alberto had to make a split-second evaluation of whether to shoot or hold his fire.
- It is a point of great personal pride for Alberto that rarely did a captive take a bullet, while stacks of the enemy were riddled with slugs from his HK-21.
- Alberto believed he was ready for the real thing and just in time to play a role in a world crisis.
- When Iranian students captured the American Embassy in Tehran, Alberto knew immediately that the rescue of the hostages was a job for Delta.

- Since the Shah of Iran was deposed by Islamic fundamentalists led by Ayatollah Khomeini, tensions against anything American escalated in Iran.
- Within days of the embassy invasions, intelligence units delivered detailed drawings of the compound where 53 American hostages were being held, as well as routes to and from the embassy through the city of Tehran.
- They also provided information on the captors, how they were armed, and their possible plans for the hostages.
- Soon Alberto and his unit were assigned to a remote training site in the North Carolina woods dubbed Camp Smoky.
- There, as new information was delivered, they trained, retrained and prepared for the mission ahead.
- Over the next three months, they were called up six times, only to be told to stand down each time.
- As frustration grew, Alberto did not know whether the military or the politicians were calling the shots, and though he tried to remain silent, he often failed.
- Daily, the newspaper and television reports made America and its military look impotent and cowardly while the 53 hostages awaited their fate at the hands of religious fanatics.
- In April, Delta got the seventh call.
- On the plane, the highly trained warriors of Delta said little; there was no need for nervous chatter—the trademark of less seasoned troops, Alberto believed.
- After the plane landed in Egypt for a short stay, Alberto's unit was flown to a small island off the coast of Oman.
- From there, six C-130 transports—three filled with troops and three loaded with fuel—flew into the Iranian desert to a site called Desert One.
- The mission was finally under way.
- There, they unloaded the transport plane and waited to be met by the eight CH-53 Sea Stallion helicopters, which were flying in from the aircraft carrier *USS Nimitz*.
- The helicopters' role was to fly two hours and 13 minutes toward Tehran and place the Delta Force to within 50 miles of their destination.
- Eight trucks were to take the Delta Force into the hostile city; once the hostages were free, the helicopters would get them and their rescuers out.

- In the heat of the desert, a force of 120 men, including 90 from Delta, 12 drivers, an interpreter and 13 other Special Forces, waited silently.
- During the final briefing, Alberto was told that only about 15 student radicals guarded the embassy compound.
- Only three or four guards would be outside, one of whom habitually leaned his rifle against the wall; stories about extensive booby traps and mines appeared to be false.
- After nightfall, he was told, his unit would first be flown by helicopter, then driven through the city to the embassy.
- The hostages would be freed and the captors taken out before sunrise.
- The rescue helicopters were to meet them either in the embassy compound or the soccer field across the road.
- Hostages and soldiers would then be flown by helicopter to a captured Iranian airfield 38 minutes away, where large transport planes would fly them to freedom in Egypt.
- That was the plan; bold, simple and logical.
- At the appointed hour, Alberto was more than ready, waiting in the desert for the first leg of the trip.
- But the helicopters were late.
- When they finally arrived, the mission was already one hour behind schedule.
- Soon, six helicopters landed instead of eight; two had been forced to turn back because of mechanical problems.
- The mission was redesigned around six helicopters.
- Alberto then heard angry voices from the officers in charge.
- As more officers gathered, the shouting increased.
- One of the six helicopters could not fly.
- His commander said the mission was aborted; without explanation, he ordered Alberto and his men to reload the C-130 transports and depart.
- The helicopters would fly empty back to the *Nimitz* in the Coral Sea.
- Disgusted and in shock, Alberto was reloading the transport when, as one of the refueled but empty helicopters attempted to lift off from the desert floor in the dark, it collided with a parked C-130 transport and exploded, shooting flames hundreds of feet into the air.

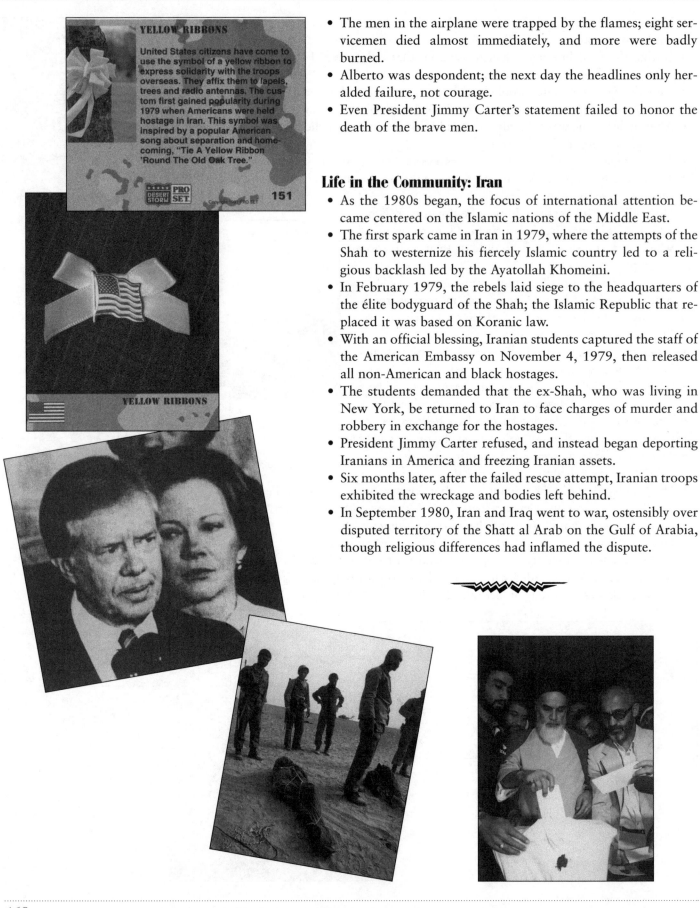

YELLOW RIBBONS

United States citizens have come to use the symbol of a yellow ribbon to express solidarity with the troops overseas. They affix them to lapels, trees and radio antennas. The custom first gained popularity during 1979 when Americans were held hostage in Iran. This symbol was inspired by a popular American song about separation and homecoming, "Tie A Yellow Ribbon 'Round The Old Oak Tree."

DESERT STORM  PRO SET

151

YELLOW RIBBONS

- The men in the airplane were trapped by the flames; eight servicemen died almost immediately, and more were badly burned.
- Alberto was despondent; the next day the headlines only heralded failure, not courage.
- Even President Jimmy Carter's statement failed to honor the death of the brave men.

## Life in the Community: Iran

- As the 1980s began, the focus of international attention became centered on the Islamic nations of the Middle East.
- The first spark came in Iran in 1979, where the attempts of the Shah to westernize his fiercely Islamic country led to a religious backlash led by the Ayatollah Khomeini.
- In February 1979, the rebels laid siege to the headquarters of the élite bodyguard of the Shah; the Islamic Republic that replaced it was based on Koranic law.
- With an official blessing, Iranian students captured the staff of the American Embassy on November 4, 1979, then released all non-American and black hostages.
- The students demanded that the ex-Shah, who was living in New York, be returned to Iran to face charges of murder and robbery in exchange for the hostages.
- President Jimmy Carter refused, and instead began deporting Iranians in America and freezing Iranian assets.
- Six months later, after the failed rescue attempt, Iranian troops exhibited the wreckage and bodies left behind.
- In September 1980, Iran and Iraq went to war, ostensibly over disputed territory of the Shatt al Arab on the Gulf of Arabia, though religious differences had inflamed the dispute.

## HISTORICAL SNAPSHOT
# 1980

- Yellow ribbons became a widely used symbol of American concern for the hostages in Iran
- The divorce rate had grown from one in three marriages in 1970 to one in two a decade later
- The World Health Organization announced that smallpox had been eradicated
- Surgeons were able to relieve coronary artery obstructions with a stretchable balloon-tipped catheter
- A 10-year study correlated fatal heart disease to the saturated-unsaturated fat ratio in the diet
- The combination of First Lady Nancy Reagan's elegance and the wedding of Lady Diana to Prince Charles stimulated a return to opulent styles
- Cordless telephones, front-wheel-drive subcompact cars, 24-hour-a-day news coverage and *Discover* magazine made their first appearance
- The prime rate hit 21 percent; gold was $880 per ounce
- Supply-side economics proposed that government increase incentives, such as tax reform, to stimulate production
- The 1980 Census reported the smallest rate of population growth in America since the Great Depression
- *Dallas, M*A*S*H, The Dukes of Hazzard, 60 Minutes, Three's Company, Private Benjamin, Diff'rent Strokes, House Calls, The Jeffersons* and *Too Close for Comfort* were the top-rated television shows of the year
- An eight-year Veteran's Administration study stated that Vietnam veterans suffered more emotional, social, educational and job-related problems than did veterans of other wars
- Top albums of the year included Pink Floyd's *The Wall,* Blondie's *Eat to the Beat, Off the Wall* by Michael Jackson and *Glass Houses* by Billy Joel
- Researchers at the University of California, San Diego, reported that "passive smoking" can lead to lung cancer
- The "Stop Handguns Before They Stop You" Committee ran an advertisement reading, "Last year handguns killed 48 people in Japan, 8 in Great Britain, 34 in Switzerland, 52 in Canada, 58 in Israel, 21 in Sweden, 42 in West Germany, 10,720 in U.S. God Bless America"
- Four hundred cases of toxic shock syndrome, caused by extended tampon use, were reported

## Selected Prices

| | |
|---|---|
| Beef Jerky | $1.99 |
| Circus Ticket, Ringling Bros | $8.50 |
| Computer, IBM, 256K RAM | $1,795.00 |
| Cranapple Juice, Oceanspray | $0.93 |
| Footlocker | $49.99 |
| Gas Grill | $179.99 |
| Golf Balls, Spalding Top-Flite | $13.99 |
| Golf Clubs, Wilson | $219.99 |
| Lawn Mower, Craftsman | $299.99 |
| Printer, Epson | $239.00 |
| Rifle, .177 Caliber | $299.50 |
| Shotgun, 12-Gauge | $1,200.00 |
| Telephone, Cordless | $139.95 |
| Truck, Dodge Ram 50 | $5,999.00 |
| Wristwatch, Seiko | $84.95 |

Technics direct-drive. The turntable 73 of the top 100 radio stations use.

Hey, Calvin Klein, Gloria Vanderbilt, Yves St. Laurent—meet our jeans Designer.

TRY ONE ON

Three body-hugging styles to choose from

THE BODY BILLFOLD
AMITY.

The Honda Passport. For all those trips that are too big for the feet and too small for the car.

The Honda Passport. Get one. It'll take you almost anywhere.

## "For Rangers in Egypt, Bunker 13 Proved a Harbinger of Future," George C. Wilson, *The Washington Post*, April 25, 1982:

"We're going to attract as little attention as possible," the army sergeant warned the group of 83 Rangers standing before him in the predawn darkness of April 22, 1980.

The Rangers knew they were at last leaving their base in Savannah, Ga., to execute their part in the complex effort to rescue American hostages in Tehran, an operation they had been practicing in America's back country for months under the tightest security.

With creaking rucksacks the loudest sound, the Rangers marched wordlessly and briskly from their barracks at Hunter Army Airfield to the strip where a C141 jet transport was waiting to fly them to the other side of the world.

The windows of the C141 were covered with paper and tape to keep the Rangers from knowing where they were going. But the troops saw and heard enough to figure out that their first stop was New Jersey's Air Force Base; their second Ramstein, West Germany, and their last, a stretch of desert in Egypt near Luxor.

Another group of troopers was going across the world with the same kind of stealth. They were part of the Blue Light elite group headquartered at Fort Bragg, N.C., and now formed a Delta team of about 90 under the command of Col. Charles A. (Chargin' Charlie) Beckwith. . . .

Egyptian President Anwar Sadat had agreed to let his friend, President Carter, use the remote base called Qena, north of the Aswan High Dam, as the launching pad for the most daring and difficult American rescue ever attempted.

The spearhead of this rescue force was to be the Delta team of Green Berets and other stealth warfare specialists from Fort Bragg. Many Delta troopers and the Rangers from Savannah found themselves sleeping side-by-side on cots spread across the floor of the No. 13 shelter at the base. They came to call it Bunker 13.

The Rangers from Georgia could tell they were with Beckwith's outfit without asking. Delta troops wore their hair long in case they had to blend in with civilian populations. They dressed in civilian clothes for the same reason. The Delta men did not look as fearsome as their reputation as they sweated out the "move out" order in Bunker 13. Dressed in shorts for the desert heat, they read paperbacks or slept on the cots most of the day. Waiting. War is waiting. Hurry up and wait. . . .

The day before launch, tensions mounted in Bunker 13. Reading and sleeping gave way to cleaning rifles; sharpening knives; checking gear lashed to jeeps, including motorcycles; and watching comings and goings of high-ranking officers, including Army Maj. Gen. James Vaught, task force commander.

The teams were read their operation orders; the men were given plastic maps showing where they were going; officers gave the "E and E" lectures: how to escape and evade the enemy if things went wrong.

If stranded anywhere near Tehran, the officers told the men, head north for Turkey under the cover of darkness. Don't try to reach American ships plying the Persian Gulf. That's too long a hike. Hide during the day. . . .

*Colonel Charles A. Beckwith*

## "For Rangers in Egypt . . ." *(continued)*

American spy satellites would be looking down on Iran during the mission, the soldiers were told. To help them spot you, make a big American letter with brush or stones that would show up in satellite photographs. . . .

Briefings over, the Delta troopers made a discreet, even polite, departure from Bunker 13 in daylight. They even folded their cots. Several Rangers smiled as they noticed the guns and ammunition bulging out of the civilian suits, overcoats and jeans of the longhaired Delta troopers.

"Good luck," a Ranger whispered to one of Beckwith's men as they shared their secret for a moment in the heat of Bunker 13. The Delta trooper winked back and bequeathed his new buddy a paperback novel.

## "Homecoming Album for a Hostage, the Year Jimmy Lopez Missed," Anne Fadiman, *Life*, December 1980:

On November 4, 1979, Sergeant James Lopez of the U.S. Marine Corps was taken hostage at the U.S. Embassy in Tehran. He was 21. Until 1977, when he joined the Marines, Jimmy Lopez had spent most of his life in Globe, Ariz., a mining town of 7,900 in the foothills of the Pinal Mountains, 80 miles east of Phoenix. He was the starting left guard of the Globe High School football team, played cornet and trumpet in the band and is remembered by his classmates as a distinguished Saturday night carouser. Once named Marine of the Month and twice offered officers' training (he declined, wishing to work his way up in the ranks), Jimmy was posted to Iran in August 1979 as an embassy guard.

Jimmy is the third of six children. His father Jesse Lopez is a timekeeper for Kennecott Copper. His mother Mary works part-time keeping accounts for the *Arizona Republic*. Like many residents of Globe, both are second-generation Mexican-Americans. Jimmy's oldest brother Rick is an officer with the Globe police force (his wife Velia is a former truck driver). Anna is 27, a training coordinator at Inspiration Copper. . . . Danny, 19, is, like Jimmy, a Marine—a lance corporal working as an avionics technician at the Marine Corps Air Station in El Toro, California. Lori, 17, is a senior at Globe High. Marcie, 10, is in the fifth grade at Holy Angels School. . . .

Mary: I found out when I was driving home from work, just driving around the block here when I turned the radio on and I heard, "Terror in Iran—Tehran embassy has been overrun!" I hadn't even realized I was driving fast, but the children said they heard the car just screech to a halt outside.

Lori: We found out that afternoon that Jimmy was one of the hostages for sure. Mom was on the phone with the newspaper and she just hit her fist down on the table and got this real blank look. It was real cold, just starting the winter season, and I remember sitting outside, looking up into the mountains, and trying to picture him there in my mind and thinking, "Oh, God, what are they doing to him?"

Velia: The night before, Rick and I had finally decided to get married, and when we came over with the good news everyone was crying. "Jimmy has been taken hostage," said Mary. So we changed our wedding plans. We'd intended to get married at Our Lady of the Blessed Sacrament, a big wedding with a long dress and everything, but instead we ended up just going to the justice of the peace.

Jesse: I started smoking that day. I'd never smoked before and now I've smoked for a year.

Mary: Jesse wouldn't eat. He didn't eat one bite until Danny came home and said, "Old man, you sit down right here and eat that chicken or I'm gonna get it and stuff it down your mouth."

Danny: When I came home I started drinking too much, got in too many fights. A friend of mine and I beat each other up right in front of the Catholic Church. At home Mom was always in tears, and that I could hack, but when I saw my father put his head in his hands and cry, I went in the bathroom and pulled the towel rack right off the wall.

Mary: I don't know what happened to us, we all started sleeping in the living room. We couldn't sleep anyway, and Marcie would keep turning up in my bed or Lori's bed, so we just spread out bedrolls together on the floor and slept that way for a month.

Anna: Two weeks after it happened Lynn and I went to a Marriage Encounter weekend, which is designed to make good marriages even better. I didn't want to go but we had it planned, so we went ahead. And it really helped me. You know,

## "Homecoming Album . . ." *(continued)*

you have so much pent up inside, you have to let it out somehow.

Mary: I stopped cooking, and yet there was always a meal on the table. People would just bring things by. But Thanksgiving Day I made turkey and all the trimmings just like I usually do. There's this special salad I always make. It's got shredded lettuce, shredded carrots, olives, green onions, pickles, all mixed up with mayonnaise, and the kids just love it. But no one really enjoyed it. When we sat down at the table, Danny said he'd say grace. But then he continued to say a prayer for his brother and that just did us all in. . . .

Lori: I used to write Jimmy a lot. I sent a lot of cards because a card has more color in it, to make it brighter—but I ran out of things to say. You feel guilty telling him about the things you're doing.

Mary: At Easter we got a message out through one of the clergymen. It's the last one we've gotten, and we hadn't known if he's gotten our letters. He said he had a terrific craving for a beef tamale. Typical Jimmy. And then we saw him in a film the militants had made. He was taking Holy Communion, and when we saw it we hardly recognized him.

Marcie: It didn't even look like him. The Jimmy I know is nice and bulky. He was so thin.

Danny: When I first heard about the rescue attempt in April, first I thought, "Damn, it didn't work." And then I thought, "Those guys, they died for my brother, trying to save my brother, and that's all that matters to me. They died for him and they didn't even know this man." And that's when I came to be proud. It takes one hell of a man to say, "Hey, I'll do it," because it's the same thing Jimmy did.

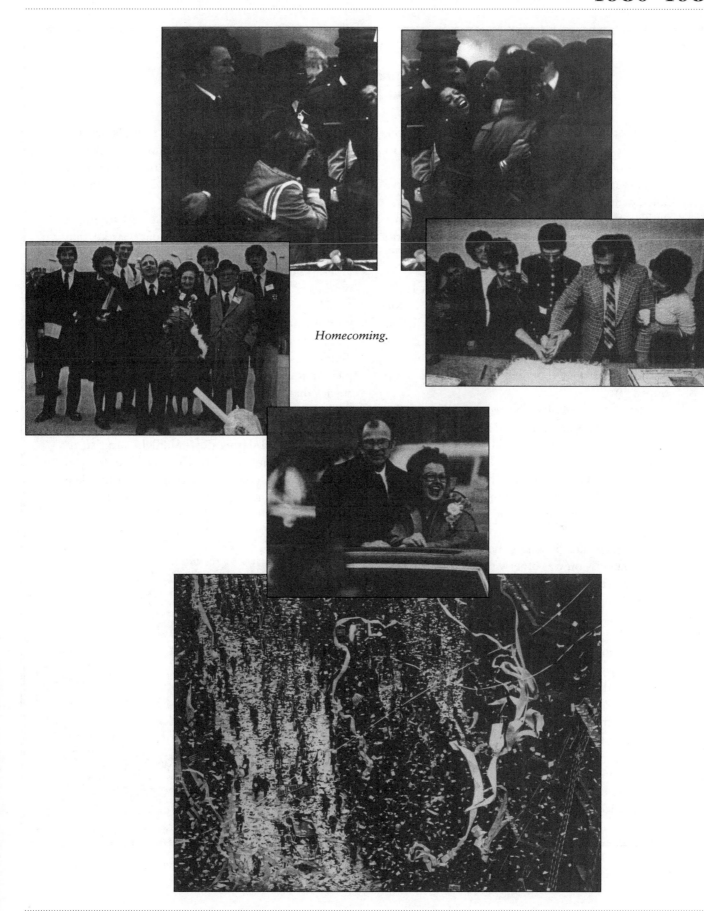

*Homecoming.*

## "Iran Rescue Bid Recalls Vietnam, *Mayaguez* Raids," Martin Weil, *The Washington Post*, April 25, 1980:

This morning's surprise announcement of the deaths of eight Americans in an aborted effort to free the hostages in Iran marked the third time in recent years that similar U.S. operations have failed or led to heavy loss of life.

The planned mission inside Iran, called off because of equipment failure, recalled two operations mounted in Southeast Asia in the 1970s. The first was the attempt to pluck prisoners of war from the camp at Sontay, North Vietnam, in 1970. The other was the effort to rescue the crew of the freighter *Mayaguez,* seized off Cambodia in 1975.

The daring Sontay raid, carried out under cover of darkness in November 1970, proved fruitless when the airborne raiders found the camp empty.

Planners were guided by reports that as many as 70 Americans had been held at Sontay, 23 miles from Hanoi, with 100 North Vietnamese guarding them.

The picked team of raiders flew into Sontay by helicopter after several months of training that employed a scale model of the North Vietnamese camp.

Although no prisoners were found in the camp, the mission was otherwise smoothly carried out. Aided by shock and surprise, the Green Beret raiders had only one man wounded in the 1970 mission.

In 1975, when U.S. Marines made an assault intended to rescue the *Mayaguez* crew from a Cambodian island, the 40-man crew was recovered, but the losses were greater. The operation cost the lives of 18 Marines who made the assault and 23 airmen whose helicopter crashed while on the way to the scene.

The operation inside Iran that was revealed in this morning's White House announcement also follows two other successful hostage rescue missions carried out by other nations.

In a celebrated raid on July 4, 1976, Israeli airborne commandos flew thousands of miles to Uganda's Entebbe airport where they freed more than 100 hostages held by pro-Palestinian hijackers.

Israeli commandos landed in C130 transport planes to launch the now-legendary strike that achieved complete surprise, cost few Israeli casualties, and provided a great boost to Israel's morale.

The possibility of conducting a raid similar to that at Entebbe had been widely discussed in the United States since the hostages were taken in Tehran last November. Many observers had argued that conditions in Iran posed far greater obstacles than were faced by the Israelis. . . .

In another successful and widely praised operation, a squad of West German antiterrorist commandos made a daring post-midnight surprise attack in Somalia on Oct. 18, 1977, to free 86 passengers and crew members aboard a hijacked Lufthansa airliner. The commandos used a specially equipped Boeing 707 jet.

FREE THE HOSTAGES

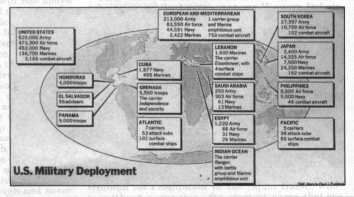

U.S. Military Deployment

# 1983 Profile

## American Invasion of Grenada

### Civilian

Alicia Burack's efforts to become a doctor have led her through two attempts at the Medical College Admission Test, life on a Caribbean island, a government coup and a military invasion.

### Life at Home

- Alicia Burack, known to all as Cia, had wanted to be a doctor since she was a small child.
- Cia grew up in a very small town high in the Rockies of southwestern Wyoming near the continental divide.
- There, everyone counted on Dr. Robert McMullen—Dr. Bob—for all their healthcare needs.
- He had been there when Cia broke her right leg, left wrist, and battled the mumps, measles and severe acne.
- Once, when heavy snow kept the vet at bay, he had even nursed Cia's mare Sally through a difficult delivery.
- The Dr. Bob tales involved late night visits, miraculous recoveries and waived fees.
- Cia felt it was her destiny to step into his shoes when he finally decided to retire.
- After graduating from high school as valedictorian, she attended the University of Wyoming, where her grades were strong, particularly in the sciences.
- Her extracurricular activities included forestry rescue, EMT training and time with the local Rescue Squad during summer breaks.
- Everything she did prepared her to become a doctor, until she took the MCAT, the Medical College Admission Test.
- She had never done exceptionally well on standardized tests, and this time was no different.
- Though she thought she could handle it if her score was not great, she wasn't ready for the dismal results.
- Two days of tears, three more months of study and another shot at the MCAT brought no improvement.

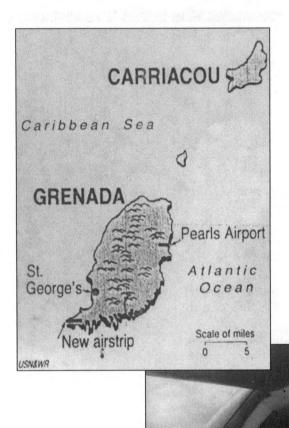

"It didn't upset my breakfast at all."
—President Ronald Reagan on UN disapproval of the Grenada invasion

- Her advisor told her to apply to her chosen medical schools anyway, but add to her list the University of St. George's Medical School in the Caribbean island nation of Grenada.
- He said the admission standards might be less rigorous and tended to consider the whole person, not just the test scores.
- Cia bristled at the idea of going to a "cop-out" school, but in the end, the only acceptance letter came from the University of St. George's Medical School; she would become a doctor after all, via Grenada.
- There, she discovered the unexpected: a beautiful island paradise controlled by a Marxist government.
- Cia settled down to work in a lush seascape far removed from the mountains of Wyoming.
- She took long swims in the morning, enjoyed rides on a rented horse twice a week, and most important, thrived in the academic, often challenging atmosphere.
- By the time her third year rolled around, she was near the top of her class.
- Dr. Bob had even proposed that he hand over his practice to her once she had the word "doctor" placed before her name.
- The stars were truly aligned this time.

### Life at Work

- In early October, third-year medical student Cia Burack heard the first rumors of major political unrest in Grenada.
- According to the stories, the conflict was pitting Prime Minister Maurice Bishop against the Deputy Prime Minister Bernard Coard and his influential wife, Phyllis Coard, Minister for Women's Affairs.
- The two were accusing the charismatic Bishop of not practicing a pure form of Marxism.
- Cia wasn't interested; her thoughts were focused entirely on finishing school.
- Even word that Bishop had been placed under arrest had little impact on her.
- On Wednesday morning, October 19, rumors began to circulate that a large crowd had freed Bishop and was marching on Fort Rupert just a few miles up the coast.
- This development brought more notice on campus; some students began checking the airline schedules.
- Then, word arrived that Bishop and several of his key supporters were dead.
- Immediately, some of the American students started packing, assuming classes would be cancelled, anyway.
- Cia decided to stay in her room, keep her head down and study.

- She was unaware that the execution of Bishop set into motion a chain of events in America; the safety of the students of the University of St. George's Medical School was now a major concern in Washington.
- On short notice, a large-scale mission was assembled, ostensibly to rescue Cia and her fellow students.
- A naval task force carrying a Marine Amphibious Unit was diverted from Lebanon to Grenada.
- Special Forces, including SEALs, Rangers and Delta Force, were called up, along with two brigades of the 82nd Airborne Division.
- Cia got her first real alert of the brewing storm after her usual morning swim, when her parents called to say they were concerned about the unrest.
- Then, Dr. Bob called, saying he had waited for retirement this long, and did not wish his replacement to be shot out of the saddle.
- Cia told everyone all was well in Grenada, and that the media were exaggerating the danger, as usual.
- The next day, she heard that Cuban or even Russian soldiers would soon be arriving to fortify the island.
- The only Cubans she had seen were construction workers near True Blue campus; most were friendly and quick to wave hello.
- By Monday, the Grenadians who worked on-campus were becoming increasingly tense, but there seemed to be no threat of violence.

*To rescue the American medical students, Navy SEALS landed at dawn, followed by parachuting Army Rangers.*

- Early Tuesday morning, when Cia heard booms and thuds to the south, she realized fighting was under way—but who was fighting whom? Were Soviets involved? The Cubans? Where were the Americans? Would she be safe?
- Later that morning, word came from True Blue campus that American troops had landed, and that the students at that campus would be first flown to Barbados and then to the U.S.

## Editorial: "Grenada's Gain, Our Loss," *Commonweal*, November 18, 1983:

Nowhere in the world are people so pleased with the American invasion of Grenada as in Grenada itself. Under the circumstances, some of the Grenadian enthusiasm should be taken with a grain of salt. Still, the reaction has been so widespread that critics of the invasion cannot ignore it. It sets the Grenada action apart from other recent Great Power interventions. In Afghanistan, for example, and in Nicaragua, the populations have hardly welcomed their "liberators." But the Grenadians' contentment was far from a conclusive answer to the disturbing questions this invasion raises. . . .

Invading another country is not a small matter; even invading a small country is not a small matter. America's action has reinforced the pattern of quick military strikes, meant to confront objecting nations with *faits accomplis,* that buys success of putting the world on hair trigger. The invasion twisted international law into a pretzel and undermined the U.S.'s own invocations of the principle of nonintervention. International law, full of loopholes as it is and frequently honored in the breach, is not absolute, nor is the principle of nonintervention. . . .

Grenada was ruled by an increasingly bizarre and fratricidal group of Marxists. Like many Third-World governments, including the one they succeeded, they are a burden on their own people. Their thuggishness, however, was scarcely in the same league with that of some of the thugs Washington has chosen generously to aid and abet for the same reason. If throwing out thugs were our concern, then the Rangers and Marines ought to be heading toward Haiti or Guatemala or perhaps El Salvador, where American Embassy officials have identified the Constituent Assembly's security chief and other ranking government officials as directing and financing death squads that have assassinated thousands of Salvadorans. The evidence that the Grenadian hard-liners were threatening American medical students has never emerged; what has emerged instead is considerable evidence that the Grenadians were assuring the Americans' safety and that obstacles to the students' evacuation came not from Grenada, but from other Caribbean states already involved in the invasion plans. All this was apparently known and conveniently ignored by Washington. It wanted this invasion.

*The Rangers encountered stiff opposition in Grenada.*

- To prepare for the invasion, Navy SEALs had landed before dawn, followed by Army Rangers parachuting into the airport, where 250 Cubans were captured.
- Shortly thereafter, they secured the 500 American students on True Blue campus on the eastern tip of the island.
- The plan was for the soldiers to secure the Grand Anse campus next, though Cia was still unsure of what she was being saved from.
- Movement off of campus was prohibited, and telephone service became intermittent; fortunately, one of the students was a hand radio operator and able to send messages through civilian operators.
- To outsiders in the states, Cia realized her situation appeared desperate.
- According to reports, as the Rangers moved northward to Frequente, west of the Grand Anse campus, they encountered stiff opposition.

- In a metal warehouse near Frequente, American soldiers discovered a large cache of Cuban and Soviet weapons.
- Cia understood little of the politics and knew next to nothing about the principal players, so she was unsure of whom to trust, and pleased that the soldiers would secure the campus in the morning.
- The students reacted in a variety of ways to the situation; two women cried quietly, several made a great production out of packing, while others were angry that anyone would threaten their safety.

*The recovery of the body of Prime Minister Maurice Bishop helped justify the invasion of Grenada.*

- While the sound of battle continued in the distance, few slept.
- Throughout the night, Cia learned about troop movements, shootings, bombings and enemy positions via the hand radio.
- She also heard that some of the medical students at True Blue campus were being asked to help treat the wounded.
- It was very confusing, but clearly American troops were battling Cuban troops, who were on the island to help defend the new Marxist government.
- Dawn brought increased excitement.
- One older student, who claimed ties to the State Department and West Point, instructed everyone to wear long pants and running shoes to make their rescue and evacuation easier.
- He then tore sheets into strips to create white armbands so all 224 students could be easily identified.
- Mattresses were placed in front of the glass doors and windows to protect against flying glass.
- As the hours passed, the rooms became hot; tempers tweaked by fear also flared.
- At 4:30 a.m., intense explosions drove shattered glass into the mattresses; the sound of frequent gunfire was shockingly loud.
- Cia, like many of the students, felt helpless, huddled in the dark waiting for a rescue team.
- Twelve students took refuge in the safest room in the dorm—the bathroom.
- Others kept up their spirits by singing, "The Star-Spangled Banner," "God Bless America" and "You're a Grand Old Flag."
- At noon, the students were instructed to move into 12 dorm rooms close to the beach.
- This required that some people lie two deep on the floor, packed body over body like canned fish.
- The air conditioning no longer functioned, and the heat was stifling.
- Thirty hours had passed since the liberation of True Blue campus.
- Suddenly, Cia could hear the faint sound of a helicopter.
- As it approached, the sound became deafening; the helicopter seemed to be on top of the dorm.

- The door shattered and a huge, fully camouflaged military man toting a giant weapon burst through the opening, fully filling the space.
- "U.S. soldier, freeze!" he barked. "Friend or foe?"
- Cia was the first to respond, "Friend, friend!"
- The soldier quickly organized the students into single-file lines of 40, directing them toward the beach and the military rescue helicopters.
- Cia helped organize the evacuation; she was the last to leave, supporting one woman who sobbed uncontrollably.
- The path to the beach was guarded by a phalanx of armed troopers.
- The 224 students piled aboard the Chinook helicopters, which took them to Point Salines, near True Blue campus; there, a C-141 transport flew them to Charleston, South Carolina.
- At Point Salines, the students paused to drink fruit juice and eat K rations, some of them captured from the Cubans.
- Only after she landed in Charleston and had an opportunity to read a newspaper did Cia understand the size and intensity of the invasion of Grenada.
- Early reports showed that 160 Grenadian soldiers and 71 Cubans died in the fighting, while American deaths totaled 18.
- When she spoke to her parents this time, she made sure everyone knew she was safe, but not as cavalier about the dangers of a Marxist revolution.

## Life in the Community: Grenada

- The University of St. George's Medical School in Grenada is located on two campuses several miles apart.
- True Blue campus is near the new airport being constructed by several hundred Cuban workers.
- The 10,000-foot airstrip is costing $71 million to build.
- Cia lived in a dorm near the beach on the Grand Anse campus.
- In addition, some students lived off-campus in an apartment complex.

# Historical Snapshot
# 1983

- Ameritech received the FCC's first cellular phone license
- Bestselling books included *In Search of Excellence* by Thomas J. Peters and Robert H. Waterman, *Megatrends* by John Naisbitt, *Jane Fonda's Workout Book* by Jane Fonda and *On the Wings of Eagles* by Ken Follet
- Over-the-counter drug packaging procedures changed in response to the 1982 cyanide tampering of Tylenol bottles in Chicago
- The U.S. Government approved the use of aspartame as an artificial sweetener in soft drinks
- The compact disk was launched, rapidly changing music production
- Hit songs for the year featured "Billie Jean," "Every Breath You Take," "Maniac," "Total Eclipse of the Heart," "Say, Say, Say," and "Islands in the Stream"
- The average tuition for four-year private colleges was $7,475; Harvard cost $8,195
- Martin Luther King, Jr. became the first person since Abraham Lincoln whose birthday was declared a national holiday
- Worldwide AIDS cases totaled 2,678, with 1,102 deaths since its first appearance in 1978
- MTV was received in 17.5 million homes
- *A Chorus Line* became the longest-running show in Broadway history at 3,389 performances on September 29
- The TV watch, dial-a-porn, fingerprinting infants, a black astronaut in space, *Vanity Fair* magazine (revived after 47 years) and the large ceiling TV screen made their first appearance
- Following the terrorist truck bombing in Beirut that killed 239 Marines, South Carolina Senator Ernest Hollings said, "If they've been put there to fight, then there are far too few. If they've been put there to be killed, there are far too many."
- Magazines reported a new phenomenon: computer widows
- The per-capita personal income in New York was $12,314; in Alaska, $16,257; and in Mississippi, $7,778
- Magazines with the highest circulation were *Reader's Digest, TV Guide, National Geographic, Modern Maturity, Better Homes and Gardens,* and *AARP News Bulletin*

## Selected Prices

| | |
|---|---:|
| Automobile, Pontiac Firebird | $6,132.00 |
| Blouse, Polyester | $12.00 |
| Cigars, Cuban Sampler | $10.90 |
| Fan | $34.99 |
| Milk, Half Gallon | $1.01 |
| Photo Finishing, per Photo | $0.14 |
| Pork Loin, per Pound | $0.99 |
| Rental Car, Budget, per Day | $44.95 |
| Roller Skates | $24.99 |
| Screwdriver, Stanley | $14.95 |
| Shirt, L.L. Bean | $18.25 |
| Sleeping Bag, Coleman | $32.00 |
| Vacuum Cleaner, Eureka MiniMite | $39.95 |
| Video Camera, Sharp | $359.50 |
| Videotape | $42.50 |

**Marlboro**

## "The Battle for Grenada, American Troops Take Charge on the Island but Face Surprisingly Stiff Opposition," *Newsweek*, November 7, 1983:

Dawn had just broken over the beaches of Grenada. At True Blue campus of St George's Medical College, an odd droning noise woke first-year student Ron Emerson from a fitful sleep. Rushing outside, he looked into the sky. Just west of the campus, two planes were circling the southern edge of Point Salines Airport. Minutes later, helicopters roared in off the ocean and flew straight into a hail of antiaircraft fire. Emerson and dozens of other students scrambled for cover. "Get down! Get down!" A. J. Quaranta, 22, screamed at his roommate, Jeff Geller.

Geller dove under his bed. After a few minutes passed, some of the students crawled to the windows. At first they could see only red tracer bullets streaking across the fading darkness. More planes swooped low. Billowing parachutes filled the air. Soldiers rushed up and cut through a chain-link fence surrounding the campus. Terrified, Karen Young, 23, wondered if Grenada's rebel military junta was sending men to take the students hostage. An eerie lull fell over the fighting. Then, at one end of the men's dorm, a menacing figure in combat fatigues, his face streaked with green camouflage paint, burst through the door. "American soldier," he barked in an unmistakable Southern drawl. "We're here to take you home."

Operation Urgent Fury had begun just a few hours earlier on the other side of the tiny island. At Pearl's Airport, 400 Marines from Amphibious Ready Group 1-84 landed aboard armed helicopters from the U.S. aircraft carrier *Guam*, part of a nine-ship task force hovering off Grenada to back up the invasion. The Marines met weak resistance from a ragtag force of Grenadian Army troops, militia and some Cuban defenders. They secured the airfield within two hours. The northern half of Urgent Fury had gone exactly according to plan.

The invasion forces didn't have as much luck in the southern half. At Point Salines, transport planes carrying 500 Army Rangers in and off the ocean flew into a storm of antiaircraft and ma-

chine-gun fire. The lead plane managed to drop its load of paratroopers. But the next two planes had to peel off, then circle back under cover from AC-130 gunships. The planes swooped so low that the Rangers had to jump from 500 feet—something U.S. troops haven't done since World War II. As some of the Rangers floated through the air, machine-gun fire punched holes through their parachutes.

The Rangers finally landed and fanned out toward True Blue campus, a compound consisting of five barracks-style dorms, a lecture hall, a cafeteria and a basketball court. As they advanced, they had to dodge through withering AK-47 and machine-gun fire. The barrage came from Cuban forces arrayed in a defensive arc north of the airstrip. By midmorning, the Rangers knew that they were up against more defending troops than expected—as many as 1,000. Most of them were Cubans—not just the airport construction workers known to be on the island, but well-armed, well-trained combat troops. "The Cubans were much tougher than expected," said Maj. James Holt, an 82nd Airborne commander. "They were professionals."

# "Grenada Syndrome," Michael T. Klare, *The Nation*, November 12, 1983:

Although it took many people by surprise, the U.S. invasion of Grenada was a logical extension of a well-established Reagan Administration defense policy. For three years, officials have suggested that the Cuba-Grenada alliance represented a severe threat to U.S. security and that extraordinary measures would be justified to overcome that threat. Indeed, what is most surprising is that the Administration did not move sooner to carry out its strategic design.

Since Reagan took office, his Administration has enunciated a clear and consistent military doctrine, holding that: (1) America's overseas economic interests are severely threatened by growing rebellion and "terrorism" in the Third World, most of it attributable to Soviet-Cuban adventurism; (2) this disorder was encouraged by the U.S. disinclination to use military force in resisting such threats (the Vietnam syndrome); and (3) it is imperative that America actively combat Soviet-inspired insurgency to restore the "credibility" of American power and thereby discourage future threats to U.S. interests. These three concerns have produced an interventionist sentiment in the Administration which can now be given a name: the Grenada syndrome.

One of the earliest articulations of the Administration's defense policy came in a speech to the American Newspaper Publishers Association by Secretary of Defense Weinberger in May 1981. Said Weinberger, "We and our allies have come to be critically dependent on places in the world which are subject to great instability." These instabilities are a significant threat in their own right, he said, and furthermore, they "present a temptation for various forms of Soviet intervention." Unless they are firmly resisted, this threat will multiply. Therefore, the United States urgently needs to develop "a better ability to respond to crises far from our shores, and to stay there as long as necessary."

Weinberger expanded on this theme the following April in a speech to the corporate members of the Council on Foreign Relations, in New York City. Contending that the Soviet Union had been "emboldened by America's post-Vietnam paralysis" to push "its traditional policy of global expansion to new dimensions," Weinberger said that the United States must not only resist Soviet incursions in the Third World but also "seek to reverse the geographic expansion of Soviet control and presence, particularly when it threatens a vital interest or further erodes the geostrategic position of the United States and its allies."

That reference to the "geostrategic position" of the United States reflects the presumption, long advanced by conservative military analysts, that the Russians seek to cripple the West by gaining control of the world's sea lanes and maritime "choke points." Because the United States and its allies are so dependent on imported raw materials, the argument goes, the Russians can gain a "stranglehold" over the Western economies by "interdicting" these key trade routes.

Clearly, the Reagan Administration views the Grenada operation as a test both of its military doctrine and of domestic political sentiment. If the reaction to the invasion is circumscribed or muted, the Administration will not be persuaded that the Vietnam syndrome has finally been overcome and that Americans will accept a policy of global intervention—the Grenada Doctrine. In the wake of the invasion, the Administration will hold an unofficial plebiscite on U.S. foreign policy. All who oppose it should make sure their votes are counted.

## "The Cuban Connection: The American Victory Deals a Blow to Fidel Castro's Ambitions in the Caribbean and Central America," *Newsweek*, November 7, 1983:

*"Grenada, we were told, was a friendly island paradise for tourism. Well, it wasn't. It was a Soviet-Cuban colony being readied as a major military bastion to export terrorism and undermine democracy."*

—*Ronald Reagan*

Did Operation Urgent Fury save Grenada from Cuban subversion "just in time"? The president thought so and said so last week. The sheer volume of captured Cuban weapons, documents and prisoners strongly suggested that Fidel Castro had something more than Grenada's national defense in mind. And the 49 Soviets, 24 North Koreans, 10 East Germans and assorted Bulgarians and Libyans who turned up under the palm trees appeared suspiciously like a comradely advisory board bent on transforming the little island into a strategically placed anti-Western base.

Castro had called his advisers a peaceful complement of doctors, teachers, construction crews, technicians—and only about 40 military trainers, none armed with more than "light infantry weapons." But on the ground, the U.S. invaders quickly came up against a hardened professional corps of about 600 Cuban troops. Their arsenal bristled with AK-47 assault rifles, 82-mm mortars, antiaircraft cannons, BTR-60 armored personnel carriers and sophisticated communications gear. The Americans said they captured an officer who may have been Col. Pedro Tortola Comas, a Castro confidant who had arrived hours before invasion day to take charge of Grenada's defenses. Tortola commanded an executive officer and two battalion commanders. In any case, the Americans confronted a Cuban force estimated at half a combat regiment.

While fighting was tougher than expected, the American victory hurt Castro badly. Operation Urgent Fury pounded Grenada hard enough to rattle his ambitions from the Caribbean beaches to the panicky streets of Nicaragua. Looking pale and weary—even his beard seemed more scraggly than usual—the Cuban leader sank into a vinyl armchair to face foreign reporters in Havana. Why had he not evacuated his Grenada garrison as the U.S. strike force closed in? That would be "demoralizing and dishonorable for our country," Castro said. Had he considered sending reinforcements? "Impossible," he snapped. "They would never compare with the air and land forces of the United States." Then how could he secure his larger stakes in Central America? "We would try to do everything possible for Nicaragua," Castro said lamely. "But we would face the same problem as in Grenada. . . . Those are the facts. We do not have any other options."

## "The Caribbean: Grenada's Palm-Tree Putsch," Steven Strasser, *Newsweek*, October 24, 1983:

The people of Grenada, the Caribbean isle of spice and revolution, have long ignored their government's warnings against the threat of right-wing mercenaries. But last week, Radio Free Grenada was spreading alarm about a very real coup attempt—engineered by the radical-Marxist left. On Thursday, Prime Minister Maurice Bishop flew home from a trip to Romania and Czechoslovakia. Shortly afterward he went on radio to deny rumors of a split between his leftist supporters and the far left. Then Bishop dropped from sight—and before long, the far left seemed to have control of the airwaves.

The palm-tree putsch was not completely unexpected. In the fourth year of his rule, Bishop has had increasing trouble holding his left-far-left coalition together. From the start, the lawyer-prime minister, 39, had paid his revolution's di-

alectical dues, established close ties with Cuba and offered support to his fellow revolutionaries in Nicaragua and Surinam. All the same, radicals led by Deputy Prime Minister Bernard Coard and his wife, Phyllis, complained that Grenada's conversion to pure-strain Marxism was proceeding too slowly. They were not reassured by Bishop's recent attempts to normalize relations with the United States. And last week, they apparently struck. The first hint came from National Mobilization Minister Selwyn Strachan, a hard-liner who advocated that Grenada offer comradely assistance to revolutions in the Caribbean. Strachan announced that Bishop stood charged with refusing to share leadership with his more radical comrades—and that Coard had replaced him.

Motives: At first neither Bishop nor Coard appeared in public to claim power. Radio Free

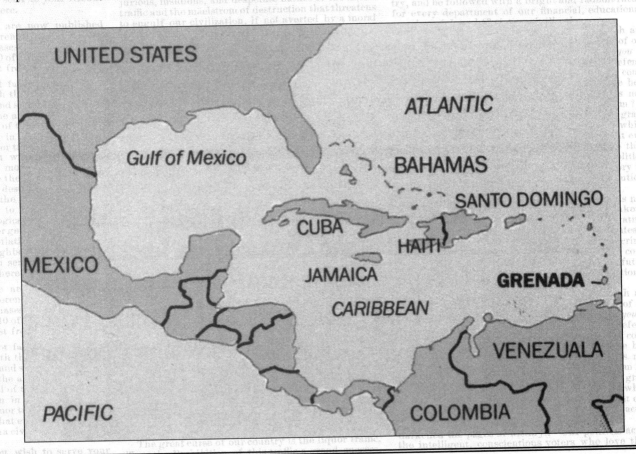

## "The Caribbean . . ." *(continued)*

Grenada only muddled things further by reporting that Coard—not Bishop—had resigned. Coard's supposed reason: to make clear that rumors of his coup plot were false. But his motives might have been less altruistic. By divorcing himself from the Bishop regime, Coard might have improved his chances to lead a new government. At the weekend, a Coard supporter, military officer Leon Cornwall, denounced Bishop in a speech for "vicious counterrevolutionary lies and rumors," an indication that Coard was prevailing. Throughout the intrigue, streets in St. George's, the island's capital, appeared quiet—with few troops in evidence, but plenty of bewildered citizens.

The United States, with no diplomatic representatives in St. George's, was just as confused at first. The Carter and Reagan administrations had bridled against Bishop's government since its own birth by coup. But lately, Bishop had openly courted better relations with Washington, and the administration was at least listening. During his unofficial June trip to Washington, Bishop was granted an audience with Deputy Secretary of State Kenneth Dam and National-Security Adviser William Clark, a meeting that produced no breakthroughs but set the precedent for further contacts. No such understandings were conceivable in Coard's case. Some Grenadians muttered that

Coard's main allegiance lies with Cuba—and in the days leading up to last week's coup attempt, Grenadians witnessed a noticeable buildup of Soviet materiel on their sunny little island.

## "How Much Can America Do? Its power is vast, but its global commitments are breathtaking," George J. Church:

"We are a nation with global responsibilities." So said President Reagan in his speech to the nation last week on the events in Beirut and Grenada. But he did not address the question that assertion raises at the most basic level: Has the nation taken on worldwide commitments for the potential use of force that its military power currently is stretched too thin to fulfill?

The answer by military experts is not altogether reassuring. Its essence: As long as trouble on opposite sides of the globe can be met by deployments the size of those in Lebanon and Grenada, there is no strain. Those two crises are engaging only two of the 12 Marine amphibious units (a total of 150,000 troops) available to be dispatched 'round the world, and, of course, there remain all the other armed services of the nation to be drawn on. But a pair of widely separated major confrontations—a Soviet threat to the Persian Gulf oilfields, say, and a blowup in Korea—would pose a real problem. General John A. Wickham, the Army Chief of Staff, fears that U.S. commitments "probably exceed the force capabilities."

The U.S. is obliged by treaty to defend Japan, South Korea and Western Europe (and Western Europe, by NATO definition, includes Greece and Turkey) from armed attack. It has a clearly enunciated pledge to use force if necessary to keep oil flowing to the free world from the Middle East. This implies a determination to defend Saudi Arabia,

*Oman,* Egypt, Jordan and Pakistan from threats external and internal. Six months of maneuvers and training exercises in Honduras, involving up to 5,000 troops at one time, underscore U.S. opposition to leftist revolution in Central America. The U.S. recently felt obliged to send AWACS planes to watch Libyan activities in the African state of Chad.

To honor these pledges and missions, the U.S. maintains enormous forces 'round the world. But bringing them to bear in trouble spots involves severe difficulties. The worst is a shortage of sealift and airlift capacity, brought on because the navy and air force for decades have preferred to spend their money on combat hardware rather than on cargo ships and planes. Since 1981, the number of U.S. "mobile logistics ships" (vessels that carry petroleum, ammunition and other cargo to resupply battle fleets at sea) has increased by exactly one, from 72 to 73. Some 50 new transport planes are on order to supplement the present fleet of 70 C-5A Galaxies and 234 C-141 Star-Lifters. But the new planes will not begin flying for two years.

For an example of what could happen, take a case that has occupied much of the attention of U.S. planners: a hypothetical Soviet invasion of Iran. Theoretically, the U.S. Rapid Deployment Force could send 3.3 army divisions (representing some 55,000 men, with tanks, armored personnel carriers, artillery, mortars, machine guns and personal weapons), 1.3 Marine amphibious forces, and seven air force fighter wings totaling 504 planes. To do so, however, would take weeks, and after that the U.S. would be hard pressed to fly or ship in the fuel, food and ammunition to sustain the R.D.F. during a long campaign.

In addition, the R.D.F. units that could be dispatched to the Middle East are also earmarked to reinforce NATO during a European crisis. European allies would surely howl that they could not be spared, since a Middle East war might spill over into Europe. Former Secretary of Defense Harold Brown warns that even in relatively minor trouble

### "How Much . . ." *(continued)*

areas like Lebanon, prolonged deployments "are manageable over a period of months—but if they go on for a year or more, they would reduce our ability to deal with a major contingency."

It is not easy to see what might be done. Commitments could be lightened, but which friendly states should be told the U.S. might not defend them? Military forces could be built up further; the U.S. may even need the draft. But Reagan is having trouble getting his present defense-spending requests through Congress (he asked for a 14.2 percent increase over fiscal 1983). Perhaps the most comforting thought is that the Soviet Union, faced by a hostile China on one flank and ringed by potentially mutinous East European allies on another, has its own worries about how much military force it could safely commit to any bloody, prolonged foreign adventure.

## "The Meaning of Grenada," *National Review*, November 25, 1983:

Amid the kaleidoscopic onrush of images and events associated with Grenada, two moments of exquisite meaning stand out. One was the emotional outpouring of gratitude and praise from the American medical students rescued from Grenada—a response that all too obviously stunned and embarrassed the establishment media. The other was when Fidel Castro sagged limply backward into an armchair, telling reporters feebly that there is nothing he could do. Grenada, evidently, pierced Fidel to his very paranoic quick.

Full well Fidel might sag, for the action in Grenada represents the first time in history that U.S. military powers have reversed a Communist revolution and liberated a people from Marxist-Leninist rule. (The only other Communist regimes that have been toppled since 1917 have been overthrown by other Communist regimes—a phenomenon akin to inter-gang warfare.) This gives the action in Grenada a historical significance even greater, by a good bit, than the strategic importance of the island. Marx and Lenin preached historical inevitability, and Brezhnev proclaimed a doctrine of the irreversibility of Communist rule. Grenada confounds this Communist pantheon. The Marines did not just take an island; they stopped the march of history dead in its inexorable tracks.

There have been rumors of Cuban retaliation and speculation about a bold Soviet response to Grenada. Almost certainly, we will see neither, for both Havana and Moscow—like anti-American regimes everywhere—partake of a bully spirit that preys on weakness, but shrinks in the face of strength.

The liberation of Grenada will have positive reverberations for U.S. foreign policy around the globe. Surinam's disinvitation of its Cuban advisors is an early case in point. Our action will deter for a time Cuban adventurism in the Caribbean, it will knock a little sense into the Sandinistas (expect temporary sweetness and light from that quarter), and it will dampen "revolutionary ardor" (bully instincts) in El Salvador. Even the Kremlin will likely beat a prudent retreat for a time; Andropov, said to be suffering from a physical ailment, more likely is in a state of acute shock. Viewed from this perspective, the U.S. operation in Grenada represents a powerful blow on behalf of the cause to which Reagan's most passionate critics fervently claim allegiance. Grenada was a blow for peace.

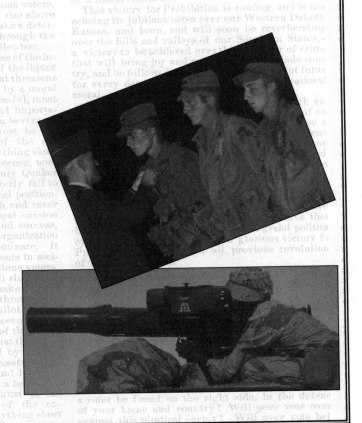

# 1983 NEWS FEATURE

### "Aftermath in Bloody Beirut," *Time,* November 7, 1983:

Days after the slaughter, the scene remained so ghastly that the eye instinctively sought out relics of life among the debris. Here was a dog tag bent out of shape by the blast, there a shred of a letter or birthday card from home. Scattered everywhere were photographs: of uniformed sons between doting parents, of laughing girlfriends and smiling wives, of babies newly born. The personal effects made the row of bodies laid out on the ground and covered with blankets more poignant, for they were reminders that each Marine pulled out of the rubble had his own private existence, peopled by all those who knew and cared about him.

The loved ones back home needed no reminders. As rescue workers clawed through the smoking ruins last week of what had once been the Battalion Landing Team Head-quarters of the U.S. Marines, and the toll grew bleaker, relatives and friends kept vigil across the country awaiting word. For most, the news came only after several wrenching days of uncertainty. All of a sudden, the dreaded figure in uniform would appear and say, "The Secretary of the Navy has asked that I inform you. . . ."

At week's end the count stood at 229 dead and 81 wounded. It was the highest number of American casualties in a single day since January 13, 1968, when 246 servicemen were killed throughout Vietnam at the start of the Tet offensive. In the heart of West Beirut, about two miles from the airport, searchers hunted through the remains of a nine-story building housing French paratroopers that had been hit minutes after the airport bombing; the French toll was 56 dead, with two missing and 15 injured.

The double act of horror left a tangle of questions. Both truck drivers blew themselves to smithereens when they swerved madly into their targets and detonated their deadly cargoes. But who was behind the attacks? Why was security not more stringent, especially after a nearly identical attack hit the U.S. embassy in Beirut last April, killing 63 people? Can the safety of the Marines now be ensured?

One goal of the attacks was clear: to drive out of Lebanon the troops of the U.S., France and the two other members of the Multi-National Force, Italy and Britain. In words and deeds, the four nations reaffirmed their intention to stay. . . . In his nationwide

address on television Thursday evening, President Ronald Reagan made the most power-ful pitch for a continuation of the U.S. presence in Lebanon. Said he: "We cannot and will not dishonor them now, and the sacrifices they made, by failing to remain as faithful to the cause of freedom and the pursuit of peace as they have been."

Throughout the week, the site of those sacrifices was slowly, even tenderly, pulled apart in the search for bodies. As bulldozers grumbled back and forth, cranes hoisted away slabs of concrete, their steel rods bent crazily and stuck with bits of uniforms. The Marines were aided in their grim task not only by Navy Seabees from ships of the U.S. Sixth Fleet off the Lebanese coast, but by Italian, Norwegian and Lebanese rescuers, most of them volunteers. The searchers clambered over the ruins with picks and shovels, but just as often they would fall to their knees and scoop out debris with their hands. Orders, screamed out in any of several languages, often went unheard. At night the wreckage looked especially eerie as workers kept digging under the harsh glare of floodlights. . . .

Efforts were quickly concentrated on separating the four floors of the building, once some 50 feet high, now crunched into about 10 feet of rubble. Once a chunk of floor had been lifted away, a team of workers would sift the debris for corpses and personal effects. Some bodies were sandwiched between floors and ceilings and could be retrieved only by cutting off an arm or a leg. Rescuers emerged carrying blood-soaked buckets filled with limbs and tattered flesh. The Marines kept insisting that several comrades might still be found alive in the basement, but such hopes seemed futile. By the end of the first day, the searchers had donned masks to ward off the stench of death. . . .

As the search went on, many Marines, stunned and angry, swapped memories of those killed. One Navy corpsman had just married a Lebanese woman. He had returned from his honeymoon early, on Sunday, just in time for a rendezvous with death. Some recalled the Marine staff sergeant who a few days before the attack was proudly showing a video-tape of his newborn son, whom he had never seen and now never would. Few could avoid pointing out that the tour of duty for most of those killed had almost ended, that they were scheduled to leave Beirut in a few weeks for the States.

The most haunting tale belonged to Lance Corporal Robert Calhoun, who was stationed on the roof of the building when the truck came hurtling across the parking lot. "The explosion hit, and everything started falling," Calhoun recalled. "I thought, 'This is how I am going to die.' " Afterward, Calhoun said, he talked with the sentry who had manned the entry gate bypassed by the truck. Said Calhoun: "He says just as the man went by, they'll always remember, the guy was smiling. . . ."

As memorial services for the fallen were held across the country, the Administration mulled over a tactical redeployment to make its forces in Lebanon less vulnerable. Secretary of Defense Caspar Weinberger hinted last week that more of the U.S.'s 1,600 men might be stationed offshore. Another option calls for moving the Marines to higher ground east of the airport, but the hills above Beirut are so crisscrossed with rivalries that the men might be at a greater risk there.

# 1989 PROFILE

## INVASION OF PANAMA

### Sergeant

Staff Sergeant Luella Sprague is part of a Military Police Battalion sent as part of the invasion of Panama, where the presence of women in combat captures headlines across the nation.

### Life at Home

- Luella Sprague enlisted in the army right out of high school in order to help pay for college; her childhood dream was to become part of the Tennessee Bureau of Investigation.
- Luella grew up in the community of Alto, Tennessee, at the foot of the Cumberland plateau.
- In high school, her report card reflected more C's than A's, but her prowess as a lead-off-hitting softball shortstop earned her several partial scholarship offers to small colleges in the area.
- Her parents' persistent struggles with debt convinced her that she would not attend college on the "borrow now, pay back later" plan; money worries, she already knew, could be a huge burden.
- Besides, the army's offer to see the world and earn money toward college was appealing.
- Before she joined the army, Luella's longest journey from home had been to Graceland on the anniversary of Elvis Presley's death.
- She knew she had made the right decision almost immediately; the army assigned her to military police training and offered additional courses toward a degree in criminal justice.
- As an MP, she not only received police training, but also was qualified with an M-16 and all other basic combat tactics.

*Luella Sprague joined the army to pay for college.*

*Traditionally, women were not allowed in combat units, but might see action as members of the 503rd Military Police Battalion.*

- Luella enjoyed the day-to-day routine of police work in the 503rd Military Police Battalion at Fort Bragg, North Carolina, but she loved the idea that her unit could be assigned in a hostile situation to keep peace.
- Traditionally, women were not allowed in combat units; military police served a support function.
- Luella thought the prohibition against women in combat ridiculous, and though many of her fellow male soldiers agreed, few were willing to speak publicly.
- A quarter of the soldiers in her company were tough and aggressive—and female.
- She could out-arm-wrestle many of the men, and out-drink all of them.
- However, she was just as wary as the men when in the spring of 1989, after more than a decade in service, her platoon got a new female commanding officer, Second Lieutenant Alice Zayicek, a Chicago native straight out of ROTC.
- Zayicek was a rigid disciplinarian who expected respect, and conducted herself with a quiet confidence not always found in new officers.
- After a few months, Luella decided that Lt. Zayicek was the best officer she had served with in over 11 years of service.

### Life at Work

- For much of 1988 and 1989, the country of Panama and its leader General Manuel Noriega had been in the headlines.
- Despite nearly 12,000 American troops in Panama, Noriega and his Panama Defense Force were exercising nearly absolute control over the country.
- Since the Panama Canal Treaty was signed during the Carter Administration, the influence of the United States in Panama had been declining.

### "Snap It, Scrap It," *Time*, March 2, 1987:

Disposable razors are one thing, but will anyone buy a throwaway camera? Fuji Photo Film and Eastman Kodak apparently think so. Their new rival models, both announced last week, combine film, plastic lens and shutter into one small box. After shooting pictures, users will take the entire camera to a photo lab for film processing. Kodak's Fling, which could be available by the summer, will sell for $6.95 and take 24 shots. It contains the 110 film used in Kodak's Instamatic cameras. Fuji will begin selling its Quick Snap this spring. It will cost less than $10 for 24 exposures and will use higher-quality 35-mm film.

These gadgets will sell for roughly two to three times the cost of comparable film for regular cameras. They are meant for use at the beach or other places where people might not want to bring more expensive cameras. They are not picture-perfect, though. Both models take outdoor shots only and cannot focus on objects that are less than three feet away.

- The treaty, which was derided by many, called for the entire American military presence to be gone by the end of 1999—just a decade away.
- Currently, 12,700 American troops are assigned to Panama; the Central American country serves as the headquarters of the U.S. Southern Command.
- In May, a national election was held, with Noriega claiming victory even though neutral observers said he had lost in a landslide.
- In early October, a failed coup attempt increased tensions and exacerbated anti-American sentiment among Noriega supporters, particularly the Panama Defense Force.
- Word circulated around Fort Bragg that U.S. military involvement was imminent, although President Bush publicly denied any plans to invade Panama.
- In mid-December, Noriega's Panama Defense Force shot an American officer and tortured another while threatening to gang-rape the officer's wife.
- Bush ordered that Noriega be captured and his rogue government taken down.
- Seven thousand troops, including Ranger, airborne and infantry, were airlifted to Panama to join the forces on the ground.
- The operation was designated "Just Cause."
- Early on the morning of December 20, a multipronged attack—the largest force in the field since Vietnam—hit targets in Panama.
- As part of the assault, 3,000 members of the 82nd Airborne Division made the largest parachute drop since World War II.
- Noriega's defense forces provided token resistance before fading into the landscape to conduct guerrilla warfare.
- Luella's company was deployed early in the attack plan.
- Approximately 2,500 troops consisting primarily of MPs landed in Panama behind the air assault.
- Although for Luella, excitement had been building all week, some soldiers were visibly nervous, while others were in a panic about childcare, since both mother and father were deployed at the same time.

- The night before she shipped out, Luella wrote her family the longest letter of her life, describing her pride at being an American, her joy of being a female soldier, and her excitement that she would be allowed to fight for her country.
- Upon landing in Panama, the MPs were immediately immersed in the thick of the fray.
- Luella's squad was assigned to join a perimeter force around the Ministry of Foreign Affairs.
- Almost immediately, she was subjected to fire; as the day progressed, the sounds of war were persistent, but not heavy.
- One soldier in her unit was hit, and although the wound was not life-threatening, he screamed in pain and fear at seeing blood gushing out of his body.
- Luella was embarrassed by his behavior as he was carried off for medical treatment.
- In the second of several firefights during the first day, she was sure she had taken down two of the enemy.
- What a rush!

- Late in the day, an exhausted Lt. Zayicek stopped at Luella's post, offering encouragement with a firm "Carry on, soldier," and moving on.
- Luella marveled at the maturity of the 22-year-old officer.
- Panamanian resistance collapsed quickly in the face of superior strength.
- In the days that followed, the MPs set up a police department, as well as a night court staffed by Panamanian magistrates.
- Luella had performed similar operations on the island of St. Croix after Hurricane Hugo struck the island in September.
- Her other concern was containing the looters trying to take advantage of the chaos; each day, she patrolled with several Panamanian policemen.
- A stickler for details, she kept those in her unit alert and aware of the dangers.
- Weapons were cleaned, oiled and on ready at all times, as the MPs were still subject to fire from burned-out buildings and looted storefronts.
- Rumors were bruited of sniper killings in the forbidding streets; every face and building were scanned for potential danger.
- Luella knew that she could die in seconds in these situations.

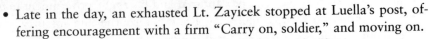

- She was amused that the stateside media was obsessed with the idea that women like her were in the line of fire, because in Panama, hundreds of women operated in the combat zone and had come under enemy fire.
- Also, for the first time, women led soldiers into action against an enemy.
- Official army policy still kept women from serving in units designated for combat; since the mid-1970s, women had served in support units such as the Military Police and the Signal Corps.
- The Panama invasion was now proving what military experts had said for years—in today's urban warfare, the line between combat and support is quickly blurred.
- Just as life began to fall into a routine—albeit still harrowing at times—word arrived that one of Noriega's chief lieutenants was hiding in a nearby apartment complex.
- Luella was beside herself with excitement as the entire unit piled in HMMWVs (high mobility multipurpose wheeled vehicles) and roared to the location.
- She leapt from the vehicle, her M-16 ready.
- As the building was quickly surrounded, a group led by Lt. Zayicek was the first inside, with Luella leading a group in right behind her.
- At each door, Lt. Zayicek knocked, producing a search warrant from the newly constituted Panamanian courts, then instructed Luella's team to fan quickly through the apartment from room to room with weapons highly visible.
- The Panamanian policemen watched in awe.
- Little was found until the fifth apartment search, where a soldier discovered a padlocked satchel from which, when slit open, tumbled out wads of U.S. bills.
- The three women occupying the apartment vehemently denied knowledge of the money as they were frisked and cuffed by Luella, who had little patience for their denials.
- She had even less patience with a soldier who began using the barrel of his gun to encourage one of the women to talk.

- "We're pros!" she barked, and the interrogation ended.
- She knew the prisoners would talk in good time.
- For the time being, it was her job to secure the money and wait for the women to be driven to the police station.
- Within weeks, she and her unit shifted from fighting to peacekeeping.
- Through a cash-for-weapons program, the U.S. paid out $60,000 for 75,000 guns collected by the police; one Panamanian received $5,000 for driving an armored personnel carrier up to the doorstep of the U.S. troops.

## Life in the Community: Washington, DC and Panama
- Critics in Washington are condemning the invasion of Panama as a "throwback to the era of gunboat diplomacy."
- Others are saying it was simply a contrived, glorious moment in the "war against drugs" for a commander-in-chief who is still suspected of being wimpish.
- The United Nations did not approve the invasion, considering it an illegal, unilateral use of force.
- Approximately 23 American and 300 Panamanian soldiers died in the assault.
- Editorial writers generally agree with President Bush that the invasion of Panama was necessary as a crusade for a democratic and drug-free hemisphere.
- The president of the Panamanian Chamber of Commerce calculates that losses from looting and damage caused by the military invasion will top $1 billion.
- Millions more, it is believed, will be needed to refurbish streets, waterworks, public buildings and other facilities long neglected by a government more obsessed with power than governance.
- To help out in the crisis, the United States has asked Japan, which extensively uses the Panama Canal, to provide aid.

## HISTORICAL SNAPSHOT
# 1989

- The longest peacetime period of economic expansion reached its eighty-fifth month in December; per-capita income was up 19 percent since 1982
- Congress passed a $166 billion legislation to bail out the savings and loan industry
- Cocaine and crack cocaine use was up 35 percent over 1985
- Sony purchased Columbia Pictures, sparking comments of Japan invading Hollywood
- Demonstrators at Tiananmen Square carried a Styrofoam Statue of Liberty as part of the protest against the Chinese government
- A private U.S. satellite, comedy cable TV, pregaphone to talk to the fetus and a girl in the Little League World Series drew national attention
- The movie *Batman* grossed $250 million, the fifth-highest-grossing film in movie history
- *Field of Dreams, When Harry Met Sally, Glory, Driving Miss Daisy, sex, lies and videotape* and *Roger and Me* premiered at movie theaters
- Baseball Commissioner Bart Giamatti banned ballplayer Pete Rose for life from the sport for allegedly betting on games
- *The Joy Luck Club* by Amy Tan, *The Satanic Verses* by Salman Rushdie, *The Temple of My Familiar* by Alice Walker, *The Oldest Living Confederate Widow Tells All* by Allan Gurganus and *A Brief History of Time* by Stephen Hawking were bestsellers
- In Chicago, U.S. veterans protested at the Art Institute where the American flag was draped on the floor
- "Wind Beneath My Wings" by Bette Midler won a Grammy Award for best song
- Americans watched live news coverage of the Chinese and Eastern European revolutions and the San Francisco earthquake
- Across America, 57 percent of households had cable TV, and 66 percent owned a VCR
- A piece of the fallen Berlin Wall could be purchased at Bloomingdale's for $12.50
- Van Cliburn made a successful comeback after 11 years, playing the Liszt and Tchaikovsky piano concertos in Philadelphia and Dallas
- Physicists agreed on three basic types of matter: up and down; charmed and strange; and top and bottom quarks
- AZT was shown to delay the onset of AIDS

## Selected Prices

| | |
|---|---|
| Azalea, Six-inch Pot | $3.99 |
| Beer, Michelob, Case | $9.95 |
| Car Phone | $995.00 |
| Cereal, Kellogg's Corn Flakes | $1.59 |
| Compact Disc | $11.99 |
| Compact Disc Player | $229.95 |
| Computer, Apple IIGS | $795.00 |
| Glue Gun | $24.99 |
| Gun Kit | $19.99 |
| Light Bulb | $4.00 |
| Microwave, Kenmore | $199.99 |
| Panty Hose, Three Pairs | $8.07 |
| Silk Azalea | $24.99 |
| Soft Drink, Coke, Two-Liter | $1.00 |
| Synthesizer, Yamaha | $188.88 |

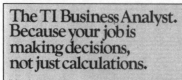

## "Instances of Use of United States Force Abroad, 1980s," Ellen C. Collier, Specialist in U.S. Foreign Policy, Foreign Affairs and National Defense Division:

1980: Iran—On April 26, President Jimmy Carter reported the use of six U.S. transport planes and eight helicopters in an unsuccessful attempt to rescue American hostages being held in Iran.

1981: El Salvador—After a guerilla offensive against the government of El Salvador, additional U.S. military advisors were sent to El Salvador, bringing the total to 55, to assist in training government forces in counter-insurgency.

1981: Libya—On August 19, U.S. planes based on the carrier *Nimitz* shot down two Libyan jets over the Gulf of Sidra after one of the jets had fired a heat-seeking missile.

1982: Sinai—On March 19, President Reagan reported the deployment of military personnel and equipment to participate in the Multinational Force and Observers in the Sinai.

1982: Lebanon—On August 21, President Reagan reported the dispatch of 80 Marines to serve in the Multinational Force to assist in the withdrawal of members of the Palestine Liberation force from Beirut.

1982: Lebanon—On September 29, President Reagan reported the deployment of 1,200 Marines to serve in a temporary multinational force to facilitate the restoration of Lebanese government sovereignty.

1983: Egypt—After a Libyan plane bombed a city in Sudan on March 18 and Sudan and Egypt appealed for assistance, the United States dispatched an AWACS electronic surveillance plane to Egypt.

1983-89: Honduras—In July 1983, the United States undertook a series of exercises in Honduras that some believed might lead to conflict with Nicaragua. On March 25, 1986, unarmed U.S. military helicopters and crewmen ferried Hon-duran troops to the Nicaraguan border to repel Nicaraguan troops.

1983: Chad—On August 8, President Reagan reported the deployment of two AWACS electronic surveillance planes, eight F-15 fighter planes, and ground logistical support forces to assist Chad against Libyan and rebel forces.

1983: Grenada—On October 25, President Reagan reported a landing on Grenada by Marines and army airborne troops to protect lives and assist in the restoration of law and order, at the request of five members of the Organization of Eastern Caribbean States.

1984: Persian Gulf—On June 25, Saudi Arabian jet fighter planes, aided by intelligence from a U.S. AWACS electronic surveillance aircraft and fueled by a U.S. KC-10 tanker, downed two Iranian fighter planes over an area of the Persian Gulf proclaimed as a protected zone for shipping.

1985: Italy—On October 10, U.S. Navy pilots intercepted an Egyptian airliner and forced it to land in Sicily. The airliner was carrying the hijackers of the Italian cruise ship *Achille Lauro* who had killed an American citizen during the hijacking.

1986: Libya—On March 26, President Reagan reported to Congress that on March 24 and 25, U.S. forces, while engaged in freedom of naviga-

## "Instances of Use of United States . . ." *(continued)*

tion exercises around the Gulf of Sidra, had been attacked by Libyan missiles and had responded with missiles.

1986: Libya—On April 16, President Reagan reported that U.S. air and naval forces had conducted bombing strikes on terrorist facilities and military installations in Libya.

1986: Bolivia—U.S. Army personnel and aircraft assisted Bolivia in anti-drug operations.

1987-88: Persian Gulf—After the Iran-Iraq War resulted in several military incidents in the Persian Gulf, the United States increased U.S. Navy forces operating in the Persian Gulf and adopted a policy of reflagging and escorting Kuwaiti oil tankers through the Gulf. President Reagan reported U.S. ships had been fired upon, struck mines, or taken other military action on September 23, October 10, and October 20, 1987, and April 19, July 4, and July 14, 1988.

1988: Panama—In mid-March and April 1988, during a period of instability and as pressure grew for Panamanian military leader General Manuel Noriega to resign, the United States sent 1,000 troops to Panama, to "further safeguard the canal, U.S. lives, property and interests in the area." The forces supplemented 10,000 U.S. military personnel already in Panama.

1989: Libya—On January 4, two U.S. Navy F-14 aircraft based on the *USS John F. Kennedy* shot down two Libyan jet fighters over the Mediterranean Sea about 70 miles north of Libya. The U.S. pilots said the Libyan planes had demonstrated hostile intentions.

1989: Panama—On May 11, in response to General Noriega's disregard of the Panamanian election, President Bush ordered a brigade-sized force of approximately 1,900 troops to augment the estimated 11,000 U.S. troops already in the area.

1989: Andean Initiative in War on Drugs—On September 15, President George Bush announced that military and law enforcement assistance would be sent to help the Andean nations of Colombia, Bolivia, and Peru combat illicit drug

producers and traffickers. By mid-September there were 50-100 U.S. military advisors in Colombia in connection with transport and training in the use of military equipment, plus seven Special Forces teams of two to 12 persons to train troops in the three countries.

1989: Philippines—On December 2, President Bush reported that on December 1, U.S. fighter planes from Clark Air Base in the Philippines had assisted the Aquino Government to repel a coup attempt. In addition, 100 Marines were sent from the U.S. Navy base at Subic Bay to protect the U.S. Embassy in Manila.

1989: Panama—On December 21, President Bush reported that he had ordered U.S. military forces to Panama to protect the lives of American citizens and bring General Noriega to justice. By February 13, 1990, all the invasion forces had been withdrawn.

## "Fire When Ready, Ma'am: The Invasion Reopens the Debate on Women in Combat," *Time*, January 15, 1990:

A dog kennel seemed an odd venue for a watershed event in U.S. military history. But when members of the 988th Military Police Company from Fort Benning, Georgia, engaged Panamanian soldiers in a firefight at an attack-dog compound near Panama City, the American platoon was commanded by a woman: Captain Linda L. Bray, 29, of Butner, North Carolina. Bray, one of 771 army women who took part in the Panama operation, had added a page to the annals of American warfare: For the first time, women, who compose almost 11 percent of the U.S. armed forces, had engaged hostile troops in modern combat. Though doubts arose over whether Bray's platoon had actually killed any enemy soldiers, her exploits rekindled a debate over whether women should be on the firing line.

American women are excluded by law and regulation from assignment to units, such as infantry, armor and artillery, that are likely to be engaged in combat. But Panama demonstrated how such distinctions blur when the shooting starts. Colorado Congresswoman Patricia Schroeder argued last week that "once you no longer have a definable front, it's impossible to separate combat from noncombat. The women carried M-16s, not dog biscuits."

Although military police like Bray are considered support troops, their duties can be hazardous. Women are among Marines guarding U.S. embassies abroad, and the Air Force employs female test pilots. Yet promotion often hinges on command experience in aircraft, fighting ships or tanks—and women's careers are circumscribed without it.

Brian Mitchell, author of *Weak Link: The Feminization of the American Military*, argues that the use of female troops in Panama proved nothing. "The sorts of things they were doing could be done by a 12-year-old with a rifle," he says. He and other critics contend that women are not capable of performing critical battlefield functions: Women Marines, for example, are not allowed to throw live grenades because the corps does not believe they can toss them far enough to avoid injury. But recent army studies indicate that women's physical strength develops rapidly during training, and as Meredith Neizer, head of a Defense Department advisory committee, notes, intelligence and technical skills are also important to a soldier: "Modern war is fought in a variety of arenas, and the slight physical differences don't have to play a role."

A greater barrier to a combat role for women is public sensitivity to possible female casualties. Yet the military knows the combat exclusion is artificial protection. "The critical point," army spokeswoman Paige Eversole said last week, "is that these women were trained for whatever contingency they encountered. They could and did fire their weapons where necessary. In war," she added, "we expect women to be casualties in direct proportion to the numbers in which they serve.

## "Gun-Barrel Democracy," *The Nation*, January 8, 1990:

When a superpower allows its satellites to arrange their own affairs, the results can be astounding: Four Eastern European regimes have been swept away, almost without bloodshed. But Moscow's renunciation of empire inspires no similar feelings in Washington. On the contrary, George Bush has taken it as carte blanche to run amok in the U.S. backyard, where in the 1980s the death toll climbed to six figures—a carnage now swelled by unnumbered Panamanians. Even heads of state are considered fair game.

A new Panamanian president has been duly sworn in, flanked by an army of occupation. In

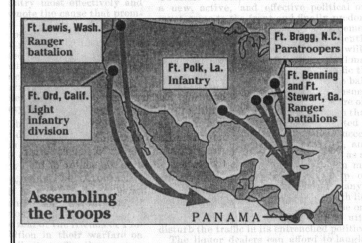

**Assembling the Troops**

Ft. Lewis, Wash. Ranger battalion

Ft. Ord, Calif. Light infantry division

Ft. Polk, La. Infantry

Ft. Bragg, N.C. Paratroopers

Ft. Benning and Ft. Stewart, Ga. Ranger battalions

PANAMA

this, he greatly resembles the country's first rulers, who were installed in 1903 as U.S. Army officers and ran up Panama's first flag while gunboats waited offshore. All, then as now, in the name of democracy—as if democracy could be shot from the barrel of a gun. The United States has trashed that honorable word as thoroughly as the German "Democratic" Republic did. Bush toasted Ferdinand Marcos for his love of democracy; Salvadoran Nazis are applauded for defending it; the assassins of Beijing are praised for moving in a democratic direction.

The United States is a country in search of enemies, and the Panama invasion is a major step toward cementing in place a new external demon—the narcotraficante—to supplant the outmoded menace of Communism. While it strips away any illusion of Bush as a foreign policy moderate, the invasion also conveniently diverts attention from his vertiginous loss of control in El Salvador and the wreckage of the "war on drugs"—his only real domestic program. And it engineers a national consensus for a facile morality play about good guys and bad guys. For Latin Americans, meanwhile, there are still only three words of English worth learning: Yankee Go Home.

## "Panama Cocked Hat," *The New Republic*, January 8-15, 1990:

*Manuel Noriega*

The American military intervention in Panama is only a few hours old as this issue of TNR goes to press, but it is already clear that it will succeed in one of its stated objectives: overthrowing the narcocratic military dictatorship of Manuel Antonio Noriega and replacing it in power with Guillermo Endara, the legitimately elected opposition leader whose 2-to-1 victory in last May's Panamanian presidential election was viciously overturned by Noriega. Whether Noriega himself will be apprehended remains to be seen. But his status is now appropriate to his character: He is no longer a "maximum leader" who is also a thug. He is simply a thug, a fugitive from justice.

The Panamanian people will not be unhappy to see the back of him. Neither will the United States' Latin American friends, whatever ritual objections they feel obliged to lodge. And the Bush Administration is likely to win broad support for this action among the American people and in both parties in Congress. Noriega was a narcotics trafficker, a murderer (he had killed more than 100 members of his own military in the weeks since the failed coup of October 3), and a strangler of democracy. And it was General Noriega, not President Bush, who had declared a "state of war."

Bush came under severe criticism, in these quarters and others, when he failed to act decisively in connection with the October 3 coup. An opportunity was lost to remove Noriega with minimal loss of life. This time the cost is going to be much higher. Noriega deserves his misfortune, but the American soldiers and Panamanian civilians who have been killed or wounded, and any American hostages seized by Noriega's grotesquely named "dignity battalions," did not deserve theirs. Still, the situation in Panama was deteriorating, and there had been incidents of violence against American personnel. The United States acted later than it should have, and at a less opportune moment. But there is a powerful case that further delay would have raised the ultimate costs even higher.

In a sense, it was our duty to overthrow Noriega: He was in many ways our creation. The United States trained and maintained the Panamanian Defense Force for years as an ally. Our Drug Enforcement Administration and CIA had specific connections with Noriega himself; he handed over small-time drug peddlers to us, and supported the *contra* cause in Nicaragua.

Cynics will say that when American policy changed, Noriega became dispensable. But the change in American policy has been for the better. Noriega was just the sort of strutting, bemedaled authoritarian the United States used to support routinely, in the name of anti-communism. Now we back elected governments, and Noriega appropriately went into alliance with the two other antidemocratic leaders of the region, Daniel Ortega of Nicaragua and Fidel Castro of Cuba.

It's not enough, though, for the United States to install a democratic regime that may be subject to continuing pressure by the military and certainly will be forced to cope with economic woes caused by U.S. sanctions against the Noriega regime. Panama does not need a "Panamanian Defense Force." Starting with Panama, it's time we began using our influence to get the officer corps of Latin America out of politics and to dismantle themselves, on the model of Costa Rica. And it's appropriate that we find the money to help repair the Panamanian economy. In ousting Noriega, we've only begun to clean up the mess we've made in Panama.

## *Newsweek*, January 1, 1990:

On the second day of the U.S. invasion of Panama, George Bush announced: "This operation is not over, but it's pretty well wrapped up." It wasn't. At noon on the third day, mortar shells began to land near Quarry Heights, the headquarters of U.S. forces in Panama, as a police station was attached by troops stubbornly loyal to the fugitive dictator, Gen. Manuel Antonio Noriega. A press briefing was about to begin when the mortars started up, followed by heavy automatic-weapons fire. Journalists and military officers alike dove to the floor. No one was hurt, but as Gen. Maxwell Thurman, chief of the U.S. Southern Command, said later, "There's a significant amount of . . . armed terroristic activity going on."

That was an understatement. Gunmen known as dignity battalions—Noriega's paramilitary forces—roved freely through Panama City from their working-class neighborhoods. They engaged the invaders, hit and run. Their strength proved "greater than expected," Thurman said. Sniper fire spooked American soldiers. Bands of baton-wielding

youths brought the capital to the brink of anarchy, smashing the windows of shops and cars, looting as they went. By the end of the week, there were shortages of food and water, and medical supplies. Meanwhile, some elements of the regular Panama Defense Forces (PDF) fought on for Noriega, in civilian clothes. And behind the sporadic but lethal resistance, Noriega still seemed to be calling the shots. At least part of the resistance, said Thurman, was "centrally controlled."

It was also unexpected. America's Operation Just Cause was supposed to sweep all before it. Massive and quick. "Just Cause" was the largest U.S. military airlift since Vietnam. It included a nighttime parachute jump by more than 3,000 men, the biggest combat drop since World War II. The main military objective was to take the stick out of Noriega's hand by destroying the PDF. The immediate political aim was to install a civilian government under Guillermo Endara, who apparently won a free election last May, only to have it stolen by Noriega. At first, the Americans made rapid progress.

"I have political power," Endara declared after swearing himself in at a U.S. base in Panama as the invasion began. American casualties were relatively modest: 21 servicemen killed in the first three days and

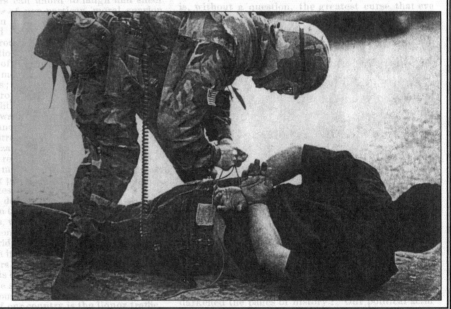

about 200 wounded. Some American civilians were taken hostage by unknown but presumably pro-Noriega forces, and at the end of the week a few were still thought to be captive. Although Bush agonized over the human cost, he had to conclude that "yes, it was worth it." At least for now, public opinion was solidly behind him. In a *Newsweek* poll, 80 percent of the people questioned said the attack on Panama was justified.

What about Noriega? U.S. commandos tried to snatch him just before H-hour. The idea was to bring him to justice in the United States, where he had been indicted for running drugs and laundering the profits. After fumbling its support for an anti-

Noriega coup last October, the administration was determined to get him this time. But Noriega escaped and dropped out of sight, a pimply-faced Pimpernel who for the moment confounded his pursuers. "He's a crafty devil, as you know," Lt. Gen. Thomas Kelly, a top Pentagon planner, said at a briefing last Wednesday. "We thought we had a pretty good idea where he was last night. We went there, and he wasn't there." Instead, Noriega's voice was heard on the government radio station, which the Americans had neglected to seize at the outset. "Our slogan is to win or die," Noriega bragged. "Not one step back." Bush was reduced to putting a million-dollar bounty on the dictator's head.

# 1990–1999

The 1990s opened in an economic recession, a ballooning national debt, and the collapse of much of the Savings and Loan industry. The automobile industry produced record losses, while housing values plummeted and factory orders fell.

Military operations involving American troops included Operation Desert Storm in response to Iraqi President Saddam Hussein's invasion of Kuwait. President George W. Bush ordered American forces to join in a coalition against Iraq that comprised Britain, France, Egypt, Saudia Arabia, Syria and several other nations. The operation took only weeks to accomplish its aim of removing Iraqi troops from Kuwait, with estimates of Iraqi military deaths ranging from 8,000 to 100,000, while the allies lost about 300 troops. Four years later, in 1995, President Bill Clinton, in concert with NATO, organized Operation Deliberate Force in Bosnia, where the Bosnian Serb army was brutalizing Muslims in an "ethnic cleansing" campaign.

By the late 1990s, the decade was being referred to by *Fortune* magazine as the "Era of Possibilities," characterized by economic expansion, low inflation, high employment and dramatic gains in technology-based products, fueled by the emerging Internet. Most of the military campaigns during the period had been successful, and the last bastion of gender segregation—the all-male military college The Citadel—finally admitted its first female cadet.

# 1990 Profile

# The Fall of Communism in Romania

## Foreign Service Officer

Grover Walton "Binky" Haddon's job in the Foreign Service provided a front-row seat during the dramatic fall of communism in Romania.

## Life at Home

- Grover Walton Haddon has been known as "Binky" since his childhood in Bennington, Vermont, where his ancestors had lived since before Vermont was even a state.
- He attended St. Paul's College at Williams, where all the Haddon men have gone, and obtained his graduate degree at the School for Advanced International Studies of Johns Hopkins University in Washington, DC.
- There, he concentrated on studying communism and Eastern Europe.
- After joining the Foreign Service, Binky was assigned as a political officer in Bucharest, Romania, where he was responsible for tracking and reporting on the communist-controlled Romanian Government.
- Although much of his work, including report writing, was often mundane, the opportunity to observe a working communist regime was fascinating.
- Romania was particularly interesting; although a member of the Warsaw Pact, Romania had gone its own way on numerous issues.
- For 24 years, the country had been under the dictatorial control of Nicolae Ceausescu and his wife Elena.
- At first, Ceausescu was supported in the west for diverging from Moscow in domestic and foreign affairs.
- He helped Richard Nixon plan his initial visit to China in 1972, and visited Jimmy Carter in Washington.
- In 1968, he refused to join the Soviet invasion of Czechoslovakia, and prohibited Soviet troops from entering Romania.
- But Ceausescu's Romania also had its brutal, dark side that included indiscriminate killings, imprisonment and laws against many freedoms that Westerners enjoyed.

*Binky Haddon was a witness to the fall of communism in Romania.*

- To pay the national debt and decrease dependence on the Soviet Union, most Romanian products, including food, were exported, leaving the population without enough to eat.
- At the same time, contraception and abortions were forbidden, causing the population to rise rapidly.
- The government employed more than 40 members of Ceausescu's family.
- The regime held on to power, thanks to the Securitate, or secret police, known for their fanatical loyalty and brutality.
- Yet rumors abounded that communism was on its last legs.
- Binky loved having a front-row seat; unlike his friends still teaching at U.S. universities, he was witnessing history being made.
- In 1989, communism in Europe was clearly beginning to crumble, especially in Eastern Europe.
- Binky was fascinated and mystified that Romania appeared to be resisting the movement, although he did file more than one insightful report indicating a growing public opposition to Ceausescu and his ability to resist the trend.
- Then, in December 1989, the direction of Romania changed.

*At first, Nicolae Ceausescu was supported by the west.*

## Life at Work

- The political sea change that Binky Haddon had been anticipating for years began on December 17, 1989, when Nicolae Ceausescu's hated Securitate fired on peaceful demonstrators in Timisoara.
- After 24 years of repression under Ceausescu, the protestors fought back, setting off a backlash of violence.
- Eventually, up to 4,000 would die, including soldiers who were summarily executed by Securitate men for refusing to fire on the demonstrators.
- Upon Ceausescu's return from a visit to Iran four days later, his attempts to address a huge, restive crowd from his balcony were unsuccessful as he was shouted down.
- That evening, as the crowd grew almost spontaneously, the Securitate attempted to maintain control and fired at the protestors, killing dozens.
- By the next day, a revolution had begun in earnest.
- Ceausescu's second attempt to address the crowd was met with an uglier response when the army aligned itself with the demonstrators.
- Binky filed reports hourly.
- Ceausescu and his wife escaped by helicopter after giving orders for the Securitate to fire at will at the citizens of Romania.

*By 1989, Communism was crumbling in Europe.*

- Within hours, a group calling itself the "National Salvation Front" declared itself in charge of the country and called for free elections.
- Units of the Securitate roamed the streets, killing indiscriminately.
- At the American Embassy, Binky was desperate to learn everything he could.
- Communism, the great enemy of the west and the motivating force behind American foreign policy for his entire lifetime, was collapsing before his eyes.
- The streets of Bucharest were crowded with people chanting slogans, while some simply sang Christmas carols, an activity banned for two decades.
- Some just wandered the streets in wonder, unable to fully comprehend the revolution taking place.
- While standing in a square in Bucharest, Binky watched a band of young people waving the Romanian flag with the communist symbol cut from its center.
- All was festive until the first shots were fired.
- Immediately, the square emptied, except for a frantic young girl about 10 years old, crying for her mother.
- As Binky watched, a rifle's crack filled the air and the little girl fell, blood blossoming from her stomach.
- With no consideration for his own safety, Binky rushed to the girl's side as others, including the girl's mother, joined him.
- Just as spontaneously, a phalanx of enraged citizens descended upon the Securitate sniper.
- Several demonstrators were shot at, but the crowd was relentless.
- They dragged the sniper from his hiding place and into the square, where they beat him.
- As Binky attempted to stop the girl's bleeding, he was only vaguely aware of the sniper's screams.
- The smell of gasoline pulled him from his work and back to the square; the crowd had set the sniper ablaze.
- Determined to report accurately the events of the day, Binky returned to the embassy, where hundreds of Americans were seeking protection from the violence.
- Russian Premier Mikhail Gorbachev sent medical aid from the Soviet Union to Romania and promised direct Soviet intervention on the side of the revolutionaries.
- On Christmas Day, it was announced that Ceausescu and his wife had been captured.
- Word circulated of a trial.
- Ceausescu was accused of the genocide of 60,000 Romanians and stealing millions in state money.
- Binky went to the hospital to find the little girl.
- In a chaotic ward filled with people of all ages, Binky discovered her with a drainage tube extending from her stomach.
- Her mother rested in a chair nearby while a jolly St. Nicholas doll observed from the little girl's pillow.
- The girl, whose name is Lulia, was doing well; her mother remembered Binky from the shooting in the square and thanked him.

*Within hours of Ceausescu's departure, the National Salvation Front declared itself in charge.*

*All was festive in the square until the first shots rang out.*

- When Binky gave Lulia two wrapped packages, she looked at him shyly, unsure of what she was allowed to do.
- When her mother nodded approval, Lulia ripped into the boxes.
- The first was a box of chocolates—a forbidden pleasure in communist Romania; the second was a jigsaw puzzle of the Manhattan skyline.
- Many patients watched silently as the awkward American and the shy Romanian talked.
- As Binky left, a Christmas carol began softly in one end of the ward and was soon taken up by the entire room.
- The next day, television broadcasts repeatedly showed a videotape of the corpses of Nicolae and Elena Ceausescu: Following a televised trial, justice had been swift in the new Romania.
- The National Salvation Front soon announced sweeping constitutional changes and set national democratic elections for April.
- At first, Binky was ecstatic, even as he worked 18-hour days to process information back to the United States.
- New Year's Day, 1990, passed almost without notice as Binky struggled to discern order from the chaos.
- Quickly, he became alarmed and saddened that the Front was largely dominated by former communists.
- By the time Binky visited Lulia in the hospital again, the puzzle was complete, the picture dominated by two tall buildings the child had never seen before.
- Her recovery was going well—the revolution, less so.
- Thousands of orphans and abandoned children, many with AIDS, filled the streets.

- Rural poverty—including malnutrition—was extensive.
- Regional conflicts concerning Hungarians in Transylvania threatened to explode.
- Binky knew from history what the transition would take; no nation knows how to govern itself the first day.
- At the close of one particularly difficult day, a package arrived.
- Inside, he found a note from Lulia's mother reading, "God Bless"; inside the box were two apples, a bottle of cold coffee, some homemade cakes and a slab of cheese.
- "God Bless, indeed," Binky reflected.

## Life in the Community: Romania

- Romanian President Nicolae Ceausescu's efforts at control were thorough.
- In addition to complete control of all newspapers, radio and television, the police kept samples from every typewriter in order to identify anonymous letters and manuscripts.

*After being shot, Lulia was taken to the hospital; throughout Romania, people celebrated a country free to sing Christmas carols again.*

- At the time of his death, plans were under way to tap every phone in the country.
- Citizens were required to report all contact with foreigners; it has been estimated that one in three Romanians informed on neighbors.
- Those who dared to criticize the government quickly found themselves under surveillance, house arrest or incarcerated.
- Some imprisoned dissidents were bombarded with radiation in hopes they would die of cancer before their release.
- Creativity in art was discouraged; ancient churches in Bucharest's historic center were dynamited to make room for monuments honoring socialism.
- Romania's two million Hungarians were prohibited from speaking their own language, and no books could mention that Transylvania belonged to Hungary before it was made part of Romania in 1921.
- Germans and Jews were sold to West Germany and Israel for hard currency; Israel paid $5,000 to $7,000 per person to free them from Romania.
- Because of its foreign policy, especially toward the Soviet Union, the United States maintained cordial relations with Romania, which enjoyed most-favored-nation status until 1987.

## HISTORICAL SNAPSHOT
# 1990

- The Food and Drug Administration approved the first low-calorie fat substitute
- The gross national product fell after eight years of growth, while housing values plummeted and consumer confidence shrank
- The Hubble space telescope was launched into orbit
- First appearances included a McDonald's in Moscow; the Infiniti, Saturn, and Lexus; gender-specific disposable diapers; Caller ID systems; and the contraceptive implant Norplant
- Census data showed that 25 percent of the population were members of a minority group; Asians and Pacific Islanders were the fastest-growing minorities
- Dieting became a $33 billion industry
- A complete edition of John J. Audubon's book, *Birds of America,* sold for $3.96 million at auction
- Television premieres included *The Simpsons, Law and Order, Twin Peaks* and *Seinfeld*
- Women constituted 11 percent of U.S. troops, up from three percent in 1973
- An EPA report claimed that 3,800 people died annually from second-hand smoke
- The 11-hour-long documentary *The Civil War* by Ken Burns was released on public television
- The timber industry of the Pacific Northwest was outraged when the northwest spotted owl was declared an endangered species
- *Dances with Wolves* was named the Academy Awards' best picture; *Pretty Woman, Total Recall, Goodfellas* and *Home Alone* were also released
- The Dow-Jones Industrial Average hit a high of 2,999.75, a low of 2,365; inflation was at 5.4 percent and unemployment at 6.1 percent
- Both President Bush and Premier Gorbachev called for Iraqi withdrawal following its invasion of Kuwait

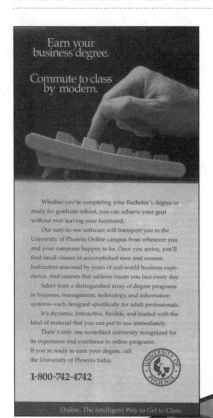
## Selected Prices

Christmas Tree, Seven-Foot Artificial...........$124.99
Coffee Maker................................................$7.99
Crackers, Ritz..............................................$1.69
Duct Tape....................................................$2.99
Easy Chair, La-Z-Boy.................................$599.00
Eggs, Dozen.................................................$0.89
Exercise Equipment, Nordic Track.............$399.95
Hibachi Grill............................................... $6.99
High School Class Ring................................$69.95
Pager Service, Motorola, per Month...........$7.95
Pistol, Smith & Wesson .38 Caliber.............$309.00
Sheet Set.....................................................$17.96
Television, Zenith 25-Inch..........................$388.00
Tennis Shoes, Nike Air................................$58.99
Vodka, Absolut...........................................$12.29

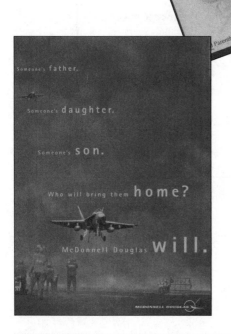

## *"Moments of Revolution," Eastern Europe,*
## *Mort Rosenblum, 1990:*

Czechoslovaks jingled their keys in the air, and 41 years of Communist Party totalitarianism fell away before their eyes. East Germans awoke one morning to find their hated wall had crumbled beneath its own weight. Romanians fought a bitter war against terror in their streets, but it was over in a week. From the Baltic to the Balkans, in a matter of months, the earth shifted. The words "freedom" and "democracy" were repeated again and again. But this was not about words.

Zdenek Machon was among a quarter-million Czechoslovaks who, on a December Sunday too cold for standing still, came back one more time to Wenceslas Square. He stood in a vast sea of arms outstretched in victory. Like the others, he made a triumphant V with his fingers. But he could not quite manage the national anthem. His voice cracked and boiled over from the heat of revolution.

"I can look people directly in the eye now, people from other countries," he told an American reporter, who was nearly as overcome as Machon. "We are a free people again. We are part of Europe again."

"Everywhere in the world, people were surprised how these malleable, humiliated, cynical citizens of Czechoslovakia, who seemingly believed in nothing, found the tremendous strength within a few weeks to cast off the totalitarian system, in an entirely peaceful and dignified manner."
—Czech playwright Vaclav Havel, New Year's Day, 1990

## "Ciao, Ceausescu," *The New Republic*, January 22, 1990:

Of all the extraordinary images that flashed out of Romania during the final days of the decade, two linger in the mind's eye. The first is Nicolae Ceausescu's final speech in front of the presidential palace in Bucharest. As the crowd's compulsory ovation turns, incredibly, to jeers, a decade-long accumulation of anger pops like a blown gasket, and Dracula's pep rally becomes a revolution. Equally unforgettable is the companion piece: Ceausescu's disheveled corpse sprawled in the dirt, next to a bullet-pocked concrete wall. The two pictures are united by the face of the dictator, frozen first in shock and then in death.

With resistance to the Securitate broken, the novelistic details of its reign of terror are finally making themselves known. Secret tunnels undergirded Bucharest, holding huge caches of food and weapons meant to enable the survivalists of socialism to hold out for months or years. Some may still be hiding, deep underground. Those captured are described as glassy-eyed robots with preternatural strength. The day after the revolution broke out, a rumor circulated that Securitate desperados were threatening to explode a nuclear device. Another made the rounds a few days later

### "Ciao, Ceausescu . . ." *(continued)*

that they had poisoned Timisoara's water supply. That these fables were widely believed testified to the ruthless sadism of Ceausescu's gangster élite.

There has been much exaggeration in the international press, both about the number of people killed by Ceausescu and about the lavishness of the life he and his wife led. It is easier to conceive of despots as mass murderers who kill for pleasure, or as sybarites who feast on caviar while the masses toil and starve. But although Ceausescu was responsible for many deaths, perhaps many thousands of deaths, and though he surrounded himself with extravagant kitsch, mass murder and luxury were not the hallmarks of his brand of despotism. He developed a personal totalitarianism that was characterized by excessive vanity, cultural vandalism, and a mad fantasy of complete control.

## "Wild in the Streets," John Borrell, *Time*, June 25, 1990:

Ever since taking over from deposed dictator Nicolae Ceausescu last winter, Romanian leader Ion Iliescu has played down his communist background and promised his countrymen a new democratic era. But actions speak louder than words. By setting club-wielding miners loose in Bucharest last week to crush antigovernment protests, Iliescu demonstrated that he was quite willing to rule by thuggery.

The Romanian leader's performance as a party boss was a brutal reminder that while the countries of Central Europe have removed communists from positions of any real power, the Balkans remain dominated by an old order dressed up in new suits. That fact was reinforced last week when the Bulgarian Socialist Party, formerly the Community Party, emerged victorious in the first free elections since 1931.

Iliescu's National Salvation Front also prevailed in elections last month, collecting an astonishing 85 percent of the vote. But even the magnitude of the win did not silence a minority that believes last December's revolution was hijacked by onetime communists. Every day hundreds of protesters gathered in Bucharest's University Square, occasionally chanting, "The final solution is another revolution!"

The government tolerated the occupation for nearly two months, but last week it lost first its patience and then much of its credibility. Just before dawn on Wednesday, more than 1,000 riot police poured into the square, setting fire to the tents of hunger strikers and beating 100 dissidents. Within hours, thousands of protestors armed with clubs and petrol bombs were battling police throughout the city. As black smoke rose over Bucharest, Iliescu appeared on television to appeal for support against "a fascist rebellion."

The next day thousands of miners, brought to the capital from towns as far as 250 miles away, took control of the city. Wielding clubs and steel pipes, they set up roadblocks and demanded identity documents, savagely beating anyone suspected of opposing the government. By the time calm returned, at least four people had been killed and hundreds wounded.

## "Watching the Babies Die: Romanian AIDS Scandal," Eloise Salholz with Theresa Waldrop in Bucharest and Ruth Marshall in Paris, *Newsweek,* February 19, 1990:

At the Victor Babes Hospital in Bucharest, 15-month-old Nicoletta Buia lies in a too-small cot, eyes blank, hands swathed in bandages, her face covered with herpes sores. In the next bed, an 18-month-old slowly rocks his head back and forth, back and forth, keeping time to a dirge only he can hear. The room itself is eerily silent: Its 15 inmates are too weak to cry. It reeks of dirty diapers and alcohol, but worst of all is the stench of death. There are five such rooms at Babes, some with as many as four little patients to a bed, a total of 70 children. All are dying of AIDS.

With the revelation last week of a pediatric AIDS epidemic in Romania, dictator Nicolae Ceausescu seemed to slip another rung in hell. Before the December revolution that led to his execution, AIDS did not officially exist in Romania—Ceausescu insisted only "decadent" countries were at risk. Now, the awful truth has begun to emerge: Because of antiquated medical procedures performed on newborns and inadequate medical supplies, AIDS has cut a deadly swath through Romania's pediatric wards and overcrowded orphanages. So far, out of 2,084 children in Bucharest and the port city of Constantsa, 706 tested positive for HIV, the virus that causes AIDS. Experts expect those numbers to increase dramatically. "Manifestly, this is an epidemic transmitted through medical acts," says Dr. Jacques Lebas, president of Doctors of the World, a French humanitarian organization assisting the Romanians. "That hurts, especially."

### "Romania Unchained: A New Coalition Government Confronted Demands for Even More Liberty," *Maclean's,* January 8, 1990:

Eyes glazed over in death, a tuft of grey hair, a puddle of blood—the picture of executed dictator Nicolae Ceausescu broadcast over Romanian TV last Tuesday marked the bloody climax to an already violent revolution. But it was a climax that had come with stunning speed. A mere week after anti-government demonstrations first broke out in the northwestern Romanian town of Timisoara, Ceausescu and his wife, Elena, fled the capital of Bucharest when army units joined the rebellion. That same day, December 22, the couple was captured and on Christmas Day went before a military tribunal that accused them of genocide and plundering more than $1 billion from the country. But during the two-hour trial, Ceausescu, the self-proclaimed Genius of the Carpathians, defiantly challenged the tribunal's authority. "I am the president of Romania," he shouted. "I will only answer to the working class." Then, with the sentence passed, he and his wife, who served as the country's deputy prime minister, were led to their deaths at the hands of a three-man firing squad.

Army officials said that about 300 soldiers had volunteered for the assignment—an indication of the deep-seated hostility towards Ceausescu unleashed by the end of his repressive 24-year regime. And after the relatively violence-free groundswell of reform that had swept through Poland, Hungary, East Germany, Czechoslovakia and Bulgaria, the Romanian uprising was a clear reminder that change is often accompanied by bloodshed. At week's end, as Romanians continued to bury the hundreds who had died, the country still faced the possibility of a drawn-out terrorist campaign by militant members of the late president's well-armed secret police force, the Securitate. And in spite of offers of aid and support from Western countries and the establishment of a provisional government that pledged an end to communist rule and free elections in April, the political future of the country remained under a cloud. But even the doubts could not dispel the joy expressed by many over the end of the Ceausescu era. Said Mihail Isaih, 40, an engineer at the Romanian national television station: "I don't think we realize yet what has happened. It is difficult to take it all in."

# 1990 NEWS FEATURE

**"The Minister Who Sparked a Revolution," Rudolph Chelminski,**
*Reader's Digest,* **1990:**

At dusk Pastor Laszlo Tokes peeped through a crack in the boards nailed over a window of his apartment in Timisoara, Romania. Outside, dozens of his parishioners stood vigil, while members of the Securitate, the dreaded security police, moved watchfully among them. Tokes, a pastor in the Hungarian Reformed Church in Timisoara, and his pregnant wife, Edit, felt an extra chill: the certainty that the madman who had sent the Securitate to their door was about to move against them.

The madman was Nicolae Ceausescu, secretary-general of the Communist Party and autocrat of the most brutally repressive regime in Eastern Europe. Ceausescu hated and feared the two million ethnic Hungarians in Romania for their independent spirit and the Christianity that bound their community. To bend the Hungarian Reformed Church to his will, Ceausescu had restricted the number of seminary students, forbade church libraries from lending books and stopped the reprinting of Bibles and hymnals.

The Reformed Church's two bishops, Gyula Nagy and Laszlo Papp—straw men appointed by the regime—took no action. Papp, a member of Parliament, is reported to have approved the arrest of ministers who raised their voices against the regime.

In 1984, the elder Tokes publicly criticized authorities of the Hungarian Reformed Church for cooperating with the government. Bishop Nagy subsequently stripped him of his church posts. Laszlo, a pastor in the small down of Dej at the time, was then suspended because he had been equally insubordinate. Two years later, Laszlo was reinstated but demoted to assistant minister and sent to Timisoara, with the warning to keep his mouth shut. Timisoara is a remote city, far from the main centers of ethnic Hungarians. The congregation of its only Hungarian Reformed Church, on the third floor of an apartment building on Cipariu Street near the Bega Canal, consisted of only a few dozen regulars.

**Sentenced to Exile.** Soon Roman Catholics, Eastern Orthodox and even nonbelievers were drawn to the new preacher with the spellbinding voice and unbending principles. Within two years, the new dozen parishioners grew to more than 2,000. Some Sundays, the crowd spilled out onto the sidewalk.

In September 1988, Tokes and a fellow minister wrote a letter to Reformed Church authorities, denouncing Ceausescu's "systematization" campaign. For six months there was no official reaction to the letter. Then, on April 1, 1989, Tokes was again suspended.

This time his suspension generated critical articles in Hungary, Western Europe and North America. Faced with this outcry, Bishop Papp reinstated Tokes but ordered him to Mineu, a remote farm hamlet reachable only over rutted wagon tracks—the perfect place to exile a man condemned to silence. Tokes refused to go. With the glare of world opinion on him, Bishop Papp could find no other recourse than a court action to evict Tokes.

**Death or a Miracle.** Soon letters of support were openly circulating within the parish. Late in May, a delegation from the congregation carried a petition to Bishop Papp, asking that their pastor stay in Timisoara. Papp refused to see them. Then, on July 24, Hungary's most popular TV news show, Panorama, aired a clandestine interview Tokes had granted a Canadian TV team. Hungarian television is received in the western half of Romania. Millions of viewers heard Tokes denounce the systematization scheme in eloquent detail.

Police squads at the entrance to his church checked the identity of parishioners. Visitors to the Tokes family were subjected to body searches and followed after they left. On October 20, the court ruled against Tokes, as expected. He responded by appealing the eviction and locking himself up in his home.

The police posted round-the-clock guards outside the church building. One day early in November, four masked thugs armed with clubs and knives burst through the locked door of Tokes's apartment. Laszlo fell to the floor under a hail of punches as his three-year-old son, Mate, stared in terror. Edit instinctively moved to shield her son and begged the police outside for help. They ignored her.

**Night Vigil.** On November 28, Tokes lost his appeal. The deadline for his departure was set at December 15. But Laszlo kept the initiative, making more people realize what kind of government they had. The Securitate didn't know how to handle this. It sent a gang armed with beer bottles to break every window in the apartment. Tokes simply boarded up the windows and sent his son away to stay with the boy's grandmother.

By Friday, December 15, an almost palpable tension gripped Timisoara. The congregation knew that Pastor Tokes would be taken away. By late afternoon, several hundred parishioners were standing vigil below the Tokes apartment. Through Friday night and all of Saturday, the parishioners kept a human chain around the church. Facing the scowling police, they read prayers and sang psalms. By 9 p.m., the crowd numbered about 5,000. Emboldened by the dark, the people let their voices ring out with words no one would have dared speak in daylight.

"Down with dictatorship!" came a shout. "Down with Ceausescu!"

Around 10 p.m., additional police squads arrived to break up the gathering. The people reacted by marching to the center of town, where they threw portraits of Ceausescu into the Bega Canal and pillaged a bookstore because it contained almost nothing but his writings. Once the crowd was dispersed from Cipariu Street, the police were free to deal with the cause of all the trouble. At 3 a.m. on Sunday, a Securitate squad battered down the apartment door, but Laszlo and Edit retreated to the church, locking that door behind them. Since the only arms he could command were symbols, Tokes used them. He donned his black cassock over his pajamas, held his Bible and waited with Edit by the altar. With a great crash, the door splintered and the Securitate set upon Tokes with a fury. Bundled into separate cars, Laszlo and Edit were driven off. Hours later they reached Mineu. Their belongings, thrown together in total disorder, arrived later.

**The Miracle.** Their little house in Mineu was surrounded by armed police with dogs and illuminated by floodlights. Every morning for three days, the Securitate spent hours grilling Tokes. He must go on television, they insisted, and admit he was in league with a foreign power. Tokes refused.

For six days and nights, hundreds of thousands of citizens demonstrated in Timisoara.

Tanks and armored personnel carriers rolled against civilians. There were many acts of heroism in those six days, and many people died. But eventually the army refused to fire on the crowds anymore.

On the morning of December 21, 1989, Ceausescu stepped to the microphones on the balcony of the Community Party building in Bucharest. The 100,000-strong crowd beneath him in Palace Square, herded in since dawn, had been given the usual instructions to cheer the words of their absolute leader. But shortly before noon, somewhere in the back of the crowd, arose the cry.

"Timisoara!"

Suddenly, the crowd was no longer obedient. "Murderer!" someone else shouted. "Assassin!" Ceausescu froze in a grotesque grimace.

Within hours, Bucharest exploded into furious, uncontrollable demonstrations. Four days later, the dictator and the second-in-command of his tyrannical regime—his wife, Elena—were tried by a special military tribunal and shot. On Tokes' sixth day in Mineu, the miracle happened: He looked out the window and saw that his jailers were gone. They had heard the news about Ceausescu and fled.

Today Pastor Tokes is Bishop Tokes—but it is still unclear where the revolution he sparked will go. "I am not a hero," he insists. "The scenario was written by God. He gave us a message, and that message was: Do not be afraid."

# 1991 PROFILE

## OPERATION DESERT STORM: KUWAIT

### Lance Corporal

Lance Corporal Raul Hernandez was just as eager to enter Operation Desert Storm as he had been to join the Marines, which offered him an escape from poverty and the chance for a better future.

### Life at Home

- Raul Hernandez discovered his future while sitting on the steps of his apartment building.
- He grew up on the rough streets of the South Bronx, where hope was just an invitation to disaster.
- Few of the men could find jobs, and drug and alcohol abuse were as rampant as violent crime; every month or so, Raul learned of someone else he knew who had been killed.
- Then, on a Saturday morning, when Raul was sitting outside, his old friend Rafael, whom Raul had not seen in years, stepped from a cab.
- Rafael had completely changed.
- He stood ramrod straight, walked with a purpose, and his Marine uniform, which was graced by three stripes on its sleeve, was spotless and crisp.
- They spoke briefly, making arrangements to meet again.
- During the next few days, they talked about Rafael's experiences, his travels, plans, and expectations for the future.
- Raul decided the Marines were his answer—and his escape.
- Because he was unaccustomed to discipline, training at Parris Island was difficult, but for the first time, he made friends with non-Hispanics.
- He began to read the newspapers and explore the greater world around him.
- By the summer of 1990, it was obvious to him and his fellow trainees that trouble was brewing in the Middle East; Iraq had invaded Kuwait without provocation.
- American troops were joining military units from countries as diverse as Great Britain, France, Bangladesh, Pakistan and Egypt, among many others.

*Once in Saudi Arabia, Raul learned one of the lessons of military life: waiting.*

- President George Bush had issued an ultimatum to Iraq's leader Saddam Hussein: Get out of Kuwait or suffer the consequences.
- Raul was excited when orders arrived in August for his entire division to ship out for Saudi Arabia.
- His girlfriend cried, and his mother said she was proud.
- Most of the officers felt Saddam would back down in the face of the overwhelming coalition of forces mounted against him.
- Once he arrived in Saudi Arabia, Raul learned another lesson of military life: waiting.
- After the initial excitement of getting settled, the days became routine.
- In a nearby warehouse, a priest held mass, which Raul attended occasionally.
- A baptized Catholic, he knew that when the shooting started he was going to need all the help he could get.
- Besides, because the base was located in Saudi Arabia, no alcohol was allowed.
- This was a hardship; Raul had grown accustomed to ending his day with a few cold beers.
- As he waited, he checked his gear, took field exercise, played touch football, and feared a Dear John letter from his girlfriend.
- The few cards he got from home were displayed on the bed above his cot.
- When Christmas in the hot desert arrived on schedule, Raul joined his few Marines in what they were told would be a traditional Christmas meal.
- As expected, his fellow Marines complained about the chow and told stories about grand, wonderful Christmas celebrations back home.
- Raul was fascinated; he and his mother normally ate a simple meal on Christmas after mass, since it was all they could afford.

## Life at Work

- As the New Year passed, Lance Corporal Raul Hernandez's anticipation began to grow.
- President George Bush had given Iraqi President Saddam Hussein until January 15, 1991, to get his forces out of Kuwait or be subject to attack.
- The coalition forces had amassed 500,000 troops, 3,300 tanks, 4,000 armored personnel carriers, 3,600 pieces of artillery, 1,900 helicopters and 2,600 combat aircraft in the region.
- More than 100 ships were stationed offshore.
- As the deadline passed, the air war began.
- Day after day, the Iraqi forces were pounded, while the Marines waited on ready.
- Raul knew the ground war was next, and that his time was coming.
- Like most Marines, he was constantly hungry for news of the war and its progress.
- After 38 days of air assaults, orders arrived to move out.
- Accompanied by a picture of his girlfriend, Raul climbed aboard a HUMVEE heading toward the Kuwait border.
- Now he could prove he was a soldier worthy of the Marine uniform.
- Raul was part of a recon force of three companies outfitted in light armored vehicles; their task was to determine the Iraqi position within Kuwait.
- The approximately 500 men were armed with M-16 rifles, machine guns, grenade launchers and antitank weapons.
- The first major battle of Raul's young life began around noon.

*Like most Marines, Raul was constantly hungry for news of the war and its progress.*

- The Iraqis attacked with mortars, artillery and machine-gun fire, then with T-55 tanks.
- To counter, the Marines' land-launched TOW missiles took out four Iraqi tanks, seven trucks and an BMP armored personnel carrier.
- Despite all his training, Raul felt unsure of his first burst of fire, but his confidence grew quickly.
- In the first wave, 73 prisoners were captured, with an additional 23 surrendering under fire early the following day.
- Raul was amazed at the fast appearance of white flags, but the officers explained that the Iraqi soldiers were eager to avoid being killed for Saddam.
- Most were not trained soldiers, and just wanted to go home.
- The next day presented Raul with a different picture of war.
- The battle unfolded against a surrealistic backdrop: more than two dozen burning Kuwaiti oil wells, each shooting orange jets of flame 50 or 60 feet into the air and throwing off vast clouds of black smoke that formed a thick curtain above the Iraqi positions.
- Both sides exchanged artillery and mortar fire, but the Iraqi fire came from a fixed position, so the Marines quickly calculated where it would land.
- Two Marines were wounded.
- During the battle, Raul and another Marine moved forward in a HUMVEE filled with ammunition.

- Only later did Raul learn that it was a mortar round which landed in the back and detonated, exploding the ordnance in the Hummer and blowing the entire vehicle to shreds.
- Both men were blasted out of the vehicle.
- The next thing Raul knew, he and the other Marine were lying on the ground.
- Both experienced ringing in their ears and a few bruises, but little else.
- The medics were amazed.
- Both Marines inscribed their helmets with "LUCKY AS HELL" and returned to battle.
- With his M-16 in hand, Raul felt like real Marine with a story to tell.

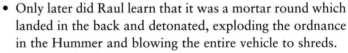

- But even though thousands of Iraqis were surrendering, the war was far from over.
- Kuwait City—and possibly Baghdad—were still ahead.

## Modern Warfare in Desert Storm

- The focus of high-tech conventional warfare has been to reduce general destruction.
- During the first five days of Desert Storm, the coalition air force delivered around 15 kilotons of high explosives—about the same as the blast power of the Hiroshima bomb—yet the civilian loss of life was considerably less and accuracy greater.
- In World War II, the typical allied bombing range was almost one mile, meaning nonmilitary targets were often hit when rail yards or airbases had been the real targets.
- By the Vietnam war, overall bombing accuracy had improved to roughly one-quarter of a mile.
- Smart bombs used in the Desert Storm raids had an accuracy of within 100 feet or less, allowing three missiles to destroy the Iraqi Ministry of Defense, while leaving a nearby hospital untouched.
- Experts say a similar raid in World War II would have required 30 planes scattering bombs over an area of several miles.
- Most of the Desert Storm weapons were launched from maneuverable, fighter-type aircraft such as the F-15E or F/A-18.
- Unlike lumbering high-altitude bombers such as the B-52, these aircraft can draw close enough to the target for it to be seen—visually or electronically—before a weapon is released.
- Destruction is also decreased because of greater explosion control.
- Though new explosive compounds are more energetic than those of World War II, in many cases the warhead of a smart weapon is not very large.
- Huge warheads are not needed if the weapon finds the target precisely.
- Now, the body of the device must accommodate engines, fuel and electronics, leaving less room for explosives.

# HISTORICAL SNAPSHOT
# 1991

- Allied forces attacking Iraq dropped 2,232 tons of explosives the first day, the largest strike in history; all regular television programming was canceled for full coverage of the Gulf War
- The economy officially went into a recession for the first time since 1982
- A record 23,300 homicides were reported nationwide
- Arlette Schweitzer, 42, acted as surrogate mother for her daughter, born without a uterus, thereby giving birth to her own twin grandchildren
- A Tufts University study showed that pharmaceutical manufacturers were the source of 92 percent of new drugs, with government and academia accounting for the rest
- Raytheon's Patriot missile defense system was deployed during the Persian Gulf War
- Compact disks outsold cassettes for the first time
- The number of single parents rose 41 percent from 1980, while the number of unmarried couples living together was up 80 percent
- The U.S. Postal Service increased the first-class postage stamp rate from $0.25 to $0.29
- The U.S. trade deficit hit an eight-year low
- The median age for first marriages was 26.3 years for men and 24.1 years for women.
- The U.S. Supreme Court ended forced busing, originally ordered to end racial segregation
- Congress approved family leave, allowing up to 12 weeks for family emergencies
- Eastern and Pan Am went into bankruptcy; Delta took over most of Pan Am routes and became the nation's leading carrier
- A single sheet of the first printing of the Declaration of Independence sold for $2.42 million; it was discovered in the backing of a painting that sold for $4 at a flea market
- School violence escalated; 25 percent of whites and 20 percent of blacks said they feared being attacked in school
- Walter H. Annenberg bequeathed a $1 billion art collection to the Metropolitan Museum of Art
- *Scarlett*, Alexandra Ripley's sequel to *Gone with the Wind*, sold a record 250,000 copies in one day
- Congress halted the nationwide rail strike after one day
- General Motors announced plans to close more than 20 plants over several years, eliminating more than 70,000 jobs
- Motorola introduced the 7.7-ounce cellular telephone
- Colloquialisms entering the language included date rape, boy toy, homeboy and living will

## Selected Prices

| | |
|---|---|
| Baseball Cap | $2.99 |
| Blank Videotapes, Three-Pack | $8.49 |
| Camcorder, RCA 8 mm | $699.00 |
| Car Seat | $80.00 |
| Cruise Ticket, Alaska, per Person | $2,395.00 |
| Exercise Bicycle | $249.99 |
| Flour, Five Pounds | $0.79 |
| Ointment, Preparation H | $2.88 |
| Plastic Reynolds Wrap | $1.99 |
| Smoke Detector | $5.99 |
| Tent, 7' x 8' | $89.98 |
| Turkey, per Pound | $0.69 |
| VCR, RCA | $294.97 |
| Weed Killer, Round-Up | $16.99 |
| Work Shirt, Man's | $15.40 |

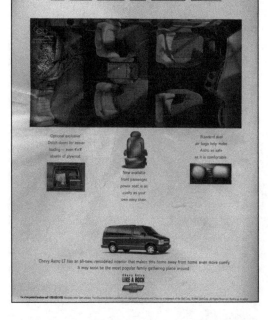

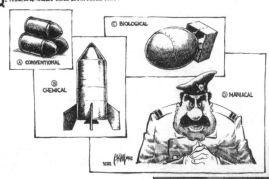

## "Allied Blitzkrieg," *Newsweek*, March 4, 1991:

With an avalanche of ordnance and phalanxes of hard-charging tanks, allied land forces finally swarmed into Kuwait and southern Iraq at 4 o'clock Sunday morning. The defeat of Saddam Hussein's army was foreordained. But confident American generals had a grander goal in mind: the greatest feat of arms since World War II. They expected tough fighting; they knew there would be allied casualties and they were prepared for Saddam to strike back with poison gas or some other terror weapon. But what unfolded in the desert on Sunday was an unequal contest between the most advanced armored divisions in the history of warfare and a large but crude Third-World army already groggy from 38 days of relentless bombing. The issue was not whether the Iraqis would be defeated, but how shatteringly. The allies were after total victory, a victory on such a scale and of such technical elegance that the campaign would be taught in military academies for generations to come, like Hannibal at Cannae or Napoleon on a very good day.

Near the end of the first day's fighting, it seemed almost too easy. The attackers achieved all their initial objectives: a 20-mile advance into Kuwait by the heavy armored columns of the U.S. VII Corps and other forces and, far to the west, a 70-mile thrust into Iraq by U.S. airborne and tank units with the French Foreign Legion as their spearhead. There was an airborne assault on Kuwait City, probably by the U.S. 82nd Airborne Division. There were reports of amphibious landings by the U.S. Marines. Allied air forces were "surging," mounting combat sorties at about their normal rate. "Friendly casualties have been extremely light. As a matter of fact, remarkably light," said Gen. Norman Schwarzkopf, the allied commander. With a new blackout in force, Schwarzkopf offered few details. . . .

Saddam lashed back with his most practiced weapon: rhetoric. "Fight them, brave Iraqis," he exhorted his army and his people in a radio broadcast, vowing to defeat "Bush and his stooges." Beating up on an easy prey, the Iraqis continued to retaliate by setting fire to Kuwaiti oil wells; about 500 were in flames by Sunday. And there were reports that their army of occupation was murdering Kuwaiti civilians and rounding up others to hold hostage against the allied attack. So far, however, Iraqi troops in the field weren't putting up much of a fight.

### "Median value of assets held by baby boomers age 35 to 44, and percent of households owning them," Census Bureau, 1991:

| Asset | Amount | Percent Owning |
|---|---|---|
| Equity in home | $31,082 | 67.4% |
| Rental prop. equity | 30,114 | 9.3 |
| Other real estate | 18,284 | 10.8 |
| IRA/KEOGH accounts | 8,634 | 25.8 |
| Equity in business | 9,703 | 16.0 |
| Other interest-earning accounts | 9,311 | 7.4 |
| Stocks/mutual funds | 4,563 | 21.3 |
| Bank interest earnings | 2,363 | 75.0 |
| U.S. Savings Bonds | 600 | 23.2 |
| Checking accounts | 481 | 48.4 |
| Other assets | 14,353 | 2.2 |
| Total net worth | 31,148 | NA |

### "On Target, How Goes the War?" *U.S. News & World Report*, February 11, 1991:

If modern air power and precision-guided weaponry have created a new kind of warfare, they also have created a new problem in military public relations: How do you demonstrate success in a war with no front line to move across a map and no outposts to seize?

Last week, as the war entered its third week, some tangible measures of success began to tell. Although only about 60 of Iraq's 700-plane air force have been confirmed destroyed, the Iraqi air force showed clear signs of disintegrating as an effective fighting force. The true measure of success, commanders said, in effect, is what you don't see: Iraqi fighters stopped even trying to intercept allied attack aircraft on their bombing runs. "In Washington, there's a preoccupation with data," said Air Force Commander Lt. Gen. Charles Horner. "What you really need are measures of success that make sense. How many of our aircraft have been lost in air combat? Zero. How many air attacks have the Iraqis made upon any U.S. forces? Zero. If the measure of our success is just how many aircraft shelters we put holes in, that's just a body count."

## "The Air War," Gen. Michael Dugan, *U.S. News & World Report,* February 11, 1991:

Operation Desert Storm opened with the most awesome and well-coordinated mass raid in the history of air power. Tomahawk cruise missiles, launched from several different ships, all were timed to hit their initial targets at precisely three in the morning. Immediately after the Tomahawks hit, air force F-111F and F-15E fighter bombers and F-117 Stealth attack aircraft based in Saudi Arabia, along with navy and Marine A-6E attack bombers from carriers 600 miles away, took advantage of the confusion the missiles created in the Iraqi air defenses to pound high-priority targets.

B-52 heavy bombers, some of which flew nonstop for more than 12 hours from Barksdale Air Force Base in Louisiana, carpet-bombed priority targets in lightly defended areas. The sun was just beginning to rise when the big planes lifted off in Louisiana: It would be another 10 hours before House Speaker Tom Foley, found at a Brooks Brothers clothing store, would be summoned to the White House and told of the operation. The B-52s were tracked on radar by three E-3 AWACS aerial-surveillance planes and were accompanied on their last leg by F-15 fighters to ward off any air attacks. Tornado fighters from the United Kingdom hit airfields. Navy EA-6B and air force EF-111 electronic-warfare planes jammed Iraqi air-defense radars, and F-4G Wild Weasel antiradar missiles destroyed enemy radar antennas. Pilotless drone aircraft that look like real planes on radar and are typically used for target practice swept in as decoys to suck up surface-to-air missiles and cause the Iraqis to reveal where their missile batteries were located. But tactical surprise was so complete that the Iraqis, who had shut down most of their early warning radars in November in the face of continued American probing, still had them turned off when the great armada arrived. . . .

The air campaign that has unfolded, with 1,800 American combat aircraft and 435 from seven other countries flying as many as 3,000 sorties a day, not only shows the might and precision of Western air power, it also demonstrates the ability of America and its partners to control this unprecedented force to achieve allied military aims—while holding casualties to a remarkably low level.

## "The Very Nervy Win of CNN: A Network That Links the Global Village Shows How to Cover a War," Matthew Cooper, *U.S. News & World Report*, January 28, 1991:

Just an hour after the bombing of Baghdad began, Bob Furnad's war was already well under way. At Cable News Network's Atlanta headquarters, the senior executive producer stood in his darkened control room amid a swirl of staffers and television monitors, making split-second decisions about what the world would see. "You gotta get touchy feely! Show some emotion!" he shouted above the din, cutting to a shot of a citizen reaction in St. Louis. From there, he took viewers to the Pentagon, to Amman and, for hundreds of coffee-logged staffers, to the sweet victory of an exclusive report from Baghdad.

**Murrow's mantle.** January 16 will be remembered as the night Furnad and his CNN colleagues carpet-bombed the competition. Overnight ratings soared to new highs, besting CBS in 25 big cities and suggesting that CNN's journalistic success might translate into even better commercial prospects. Former CBS News president Fred Friendly predicts that the Gulf War will mark CNN's broadcasting preeminence, just as Edward R. Murrow's reports during London air raids signaled CBS's reign after World War II. Indeed, before Iraqi authorities cut off their transmission, CNN Baghdad correspondents Bernard Shaw, John Holliman and Peter Arnett offered harrowing Murrowesque reports from their hotel, using his microphone-out-the-window technique to capture the sounds of battle. And while some competitors trained their cameras on pundits, CNN offered the best live-TV transmissions from Israel during the first moments of the attack on that nation. Across the country, more than 200 news directors at local affiliates often abandoned their own network's feed to get CNN material. Ron Bilek of NBC's Atlanta station said he switched to take advantage of CNN's "fresh stuff." And NBC anchor Tom Brokaw interviewed Shaw to find out the situation in Baghdad.

In fact, the Gulf War established CNN as an entirely new kind of global information system—an intelligence network that serves not only 70 million households, but also world leaders. Both Defense Secretary Dick Cheney and Joint Chiefs of Staff Chairman Colin Powell dubbed CNN the best source for discovering the extent of the Baghdad bombing, and Air Force Lt. Gen. Charles Horner, architect of the air war, said reports of CNN prowess convinced him that he needed a TV at his command post. It was no small irony that military officials were relying on and praising CNN; they had tried to get its correspondents and all reporters out of Baghdad before the bombing began, partly out of fears they could be used for propaganda purposes by Saddam Hussein.

CNN has also become "the most efficient way for one government to speak to another during a crisis," says Peter Tarnoff, president of the Council on Foreign Relations. Saddam Hussein reportedly has all his bunker TVs tuned to the network. Iraqi officials often delay press conferences until CNN reporters arrive. Jordan's King Hussein has ordered his royal staff to monitor CNN around the clock and to awaken him when it breaks big news. Margaret Thatcher became a fan after the Gulf crisis began in August—and she was finally convinced that the network, contrary to her suspicions, did not air pornography.

# "Hussein's Many Miscalculations," Mortimer B. Zuckerman, *U.S. News & World Report*, January 28, 1991:

IRAQI WARHEADS

SCUD

DUD

America is now in a war it did not want with a man we do not understand. Saddam Hussein still mystifies us. What could be going on behind that old-fashioned mustache, those flat eyes, that eerily calm demeanor? What kind of man wears those preposterous military uniforms, rides a white horse and performs in those stilted TV photo opportunities? How could a man facing certain defeat and quite possibly his own annihilation choose war in defiance of world opinion? We cannot imagine or understand his actions.

Clearly, he miscalculated the overwhelming superiority of U.S. military technology—particularly the lethal precision of our air power. Who wasn't amazed by the videotape of a bomb put through the door of a redoubt? He must have imagined a political victory for having been the first Arab leader who stood up to a superpower. Or perhaps he felt that withdrawal would lead to his death at the hands of Iraqis or others who would have considered him a coward or a traitor. Maybe he was convinced that if he had to die, Iraq would die with him and he would become an inspirational martyr.

Perhaps his biggest miscalculation was that we would swallow his corruption of the language of peace. But we understood what the military thinker Clausewitz wrote: "The aggressor is a man

of peace. He wants nothing more than to march into a neighboring country unresisted." Hussein even corrupted, through political use, the religious language of the Islamic faith. He sought to stir up Muslim hatred and violence and direct it against the West—the "enemies of God." Yet the holy war he wants to create is not the wave of the future. It is the legacy of the frustration of the past.

Hussein asserted that he wished to create a technologically advanced, economically sophisticated "Arab Nation" led by Iraq, recapturing the Muslim greatness that was lost almost three centuries ago in what the historian Gibbon called "the Great Debate" between Christianity and Islam; the debate ended with the rise of European and Christian world dominance and the Arab fragmentation of the Ottoman Empire. Yet Iraq's military actions had been exclusively against other Arabs and Muslims, in Iran, Kuwait and even Lebanon—dividing rather than unifying the "Arab Nation."

The calculation of this cruel zealot was manifest on the evening of January 17, when the Scud missiles hit Israel, threatening a wider war and the subversion of the coalition. Here was an attack without military justification, on a country not involved in the confrontation, aimed not at bases or soldiers but at civilians. It was an attack on Arab as well as Jew in Israel—even though the Pales-

DADDY, WHY'S THE U.S. AND ITS ALLIES BOMBING?..

UM, TO RID THE WORLD OF THAT IRAQI GUY?...

© 1999 LUCKOVICH—ATLANTA CONSTITUTION

## "Hussein's Many Miscalculations . . ." *(continued)*

tinians in Jordan rejoiced. Its only purpose was to sow terror and confusion and enrage Israel to a response with incalculable consequences.

The unprovoked attack on Israel is not just a present horror. It was a telescoping of the future. Had the coalition not moved, we would have been assured more devastating wars when Hussein would have been stronger and the coalition weaker. The only question would have been, "Who would he strike first?" No wonder the peacemakers who sought ways other than war to contain him lost out.

An America resigned to war went to war, knowing it was necessary but not welcoming it. This is not another Vietnam to which the phrase "never again" was applied. For some, "never again" meant that the United States would fight only if directly attacked. For others, "never again" meant not to be drawn easily into conflict, but when conflict is unavoidable, to use whatever military power was necessary to win quickly and decisively.

America was not driven into this conflict lightly. If ever a political leader had gone down the list of preconditions for a just war, seeking alternatives short of rewarding the aggressor, it was George Bush. Hussein would not budge one inch. The result? America accumulated and is now using that necessary military power, especially air power, for a quick and decisive result, demonstrating the effectiveness of this new strategy.

In the end, President Bush has managed this whole complicated process brilliantly. He formed and led an international coalition. He retained and built popular support at home. He carried enough bipartisan support in Congress. He gave appropriate leeway and support to America's military planners and our fighting men and women. They all deserve our thanks and prayers.

## "I Don't Want Any Tears," *Newsweek*, March 4, 1991:

With the ground war approaching, American troops delivered what they believed might be their final messages home. Some sent letters or tape recordings. Others stood in line at pay phones for hours, waiting for a line to the United States. Their contacts with home were marked by words of courage, hope, fear and, above all, love.

Rose Buchanan of San Diego was delighted when she received five letters from her husband, Marine Cap. Larry Buchanan, one day last week. But as she read the missives, she grew increasingly somber. "Dear Snookums," one of them read: "I am not speaking negatively, honey, in saying that I don't know how this thing is going to end. . . . I am hopeful and confident that God will see me through. . . . The last thing in this world that I want is to be separated from you in any fashion, especially death. But at some time when you can, try to imagine what you would do if someone showed up at your door in dress blues with a chaplain. To have things in order now would ease [the effect of] my passing on you later. Such things as getting a copy of our marriage certificate and placing it with the will; going over the will we made a few years back to see if we still agree with what is in it. . . . And here is one [question] I'm not sure of: Does my [insurance] policy pay if I'm killed in war?"

Ryan Anderson's latest letters to his mother, Ann, in Atlanta have been upbeat, detailing life in the Saudi culture. The 19-year-old artillery-unit soldier has written about the desert beauty, rocks he has found and those "stinking, smelly, clumsy" camels. He says one package of Snickers minibars can fetch $15. And he asked for something that puzzled his mother: tins of sardines. "It's the oil," he explained in a phone call. "It keeps the bugs off me." But what he wanted in one recent letter was reassurance. "If I kill anyone over here, will that change anything between us?" he asked. She wrote back immediately. "Nothing you ever do will make me not love you," she answered. "I am your mother."

A letter from Specialist Herbert Plummer, son of Mary Plummer of Springfield, Massachusetts, finally confirmed the receipt of a gift—a volleyball with "Hi From Mom" written on it. But Herbert was writing to say thanks for more than the ball. "You have always taught me . . . when I was young that paying attention to detail is most important," it read. "Believe me when I say that it's proving itself more worthwhile than ever. . . . Your love and support have brought me a long way—especially in this situation. God has totally blessed me with you. I love you, mom. Your son, Herbert."

Jim Ives had something to say to his wife on Valentine's Day that he felt no printed card would capture. So he climbed into his Jeep and drove to the nearest telephone—400 miles away. But when the Ft. Lauderdale, Florida, policeman and reservist tried to call his wife, Judy, no one answered. He tried again and again. But after hours of dialing, he wasn't successful. So he called a man's very first love—his mother. Jim told her about life in the desert and said he hadn't had a bath in seven weeks. He seemed optimistic, but his mother was upset nonetheless. "I broke down," she recalls, "and he told his sister, Meredith, 'Look, take care of Mom. . . . I know what I have to do and I'm coming home. Tell Mom the worst thing that's going to

## "I Don't Want . . ." *(continued)*

happen to me in this war is I broke my nose playing football.'" In his last call to his wife, however, Jim Ives told the answering machine a different story. He said he was at the front, she recounted, and "he didn't know if he could call again."

"I've taken advantage of the endless hours of waiting," Army Specialist Brad J. White wrote his wife, Kit, in El Paso, Texas. "I've been going to a Bible study a couple of nights a week. It's really enlightening. I can fully understand now why God placed key figures of biblical times into the desert

for days, months, even years at a time. In some ways, it's very cleansing. With no TV, little radio, and newspapers that are days or weeks old, I've had more time to work out how I feel and deal with our situation. I believe that I've fully adjusted physically, accepted mentally and have realized that I have faith that I'll be home. The difficulty for me at this point is simply homesickness."

Test-pilot Oswald Ingraham is one of three Ingraham brothers stationed in the gulf. "I've been into a mission a couple of times, and we've all made it back alive," he wrote his wife, Regina, in Clarksville, Tennessee. "I won't lie; it's scary. Your stomach muscles tighten. . . . I think of how nice it would be to be home again. I don't like killing people and may God forgive me."

## "Reshaping the Mideast: After the Fall of Saddam," Eliahu Salpeter, *The New Leader*, January 28, 1991:

Almost from the start of the fighting in the Persian Gulf, one could discern the outlines of major changes likely to result in the geopolitics of the Middle East, in relations between the region and the outside world, as well as in maneuverings among the U.S., Europe and the Soviet Union. For although technically the war was launched to liberate Kuwait, it soon became clear that the destruction of Saddam Hussein's regime in Iraq was Washington's ultimate objective—and that rarely, if ever, had the conduct of a military conflict been as strongly influenced by potential postwar policies.

President George Bush's firm insistence upon sticking to the January 15 United Nations deadline for Iraq to quit Kuwait or face the consequences sharply enhanced U.S. credibility in this part of the globe and beyond. So did his speedy dispatch of American-manned Patriot missile batteries to Israel after the first Scud attack. In part, this explains Jerusalem's willingness to go along with Washington's request that it exhibit restraint and not pursue its traditional practice of instant retaliation.

It should quickly be noted, though, that the enthusiastic support of the Palestine Liberation Organization (PLO) for Saddam, and the cheers sent up by the Palestinians in Jordan and the occupied territories when Iraqi missiles began to come down on Israel, have reinforced the hawks' opposition to establishing a Palestinian state 20 miles from Tel Aviv. What is probably more important, doves now have grave doubts about such an entity, too. The Scuds confirmed the feelings of many here that the refusal of most Arab countries to accept the Jewish State's existence is a greater threat than the intifada.

Israelis will, in short, be much more reluctant than in the past to make groundbreaking concessions to the Palestinians. Most of them believe the experiences of the war will have a positive impact on Washington's attitude when attention turns to settling longstanding Middle East disputes, yet they may be deluding themselves because of their belief that relations with the U.S. are close again.

## "The Bear: Gen. H. Norman Schwarzkopf Knows Soldiers and Loves Them, Knows War and Hates It," *U.S. News & World Report,* February 11, 1991:

The general's personal quarters, in an alcove just off his office, are neither large nor luxurious; Spartan is the word. The nightstand next to the bed is piled with books, magazines and a frame full of photos of his wife and children. One of the books is William Tecumseh Sherman's memoirs, sent to him by an old friend and classmate at West Point. It is well-thumbed and marked. One passage stands out: "Some men think that modern armies may be so regulated that a general can sit in an office and play on his several columns as on the keys of a piano; this is a fearful mistake. The directing mind must be at the very head of the army—must be seen there, and the effect of his mind and personal energy must be felt by every officer and man. . . ." The mind and personal energy at the head of Operation Desert Storm are those of H. Norman Schwarzkopf, a general who knows soldiers and loves them, who knows war and hates it.

Norm Schwarzkopf is 56 years old, a four-star army general, commander in chief of the U.S. Central Command. On August 2, 1990, when Saddam Hussein invaded Kuwait, Schwarzkopf's command existed largely on paper and in the minds of several hundred staff people at MacDill Air Force Base, Florida. Today, he commands more than 500,000 American troops and co-commands an additional 200,000 allied forces poised on the Saudi-Kuwaiti border awaiting the order to attack. Schwarzkopf and his staff brought this force together in the desert, planned and coordinated the mission of a polyglot multinational force, and soon will command the attack that sends some 2,000 tanks crashing into the Iraqis. If Desert Storm goes according to plan, senior Pentagon officials say, Schwarzkopf has a clear shot at becoming the next army chief of staff.

The largest American military operation since

Vietnam is no ordinary mission, but then H. Norman Schwarzkopf is anything but an ordinary man. Regarded as hot-tempered and demanding by some of his peers, he is both a product of his times, turbulent and troubled, and a throwback to a more innocent era when the words *duty, honor, country*—not career—were engraved on the hearts of graduates of West Point.

The famous son of a famous father, Schwarzkopf knew from the age of four that he would follow his father to West Point. His father told him so, and he never doubted it. At the age of eight, he was devouring the letters his father, Maj. Gen. Herbert Norman Schwarzkopf, sent home from Iran, where he was building a national police force for the shah. They were long letters filled with fascinating accounts of the culture, art and politics of Iran and Saudi Arabia. His father sent for young Norm at age 12, plucking him out of Trenton, New Jersey, and permitting him for one glorious year to live the adventures of those letters in Tehran. Nothing—not boarding school in Switzerland, not the rigors of life at the U.S. Military Academy, not even 30 years of the pain and pride of an army career—would kill the romantic who lives inside Norm Schwarzkopf's heart.

### "America's Place in the World," Lane Morrow, *Time*, March 18, 1991:

The war was a defining moment, everyone thought. What exactly did it define?

- The end of the old American depression called Vietnam syndrome—the compulsive pessimism, the need to look for downsides and dooms?
- The birth of a new American century—onset of a unipolar world, with America playing the global cop?
- Another chapter in an age of astonishments that has brought down the Berlin Wall, ended the Cold War and begun preliminary work on the disintegration of the Soviet Union?
- The first post-nuclear big war, almost as quick and lethal as one with nukes, but smarter, fairer, precisely selective in its targets, with no radioactive aftereffects?
- The first war epic of the global village's electronic theater?
- The apotheosis of war-making as a brilliant American package—a dazzling, compacted product, like some new concentrate of intervention: Fast! Improved! Effective!
- The dawn of a new world order?

All of those and much, much more. Or somewhat less.

The enterprise is still surrounded by a daze of astonishment: that it should have been so quick, so "easy," so devastating in effect. That coalition casualties should have been so light. That the cost to American taxpayers will be relatively small ($15 billion or less if Japan, Germany and others honor their pledges of financial support). That Saddam Hussein should have been so cartoon-villainous (and incompetent as a military leader). That his soldiers should have committed atrocities that took the moral onus off the carnage that the coalition left in the desert.

The American mind may have sought out an innocent analogy: George Bush had—unexpectedly, miraculously—found the sweet spot. He and his men (Powell, Schwarzkopf, Scowcroft) had performed a miracle of American concentration and grace under pressure, after years when those seemed almost archaic American talents. Now, Bush was rounding the bases while the baseball he hit was still rising in the air and might yet—who knows?—go into some orbit of higher historical meaning.

# 1995 Profile

## Operation Deliberate Force: Bosnia

### Air Force Major

For as long as he could remember, Major Jimmy Tittle, from Phoenix, Arizona, wanted to attend the Air Force Academy, which trained him to fly an F-16—straight into Operation Deliberate Force in Bosnia.

### Life at Home

- Major Jimmy Tittle was a physical fitness machine; even the younger pilots were in awe of his conditioning and discipline.
- A native of Phoenix, Arizona, he had always taken great pride in his skills, precision and ability to perform under pressure.
- Early on, two things were clear: His older brother Matt was going to take over the family land surveying business, and Jimmy was obsessed with flying and physical fitness.
- While still in junior high school, he wrote an essay called, "Why I should attend the Air Force Academy."
- Privately, his father thought this obsession would pass; one tour of service duty and then his youngest son would enjoy a lifetime of good pay and good living as a commercial airline pilot.
- Upon graduating from the Air Force Academy in Colorado Springs, Jimmy got to live his real dream—a chance to train in jet fighters.
- At flight training school, he also found a wife; Kim, the daughter of a retired colonel, fully understood the unconventional and transient life of an air force wife.
- Three daughters followed, though Jimmy was careful never to mention his hunger for a son.
- The Tittle family was stationed at Ramstein Air Force Base when he learned that his squadron would be shipped to Aviano, Italy.
- There, his F-16C fighters would be deployed to his new assignment: Bosnia.

*Jimmy Tittle takes pride in his skills, precision and coolness under fire.*

- Four years earlier, in 1991, when he had flown in the Gulf War, he had seen relatively little actual combat.
- This time, after a dozen years in the air force, it looked as if he would be in the middle of a real shoot-out.
- Jimmy's family loved having a duty station in Europe and often took trips together; the girls were learning to speak German.
- Alex, the oldest, was mesmerized by the Alps and covered her bedroom walls with Alpine scenes.

### Life at Work

- When Major Tittle's squadron arrived in Aviano, Italy, their mission was described as "routine patrols" over Bosnia.
- It did not work out that way.
- The flights were often harrowing and included hostile fire.
- In May, NATO planes returned fire, hitting a Serb ammo depot, just to prove that the patrols were not to be taken lightly.
- In June, Captain Scott O'Grady, a pilot in another air force squadron, was shot down by a Serb missile and forced to live off the land for several days until he was rescued by Marines.
- This highly publicized incident caused Kim and the girls considerable concern.
- Julia, who was too young to write, sent a smiling yellow sun to cheer up her dad.

- By the time NATO and the U.S. were prepared to make an aggressive commitment to peace by waging war on the Serbs, Jimmy had flown 50 peacekeeping missions over Bosnia.
- His F-16 squadron was called upon to play a lead role.
- He enjoys flying the F-16, which has a single seat, making the pilot alone responsible for all aspects of flight, from navigation to weapons systems.
- His adrenaline would pump his heart harder every time he entered Bosnian air space, even as he struggled to fully understand the conflict.
- After the death of the dictator Tito in 1980, the various nations of Yugoslavia dissolved into warring factions.
- Many ethnic groups saw this as an opportunity to reclaim land or capture power lost decades earlier.
- United Nations peacekeepers tried to keep order, but generally, they were ineffective—sometimes embarrassingly so.
- The Bosnian Serbs continued to be hostile; thousands of Muslims were murdered and the boundary line redrawn.
- After more than three and a half years of measures intended to resolve the fighting, President Bill Clinton felt the United States—acting in concert with NATO—had few options but to take charge.
- Peace would only come, he concluded, through the threat of war, to include a massive NATO bombing campaign against the Bosnian Serbs and a multilateral effort to arm and assist the Muslims.
- Led by American fighter planes, NATO launched its most massive military operation to date.

- This decision came after the Bosnian Serb Army captured the town of Srebrenica, 50 miles northeast of Sarajevo.
- Dutch peacekeepers were held at gunpoint while the Muslim population was brutalized by the Serbs, who murdered the men and raped the women.
- In all, 8,000 men were taken from the town and gunned down in a nearby field.
- The world was outraged, but little changed for another month.
- In late July, the Bosnian Serb Army fired a mortar shell into a marketplace in Sarajevo, a once-glorious city that had been under siege for three years.
- Over 37 people were killed and dozens wounded.
- Finally, NATO and the U.N. demanded retaliation against the Serbs; thus, Operation Deliberate Force was unleashed.
- In its first wave, U.S. F-15Es, F-16s and F/A-18s attacked the Serb air-defense installations in Mostar, Gorazde and Tuzla.
- In subsequent waves, the allies went after command and control centers, ammunition dumps and surface-to-air missile sites.
- At the same time, A-10 Warthogs and AC-130 gunships pounded heavy-artillery installations around Sarajevo.
- On the ground, four-star admiral Leighton Smith, Jr. led the 60,000-member NATO force in the Balkans.
- Jimmy was proud to be in the center of the assault.
- Before each flight, he read the latest letter from home.
- Over three days, the NATO allies—Spain, France, Britain, Germany, Turkey and the Netherlands—flew hundreds of sorties.
- During Jimmy's initial flight, he had a clear shot at his target and dropped his bomb accurately, helping eliminate an ammunition depot near Sarajevo.
- His squadron struck again the next night and the day after that, while the U.N.'s Rapid Reaction Force fired more than 1,000 shells on Serb positions near Sarajevo.
- On the fourth day, they stopped to assess the situation.
- Jimmy used that time to write home and thank little Julia for her picture.
- Unfortunately, the Bosnian Serb Army did not pull back, and he was in the air bombing targets again the next day.
- For days, the NATO force pounded the targets.
- Jimmy was beginning to wonder what kind of fanatical, stubborn force they were fighting, when word came that the Bosnian Serb Army had been broken.
- Two days later, when the siege of Sarajevo was lifted, thousands celebrated in the streets.
- Clearly, NATO was going to stop short of a full-scale military solution.
- Jimmy was pleased and disappointed; now, his life would become routine again.

### Life in the Community: Yugoslavia

- As communism declined in the late 1980s, Yugoslavia was believed to be better positioned than any other communist state to make the transition to multiparty democracy.
- Below the surface lurked a problem, however: For decades under communism, ethnic grievances had been suppressed.
- Even as the presidents of Yugoslavia's six republics—Bosnia-Herzegovina, Croatia, Macedonia, Montenegro, Serbia, and Slovenia—quarreled in public about the country's future structure, some were plotting a path to disintegration.
- The most visible of these powers was Serbia's Slobodan Milosevic, who carefully used nationalism to strengthen his role, first over Serbia, then Yugoslavia.

> "The objective is not simply to retaliate for the barbaric attack on Sarajevo, but to send a very strong deterrent signal to the Bosnian Serbs that this time around, the international community means business."
> —NATO spokesman Jamie Shea

- His dream was to step into the shoes of Josip Broz Tito as leader over all of Yugoslavia.
- By 1991, when he found this impossible, he focused on the creation of an enlarged Serbian state, encompassing as much of Yugoslavia as possible.
- This action helped convince the other states that the Yugoslav federation would fail and set them on the road to independence, and then war.
- The first Yugoslav state was created after World War I from the ruins of the Ottoman and Hapsburg empires.
- At its founding, it was called the Kingdom of Serbs, Croats and Slovenes, and only later rechristened Yugoslavia.
- The country embodied a dream of unity for southern Slavic people, and freedom from Austrian and Ottoman domination.
- In 1941, the Axis powers invaded the country, and communist Yugoslavia was founded in 1943 by Tito.
- When in 1945 the Soviet Army installed communist governments throughout Eastern Europe, Yugoslavia stood alone, already communist but not under the control of Russia.
- From Moscow's viewpoint, Tito and his country were dangerously independent and were expelled from the common institutions of the Eastern Bloc in 1948.
- After his split with Moscow, Tito used his country's unique position to secure backing from both the East and the West.
- Throughout his rule, Tito prevented the biggest faction—the Serbs—from dominating the Croats through constitutional balancing and brute force.
- For all its faults, Tito's Yugoslavia enabled the country's many peoples, cultures and traditions to live side-by-side.
- Upon Tito's death in 1980, the framework known as Yugoslavia began to disintegrate.
- Yugoslavia formally ceased to exist in January 1992 when all 12 members of the European Community (EC) officially recognized Slovenia and Croatia as independent states.
- Preoccupied with the Gulf War and the future of the former Soviet Union in 1991, the U.S. left the handling of the conflict to the EC.

"Yugoslavia had tourism, heavy industry; it was a food-surplus nation. Its new freeways linked the rest of the European Community with Greece, Turkey, and the export markets of the Middle East. The totems of an emerging consumer society were everywhere: new gas stations, motels, housing developments, and discos and sidewalk cafés in the villages. Most impressive were the large private houses covering the roadside hills. Before the killing started practically everyone, it seems, was just finishing a new house, or had just bought a new car."
—T. D. Allman, *Vanity Fair*, 1992

- Several months later, as war engulfed Croatia, the United Nations entered the diplomatic search for peace.
- Reports of widespread killings, rapes and other atrocities, despite the presence of U.N. and European peacekeepers, captured worldwide attention.
- More than 300,000 people would die in the next three years.
- The U.S. entered the conflict as part of NATO in 1995.

## HISTORICAL SNAPSHOT
## 1995

- The Dow-Jones Industrial Average reached 5,216; the low for the year was 3,832
- The movies *Braveheart, Apollo 13, Leaving Las Vegas,* and *Dead Man Walking* premiered in theaters
- America boasted 720,000 physicians and 190,000 dentists
- Fifty-seven million viewers watched the murder trial of O. J. Simpson, accused of killing his estranged wife Nicole Brown Simpson and her friend Ron Goldman
- The 500-year-old frozen body of an Inca girl, bundled in fine wool, was found in the Peruvian Andes
- On television, *ER, Seinfeld, Friends, Caroline in the City, NFL Monday Night Football, Single Guy, Home Improvement, Boston Common, 60 Minutes* and *NYPD Blue* led in the Nielsen ratings
- Research showed that three ounces of salmon a week reduced the risk of fatal heart arrhythmias by 50 percent
- Two Americans were arrested for the Oklahoma City bombing, which killed 169 people and left 614 injured
- The all-male college, The Citadel, finally admitted its first female cadet, who withdrew after only a few days
- Louis Farrakhan led a "Million Man March" on Washington, attracting 400,000 men who pledged greater social and family responsibility
- Hollywood's most expensive film, *Waterworld,* which cost $200 million in make, was a flop
- More than seven million people subscribed to online computer services such as America Online, CompuServe and Prodigy
- Blue M&Ms, custom-made coffins, Pepcid AC and the computer language Java made their first appearance
- The Centers for Disease Control reported a leveling-off of teen sexual activity; reportedly, 52.8 percent used condoms
- Businesses nationwide introduced casual Fridays, which allowed employees to wear more comfortable attire
- Physicists discovered the megaparticle, predicted by Einstein and consisting of a few thousand atoms
- After 139 years, Mississippi lawmakers ratified the 13th Amendment abolishing slavery
- Coffee bars, led by companies such as Starbucks, spread rapidly, providing an inexpensive, safe dating haven
- Singer Kurt Cobain's blood-stained guitar sold for $17,000 after his death by suicide

## Selected Prices

| | |
|---|---|
| Answering Machine | $250.00 |
| Battery, Two-pack | $6.00 |
| Bra, Olga | $20.63 |
| Cat Food | $7.99 |
| Dental Services, Tooth Extraction | $25.00 |
| Deodorant, Old Spice | $1.79 |
| Field Jacket | $69.50 |
| Garage Door Opener | $275.00 |
| Notebook Computer, Compaq Presario | $1,199.00 |
| Olive Oil, Extra Virgin | $32.00 |
| Purse, Kenneth Cole | $148.50 |
| Rollerblades | $34.97 |
| Toilet | $49.00 |
| Videotape, Disney's *Lion King* | $29.97 |
| Water, 1.5 Liters | $0.49 |

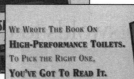

## "In Hot Pursuit of the War Criminals: The Chase Could Threaten the Peace Process," Russell Watson and Rod Nordland, *Newsweek,* February 19, 1996:

Kadira Mesanovic refuses to believe that her husband and son are dead. "It's never too late for me to hope," she says. She left the besieged enclave of Srebrenica last July when it fell to the Serbs, and her menfolk are among the 8,000 Muslims listed by the Red Cross as dead or missing. Despite considerable evidence that thousands of Muslims were massacred by the Serbs, she insists it would have made no sense for them to execute her 16-year-old son. "Mirza was too young to be killed," she says. "It's not possible to kill so many, even for the Serbs." Her cousin Oric Mevludin was one of the few men to escape from Srebrenica. He says he hid among the bodies in a field where Serbs were systematically slaughtering Muslims. "I don't think any of the (missing) men are alive," he says. "Perhaps some small group is being used for slave labor. They'll kill them, too, when they're done. But you can't tell the women that. They don't want to know."

The women of Srebrenica were out in force last week. Demonstrating in Tuzla, near the headquarters of U.S. troops in Bosnia, they demanded to know the fate of their men and boys. For once, they could not be ignored. Suddenly, the issue of alleged Serbian war crimes threatened to stall the entire Bosnian peace process.

Last month, Bosnia's Muslim-dominated government arrested 20 Serb soldiers, claiming they were suspected of war crimes. The international war-crimes tribunal in The Hague said it would investigate the two senior soldiers, a general and a colonel, and might indict them. In an effort to get the men released, the military commander of the Bosnian Serbs, Gen. Ratko Mladic, ordered his forces to cut off all contacts with the NATO units implementing the Dayton peace agreement. If it holds, the boycott could prevent the parties from resolving crucial remaining issues, including postwar political arrangements. That, in turn, could even delay the withdrawal of some U.S. forces from Bosnia.

## "Snooping around in Bosnia," Colin Soloway in Sarajevo, *U.S. News & World Report*, April 15, 1996:

Dispatches: Captain Aleksandar Milutinovic is from the second generation of his family to see military duty in the Balkans; his father was a Serbian soldier in the Royal Yugoslav Army during World War II.

Milutinovic spoke with *U.S. News*'s Colin Soloway near Srebrenica, where he utilizes his knowledge of Serbo-Croatian as a liaison officer with Serbs and Muslims.

**Eastern Bosnia.** My father finds it ironic that I am here, because he fought through these hills back in '44, '45 against the communists and protecting the Americans who bailed out over Yugoslavia at the time.

I'm quite well received on all sides, because they view me first as an American. But there's hate here that you can't comprehend in the United States, that Americans can't even begin to understand. And the former Yugoslavs cannot even grasp the concept of what being an American is, of what tolerance is, and what human rights are. They tend to hide in self-righteous indignation and to see themselves as faultless.

What you have is the worst of communism combined with the worst of Western materialism. There is a scramble by the former ruling classes to preserve power. People really don't have anything to believe in. There are no noble causes to fight for here, except for peace.

The Republika Srpska (Bosnian Serb) Army cannot comprehend the American concept of leadership, that our officers always set the example and that we will never have anything better than our own soldiers. We took some (Serbian) commanders on a tour, and they were amazed that Colonel Batiste, our brigade commander, was living in a simple hex tent. When we go to dinner, our officers stand with their men.

I figure if not me, then who? In essence I'm an embodiment of America, the son of immigrants. Who's more appropriate than an individual who understands the language and history of this place to come and represent America?

## "Louder Than Words," Kevin Fedarko, *Time*, September 11, 1995:

After years of bluffing, NATO responds to a Serb atrocity with force, and chances for a settlement in the Balkans seem better than they have since the wars there began.

"A man with no arm came into my shop, the blood gushing from his stump. Then he ran away. I saw the torso of a woman. She was still moving, but her legs were gone. The other day I saw something similar in a film. A beast cut a young man in two, torso and legs. One was a movie, the other is our reality here in Bosnia. We are like a block of little chickens squeezed into this cage of a town, chirping for help."

Those were the reflections of Ferid Durakovic the day after a Serb mortar shell landed near his food store in Sarajevo last week, killing 43 people and wounding more than 80. Others recalled hands and feet tossed among odd bits of clothing, torsos strewn amid fresh vegetables, wet scraps of flesh clinging to the stone walls of nearby buildings. It was another savage attack on a city that has seen too many, and everyone in Sarajevo knew it would go unavenged, like all the rest.

"After I pickle (fire) the bomb off, I don't have to worry about watching the FLIR (forward-looking infrared system) because I can watch for triple-A (antiaircraft artillery) and other things as my whizzo (weapons system officer) holds the laser on the target all the way in." U.S. Marine Captain Erik Swenson, speaking here, is the pilot of an F/A-18 Hornet (call sign: "Lumpy"), and he could hardly be more different from a Sarajevo shopkeeper. But he and Ferid Durakovic are intimately linked. Starting last Wednesday morning, Captain Swenson—in his first taste of combat—and dozens of other NATO pilots began bombing the Serbs in retaliation for the massacre Durakovic had witnessed. "I saw explosions 30 or 40 miles away," said Swenson. "They seemed to be everywhere, like popcorn going off." What no one thought would ever happen finally had.

Last week was one of the most remarkable in the 41-month-old Bosnian struggle. On Monday, the Serbs committed their atrocity. Then, from Wednesday through Friday, NATO conducted the largest combat operation in its history, finally pounding the Serbs after endless bluffing. By Friday, a diplomatic breakthrough had occurred, with all parties agreeing to meet in Geneva this week for preliminary peace talks. After years of war and "ethnic cleansing," the brutal dialectic of aggression, retaliation and reconciliation seemed to have been telescoped into a matter of days. There is still a long way to go, and all hope could yet be dashed—on Saturday, the Bosnian Serbs' continued recalcitrance triggered a new NATO ultimatum: Lift the siege of Sarajevo, or be subjected to yet another round of air strikes. But all of a sudden, the chances for a settlement in Bosnia seem better than they have been since the wars there began.

## "The Costs of Peace," *Commonweal*, January 12, 1996:

Peacemaking is not peaceful. In Somalia, violence dogged every peacemaking step, finally driving the United States to withdraw from what began as a humanitarian mission to feed the hungry. Haiti has been more complicated and the outcome more ambiguous. Short-term peace has prevailed—more or less: Political agreements have been kept and elections were quiet. Still, development and real peace exist only in an elusive future.

No doubt sending U.S. troops to Bosnia is a risk, not the least because the very presence of Americans may invite terrorist attacks from all of the belligerents: recalcitrant Bosnian Serbs; the Islamic fighters whose presence helped to fortify the Bosnian army, but whose future plans remain obscure; the Croats, should their territorial hopes be thwarted; and the unofficial militias who have operated outside of official chains-of-command. As 60,000 NATO troops, including 20,000 Americans, move to impose a rough calm on a still-simmering Bosnia, simply enumerating the potential terrorists begins to suggest the explosive costs of peace.

In Bosnia, two million people are displaced from their homes, 250,000 killed, 200,000 wounded. Yielding, negotiating, repenting and reconciling all demand more of us humans—spiritually, psychologically and materially—than most of us have much experience at giving. How much more it asks of those who have raped, tortured, murdered, burnt and pillaged, those who have been victims, and those who have been witnesses of these crimes. Healing these wounds, of course, is not the mandate of NATO, which has been given a year to separate armies, patrol borders, provide security. Armies can only protect a peace that the belligerents themselves must pursue. This

in the midst of a devastated economy in which infrastructure, homes, schools, businesses have been ruthlessly destroyed and international funds for resettlement and reconstruction are in short supply. A year seems pitifully brief.

Thus, the chief source of uneasiness about NATO troops in Bosnia: Are they guarding a peace that will take hold or enforcing a cease-fire that Serbs and Croats will use to prepare a final offensive against the vulnerable remains of Bosnia? Neither Franjo Tudjman of Croatia nor Slobodan Milosevic of Serbia, signers of the Dayton Peace Accord, is to be trusted. Many Americans, certainly many in Congress, do not trust that President Bill Clinton and his chief negotiator Richard Holbrooke know what they are getting into—and more critically, know how to get out. Every possible argument against sending American soldiers to Bosnia has been made; some are plausible, some reek of mere political calculation.

All things considered, one thing is clear: In Bosnia, a year of peace is better than another year of war. A cease-fire is better than slaughter. The Bosnians did not start this war; they resisted defeat and international indifference; now they are ready to pursue peace despite the looming threat of a greater Croatia and a greater Serbia. For them, the cost of war has been enormous, and peace, if it is achieved, will exact a further price. The cost to the United States, in contrast, seems relatively modest. We should pay it.

## "The Russians Are Coming," Kenneth Miller, *Life*, April 1998:

General Gennadi Kotenko begins his interrogation. "So. You have a computer?" Across the table, Nathan Rice nods. "How much time do you spend on it?" Nathan answers cautiously, "I mostly play games on it. . . ." He takes a breath. "So it depends on how bored I am." General Kotenko, who has a grown son of his own, grins and digs into his ham and eggs.

Similar debriefings are being held throughout the lemon-yellow cafeteria of the Galvin Middle School in Wakefield, Massachusetts, where Nathan is a seventh-grader. Aided by translators, 20 Russian officers—12 generals, seven colonels and an admiral—are collecting data on the habits and hobbies of students and teachers, moms and dads. But the hum of cultural transmission is broken when Gerry Scott, a businessman unaccountably dressed as a cowboy, steps to the podium. "I will now teach you two very important words," Scott announces: "Howdy, partner!" *Haww-dee, part-nehr,* the Russians reply, and laughter rocks the room.

For more than three centuries, Wakefield (pop. 23,939) was the kind of town where nothing much happened. Its factories turned out chairs and slippers, its lakes supplied New Englanders with ice, and then the icehouses failed and the mills shut down and folks went to work in malls. But Wakefield has changed. Once a year, the town transforms itself into a capital of reconciliation—a place where ordinary Americans, in an effort to heal five decades of hatred and mistrust, spend a Saturday hanging out with members of Russia's military élite.

After breakfast, sporting new black Stetsons (gifts from Scott), the Russians troop down snowy Main Street. Except for their outfits, they could be replaying a scene from *Red Dawn*—a horde of Slav warriors trampling triumphantly on America's small-town heart. In reality, they are here on a field trip from Harvard's John F. Kennedy School of Government, where they're attending a two-week program in global affairs. Accompanying them are a hundred locals, Harvard people and U.S. officers—their classmates—all led by Wakefield's most illustrious son. John R. Galvin, who nearly flunked out of the school that now bears his name, is a slight, gentle-voiced man of 68. In his Elmer Fudd cap and duck boots, he might be taken for a dairy farmer. But during the waning days of the Cold War, he was one of NATO's two supreme allied commanders, the general in charge of countering Moscow's moves in Europe. Later, he became dean of Tufts University's Fletcher School of Law and Diplomacy. And in 1993, when he heard about the Harvard program for high-ranking Russians, he decided to give the participants a tour of his hometown. After sitting through days of lectures on geopolitics and geoeconomics, they would learn about Wakefield—and, by extension, about ground-level capitalism, grassroots democracy and the people who were once Russia's mortal enemies.

The tour's first stop is Hart's Hardware, where a trio of colonels exclaim over a rack of chains. Such an assortment! Light, medium and heavy-duty! Plain, brass-plated and plastic-coated! At Smith Drugs, General Boris Karpovich, a barrel-shaped man in a fur-trimmed coat, buys salve for his sore feet. "The selection is better than in Moscow," the general says, "and the prices are cheaper." Colonel Aleksandr Gurvich is less impressed. "I prefer another kind of medicine," he quips. "Russian vodka."

At *The Wakefield Daily Item*, the interrogations resume. The Russians want to know the paper's yearly profit. (Editor Peter Rossi pleads ignorance.) In the selectmen's office, they grill town official Tom Butler on the mechanics of tax collection. At the First Parish Congregational Church, they inquire about relations among Wakefield's religious groups; when Pastor Richard Weisenbach confides that a rabbi acts as guest preacher on Thanksgiving, there are gasps of amazement. In the office of attorney Mark Curley, the O. J. enigma is raised: If your system is so good, how could he have walked? At Liberty

## "The Russians Are Coming . . ." *(continued)*

Chevrolet, the Russians gleefully honk the horns of sleek Corvettes and Camaros. But on a typical general's salary of $400 a month, such vehicles are out of reach, and the diesel-repair company out back holds more real estate. "What's the fuel mileage on that bus?" someone asks president Jeff Manning. Over lunch at the Best Western Lord Wakefield, as Galvin and Kotenko compare notes on military family life (the constant moves!), General Dmitri Gavrilov questions the sanity of American smoking laws. "And what is this tradition," he asks Curley, "of letting the fish go after you've caught it?"

After the mystery is solved, it's time for some plain American fun. At the Wakefield Bowladrome, owner Sal Orifice—a World War II vet who remembers when the Japanese were the enemy—has reserved half the lanes for the Russians, free of charge. The first balls charge straight for the gutter, but soon candlepins are flying and generals are leaping. Appetites whetted, the Russians head off to dinner at the Bear Hill Golf Club. Then comes the day's finale: visits to real American homes.

In their gingerbread Victorian, Richard and Phyllis Bayrd host Gavrilov, Karpovich and General Mikhail Sautin. A retired missile engineer and a Narragansett Indian, Richard crowns each guest with a headdress. "We have always identified with Indians," say Karpovich. A peace pipe is passed, followed by vodka. Richard's toast reveals what Wakefielders have learned from spying on the Russians: "We're no different from you, except you guys talk funny." To which the generals reply, "Nazdarovye!"

### "Make War, Make Peace," *Newsweek*, September 11, 1995:

What shaped this radical turn of events? Mostly, American determination to take the lead—and changing conditions on the ground. Last month's Croatian offensive in the Krajina region and western Bosnia surprised and weakened Serb forces. The coup de grace came from Serbian President Slobodan Milosevic, who, despite repeated promises of assistance, declined to help his ethnic cousins when they most needed it. Having thrown over communism, nationalism and the dream of Greater Serbia, Milosevic eventually decided to hang his political future on cooperation with the West.

Bill Clinton didn't want Bosnia in his political future either—and resolved in July to take decisive action. The GOP Congress decried his Balkan policy. After the humiliating display of U.N. hostages handcuffed to strategic Serb sites, and the brutal conquest of two Muslim safe areas, GOP leaders voted to lift the arms embargo against the Bosnians. That would ultimately have forced Clinton to send U.S. troops—a politically disastrous move.

The president's frustration boiled over one humid evening in July on the private putting green in back of the White House. Clinton, says a top aide, demanded a progress report on the Balkans, saying, "The status quo in Bosnia is unacceptable," and then angrily flubbed several shots. Days later, an Oval Office meeting with Clinton's foreign-policy team produced poignancy, but little sharpening of purpose. Srebrenica had just fallen, and U.S. officials seemed haunted by reports of Serb atrocities. Vice President Al Gore, says a senior official, was particularly appalled by the picture of a young Muslim woman who fled into the woods and hanged herself. "My daughter asked me the other day why we weren't doing something about it," Gore said. None of the assembled had an answer. "Everyone around the room was very, very quiet," says the administration official.

# 2000–2009

The first decade of the twenty-first century began with record prosperity, and ended with recession and record unemployment. By 2009, 6,259 coalition troops had been killed in wars in Afghanistan and Iraq, including 5,318 Americans.

Relative peace was shattered when, on September 11, 2001, terrorists hijacked four American commercial airliners and crashed them in New York; Shanksville, Pennsylvania; and the Pentagon. Two planes were crashed into the twin towers of the World Trade Center, bringing both down in clouds of as a shocked and horrified nation watched.

Americans felt vulnerable to a foreign invasion for the first time in decades and citizens all over the country begain questioning their safety.

U.S. forces were dispatched around the world in a War on Terror. United in grief and outrage, the nation mobilized its military, intelligence, law enforcement, diplomatic, and financial resources. The first stop was the mountains of Afghanistan, where a new breed of suicidal terrorists, al-Qaeda, were collected into an army of self-styled Islamic warriors determined to destroy America. America's military response was swift and uncompromising. The initial fighting force combined billion-dollar U.S. technology, and the Taliban was quickly routed, although al-Qaeda leader Osama Bin Laden escaped capture. Within months of the invasion, more than 2,400 suspected terrorists in 90 countries were detained and the messy process of rebuilding Afghanistan began.

The United States shifted from the war in Afghanistan to Iraq, home of leader Saddam Hussein and his "weapons of mass destruction." As in the invasion of Afghanistan, the U.S. achieved a rapid victory, but were unable to find Saddam's weapons of mass destruction. Waging peace and establishing stability proved to be far more complex than fighting the Iraqi Army.

As 2003 was drawing to a close, the U.S. found itself struggling with multibillion-dollar deficits, continued job loss, and a price tag for the invasion of Iraq nearing $100 billion in aid alone. President George Bush's approval rating for his handling of the war in Iraq fell to 49 percent.

The U.S. economy stagnated in most areas in the mid-2000s with one exception—housing. As home prices soared, small investors began a cycle of flipping houses for a quick profit. Investors fueled the frenzy by selling mortgages that carried high interest costs. At first, the mortgages were highly profitable, and banks bundled them into complex securities sold to investors. However, as record numbers of families crumbled into foreclosure on these shaky "subprime" loans, the housing bubble burst, and by late 2008, the United States was at the edge of a financial collapse that rivaled the Great Depression of the 1930s.

An outright collapse was avoided by a massive infusion of government money in the form of a "bank bailout" and financial interventions by the Federal Reserve. But the resulting recession cost more than seven million Americans their jobs, as unemployment doubled to 10 percent. Americans living below the poverty line grew from 11.3 percent in 2000 to 13.2 percent in 2008.

Meanwhile, the cost of war—mostly the Iraq war—continued to soar. The Associated Press estimated that 110,600 soldiers and civilians were killed in the conflict in Iraq from March 2003 to April 2009. Direct U.S. government spending reached about $612 billion by April 2009. Indirect costs would total billions more, including caring for soldiers with long-term injuries, such as the traumatic brain injuries caused by roadside blasts.

Politically, the Republican Party's support began ebbing from its high water mark of 2003 when the number of Americans supporting the GOP finally matched support for the Democratic Party. Dissatisfaction with the Iraq war and George Bush eroded the Republican Party's ranks throughout the rest of the decade.

The war and economic disintegration also played a major role in the election of Barack Obama as president on November 4, 2008. Not only did the Democratic Party regain the White House for the first time since 2000, but voters also had chosen, for the first time, an African American for the nation's highest office.

The first year of the Obama presidency saw political divisions deepen even as the United States began pulling troops out of Iraq and hints of an economic recovery appeared by the year's end.

# 2001 NEWS FEATURE

**"Terrorists Hijack 4 Airliners; Destroy World Trade Center; Hit Pentagon; Hundreds Dead," Steve Twomey and Arthur Santana, *The Washington Post*, September 12, 2001:**

Rescuers fought through tons of debris in quest of victims at the Pentagon last night after terrorists seized an airliner outbound from Dulles International Airport and plunged it into the heart of American military power, killing an estimated several hundred people.

Hampered by fires that still raged as evening fell, emergency teams had carried out only six bodies, but they were preparing to remove many more, and rescuers were using dogs and listening devices to search for people they believed might be trapped alive.

Precise figures were hard to come by because portions of the building were under construction, and many of the military and civilian personnel had been temporarily relocated, according to Arlington Fire Chief Edward P. Plaugher.

Coming less than an hour after two hijacked passenger jets slammed into the twin towers of New York's World Trade Center, the assault on the Pentagon began an unprecedented day of office and school closings, panicked phone calls, wild rumors and extraordinary security in the Washington area.

Last night, downtown streets were largely deserted as D.C. National Guard units joined police in patrolling the city. D.C. Mayor Anthony A. Williams (D), Maryland Gov. Parris N. Glendening (D) and Virginia Gov. James S. Gilmore III (R) declared states of emergency that broadened their power to govern without legislative authority.

Most of the region's school systems will be closed today, although President Bush announced that the federal government would reopen, after having shut down within an hour of yesterday's Pentagon attack.

At a late-evening news conference, D.C. Police Chief Charles H. Ramsey said that the attacks here and in New York would forever change security operations in Washington, and that there was no longer such a thing as "business as usual" here.

Originally headed for Los Angeles, the American Airlines Boeing 757—carrying 64 people and loaded with 30,000 pounds of fuel for the long flight to the West Coast—smashed into the five-story Pentagon's west facade about 9:40 a.m. after skimming above Arlington at breakneck speed.

Cmdr. Thomas P. Van Leunen, Jr., director of the navy's media operations, said the explosion was "similar to shooting a five-inch gun, only a little bit longer and louder."

The impact rocked the immense building, gouging a wedge deep into its interior, collapsing floors and touch-

ing off fires. Stunned, often disheveled employees stumbled from their offices and into the acrid smoke of what had been a perfect late-summer morning.

"People were yelling, 'Evacuate! Evacuate!' And we found ourselves on the lawn looking back on our building," Air Force Lt. Col. Marc Abshire said. "It was very much a surrealistic sort of experience. It was just definitely not right to see smoke coming out of the Pentagon."

At least 1,000 law enforcement officers, firefighters and Pentagon employees searched for victims and evidence, even as flames shot out of the building. Military helicopters and fighter aircraft prowled the skies, at times frightening those below, who believed another air assault might be under way.

Officials said most of the damage was in the E Ring, inflicted by an aircraft that disintegrated on impact. Parts of the wings were reportedly found outside the building.

The region's emergency medical system prepared for massive casualties, but by late afternoon, hospitals in Northern Virginia and the District had been able to cope easily with the approximately 70 brought to them. The busiest by far was Virginia Hospital Center-Arlington, where 36 patients were taken. Inova Alexandria Hospital treated 18, and 13 went to Washington Hospital Center, which has the region's only advanced burn-care center. Many patients were later released.

As rescue workers streamed toward the Pentagon, the federal government closed its offices in the area, telling its 260,000 local workers they were free to leave, and the D.C. government and many businesses followed suit. That unloosed an army of homebound drivers upon downtown's streets, causing temporary paralysis that, once cleared, was followed by the kind of emptiness and silence usually limited to snowstorms.

In the District, hundreds of members of the National Guard reported for duty in camouflage and took an oath to defend District streets. They patrolled in Humvees.

Cell phone networks stopped working as their patrons all tried to check on loved ones at once. Some school systems decided to send children home early, but even before they could be dismissed, parents showed up in droves to pick up their youngsters.

Historian David McCullough, author of the bestselling book on President John Adams, was staying at the Hay-Adams Hotel downtown, where he climbed to a high point in the building to view the smoke rising across the Potomac River at the Pentagon.

"This is going to be a dividing point in history," said McCullough, who was turned away when he went to George Washington University Hospital to try to give blood. "If they still teach history 100 years from now, children will still be reading about this day," he said, adding, "We haven't seen such destruction on our own soil since the Civil War."

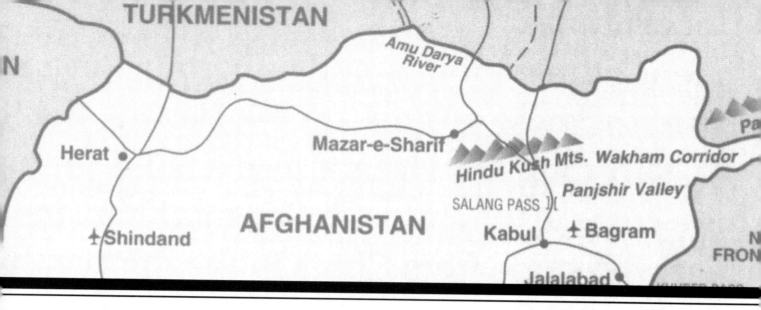

# 2001 PROFILE

## WAR IN AFGHANISTAN

### Sergeant

Sergeant Stanley Macauley thought he was a tough guy when he was growing up in Texas, but changed his mind after joining the U.S. Special Forces in Afghanistan.

### Life at Home

- Stanley "Mac" Macauley was broke, alone and desperate when he joined the army.
- The son of a truck driver, he grew up on the edge of suburban San Antonio, Texas.
- Because of emphysema, his father was often reduced to long stretches of TV watching, while his mother helped support the family by earning tips as a waitress.
- Mac considered himself a tough guy, capable of taking care of himself; he stayed in school primarily to play tight end on the football team.
- He boxed in the Golden Gloves program because he loved to see fear leap into the eyes of his opponent.
- After high school, he got married, agreed to attend community college, worked at the local garage and began to run with the nightclub crowd—with an impromptu brawl tossed in every once in a while for good measure.
- It was a plan that worked for 13 months, until he flunked out of school, showed up drunk for work and found out his wife was leaving him for another man.
- Suddenly, escape and the military looked good.
- Immediately, he discovered that he liked the structure of military life, and enjoyed learning practical things.
- In the army, he also discovered a goal: joining the Special Forces, reputed to be the toughest, smartest, trickiest soldiers around.
- He finally got his shot on the Special Forces Qualifying Course, but realized the competition was stiff, and felt no more than average.
- When it came time to swim the length of the pool and back wearing fatigues, boots and a 40-pound pack, he knew this was the way to set himself apart from the crowd.
- He dove in and breast-stroked the length of the pool underwater and back before resurfacing, though he was ready to pass out.

## Afghanistan: In For the Long Haul

HAS THE WAR ON TERROR been a success? Well, yes and no. "I think it's bumbling along in the right direction," says a Western diplomat in Kabul. "Probably, things will be all right." Osama bin Laden and Ayman al-Zawahiri, al-Qaeda's two top leaders, remain unaccounted for, and U.S. intelligence sources suspect that both are still alive. So is Mullah Mohammed Omar, the leader of the Taliban. Sources tell TIME that Omar may be forging an alliance with Gulbuddin Hekmatyar, a particularly dangerous former *mujahedin* leader—and briefly Prime Minister of Afghanistan—who slipped back into the country around February. "Hekmatyar should be seen as quite as much a worry as Omar," says a Western intelligence official in Kabul. "If the two are cooperating, then the danger of a growth in terrorist attacks and assassinations is very real."

What's more, al-Qaeda seems to be having little trouble funding its continuing operations. According to a draft of a report by a United Nations group charged with monitoring international controls on terrorist groups, only about $10 million of identified terrorist assets have been frozen since the beginning of the year, compared with $112 mil-

**MUDDLED VICTORY A special-forces soldier in Afghanistan**

lion in the immediate aftermath of Sept. 11. In Washington, the Treasury Department challenged the report's conclusions on the ineffectiveness of the effort to clamp down on terrorists' assets. But the U.N. document also detailed the relative ease with which terrorists can cross international boundaries and replenish their supplies of weapons. Al-Qaeda, said the report, "is by all accounts 'fit and well' and poised to strike again at its leisure."

In the year since 9/11, the war against terrorism has also had some clear victories. In Afghanistan itself, says Lieut. Colonel David Gray, director of operations for the 10th Mountain Division, "we have certainly defeated if not destroyed the al-Qaeda network as it existed before the war." Military and intelligence analysts agree that the combined power of Taliban and al-Qaeda forces in Afghanistan has been reduced to not much more than several hundred men, none of them assembled in large groups. Another few hundred al-Qaeda fighters are thought to be across the border in Pakistan. One by one, two by two, they are being hunted down.

- The commanding officer was impressed.
- Within the Special Forces environment, Mac began to grasp his full potential, taking college courses and becoming fluent in Arabic, Russian and Dari.
- He also became proficient in a variety of light weapon and hand-to-hand combat techniques.
- His particular specialty was his ability to work with horses, which quickly became an off-duty passion.
- Each 14-man Special Forces team included two specialists in intelligence, medicine, demolition, communications, weapons and, thanks to a recent change, two air force "targeteers" to help call in air strikes.
- Mac's area of expertise was intelligence.
- Two of each specialty were employed to allow the team to be divided into two equally qualified groups, if necessary.
- Since his team was part of the 5th Special Forces Group that specialized in the Middle East and Central Asia, he observed the tragedy of September 11 with special insight.
- The fight ahead was the one for which he had been trained.

### Life at Work

- Sgt. Macauley was on his way back from a visit with his sister, brother-in-law and two adoring nieces in Texas when his cell phone rang.
- "Stop shaving immediately and report to the base for deployment," he was told.
- Shortly thereafter, with his beard just beginning to look respectable, he and the rest of his team shipped out for Central Asia.
- Soon, they were helicoptered into a remote spot high in the mountains—far behind enemy lines.

- Their mission was twofold: to direct American air assaults from the ground, and assist and support the Northern Alliance, which would be conducting the ground war.
- The Northern Alliance was a loose confederation of tribal chiefs, often called warlords in the American press, who were opposed to the Taliban.
- The Bush administration did not feel that domestic policy would allow for the insertion of large numbers of ground troops, especially if U.S. casualties resulted, so small Special Forces teams and native forces—some of questionable reliability—were selected to carry the brunt of the combat burden.
- Mac and his team were assigned to a particularly unsavory warlord, known for shifting sides and for his creative ways of killing those who displeased him.
- The entire U.S. team, now sporting beards, wore clothing similar to that of the Northern Alliance, including the round wool hats, or "pakols," and long checked scarves.
- Each person also carried a pack with approximately 200 pounds of equipment and supplies.
- To help them move through the mountain trails to the warlord's camp, they arranged for a string of sturdy mountain horses.

- Since it was Mac's responsibility to supervise the loading of the animals, he also brought up the rear in case any of the team members, less accustomed to mountain horseback riding, ran into trouble.
- Ahead were 24 hours of difficult riding without rest.
- When they finally arrived exhausted and sore into camp, Mac, as the team's only Dari speaker, was pressed into service as a translator.
- One of the first orders of business was the treatment of Afghan wounded and injured; Mac's team included two medics.
- Unfortunately, one of the most seriously wounded required the amputation of his leg just below the hip.
- To bolster the fighting morale of the native fighting force, long deprived of supplies, the captain ordered food and medical supplies air-dropped to the site as soon as possible.
- The warlord claimed to have 2,000 men in his command, though Mac figured his strength to be no more than 1,200, many without much training.
- When they moved out toward a Taliban stronghold to the south, progress through the mountains was slow, taking two days.
- The enemy position was a seemingly impregnable fortress atop a crag, where Taliban soldiers were reported to be armed with machine guns, some light artillery, mortars and several Russian-made shoulder-mounted rocket launchers.
- While Afghan soldiers surrounded the crag, the Special Forces team divided into two groups.
- Mac and his team members carried the M-4, a shorter M-16 with collapsible stock, scope and laser designator.
- He helped pepper the enemy soldiers with automatic fire, while the second team used satellite radios to guide the first of the air strikes.
- The first to arrive were the F-14s with rockets and bombs to soften the enemy position.

- As they approached, Mac's team picked out targets and "painted" them with a laser beam capable of guiding the smart munitions to their targets.
- The Afghan allies watched in amazement as a cave entrance was first marked by a mysterious red beam followed by a pinpoint explosion on that exact spot, sending debris and bodies into the air.
- An AC-130 Spectre gunship followed the bombing run, making several passes designed to further pummel the Taliban position.
- The crag was quiet for only a few minutes before small-arms fire erupted again.
- Mac and his team were enthusiastically returning fire, when Warrant Officer Stephen Amato called out, "Here comes the big girl!"
- Overhead, the shape of a B-52 bomber emerged in the sky and released a dozen 500-pound bombs.

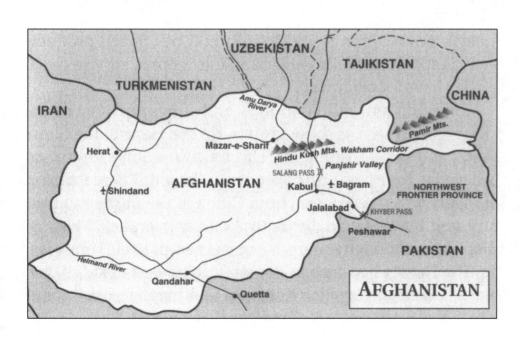

- The crag, nearly flattened by the explosions, took on an eerie silence, and the Northern Alliance headed up the rise.
- The few remaining Taliban surrendered immediately, and Mac wondered what plans the warlord had for these men.
- Mac and his team were surveying the beautiful brutality of modern weaponry when the captain took a radio call.
- Several hundred Taliban troops had been spotted to the southeast.
- All around him, the Afghan fighters were talking about the powerful explosions they had seen; surely the Taliban could not withstand this force for long, they remarked to him in a mixture of Russian and Dari.

- He had heard that about 100 Special Forces men were on the ground in Afghanistan—more than enough, he thought, to teach the Taliban not to mess with the U.S.A.

## Life in the Community: Afghanistan

- Afghanistan's geographic location between the Persian Gulf, Central Asia and the Indian subcontinent made it a significant world player, and created the potential for Afghan rulers to spread their authority east and west.
- It also made the country a target for international powers focused on global control.
- Of the 25 million people in Afghanistan, 20 percent live in urban areas, the rest in the vast rural stretches.
- The mountainous features of the country make it necessary for many villages to be self-sufficient.
- The population comprises eight major ethnic groups: Pashtuns (38 percent); Tajiks (25 percent); Hazaras (19 percent); Uzbeck (six percent); Turkmen, Aimaqs, Kirghiz, and Baluchis (12 percent).
- Eighty-five percent is Sunni Muslim, 15 percent Shiite Muslim.
- The main national languages are Dari and Pushto; in addition, there are 20 languages and 40 dialects spoken.
- The modern state of Afghanistan emerged in 1747.
- The establishment of the first Republic of Afghanistan took place from 1973 to 1979.
- The People's Democratic Party of Afghanistan led a coup d'état in April 1978.
- The Soviet invasion began in December 1979, and lasted for almost 10 years.

- The Islamic State of Afghanistan existed from 1992 to 1996, followed by the rise of the Taliban movement and the establishment of the Islamic Emirate of Afghanistan.
- The rise of the Taliban was unanticipated, springing from the southern villages of Qandahar and the refugee camps in Pakistan.
- Many ex-military officers participated in the Taliban, whose supreme leader had a combined spiritual and political status in the high council and the affairs of the people.

## HISTORICAL SNAPSHOT
# 2001

- The number of U.S. golf courses had increased from 13,353 in 1986 to 17,701
- The number of unmarried couples heading U.S. households increased from 3.2 million in 1990 to 5.5 million in 2000
- The price paid for a typical set of childhood vaccinations was now $385, up from $10 in 1971
- Education reform was approved, requiring annual standardized tests in grades three through eight by 2005-6
- Former President Jimmy Carter was honored with the Nobel Peace prize
- The War Against Terrorism legislation, authorizing the president to use force against those who perpetrated or assisted in the September 11 attacks, passed the House and Senate without objection
- After a letter containing anthrax was sent to Senator Tom Daschle's office, the Hart Senate Office Building was closed for three months
- During the last three months of the year, after nearly a million jobs had been lost, unemployment stood at nearly six percent, up from 3.9 percent a year earlier
- The USA Patriot Act expanded the powers of the police to wiretap telephones, monitor Internet and e-mail use, and search the homes of suspected terrorists
- President George W. Bush said during his 2002 State of the Union address: "States like those (Iraq, Iran and North Korea) and their terrorist allies, constitute an axis of evil, aiming to threaten the peace of the world"
- Enron, a $50 billion energy-trading company, became the largest U.S. company ever to file for bankruptcy
- The Dow-Jones Industrial Average reached a high of 11,337 (May) for the year and low of 8,235 (September)
- The much-anticipated movie version of the book *Harry Potter and the Sorcerer's Stone* grossed $150 million in five days
- China was formally granted permanent normal trade status, reversing a 20-year policy of requiring an annual review for the country to expand its human rights activities
- U.S. forces continued to search for terrorist mastermind Osama bin Laden; hundreds of al-Qaeda forces were believed to have escaped into Pakistan
- The United States withdrew from the 1972 Antiballistic Missile Treaty, thereby allowing the military to test and deploy missile-defense systems without restraints

## "Green Berets up Close," Donatella Lorch, *Newsweek*, January 14, 2002:

They landed in darkness on an early November night, deep in the mountains of northern Afghanistan. For six hours, they'd hunkered down in the freezing hold of the transport helicopter, tossed by heavy winds, before setting down 6,000 feet above sea level. Shouldering 200-pound packs stuffed with weapons, ammunition and communications gear, the U.S. Army's 1st Battalion 5th Special Forces A-Team piled out of the chopper and onto the snowy turf. The helicopter retreated, a roar of roto wash kicking dirt and ice into the men's faces. Then, silence. For weeks, the 13-man Green Beret team had trained and studied and obsessed about their mission. They were a tight-knit group, each man trusting the others with his life. Yet it wasn't until the chopper faded from view and the vastness of the landscape came into focus that they realized how far from home they were, and how alone: 90 miles behind enemy lines, in the heart of Taliban territory.

To the men, standing in the blackness that night, the mission ahead seemed almost impossible. The team was to find and win the trust of an elusive Northern Alliance commander they knew virtually nothing about and whose language they did not speak, supply his ragtag team of fighters and then, with his help, storm a key Taliban stronghold, the northern city of Mazar-e Sharif. After wrestling control from the enemy, they were to restore order and help local leaders begin rebuilding the ravaged city. Along the way, they were to sneak up on armed Taliban camps and caves, helping to laser-guide U.S. bombers to their targets.

In the harrowing, heroic days that followed, they did just that. The fall of Mazar-e Sharif turned out to be a critical moment in the Afghan war, setting off a domino effect that quickly led to the fall of the major cities of Kabul and Qandahar, and the collapse of Taliban rule. It also provided a dramatic victory for the élite Special Forces, whose daring missions in the past had sometimes gone disastrously wrong.

### "Buddy System, for the Air Force, Structured Mentoring Beats On-the-Fly Programs," Peter Economy, *Gallup Management Journal*, Fall 2001:

KEN ALEXANDER
Courtesy San Francisco Examiner

THE U.S. ARMY WILL GIVE YOU $1,500.00 BONUS TO ENLIST IN THE COMBAT UNIT OF YOUR CHOICE

U.S. ARMY RECRUITING

KEN ALEXANDER

"I see the Marines got one"

Like most organizations today, the United States Air Force is having a tough time retaining its best people. It invests a considerable amount of time and money—estimated by a congressional source at more than $6 million per person—to train its pilots. Still, in 1997, only 36 percent of pilots who had reached the end of their initial nine-year service commitment agreed to stay on—far short of the organization's goal of 50 percent. That same year, more than 800 pilots refused $60,000 bonuses to stay an additional five years, choosing instead to separate from the service. The result is a chronic shortage of qualified pilots that places additional pressure on those who remain and threatens the air force's ability to execute its missions.

The air force has tried a variety of approaches to address this crisis, including increased salaries and cash incentives. But according to Captain Edward "Buzz" Haskell, assistant professor at the U.S. Air Force Academy, increasing compensation for air force personnel has not had the desired effect. "Many people are not satisfied with current conditions. Senior leaders in the air force talk about raising bonuses and retention incentives, but so far, money has not been an indicator for people staying," he says. Instead, says Haskell, quality-of-life issues, including how people feel about their careers, their workplaces and their families, have a much greater impact on retention.

These facts weren't lost on the air force's top brass. In 1997, mentoring was targeted as a key process for enhancing career development and communications within the air force, and then–Secretary of the Air Force Sheila Widnall mandated that the organization implement mentoring programs throughout its operations. But because Widnall's edict did not spell out a strategy, figuring one out became the first order of business for officers like Haskell.

Haskell had already conducted research on mentoring as part of his doctoral dissertation, and knew it could be problematic. "Mentoring has been traditionally viewed as top-down," says Haskell. That approach, he says, has led to assigned mentorships, or "forced matching," which Haskell believes does not always work. "The protégés can easily feel stuck with a person they do not respect or wish to emulate."

Haskell turned to Gallup's research on mentoring programs because, he says, "Gallup has the only mentoring research I've ever seen that encourages non-forced matching." By non-forced matching, Haskell means that, according to Gallup, organizations allow protégés to select their own mentors, based on criteria established by a mentor-match instrument, which consists of two questionnaires—one for prospective mentors and another for prospective protégés. The questionnaires assess a variety of areas, including coaching style and experience. For example, protégés are asked to choose between pairs of characteristics that most closely reflect what they would like from mentors. The results are run through a computer program that provides protégés with scores indicating their compatibility to mentors in each of the assessed areas. A

## "Buddy System . . ." *(continued)*

protégé who, for example, prefers a challenging coaching style—one where his or her coach continually raises the bar for performance—can be matched with a mentor whose coaching style is challenging. . . .

To assess the effectiveness of the mentoring program in a military environment, Haskell conducted a survey of pilots, navigators and electronic warfare specialists in the 55th Wing at Offutt Air Force Base in Nebraska. In this three-month study, he used the mentor match instrument to pair 24 junior officers with 24 senior officers in the same job specialty. In a twist on the top-down approach, protégés in Haskell's study used the mentor-match instrument to choose with whom they would be paired. He provided protégés with workbooks and had them meet twice a month with their mentors. "For that one hour that

they met, it was 100 percent about the protégé—tell me about your career, what do you want to do, what do you think you can do, let me help you with that. It was geared toward the protégé's professional development," says Haskell.

The results were dramatic. According to written questionnaires given to all participants before and after the mentoring program, protégé post-study performance improved over pre-study performance in preparation to supervise enlisted personnel (81.8 percent reporting above average or excellent versus 63.6 percent before) and decision-making ability (95.5 percent above average or excellent versus 81.9 percent before). Furthermore, participants reported a higher probability of retention, with 95.5 percent planning to serve 20 years or more versus only 72.7 percent before the study commenced.

## "The Manhunt," Josh Tyrangiel, *Time*, December 24, 2001:

The 12 bearded soldiers making their way up a pass in the White Mountains of Tora Bora were decked in flat-topped Afghan caps and flowing *shalwar kameezes*. From a distance, only one detail gave them away as Americans. Afghan alliance fighters—dedicated but largely untrained—walk upright, making themselves easy targets for enemy fire. The Americans were shimmying up the hill on their bellies.

Late last week, American special operations forces quietly made their way to Tora Bora, to the very front of the front lines. The dozen U.S. soldiers used a translator to coordinate with an Afghan commander. To the Afghan fighters at their side, the Americans made it clear they were on a search-and-destroy mission. "We and the Americans had the same goal," said Khawri, an Afghan who was shoulder-to-shoulder with U.S. troops. "To kill all the al-Qaeda people." By Sunday, the Afghans were claiming victory, though the U.S. remained guarded.

The war in Afghanistan began nine weeks ago on a battlefield the size of Texas, and it may end in a high, narrow valley smaller than the city of Austin. After weeks of playing Where's Osama?, military officials believe they have overheard bin Laden on handheld radios in the White Mountains, giving orders to his dwindling al-Qaeda forces. Afghan fighters said they had killed 200 and routed al-Qaeda, but the U.S. said too many nooks had yet to be searched. If bin Laden is in Tora Bora, he and his soldiers are trapped in a box: Snow-covered peaks loom on two sides, Afghan and American soldiers await on a third,

and Pakistani border patrols stand guard on the fourth.

The cornered fighters have little room to maneuver. With no enemy antiaircraft fire, U.S. spy planes circle the sky, daring al-Qaeda fighters to step out of their caves and become glowing infrared targets. Few have done so. Bin Laden has resorted to giving orders on shortwave radio, U.S. authorities suggest, because there's no one else left to do so.

But inevitability almost slipped away last week. The three Afghan warlords in control of alliance forces began the week with a successful assault on the Milawa Valley, the lone entrance to Tora Bora from the north. Al-Qaeda soldiers fled quickly, though they did manage to kill a few alliance troops. Having taken the territory, the warlords committed a major tactical error: They withdrew from the valley. When alliance forces returned the next day, they were greeted by three al-Qaeda fighters armed with machine guns who opened fire from 200 meters. No alliance soldiers were killed, but the morning was spent fighting a battle for territory that had already been won.

The follies had only just begun. As al-Qaeda fighters scampered up the mountains in search of a safe haven, one of the warlords, Haji Zaman, agreed to a ceasefire without bothering to consult the other two Afghan commanders or the U.S. Zaman claims the Arab-speaking fighters reached him via wireless and offered to surrender on the condition that they be turned over to the United Nations. "They said they had to get in contact with each other and would surrender group by group," Zaman says. He then announced the ceasefire, halted his troops' advance and gave the opposition until 8 a.m. to give themselves up.

Zaman's fellow Afghan commanders were outraged, while U.S. officials appeared shocked. The Americans did not object to an al-Qaeda surrender, but any surrender had to be unconditional. As for the ceasefire, Air Force General Richard Myers, the Chairman of the Joint Chiefs of Staff, simply ignored it. "Just for the record," said Myers,

## "The Manhunt . . ." *(continued)*

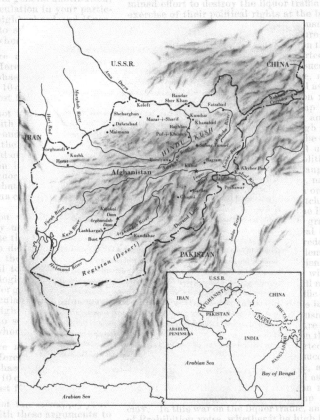

"our military mission remains to destroy the al-Qaeda and the Taliban networks. So our operation from the air and the ground will continue until our mission is accomplished."

The U.S. ignored the ceasefire and bombed relentlessly. Sure enough, the next day, the surrendering al-Qaeda troops had vanished. Zaman's aides insist that they were probably "confused" when the U.S. broke the ceasefire and scampered back into their holes. But other Afghan leaders thought Zaman had been duped. "It was a trick," said Haji Zahir, one of the warlords commanding Afghan troops in Tora Bora. "They were buying time."

The arrival of Western troops at the front lines had the added advantage of giving the Afghan fighters new resolve. During previous weeks, the Afghans withdrew from their positions during the day in time to break their Ramadan fasts at dusk.

With the end—and the Americans—in sight, they held their positions.

From the start of the war, the U.S. has relied heavily on Afghan ground forces rather than deploy a sizable contingent of American troops. But the ceasefire screw-up was a reminder that the Afghans might be useful proxies for some jobs, but were perhaps not quite professional enough to finish this one. On Sunday, Zaman managed to get back into the U.S.'s good graces—and back into the race for the $25 million bounty on bin Laden's head—as he ferried Western commandos to the front. By then, U.S. warplanes were pounding al-Qaeda positions with hundreds of bombs and missiles, and more than 100 U.S. and British special-ops soldiers had moved in, signaling to the Afghans and al-Qaeda that the time for mistakes was over.

"Al-Qaeda is finished," crowed Afghan commander Hazrat Ali from his battlefield perch below the caves on Friday afternoon. "They are surrounded." American military leaders were more cautious. "'Surrounded' probably is not a terribly good word," said General Tommy R. Franks, the regional commander of American forces. "But the view of the opposition leaders on the ground is that this al-Qaeda force is contained in that area."

## "Inside the Battle of Shah-i-Kot, Where the Enemy Has Nothing to Lose and U.S. Soldiers Had to Fight for Their Lives," Michael Elliott, *Time*, March 18, 2002:

In the TV commercials, they call it "An army of One," and the phrase is intended to send a message: In the U.S. armed forces, every person counts. If you take a round, your buddies will come and get you. "The Ranger creed is that you do not leave a fallen comrade on the field of battle," says David Anderson, of Jacksonville, Fla., a former Ranger whose son, Marc Anthony Anderson, followed him into the army. "I really believed in what the creed says, and Marc did. He said, 'If something happens to me, don't worry, because you'll have a body.'"

Last week Marc's body, along with those of seven other American soldiers, was flown from Afghanistan to Ramstein Air Force Base in Germany before coming home for those proud, sad ceremonies that mark the death of young men in battle. The army had once more been asked to live up to the promise it makes to those who serve. "We don't leave Americans behind," says Brigadier General Jon Rosa, Jr., deputy director of operations for the Joint Chiefs of Staff. Last week, that word was kept. But the price for doing so was high.

For weeks, U.S. forces had been watching as Taliban and al-Qaeda fighters gathered south of Kabul. Code-named Operation Anaconda, the battle plan aimed at this force was a hammer-and-anvil strategy. Friendly Afghans, assisted by U.S. special forces, would flush the enemy from the north and northwest toward three exits of the Shah-i-Kot valley, where American troops waited. To the south, battle positions Heather and Ginger were divided by a hill christened the Whale, while to the east, battle position Eve guarded escape routes over the high mountains to Pakistan. But after two days of fierce combat, the al-Qaeda and Taliban fighters were still in place; one American had already been killed.

Before dawn on Monday, two huge MH-47 Chinooks, double-headed flying beasts like something out of Tolkein, chugged through the frigid air. They were on their way from Bagram Air Base, north of Kabul, to Shah-i-Kot and the most intense battle so far of the Afghan war. A force that would eventually grow to more than 1,000 Americans, drawn mainly from the 10th Mountain and 101st Airborne divisions, together with Afghan militias and about 200 special forces from allied nations, was engaged with perhaps 1,000 al-Qaeda and Taliban fighters—four times as many enemy men as the U.S. had expected. The battlefield spread over 70 square miles, at altitudes that ranged from 8,000 to 12,000 feet and temperatures that dipped at night to 15 degrees.

The Chinooks headed for Ginger, at the southeast corner of the valley, where American forces had met intense opposition two days before. As the choppers prepared to set down, they came under heavy fire from small-arms and rocket-propelled grenades, one of which bounced, without exploding, off the armor of a Chinook. In the same bird, a hydraulic line was cut, and the pilots radioed back to Bagram that continuing with the mission would be suicide. Major General Frank (Buster) Hagenbeck, the force commander, agreed, and the choppers veered away to the north, climbing steeply. They found a place to set down and did a head count. On the damaged Chinook, one man was missing. They counted again. Navy SEAL Neil Roberts, the rear gunner who had been returning fire from the open back hatch, was no longer with his team. Roberts had apparently been

## "Inside the Battle . . ." (continued)

jolted out when the chopper banked hard to the north.

The Rangers radioed Bagram for permission to go after their man. Hagenbeck agreed, and the undamaged Chinook dropped off six commandos to search for Roberts; then both helicopters returned to base. Unmanned surveillance aircraft searched for the missing man and found him moving across the valley. Images beamed from the drones to video monitors at Bagram showed three men approaching Roberts. They were at first thought to be friendly. Then Roberts was seen trying to flee. About three hours after the first incident, two more Chinooks set off from Bagram on a dual mission: to rescue Roberts and

to insert more troops at Ginger. One of the choppers took heavy machine-gun fire. It shuddered and spiraled toward the ground but managed to crash-land less than a mile from the place the first pair had come under attack. As the troops clambered out of the wrecked MH-47, they were ambushed. Hagenbeck ordered AC-130 gunships to the battle to provide close air support, but the al-Qaeda barrage was so intense that U.S. troops couldn't be lifted out during daylight. Fighting continued throughout the day, as the first team searching for Roberts fought its way to the downed Chinook. It was not until midnight that the last U.S. soldier was evacuated. The choppers also carried 11 wounded and the bodies of seven Americans—Roberts and six of his would-be rescuers. Roberts had died at the hands of his three pursuers.

Soldiers know the nature of their business. But death in war is no less painful to those left behind just because it goes with the mission. Roberts, 32, from a suburb of Sacramento, Calif., left a wife and two-year-old daughter. "He was a great guy," said his sister-in-law Denise Roberts. "His mother said at least she knew he died doing what he loved to do." Valerie Chapman, widow of Air Force Technical Sergeant John Chapman, 36, who lived in Fayetteville, N.C., had the same thought. "You have to love it to do what they do," she said of her husband, who died with Anderson and four others in the firefight after the Chinook crash-landed. "And he loved his job."

## "Not-So-Special Operation: Bush Adopts the Clinton Way of War," Andrew J. Bacevich, *National Review,* November 19, 2001:

When it comes to America's ongoing war to destroy al-Qaeda and topple the Taliban, any outcome short of decisive victory is simply unacceptable. But as President Bush and other members of his administration have repeatedly emphasized, the present conflict is not simply an isolated challenge to be confronted and overcome so that life can return to normal. There will be no such return. Colin Powell has rightly noted that, after just slightly more than a decade, the prodigal era that began with the fall of the Berlin Wall has ended. The events of September 11 plunged the United States into a menacing new age of insecurity, in which we are destined to live out our days.

Thus, the ongoing Afghan war not only marks the Pentagon's response to the attack of September 11; it also provides a preliminary assessment of the nation's capacity to address the dangers awaiting it in this new era. In that regard, the war's first weeks offer little cause for comfort. Based on the available evidence, it appears that the world's most generously endowed and best-trained military forces lack the tools—conceptual as well as material—to deal effectively with the enemies we face. The conceptual deficit may be greater than the material one; it is not our weapons that have been found most seriously wanting in Afghanistan, but the ideas underpinning a deeply flawed "American Way of War."

President Bush has labeled the present struggle the "first war of the twenty-first century." Yet his administration's approach to waging this war does not differ appreciably from the methods on which the U.S. relied to wage the last wars of the previous century—namely, the sundry minor military adventures concocted by the Clinton administration during the '90s. In Operation Enduring Freedom, the Clinton legacy at its most pernicious lives on.

Beginning in 1993 with its failed war in Somalia and continuing until Bill Clinton's last day in office—an occasion coinciding with U.S. air strikes against Iraq, all but unnoticed because they had become so commonplace—the Clinton administration evolved a distinctive way of employing U.S. military power. The hallmarks of this Clinton Doctrine included the following: inflated expectations about the efficacy of air power, administered in carefully calibrated doses; a pronounced aversion to even the possibility of U.S. casualties, combined with an acute sensitivity to "collateral damage" (the media converted these into the chief criteria by which to "grade" any operation); a reliance on proxies to handle the dirty work of close combat (Croats in Bosnia, for example, or the Kosovo Liberation Army in the war against Yugoslavia); vagueness when it came to defining objectives (for example, bombing campaigns conducted not with expectations of actually achieving a decision, but with an eye toward "diminishing" an adversary's capabilities); and a tendency to convert limited commitments into permanent obligations (remember the solemn

### "Not-So-Special Operation . . ." *(continued)*

promise that the troops would be out of Bosnia within a year?).

Republicans found much to dislike about this doctrine. Adding to their irritation was the fact that the Clinton administration—its upper echelons salted with Vietnam-era draft evaders and antiwar protesters—had blithely discarded the hard-learned precepts regarding the use of force that had emerged from Vietnam and codified during the Reagan years. Clinton and his lieutenants routinely violated the tenets of the Weinberger Doctrine, or the Weinberger-Powell Doctrine as it became known after the Gulf War had seemingly demonstrated its validity for all time. The conviction that force should be reserved for vital interests, the emphasis on overwhelming force, the crafting of precise military objectives, the attention paid to "end states" and "exit strategies"—all of these Commander-in-Chief Clinton chucked overboard during his peripatetic journey from Somalia to Haiti to Bosnia to Kosovo, with periodic excursions against Iraq.

Among the benefits expected to flow from the return of the Republican national security professionals to power in January 2001 was that this silliness would end. A rational and principled use of force would once again become a hallmark of U.S. policy.

In point of fact, this has not occurred. Rather, seized by the notion that the war against terror is completely "different" and utterly "new," members of the Bush administration have themselves driven the last nails into the coffin bearing the remains of Weinberger-Powell.

Thus, for example, in the aftermath of September 11, Defense Secretary Donald Rumsfeld instructed Americans to "Forget about 'exit strategies': We're looking at a sustained engagement that carries no deadlines. We have no fixed rules about how to deploy out troops." How will we know when we have won this sustained engagement? According to Rumsfeld, "Victory is persuading the American people and the rest of the world that this is not a quick matter that is going to be over in a month or a year or even five years." That is, success lies in convincing Americans that real success will be a long time coming.

As a practical matter, the military bureaucracies that conduct wars cannot function without rules. If political leaders rocked back on their heels by the events of September 11 and its aftermath abdicate their responsibility to provide these rules, the generals will find them elsewhere—typically by adverting to the familiar. In short, they will fight the next war—whatever its character—by adhering to the routines they grew comfortable with in the last.

# 2003 Profile

# War in Iraq

### Lieutenant Colonel

Lieutenant Colonel Joshua Cohen, who has modeled himself on General George S. Patton, believes he is leading an assault in Iraq that will be an example of superb tactical warfare, taught in schools for years to come.

### Life at Home

- When asked his profession by civilians, Lieutenant Colonel Joshua Cohen always replied, "Warrior."
- The term "soldier" might apply to people in the Quartermaster Corps, but not to the commander of a tank battalion spearheading the drive to root out Saddam Hussein and his regime.
- The Cohen family was deeply religious, patriotic and dedicated to doing well.
- Joshua's straight "A" report card was an expectation; he also pushed himself to excel at wrestling, debate and military history.
- He had seen the movie *Patton* too many times to count and, well aware of the origin of his name, knew all the great warriors of scripture.
- Graduating in 1986 from West Point near the top of his class, he was known for his keen intelligence, salty language and stentorian voice.
- In the evenings, he often circulated among the troops, blending bawdy stories with quotes from the Classics.
- A company commander in Desert Storm, he had been outraged at President George Bush when his troops were not allowed to proceed into Baghdad and take out Saddam.
- Now, with Gulf War II declared, that mistake was about to be rectified, ironically by a second President Bush.

### Life at Work

- Lieutenant Colonel Cohen is extremely proud of his unit and very protective of his men.

- He hates that the modern army includes women and homosexuals, and thinks that only men—real men—are suited for combat.
- His current object of anger is Captain Rachael Greene, who joined the military for all the wrong reasons.
- Not only is she National Guard, but her motivation for going into the military was extra money for graduate school.
- Yet she commands a five-person team of Arabic linguists in the Guard's 300th Military Intelligence Brigade.
- He is particularly irritated by the sign she and one of the other women had drawn and placed in front of her Humvee, reading "One weekend a month, my butt!" referring to the customary terms of her National Guard service.

- When word came down for Joshua's battalion to move out in the opening wave of the war, he was jubilant.
- His unit was to be at the tip of the spear on the army's drive to Baghdad.
- During the first Gulf War a decade earlier, all of the foreign allies had wimped out when it came time to eliminate Saddam, but nothing could stop America this time.
- Joshua could feel victory in his bones.
- When he addressed his troops in preparation for battle, he was clear: Confront the enemy and kill with extreme prejudice.

*Joshua was extremely proud of his unit.*

SHOWDOWN IN IRAQ

- When he finished his talk with a monologue from Shakespeare's *Henry V*, several rolled their eyes.
- As the battalion's M1A1 Abrams tanks moved through the scrubland of Iraq, they met only token resistance.
- All enemy soldiers were quickly vanquished in the assault.
- As in the previous Gulf War, others quickly surrendered—so many that the column's progress was slowed.
- Those Iraqis with command seniority were sent back to division HQ for interrogation by Captain Greene and her team.
- As they proceeded, the U.S. tanks drew fire.
- At one point, Joshua's tank was hit, though he was not badly hurt.
- The tanks annihilated the Iraqis.
- Afterwards, Joshua stood among the smoldering remains of the Iraqi position and told his men, "God has been good to us this day," echoing the words of Confederate General Stonewall Jackson following the battle of Antietam.
- But the lightning pace of the attack left little room for reveling in victory.
- Soon, the column of tanks and Bradley fighting vehicles were thundering into the farmlands of Iraq near the Euphrates River.
- As they prepared to cross the river, an Iraqi military contingent offered stiff resistance.
- Rapidly, Joshua's men counterattacked, firing shell after shell into the Iraqi positions.
- When several Iraqi vehicles appeared disabled, Joshua ordered an all-out attack, destroying everyone.
- The remaining Iraqis fled.

*The rules of combat were clear: confront the enemy and kill with extreme prejudice.*

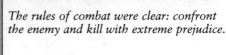

"Making Congress look even sillier than it sometimes looks would not be high in my priority list."
—Representative Barney Frank, (D), after French fries were replaced by "freedom" fries on the House menu

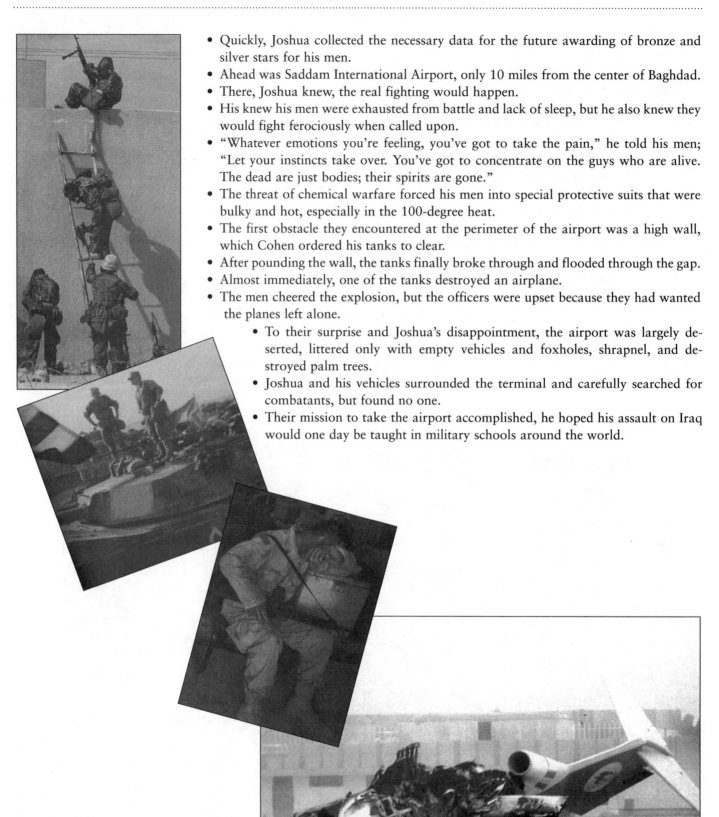

- Quickly, Joshua collected the necessary data for the future awarding of bronze and silver stars for his men.
- Ahead was Saddam International Airport, only 10 miles from the center of Baghdad.
- There, Joshua knew, the real fighting would happen.
- His knew his men were exhausted from battle and lack of sleep, but he also knew they would fight ferociously when called upon.
- "Whatever emotions you're feeling, you've got to take the pain," he told his men; "Let your instincts take over. You've got to concentrate on the guys who are alive. The dead are just bodies; their spirits are gone."
- The threat of chemical warfare forced his men into special protective suits that were bulky and hot, especially in the 100-degree heat.
- The first obstacle they encountered at the perimeter of the airport was a high wall, which Cohen ordered his tanks to clear.
- After pounding the wall, the tanks finally broke through and flooded through the gap.
- Almost immediately, one of the tanks destroyed an airplane.
- The men cheered the explosion, but the officers were upset because they had wanted the planes left alone.
  - To their surprise and Joshua's disappointment, the airport was largely deserted, littered only with empty vehicles and foxholes, shrapnel, and destroyed palm trees.
  - Joshua and his vehicles surrounded the terminal and carefully searched for combatants, but found no one.
  - Their mission to take the airport accomplished, he hoped his assault on Iraq would one day be taught in military schools around the world.

## The 300th Military Brigade

- The 300th Military Intelligence Brigade (linguist) comprises trained and ready linguists and military intelligence soldiers.
- The organization is built from the bottom up with five-soldier teams possessing unique language skills.
- The brigade has 1,400 documented linguist team positions covering 19 languages.
- Arabic, Persian-Farsi and Korean are heavily represented; other languages include Russian, Chinese, Vietnamese, Thai, Spanish, French, Turkish, Serbo-Croatian and German.

## HISTORICAL SNAPSHOT
# 2003

- Surveys indicated that 80 percent of Americans were unwilling to sacrifice taste for more healthful, less flavorful foods
- Iraq's oil ministry, which produced 3.5 million barrels of oil a day only five years ago, produced only five percent of that number
- Despite the dot-com implosion, consumers purchased more than $2 billion worth of groceries online—three times the volume of 2000—leading to the sale of traditional grocery store chains such as Safeway and Albertson's
- School districts dominated by blacks and Hispanics spent $902 less per student on average than mostly white school districts
- The book *Harry Potter and the Order of the Phoenix* sold more than five million copies in the first week
- Surveys showed that 40 percent of all U.S. e-mail was spam
- Thanks in part to file swapping, the sale of CDs was down 20 percent from the year 2000
- Surveys indicated that 83 percent of children believed they would go to college, 68 percent thought they would get married, and 12 percent thought they would join the armed forces

### Cost of Past Wars in 2002 Dollars:

| | | |
|---|---|---|
| Revolutionary War, 1775-83 | | 1.7 million |
| War of 1812, 1812-15 | | 975 million |
| Mexican War, 1846-48 | | 1.5 billion |
| Civil War, 1861-65 | (Union) | 38 billion |
| | (Confederacy) | 23.8 billion |
| Spanish-American War, 1898 | | 8.8 billion |
| World War I, 1917-18 | | 564.5 billion |
| World War II, 1941-45 | | 4.6 trillion |
| Korean War, 1950-53 | | 391.8 billion |
| Vietnam War, 1964-73 | | 840 billion |
| Gulf War, 1990-91 | | 8.6 billion |

## VIEWPOINT ■ Daniel Benjamin and Steven Simon

# The Real Worry

### In Iraq we have created a new "field of jihad"

EXACTLY WHO BOMBED THE U.N. IN BAGHDAD IS THE QUESTION EVERYONE wants answered. But in some ways it misses a point that is already clear—that there is a growing abundance of potential suspects, ranging from radicalized locals to al-Qaeda émigrés. What's worrisome is that they may be coalescing around the same cause, which is to turn Iraq into a showplace of terrorism.

For militants who share al-Qaeda's ideology, the target of the bombing was a natural one. For years, jihadists have reviled the U.N. as an arm of world infidelity. They have depicted the organization as a tool America relied on to allow the slaughter of Muslims in Bosnia and to kill innocent Iraqis through the sanctions that were Saddam's punishment for noncompliance with U.N. resolutions. Islamist militants had already tried once to bomb U.N. headquarters. That 1993 effort grew from the same jihadist circle that provided the manpower for the first World Trade Center attack, which killed six.

In Iraq the old regime wanted to avoid military retaliation or invasion, so it made sense to shun collaboration with Osama bin Laden's maximal terrorists. But since Saddam and his loyalists have lost their state, the prudence that deterred them from working with the jihadists is gone. Together or alone, the radicals must strike in Iraq, the newest "field of jihad." That phrase, redolent of Scripture, is actually a modern coinage to refer to a theater of operations for the Islamist insurgency. There are many: the U.S. and Europe have emerged as central fields of jihad, along with Egypt, Algeria, Saudi Arabia, Chechnya, Kashmir, Indonesia and others. The extremists will fight and die to evict "infidel" forces from those places, including any Muslim government they consider apostate.

For these God-obsessed terrorists, the imperative to free Iraq is profound. The country is in the heartland of Dar al-Islam, the true realm of the faith, not some backwater like Afghanistan. For 500 years, Baghdad was home to the Caliph, the leader of all Muslims, the equivalent of both Pope and King. For them, U.S. occupation of this land is an existential affront. Now they must prove their core claim that they, not the corrupt potentates of the region, are the true defenders of the faith. That requires the radicals to bloody the Americans—the more savagely, the better.

A continuing wave of terrorism in Iraq will have real consequences. America's relationship with the Muslim world is staked to our success in reconstructing and stabilizing the ruined country. As long as our troops must attend to protecting themselves and tracking insurgents instead of setting the country aright, the U.S.'s claims of being a beneficent liberator will ring hollow in the ears of many Muslims. And they in turn may find the al-Qaeda view of the universe increasingly attractive. ■

*Daniel Benjamin is senior fellow at the Center for Strategic & International Studies, and Steven Simon is senior analyst at the Rand Corp. They are the authors of* The Age of Sacred Terror *(Random House, 2002)*

## "The Sand and the Fury," Arian Campo-Flores, *Newsweek,* April 7, 2003:

Last Wednesday at around 3 p.m., in a patch of Iraqi desert where the 3/7th Infantry Battalion is camped, the wind whipped into a frenzy and the air began to glow a seemingly radioactive red. Tents strained against their poles, and any loose object fired away like a projectile. Minutes later, the sky turned dark and we were fully enveloped in dust. Then, thunder cracked the sky and it began to rain mud as moisture in the air gathered particles on its way to earth. It was the worst sandstorm I've yet experienced here—a three-day tour de force that battered the soldiers' morale as much as their equipment.

Despite the conditions, our unit had to embark on a mission to clear a militia compound that night. Before leaving, soldiers lined up for a hot meal—their first since the war started—and ended up eating ham and rice suffused with sand. Others scrambled to tie down equipment and shroud electronics tightly in plastic. For some, simply walking 100 feet to an adjacent squad required using a Global Positioning System. Those attempting to defecate in the field had to contend with dust surging at their backsides—and toilet paper being yanked from their hands by the howling wind.

When our Bradley fighting vehicle set off, visibility was practically zero. Through his night sight, Pfc. Giovanni Garcia, the driver, could only see a fuzzy, swirling mass and two lonely dots: the taillights of the vehicle in front of him, his only navigational reference along precarious terrain. A Bradley he trailed behind at one point threw him

into a panic; only one of its taillights was working and Garcia couldn't tell if it was the right or left one. The difference mattered; drivers ride in each other's tracks to avoid potential mines and other hazards (one Bradley last week plunged into a deep crevice, killing one soldier and injuring another). Further along, we nearly crashed head-on with a Humvee that emerged suddenly from the murk. We arrived at our destination five hours later—after traveling just five miles. Once there, Staff Sgt. José Espada, the master gunner, exited his hatch to relieve himself from the Bradley's roof and was nearly knocked off by 60-mile-an-hour winds.

The sand—much of it as fine as flour—is inescapable. It infiltrates every sealed container and every orifice. It costs crucial pieces of equipment—guns, ammunition, engines, radios—rendering them useless if they aren't quickly and thoroughly cleaned. Worse yet, the lubricant necessary to keep guns functioning smoothly traps dust like flypaper, clogging machinery with gritty goo. Sandstorms exact a physical and psychological toll. Your breathing becomes labored (imagine enclosing your head in a discarded vacuum cleaner bag). Goggles and bandannas are *de rigueur*. Bombarded with fine particles, your body responds by emitting copious amounts of fluids. Your nose seeps brown snot. Your throat discharges dark phlegm. Your eyes—which quickly turn scarlet from irritation—shed tears continuously, releasing

## "The Sand and the Fury . . ." *(continued)*

muddy rivulets down your face. Sgt. Brian Torres, the gunner, woke up the following morning with his eyelids welded shut from crust. Maj. Frank McClary, the 3/7th's operations officer, who often travels with his head poking out of the Bradley's turret, had the skin on his eyelids and cheeks seared by the sand and wind. He now carries two sticks of lip balm—one for his lips and one for his face. Our only refuge that night was our sealed-up Bradley. All we could do was wait for the storm to pass. And wonder aloud, like many a soldier did: "Why would anyone want to fight over this place?"

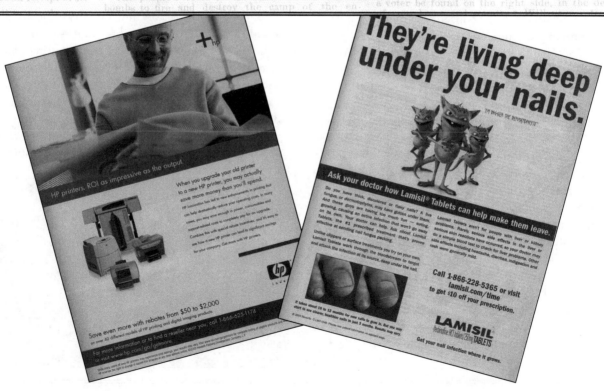

## "A Plan under Attack," Evan Thomas and John Barry, *Newsweek*, April 7, 2003:

The Abrams M1A1 tank is a magnificent instrument of war. It can move faster across country (more than 40 mph) and shoot farther (almost two miles) than any tank ever built. In the first Gulf War, its scorecard against Russian-built Iraqi tanks was, approximately measured, 1,245 to zero. But like a great mythic warrior, the Abrams has an Achilles' heel. It can be killed from behind by a well-placed antitank missile aimed at a small chink in its armor.

So far in Operation Iraqi Freedom, the American military has lost two Abrams tanks. The first M1s ever destroyed by enemy fire in battle, they were caught in an ambush of the U.S. Army's 3/7th Cavalry near As Samawah, on the west bank of the Euphrates River. Two is not a large number, and the Coalition forces have at least 650 tanks in Iraq with more on the way. But U.S. officials are worried about the skill or at least the fanaticism of the guerrilla fighters who sneaked up on the tanks driving a "technical," a jeep, under cover of a sandstorm. More worrisome are the type and the source of the weapon apparently employed, a Russian-made Kornet antitank missile.

The Iraqis have secretly bought as many as a thousand of these lightweight, very powerful, easy-to-use weapons. The sellers, according to Pentagon officials, are Ukrainian arms dealers (who reportedly sent Baghdad some 500 Kornets in January) and possibly some entrepreneurial Syrian generals, or the Syrian government itself. Last week, Defense Secretary Donald Rumsfeld pointedly warned the Syrians to stop shipping military equipment, like night-vision goggles, to the regime of Saddam Hussein. The Syrian Government, Rumsfeld said, would be held "accountable."

Less than two weeks into the second Gulf War, does Operation Iraqi Freedom risk blowing up into a Middle East war? That scenario, once very remote, is no longer unthinkable. Some neoconservative hawks might even wish a wider war ("On to Damascus!"); more restrained Bush administration officials dread an inflamed "Arab Street" turning on its pro-U.S. governments—a conflagration that could force a regime change in say, Amman, Jordan, before Baghdad. Barring a sudden collapse of the Baathist regime—still a possibility, senior administration officials insist—the war in Iraq is about to get bloodier. Saddam's regime is doomed, almost certainly. But at what cost?

Bush administration and military officials insisted that Operation Iraqi Freedom was still "on plan." They pointed out that Coalition forces had seized the rich oilfields of southern Iraq before Saddam could torch more than a few wells; that Coalition forces, in a remarkable feat of arms, had driven some 300 miles into Iraq in less than a week; that U.S. Special Operations Forces were scoring successes in the western desert and north-

### "A Plan under Attack . . ." *(continued)*

ern mountains. Pentagon officials hinted that a decisive battle to crush Saddam's Republican Guard on the outskirts of Baghdad was coming soon. The woeful TV chorus of pundits and retired generals lamenting the unexpectedly slow progress of the war was "silly," said President George W. Bush.

Determined to show that President Bush is not "micromanaging" the war like LBJ in Vietnam, his aides pictured the commander in chief as lofty and resolute. When he's presented with a list of possible targets, his general reaction, says one adviser, is "I don't know why you are bringing this to me." Bush insisted that he would not "second-guess" his ground commander, Gen. Tommy Franks. And how long would the war last? "However long as it takes," Bush replied. "It isn't a matter of timetable, it's a matter of victory. And the Iraqi people have got to know that, see?" said the president, sounding less like Winston Churchill than Jimmy Cagney.

If the president seemed a little testy and defensive at times, the press was also guilty of what Rumsfeld described as "mood swings." Pentagon officials noted that during the Afghanistan War in the fall of 2001, the pundits began predicting a "quagmire"—right before the Taliban broke and al-Qaeda fled for the hills. The gloomy press accounts did nothing to shake public support. According to the new Newsweek Poll, 58 percent of U.S. adults say they would support a military ac-

tion that lasts for a year or more, and an additional 13 percent would back a war lasting several more months. Three out of four said that the U.S. war plan was well thought out.

Still, the second-guessers included some very high-ranking generals. "The enemy we're fighting is different from the one we war-gamed against," said Lt. Gen. William Wallace, the army's ground commander in Iraq. Because of the fierceness of the resistance and overextended supply lines, the war is going to take longer than predicted, Wallace told reporters. Wallace has a reputation for shooting off his mouth; also, for speaking plainly.

His remarks brought to a boil long-simmering tensions in the Pentagon over the best way to defeat Saddam. The classic American way, favored by most army generals, is to grind down the enemy with overwhelming firepower. Rumsfeld, however, prodded the war planners for more creative approaches, taking advantage of high technology and using surprise and agility. The result was a compromise: Most generals wanted to send at least four armored divisions after Saddam; the plan worked out by Rumsfeld and Franks called for three, the army's 3rd and 4th Mechanized Divisions and the Marines' First Expeditionary Division, with the 101st Air Assault Division for mobility. The 4th Infantry Division got hung up when the Turks balked at allowing American forces to use their bases. It is only now arriving at ports in Kuwait.

## "The March to War," Kevin Whitelaw, *U.S. News & World Report*, March 24, 2003:

One way or another, the time for diplomacy is just about over.

Diplomacy, at its best, looks as effortless and choreographed as a Viennese waltz. The scene at the United Nations last week was anything but. It looked more like a junior high school dance—painfully awkward, with everyone self-consciously trying to score points with the same newly popular countries. The great powers spent the week cajoling and pressuring the six developing countries that just happened to be undecided nonpermanent members of the Security Council. For their part, Angola, Cameroon, Guinea, Chile, Mexico and Pakistan all seemed a little dazed by all the sudden attention.

Chaotic as it was, the situation could not be more serious. But to many, the United Nations debate seemed almost beside the point. The resolution that Washington was hawking would, if passed, signal imminent war. If it failed or was withdrawn, however, it could bring even more imminent war. "One way or the other, we're ready to do this," says a senior State Department official.

Far away from the diplomatic maneuvering in the landmark U.N. tower, a different kind of maneuver is under way. American and British troops in their sand-blasted desert encampments in Kuwait continue to roll out perhaps the most potent and technologically advanced fighting force ever assembled. U.S. warships are steaming from the Mediterranean to the Red Sea to get a clear shot at Iraq for their Tomahawk cruise missiles, and Air Force Stealth bombers are moving into striking range. In northern Iraq, Kurdish militia fighters widen remote airstrips, anticipating the arrival of U.S. forces. "When I see what the Amer-

icans are preparing for us . . . these huge armaments, I can't be optimistic," Iraq's ambassador to the U.N., Mohammed al-Douri, tells *U.S. News*.

Back in the desert, America's war machine is more than ready. The soldiers who have spent months preparing supply lines now waste away their off hours at Camp Arifjan, Kuwait, playing marathon games of Risk, releasing boredom and frustration by marching their plastic armies into Iraq and across the world. One sure sign of impending war: the arrival at Arifjan last week of the 883rd Combat Stress Control Medical Detachment, or, in the words of one specialist, "the head doctors." Soon the group of psychologists, psychiatrists and social workers will be looking for soldiers already exhibiting the haunted "1,000-yard stare" and preparing to help those freaked out by the violence and modern warfare—treating them within 72 hours and then sending them back out to fight.

Meanwhile, at the Marines' Camp Commando, military cooks on Friday dished up something special: a dinner of lobster tails, better food usually being another sign that combat may be only days away.

## "The Face of Our Forces: A Demographic Profile," *Newsweek*, April 14, 2003:

The 1.4 million American military personnel serving on active duty around the world represent a racial and ethnic cross-section of the United States. An overview of the troops:

### Race and Ethnicity
### All Active Duty

| | |
|---|---|
| Caucasian | 64% |
| African-American | 20 |
| Hispanic | 9 |
| Asian | 4 |
| Native American | 1 |
| Other | 2 |

### Military Compensation

| | |
|---|---|
| Base pay for army private with one-year contract | $15,480 |
| Starting salary for second lieutenant | $26,200 |
| Average combat pay | $150/month |
| Death gratuity | $60,000 |
| Life insurance | $250,000 |
| Dependency compensation | Child: $247/month<br>Spouse: $948/month |

### Education

| | Officers | Enlisted |
|---|---|---|
| College graduate | 94.7% | 3.5% |
| Two or more years college | 96.9% | 9.4% |
| Some college | 97.4% | 10.1% |
| High school graduate | 100.0% | 99.1% |

## "How to Survive Double Deployment," *USA Magazine*, March 2003:

Twelve-year-old Chris Newman looked at the family photo on his nightstand every evening. Although seeing it sometimes made him sad, it also helped him remember what his mom and dad looked like.

For his brother William, 7, it was being tucked in at bedtime that he missed the most. "It was hard to live without my mom and dad for all those days. I really missed them a bunch," the second-grader says.

Having both parents deployed at the same time for five and a half months called for a lot of adjusting from the Newman brothers—not to mention a few tears.

Just as thousands of troops are deploying now to the Middle East, Chris' and William's parents knew right after September 11 that they both might be deployed.

Army Lt. Col. Carol Newman is assistant chief nurse at Blanchfield Army Community Hospital at Fort Campbell, Kentucky. Her husband, Chief Warrant Officer Ryan Newman, is a Black Hawk helicopter pilot and aviation safety officer for the 6th Battalion, 101st Aviation Regiment, there.

The couple had discussed the possibility of deployment with their children ever since they were very young, Carol says, and the boys were used to one parent or the other being gone several weeks or months at a time for training. But this was different.

Notified in October 2001 about an impending

deployment, Carol had only seven weeks to prepare her children for her departure in December as deputy commander for nursing with the 86th Combat Support Hospital. Located in Uzbekistan, it was the only Level 3 trauma hospital in the Afghanistan area of operations. Carol wouldn't return until the following summer.

Meanwhile, in February 2002, Ryan had the opportunity to command the airfield in Qandahar, Afghanistan, when the former airfield manager had a medical emergency. Even though it was difficult to leave his sons behind, Ryan notes that wartime is what being a soldier is all about. "Forty-eight hours later I was on an airplane headed for Afghanistan."

While it was hard to be apart, the family kept in touch through letters, e-mails and weekly phone calls.

Fortunately, the Newmans began preparing for a possible double deployment right after September 11, and they keep their plan updated today. Carol ordered a USAA Deployment Guide and the couple reviewed their legal and financial issues, as well as their Family Care Plan. The military services require dual-career couples, as well as single-parent service members, to complete a Family Care Plan.

"We asked a civilian family we knew through Boy Scouts here in Clarksville (Tenn.) to take care of the boys," Carol says. "We wanted to keep our children here so they could stay in the same school system. We felt it would be the least disruptive for them."

While it's complicated and time-consuming for couples to prepare a Family Care Plan that addresses every contingency, Ryan says, "When you need it, you'll be glad you've got one that really works."

Regarding their financial and legal issues, the Newmans set up automatic electronic payments for their insurance policies and other bills.

They opted to use debit cards instead of credit cards to avoid generating bills while they were gone. They also set up a special bank account that

## "How to Survive . . ." *(continued)*

the care-giving family could access to provide for ongoing expenses for their children and pets.

The Newmans put their cars in storage and reduced auto insurance coverage until they returned. They also updated their wills, powers of attorney and other legal documents, and set up a home security system, since their house would be unoccupied.

When Carol returned July 14, 2002, it didn't take long to become a family again, says Chris. "Mom was in such a good mood, nothing made her mad!" he recalls with a grin. "She would bake cakes and cookies and brownies. She was just so

happy to be back!" The family was pleasantly surprised by Ryan's early arrival a week later on July 21.

"We're back to normal," says Carol smiling. "I'm yelling at them to take out the trash. You know, all those little things that family life is all about."

"But we are so proud of the boys," she continues. "They both maintained straight A's while we were gone. They also did very well in scouting. Christopher just received his Life award, so he's one step away from Eagle Scout."

## "Counting Heads," Peter Beinart, *The New Republic,* April 7, 2003:

It's dangerous to generalize about this war. America's attack on Iraq is moving so fast that basic assumptions about its course can flip in the course of one day. But, as of this writing, the war's conduct suggests at least one irony: This supposedly cold-blooded administration is making a remarkable, some might even say militarily dangerous, effort to spare Iraqi lives. Conservatives once attacked Bill Clinton for being too squeamish about civilian casualties. But compared with George W. Bush—at least so far—Clinton didn't even come close.

The right has long attacked the left as insufficiently concerned with national interest. Liberals, the argument goes, only support humanitarian wars untainted by America's need for security. But, if the rationale for this war is U.S. security, you'd hardly know it from listening to the Bush administration over the last few days. Consider the attack's name: "Operation Iraqi Freedom." The campaign to topple the Taliban, you'll remember, was dubbed "Operation Enduring Freedom." But that referred to *American* freedom, attacked on September 11, 2001. For this war, the military reportedly favored "Operation Desert Freedom," which would have harkened back to "Desert Storm." But Bush administration civilians evidently considered that too morally vague (after all, we weren't freeing the desert) and thus settled on a name that could have been cooked up by Human Rights Watch. As one writer on *National Review Online* recently joked, "Whatever happened to all those in-your-face, aggressive names for military ops—the ones with words like 'storm,' 'sword,' 'lightning,' and so on?"

In fact, the Bush administration hasn't only

vowed not to make this a war against the Iraqi people; it has practically promised not to make it a war against the Iraqi military, either. In his March 17 speech giving Saddam Hussein a 48-hour ultimatum, President Bush said, "It is not too late for the Iraqi military to act with honor and protect your country by permitting the peaceful entry of coalition forces," and urged "every member of the Iraqi military and intelligence services, if war comes, do not fight for a dying regime." In the months leading up to the war, the United States dropped millions of leaflets urging Iraqi soldiers to surrender and be spared. And Pentagon officials have talked openly about their desire to negotiate with Iraqi generals rather than destroy them. The clear implication is that the United States considers most of the Iraqi military a victim of Saddam's government rather than a manifestation of it.

The Bush administration's extremely narrow definition of the enemy has guided the war's conduct as well as its rhetoric. First, there was the decision to scramble war plans by going for an early knockout punch on Saddam's bunker. Sticklers for international law muttered that the Bushies were circumventing traditional prohibitions on assassinating another country's leader. But, viewed more broadly, the effort to get Saddam and sons was clearly a humanitarian decision—an attempt to spare virtually all Iraqis from conflict.

In less obvious ways, that logic continued to guide the entire first week of the war. In 1991, the United States bombed Iraq for 38 days before beginning its ground offensive; this time it bombed for one day. And the Pentagon avoided strikes against Baghdad's electrical grid, water system, bridges and power plants in order to reduce civilian suffering. That decision has so far limited Iraqi casualties. But the decision to send U.S. Marines and infantrymen into Iraq before "preparing the battlefield" with extended air attacks also exposed American troops to greater danger. According to National Public Radio, American commanders even ordered helicopters to fly low over tanks,

## "Counting Heads . . ." *(continued)*

minimizing the chances of collateral damage but exposing them to Iraqi ground fire. In Kosovo, some liberal humanitarians charged that the Clinton administration's obsession with preventing U.S. combat deaths—it ruled out a ground war and instructed pilots to fly so high that they were impervious to Serb antiaircraft fire—led to higher Serb and Kosovar civilian casualties. Today, the supposedly ruthless Bush administration has reversed the moral calculus. Some American troops will probably die because some Iraqis were spared.

The moral calculus has also shaped the Bush administration's decision to send ground troops straight to the Iraqi capital. The American forces surging toward Baghdad bypassed as many Iraqi units as possible and operated under orders to fire only when fired upon. Critics charge that, by not destroying Iraqi troops, the United States left its lightly armed logistical "tail" vulnerable to the kind of counterattack suffered by the 507th Maintenance Company on March 24. As Peter Feaver, director of Duke University's Triangle Institute for Security Studies, told *The Washington Post*'s Thomas Ricks this week, "The really important thing about the [U.S. war] plan is that it has put mission accomplishment ahead of force protection." And that mission isn't only to take Baghdad; it's to minimize the killing of Iraqis along the way.

Does all this make the Bush team pure? Of course not. But it does suggest that they recognize that this war's grand moral aims—to implant democracy in the Middle East—must guide its means as well. The imperviousness to public opinion and the hypocrisy about human rights that have at times blemished this administration have so far been blessedly absent from its war in Iraq. That could all change in a heartbeat, of course. But, if it doesn't, there is at least some hope that the United States may actually win this terrifying war, not only militarily, but politically as well.

## "Rebuilding Iraq: An Assessment at Six Months," *The New York Times*, Tuesday, November 4, 2003

Attacks against soldiers and occupation targets continue.
Here are the numbers as of Sunday [November 2, 2003]:

Average number of U.S. soldiers killed per week since major combat ended: 5
Number of U.S. soldiers wounded since major combat ended: 1,285
Number of U.S. soldiers killed since major combat ended: 135
Estimated bounty, in U.S. dollars, paid to Iraqis who kill U.S. soldiers: $300-$1,000
Tons of weapons and munitions found and destroyed, per day: 100
Average price of an Iraqi-made hand grenade in early May: 10 cents
Average price now: $2.50
Average price of a fully automatic Kalashnikov assault rifle in May: $5.
Average price now: $80.

## "2 Soldiers, 6 Kids, 1 Exhausted Grandmother," Richard Jerome, Jason Bane, Cathy Free and Jane Sims Podesta, *People,* September 8, 2003:

Major conflict in Iraq may have ended, but for families like the Holcombs, with both parents overseas, the battle continues at home and abroad.

Fort Carson, Colo., 6:25 a.m.: Inside a condominium on this dusty army base, Sue Bearer savors her last few moments of peace, sipping coffee and taking a drag from her cigarette.

6:35 a.m.: All hell breaks loose. It starts benignly enough, as nine-year-old Dustin trots downstairs and with a "Hi, Grandma!" and plants a kiss on Bearer's cheek. Then, the ceiling rumbles as if a *Riverdance* road company were rehearsing upstairs, and five other children tumble down to the kitchen. The boys—Tristan, 6, Skylor, 7, Forest, 11, and 12-year-old Jon—chatter and tease as they fix cereal and make bologna sandwiches for school; Taylor, 7, the only girl, plops down for Bearer to brush her strawberry-blond hair. Meanwhile her brothers—amped up over the new *Freddy vs. Jason* flick—taunt their sister for her loyalty to *Barney.* "Leave Taylor alone!" orders Bearer, 59. At 7:25, the backpacked brood moves out for school, and Bearer calls, "Hey, kisses!"

Then, silence.

This is the unseen Iraqi war, the quiet, unheralded heroism of the home front. For seven months now, since early February, Sue Bearer has been mother and father to her six grandkids because both their parents are on active duty in Iraq. For many, the war may have entered its final stage on April 9, when U.S. Marines helped topple Saddam Hussein's statue in central Baghdad. But the coda has been long and brutal—for the 140,000 U.S. troops still deployed in sweltering temperatures (up to 120 degrees F in some places) and under constant threat, and for their families back home for whom it won't end until they meet safely again.

Bearer's son Vaughn Holcomb, 40, and his wife, Simone, 30, don't know when they will be home; perhaps next spring. Vaughn, who left in March, is an army sergeant in the 3rd Armored Cavalry Regiment in charge of a tank platoon located outside the northern town of Al Quaim. Simone, a nursing student in civilian life, left home in January to serve as a National Guard medic stationed in Baghdad. Though husband and wife talk to each other by phone once a week, calls home are much rarer, and the uncertainty is beginning to take a toll. "It's hard. I miss my children," Vaughn told *People* via e-mail from Iraq. "Oh, and it's hot, sandy—and did I say hot?" Adds Simone, over a scratchy phone line: "It's beyond frustrating. At least if we had a [homecoming] date to look forward to, it would be much easier."

Bearer had been preparing since last fall to assume legal guardianship of the children (two are Vaughn's and four are Simone's, all from previous unions) just in case. "I volunteered," she says, "but I never thought it would happen. My whole life has been put on hold." A successful real estate agent, she had been living comfortably in Akron with her husband, Joe, 76, a retired postal worker, eating out for breakfast and dinner every day and enjoying her rose garden. Now, she has quit her job, cooks for seven every night and endures a wrenching separation: Joe is staying in Akron to mind the couple's two rental properties. "Joe and I went everywhere together," she says, tearing up. Back home in Akron, her husband's feelings run just as deep. "In the evening is when it hits you," he says. "Man, oh man, is it lonely."

Most of Bearer's time, however, is spent dealing with a greater separation: two parents and six young children, 7,000 miles apart, living under the ever-present spectre of tragedy—brought home when one of Jon's classmates lost a parent in the conflict. The stress weighs heavily on the kids, manifested in occasional bed-wetting, mood swings and sleepless nights. "I've just had nightmares all the time, that my mom blew up; it's horrible," says Forest, softly. "It stinks," adds Jon, looking at the floor. "I don't think it's fair that they left us."

# 2007 News Feature

**"The War as We Saw It," Buddhika Jayamaha, Wesley D. Smith, Jeremy Roebuck, Omar Mora, Edward Sandmeier, Yance T. Gray and Jeremy A. Murphy, *The New York Times*, August 19, 2007** (excerpt)

BAGHDAD—Viewed from Iraq at the tail end of a 15-month deployment, the political debate in Washington is indeed surreal. Counterinsurgency is, by definition, a competition between insurgents and counterinsurgents for the control and support of a population. To believe that Americans, with an occupying force that long ago outlived its reluctant welcome, can win over a recalcitrant local population and win this counterinsurgency is farfetched.

As responsible infantrymen and noncommissioned officers with the 82nd Airborne Division soon heading back home, we are skeptical of recent press coverage portraying the conflict as increasingly manageable and feel it has neglected the mounting civil, political, and social unrest we see every day. (Obviously, these are our personal views and should not be seen as official within our chain of command.)

The claim that we are increasingly in control of the battlefields in Iraq is an assessment arrived at through a flawed, American-centered framework. Yes, we are militarily superior, but our successes are offset by failures elsewhere. What soldiers call the "battle space" remains the same, with changes only at the margins. It is crowded with actors who do not fit neatly into boxes: Sunni extremists, Al Qaeda terrorists, Shiite militiamen, criminals, and armed tribes. This situation is made more complex by the questionable loyalties and Janus-faced role of the Iraqi police and Iraqi Army, which have been trained and armed at United States taxpayers' expense.

A few nights ago, for example, we witnessed the death of one American soldier and the critical wounding of two others when a lethal armor-piercing explosive was detonated between an Iraqi Army checkpoint and a police one. Local Iraqis readily testified to American investigators that Iraqi police and Army officers escorted the triggermen and helped plant the bomb. These civilians highlighted their own predicament: had they informed the Americans of the bomb before the incident, the Iraqi Army, the police, or the local Shiite militia would have killed their families.

As many grunts will tell you, this is a near-routine event. Reports that a majority of Iraqi Army commanders are now reliable partners can be considered only misleading rhetoric. The truth is that battalion commanders, even if well meaning, have little to no influence over the thousands of obstinate men under them, in an incoherent chain of command, who are really loyal only to their militias.

Similarly, Sunnis, who have been under-represented in the new Iraqi armed forces, now find themselves forming militias, sometimes with our tacit support. Sunnis recognize that the best guarantee they may have against Shiite militias and the Shiite-dominated government is to form their own armed bands. We arm them to aid in our fight against Al Qaeda.

However, while creating proxies is essential in winning a counterinsurgency, it requires that the proxies are loyal to the center that we claim to support. Armed Sunni tribes have indeed become effective surrogates, but the enduring question is where their loyalties would lie in our absence. The Iraqi government finds itself working at cross purposes with us on this issue because it is justifiably fearful that Sunni militias will turn on it should the Americans leave.

In short, we operate in a bewildering context of determined enemies and questionable allies, one where the balance of forces on the ground remains entirely unclear. (In the course of writing this article, this fact became all too clear: one of us, Staff Sergeant Murphy, an Army Ranger and reconnaissance team leader, was shot in the head during a "time-sensitive target acquisition mission" on August 12; he is expected to survive and is being flown to a military hospital in the United States.) While we have the will and the resources to fight in this context, we are effectively hamstrung because realities on the ground require measures we will always refuse—namely, the widespread use of lethal and brutal force.

•••

*Buddhika Jayamaha is an Army specialist. Wesley D. Smith is a sergeant. Jeremy Roebuck is a sergeant. Omar Mora is a sergeant. Edward Sandmeier is a sergeant. Yance T. Gray is a staff sergeant. Jeremy A. Murphy is a staff sergeant. From The New York Times, August 19 © 2007 The New York Times. All rights reserved. Used by permission and protected by the Copyright Laws of the United States. The printing, copying, redistribution, or retransmission of this Content without express written permission is prohibited.*

## 2 G.I.'s, Skeptical but Loyal, Die in a Truck Crash in Iraq
### By David Stout, *The New York Times*, September 13, 2007

WASHINGTON, Sept. 12—"Engaging in the banalities of life has become a death-defying act," the seven soldiers wrote of the war they had seen in Iraq.

They were referring to the ordeals of Iraqi citizens, trying to go about their lives with death and suffering all around them. But sadly, although they did not know it at the time, they might almost have been referring to themselves.

Two of the soldiers who wrote of their pessimism about the war in an op-ed article that appeared in *The New York Times* on August 19 *[Ed. note: article above]* were killed in Baghdad on Monday. They were not killed in combat, nor on a daring mission. They died when the five-ton cargo truck in which they were riding overturned.

The victims, Staff Sgt. Yance T. Gray, 26, and Sgt. Omar Mora, 28, were among the authors of "The War as We Saw It," in which they expressed doubts about reports of progress.

"As responsible infantrymen and noncommissioned officers with the 82nd Airborne Division soon heading back home, we are skeptical of recent press coverage portraying the conflict as increasingly manageable and feel it has neglected the mounting civil, political and social unrest we see every day," the soldiers wrote.

Sergeant Gray's mother, Karen Gray, said by telephone on Wednesday from Ismay, Montana, where Yance grew up, "My son was a soldier in his heart from the age of five," and she added: "He loved what he was doing." The sergeant's father, Richard, said of his son, "But he wasn't any mindless robot."

Sergeant Gray leaves a wife, Jessica, and a daughter, Ava, born in April. He is also survived by a brother and a sister.

Sergeant Mora's mother, Olga Capetillo of Texas City, Texas, told The Daily News in Galveston that her son had grown increasingly gloomy about Iraq. "I told him God is going to take care of him and take him home," she said. A native of Ecuador, Sergeant Mora had recently become an American citizen. "He was proud of this country, and he wanted to go over and help," his stepfather, Robert Capetillo, told The Houston Chronicle.

Sergeant Mora leaves a wife, Christa, and a daughter, Jordan, who is five. Survivors also include a brother and a sister.

While the seven soldiers were composing their article, one of them, Staff Sgt. Jeremy A. Murphy, was shot in the head. He was flown to a military hospital in the United States and is expected to survive. The other authors were Buddhika Jayamaha, an Army specialist, and Sgts. Wesley D. Smith, Jeremy Roebuck, and Edward Sandmeier.

"We need not talk about our morale," they wrote in closing. "As committed soldiers, we will see this mission through."

*Olga Capetillo mourns the death of her son, Sgt. Omar Mora, with her cousin, Bertha Oaks. Photo: Pat Sullivan/Associated Press*

*Staff Sgt. Yance Tell Gray of Ismay, Montana, with his wife, Jessica, and their daughter. Photo: www.pbs.org*

## 2008 Profile

# Training Soldiers to Think and Fight

### Brigadier General

Jim Schwitters was among the early recruits to the all-volunteer military. In a career that took him from private to brigadier general, he learned the value of initiative and critical thinking, and he applied those lessons to recruits training at Fort Jackson for combat in Iraq and Afghanistan.

### Life at Home

- Jim Schwitters was in high school as the Vietnam War's death toll was accelerating.
- While just under 2,000 Americans were killed in 1965, when Jim was a sophomore, the death toll rose to 6,350 in 1966 and 11,363 in 1967.
- In 1968, the number of Americans killed, many of them the same age as Jim, rose to a peak of 16,899.
- Most young people of Jim's age were patriotic, but few wanted to go to Vietnam.
- Since 1940, young men had been forced into the military through the draft.
- Some sought exemptions, such as enrolling in a seminary to become a minister, while others had deferments, most commonly by being enrolled in college.
- Jim was among the latter.
- He enrolled at LeTourneau College in Longview, Texas, but in his junior and senior year, the U.S. government started the lottery.
- He had a high number (348, birthday November 3), "So I didn't have to worry about being drafted," he recalled.

*U.S. Army Brig. Gen. James Schwitters, above right, and opposite.*

*Brig. Gen. Schwitters accepts flag during retirement ceremony.*

- He worked summers and during the school year, graduating in 1972 with an engineering degree and working for the next three years for John Deere.
- In 1975, he enlisted in the Army for a four-year stint.
- "It sounds corny, but it was a sense of duty that every male needed to serve," he said.
- Jim joined the military at one of its lowest points.
- The long war in Vietnam ended swiftly in the spring of 1975.
- The South Vietnamese army, which had absorbed billions of dollars of U.S. aid, had been fighting without U.S. troops for the prior three years but retreated in the face of a North Vietnamese offensive, and then the retreat became a rout with some commanders abandoning their troops in the field.
- The United States, whose president had resigned in disgrace less than a year earlier, looked weak.
- Then things got worse about two weeks after the fall of Saigon, South Vietnam's capital.
- Cambodian communists seized the U.S.-crewed cargo ship *S.S. Mayaguez* off the coast of Cambodia, to which the U.S. responded with a bungled rescue attempt.
- Even as the Cambodians were returning the crew unharmed, a force cobbled together of Marines and Air Force police were invading the Cambodian island where the hostages were no longer held.
- Ten U.S. soldiers were killed, and three Marines were abandoned on the island to be captured and killed by the Cambodians over the next few days.
- The American public knew little about the *Mayaguez* incident at the time, but it was one of the signals to military leaders that the United States needed a hostage rescue force.
- An example of what such a force might look like came in 1976 when the Israeli military carried out a stunning rescue mission.
- After a week of planning, 100 Israeli commandos flew 2,500 miles to the Entebbe Airport in Uganda to rescue 94 hostages from a hijacked airplane; three hostages and one Israeli commando died in the mission, with the rest of the hostages freed.
- The mission was carried out in 90 minutes on the ground.
- U.S. military leaders decided they needed that kind of swift strike capability.
- The secretive Delta Force was started in November 1977 by Colonel Charles Beckwith, a Vietnam combat veteran who had been advocating for such a unit since working as an exchange officer with the British Special Air Service in 1962.
- When Jim joined the Army, his first stop was Fort Jackson, South Carolina, where he was given his physical, issued a uniform, and sent to basic training at Fort Gordon near Augusta, Georgia.
- From there he went to advanced individual training, a three-week jump school, and was assigned to the 2nd Battalion Rangers at Fort Lewis, near Tacoma, Washington: "They were the Army's elite light infantry. They took pride in their training and standards," he explained.
- In winter of 1976-1977, he was sent to a communications course at Fort Bragg, North Carolina.
- "Some of my instructors at that course were later hired at Delta. They recalled me going through the course," he said.

- In the late summer of 1977, Jim was recruited for Delta Force; after discussing it with his wife, Rebecca, he decided to join as a radio operator and was assigned to the Fort Bragg-based unit in 1978.
- "I found the job at Delta was very rewarding. We were literally writing the book on our mission profile. We were developing the tactics," he noted.
- Jim was among the first cadre of Delta Force operational unit members.
- Like Beckwith, a great number of the members had combat experience in Vietnam and Special Forces training.
- Delta Force developed a selection system to ensure the unit kept the personnel with the right character, skills, and abilities to serve successfully.
- In the fall of 1979, Delta Force began a weeklong exercise to test the unit's abilities while senior officers, many of them highly skeptical, watched.
- "Those on the fence were gobsmacked on how well the organization performed," Jim said.
- Literally hours after that exercise, students in Iran who had supported the overthrow of the American-supported dictator stormed the U.S. embassy in Tehran on November 4, 1979, and took hostage 52 American diplomats and citizens.
- Delta Force began preparing for a rescue mission, which underwent numerous revisions as they practiced worst-case scenarios, in which the prisoners were difficult to find and heavily guarded, and best-case scenarios, where they were found quickly and lightly guarded.
- After the U.S. planes and helicopters took off on April 24, 1981, they met in the desert for the final leg, but a series of mishaps led the mission's leaders to decide to abort.
- Before taking off to return, one of the C-130 planes was hit by a helicopter and caught fire.
- Jim was among the 60 soldiers and crew aboard the plane.
- The exit on one side was blocked by a wall of flames, but the other side was clear.
- Jim and most of those aboard made it out, but eight men died, and many more were burned.
- Jim realized more coordination was needed between the air and ground forces, and saw that the steps in training for the mission were insufficiently detailed.
- Lesson No. 1: "Pay attention to the details."
- Lesson No. 2: "You can't just assume it will all work."
- The failure of the mission was all the more painful when intelligence later showed the hostages had been right where they were expected to be and lightly guarded.
- "Their guards didn't even have ammunition in their weapons," Jim related.
- Later in 1981, Jim became an officer through direct appointment—an unusual method.
- "Colonel Beckwith kind of wanted to see if he could do it," Jim explained. "He thought I should be an officer. He told his adjutant to make it happen, and I was the victim."
- From 1982 to 1984, Jim served as a captain of an infantry battalion in Germany.
- He was back with Delta Force from 1984 to 1995, when he was promoted to lieutenant colonel.
- He commanded a training brigade at Fort Jackson from 1996 to 1998.

- "I became very familiar with how training was done. I saw how we trained in peacetime," he said.
- He was Delta Force commander in 2000-2002, and after the terrorist attacks of September 11, 2001, he oversaw units that were sent to Afghanistan.
- He was promoted to brigadier general in 2002 and sent to Iraq where, in the summer of 2004, he was assigned to help train a new Iraqi army, since its old military had been dismantled after the U.S. invasion in 2003.
- "At the institutional level, they were captives of their recent history. The institutions in their military were all limited by the regime in their scope of capability. Many were hobbled to support the regime instead of being a national asset," Jim remarked.
- The Iraqis developed a culture of self-serving officers and failed to develop a level of professional non-commissioned officers; they also treated their common soldiers like consumables.
- Under those conditions, the Americans were trying to help the Iraqis create a professional army that served the nation.
- "That was the hardest nut to crack, and frankly we didn't," Jim admitted.

*Basic Combat Training, above and right.*

## Life at Work

- Jim Schwitters returned in 2005 to Fort Jackson as the 42nd commander in the fort's history; he is spending his last three years in the Army there before retiring.
- The year before he arrived, basic training at Fort Jackson and other posts was made tougher, especially for cooks, clerks, truck drivers, and others usually outside of combat.

- The irregular nature of the wars in Afghanistan and Iraq, where there are no "front lines," means all personnel need to be ready for combat.
- Also, the training needed to become more intense because many soldiers had little or no time for extra training before being deployed.
- Jim's assignment gives him the chance to apply the lessons of his career to new generations of soldiers, his goal being to change training to develop soldiers who are self-starters and self-disciplined.
- He wants to cultivate "thinking soldiers" as opposed to soldiers who are robotic, simply obedient, and reliant upon leaders to do their thinking for them.
- "The opposite of that is you're taught a whole bunch of procedures," Jim explained. "We're not going to be able to train for every situation that occurs. There will be millions of situations, and we can't foresee each one."
- Jim had the honor of escorting President George W. Bush when he visited Fort Jackson on November 2, 2007; Bush was the first president to visit the installation in more than 50 years.
- While Bush was there, he met with family members of some of the soldiers killed in Afghanistan and Iraq.
- "Bush did a significant amount of that. He downplayed it in the press. He didn't want to make it a spectacle," Jim asserted.
- Bush delivered a 20-minute speech to 1,300 graduates of basic training, opening his remarks with a loud "Hooah!"
- The president gave a progress report on Iraq, saying the number of roadside bomb attacks had fallen in half in the last five months, and the number of American military deaths had fallen to its lowest level in 19 months.
- He said American troops and Iraqi allies had killed or captured an average of more than 1,500 "enemy fighters" per month since January.
- Moreover, he surmised that there were signs that internal divisions were healing as Shiite and Sunni leaders were beginning to cooperate with one another to fight against Al Qaeda.
- Bush told the graduates, "You have stepped forward and volunteered in this time of danger. You need to know you make Americans proud. Soldiers who have marched on this field have battled fascists, dictators, and terrorists. Our soldiers have brought freedom to millions of people they never knew. Because of their efforts, America is stronger; America is safer; and America is free."
- He ended the speech with Fort Jackson's motto, "Victory Starts Here!"

*President George Bush at the Army's training camp at Fort Jackson, Columbia, South Carolina.*

## Life in the Community

- Fort Jackson in Columbia, South Carolina, is the Army's largest training base, with more than 45,000 soldiers graduating each year from basic combat training or advanced schools.
- Camp Jackson first opened in 1917 as the United States entered World War I and was named for Andrew Jackson, president from 1829 to 1837.
- The camp was reactivated at the outbreak of World War II in Europe in 1939 and renamed Fort Jackson
- Active ever since then, it sprawls over 52,000 acres and is home to 3,600 active-duty soldiers and their 10,000 family members.
- The base directly supports nearly 8,000 full-time jobs, drawing $469 million in wages and benefits.
- The base has 1,150 buildings, including housing.
- In 2005, the Army began an eight-year, $1 billion plan to upgrade quarters.
- The Fort has one elementary school, one middle school, two bowling alleys, several park and picnic areas, a sport-shooting range, a miniature golf course, hunting and fishing grounds, a recreational water park, and a 36-hole golf course.
- A $4.5 million family water park opened in the summer of 2004.
- The base's mission has been expanding; in 2007 the Army consolidated all of its training facilities for drill sergeants at Fort Jackson.
- In 2008, Fort Jackson became the site of the first of six national cemeteries to open under legislation signed by President Bush in 2003.

*Mazie Winter trained as an Army nurse at Camp Jackson, Columbia, South Carolina. Photo: Collection of Jim DuPlessis*

# HISTORICAL SNAPSHOT
# 2008

- Americans elected Barack Obama president, the first African American elected to that office.
- An economic recession began that rivaled the Great Depression of the 1930s and caused in large part by banks pushing securities backed by shaky, high-interest loans to homebuyers.
  - President George W. Bush signed a $700 billion bill on October 3 to bail out banks and stem a financial crisis.
  - Television shows winning an Emmy award included NBC's *30 Rock,* Comedy Central's *The Daily Show with Jon Stewart,* and the first season of AMC's drama, *Mad Men.*
  - Seth MacFarlane signed a $100 million deal with the Fox television network to keep *Family Guy* and *American Dad* on the air until 2012, making MacFarlane the world's highest paid television writer.
- *Good Masters! Sweet Ladies! Voices from a Medieval Village* won the 2008 Newbery Medal for children's literature. The book, written by Laura Amy Schlitz and illustrated by Robert Byrd, tells the stories of 21 young inhabitants of a thirteenth-century England village and manor.
- Bernard Madoff was arrested and charged with securities fraud in a $50 billion Ponzi scheme.
- California became the second state to legalize same-sex marriage after the state's own Supreme Court ruled a previous ban unconstitutional. The first state was Massachusetts in 2004.
- *Slumdog Millionaire,* a movie about a young man from the slums of Mumbai, India, won the Academy Award for the best film of 2008. Altogether, the film won eight Oscars, the most of any 2008 film.
- Australian actor and director Heath Ledger died from an accidental overdose at age 28, a few months after finishing filming for *The Dark Knight.* Ledger was posthumously awarded the Oscar for Best Supporting Actor for that role.
- The British alternative rock band Coldplay won the Grammy award for Song of the Year for "Viva la Vida," a Spanish phrase that can mean either "long live life" or "live the life."
- Pope Benedict XVI visited the United States.
- Bill Gates stepped down as chairman of

*Keith Ledger, left, and as* The Dark Knight.

Microsoft Corporation to work full-time for the nonprofit Bill & Melinda Gates Foundation.
- Toshiba recalled its HD DVD video formatting, ending the format war between it and Sony's Blu-Ray Disc.
- Gold prices on the New York Mercantile Exchange hit $1,000 an ounce for the first time on March 13.
- Greg Maddux pitched his 5,000th career inning against the San Francisco Giants on September 19.
- The New York Yankees played their final home game at Yankee Stadium against the Baltimore Orioles on September 21.
- Colombian armed forces rescued politician and activist Ingrid Betancourt and 14 others after six years as hostages of the Revolutionary Armed Forces of Colombia (FARC).
- The Detroit Lions finished the football season 0-16, the first time in National Football League history that a team went winless in a 16-game season.

## Selected Prices

*Cold War Kitchen*, eds. Ruth Oldenziel and
  Karen Zachmann .................................................. $36.00

Talking atomic watch ...................................... $89.95

Red Hot Chili Peppers concert ticket .......................... $57–$68

Designer-inspired amethyst ring .............................. $35.00

DNA testing to determine ancestry ......................... $95–$399

Build-A-Bear, deluxe ...................................... $25.00

Bushel of feed corn .......................................... $3.50

Online *Wall Street Journal* annual subscription ............ $103.00

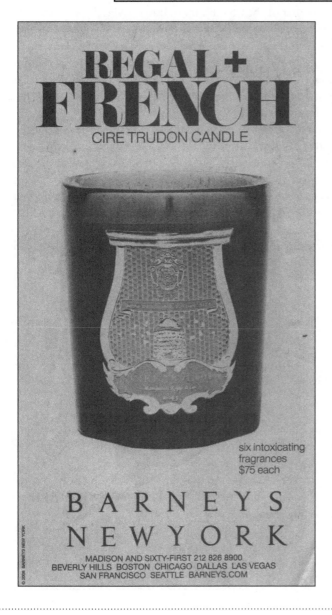

REGAL + FRENCH

CIRE TRUDON CANDLE

six intoxicating
fragrances
$75 each

B A R N E Y S
N E W Y O R K

MADISON AND SIXTY-FIRST 212 826 8900
BEVERLY HILLS BOSTON CHICAGO DALLAS LAS VEGAS
SAN FRANCISCO SEATTLE BARNEYS.COM

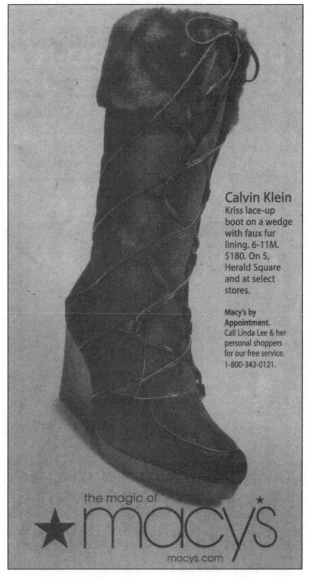

Calvin Klein
Kriss lace-up
boot on a wedge
with faux fur
lining. 6-11M.
$180. On 5,
Herald Square
and at select
stores.

Macy's by
Appointment.
Call Linda Lee & her
personal shoppers
for our free service.
1-800-343-0121.

the magic of
★ macy's
macys.com

# From the Blog of Major P. Alston Middleton, Jr., USMC

### Thursday, July 3, 2008—Current Challenges in Iraq

Dear Friends, Family and Fellow Marines,

I hope this email finds you all well. I guess we, those of us in my command, are victims of the Iraqi's success. The Ministry of Defense and the Iraqi Army are swelling with confidence and challenging us as a staff to stay up with them. The Iraqis are making major changes in their army on a weekly basis that would take us years to enact within our own force, yet they are having trouble getting approval to spend small sums of money. Much of the Iraqi leadership still tries to do things the old way while the lower ranking officers and younger staff seem to understand the need to modernize and improve their procedures.

It is both fascinating and frustrating. I must say that the future of Iraq is very bright. As long as the Iraqi Army/Police can maintain the security gains within Iraq, the potential is huge. This country has vast amounts of oil, is centrally located in the middle east, and has a very rich cultural heritage. In short, the only question remaining is how do we inform the citizens of the US of our success.

It has now been about 100 days since we lost the 4000th member of the US military in Iraq on March 24th. It was the day after Easter and Easter was the start of over 2 months of rocket attacks on the International Zone (IZ). Fortunately, we have not had any attacks in the past 3 to 4 weeks and life seems to be returning to some sort of normalcy. The current count of US military deaths is 4113, which has been slowing over the past 2 months. Each loss is very painful including COL Scott, MAJ Wolfer and SSgt Frost, but the sacrifice being made over here must not be in vain. Afghanistan is now starting to surpass Iraq in the number of coalition losses. The fight and focus of the enemy seems to be shifting from Iraq to Afghanistan which is good news for this country.

The news over here is very encouraging, but will it sell in an American election year? I would expect the criminal elements of Al Qaeda and the Shi'ia "Special Groups" to possibly ramp up their attacks sometime in August through October in an attempt to sway public opinion of this war in the US press. Time will tell. Honestly, the biggest challenge is how do we back down and let the Iraqi government take the lead. The biggest trap over here is the temptation of performing tasks the American way. This temptation often creeps into play, and the Iraqis do the natural thing of stepping back and watching the US forces do the heavy lifting. Basically, it is a cultural difference that requires us to make a conscious effort to adjust.

I am very grateful for your continued support and I am looking forward to returning home in about 100 days, early to mid October.

Sincerely,

Alston
P. Alston Middleton, Jr.
Major, USMC

### Monday, July 21, 2008—A Poolside Baptism

Dear Friends, Family and Fellow Marines,

I hope this email finds you well. Life in Iraq has been churning on at a very intense pace with the weeks flying by but the days sometimes are painfully slow. It is becoming more and more apparent to those of us over here that the Iraqi leadership and the Ministry of Defense have their own ideas about Iraq and its future. Honestly, it is good to see them approaching these problems with their determination and grit. However, we are two different cultures with different ideas about communications, logistics, maintenance and supply. So, it appears that the coalition is now having less and less influence over Iraqi problems which may be a natural progression - but a difficult one.

On another note, last Saturday, I went to the liberty pool for a baptism. This pool was the hangout for Sadam's sons, Uday and Quesay.

## From the Blog of Major P. Alston Middleton, Jr., USMC *(continued)*

It is now a nice facility run by the State Department. Seven of the Ugandan security guards in the IZ were baptized in a spirit filled ceremony. It was an amazing site which was made possible through one of the bible studies that occur locally. The singing and dancing during and after the baptism was incredible. I was truly impressed by their commitment and the musical talent of the other Ugandans attending.

I am now close to 80 days from heading home and I can't wait. A year-long tour over here gives you a new outlook on life. I really do appreciate the small things like a hug from my wife and children, the chance to go for a run down the beach or to watch a sunset over the Pacific Ocean.

Please join me in praying for the Coleman family which has experienced an unexpected loss last week. I will truly miss Walker, he was a Saint.

Sincerely,

Alston
P. Alston Middleton, Jr.
Major, USMC

### Monday, August 11, 2008—A Chance Encounter

Dear Friends, Family and Fellow Marines,

The latest news from Iraq is truly amazing. In the month of July, there were a total of 11 US military fatalities in all of Iraq.

The number of combat related deaths was only five. While these low numbers are very encouraging, each of these fatalities have given the last full measure in order to bring peace to this nation and the region.

The Iraqi Army is still taking the fight to the enemy and going on the offense with strong support from the coalition.

One of the six noncombat related fatalities was a soldier named Specialist Andre D. Mitchell, 25, Elmont, NY assigned to the 2nd BN, 3rd Armored Cavalry Regiment, Fort Hood, TX. I was honored to be on the C-130 flight that carried Andre from Mosul to Kuwait International Airport. This redirected flight was originally scheduled to go from Baghdad International Airport (BIAP) to Al Udeid Air Base in Qatar; I was going on a 4 day pass at Camp As Sayliyah in Qatar. I have to credit the Air Force with making sure that this soldier was given what I perceived to be a very dignified entrance and exit on the C-130. Again, I was honored to be a Marine in the formation at 0300 in the morning on 1 August as he was carried off of the plane in Kuwait International Airport. I will never forget that moment.

I had a chance encounter on my trip to Qatar with a fellow Charlestonian at BIAP and at Camp As Sayliyah. Mr. Gibson, the incoming CEO for the USO, came over to the middle east to see how his organization can best support the troops in the field with tailored, deployable USO care packages. If you are looking for an organization to support that directly impacts deployed US military forces, give to the USO. It is hard to believe that our encounters were pure chance. I believe that my delayed departure from BIAP was directed by the good Lord in order to help him and one of his colleagues get to the MNC-I Headquarters at the Al Faw Palace on 31 July. We were able to link up with their POC by 0800 that morning. I also saw Mr. Gibson on 7 August at Camp As Sayliyah in Qatar as I was trying to get back to Iraq. My original flight from Al Udeid to BIAP on 6 August was canceled late that evening which gave me two extra days in Qatar. We had a nice meeting and I enjoyed the beer and spending time with 2 Navy LCDRs and an Air Force Major.

I am recharged and back at work pulling my MNSTC-I oar for the next 50 to 60 days as hard as I can. I need to stay focused on the mission and not redeploying, but I must say planning my redeployment is great.

Sincerely,

Alston
P. Alston Middleton, Jr.
Major, USMC

# 2010-2015

The second decade of the twenty-first century suffered from the results of the Great Recession of 2008. Officially, the deepest economic crisis since the Great Depression ended in June 2009, yet its shadow lingered for years. Unemployment remained high, and the underemployment of millions diminished the expectations of American families. This economic calamity temporarily pushed the wars in Iraq and Afghanistan off the front page but, despite a growing lack of interest in waging war and losing lives, the twin wars continued, eventually spanning more than a decade. By 2015 the fighting was still underway in both countries even though American role had been radically diminished.

America experienced a jobless recovery. Surveys showed that half of Baby Boomers aged 45 to 75 were being forced to delay retirement, thus decreasing the number of jobs available to the younger generation. By 2014 a languid recovery was underway. The stock market established record highs, and the housing market came back to life as building permits and housing prices both grew. Consumer confidence surged to its highest level in nearly six years. New car sales increased. The jobless rate, which hovered around 10 percent in October 2009, fell to 5.5 percent by March, 2015, another sign of business confidence.

Despite the poor economy in 2012, incumbent President Barack Obama won re-election, proudly promoting the first-term passage of the Affordable Care Act, designed to make healthcare insurance available and affordable to all Americans. The new law drew the ire of the right wing of the Republican Party and was forced to survive four dozen repeal votes in the U.S. House of Representatives. This signature achievement of the Obama administration was credited with bringing health care to millions of previously uninsured individuals.

Politically, the decade will be recognized for the rapid rise and resilience of the Republican-based Tea Party movement, known for a no-compromise approach to a reduction in the national debt and federal budget deficit through dramatic cuts in government spending and taxes. Frustrated by a divided government, American's approval rating of Congress plunged into the single digits.

The Occupy Movement spontaneously held national demonstrations to protest the shrinking middle class and the concentration of wealth in the nation's top one percent. The first Occupy protest to receive widespread attention was Occupy Wall Street in New York City's Zuccotti Park, begun on September 17, 2011. By October 9, Occupy protests were underway in 600 communities in the United States.

Meanwhile, concerns mounted during the decade over deaths of unarmed black men at the hands of police, or a vigilante. Unarmed African Americans killed in such a manner between 2012 and 2014 included Trayvon Martin in Florida, Ramarley Graham in the Bronx, Eric Garner in Staten Island, and Michael Brown in Ferguson, Missouri.

Same-sex marriage rapidly gained acceptance. By early 2015, marriages licences were being given to same-sex couples in 36 states and the District of Columbia. Gay marriages became legal in 32 of those states since 2010.

The years 2010 to 2015 also saw the emergence of self-appointed cyber watchdogs who exposed U.S. government secrets through massive data dumps via the internet. Julian Assange of WikiLeaks was hailed as both a traitor and a hero when he released thousands of secret documents concerning the Iraq War and private diplomatic State Department cables. The releases ignited strong disapproval and condemnation from many governments, which criticized WikiLeaks for potentially jeopardizing international relations and global security. A similar firestorm erupted in 2013 when NSA whistleblower Edward Snowden exposed the on-going operational details about the U.S. National Security Agency's global surveillance of foreign nationals and U.S. citizens.

On the energy front, the United States became a leader in the production of natural gas by employing a controversial water injection technique known as fracking. This brought the country greater oil independence, as did an expanded search for off shore oil. The search turned tragic when, on April 20, 2010, a British Petroleum oil drilling rig exploded in the Gulf of Mexico, causing the worst oil spill in U.S. history, surpassing the damage done by the Exxon Valdez in the environmentally sensitive Cape William sound in 1989.

# 2010 News Feature

### THE COST OF WAR: 'It Changes Who We Are,' Christian Davenport, *The Washington Post*, October 3, 2010

The doctor begins with an apology because the questions are rudimentary, almost insultingly so. But Robert Warren, fresh off the battlefield in Afghanistan and a surgeon's table, doesn't seem to mind.

Yes, he knows how old he is: 20. He knows his Army rank: specialist. He knows that it's Thursday, that it's June, that the year is 1020. Quickly, he corrects the small stumble: "It's 2010." He knows that his wife is Brittanie, that she's due with their first child any day now, and that they "got married two to three weeks before I went to that country."

Stumble No. 2: "That country."

David Williamson doesn't let it slide. "Which country?"

"Whatever country it was that I got blown up in," Warren says.

In a conference room at the National Naval Medical Center in Bethesda, he purses his lips, and as he searches for the word "Afghanistan," he slides his hand over the left side of his head, which is cratered, like an apple with a bite taken out of it.

"Crap, I can't remember," he says finally.

Warren has trouble remembering a lot of things. Which isn't surprising, considering that several pieces of shrapnel tore through his skull after insurgents outside Kandahar blew up his truck with a rocket-propelled grenade in May. One piece came to rest in the center of Warren's brain two millimeters from his carotid artery where it remains, suspended like a piece of fruit in a gelatin mold, too dangerous to extract.

"I'm going to say three words and then have you say them back to me, okay?" says Williamson, a neuropsychiatrist who runs Bethesda's traumatic brain injury unit. "Apple. Desk. Rainbow." Warren doesn't hesitate: "Apple. Desk. Rainbow."

He seems satisfied to have answered a question correctly. But repeating the words immediately isn't the point of the exercise; it's being able to repeat them in 10 minutes or so, after some other tests. A person with normal cognitive function will probably remember all three words. Patients with mild Alzheimer's might recall two. People with advanced dementia might remember only one, or none at all.

At the Bethesda hospital, the flow of brain-injured patients is constant. For nearly a decade, the United States has been fighting wars in which soldiers are routinely exposed to brain-rattling blasts that can send ripples of compressed air hurtling through the atmosphere at 1,600 feet per second. Now, the military is struggling to come to terms with an often-invisible wound.

The military brass are discovering that what used to be shrugged off as "getting your bell rung" can lead to serious consequences. In some cases, even apparently mild brain injuries can leave a soldier disqualified for service or require lifelong care that critics say the Department of Veterans Affairs isn't equipped to handle. Since 2000, traumatic brain injury, or TBI, has been diagnosed in about 180,000 service members, the Pentagon says.

But some advocates for patients say hundreds, if not thousands, more have suffered undiagnosed brain injuries. A Rand study in 2008 estimated the total number of service members with TBI to be about 320,000.

A small percentage of those injuries are as serious as Warren's. To let his brain swell and keep the blood flowing, thereby preventing the damage from worsening, doctors removed virtually the entire left side of his skull, a procedure known as a craniectomy.

Warren's physical wounds will heal, but three weeks after he was hit, military doctors are still discovering the extent of the damage.

Williamson plows ahead with other tests, revealing that Warren doesn't know where he is. "This is the U.S.A.?" he says.

Warren cannot subtract seven from 135, but he can spell "world" though not backward. He can recite the days of the week but can't come up with the words for necktie or button.

Finally, Williamson asks whether he can remember those three words he had to repeat. Sixteen minutes and 19 seconds have passed.

"Which words?" Warren says.

No two traumatic brain injuries, signature wounds of the wars in Iraq and Afghanistan, are the same, but the patients on 7 East, Williamson's TBI unit, demonstrate what life is like when the organ that turns a body into a person is damaged.

There's the Marine whose injury robbed him of the ability to understand speech even though he could still read, another who could no longer laugh, one who could see out of both eyes but only to the left, and one soldier who became dangerously impulsive and started spending thousands of dollars on junk he didn't need.

Although their injuries might not be as visible as a severed limb, TBI victims' damaged neurons and altered brain chemistry can cause all sorts of behavioral problems. Those injuries are about much more than a lump of tissue sitting between the temples. "It's about who they are," Williamson says. "How they see the world. How they process different experiences. It's about how their personality changes. It's about their humanity."

Many patients on 7 East suffer from little more than the general haziness that comes from having been too close to an explosion. Those concussions, often referred to as mild TBI, are the most common brain injuries in wars in which the enemies' weapon of choice is the makeshift bomb.

Severe TBI, such as Warren's, can lead to wholesale personality changes. But doctors now know that even mild TBI can have serious consequences. A blast "causes a change in how your brain functions," said Vice Adm. Adam M. Robinson Jr., the Navy surgeon general. "People have been very, very slow to come to that conclusion, but it's true."

# 2010 Profile

# Treating War's Invisible Wounds

## Wounded Warrior

Tony Saxton was the son of Army veterans. He joined shortly after high school and planned to make it a career. Instead, he was medically discharged in 2010 after nine years because of the toll to his mind and body from a tour of duty in Afghanistan and two tours in Iraq. Now, at age 28, he's tending to his wounds.

## Life at Home

- Tony Saxton was born on November 13, 1982, in Mount Clemens, Michigan, and grew up in Wisconsin.
- Both his parents had been in the Army. His mom, Margaret, spent four years in the Army as a dental hygienist.
- His dad, Robert Saxton, was career Army, serving 24 years in the infantry; his career included two tours in Vietnam: 1966-1967 with the 7th Cavalry, and 1967-1968 with the 101st Airborne.
- In 1966, he was wounded over 60 percent of his body from grenade shrapnel.
- Tony joined the Army in March 2001; "I knew pretty much from the git-go I was going to join," he said. "My whole life I grew up with it."
- He was home on leave on September 11, 2001, when terrorists hijacked jets and flew them into the World Trade Center in New York and the Pentagon in Washington, D.C.
- He knew he would be in action now.
- Tony was in the 505th Regiment, one of the most deployed units in the Army.
- It was the only unit of the 82nd Airborne deployed in the first Gulf War in 1990-1991.
- The 505th Regiment made four combat jumps in World War II and was part of the U.S. invasions of Grenada in 1983 and Panama in 1989.

*Tony Saxton after returning from war. Photo: Jim DuPlessis*

- It was also deployed to Kuwait and Iraq in 1991 as part of Operation Desert Storm.
- Tony's first deployment was to Afghanistan from January to October 2003.
- Six months earlier, he had married Nichole, a woman from his hometown.
- During his deployments, she stayed with her parents in Wisconsin.
- Tony was sent to a primitive camp in the mountains on the Afghanistan-Pakistan border, where fewer than 200 soldiers lived in tents and rotated duty manning four observation posts.
- Their chow hall was a trailer, and they burned all of their trash and other waste—all of it.
- Burning waste from the latrines was accomplished by mixing a stew of latrine waste, diesel oil, and gasoline; to burn the entire contents, Tony and other soldiers stood by to occasionally stir the pot with an old shovel handle.
- The observation posts were about one to four miles from the base, with each manned by a team of six to 10 soldiers who had to carry all of the food, water, ammunition, and other supplies needed to maintain themselves for their week-long rotation at the observation post.

- Each man carried 100 to 150 pounds of gear.
- "We lived off of whatever we could carry up there," Tony said.
- The elevation was high, and it took soldiers a while to adjust to the lower oxygen content of the air.
- Tony's first assignment was to man the closest observation post.
- It took his team about three hours to hike the one mile uphill to the post; after getting used to the altitude, his team did the same climb in about 45 minutes.
- They had no close contact with the enemy: "We got rocketed every day or every other day," Tony recalled.
- He had hardly been back home four months when his unit was called up to go to Iraq because a National Guard unit out of California wasn't ready.
- "We weren't even supposed to be deployed," Tony explained. "We found out on the news."
- He was deployed to Iraq from January to July 2004.
- His unit was assigned to Forward Operating Base Kalsu, built in May 2003 near Iskandariya, 20 miles south of Baghdad.
- The base was named after Bob Kalsu, a football player for the University of Oklahoma and the Buffalo Bills, who was killed when his unit came under mortar fire in Vietnam.
- Three soldiers from Tony's unit were killed by a roadside bomb on January 27 near Fallujah, about 50 miles west of Baghdad.
- Another bombing on February 4 killed another soldier.
- Tony was back at Fort Bragg before his son was born in July 2004.
- In March 2006, he was promoted to Staff Sergeant (E6).
- Soon afterward, he learned he was being deployed again to Iraq.

- From August 2006 to October 2007, he was at Forward Operating Base Brassfield-Mora, named for Army Specialists Artimus Brassfield and Jose Mora, who were killed in separate mortar attacks in October 2003.
- The base housed a battalion, or about 1,500 troops, and was located about 84 miles north of the Iraqi capital of Baghdad and six miles north of Samarra, a city of about 350,000 people.
- Samarra is a key city in Salahuddin province, a major part of the so-called Sunni Triangle where insurgents were active during the Iraq War.
- Samarra has several holy sites for Shia Muslims, who constitute the majority of Iraq's population but who are a minority in Samarra.
- Terrorist groups, who considered themselves allied with Sunni Muslims, attacked Shiites and their shrines.
- Sunnis bombed one of the holy sites, the al-Askari Mosque, on February 22, 2006, destroying its landmark golden dome and setting off a chain of violence across Iraq that claimed hundreds of lives.
- Tony's unit arrived in the Samarra area six months after that bombing.
- Conditions had worsened in Iraq, and Tony knew this would be harder than his last two deployments.
- "Every deployment I went on progressed," he said. "My first tour to Iraq, we were rolling around with no doors on the Humvees. The IED threat just wasn't really there. By the time I went back, they had the Generation 4 up-armored Humvees. When you closed the door, it sounded like a vault closing behind you."
- He continued, "I lived it a day at a time and kept my mind focused on the mission. I didn't want to have my mind somewhere else when I was supposed to be doing something. I just wanted to bring all my guys back in one piece."

- As staff sergeant, he was third in command in his platoon, outranked by the platoon sergeant and the lieutenant.
- Tony often commanded Quick Reaction Force missions that were a few minutes to an hour away from the base.
- When a roadside bomb went off, their job was to rescue vehicles and gather information from locals, Iraqi police, or U.S. troops on the scene.
- They also provided security for an explosive ordnance disposal team of three Navy specialists.
- Brassfield-Mora was along a main supply route, so the Quick Reaction Force was called out frequently.
- In April 2007, Tony was called on to respond to a roadside bomb that had destroyed an armored vehicle and injured three soldiers in the 2nd Platoon who were hit about five to 10 miles north of the base along the main supply route.
- A good friend of his was among the wounded; he was the truck commander sitting in the passenger seat—the same position Tony sat.
- Tony was in command of 16 men in four gun trucks—up-armored Humvees.
- On the way out to the scene, his truck was struck three times by roadside bombs.

- "Of course, we just drove through them," he said. "We didn't stop."
- "Once it happens, your adrenaline kicks in," he explained. "If it's not that close, the truck will rock a little bit, and you blow right through it. Or you hear a bunch of dirt and shrapnel hit the side of the truck."
- When Tony's unit arrived, they saw that the bomb had blown off the front half of the armored vehicle.
- Investigators later determined the bomb was fashioned from three 155 mm artillery rounds.
- Two of the three troops were medevaced out; the third was manning a 50-caliber machine gun atop the Humvee.
- "The gunner refused to get out from behind his 50-caliber until the other two were medevaced out," Tony said. "The gunner had scratches, bruises, and a couple of cuts."
- After the two soldiers were evacuated, the rest of the platoon moved into security positions.
- Tony's unit moved in to support them: "We started to go through the surrounding houses," he said. "We didn't find the trigger man."
- Tony didn't know it at the time, but he had suffered a blast concussion on the way out.
- He just kept on.
- In June, Tony's unit was called into Samarra after insurgents set off another set of bombs that destroyed the two minarets and a clock tower at the ruins of the golden dome at the al-Askari Mosque.
- Shiite cleric Muqtada al-Sadr called for peaceful demonstrations and three days of mourning, while Iraqi police placed a curfew on the city, and Tony's unit provided crowd control around the mosque.

## Life at Work

- By the time Tony Saxton left Iraq, he had been exposed to eight roadside bomb blasts.
- He still wanted to make the Army a career, but he knew the deployments were taking a toll.
- He had returned home briefly in October 2006, three months into his last deployment, to be with his wife for the birth of their daughter.
- "I came back and she was a year old," he recalled.
- He re-enlisted to get out of the 82nd Airborne—"to give me a break from deployments," he said. "You can only go through so much before you realize you're not going to come out of it unscathed. No matter what you do over there, when you come back, you're changed."
- Tony was transferred to Fort Jackson, South Carolina, where he served as a range cadre, maintaining a course where recruits practiced map reading.
- He soon realized he was suffering from recurrent severe headaches and bouts of dizziness, but, he said, "I basically just blew it off."

- Eventually, doctors sent Tony to a poly-trauma unit at the Veterans Administration hospital in Tampa, Florida, where specialists performed CAT scans, MRIs, and other tests.
- Doctors diagnosed Tony as having a traumatic brain injury.
- In 2010, he was given a medical discharge.
  - Because of the brain injury, he also had an auto-processing disorder that acts like hearing loss.
  - "My brain doesn't process words if there's a lot of background noise. I have to physically look at people. That's something I'll have to live with," he said.
  - He was also diagnosed with post-traumatic stress disorder (PTSD) and was treated for an alcohol problem.
  - "After I got back from my last deployment, I was basically self-medicating with alcohol."
  - He had graphic scenes and personal losses that came back to him.
  - "I lost 12 friends while I was overseas. It was partly like survivor's guilt," he said. "I can try to forget about it and push it to the back of my head, but it always finds a way to come back out."
  - He joined a support group of about 15 soldiers and combat medics with PTSD who met for an hour about once a week.

*Sgt. Tony Saxton in Iraq during his third deployment.*

- They talked about common problems like nightmares, reacting to gunfire at the base ranges, and having trouble reconnecting with their families.
- In that regard, Tony was lucky.
- "My wife's been right there for me. She can tell when something's off," he said.
- He was being treated with medication.
- What do his doctors say about his prognosis?
- "I don't even think they know," he said. "With each individual, it's a learning process, basically."

## Life in the Community

- The military counted 25,353 blast injuries from October 7, 2001, through August 1, 2009—the single highest source of U.S. casualties in the wars in Iraq and Afghanistan.
- Ninety percent survived, largely because of better armor and better medical treatment than had been available in past wars.
- Tony Saxton was among thousands of others who had been exposed to blasts but whose injuries were invisible at the time; they did not get counted on casualty reports and did not get medical treatment at the time.
- A Rand Corporation study in 2008 estimated that 160,000 to 320,000 service members had experiences from the wars in Iraq and Afghanistan that may have resulted in a traumatic brain injury.
- Blast injuries happen from waves of air pressure often powerful enough to throw a soldier dozens of feet in the air.
- Even with a helmet, the jolt can cause the brain to crash against the inside of the skull.

- Repeated brain trauma among some football players and boxers has been linked to the later appearance of a disease known as chronic traumatic encephalopathy.
- Many athletes who were found after death to have had the disease experienced memory loss, depression, and oncoming dementia as early as their thirties, decades before afflictions such as late-onset Alzheimer's appear in the general population, according to *The New York Times*.
- Researchers have linked some athletes' later-life emotional problems to their on-field brain trauma.
- So, too, the research on military personnel was trying to determine whether some soldiers with PTSD—a psychological diagnosis—actually had physical brain damage from battlefield blasts.
- Some signs of PTSD, particularly depression, erratic behavior, and the inability to concentrate, appear similar to those experienced by concussed athletes.
- Boston University's Dr. Robert Stern, a leader in brain disease research, said that blast injuries could be seen as this generation's version of exposure to Agent Orange, the herbicide used in the Vietnam War and later linked to widespread health problems among returning veterans.
- "During exposure to Agent Orange, it wasn't known what long-term effects there would be, but through long-term scientific study of veterans, those effects have been more clearly understood," he said. "We need to know if these individuals with blast injuries are going to require long-term care and treatment."

# HISTORICAL SNAPSHOT
# 2010

- A 7.0-magnitude earthquake devastated Port-au-Prince, Haiti, killing 200,000 people. It was the region's worst earthquake in 200 years.
- On April 20 an explosion occurred on a BP oil drilling rig off the coast of Louisiana, killing 11 people and shooting an estimated 42,000 gallons an hour of crude oil into the Gulf of Mexico. BP capped the oil spill 86 days later.
- *The Hurt Locker,* which portrays bomb disposal experts in Iraq, won six Academy Awards, including Best Picture and Best Director for Kathryn Bigelow, the first woman to win the Best Director award. *Avatar* won three awards. *Crazy Heart, Precious,* and *Up* each won two awards.

*Chaos following the Haiti earthquake.*

- The movies raking in the most money at the box office in 2010 were *Toy Story 3* ($415 million); *Alice in Wonderland* ($334 million), *Iron Man 2* ($312 million), *The Twilight Saga: Eclipse* ($301 million), and *Harry Potter and the Deathly Hallows: Part 1* ($295 million).
- The 2010 Winter Olympics opened in Vancouver, British Columbia, on February 12.
- Beyoncé won a total of six Grammy awards, breaking the record for most wins by a female artist. Taylor Swift won five.
- The Grammy Award for Best New Artist went to the Zac Brown Band, an American country music band from Atlanta.
- Eminem's comeback album, *Recovery,* was the United States' best-selling album of the year, with 3.42 million copies sold.
- Liu Xiaobo (China) won the Nobel Peace Prize "for his long and non-violent struggle for fundamental human rights in China."
- A painting by Picasso sold for a record-breaking $106.5 million at a Christie's auction. The painting, *Nude, Green Leaves and Bust,* depicts Picasso's mistress and was painted in just one day in 1932.
- The United Kingdom got its first coalition government since World War II when Conservative Party leader David Cameron became prime minister and formed a government with the ideologically opposed Liberal Democrats.
- Yukio Hatoyama resigned in June as Japan's prime minister after just nine months in office. He was succeeded by Naoto Kan, the country's fifth prime minister since 2006.
- The U.S. discovered 10 Russian spies masquerading as civilians in the United States and then agreed to swap them for four alleged spies captured by the Russians.
- Spain beat the Netherlands in soccer for the World Cup.
- Iran released three American hikers charged with espionage and imprisoned for more than a year: Sarah Shourd, Shane Bauer, and Joshua Fattal.
- Thirty-three Chilean miners were rescued after spending 68 days trapped in a mine half a mile underground.
- Julian Assange, the Australian-born co-founder of WikiLeaks, was arrested in England on charges of sexual assault.
- The United States, Russia, China, and others agreed to impose a fourth set of sanctions to stem Iran's nuclear weapons program.
- *Call of Duty: Black Ops* was the year's most popular video game.

## Selected Prices

| | |
|---|---|
| Coaster set | $13.00 |
| Cordless wine opener/chiller | $27.97 |
| Picture frame, 8" x 10" | $10.98 |
| Shower cap, set of three | $14.85 |
| Men's bath and shower gel | $11.19 |
| Coffee grinder | $27.99 |
| Tilex mold and mildew remover | $9.05 |
| Corded telephone | $29.44 |
| HP All-in-One printer | $590.00 |
| CD | $13.97 |

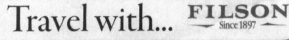

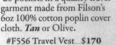

## A Chance for Clues to Brain Injury in Combat Blasts
### By Alan Schwarz, *The New York Times*, June 23, 2009

No direct impact caused Paul McQuigg's brain injury in Iraq three years ago. And no wound from the incident visibly explains why Mr. McQuigg, now an office manager at a California Marine base, can get lost in his own neighborhood or arrive at the grocery store having forgotten why he left home.

But his blast injury—concussive brain trauma caused by an explosion's invisible force waves-is no less real to him than a missing limb is to other veterans. Just how real could become clearer after he dies, when doctors slice up his brain to examine any damage.

Mr. McQuigg, 32, is one of 20 active and retired members of the military who recently agreed to donate their brain tissue upon death so that the effects of blast injuries—which, unlike most concussions, do not involve any direct contact with the head—can be better understood and treated.

The research will be conducted by the Sports Legacy Institute, a nonprofit organization based in Waltham, Mass., and by the Boston University Center for the Study of Traumatic Encephalopathy, whose recent examination of the brains of deceased football players has found damage linked to cognitive decline and depression.

Whether single, non-impact blasts in battle can cause the same damage as the years of repetitive head bashing seen in football is of particular interest to researchers. The damage, primarily toxic protein deposits and tangled brain fibers, cannot be detected through noninvasive procedures like MRIs and CT scans.

"We don't know much about the medium- or long-term effects of head trauma experienced by our military," said Robert Stern, co-director of the Boston University center as well as its Alzheimer's Disease Clinical and Research Program. "We know that there are some immediate effects in terms of blast injury on cognition and behavior. But we do not yet know whether there are any long-term effects.

"Does that single blow result in something that doesn't go away," he added, "or perhaps sets off a cascade of events that leads to a progressive degenerative brain disease?"

Mr. McQuigg may be finding out the cruelest way. In February 2006, he was on combat patrol when his Humvee was hit by a roadside bomb, knocking him unconscious, shattering his jaw, and damaging his right eye. His helmet could not protect him from a severe concussion that doctors told him was caused solely by the bomb's force waves, not direct impact.

Now he is experiencing headaches, short-term memory problems, and trouble with balance that have only worsened. "With prosthetics, you can replace an arm or a leg and can still throw a football with your kid," said Mr. McQuigg, who works at Camp Pendleton, north of San Diego. "If you have a severe brain injury, you might not be able to live on your own."

"And people don't know what's wrong with you," he added. "People know if you're missing an arm, something happened. If it happened to your brain, they can't tell."

Benefits of the research on military personnel could extend to the general population, said Dr. Daniel P. Perl, director of neuropathology at the Mount Sinai School of Medicine in New York. Even though civilians are rarely subjected to anything close to the devastating waves that burst from battle explosions, the characteristics of blast injuries could lend insight into brain damage caused by single impacts in automobile accidents, for example.

If protein deposits and tangles appear in the hippocampus area of the brain, for instance, then they would affect short-term memory; appearance in the frontal lobes could impair executive function; and in the cerebellum, coordination and balance. The researchers will also be looking at possible genetic factors.

"I wouldn't be surprised if there was a great deal of overlap between examples of this from the sports arena and the military, but we don't know," Dr. Perl said. "The forces are different, and presumably the mechanisms are somewhat different. If this research and the examinations are done right, they have the potential to contribute significantly. It could tell us what happens, which we're not going to get otherwise."

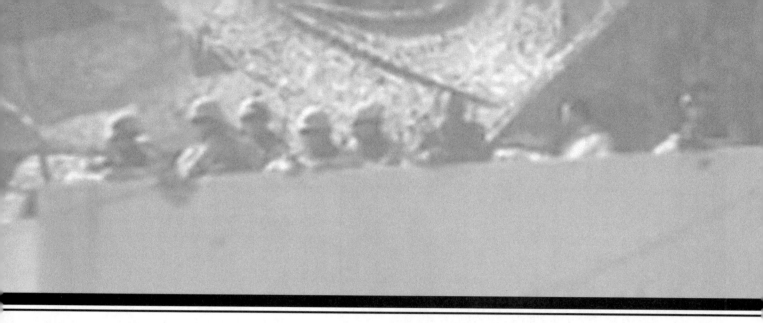

## 2012 Profile

## American Returns Home as a Stranger

### Sergeant

Karl Zeithammel followed his father's footsteps into the Marines—and combat. But unlike his father's generation, Karl came home realizing that few of his peers understood the sacrifices he made.

### Life at Home

- Karl Zeithammel has gone to war three times in the past 10 years, and despite the U.S. Marine recruiter's promise that he would see the world, each mission has been to the same place: Iraq.
- During all those years, Karl has broken two engagements, married once, missed the birth of his first child, and witnessed firsthand the slow—very slow—Initial steps of an ancient nation simultaneously reaching for the future while holding tightly to the past.
- During his time in a country mentioned prominently in his Sunday School classes, he fell in love with the people, some of the countryside, and the role he was playing to build a new country.
- Born in Battle Creek, Michigan, Karl had just turned 19 with one year of community college under his belt when the president called upon the nation to attack Iraq and topple the brutal government of Saddam Hussein.
- The media hoopla about weapons of mass destruction was not of Karl's concern; he signed up to follow orders and make the world safe.
- Besides, the training required to build a marine, conducted at the hot, swampy, humid Paris Island, South Carolina, was not the stuff of Shakespeare's sonnets and Sunday morning political talk shows.
- Karl was prepared to be a fighting machine, at least the first time he was shipped to Iraq.

*Karl Zeithammel, right, in Iraq.*

- Each time he returned, the training had evolved to both include the latest defenses against fearsome weapons such as IEDs and a greater emphasis on diplomacy and winning the trust of the Iraqi citizens.
- Communications also evolved at the speed of sound from letter writing to Skyping with his wife and eager young son, who could recognize daddy on the screen.
- Groomed by his father to be a state champion high school football lineman and a wrestler, Karl loved the physical aspects of the military training—no matter how brutal the demands or militant the Southern mosquitoes.
- His father had been a Marine in Vietnam in the mid-1960s, when the U.S. still marginally backed the war; this time, Karl was convinced the nation was very happy to ignore the wars of his generation in Iraq, Afghanistan, and other hotspots nearby.
- After World War II, the standing force remained so large that most Americans had a direct military connection and the draft was still in place.
- Among older Baby Boomers, those born before 1955, at least three-quarters had an immediate family member—sibling, parent, spouse, child—who served in uniform.
- Of Americans born since 1980, the Millennials, about one in three was closely related to anyone with military experience, in part because America had moved to an all-volunteer army.
- Dinner table talk was rarely about the military and never about politics, although cereal—its manufacture, sales, and annual consumption—was regularly on the agenda.

- Karl's father worked in middle management with one of Kellogg's more established brands; his mother also worked for Kellogg, in the same building but in another department, as an executive secretary.
- The city's largest employer was formed in 1906 by William Keith Kellogg based on his brother's conviction that cold cereal was better for the human body than a large, hot breakfast of eggs, sausage, and bread.

## Life at Work

- The initial 2003 invasion of Iraq lasted 21 days and signaled the start of the conflict dubbed Operation Iraqi Freedom by the United States.
- The invasion consisted of a combined force of troops from the United States, the United Kingdom, Australia, and Poland that invaded Iraq and deposed the Ba'athist government of Saddam Hussein.
- The invasion phase was primarily a conventionally fought war which concluded with the capture of the Iraqi capital of Baghdad by American forces.
- Then the hard work of establishing a peace began.
- Iraq had a population of 24 million scattered over a land mass the size of California with porous borders.
- Karl was unprepared for the wide contrast—the sky-high adrenaline of fighting and the absolute boredom of undirected peacekeeping—or the lack of clarity of mission.
- For example, the chaos of Kirkuk was astounding.
- "The Kurds were vandalizing and stealing everything they could get their hands on in revenge. It was obvious they intended on pillaging the city," explained Karl.
- He continued, "As there were only a few U.S. troops on the scene in those first few days, there wasn't much we could do about the whole scenario."
- One Peshmerga drove by in a forklift.
- "I am not sure what he intended on doing with it, but it was his, by God, and he was driving it home," said Karl.
- Later, Karl saw a full-sized and operational fire truck heading back north.
- A few weeks later he saw this same fire truck abandoned on a mountain road with no wheels or battery. "It must have run out of fuel, and they stripped whatever was valuable," he noted.
- During the first tour, he experienced some fighting that he refuses to discuss, but one night he was called upon to move some of his fellow wounded and killed soldiers.
- One Marine he found dead was carrying a note to ask his mother to send Skin So Soft to keep the fleas away.
- The duty was gruesome, but even worse was the smell.
- For Marines in Iraq at that time, laundry services only occurred every couple of weeks, so even if Karl was careful and very clean, the smell of death seemed to cling to him.
- After his first tour, he planned to get out and maybe take a job with Ace Hardware, where an old high school buddy was manager.
- When he got back stateside, life was not as he had expected; he felt a certain awkwardness back in the States that he had trouble articulating.

- Karl had experienced some hearing loss, but otherwise he was healthy and intact, yet in many subtle ways, life was not at all the same.
- There was the awkwardness at bars and parties when acquaintances danced around his war experience, avoiding the topic as if he had cancer.
- Mostly, there was the painful disconnect between the very real war in which he had fought and the one Americans read about or glimpsed while channel surfing.
- He felt a profound bond with the Marine Corps and found himself wishing that the American public displayed more support for the military.
- As an example, during a phone conversation with a friend, he mentioned that he had heard on the news that a dozen soldiers were killed in Iraq that day.
- The friend replied, "Oh, man, that sucks. What are we going to do later?"
- "There was no sacrifice being demanded of the American people," Karl observed;
- "I think I romanticized the idea, but I had a feeling that if I didn't go and do it, I would regret it in the future."
- It was during his second tour that IEDs became a deadly fact of life.
- He also came to fully understand the military saying, "Amateurs talk strategy, professionals talk logistics."
- Every aspect of his day needed to be considered, from which vehicle to use, which vest to wear, and which roads to run.
- The confusion he felt during his second rotation was similar to his father's oft-repeated comments about the Vietnam War: "Hell, there was no way to tell the good actors from the bad actors—what were we to do?
- I'll tell you what we did: we survived—whatever it took."
- They had a son who was named Karl Jr., who seemed delighted to visit with daddy over Skype several days a week.
- Karl also learned—against his will—how to text, tweet, and, most of all, talk long distance from Iraq without constantly counting up the cost.
- The third tour was awkward: after years of being taught how to break things, suddenly the military wanted him to become a diplomat and talk soothingly to the people who had been both allies and enemies.
- This mission gave him a real sense of how much destruction the Saddam Hussein regime had wrought and why the invasion was necessary; the man was a monster.
- He also came to understand that being a soldier requires taking personal responsibility for representing one's country, and protecting allies and comrades around you at all times, under all orders.
- Service was something a majority of young Americans appeared comfortable letting others do for them.
- Since the end of the military draft system in 1973, most young people have had little motivation to serve.
- "A military that is disconnected from the rest of society is a condition that does not bode well for the future of military-civilian relations," Karl said.
- In 2012, he began considering running for political office, noting, "We need people making decisions who have been separated from their families in combat; I wonder what this country would be like if our ancestors were not willing to run toward danger in defending America, while leaving that task to others."

*Battle Creek, Michigan, 1907.*

## Life in the Community

- Battle Creek, Michigan, was named for a skirmish that took place almost two centuries ago between a government land surveyor and two Indians.
- During that 200 years, the city has picked up a variety of names: the Queen City, the Health City, and the International City.
- Today, according to the Chamber of Commerce, the Cereal City is the "best known city of its size in the country."
- The village of Battle Creek began as a market and mill center for prairie farmers.
- By the late nineteenth century, the town developed into a major industrial center, supplying a variety goods including agricultural machinery, steam pumps, violin strings, and newspaper printing presses.
- Since its earliest days, Battle Creek has welcomed social and religious non-conformists.
- Quaker pioneer Erastus Hussey operated a station on the Underground Railroad, helping escaping slaves reach freedom in Canada.
- In the last years of the nineteenth century, the town became a Spiritualist center, where séances and "table knocking" were common, if inexplicable, phenomena.
- Sojourner Truth, nationally known as a charismatic speaker for abolition and women's rights, visited Battle Creek in 1856, and for the next 27 years, the ex-slave made Battle Creek her home.

*Field Hospital 338, Camp Custer near Battle Creek, 1917. Photo: Collection of Jim DuPlessis*

*Ex-slave Sojourner Truth, outspoken advocate for women's rights, lived in Battle Creek.*

- The economy of the community is now bolstered by an international business center and is an amateur sports capital, but the name Battle Creek will be forever linked to health and diet reform, thanks to the pioneering research of Dr. John Harvey Kellogg into food health and safety.

- In addition to its reputation as the birthplace of the cereal industry, Battle Creek served as a basic training site for American soldiers during both world wars, and the home of the famous Percy Jones Orthopedic Hospital.

- During the final years of the nineteenth century, W. K. Kellogg was working diligently for his older brother at the sanitarium, but by 1906 he decided he was ready to form his own cereal business: the Battle Creek Toasted Corn Flake Company.

- Kellogg used extensive and innovative advertising to make his distinctive signature and the Sweetheart of the Corn universally recognizable.

- To families everywhere, "Kellogg's of Battle Creek" meant cereal.

- Most of the small cereal companies in the U.S. had disappeared by 1910, but Battle Creek remained the cereal capital of the world as Kellogg, Ralston, and Post products became staples on breakfast tables around the globe.

- During World War I, Battle Creek was the second home to the "doughboys" who passed through the Army training center at Camp Custer.

- Thousands of young American men received their first taste of military life here and sampled the generous hospitality of the townspeople.

- Renamed Fort Custer, the base was reactivated during World War II.

- In addition to serving as a basic training location, the fort was an internment center for German prisoners of war.

## HISTORICAL SNAPSHOT
# 2012

- Utah banned discounts or specials on alcoholic drinks, essentially outlawing Happy Hour.
- San Francisco raised the minimum wage within its jurisdiction to over $10 per hour, making it the highest minimum wage in the country.
- The Supreme Court ruled unanimously that telephone consumers can gain standing in federal courts to sue abusive telemarketers based on the Telephone Consumer Protection Act (TCPA) of 1991.
- Photography pioneer Kodak filed for bankruptcy protection, no longer able to compete in the digital age.
- Approximately 111.3 million viewers—approximately one-third of the total population of the U.S.—watched the Super Bowl.
- The Kellogg Company purchased snack maker Pringles from Procter & Gamble for $2.7 billion.
- At the 84th Academy Awards, The Artist won Best Picture—the first silent film to win that award since Wings in 1927.

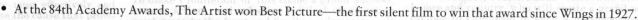

Trayvon Martin, left, was shot to death by George Zimmerman, right.

- The shooting of Trayvon Martin, an unarmed black 17-year-old, by George Zimmerman in Sanford, Florida, ignited nationwide discussion of the role of race in America.
- The *Encyclopædia Britannica* announced that it would no longer be producing printed versions but would continue online editions.
- The United States, Japan, and the European Union filed a case against China at the WTO regarding export restrictions on rare earth metals.
- American golfer Bubba Watson won the U.S. Masters, defeating Louis Oosthuizen of South Africa in a playoff.
- The Guggenheim Partners purchased the Los Angeles Dodgers for $2.1 billion, the most ever paid for a professional sports franchise.

- The first licenses for autonomous cars in the U.S. were granted in Nevada to Google.
- Goldman Sachs director Rajat Gupta was convicted of three counts of securities fraud and one count of conspiracy related to insider trading in 2011.
- Connecticut repealed the death penalty.
- Former American Major League Baseball player Roger Clemens was acquitted on all charges of perjury.
- Moody's downgraded the credit rating of 15 major world banks.
- NBCUniversal bought full control of the U.S. news website MSNBC.com and rebranded it as NBCNews.com.
- In swimming, Michael Phelps of the United States won his 19th career Olympic gold metal, with gold in the 4 x 200-meter freestyle relay.
- The first presidential debate of 2012 was held at the University of Denver in Colorado.
- Two American scientists, Robert Lefkowitz and Brian Kobilka, won the 2012 Nobel Prize in Chemistry for their discoveries of the inner workings of G protein-coupled receptors.
- Felix Baumgartner broke the world human ascent by balloon record before space diving out of the *Red Bull Stratos* helium-filled balloon over Roswell, New Mexico.
- The Walt Disney Company purchased Lucasfilm Ltd. from George Lucas for $4.05 billion; included in the deal were the rights to the Star Wars and Indiana Jones franchises.
- Washington became the first state to legalize marijuana.
- Hostess, which includes such brands as Twinkies, announced it would file for bankruptcy, liquidate its assets, and lay off 18,500 workers.

## Selected Prices

| | |
|---|---|
| Super Heavyweight Hangers Light-Gray, 18-Pack | $22.99 |
| Panasonic RX-D55GC-K Boombox | $177.83 |
| Men's slippers | $31.15 |
| Electro-Luminescent Sport Watch | $88.94 |
| Bamboo placemat coaster chopstick set | $28.19 |
| Dental floss, pack of six | $19.81 |
| 25 Watt A15 Incandescent Light Bulb, 4 | $6.39 |
| 7 Day, 7 Sided Pill Reminder | $4.29 |
| Belle Hop ID Document Organizer | $21.29 |
| Flannel Nightshirt | $22.43 |

# Timeline for The Kellogg Company

- 1898: While attempting to make granola, the company's founder, W. K. Kellogg, and his brother Dr. John Harvey Kellogg, accidentally flaked wheat berry. W.K. kept experimenting until he flaked corn and created the recipe for Kellogg's Corn Flakes.
- 1906: W. K. Kellogg opened the "Battle Creek Toasted Corn Flake Company" and hired 44 employees who created the initial batch of Kellogg's Corn Flakes and brought to life W. K.'s vision for healthier breakfast foods.
- 1914: Kellogg's Corn Flakes was introduced to a new country: Canada.
- 1915: Kellogg introduced Bran Flakes, the first high-fiber cereal, followed by Kellogg's All-Bran one year later.
- 1923: The Kellogg Company became the first in the food industry to hire a dietitian.
- 1930: Kellogg founded the W. K. Kellogg Foundation, whose mission was to help children realize their potential, and became one of the first companies to display its cereals' recipes and nutritional information on its boxes
- 1942-1945: Kellogg's employees produced K-rations for the U.S. Armed Forces overseas during World War II and introduced a new, whole-grain cereal—Kellogg's Raisin Bran.
- 1969: The Kellogg Company was selected to provide breakfast for the legendary Neil Armstrong, Buzz Aldrin, and Michael Collins during their groundbreaking Apollo 11 trip to the moon.
- 1997: The W. K. Kellogg Institute for Food and Nutrition Research was opened.
- 2009-2010: Kellogg increased the fiber in many of its popular cereals, including Kellogg's Froot Loops

*W.K. Kellogg founded The Kellogg Company in Battle Creek, Michigan.*

# 2013 NEWS FEATURE

### "Still Shooting After the End of War," Andrew W. Lehren, *The New York Times*, May 15, 2013:

Stacy Pearsall never wanted to stop being a combat photographer. When her job ended, she wondered whether life was worth living.

Ms. Pearsall joined the Air Force at age 17 and soon grew eager to photograph American military efforts around the world. But the odds of covering combat were slim, and she knew it.

"Somebody had to either die or retire," she recalled. When a position opened up, it changed her whole world.

The Air Force staff sergeant began training in a program for war photography at Syracuse University. She traveled to more than 40 countries, including places like South Korea and the Horn of Africa. But it was her two rotations in Iraq where she made her deepest mark. Among her many honors include twice being named the National Press Photographers Association's military photographer of the year. The Pentagon handed out her work documenting the military efforts in Iraq to the media and public on a daily basis. They were republished online, and in newspapers and magazines.

*Air Force Sergeant Stacy Pearsall was named Military Photographer of the Year. Photo: U.S. Air Force*

During her first stint, which began in September 2003, assignments varied widely. "One day we were on a raid hunting down one of the face cards," she recalled, referring to the deck of cards identifying the most wanted officials of Saddam Hussein's government. "The next day we were shooting a school opening."

*Stacy Pearsall, left, ready to document a raid in Iraq. Photo: U.S. Army*

Her second stint centered on 2007's battle of Baquba. "The fighting I experienced was very extreme," she said. "In my last deployment, it was an everyday occurrence."

She had started her military photo career inspired by noted war photographers like James Nachtwey, Carolyn Cole, and Eddie Adams. Ms. Pearsall worked to get into the right spot, take a moment, and plan the shot.

"I'm definitely as deliberate as I can be in the circumstances," she said. "Instead of chasing the action, I'm kind of anticipating where that action is going to happen, taking risks, and getting in front of the action so you can be there when it happens." She tells more about her craft in her newly published second book, *A Photojournalist's Field Guide.*

Her work took her to the front lines, not common for female soldiers, and where the United States only recently lifted its ban on women in combat despite 20 percent of its ranks being female. "Being a woman, it was a really unique opportunity," she said.

Not everyone understood. Sometimes soldiers would yell at her. But she felt, "If you don't take those pictures, then how will anybody know what sacrifices were made?" Sometimes Ms. Pearsall was capturing images of soldiers she barely knew. Other times it was of her closest friends. She recalled the death of Capt. Donnie R. Belser, killed by sniper fire mere hours after she had heard him singing "Happy Birthday" to his son.

And at times she set down her cameras to help her fellow soldiers in battle. While riding along with a unit caught in an ambush, she picked up an M240 machine gun and provided cover fire as others brought back wounded soldiers. Amid flying bullets, she hauled the wounded into the armored vehicle, including a soldier almost twice her size, placing her hand on his neck to stop the blood pumping out of his carotid artery.

But her two rotations in Iraq exacted an enormous physical toll. During her first tour, she suffered injuries from a roadside bomb that tore through her Humvee, and a similar IED blast occurred during her second tour. She suffered concussions, traumatic brain injuries, and a ruptured disc in her neck.

By February 2007, Ms. Pearsall began to feel tremors in her hands, and it was difficult to hold her head up straight. One morning she could not get out of bed. Her bunkmate, Kathryn Robinson, a videographer, got her to go to the doctor, where she learned the injuries were worse than she suspected. About three months later she was flown out of Iraq for medical care in Charleston, South Carolina.

Her job prospects dimmed. She was awarded a Bronze Star, but photojournalism was no longer an option in the military. She felt the Air Force did not take her injuries seriously, including her post-traumatic stress, and they questioned why she did not report her problems sooner. But she knew that if she had reported them, she would lose the job she loved so much. "The military had trained me this way—to suck it up," she said.

Ms. Pearsall reluctantly took a medical discharge in one of the most difficult times in her life. Even worse, she said, was the psychological toll. She was reluctant to say anything about PTSD, fearful that few of her colleagues would take her seriously.

"The one thing about PTSD is it's the war that never ends" she said. "Suicide might seem like a viable option. It's a permanent solution to a temporary problem."

Driving in South Carolina one day, she wondered whether she should just steer her car into an overpass. Nearly a thousand active duty military personnel have attempted suicide in 2011, the most recent year for which there are official statistics. While Ms. Pearsall did not, she is among an untold number who engage in what is termed suicidal ideation, contemplating how they might kill themselves.

Ms. Pearsall sought help from a local Department of Veterans Affairs clinic. Now she is active in a variety of efforts to help veterans, including photography workshops and her work as a spokeswoman for the Real Warriors Campaign. She's spoken about her path on Oprah's television show, and the role of women in combat.

But photography still remains her passion. She runs a photo studio in Charleston with her husband, who was also a military photographer, and highlights work by her students on her studio's walls. Her military experience has led to commercial assignments for products like body armor.

Ms. Pearsall continues to ensure that the sacrifices made by veterans are not forgotten. She started the Veterans Portrait Project, capturing images of those who served in conflicts stretching back to World War II, which hang on the walls of the local Department of Veterans Affairs hospital. She is currently at work on several photo essays about the lives of veterans.

She worries about the plight of veterans and sees her work as a continuation of her job in the military. "That story isn't over for them," she said. "I just don't want people to forget that."

# 2014 Profile

# Navy Salt Still at Sea in the Army Reserve

### Army Reservist

Jasper Peterson grew up in the shadow of World War II, the son of a Pearl Harbor veteran. Jasper followed his dad's lead, first into the Navy and then into a military career that has lasted 35 years—so far. Since 2004 he has served as a chief warrant officer in the U.S. Army Reserve. He serves as a marine engineer aboard Army cargo transport ships that dock at Morehead City, North Carolina. He engages in "battle assemblies" one weekend each month, plus an annual training that lasts 14 to 45 days.

### Life at Home

- Jasper Peterson was born in New Jersey in 1960 to Claude and Jessica Peterson.
- Claude was a Navy aircraft mechanic who was at Pearl Harbor on December 7, 1941, when the Hawaiian navy base was bombed in a surprise attack by Japanese aircraft carriers.
- Claude spent 20 years in the Navy, retiring just before Jasper was born.
- The Petersons moved in 1965 from New Jersey to Durham, North Carolina, where other family members lived. From the time Jasper can remember, he has heard of his father's exploits through World War II and Korea.
- Claude's training and Navy retirement income meant the family had a secure income: "We didn't have to worry about a meal at the table," Jasper said.
- On the other hand, serving in the Navy required sacrifices.

*Chief Warrant Officer, U.S. Army Reserve, Jasper Peterson, front left.*

*Peterson worked as a pilot on the* Atlantis, *a passenger submarine that offered tours off the coast of Hawaii. Photo: State of Hawaii, Office of Environmental Quality Control*

- In 1957, when his oldest son died at age two, Claude was on an aircraft carrier in the South Pacific and couldn't get back in time for the funeral.
- Jasper had a brother who was four years older than he, an older sister born in 1958, and a younger brother born in 1967.
- John taught Jasper how to hit a baseball and drive through a basketball court to make a layup.
- When John joined the Navy after high school, Jasper decided to do the same.
- Jasper graduated from high school in 1978 and joined the Navy the next year under the delayed entry program.
- Since he was scheduled to begin basic training a year later, he used the time off to go to a few concerts and hang out with his buddies.
- In January 1980, playtime was over.
- After eight weeks of basic training in San Diego, he was accepted into the six-week submariner school in Groton, Connecticut, to learn how to operate and repair a submarine's interior communications systems.
- This included the sound-powered phones, which don't require outside electricity; instead, they operate by using microphones that use voice pressure to generate tiny amounts of current strong enough to carry voices to several stations on a ship.
- They're important because they can be used even when a ship loses all power, including its batteries.
- Jasper also completed an eight-week course for basic electronics and electricity.
- From 1981 to January 1984, he was aboard the USS *James K. Polk* (SSBN 645), a Benjamin Franklin-class nuclear submarine launched in 1965.
- On his first mission, the "Jimmy K" completed the Navy's 2,000th strategic deterrent patrol since the Navy began them in 1960, beating the USS *Francis Scott Key* (SSBN-657) for the honor.
- The 41 participating submarines spent an average of 50 days underwater for each mission, carrying nuclear missiles that could be launched against the Soviet Union or another nuclear adversary as a reprisal.
- The presence of nuclear-armed subs offshore was meant to deter an enemy from making a first strike by the knowledge that both countries would be annihilated.
- This type of deterrence was sometimes referred to as "Mutually Assured Destruction (MAD)."
- Jasper remembers U.S. Sen. Strom Thurmond speaking at a ceremony celebrating the 2,000th patrol in Charleston, South Carolina, after the sub returned to its home base there in June 1981.
- But Jasper was more impressed at the time by the feeling of emerging after two months underwater.
- "It was wonderful to breathe fresh air and feel the sunshine," he remarked.
- In addition to internal communications, he also monitored and maintained the ship's central air system, which monitored the level of gases in the ship's atmosphere.
- The system could detect levels of oxygen and potentially dangerous levels of Freon, carbon monoxide, and carbon dioxide.
- Jasper left the Navy in 1984, but re-enlisted a year later, deciding he would try to retire from the Navy.
- "It's a good pension," he noted.
- When he re-enlisted he went aboard the USS *Proteus* (AS 19), a submarine tender, with a crew of about 1,500 working on a ship with several layers of decks.

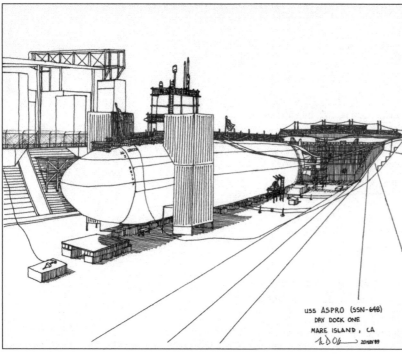

USS ASPRO (SSN-648)
DRY DOCK ONE
MARE ISLAND, CA
20 MAY 89

*Jasper Peterson served on several submarines, including the* USS Aspro, *above, and the* USS Proteus, *below.*

- He was on the *Proteus* from 1985 to 1987.
- On a voyage from Hong Kong, the *Proteus* ran into the eye of Typhoon Lola, May 20-21, 1986.
- Even though the ship experienced rolls of 40 to 50 degrees, Jasper was an old salt by then and didn't even get seasick.
- His last ship was the USS *Aspro* (SSN-648), a fast-attack Sturgeon-class submarine often used by the Navy during the Cold War to stalk Soviet submarines.
- The ship went into dry dock in Vallejo, California, near San Francisco, in 1986.
- Its refitting, which made it one of the quietest subs in the fleet, was finally completed in 1989.
- Jasper was aboard the *Aspro,* leaving the San Francisco Harbor at 5 p.m. on October 17, 1989, and listening with his crew mates to Game 3 of the World Series between the Oakland A's and the San Francisco Giants.
- Suddenly, they saw Candlestick Park shaking from an earthquake.
- The Loma Prieta earthquake collapsed a section of the San Francisco-Oakland Bay Bridge less than 30 minutes after the *Aspro* had cleared it.
- The *Aspro* returned to her home base in Pearl Harbor in late October.
- As she approached the submarine base, the other moored submarines welcomed her back to port by sounding their whistles for over four minutes.
- Jasper stayed in Hawaii when he left the Navy in March 1990.
- That year, he met his future wife, Carolyn, and found a job as a pilot and diver for a submersible tourist vessel that operated off the coast of Hawaii's Kona Island.
- Using tugboats, the tourist company would tow the submarine out to a mooring about a mile offshore, where the sub would take 46 passengers at a time on dives from about 8 a.m. to 4 p.m.
- The water was about 45 feet deep in coral.
- Passengers saw angelfish, barracuda, eel, and other species.
- Divers fed fish with dog food, which was sometimes hazardous—once, a 60-foot-long whale shark showed up.
- Each night the mooring lines for the submarine were dropped to the ocean bottom.
- One of the jobs of divers each morning was to dive to the ocean bottom to raise the mooring lines by attaching empty balloons to the lines and then filling them with air from their ventilators.
- The air-filled balloons would then carry an end of the line to the surface.
- Once, when Jasper was diving in about 60 feet of water to bring mooring lines to the surface, he thought he was having a dizzy spell because the ocean floor seemed to be moving.

- Then he realized he was watching a manta ray with a 45-foot wingspan rising from the ocean bottom.
- He had other moments of excitement, such as meeting Harrison Ford and Ozzie Osborne, but overall, "it got monotonous."
- He needed a better paying, more secure future.
- In 1995, he joined the Army Reserve to become an X-ray technician.
- The Army sent him to school in San Antonio, Texas, with two dozen other soldiers.
- A year later, he passed the board examinations and became a registered X-ray technician.
- He worked at Tripler Army Medical Center in Honolulu from 1996 to 2001, when he moved with his young family back to Durham to be close to family and to improve his income.
- There, he began working at the Veterans Administration hospital.
- A year later he completed training to perform computerized axial tomography (CAT) scans, which produce cross-section views of a patient's anatomy.
- His CAT scan training meant a $10,000 pay raise, but he wanted to improve his Army Reserve income, so he decided to apply for warrant officer training with an assignment that would allow him to go back to sea.
- In 2003, he was accepted into warrant officer candidate school in Rucker, Alaska.

*Soldiers take their places as fuel trucks prepare to load. Photos: U.S. Army*

- He passed, allowing him to go to warrant officer basic training in Newport News, Virginia, in 2004.
- During the 10-month course he learned how to repair the large diesel engines used on Army vessels— Detroit Diesel and Cummins engines with more than 1,000 horsepower.
- These engines are about 20 feet long and approximately 10 feet in diameter.
- When he graduated, his Army Reserve assignment was transferred to Morehead City on the North Carolina coast, where several Army vessels are based.
- Jasper was deployed to Kuwait from August 2006 to November 2007.
- His unit was part of a logistics center that helped moved tanks, Humvees, generators, and cargo containers to Iraq and Afghanistan.

## Life at Work

- Jasper Peterson now spends one weekend per month on training exercises at Morehead City, North Carolina, and one annual exercise lasting 14 to 45 days, as part of his duties as a member of the Army Reserve.
- He works on Landing Craft Utility boats, or LCUs.
- These special ships have a crew of about 16 people and carry personnel and military equipment from Humvees to tanks.
- The boats are 174 feet long and can carry up to three M1 main battle tanks, or 24 20-foot standard shipping containers.
- Loaded LCUs have a range of up to 6,500 miles and a fuel tank capacity of 92,000 gallons.
- Each vessel even makes its own water with two machines to distill ocean water at a combined rate of 800 gallons a day.

- His exercises vary: one spring weekend in 2014 the boat took out a group of scientists from the National Oceanic and Atmospheric Administration to catch fish samples.
- About 100 fish were put in large tanks on deck for further study.
- A few weeks later, the unit went on its annual exercise.
- Jasper packed his garment duffle bag the night before and left home after work on Friday, driving six hours to the Army Reserve Center at Morehead City where his boat, the *Matamoros,* was docked.
- He wasn't allowed on the boat yet, so he slept in his car until shortly before the crew mustered at 6:30 a.m.
- Most of the 17-member crew share a cabin, or sleeping quarters.
- Only Jasper, as chief engineer, and the skipper have their own "stateroom," or private cabin.
- Jasper's room is small, with just enough room for a desk, recliner, locker, small refrigerator, and his bunk—a single bed with drawers below.

*Peterson's fellow Warrant Officers Douglas Fuchs, right, and Kyle Oga. Photo: U.S. Army*

- A bathroom with a shower is built between the two staterooms and shared by Jasper and the skipper.
- Most of the crew sleep in group quarters on bunks stacked two high.
- Sometimes an Army nurse is aboard, but usually there is only a medic.
- There is a room for treating crew and an extra three-bunk cabin that serves as a sickbay.
- The crew readied the boat, which didn't carry much this trip, so it didn't take long to load the cargo: a military generator, a Humvee, and a few 40-foot containers.
- They pulled out of the bay on time Sunday afternoon.
- There's no reveille on board an LCU.
- "We know when breakfast is served, and we know when we stand watch," explained Jasper.
- Breakfast is served 6:30-8 a.m., lunch is 11:30 a.m.-1 p.m., and dinner is 4:30-6 p.m.
- The crew uses military time, so a civilian 1 p.m. is called 13:00 in military time.
- "A good meal is steak and lobster. A bad time is a cook who has a hard time cooking eggs," Jasper said.
- Most of the crew serve four-hour watches, while Jasper and the assistant chief engineer serve alternating 12-hour watches.
- The engine crew consists of about seven engineers who check the engine for problems like high water temperatures.
- Everyone else on the boat, except the cook, is part of the deck crew, or deckies, under the command of the skipper and the first mate.
- Sometimes the seas are rough, but this trip was smooth with normal swells of three to five feet.
- After several days, they arrived in Puerto Rico, where it took only about half an hour for the Army dock workers to unload the cargo.
- The crew began routine maintenance, such as changing the engine oil.
- They also spruced up the *Matamoros* for a visit by their commanding general.

- They ran special nautical signal flags along a line from the superstructure to the bow that read: "Welcome aboard general."
- Ship's work was usually completed by 2 p.m.
- After that, some crew members went into San Juan to visit casinos, restaurants, or stores; weekends were often spent at festivals that served local foods.
- From Puerto Rico, they sometimes sail to St. Thomas in the Virgin Islands for exercises or a "liberty" port, which means there is no scheduled work.

- "That's what we always hope for," said Jasper.
- No such luck on this trip.
- Instead, they sailed for three days to Miami.
- The route took them along the southern edge of the Bermuda Triangle, where, according to lore, ships and planes have disappeared mysteriously.
- Studies have found there is no greater chance of a ship being lost there than in other parts of the ocean.
- "You have people who it bothers, so you don't even talk about it," Jasper said.
- On their second day at sea, the engine gauges showed high water and oil temperatures.
- "We began to hear a tapping in the starboard main [engine] that told us maybe a piston was going," explained Jasper.
- He reported the problem to the skipper and shut down the engine.
- They were now traveling on the port engine at about seven to eight knots—half their normal speed.
- Jasper had been trained in engine repair, but he was smart enough to realize that the real expertise was among his crew, some of whom had extensive experience maintaining diesels in their civilian work.
- The crew reported that the engines needed to have two cylinders replaced—a big job at sea, even with an experienced crew.
- "We had everything we needed in our parts bins." More importantly, Jasper said, "We had some excellent personnel on board who knew how to repair it."
- Jasper split the crew into two rotating groups with at least two engineers working on the engine and one standing regular watch on the port engine.
- After 29 hours, the engine was back in commission.
- Only when the job was almost finished did the crew joke about breaking down in the Bermuda Triangle.
- After another day, they sailed into Miami, where they stayed about two days on liberty, going to the beach, fishing, swimming at the Coast Guard base pool, or working out at the base gym.
- "The military is one of the best-kept secrets," Jasper said. "It's not a bad gig."

## Life in the Community

- The U.S. Army Reserve exists to help the Army ramp up strength quickly in wartime.
- People enlist in the Army Reserve for three to six years, committing themselves to one weekend a month in training and two weeks a year in a field training exercise.
- The part-time arrangement allows people to serve while pursuing higher education or a career in a full-time job.
- However, they can also be called to active duty.
- Yearly pay in the Army Reserve starts at about $3,600 for privates (E1), $5,000 for staff sergeants (E6), and $8,100 for captains (O3).
- The Reserve is part-time, but it can be more time than the official hours.
- Sgt. 1st Class Ann Marie Schult-Slosser said two days a month isn't enough to complete tasks: "Not the administrative tasks, not your job tasks. A lot of Guardsmen think nothing of spending their personal time to get things accomplished. They use their personal vehicles, their personal computers. That was a surprise to me."
- The Army Reserve represented about a fifth of the Army's total strength of 1.1 million soldiers in 2011.
- The regular Army had 546,057 troops, the Army National Guard had 358,078 troops, and the Army Reserve had 201,166 troops.
- The Pentagon began cutting active-duty troops in 2010, responding to unplanned budget cuts and the end of large-scale U.S. involvement in the Afghanistan and Iraq wars.

- The regular Army had close to 514,000 soldiers in August 2014, but was expected to shrink to 490,000 by October 2015 and 450,000 by 2019.
- The Army might eventually have to skinny down to 420,000 troops—a size that leaders say may not allow them to wage even one major, prolonged military campaign, according to The Associated Press.
- Since the Vietnam War ended in 1975, Reserve component soldiers have taken a more active role in U.S. military operations.
- For example, Reserve and National Guard units took part in the Gulf War, peacekeeping in Kosovo, Afghanistan, and the 2003 invasion of Iraq.

## HISTORICAL SNAPSHOT
# 2014

- The Ebola virus epidemic in West Africa broke out in February, infecting over 21,000 people and killing at least 8,000.
- Malaysia Airlines Flight 370 disappeared over the Gulf of Thailand with 239 people on board on March 8. The aircraft was presumed to have crashed into the Indian Ocean.
- Malala Yousafzai, a 17-year-old Muslim from Pakistan, became the youngest person to win the Nobel Peace Prize. She shared the prize with Kailash Satyarthi, a Hindu from India, for their struggle against the repression of girls and women.
- Macklemore & Ryan Lewis won the Grammy Award for Best New Artist.
- The Disney movie soundtrack *Frozen* was the most popular U.S. album for 13 weeks in early 2014.
- A Sunni militant group called the "Islamic State in Iraq and the Levant" began an offensive through northern Iraq on June 5.
- Colorado allowed the sale of recreational marijuana from legally licensed businesses.

- *12 Years a Slave* won the Oscar for Best Picture; it grossed just under $188 million.
- *Transformers: Age of Extinction* was the top grossing movie of 2014, drawing more than $1 billion in box office receipts.
- The XXII Olympic Winter Games were held in Sochi, Russia.
- Belgium became the first country in the world to make euthanasia legal for terminally ill patients of any age.
- Russia annexed the Ukrainian territory of Crimea and began a covert military offensive against the Ukraine.

- The American science educator known as "Bill Nye, the Science Guy" defended evolution in the classroom in a debate with creationist Ken Ham.
- The song "Happy" by Pharrell Williams was No. 1 on the pop charts for 10 consecutive weeks.
- President Barack Obama announced the resumption of normal relations between the United States and Cuba on December 17.
- "Black Jeopardy!" became one of *Saturday Night Live's* most popular skits in 2014's Season 39 with cast member Kenan Thompson as game show host "Alex Treblack."
- On April 14, an estimated 276 girls and women were abducted from a school in Nigeria and held hostage.
- The Catholic Church simultaneously canonized Pope John XXIII and Pope John Paul II on April 27.
- Sony Pictures canceled its planned December 25 theater release of *The Interview* after threats from North Korea against the Seth Rogen-Evan Goldberg comedy that depicts the assassination of North Korea's dictator by a talk show host and his producer. Howls of criticism against Sony's backing down led the studio to release the film on video on demand.
- The 2014 FIFA World Cup was held in Brazil June 12-13. The cup was won by Germany in a 1-0 defeat of Argentina.

## Selected Prices

Women's leather ankle boots ...................................................$43.13

Floor Lamp with Alabaster Glass Shade .............................$58.52

Duraflame logs, six-pack .......................................................$29.09

Men's Hooded Sweatshirt .....................................................$59.99

CD, Memphis Minnie .............................................................$13.35

Marcato Atlas Pasta Maker ...................................................$79.95

Butcher Block Mineral Oil, 12 ounces ...............................$11.50

Wellness Canned Cat Food, 24-Pack ..................................$39.30

Self-Adhesive Removable Labels, 600 .................................$4.09

Stainless Steel Sauce Pan with Glass Lid, 3-Quart ...........$23.51

# Army to Force Out 550 Majors; Some in Afghanistan
## By The Associated Press, August 1, 2014

WASHINGTON—About 550 Army majors, including some serving in Afghanistan, will soon be told they have to leave the service by next spring as part of a budget-driven downsizing of the service.

Gen. John Campbell, the vice chief of the Army, acknowledged Friday that telling troops in a war zone that they're out of a job is a difficult task. But he said some of the soldiers could join the National Guard or the Army Reserve. The decision to cut Army majors comes on the heels of a move to slash nearly 1,200 captains from the ranks. Army leaders were criticized at the time for giving 48 of them the bad news while they were deployed to Afghanistan. The Army declined to say how many majors will be notified while they are at the battlefront.

"The ones that are deployed are certainly the hardest," Campbell told reporters. "What we try to do there is, working through the chain of command, minimize the impact to that unit and then maximize the time to provide to that officer to come back and do the proper transition, to take care of himself or herself, and the family."

Campbell said it's difficult to avoid cutting deployed soldiers because of the timing schedules. All the soldiers being forced to leave have probably already been given a heads-up that they were at risk of the job cut and will meet with a senior officer, according to the Army.

Those who are cut have nine months to leave the Army. And the soldiers who are deployed, including those in Afghanistan, will generally have about a month to move out of that job and go home to begin to transition out of the service.

The cuts have been difficult for many young officers, particularly captains, who tend not to have enough years in service to retire.

To make the cuts, the Army looked at about 8,500 majors who joined the service between 1999 and 2003. Some may have about 15 years of service, depending on all factors that go into credit for years of service, and might be able to retire, but many won't have enough time in the job, Campbell said Guard and Reserve leaders are looking for officers, especially captains, so there could be opportunities for the soldiers to continue to serve, he said.

After 13 years of war that forced a significant and rapid buildup of the Army to about 570,000, the military now has to reduce its combat forces to meet budget cuts.

The Army has close to 514,000 soldiers now, but will have to be down to 510,000 by October, shrink to 490,000 by October 2015, and be down to 450,000 by 2019. In addition, if Congress doesn't act to prevent automatic budget cuts from resuming, the Army may eventually have to get down to 420,000—a size that leaders say may not allow them to wage even one major, prolonged military campaign.

The Army tried to avoid some cuts by slowing enlistments and using attrition and some voluntary separations. It also has been combing through files looking for soldiers with disciplinary or other problems in their annual evaluations to weed out lower-performing officers first, officials said.

# EDITORIAL-OPINION
## By Gian P. Gentile, *The Washington Post*, April 18, 2014

The U.S. Army must remain prepared for battle.

*Having a force for only homeland or humanitarian missions could be disastrous.*

Gen. Matthew Ridgway, who took command of U.S. forces in Korea in December 1950, famously wrote that the "primary purpose of an army [is] to be ready to fight effectively at all times."

Ridgway arrived in Korea at a low point in the war: the Chinese had launched a counteroffensive across the Yalu River and pushed a dispirited and disorganized U.S. Army all the way south past Seoul.

How had the force that had driven the German army across France and back into Germany just five years earlier, at the end of World War II, lost the ability to fight effectively?

The answer: During those few years, U.S. political leaders had concluded that with the advent of nuclear weapons, land wars were a thing of the past. Taking this cue, generals had allowed the armored brigade combat teams from World War II to atrophy. In their place were skeletal divisions of poorly trained U.S. infantry on constabulary duty in Germany and Japan.

Slightly more than 40 years later, a very different U.S. Army evicted Saddam Hussein's military-a far more formidable foe than the North Korean army of 1950-from Kuwait. In 1991, the U.S. Army was not only better trained and had better resources, but it was also working as part of a joint force.

Virtually no Americans anticipated either the North Korean attack in 1950 or Iraq's invasion of Kuwait 40 years later. That seems to be the pattern: U.S. presidents send the Army to resolve unexpected crises, ready or not.

The world today presents a wide array of potential threats to U.S. interests, including a failed North Korean state losing control of its weapons of mass destruction, the morass of civil war in Syria, an aggressive and expansionist Russia or China, or still-unforeseen humanitarian crises in Africa and other areas. If called upon, the U.S. Army would deploy and engage in peacekeeping operations or major combat between state and non-state actors. In any event, it needs to be ready.

Some have argued that after the frustrating wars in Iraq and Afghanistan, there is little American appetite to send the Army into foreign lands, whether to fight, build nations, or distribute humanitarian supplies. This line of thinking holds that the U.S. Air Force, Navy, or Marine Corps can handle most of the security problems the world throws our way.

Defense expert Kori Schake and retired Navy Admiral Gary Roughead, for example, argued last year that the Army should be reduced to about 290,000 soldiers and have a large part of its capacity for ground combat moved to the National Guard and Reserve, in effect, turning it into a constabulary force capable of humanitarian missions-in other words, an army that can't fight. A more recent recommendation is for the Army to be reduced to 125,000 soldiers who are highly trained and backed up by the National Guard and Reserve.

These arguments resemble those made in the years leading up to North Korea's invasion of South Korea. Then, too, it seemed that the world did not need an army that could fight; it was assumed that American ownership of atomic bombs would somehow do the trick. The result was a near disaster on the Korean Peninsula. Even though Ridgway's forces held, American casualties were higher than if the Army had been prepared to fight.

Will the U.S. Army be reduced in size in the coming years? Budget reductions and a changing strategic environment demand a smaller, reorganized army. However, converting it into a force suited only for homeland defense or humanitarian missions abroad, without the ability to fight sophisticated foes as part of a joint force, would result in an unprepared Army likely to experience high casualties when called on to fight a war.

If history is any guide, the Army will inevitably be deployed again as a fighting force. The American people should invest in preparing for that event and avoid the near-catastrophe that occurred in South Korea decades ago.

*Gian P. Gentile is a senior historian at the RAND Corporation. He is a retired U.S. Army colonel and former history professor at the U.S. Military Academy at West Point. Reprinted with permission. All rights reserved.*

## More PT Testing Ideas
### This week's letters to the editor: PT, Tops in Blue, August 5, 2014

[Regarding "Fix the PT test," July 7 issue:]

Why are gym rats taking over the Air Force? This is not the Army nor is it the Marine Corps.

My take on the PT test: Get rid of it entirely. Just use the most basic metric available: Can this airman perform his/her Air Force duties? If a person fails that test, then by all means place him/her on a fitness improvement program until he/she can perform satisfactorily.

People say that obesity would cost the Air Force money in both the long and short term, but I sincerely doubt it would cost as much as we currently pay to treat physical training-related injuries, especially when you start to consider lost man-hours. In the long term, such a small percentage of the force retires with benefits that obesity-related health costs are a non-factor.

I hear we want people to present a professional image. Have you seen the corporate sector? I would have brilliant, overweight airmen in admin and intel fields than less intelligent, physically fit specimens. I hate seeing talented individuals being forced out of the service in favor of skinny ones.

Bottom line: The Air Force mission is to fly, fight, and win-not to look sexy in uniform. And deprioritizing physical fitness in favor of more relevant pursuits isn't "lazy."

This is from someone scoring in the 90s.

—*Master Sgt. Gordon Childs | Fort Meade, Maryland*

## The Song Doesn't Remain the Same
## By Neil Gussman, February 11, 2014

In January, the U.S. military and I celebrated our 42nd anniversary. Sort of. I am one of those modern soldiers with commitment issues. I enlisted in the Air Force Jan. 31, 1972.

My current and final enlistment in the Army National Guard will end May 31, 2015, the month I turn 62. In between, I switched to the Army in 1975, the Army Reserve in 1981; then I took 23 years off between 1984 and 2007 before re-enlisting in the Guard.

To say a lot has changed since I flew to Lackland Air Force Base 41 years ago hardly begins to describe the difference between serving at the end of an unpopular war and serving today.

My military career started with a wicked hangover from pitchers of beer in Boston bars the night before an early flight to San Antonio, Texas. My shoulder-length hair was shorn by a gleeful redneck. My first drill sergeant was what the Air Force called a BB Stacker. His Vietnam War service had been in Thailand loading bombs on B52s and living off base in a hooch that came with food, laundry, housecleaning, and companionship for $50 per month.

This married-with-kids master sergeant loved telling us stories of loading bombs and getting loaded himself. Though I can't remember that drill sergeant's name, I thought of him several times during a 90-day military school I attended at Fort Meade, Md., from August to November of last year.

The majority of the soldiers in the Army Student Company had just finished basic training. The rest of us shared their training schedule and their leaders.

In 1972, when we marched in formation, we sang songs about killing Viet Cong. We sang songs about the sex and heroism in our future. Most of all, we sang about Jody. Marching songs used to be referred to as Jody Calls. Jody is the guy who is back home sleeping with your wife, eating your food, driving your car, emptying your bank account, and, in the saddest versions, turning your own dog against you.

The songs we sang at Fort Meade during this summer and fall were more thoroughly bowdlerized than Sunday school stories. Cub Scouts could sing these songs in front of their mothers. No sex. No death. No cheating, lying, drinking, or drugs. Certainly no songs with refrains like "Jody got your girl and gone" or "Napalm sticks to kids."

When we ran in formation at Fort Meade, we almost always sang:

*When my granny was 91, she did PT just for fun,*
*When my granny was 92, she did PT better than you...*

and so on up to age 97. The song is clean, affirming of 90-year-old women, and mildly insulting to the wheezing 20-year-old struggling to keep in step at a run.

We also sang Airborne running songs:

*C130 rollin' down the strip,*
*Airborne Daddy gonna take a little trip,*
*Stand up, hook up, shuffle to the door,*
*Jump on out and count to four....*

The songs we sang at Fort Meade never varied.

In Army tank training in 1975, we sometimes sang the version above and sometimes this:

*C130 rollin' down the strip,*
*Blew a tire and the [two-word expletive deleted] flipped....*

We were really loud on the second line of the verse. This version goes on to insult the Air Force.

When my daughters were in preschool, I taught them some very sanitized marching songs. The girls learned "They Say That in the Army," which is a complaint song about food, coffee, and Army life in general. It has many verses, such as:

*They Say That in the Army the coffee's mighty fine,*
*It tastes like muddy water and smells like turpentine....*

## The Song Doesn't Remain the Same... *(continued)*

Each of the various verses ends:

*Gee Mom I wanna go, but they won't let me go.*

The girls also learned the "Yellow Bird" song:

*A yellow bird,*
*With a yellow bill,*
*Just landed on,*
*My window sill,*
*I lured him in,*
*With crumbs of bread,*
*And then I crushed his* (slam left foot to the ground) *little head.*

The word emphasized with a stomp was not "little" when we sang the song. And just that one word makes a lot of difference.

A decade later, my youngest daughter and some of her high school friends saw the movie *Jarhead*. Lisa came home and said with a smile, "Dad, you never told us the real words to those songs."

Lisa also wanted to know who Jody was. The older guys in the audience were laughing at places she and her friends did not get the joke. I explained Jody. Lisa and her friends went back to the movie now that they had Jody decoded.

Most of the soldiers I marched with at Fort Meade were in their early 20s, around the age my daughters are now. They had no idea who Jody was and had never sung a marching song laced with sex, violence, and words they use every five seconds in the barracks. Those words make for very loud cadence. But we sang no bad words at Fort Meade.

When the Army fights wars without enemies, we have to sing about running, old ladies, jumping out of airplanes, bad food, or wanting to visit Mom. Winning hearts and minds may be good policy, but it makes for lousy marching songs.

*Sgt. Neil Gussman enlisted in the Air Force in 1972. He first served on a live-fire missile test range in Utah until he was blinded in a test explosion. When he recovered, he re-enlisted in the Army in 1975 serving as a tank commander on active duty and in the reserves until 1984. He re-enlisted in the Pennsylvania Army National Guard in 2007, serving with the 28th Combat Aviation Brigade. He deployed to Iraq in 2009-2010 with the 28th CAB and still serves with the unit today. He blogs about life in the Army. He lives with his wife and six children in Lancaster, Pa.*

# FURTHER READING

Gwynne, S. C. (Samuel C.), *Empire of the Summer Moon: Quanah Parker And The Rise And Fall Of The Comanches, The Most Powerful Indian Tribe In American History*, Tantor Audio: Made available through hoopla, 2010.

Keenan, Jerry, *Encyclopedia of American Indian Wars, 1492-1890*. Santa Barbara: ABC-CLIO, 1997.

Tebbel, John William, *America's Great Patriotic War with Spain: Mixed Motives, Lies, and Racism in Cuba and the Philippines, 1898-1915*. Manchester Center, Vt.: Marshall Jones Co., 1996.

Lord, Walter, *The Good Years: From 1900 to the First World War*. New York: Harper, 1960

Atwood, Kathryn J., *Women Heroes of World War I: 16 Remarkable Resisters, Soldiers, Spies, and Medics*. Chicago, Illinois: Chicago Review Press, Incorporated, 2014.

Fussell , Paul, *The Great War and Modern Memory*, Oxford University Press, 1975.

*All Quiet on the Western Front*, the 1930 movie adapted from the 1929 novel by Erich Maria Remarque, directed by Lewis Milestone and produced by Carl Laemmle, Jr., Universal Pictures Corp. http://www.veoh.com/watch/v1486715efNPr68g?h1=All+Quiet+on+the+Western+Front+%281930%29

Tuchman, Barbara Wertheim, *The Guns of August* (A Pulitzer Prize-winning recreation of the powderkeg that was Europe during the crucial first thirty days of World War I traces the actions of statesmen and patriots alike in Berlin, London, St. Petersburg, and Paris). New York: Presidio Press, 2004, 1962.

*America Goes Over,* (A collection of silent films shot by the U.S. Army Signal Corps and housed at the Internet Archive), https://archive.org/details/AmericaG1918_2

Zinn, Howard, *A People's History of the United States*. Harper & Row, HarperCollins, 1980 (1st edition); 2009, http://www.historyisaweapon.com/zinnapeopleshistory.html

Lord, Walter, *Day of Infamy*. Ware, Hertforshire [England]: Wordsworth Editions, Ltd., 1998.

Moye, J. Todd, *Freedom Flyers: the Tuskegee Airmen of World War II*. New York: Oxford University Press, 2010.

Knox, Donald, 1936-, *The Korean War: Pusan to Chosin: An Oral History*. San Diego: Harcourt Brace Jovanovich, ©1985.

Karnow, Stanley A., *Vietnam: A History*. (first edition 1983). 2nd rev. and updated (New York, NY: Penguin Books, 1997).

*Pentagon Papers* online, U.S. National Archives and Records Administration, http://www.archives.gov/research/pentagon-papers/

(The Pentagon Papers, officially titled "Report of the Office of the Secretary of Defense Vietnam Task Force," was commissioned by Secretary of Defense Robert McNamara in 1967. In June 1971, small portions of the report were leaked to the press and widely distributed. However, the publications of the report that resulted from these leaks were incomplete and had quality issues. In 2011, on the 40th anniversary of the leak to the press, the National Archives, along with the Kennedy, Johnson, and Nixon Presidential Libraries, released the complete report—48 boxes and approximately 7,000 declassified pages, approximately 34% of which was never before available.)

Kyle, Col. James H., USAF (Ret.), *The Guts to Try* (An insider tells the story of the failed 1981 Iran hostage rescue). New York: Orion Books, 1990.

Beckwith, Col. Charlie A., US Army (Ret.), *Delta Force: The Army's Elite Counter Terrorist Unit*. Avon, 2000.

Hutchison, Kevin Don, *Operation Desert Shield/Desert Storm: Chronology and Fact Book*. Westport, Conn., Greenwood Press, 1995.

Cohen, Roger, *Hearts Grown Brutal: Sagas of Sarajevo*. New York: Random House, ©1998.

Bingham, Jane, *The Gulf Wars with Iraq* (This book briefly examines the military and political impact of the Gulf wars, along with their impact on civilian populations). Chicago, Ill.: Heinemann Library, ©2012.

Bergen, Peter L., *The Longest War: The Enduring Conflict Between America and al-Qaeda* (An account of al-Qaeda's evolution since 9/11 and the U.S. government's responses.). New York: Free Press, ©2011

# INDEX

# 2015 Title List

Visit www.GreyHouse.com for Product Information, Table of Contents, and Sample Pages.

## General Reference

An African Biographical Dictionary
America's College Museums
American Environmental Leaders: From Colonial Times to the Present
Encyclopedia of African-American Writing
Encyclopedia of Constitutional Amendments
Encyclopedia of Gun Control & Gun Rights
An Encyclopedia of Human Rights in the United States
Encyclopedia of Invasions & Conquests
Encyclopedia of Prisoners of War & Internment
Encyclopedia of Religion & Law in America
Encyclopedia of Rural America
Encyclopedia of the Continental Congress
Encyclopedia of the United States Cabinet, 1789-2010
Encyclopedia of War Journalism
Encyclopedia of Warrior Peoples & Fighting Groups
The Environmental Debate: A Documentary History
The Evolution Wars: A Guide to the Debates
From Suffrage to the Senate: America's Political Women
Global Terror & Political Risk Assessment
Media & Communications 1900-2020
Nations of the World
Political Corruption in America
Privacy Rights in the Digital Era
The Religious Right: A Reference Handbook
Speakers of the House of Representatives, 1789-2009
This is Who We Were: 1880-1900
This is Who We Were: A Companion to the 1940 Census
This is Who We Were: In the 1910s
This is Who We Were: In the 1920s
This is Who We Were: In the 1940s
This is Who We Were: In the 1950s
This is Who We Were: In the 1960s
This is Who We Were: In the 1970s
U.S. Land & Natural Resource Policy
The Value of a Dollar 1600-1865: Colonial Era to the Civil War
The Value of a Dollar: 1860-2014
Working Americans 1770-1869 Vol. IX: Revolutionary War to the Civil War
Working Americans 1880-1999 Vol. I: The Working Class
Working Americans 1880-1999 Vol. II: The Middle Class
Working Americans 1880-1999 Vol. III: The Upper Class
Working Americans 1880-1999 Vol. IV: Their Children
Working Americans 1880-2015 Vol. V: Americans At War
Working Americans 1880-2005 Vol. VI: Women at Work
Working Americans 1880-2006 Vol. VII: Social Movements
Working Americans 1880-2007 Vol. VIII: Immigrants
Working Americans 1880-2009 Vol. X: Sports & Recreation
Working Americans 1880-2010 Vol. XI: Inventors & Entrepreneurs
Working Americans 1880-2011 Vol. XII: Our History through Music
Working Americans 1880-2012 Vol. XIII: Education & Educators
World Cultural Leaders of the 20th & 21st Centuries

## Education Information

Charter School Movement
Comparative Guide to American Elementary & Secondary Schools
Complete Learning Disabilities Directory
Educators Resource Directory
Special Education: A Reference Book for Policy and Curriculum Development

## Health Information

Comparative Guide to American Hospitals
Complete Directory for Pediatric Disorders
Complete Directory for People with Chronic Illness
Complete Directory for People with Disabilities
Complete Mental Health Directory
Diabetes in America: Analysis of an Epidemic
Directory of Drug & Alcohol Residential Rehab Facilities
Directory of Health Care Group Purchasing Organizations
Directory of Hospital Personnel
HMO/PPO Directory
Medical Device Register
Older Americans Information Directory

## Business Information

Complete Television, Radio & Cable Industry Directory
Directory of Business Information Resources
Directory of Mail Order Catalogs
Directory of Venture Capital & Private Equity Firms
Environmental Resource Handbook
Food & Beverage Market Place
Grey House Homeland Security Directory
Grey House Performing Arts Directory
Grey House Safety & Security Directory
Grey House Transportation Security Directory
Hudson's Washington News Media Contacts Directory
New York State Directory
Rauch Market Research Guides
Sports Market Place Directory

## Statistics & Demographics

American Tally
America's Top-Rated Cities
America's Top-Rated Smaller Cities
America's Top-Rated Small Towns & Cities
Ancestry & Ethnicity in America
The Asian Databook
Comparative Guide to American Suburbs
The Hispanic Databook
Profiles of America
"Profiles of" Series – State Handbooks
Weather America

## Financial Ratings Series

TheStreet Ratings' Guide to Bond & Money Market Mutual Funds
TheStreet Ratings' Guide to Common Stocks
TheStreet Ratings' Guide to Exchange-Traded Funds
TheStreet Ratings' Guide to Stock Mutual Funds
TheStreet Ratings' Ultimate Guided Tour of Stock Investing
Weiss Ratings' Consumer Guides
Weiss Ratings' Guide to Banks
Weiss Ratings' Guide to Credit Unions
Weiss Ratings' Guide to Health Insurers
Weiss Ratings' Guide to Life & Annuity Insurers
Weiss Ratings' Guide to Property & Casualty Insurers

## Bowker's Books In Print® Titles

American Book Publishing Record® Annual
American Book Publishing Record® Monthly
Books In Print®
Books In Print® Supplement
Books Out Loud™
Bowker's Complete Video Directory™
Children's Books In Print®
El-Hi Textbooks & Serials In Print®
Forthcoming Books®
Large Print Books & Serials™
Law Books & Serials In Print™
Medical & Health Care Books In Print™
Publishers, Distributors & Wholesalers of the US™
Subject Guide to Books In Print®
Subject Guide to Children's Books In Print®

## Canadian General Reference

Associations Canada
Canadian Almanac & Directory
Canadian Environmental Resource Guide
Canadian Parliamentary Guide
Canadian Venture Capital & Private Equity Firms
Financial Services Canada
Governments Canada
Health Guide Canada
The History of Canada
Libraries Canada
Major Canadian Cities

# 2015 Title List

Visit www.SalemPress.com for Product Information, Table of Contents, and Sample Pages.

## Science, Careers & Mathematics

Ancient Creatures: Unearthed
Applied Science
Applied Science: Engineering & Mathematics
Applied Science: Science & Medicine
Applied Science: Technology
Biomes and Ecosystems
Careers in Business
Careers in Chemistry
Careers in Communications & Media
Careers in Environment & Conservation
Careers in Healthcare
Careers in Hospitality & Tourism
Careers in Human Services
Careers in Law, Criminal Justice & Emergency Services
Careers in Physics
Careers in Technology Services & Repair
Computer Technology Innovators
Contemporary Biographies in Business
Contemporary Biographies in Chemistry
Contemporary Biographies in Communications & Media
Contemporary Biographies in Environment & Conservation
Contemporary Biographies in Healthcare
Contemporary Biographies in Hospitality & Tourism
Contemporary Biographies in Law & Criminal Justice
Contemporary Biographies in Physics
Earth Science
Earth Science: Earth Materials & Resources
Earth Science: Earth's Surface and History
Earth Science: Physics & Chemistry of the Earth
Earth Science: Weather, Water & Atmosphere
Encyclopedia of Energy
Encyclopedia of Environmental Issues
Encyclopedia of Environmental Issues: Atmosphere and Air Pollution
Encyclopedia of Environmental Issues: Ecology and Ecosystems
Encyclopedia of Environmental Issues: Energy and Energy Use
Encyclopedia of Environmental Issues: Policy and Activism
Encyclopedia of Environmental Issues: Preservation/Wilderness Issues
Encyclopedia of Environmental Issues: Water and Water Pollution
Encyclopedia of Global Resources
Encyclopedia of Global Warming
Encyclopedia of Mathematics & Society
Encyclopedia of Mathematics & Society: Engineering, Tech, Medicine
Encyclopedia of Mathematics & Society: Great Mathematicians
Encyclopedia of Mathematics & Society: Math & Social Sciences
Encyclopedia of Mathematics & Society: Math Development/Concepts
Encyclopedia of Mathematics & Society: Math in Culture & Society
Encyclopedia of Mathematics & Society: Space, Science, Environment
Encyclopedia of the Ancient World
Forensic Science
Geography Basics
Internet Innovators
Inventions and Inventors
Magill's Encyclopedia of Science: Animal Life
Magill's Encyclopedia of Science: Plant life
Notable Natural Disasters
Principles of Chemistry
Science and Scientists
Solar System
Solar System: Great Astronomers
Solar System: Study of the Universe
Solar System: The Inner Planets
Solar System: The Moon and Other Small Bodies
Solar System: The Outer Planets
Solar System: The Sun and Other Stars
World Geography

## Literature

American Ethnic Writers
Classics of Science Fiction & Fantasy Literature
Critical Insights: Authors
Critical Insights: New Literary Collection Bundles
Critical Insights: Themes
Critical Insights: Works
Critical Survey of Drama
Critical Survey of Graphic Novels: Heroes & Super Heroes
Critical Survey of Graphic Novels: History, Theme & Technique
Critical Survey of Graphic Novels: Independents/Underground Classics
Critical Survey of Graphic Novels: Manga
Critical Survey of Long Fiction
Critical Survey of Mystery & Detective Fiction
Critical Survey of Mythology and Folklore: Heroes and Heroines
Critical Survey of Mythology and Folklore: Love, Sexuality & Desire
Critical Survey of Mythology and Folklore: World Mythology
Critical Survey of Poetry
Critical Survey of Poetry: American Poets
Critical Survey of Poetry: British, Irish & Commonwealth Poets
Critical Survey of Poetry: Cumulative Index
Critical Survey of Poetry: European Poets
Critical Survey of Poetry: Topical Essays
Critical Survey of Poetry: World Poets
Critical Survey of Shakespeare's Sonnets
Critical Survey of Short Fiction
Critical Survey of Short Fiction: American Writers
Critical Survey of Short Fiction: British, Irish, Commonwealth Writers
Critical Survey of Short Fiction: Cumulative Index
Critical Survey of Short Fiction: European Writers
Critical Survey of Short Fiction: Topical Essays
Critical Survey of Short Fiction: World Writers
Cyclopedia of Literary Characters
Holocaust Literature
Introduction to Literary Context: American Poetry of the 20th Century
Introduction to Literary Context: American Post-Modernist Novels
Introduction to Literary Context: American Short Fiction
Introduction to Literary Context: English Literature
Introduction to Literary Context: Plays
Introduction to Literary Context: World Literature
Magill's Literary Annual 2015
Magill's Survey of American Literature
Magill's Survey of World Literature
Masterplots
Masterplots II: African American Literature
Masterplots II: American Fiction Series
Masterplots II: British & Commonwealth Fiction Series
Masterplots II: Christian Literature
Masterplots II: Drama Series
Masterplots II: Juvenile & Young Adult Literature, Supplement
Masterplots II: Nonfiction Series
Masterplots II: Poetry Series
Masterplots II: Short Story Series
Masterplots II: Women's Literature Series
Notable African American Writers
Notable American Novelists
Notable Playwrights
Notable Poets
Recommended Reading: 500 Classics Reviewed
Short Story Writers

# 2015 Title List

Visit www.SalemPress.com for Product Information, Table of Contents, and Sample Pages.

## History and Social Science

The 2000s in America
50 States
African American History
Agriculture in History
American First Ladies
American Heroes
American Indian Culture
American Indian History
American Indian Tribes
American Presidents
American Villains
America's Historic Sites
Ancient Greece
The Bill of Rights
The Civil Rights Movement
The Cold War
Countries, Peoples & Cultures
Countries, Peoples & Cultures: Central & South America
Countries, Peoples & Cultures: Central, South & Southeast Asia
Countries, Peoples & Cultures: East & South Africa
Countries, Peoples & Cultures: East Asia & the Pacific
Countries, Peoples & Cultures: Eastern Europe
Countries, Peoples & Cultures: Middle East & North Africa
Countries, Peoples & Cultures: North America & the Caribbean
Countries, Peoples & Cultures: West & Central Africa
Countries, Peoples & Cultures: Western Europe
Defining Documents: American Revolution (1754-1805)
Defining Documents: Civil War (1860-1865)
Defining Documents: Emergence of Modern America (1868-1918)
Defining Documents: Exploration & Colonial America (1492-1755)
Defining Documents: Manifest Destiny (1803-1860)
Defining Documents: Post-War 1940s (1945-1949)
Defining Documents: Reconstruction (1865-1880)
Defining Documents: The 1920s
Defining Documents: The 1930s
Defining Documents: The American West (1836-1900)
Defining Documents: The Ancient World (2700 B.C.E.-50 C.E.)
Defining Documents: The Middle Ages (524-1431)
Defining Documents: World War I
Defining Documents: World War II (1939-1946)
The Eighties in America
Encyclopedia of American Immigration
Encyclopedia of Flight
Encyclopedia of the Ancient World
The Fifties in America
The Forties in America
Great Athletes
Great Athletes: Baseball
Great Athletes: Basketball
Great Athletes: Boxing & Soccer
Great Athletes: Cumulative Index
Great Athletes: Football
Great Athletes: Golf & Tennis
Great Athletes: Olympics
Great Athletes: Racing & Individual Sports
Great Events from History: 17th Century
Great Events from History: 18th Century
Great Events from History: 19th Century
Great Events from History: 20th Century (1901-1940)
Great Events from History: 20th Century (1941-1970)
Great Events from History: 20th Century (1971-2000)
Great Events from History: Ancient World
Great Events from History: Cumulative Indexes
Great Events from History: Gay, Lesbian, Bisexual, Transgender Events
Great Events from History: Middle Ages
Great Events from History: Modern Scandals
Great Events from History: Renaissance & Early Modern Era

Great Lives from History: 17th Century
Great Lives from History: 18th Century
Great Lives from History: 19th Century
Great Lives from History: 20th Century
Great Lives from History: African Americans
Great Lives from History: Ancient World
Great Lives from History: Asian & Pacific Islander Americans
Great Lives from History: Cumulative Indexes
Great Lives from History: Incredibly Wealthy
Great Lives from History: Inventors & Inventions
Great Lives from History: Jewish Americans
Great Lives from History: Latinos
Great Lives from History: Middle Ages
Great Lives from History: Notorious Lives
Great Lives from History: Renaissance & Early Modern Era
Great Lives from History: Scientists & Science
Historical Encyclopedia of American Business
Immigration in U.S. History
Magill's Guide to Military History
Milestone Documents in African American History
Milestone Documents in American History
Milestone Documents in World History
Milestone Documents of American Leaders
Milestone Documents of World Religions
Musicians & Composers 20th Century
The Nineties in America
The Seventies in America
The Sixties in America
Survey of American Industry and Careers
The Thirties in America
The Twenties in America
United States at War
U.S.A. in Space
U.S. Court Cases
U.S. Government Leaders
U.S. Laws, Acts, and Treaties
U.S. Legal System
U.S. Supreme Court
Weapons and Warfare
World Conflicts: Asia and the Middle East

## Health

Addictions & Substance Abuse
Adolescent Health
Cancer
Complementary & Alternative Medicine
Genetics & Inherited Conditions
Health Issues
Infectious Diseases & Conditions
Magill's Medical Guide
Psychology & Behavioral Health
Psychology Basics

**Grey House Publishing | Salem Press | H.W. Wilson** | 4919 Route, 22 PO Box 56, Amenia NY 12501-0056

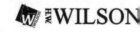
## Current Biography
Current Biography Cumulative Index 1946-2013
Current Biography Monthly Magazine
Current Biography Yearbook: 2003
Current Biography Yearbook: 2004
Current Biography Yearbook: 2005
Current Biography Yearbook: 2006
Current Biography Yearbook: 2007
Current Biography Yearbook: 2008
Current Biography Yearbook: 2009
Current Biography Yearbook: 2010
Current Biography Yearbook: 2011
Current Biography Yearbook: 2012
Current Biography Yearbook: 2013
Current Biography Yearbook: 2014
Current Biography Yearbook: 2015

## Core Collections
Children's Core Collection
Fiction Core Collection
Middle & Junior High School Core
Public Library Core Collection: Nonfiction
Senior High Core Collection

## The Reference Shelf
Aging in America
American Military Presence Overseas
The Arab Spring
The Brain
The Business of Food
Conspiracy Theories
The Digital Age
Dinosaurs
Embracing New Paradigms in Education
Faith & Science
Families: Traditional and New Structures
The Future of U.S. Economic Relations: Mexico, Cuba, and Venezuela
Global Climate Change
Graphic Novels and Comic Books
Immigration in the U.S.
Internet Safety
Marijuana Reform
The News and its Future
The Paranormal
Politics of the Ocean
Reality Television
Representative American Speeches: 2008-2009
Representative American Speeches: 2009-2010
Representative American Speeches: 2010-2011
Representative American Speeches: 2011-2012
Representative American Speeches: 2012-2013
Representative American Speeches: 2013-2014
Representative American Speeches: 2014-2015
Revisiting Gender
Robotics
Russia
Social Networking
Social Services for the Poor
Space Exploration & Development
Sports in America
The Supreme Court
The Transformation of American Cities
U.S. Infrastructure
U.S. National Debate Topic: Surveillance
U.S. National Debate Topic: The Ocean
U.S. National Debate Topic: Transportation Infrastructure
Whistleblowers

## Readers' Guide
Abridged Readers' Guide to Periodical Literature
Readers' Guide to Periodical Literature

## Indexes
Index to Legal Periodicals & Books
Short Story Index
Book Review Digest

## Sears List
Sears List of Subject Headings
Sears: Lista de Encabezamientos de Materia

## Facts About Series
Facts About American Immigration
Facts About China
Facts About the 20th Century
Facts About the Presidents
Facts About the World's Languages

## Nobel Prize Winners
Nobel Prize Winners: 1901-1986
Nobel Prize Winners: 1987-1991
Nobel Prize Winners: 1992-1996
Nobel Prize Winners: 1997-2001

## World Authors
World Authors: 1995-2000
World Authors: 2000-2005

## Famous First Facts
Famous First Facts
Famous First Facts About American Politics
Famous First Facts About Sports
Famous First Facts About the Environment
Famous First Facts: International Edition

## American Book of Days
The American Book of Days
The International Book of Days

## Junior Authors & Illustrators
Tenth Book of Junior Authors & Illustrations

## Monographs
The Barnhart Dictionary of Etymology
Celebrate the World
Guide to the Ancient World
Indexing from A to Z
The Poetry Break
Radical Change: Books for Youth in a Digital Age

## Wilson Chronology
Wilson Chronology of Asia and the Pacific
Wilson Chronology of Human Rights
Wilson Chronology of Ideas
Wilson Chronology of the Arts
Wilson Chronology of the World's Religions
Wilson Chronology of Women's Achievements